RELIGION, LANGUAGE, AND THE HUMAN MIND

Edited by Paul Chilton

   and

Monika Kopytowska

OXFORD
UNIVERSITY PRESS

Oxford University Press is a department of the University of Oxford. It furthers
the University's objective of excellence in research, scholarship, and education
by publishing worldwide. Oxford is a registered trade mark of Oxford University
Press in the UK and certain other countries.

Published in the United States of America by Oxford University Press
198 Madison Avenue, New York, NY 10016, United States of America.

CIP data is on file at the Library of Congress
ISBN 978-0-19-063664-7

9 8 7 6 5 4 3 2 1

Printed by Sheridan Books, Inc., United States of America

CONTENTS

PREFACE

At the present time in human history religious thinking, religious feeling, and religious behaviours pose more questions than they have for 500 years. This collection of papers by distinguished and innovative scholars and scientists is not, however, aimed directly at the social and political manifestations of these problems. It is aimed at a more fundamental understanding of the complex phenomenon of the human religious consciousness coupled with a drive to form religious institutions and movements. What we need are fresh insights into the individual and collective dimensions of both the ever-existing cognitive-behavioural patterns and new emerging forms of religion, faith, and spirituality. In order to pursue such goals, it is necessary to attend to the human capacity of language; without it human religions are scarcely imaginable.

This volume aims to be yet another step in furthering the understanding of religious minds and behaviours. The contributors come from a range of disciplinary backgrounds that include linguistics, religious studies, literary studies, communication science, cognitive science, neuroscience, and psychiatry. The examples of religious practice range across the major world religions: Buddhism, Christianity, Hinduism, Islam, Judaism. This volume is intended to offer a range of analytic and potentially explanatory frameworks: the implications for religious belief in general are left to the reader. In this connection, we should mention that in a number of chapters, original languages and original scripts are used. This is not simply a matter of scholarly detail: it reflects an important aspect of the relationship between language and religion—the very shape of the written word has major religious, cultural, and indeed political significance. This fact is mentioned in chapter 1 in connection with English, but it is of even greater symbolic significance for Arabic, as well as other languages that have liturgical and other religious functions. We also want to mention here that in a number of chapters that deal with mental constructs, small capitals are used to indicate concepts and metaphorical mappings (not for emphasis).

We open the volume with an Introduction that attempts to take an overview of the different strands of overlapping and convergent research on religion. Let us say at the outset that this vast task can only be engaged in by precisely that—engaging in it, as an ongoing process of scholarly and scientific interaction that will run into the future. We seek only to give an idea of how language might fit into a picture that tries to understand religion as a human phenomenon.

The volume is organised in three parts. The first introduces descriptive and theoretical approaches to religion in several paradigms. The second focuses on the role of metaphorical language and thought across religious traditions. The third brings in new perspectives and theoretical frameworks that include developments in cognitive linguistics and pragmatics, multimodal phenomena, and the role of the media.

ACKNOWLEDGEMENTS

This is an interdisciplinary volume, and the whole project has been a collective intellectual experience rather than a mere collecting of papers. So first and foremost we thank all our authors for sharing their different points of view and their diverse fields of expertise in ways that have enabled us to explore the interfaces of the cognitive, the social, and the linguistic and to make links across the chapters. We want to acknowledge all those who have made it possible for the volume to appear. Since Monika's initial inspiration for a cross-disciplinary monograph on language, discourse, and religion, a number of people have supported the project. The contributors themselves patiently encouraged us by believing in this innovative undertaking when the going was slow and new chapters were still emerging. At OUP, John Davey, Peter Ohlin, Tom Perridge, Hannah Doyle, Hallie Stebbins, and Julia Steer gave essential early encouragement and guidance. During production, Hannah Doyle and Sivaranjani Chandramouliswaran kept us on track and up to speed, while our patient copyeditors made sure the book would take its current shape.

Intellectual influences are always hard to track, and ours are certainly too numerous to mention individually here. The colleagues who have offered their thoughts and support have come from far and wide, and from many different disciplines. We are immensely grateful to those linguists and discourse analysts who have shown interest, and to the numerous scholars and scientists from cognitive science, neuroscience, religious studies, and theology who have contributed comments and criticisms. We would also like to express our appreciation of the wealth of suggestions provided by the external reviewers.

In addition we acknowledge the part played, directly and indirectly, by our home institutions—Lancaster University, University of Warwick, and University of Łódź—whose academic environment and resources became a springboard for our research and collaboration. Monika's research stay in the Department of Linguistics at Lancaster University in 2012 and 2013, during which the idea of this book was born and discussed at great length, would not have been possible without the support of Ruth Wodak, Veronika Koller, Piotr Stalmaszczyk, Łukasz Bogucki, and Piotr Cap.

The jacket design is an important part of the book as a whole. We thank all those at OUP who have been involved in its production. The image we used to reflect the themes of the book without reflecting particular religions is a painting by the British artist, David Chick (1947-2009). We thank its owner, Martin Norfield, for permission to use it, and also for his assistance in preparing our jacket notes about it. We also thank the photographer, John Alsop, who made it possible to reproduce this extraordinary work in a professional manner.

Finally, we would like to thank all the institutions and individuals who granted their permissions for the copyright material used in this book, and in particular the following.

We wish to acknowledge, with thanks, Rev. James Francis and Prof. Ralph Bisschops, the co-editors of the Religions and Discourse series published by Peter Lang, for their approval of our re-use, with significant extension and development by the authors in Chapter 3, of an article by Lieven Boeve and Kurt Feyaerts, "Religious metaphors in a postmodern culture: transverse links between apophatical theology and cognitive semantics". The article originally appeared in the Religions and Discourse series volume 2 (1999), Metaphor and God-Talk (pp. 152-84), which was also edited by Lieven Boeve and Kurt Feyaerts. Concomitantly, we thank Lucy Melville of Peter Lang Ltd. for granting the publisher's formal permission.

For Chapter 14 we wish to acknowledge the following for their kind permission to reproduce important pictorial images: The Museum of Fine Arts. Budapest; The Museo Blaisten, Mexico DF; The Tretyakov Gallery, Moscow; The Church of the Saints Justus and Pastor. Cuenca de Campos, Valladolid, Spain; The Church of the Virgin of the Pillar, San Isidro, Lima; The Saint Elizabeth Monastery. Medinaceli, Soria, Spain; The Museo del Prado, Madrid; The Bibliothèque Nationale, Paris; Monastery of Santa María de la Caridad, Tulebras, Navarre, Spain.

For materials used in Chapter 16, we are grateful to Rev. Scott Haynes, Director of Biretta Books for extracts from The Rubrics of the Missale Romanum (1962). For an extract from the Tridentine Ordo, also used in Chapter 16, we thank Prof. D. Giuseppe Costa and Dr. Francesca Angeletti of the Libreria Editrice Vaticana. Thanks are due also to Fordham University Internet History Sourcebooks Project: http://sourcebooks.fordham.edu/basis/latinmass2.asp, and for their advice to Prof. Paul Halsall of Fordham University, and to Colin O'Brien, Permissions Assistant of the United States Conference of Catholic Bishops. We are grateful to Allison Girone for permission to use a photograph of the elevation of the Sacred Host taken at the Cathedral Basilica of Philadelphia, again in Chapter 16.

CONTRIBUTORS

Mihailo Antović (PhD), associate professor, teaches cognitive linguistics in the Department of English, Faculty of Philosophy at the University of Niš, Serbia. He has presented papers on music, language, meaning, and cognition at more than twenty conferences in Austria, Greece, Germany, Italy, Hungary, Poland, Slovenia, Sweden, the United Kingdom, and the United States. He was a Fulbright visiting scholar at Case Western Reserve University and research scholar at the University of Freiburg. His articles have appeared in a number of journals, including *Metaphor and Symbol; Language and History; Musicae Scientiae, Language and Communication*; and *Music Perception*. In addition to several contributions to international edited volumes, he has also recently coedited a volume on oral poetics and cognitive science for De Gruyter. He currently heads the Center for Cognitive Sciences, University of Niš.

Antonio Barcelona is full professor in the Department of English and German, University of Córdoba, Spain (formerly at University of Murcia, Spain), He has lectured extensively on metaphor, metonymy, and cognitive linguistics in Spain and elsewhere. Author of nearly a hundred articles and author or editor of several books on these topics, he is head researcher or member of the research team in fourteen government-funded research projects, mainly on cognitive linguistics. Antonio Barcelona was founder and first president of the Spanish Cognitive Linguistics Association (AELCO) and has been a board member of the International Cognitive Linguistics Association (1997–2001), as well as Associate Editor of *Cognitive Linguistics* (2009 and 2011), of the *Review of Cognitive Linguistics* (since 2010), and of *Cognitive Linguistic Studies* (since 2013). He has also served on the editorial boards of several other international journals and book series. His two most recent books (as coeditor) are *Metonymy and Metaphor in Grammar* (2009) and *Defining Metonymy in Cognitive Linguistics* (2011).

Ralph Bisschops received his PhD in 1992 at the Vrije Universiteit Brussel, where he is now research associate in the Philosophy Department; he is also retired staff member of the Brussels Education Center. He was formerly visiting professor at the University of Duisburg (Germany) and research associate at the University of Ghent. He is the author of a book on metaphorical language and ethics, *Die Metapher als Wertsetzung* (1994), and with James Francis he is co-editor of *Metaphor, Canon and Community: Jewish, Christian and Islamic Approaches* (1999). He has published about a hundred articles, essays, and reviews on theory of metaphor, biblical exegesis, Judaism, literary criticism, and philosophy.

Lieven Boeve is Professor of Fundamental Theology at the Faculty of Theology and Religious Studies, Katholieke Universiteit Leuven, Belgium. As of August 1, 2014, he was appointed the Director-General of the general office of Catholic Education in Flanders (Katholiek Onderwijs Vlaanderen). His research concerns theological epistemology, philosophical theology, truth in faith and theology, tradition development, and hermeneutics. From 2005 till 2009 he served as president of the European Society for Catholic Theology. He is the author of *Interrupting Tradition: An Essay on Christian Faith in a Postmodern Context* (2003); *God Interrupts History: Theology in a Time of Upheaval* (2007); *Lyotard and Theology* (2014); and *Theology at the Crossroads of University, Church and Society* (2016). He has coedited various volumes, of which the most recent are *Questioning the Human: Toward a Theological Anthropology for the Twenty-First Century* (2014) and *The Normativity of History: Theological Truth and Tradition in the Tension between Church History and Systematic Theology* (2016). In 2015, the European Society for Catholic Theology awarded him the biennial prize for the best theological book of the past two years for his monograph *Lyotard and Theology*.

Paul Chilton is an Emeritus Professor of Linguistics at Lancaster University and a visiting Professor at the Centre for Applied Linguistics, University of Warwick, UK. His current research lies in the field of cognitive linguistics and in cognitive approaches to discourse analysis. His most recent book is *Language, Space and Mind* (2014), which develops a theory of language structure based on spatial cognition. He has also published on religious literature in the Reformation and Counter-Reformation period.

David Cram is an Emeritus Fellow of Jesus College, Oxford, UK. By background and training he is a theoretical linguist, but the bulk of his research has concerned the history of ideas about language in the seventeenth century on topics ranging from philosophical language schemes to theories of the origin of language. Of relevance in the immediate context is his paper 'Linguistic Eschatology: Babel and Pentecost in Seventeenth-Century Linguistic Thought' (*Language and History*, 2013, vol. 56, pp. 44–56).

David Crystal is Honorary Professor of Linguistics at the University of Bangor, UK, and works from his home in Holyhead, North Wales, as a writer, editor, lecturer, and broadcaster. He read English at University College London; specialised in English language studies; then joined academic life as a lecturer in linguistics, first at Bangor, then at Reading, where he became professor of linguistics. He received an OBE for services to the English language in 1995. His many books include *Linguistics, Language and Religion* (1965); *Begat: the King James Bible and the English Language* (2010); and anthologies of the prolific missionary poet John Bradburne (selected from his edition of the complete works at <www.johnbradburnepoems.com>).

William Downes is a Senior Fellow in the School of Politics, Philosophy, Language and Communication Studies at the University of East Anglia (Norwich, UK); and Adjunct Professor of English and Linguistics at Glendon College, York University (Toronto, Canada). Educated at Queen's University, Kingston (Ontario), the University of Toronto; and University College London, he taught at York

University, Toronto, and in England at the London School of Economics and the University of East Anglia. He has been a Northrop Frye Fellow at Victoria College and Resident at Massey College, Toronto, and Fellow at the Institute of Advanced Study at Durham University. His research employs linguistics, broadly understood to include cognition, pragmatic theory, and philosophy, as a method for understanding culture. He is the author of a major sociolinguistics textbook, *Language and Society* (1998). His most recent book is *Language and Religion: A Journey into the Human Mind* (2011).

Ahmad El-Sharif is an Assistant Professor of Linguistics in the Department of English Language and Literature at Al al-Bayt University, Jordan. He obtained his PhD in linguistics from Queen Mary University of London in 2011. In his PhD thesis, from which his chapter is extracted, El-Sharif embarked upon the implications of using conceptual metaphors in Prophet Muhammad's discourse and its persuasive power within the framework of Islamic religious discourse. Currently, El-Sharif's research interests and academic contributions are mostly oriented toward the applications of contemporary approaches to critical discourse analysis, language and identity, and persuasion in different genres of discourse.

Kurt Feyaerts is Professor of German Linguistics in the Faculty of Arts, Katholieke Universiteit Leuven, Belgium. His research interests lie at the intersection between cognitive and interactional linguistics and include aspects of multimodal, interactional meaning making; aspects of music and cognition; aspects of humour and creativity; and metaphor, metonymy, and blending. He has authored several articles and coedited various volumes on these topics: *Cognitive Linguistic Humor Research. Current Trends and New Developments* (2015); *Creativity and the Agile Mind: A Multidisciplinary Approach to a Multifaceted Phenomenon* (2013); *Cognitive Linguistic Approaches to Humor* (2006); *The Bible through Metaphor and Translation: A Cognitive Semantic Perspective* (2003); *Metaphor and God-talk* (1999, with Lieven Boeve).

Xiuping Gao is a lecturer of English at Beijing Language and Culture University and a PhD candidate in cognitive linguistics at Beijing Foreign Studies University, China. His PhD project compares the conceptual metaphors in the Christian Bible and the Buddhist *Lotus Sutra*, with an emphasis on five pairs of concepts: Christian SPACE vs. Buddhist SPACE, Christian TIME vs. Buddhist TIME, Christian LIFE vs. Buddhist LIFE, KINGDOM OF HEAVEN vs. NIRVANA, and GOD vs. BUDDHA.

Magda Giordano is a researcher at the Instituto de Neurobiología-Universidad Nacional Autónoma de México (UNAM), Juriquilla, México. The focus of her research has been the study of changes in behaviour as a result of insult or injury to the central nervous system; the search for reparation strategies, such as neural transplants; and the evaluation of the effects of environmental toxicants. The basal ganglia have been her model of study. She is currently interested in the possible participation of these nuclei in cognitive function in humans, in particular in the neural and cognitive basis of pragmatic language use, employing behavioural and neuroimaging techniques. With her fellow researchers in neuroscience, she has published on in vivo

GABA release; dopaminergic markers; and, in the field of philosophical psychology, aspects of historical consciousness.

Ellen Haskell is Associate Professor of Religious Studies and Director of Jewish Studies at the University of North Carolina at Greensboro, United States, as well as the Herman & Zelda Bernard Distinguished Scholar of Jewish Studies. She received her doctorate from the University of Chicago Divinity School, and has been honoured with an AAUW American Postdoctoral Research Leave Fellowship. She is the author of *Mystical Resistance: Uncovering the Zohar's Conversations with Christianity* (2016) and *Suckling at My Mother's Breasts: The Image of a Nursing God in Jewish Mysticism* (2012).

Glen Alexander Hayes is Professor of Religion at Bloomfield College in Bloomfield, New Jersey, United States He received his PhD in History of Religions from The University of Chicago in 1985, where he studied Sanskrit with J. A. B. van Buitenen and Bengali with Edward C. Dimock, Jr. His dissertation examined body symbolism and cosmology in medieval Bengali Tantric traditions. Author of numerous essays on the Vaiṣṇava Sahajiyā Tantric traditions of Bengal, he has published several collections of original translations of Bengali Tantric texts. In addition to his specialisation in medieval Bengali Tantra, his research interests include contemporary metaphor theory and the cognitive science of religion. He is author of 'Conceptual Blending and Religion,' in *Religion: Mental Religion* (2016). He serves as chairperson of the Steering Committee of The Society for Tantric Studies (STS), and was a founding co-chair of the Tantric Studies Group of the American Academy of Religion (AAR).

Monika Kopytowska is Assistant Professor in the Department of Pragmatics at the University of Łódź, Poland. Her research interests revolve around the interface of language and cognition, identity, and the pragma-rhetorical aspects of the mass-mediated representation of religion, ethnicity, and conflict. She has published internationally in linguistic journals and volumes (e.g. *Contemporary Discourses of Hate and Radicalism across Space and Genres* (2017); with Yusuf Kalyango, *Why Discourse Matters* (2014); and with Christian Karner, *National Identity and Europe in Times of Crisis* (2017). She is also the coeditor of *Lodz Papers in Pragmatics* (de Gruyter), the assistant editor of *CADAAD Journal,* an editorial board member of *The University of Nairobi Journal of Language and Linguistics*, and a board member of the European Network for Intercultural Education Activities.

Hubert Kowalewski is an Assistant Professor in the English Department at Maria Curie-Skłodowska University in Lublin, Poland. His main professional interests include cognitive linguistics, non-linguistic semiotics, methodology of linguistics, and philosophy of science. He has published papers on motivation in language and visual signs, Conceptual Blending Theory, and speculative fiction.

Chun Lan is Professor of Linguistics at Beijing Foreign Studies University, China, where she teaches courses in linguistics and English language. Her main research interests are in cognitive linguistics, pragmatics, and rhetoric. Her books include

A Cognitive Approach to Spatial Metaphors in English and Chinese (2003), *Cognitive Linguistics and Metaphorical Studies* (2004), *A Pragmatic Approach to* A Dream of the Red Chamber (2007), *Towards an Understanding of Language and Linguistics* (2009), and *Rhetoric: Theories and Practice* (2010).

Iain McGilchrist is a former Fellow of All Souls College, Oxford; a Fellow of the Royal College of Psychiatrists; a Fellow of the Royal Society of Arts; and former Consultant Psychiatrist and Clinical Director at the Bethlem Royal & Maudsley Hospital, London, UK. He was a Research Fellow in neuroimaging at Johns Hopkins Hospital, Baltimore, United States, and a Fellow of the Institute of Advanced Studies in Stellenbosch, South Africa. He delivered the Samuel Gee lecture at the Royal College of Physicians in 2014. He has published original articles and research papers in a wide range of publications on topics in literature, medicine, and psychiatry. He is the author of *Against Criticism* (1982), *The Master and his Emissary: The Divided Brain and the Making of the Western World* (2009), and *The Divided Brain and the Search for Meaning: Why Are We So Unhappy?* (e-book short); and he is currently working on a book entitled *The Porcupine is a Monkey, or, Things Are Not What They Seem*, to be published by Penguin Press. He lives on the Isle of Skye.

Patrick McNamara is Associate Professor of neurology in the Department of Neurology, Boston University School of Medicine and School of Business and Technology Management, Northcentral University, United States. He has authored dozens of papers and several books on the neurology of religious experiences, including his 2009 *Neuroscience of Religious Experience*, as well as *Spirit Possession and History: History, Psychology, and Neurobiology* (2011), and *The Cognitive Neuropsychiatry of Parkinson's Disease: A Theory of the Agentic Self* (2012). He co-founded the Institute for the Biocultural Study of Religion (www.ibcsr.org) and the journal *Religion, Brain and Behavior*.

Christoph Unger is a Postdoctoral Fellow in linguistics at the Norwegian University for Science and Technology (NTNU) in Trondheim, Norway. His research focuses on pragmatic theory and its implications for natural language semantics, stylistics, and cross-cultural communication. He was previously affiliated with SIL International, where he was involved in training and consulting Bible translators. He is the author of *Genre, Relevance and Global Coherence* (2006).

Anna Wierzbicka, born and educated in Poland, is a Professor (Emerita) of Linguistics at the Australian National University, Canberra. She is a Fellow of the Australian Academy of the Humanities, of the Academy of Social Sciences of Australia, of the Russian Academy of Sciences, and of the Polish Academy of Arts and Sciences. Her work spans a number of disciplines, including anthropology, psychology, cognitive science, philosophy, and religious studies as well as linguistics, Slavic studies, and English studies. She is the author of many books, including *Understanding Cultures Through Their Keywords* (1997); *Emotions Across Languages and Cultures: Diversity and Universals* (1999); *What Did Jesus Mean? Explaining the Sermon on the Mount and the Parables in Simple and Universal Human Concepts* (2001); *English: Meaning and culture*

(2006); *Experience, Evidence and Sense: The Hidden Cultural Legacy of English* (2010); *Imprisoned in English: The Hazards of English as a Default Language* (2014); and, with Cliff Goddard, *Words and Meanings: Lexical Semantics Across Domains, Languages, and Cultures* (2014).

INTRODUCTION

Religion as a Cognitive and Linguistic Phenomenon

PAUL CHILTON AND MONIKA KOPYTOWSKA

Religion exists externally as bodily and linguistic practices and internally as experiences, mental operations, and emotions in the mind-brain, interacting internally in a complex relationship and externally with other brain-minds, often but not always in particular spatial and social settings. The use of language is manifestly part of those practices, experiences, and mental operations. With a view to exploring these relationships, the present volume brings together scholars from linguistics, from theology and religious studies, as well as from cognitive science and neuroscience. We are not the first to explore these relationships. The aim is to stimulate broad cross-discipline, cross-religion, and cross-culture work in the future, while reflecting a context in which the study of religious experience, of language, and of mind converge. In this introduction, we seek to outline and contextualise a number of themes and questions arising across these different approaches. The aim is not only to introduce some of the topics, theories, and techniques used in the chapters of this volume, but also open horizons for future research into religion that will combine linguistics with other cognitive and social sciences.

1 LINGUISTIC APPROACHES TO RELIGION PAST AND PRESENT
1.1 Language in the religious traditions

The exegetic strands of religious institutions, especially in the Christian tradition, have long taken varieties of non-literal meaning to be crucial (indeed, they have needed to do so, in order to maintain religious authority and the validity of sacred text). Feyaerts and Boeve (this volume, chapter 3; also Boeve and Feyaerts 1999b and Feyaerts 2003) discuss this tradition and bring out in some detail how cognitive linguistics relates to it. A brief excursus here may help to contextualise philosophical and philosophic-religious interest in the phenomenon of metaphor.

The earliest known contribution to the systematic and objective study of language, within any religious institution, is not Christian but Hindu: the detailed descriptive work of Pāṇini, who flourished in the fourth century BCE in what is now Pakistan and produced analytic descriptions of language on the Vedic scriptures. His structure-oriented analyses are often said to have been in advance of Western linguistic speculations till the twentieth century. The European Middle Ages had, however, independently produced sophisticated philosophies of grammar and meaning among Christian, Hebrew, and Arabic scholars working on meaning as well as grammatical structure, with reference to sacred text and ritual. The *modistae* (Thomas of Erfurt is the best known), for example, developed logico-grammatical tools, later picked up and developed by the Port Royal grammarians of seventeenth-century France, which were used to analyse (and justify) ritual and text (see Chilton and Cram, chapter 16 of this volume).

Language and meaning, however, occupy a paradoxical status in religious thought. In religious traditions, what in the Christian religion is known as *apophatic* theology or *via negativa* (exemplified in sixth-century writings ascribed to Dionysius the Areopagite) testifies to the idea that the divine is beyond the human and thus beyond the human mind and human language. Yet, given the impulse to communicate intimations of the divine, both mind and language have to be resorted to. Moreover, religious traditions give central importance to sacred text as well as to oral tradition and to ritual; they also often claim direct communication to and from a god. Central here is the problem of meaning. Are the referents of human words literal and direct or indirect and metaphorical? Christian theologians of the patristic and medieval periods developed a theory of scriptural exegesis, which distinguished several different types of non-literal meaning, in certain respects overlapping with what in modern linguistics might be called metaphor. It is metaphor and related linguistic forms that somehow 'go beyond' the literal or everyday meaning of words.

In Europe, Enlightenment thinkers distrusted metaphor (not to mention religion) in all contexts, but especially in science and philosophy. By the twentieth century, increasingly sophisticated argumentation about language meaning developed in a one-sided way. Gottlob Frege and subsequently the logical positivists insisted on a referential and truth-conditional theory of meaning. Only reference of word to thing in a propositional structure was meaningful. Thus metaphor was left stranded, and so were theological questions of meaning. By the second half of the twentieth century, philosopher-theologians had to face the inference that theological and religious language was meaningless (as asserted by A. J. Ayer and other logical positivists). Further, metaphor was also meaningless since it apparently contradicted truth-conditional semantics. Max Black, however, while he was influenced by Frege's work, realised the importance of metaphor and worked on analytical definitions (Black 1962) that were drawn on by theologians, and to a degree by linguistic semanticists, into the 1990s.

Among twentieth-century theologians, the work of Sallie McFague (1982), Janet Soskice (1985), and Richard Swinburne (1992, 1999) reflects the increased recognition of the role of metaphor in human language. They were working in the context of analytical philosophy and variously drew on Black's ideas. Black's theory of associated and implied meanings in what he called 'models' made it possible to engage in critical argument about the meanings of Christian metaphors and their entailments (including feminist critiques of paternalist language). Contemporaneously, linguistic semantics, which also had Fregean roots and truth-conditional theories, was developing a counter-theory of metaphor that connected with empirical psychology, cognitive science, and a neo-Kantian epistemology. In philosophical theology, Richard Swinburne's (1999) paper on analogy, metaphor, and language in religion is an important representative of a turning point that was emerging in the 1980s, one in which the argument is driven toward a rethinking of metaphor. In Swinburne's case, this included a rethinking of Aquinas's concept of analogy (Swinburne 1992).

1.2 Modern linguistics and religious language

Philosophy, anthropology, sociology, cognitive science, and neuroscience have all taken religion as an object of systematic rational enquiry, to varying degrees, and their interest has always included, and continues to include, language. For theologians too, language has been a major concern, not only in pursuit of their theist commitments but also in an objective and rational form of enquiry. Modern linguistics, however, for all its theoretical rigour and sophisticated analyses of actual uses of language, has not given sustained attention to religious language, despite sporadic insights and efforts on the part of some important scholars. In the field of cognitive linguistics in particular (about which more below), with its focus on mental processes and the meaningfulness of linguistic form, has shown little interest in religious language.

There are some exceptions, however, that point the way. In particular, David Crystal's (1965) *Linguistics, Language and Religion* showed how linguistics could be applied descriptively within a religious framework. As Crystal shows in chapter 1 of the present volume, there was an increase of interest in the 1970s, 1980s, and beyond, when a group of scholars developed the idea of 'theolinguistics', leading figures being, amongst others, Jean-Pierre van Noppen (1981, 1983, 1988, 1999, 2011), Ralph Bisschops (1994, 1999, 2003), and Bisschops and Francis (1999). While the topic more or less disappeared from mainstream linguistics, some of the advanced linguistic work in semantics and cognition merged with theological interests in language. Boeve and Feyaerts (1999a) are witness to that overlap, and their contribution to this volume is a recapitulation and development of that trend. In 2001, George Lakoff gave the Gifford Lectures, a prestigious lecture series presented at the Scottish universities for over a century, in which distinguished scientists and scholars discuss theological and philosophical topics ('natural theology'). In these lectures he outlined the metaphorical nature of abstract concepts such as 'God'. In the same year, Wierzbicka, bringing together biblical criticism and recent developments within linguistics, anthropology, and cultural psychology, offered a new perspective on the universal meaning of Jesus' key sayings and parables. There are signs of growing interest, for example, in the work of Jäkel (1999, 2002, and 2003), Feyaerts (2003), DesCamp and Sweetser (2005), Sweetser and DesCamp (2014), and the collection by Howe and Green (2014). Charteris-Black (2004) deploys computer-aided quantitative methods to look at metaphors in the Bible and in the Quran, and this approach is used in two of the chapters in the present volume (Xiuping Gao and Chun Lan chapter 10, and El Sharif chapter 11). In parallel, some historians of religion (e.g. Bisschops 1994, 1999, 2003; Haskell 2008, 2012, 2013; Hayes 2003, 2005, 2008, 2012, 2014 and present volume chapter 8; Kowalewski this volume chapter 9) have applied conceptual metaphor theory (CMT), a theory initially outlined by Lakoff, Johnson, and Turner (Lakoff and Johnson 1980, 1999; Lakoff 1987; Lakoff and Turner 1989), some comparative scholars of religion using aspects of it to argue against a cultural-relativist stance (e.g. Egge 2013; Slingerland 2004a, 2004b, 2011). Some scholars in this current of thought describe religious metaphors within a more literary poststructuralist framework (Pathak 2013).

2 THE COGNITIVE TURN IN APPROACHES TO RELIGION

That there has been a 'cognitive turn' across the human sciences is a commonplace. It is abundantly apparent in linguistics, where it has been predominantly associated with the paradigm-changing work of Noam Chomsky in the 1950s and 1960s. As is well known, Chomsky proposed the existence in the human mind-brain of a species-specific module that handled language. Reconciling that claim with evolutionary and neurological evidence is highly controversial; we do not need to address it here. What needs to be pointed out is that the Chomskyan language module was postulated to handle only syntax, merely having an 'interface' with what is ordinarily understood by 'meaning'. However, once the attention of linguists switched to the workings of the mind, it was hard to exclude semantic phenomena from research into the general nature of human language; furthermore, some researchers found that explaining syntax also required bringing meaning into the picture. Linguistics and cognitive psychology found convergent interests. The various findings of what is now known as cognitive linguistics suggest that the human ability for language is massively connected with other cognitive dispositions, including social cognitions and emotions, of the species. Alongside cognitive pragmatics, the discipline of cognitive linguistics has opened up systematic empirical research into what was once the 'black box' of meaning.

2.1 Religion as a product of the human mind

The cognitive turn was certainly not confined to linguistics. In recent decades, at least since Guthrie (1980), there has emerged a coherent research paradigm known as cognitive science of religion (CSR), a confluence of thought flowing from advances in cognitive science, evolutionary psychology, archaeology, social anthropology, philosophy, and related disciplines (Andresen 2001; Barrett 2000, 2004, 2011; Slone 2006; Atran 2002; Dennett 2006; Mithen 1996; Sperber 1975, 1994, 1996, 2006; Boyer 1994a, 1994b, 2001; Hirschfeld and Gelman 1994; Whitehouse and Laidlaw 2007; Smith 2014), running parallel to the traditional scholarly pursuits within theology and religious studies. This highly productive current of thought has, as noted above, contributed to some of the work collected here; conversely, much of the work collected here, flowing from other sources, may contribute to the stream.

CSR has an explanatory orientation. It asks, why does the human mind develop religious concepts and cultures across time and populations? This approach encourages theory building, drawing on experimental psychology and, increasingly, on neuroscience, to test hypotheses (for an overview, see Lawson 2000; Andresen 2001; and Slone 2006, for a sample of foundational papers). A number of CSR scholars explain religious concepts on the basis of what is known as 'modularity of mind' (Fodor 1983, 2000) or the related idea of 'domain specificity' (see the papers collected in Hirschfeld and Gelman 1994).

Modules are cognitive systems based in neural structures of the brain that have specific functions in relation to human interaction with the environment. Examples well known to biologists, neuroscientists, and psychologists are the sympathetic and parasympathetic systems; the visual system with its two neural 'streams'; face recognition ability; the spatial perception systems relating to personal, peripersonal, and extra-personal space; sensory-motor systems and the metacognitive attentional systems that automatically monitor them; and so forth. Cognitive scientists, evolutionary psychologists, and philosophers of mind have hypothesised the existence of other modular systems of the brain: intuitive 'folk physics', 'folk biology', 'machiavellian intelligence', an affective-motivational system, and more (see Barkow, Cosmides and Tooby 1992; Hirschfeld and Gelman 1994; Sperber 1994, 1996; Pinker 1997; Carruthers 2006). Of particular interest to CSR have been agency detection, the ability to form mental representations and meta-representations, and the ability to accept the existence of other minds and infer intentions. Normativity—the formation of socially binding values, whatever the specific cultural content—as a fundamental ingredient has also been impossible to ignore, though whether this qualifies as module is open to debate. These are evolved abilities adapted to survival in a particular environment. An important CSR claim is that religious cognition is rooted in these natural modules, in the sense that they accommodate 'minimally counterintuitive' variants. For example, concepts of supernatural agents seem cross-culturally to have characteristics of human agents with some counterintuitive additions that also recur cross-culturally, for example, omniscience, and having no physical properties or spatial location. Religious concepts are thus thought to be 'natural' in the sense that they are easy to acquire and accept (Boyer 1993, 1994a, 1994b; Barrett 2000, 2004). They are all the more natural if several modules interact in producing them. In the case of supernatural agents, humans seem to have a spontaneous cognitive mechanism for detecting agents (an evolutionary adaptation with obvious survival advantages), and it has been proposed that the readiness to sense the presence of supernatural agents is linked to a 'hyperactive agency detection device' (Guthrie 1980). There is a further element in this cognitive account: the attention systems of the human brain. Since supernatural agency is indeed counterintuitive, it is cognitively salient and attention-grabbing. This whole approach thus seeks to explain both why religious concepts take root in a natural way and why they are also extraordinary; this further would explain why they are of interest, or have relevance (in the sense of Sperber and Wilson 1995), for communicative 'epidemiological' spread (in the terms of Sperber 1994; Atran 2002; cf. Downes 2011, p. 35).

The postulated cognitive modules should not be regarded as isolated sealed units; their interaction is crucial to the view of mind adopted in CSR. The most important contribution to this framework comes from the work of the cognitive archaeologist Steven Mithen (1996). According to Mithen, the explosion of creativity in the development of Homo sapiens during a period around 50,000 years ago (Upper Palaeolithic), abundantly evidenced in the archaeological record, can be explained by a hypothesis concerning cognitive capacities—the emergence of increased connections among modules that had been separate at earlier stages. This 'cognitive fluidity' proposal is perhaps the most important hypothesis for understanding the nature of human conceptualisation, including linguistically guided creativity, speculation, and counterfactual representation. The central argument of the cognitive science of religion—that religious conceptualisation, emotion, and practice derive from natural modules in the human mental architecture—does not say a great deal about the actual mental mechanics by means of which these postulated modules 'project' onto the abstract notions of religion and its concrete practices. How do we get from mental modules to the thoughts, feelings, utterances, gestures, and so forth of religious individuals and groups? What drives the recruitment of these already evolved and present modules in the first place? A related question is how religious concepts and practices are transmitted, as they clearly are. A cognitively and pragmatically based linguistics may provide some answers. More generally, the fact that language is a feature of religion, interwoven into all its manifestations, needs to be accounted for in any explanatory model. This important lack in theoretical explanation is to a considerable degree filled by cognitive-linguistic models and their application. It is why the particular cognitive-linguistic theories of conceptual metaphor and conceptual blending play a powerful part in the papers in the present collective volume, alongside pragmatic-cognitive explanations of the way humans make meaning through language-based communication.

2.2 A cognitive-linguistic anthropology of religion?

Sperber's work in particular has created a bridge to linguistic pragmatics within CSR and anthropological studies of religion more widely. Sperber's *Rethinking Symbolism* (1975) challenged symbolic interpretive anthropology, and shifted to a cognitive perspective that included a concept of 'relevance', a perspective which Sperber saw, interestingly, as continuous with Lévi-Straus's notion of myth as *bricolage* (Sperber 1975, pp. 110–113). This perspective abandons the structuralist notion that myth, religious narratives, rituals, and religious commentaries on these are codes, and is concerned to show differences between code-like systems, to the extent they exist, and human language as such. Perhaps the most important theoretical point made by Sperber is that both language *and* symbolic systems draw on the *same* cognitive resources, despite some specialised features of language. Both draw on human cognitive representations of the physical world, and human affective responses within it. Moreover, especially in ritual, the linguistic and the non-linguistic work together and interact.

Sperber worked with the linguist Deirdre Wilson to produce a cognitive theory of linguistic meaning production Relevance Theory (RT), which explicitly moves beyond the code notion. RT proposes that humans make sense of linguistic input by means of a principle of relevance. In practical communication, hearers use, speakers expect hearers to use it, and vice versa. A corollary is that linguistically communicated meaning is inferential another is that linguistically conveyed meaning is underspecified, not determinately encoded, and is dependent on mutual cognitive context. In this perspective, the hearer's recovering the speaker's *intended* meaning is central, a process that depends on 'theory of mind' (mentalising, perspective taking), the cognitive ability to recognise another mind's view on the world. The relevance principle itself includes the following: the presumption that utterances are worth the cognitive effort of processing, that is, yield cognitive effects that justify a degree of cognitive effort to get them. RT is thus focussed on cognitive effects perceived as advantageous or desirable by processors of linguistic (and some non-linguistic) input. Such an approach implies a critical refocusing of the effort to make sense of religious behaviours and discourses. It is an approach that makes it possible to explain the relatively costly religious behaviours not only in social-functional terms but also in terms of cognitive effects desired or needed by their human processors.

Downes (2011 and chapter 4 in the present volume; cf. Unger 2006, 2012, and this volume chapter 13) is a groundbreaking cross-disciplinary work, since it makes direct links with cognitive science and anthropology. In particular, Downes builds on theories of culture originating in Atran, Boyer, and Sperber, taking RT even further and making relevance the essential principle of cognition itself as well as of the theological, philosophical, and scientific rationalisation built upon it. Without the work of the cognitive scientists and social anthropologists, Downes's breakthrough on religious language would not have been possible. Equally, without input from linguistics, the cognitive science and social anthropological approach to the inter-relationship between language and religion will, we would like to suggest, remain underdeveloped. We have here the basis for further interdisciplinary research into the nature of religion involving linguistics and neighbouring sciences--as is illustrated in chapters 4, 5, 6 and 16, which explore the neuroscience of religion and religious language.

It is not that anthropologists and cognitive scientists are unaware of the importance of language for religion, but for one reason or another, language is not incorporated into their theory building, or at least not to the extent that it deserves. It is not simply a matter of incorporating hypotheses and claims about language and religion into abstract theoretical frameworks. We also need primary data, and analyses of the data, as in any ordinary scientific paradigm. This is why this edited volume aims to encourage the detailed exploration of the workings of the language element that is part and parcel of religious experience, practices, teachings, and organisations. None of this is unfamiliar across the organised study of religion in human affairs, but it is not, we think, clearly in focus within the cognitive perspective on religion as it stands at present. While CSR is important for the general framework and stance of our book, it is only indirectly represented in the chapters. The volume as a whole does not espouse any particular epistemological or methodological framework, but it does take for granted rationally and empirically testable methodologies that enquire into the nature of the human mind-body embedded in society and culture (and potentially, though this is not the focus here, politics). There are two dimensions—on the one hand, theory building, or better, speculative hypothesis formation, and on the other hand, detailed data description and analysis. The overarching focus of attention is the human mind, studied in several disciplines at different levels of description. In one way or another, cognitive science, neuroscience, sociology, and anthropology are all concerned with thoughts, beliefs, feelings, interaction, and communication: and thus also with language. Linguistics needs to take account of what these disciplines say. Equally, linguistics needs to feed back into these disciplines. From within linguistics it is the relatively recent branch of cognitive linguistics that is most promising, alongside the theory of speech acts and various techniques of discourse analysis. As will be seen, the cognitive theory of metaphor is particularly important for studying religious conceptualisation.[1]

At the present time, what ritual does to or with the mind is only beginning to be understood. Though the centre of gravity in the present collection of research papers is human cognition, there is no programmatic adherence to CSR as a research paradigm. One reason for this is that the question of human language seems as yet not well theorised within that paradigm. What we want to do in the present work is to open a space in which the relationship between language and religion—a relationship so obvious that in some disciplines it has been overlooked—is opened up for probing research from a broad cognitive perspective that includes, as cognition studies should, a neurological perspective. This has meant that the sociological perspectives are not intensively represented in the chapters. But this does not mean they are in principle excluded, since the cognitive-linguistic perspective certainly includes and necessitates grounding in context—and thus perforce in social experience, structure, and process.

2.3 Religious ritual

Collectively recognised rituals probably emerge within populations over lengthy time periods as a result of largely unreflective practice and intersubjective feedback. Dennett (2006) suggests that 'folk religions' emerged in early human history and were elaborated and codified only under appropriate conditions in which the human cognitive capacity for 'reflection' emerged. Some such process leads to a core of repeated but slowly changing practices that 'work' for human minds and communities. This is approximately the view taken by cognitive anthropologists such as Boyer (2001) and Sperber (1994, 1996, 2000, 2006). Boyer, Dennett, and others seeking to explain the spread of religious practices and beliefs elaborate Dawkins's (1976, 1989) notion of the 'meme'—which can apply to the transmission of religious belief or practice. For Dawkins there is a strict analogy with biological genes: cultural memes transmit themselves by blind replication, with random mutations accounting for evolutionary change. Sperber, while endorsing an evolutionary perspective, has challenged the strict replication model, arguing instead that some patterns transmit better than others because they have a cognitively better fit with stable and perhaps innate properties of the human brain-mind. Using a different metaphorical model, he has hypothesised that cultural (e.g. religious) practices spread 'epidemiologically' and that to do so they not only copy existing ones but also cognitively latch onto existing properties of the human mind-brain (Sperber 1994, 1996, 2000, 2006; cf. also Boyer 2001; Downes 2011 and present volume chapter 4). It is important to note that ideological spread is not only a matter of individual cognition. Social factors such as group identity, power, and control are also likely to be involved; these also involve the structures and processes of the human mind.

Within anthropology, ritual has relatively recently been re-scrutinised under the banner of cognitive science (see Seaquist 2006; Whitehouse and Laidlaw 2007)—but with hardly any study of the language component of ritual. There have been two related but rival theories in CSR, which we will consider now, before moving on to suggesting a framework within which language is more fully integrated.

Let us start with the theory expounded in Lawson and McCauley (1990) and McCauley and Lawson (2002). Conceptual representations of gods—'culturally postulated supernatural agents' or 'CPS-agents'—include the attribution to CPS-agents of agency, a mind, and the ability to read the minds of others. These attributes, it is argued, come from cognitive mental abilities that humans possess naturally, and attribute to other humans: agency, mind reading, or 'theory of mind' (Baron-Cohen 1995; Tomasello 1999). What humans attribute to their conspecifics they also attribute to their CPS-agents. This explanation is accepted by other CSR theorists. But how do we model agency? Interestingly, the main basis of their 'action representation system' is analogous to linguistic theories, especially cognitive-linguistic theories, of sentence structure. These are theories that model grammatical structure in relation to generalised schematic representations of action. In the simplest form, such schemas (also known as templates, frames, or scripts) consist of slots (or 'roles') with the labels *agent, patient* (the impacted entity), and *instrument*. This technical idea goes back to the work of computer scientists working in AI (Minsky, Schank, Abelson, and others). Among linguists and philosophers of language the idea has been elaborated by Dowty, Halliday, and Chomsky (whose term is 'theta roles'). Fillmore's 'semantic frames' (1982) are actually cognitive entities, and are important for the development of cognitive linguistics. Essentially, Lawson and McCauley claim that these are natural structures that are analogous to roles and relations in ritual forms; rituals are *like* sentences.

Linguistic structures go far beyond agent-instrument-patient structures, but this is the one applied by Lawson and McCauley to rituals. They propose that rituals are like ordinary actions and further propose to treat rituals as a single ritual and a single action—then, in a highly questionable move, they propose to reduce a single ritual action to a single *sentence* in English (main clause possibly plus subordinate clauses), which they call the 'action sentence'. For one thing, this move leads to overlooking entirely the fact that rituals include sentences (actually, utterances); sentences are integral parts of the action and go unanalysed in this approach. Incidentally, the sentence structure-action structure relation is probably the reverse, in the sense that actions certainly are cognised in terms of agent, patient, instrument, and so forth. But it is non-linguistic action structure whose conceptualisation informs the structure that appears in lexico-grammar. These are issues that need to be clarified within the CSR framework.

The main point of the Lawson-McCauley analysis may stand, however. Their point is that the human understanding of rituals uses the natural cognitive action schemas used in ordinary non-ritual life—with the crucial difference that a culturally postulated supernatural agent, or some human agent associated with one such, can fill one of the conceptual slots. On this basis, Lawson and McCauley build a theoretical typology of ritual that we need not go into here. What is interesting from our point of view is that the Lawson and McCauley model does not analyse the language element that is part and parcel of rituals (we do not mean 'the language of ritual' in some metaphorical sense here) they examine. Yet the ritual actions they examine are almost always accompanied by, in fact integrated with, linguistic ritual formulae, as Rappaport recognised (1979, pp. 202–206). Most importantly, many such ritual linguistic formulae are in fact actions—speech acts, the theory of which is well developed in linguistics. Although Lawson and McCauley (1990) acknowledge that 'some anthropologists and historians of religion have found Austin's [speech act] theory suggestive enough to use it in their analyses of the language of ritual systems'(p. 51) and briefly discuss a study by Ray (1973) looking at the performative use of language in Dinka and Dogon religious practices, they clearly distance themselves from treating language 'as action' and opt to look at it rather 'as the communication of information' (Lawson and McCauley 1990, p. 52). Contrariwise, McNamara (2009, pp. 208–210) as well as McNamara and Giordano (chapter 5 this volume) give a crucial role to speech acts within a neuroscientific account, as does Downes (chapter 4 this volume) within what is in many respects a CSR framework.

The rival to the Lawson-McCauley theory is the 'modes of religiosity' theory, developed by the social anthropologist Harvey Whitehouse (1995, 2000, 2004). In this theory a distinction is made between high-intensity ritual, which has high impact on individual subjectivity, and the 'exegetic' mode, which communicates beliefs considered as propositions. This distinction emerges in two types of religious manifestation: doctrinal types in which ritual is frequent but has low subjective arousal alongside publicly verbalised doctrine; and 'imagistic' forms, where ritual is infrequent but highly arousing, and exegesis is individually generated. Now, while Lawson and McCauley agree with Whitehouse that there are two attractor modes— low frequency/high arousal imagistic mode on the one hand and on the other hand high frequency/low arousal doctrinal mode—the divergence concerns the motivation of frequency. It may be that this is more a matter of emphasis and perspective, but the difference appears to be that Whitehouse starts from frequency: low frequency leads to high-arousal, high 'sensory pageantry' (the term used by Lawson and

McCauley) ritual practices, while high frequency leads to low-arousal, low sensory input ritual. Both are regarded as assuring transmission of the ritual and religious knowledge. Contrariwise, the Lawson-McCauley model starts from their 'ritual form' hypothesis: whether of you have high 'sensory pageantry' depends on whether the special actor fills the agent or the patient (or instrument) slot in the action model of ritual (outlined above).

These two rival theories, important though they are, for theorising the wide variation of ritual forms within a unified framework of similarity, leave out systematic analysis of language. True, Lawson and McCauley (1990, chapter 3) discuss linguistics and mention cognitive linguistics, but their theory takes linguistics as *a model for* the theory of symbolic-cultural systems, including religious ritual, not as a means of investigating language as *integral to* such systems, as surely it is in the case of ritual. Inclusion of language as part of religious thought and behaviour could alter the entire theoretical framework; excluding it seriously limits our understanding of religious ritual.

We need not go into further detail here. The point is to note that while they are both grounded in plausible and well-established cognitive psychology, both theories seem to be incomplete, in two respects. First, both the Lawson-McCauley theory and the Whitehouse theory, whatever their differences, seem to regard both ritual modes (the doctrinal and the imagistic) primarily as serving the function of transmission. But this is not the only hypothesis one might propose to explain ritual. A different approach might be to consider rituals as having a function *in themselves*, independently of exegesis, doctrine and even of credal commitment to a supernatural being, in other words, independently of any transmission of theological *information*.[2] Perhaps rituals are intrinsically self-rewarding, mood-changing, and even addictive. Such factors would in themselves explain the self-replication of ritual forms. Second, neither the Lawson-McCauley nor the Whitehouse approaches give any analytic attention at all to the involvement of language in rituals, whether high- or low-frequency/pageantry. Consider the following points. The two modes involve divergent uses of language, qualitatively and quantitatively. If rituals are self-rewarding, as just suggested, then ritual *language* would, in this view, require detailed investigation. Language is certainly not simply for transmission of *information*, as is well known from the study of speech acts, literary genres, and rhetoric, as well as from linguistic pragmatics. Further, and most significantly, language in ritual is not just an add-on but constitutive: certain rituals do not work if certain prescribed words are not used in the right way. The choice of words is not arbitrary, since the words and the grammatical constructions they appear in are formulated because of their cognitive and pragmatic effects. If the words are not 'right' in this sense, then the relevant cognitive and pragmatic effects are not produced (processed in the mind of participants). One example of this is analysed by Chilton and Cram in chapter 16 of this volume, and in a similar vein Kopytowska in chapter 17 discusses the performative potential of both linguistic and visual sequences in mediatised religious practices.

In general, anthropology has been restricted in accounting for the role of language in religion and religious ritual by using theoretical notions of language indirectly as a model or analogy for myth and ritual. A lot depends on the model of language assumed—if language is a code, then religions, myths, and rituals are treated as codes to be deciphered. McCauley and Lawson have assumed a version of Chomsky's transformational-generative grammar, so they look for generative rules and 'transformations'. This is not the central problem, however. Rather the mistake is to think of religious practices and doctrines as 'like' language rather than as involving language as a constituent element.

2.4 Religious ritual: A cognitive language-based account

Approaching religion in its various manifestations from the point of view of linguistics, particularly a discourse-oriented linguistics, three major types of discourse are salient across religious traditions and over their historical development: ritual, sacred text, and exegesis. To be sure, there are sub-genres that stand out, for example, sermons and related kinds of indoctrination and exhortation, as well as public and private prayer in its various forms. Here we take a brief look at ritual, which on various grounds seems fundamental and in all likelihood historically prior.

Here we can only sketch a linguistic and discourse-analytic hypothesis. Ritualised behaviour (not necessarily the same thing as socially coordinated ritual) is observable across species, is frequently related to bonding behaviour, is often an exaptation of evolved behaviours, and is some kind of communication to other members of the species (cf. Sørensen 2003, p. 215). This need not imply a very early evolution underlying such behaviour in all animals where it seems to occur; it could have evolved independently in a similar pattern, but for different reasons (cf. Boyer and Liénard 2006, p. 18).[3] In obsessive-compulsive disorder (OCD), it is not primary but a response to fear; in cultural rituals, it is most probably group bonding. Even the cautious view offers ritualised bonding behaviour as an evolved biological basis on which to build a hypothesis about specifically human forms of ritual. Since humans are uniquely a symbolising species that has uniquely developed language, anthropologists should expect language to play a major role in ritual behaviour and in religious ritual in particular. What is needed is more detailed investigation of not only the involvement of the language capacity itself but of the details of language structure that are involved.

Language would become intrinsic to ritual, conceivably beginning with emotional vocalisations (e.g. pain, pleasure, fear . . .) and group chanting (still essential in religious rituals), especially if one entertains the theory that 'musical' origins play at least some part in the evolution of language itself (cf. Hurford 2012, pp. 19–24, for a review). With the emergence of human language structure and function, repeated verbal formulae, associated with specific prosodic features, would become a feature of developed public ritual.[4] The distinctive feature of religious ritual is of course the involvement of CPS-agents. We have more to say on this below.

We turn briefly to the other two salient religious genres, sacred text and exegesis. Sacred texts appear in many religions. They may have developed initially as memorised oral genres of two possible kinds: narratives and/or moral or social prescriptions or laws, which may have developed in parallel with, or in interaction with, ritual. It is difficult to demonstrate in general terms that ritual precedes or follows the other genres, but it seems clear that in many cases the genres are combined at some stage, conceivably to fill out the social bonding function of ritual and possibly justify ritual performances themselves. Literacy would mark a qualitatively different stage in the role of narrative and prescription. Written text itself may appear mysterious: it is not self-evidently uttered by a present and perceptible speaker, nor is the time and place of utterance manifest, and initially it is the preserve of elites. With print technology, mass dissemination of central sacred texts, and texts related to them, creates further cognitive and social phenomena in the religious domain—consider the European religious expansions and conflicts of the Reformation period. The genre of exegesis can also be seen in terms of human linguistic and discursive competences. Humans possess meta-representational abilities that are facilitated further by certain structural properties of languages, which thus contribute to fixing them and disseminating them. It also seems likely that they emerge as a result of the human epistemic ability, the critical and questioning ability that invites response and justification. Again, these capacities are expanded and fixed by the structural and functional properties of languages. Further, the meta-representational and epistemic abilities result in the sort of speculative expansion, both logical and imaginative, that we call theology. Because one of the key structurally manifest functions of language has to do with commands and obligations (dependant of course on cognitively represented social structures and roles), there is overlap between such texts and the control of group norms, a form of social binding (and bounding) that ritual bonding cannot itself completely achieve.

So how might the supernatural agents get into a bonding ritual? Once the human language module enters the picture, a novel answer suggests itself. The human language ability is more than a predisposition to acquire the special structural characteristics (grammar) of human languages and their relation to conceptualisation (meaning). Human language ability is, before anything else, the ability to engage in dialogue; it is inherently oriented to communication with conspecifics. We may suppose there is a possibly innate template (or frame) for two-way human communication with which the very structure and meaning of languages are necessarily bound up—language is not a code simply for the sending of information but also for establishing, maintaining, and exploiting relationships. Human brains are built for speaking and hearing, for inferring what another speaker intends. Now, rituals are not monologues, they are dialogues in which people or their religious representatives address a CPS-agent and get messages or meanings back. In CSR terms, such ritual 'dialogues' are minimally counterintuitive: they are like the two-way communication that humans naturally engage in, but lack one feature, namely, the actual presence of an interlocutor. Since the interlocutor expected in the dialogue frame is not physically present, he or she has to be conjured up. That is to say, a supernatural agent—an interlocutor—has to be postulated, a collective cognitive process that may involve cognitive effects produced within the ritual (cf. Chilton and Cram, chapter 16 in this volume), or supplementary discourse such as sacred and exegetic texts within the discourse community that constitute the cultural postulation of agents process. The role of language and discourse here is clear, though non-linguistic cognitions are also engaged. Most kinds of the mental and vocal activity known as 'prayer' follow the same model, whether inside or outside ritual. Prayer may look one-sided to an observer; in the mind of a praying person, the activity of (silent or vocal) speaking or perhaps non-linguistic ideation ('feeling' a presence) is necessarily dialogic—it follows a cognitive template (frame) that all humans have and that is reinforced in daily social interchange. The virtual addressee in this frame also has a theory of mind, also reads the mind of the person praying or engaged in a ritual.

A number of other features of ritual viewed as bonding also follow from this approach. Unison in ritual is crucial: aligned focus, joint attention (also crucial for dialogue) that is not reciprocal among participants but is focussed on an action or object. The ritual 'dialogue' is not between human participants but between participants focussed in unison (musically, spatially, linguistically . . .) on a single action—thus replacing the normal speaking self as individual with a group as 'self', dialoguing with an absent speaker/hearer (who has to be made present, or 'proximised', as Kopytowska puts it in chapter 17 of this volume). Losing of the self here in this sense involves alignment of cognitive states in spatially aligned brains and bodies and comes with altered affect—an embodied condition created physically and physiologically, perhaps minimally in restrained cultures, ecstatically in others. This linguistically based account seems to correspond with McNamara's theory of religious states of mind in which the routine sense of agentive self is suspended. We note, further, that this approach implies that ritual itself may, in some cases at least, be the source of concepts of supernatural agents, preceding religious statements in doctrine or theology, individually or collectively (cf. Sørensen 2007, p. 290, for a similar suggestion).

3 RELIGION IN THE BRAIN: NEUROSCIENCE AND RELIGION

Unlike Barrett (2011), who is sceptical of collaboration between CSR and neuroscience, the editors of the present volume take the view that neuroscientific research into religion, and into the involvement of language in religion and cognition, can be fruitfully shared. William James's *Varieties of Religious Experience* (1902/1982) is testimony to the fruitfulness of thinking across disciplines in the pursuit of an understanding of what human religions are about. Relating religious experience and activity to the brain is an enormously complex and hazardous business, but it is one that is unavoidable if we wish to understand our species. In this section we briefly and inadequately consider first some questions of method and second some of the indicators as to the nature of religion, which, like it or not, has links with pathologies of the mind-brain.

3.1 Reflections on methods

The relationship between mind and brain is not something we can treat with the detail it deserves, but in general terms our position is that mind is *supervenient* on the material brain (for the terms 'supervenient' and 'supervenience' see the philosopher Donald Davidson 1970 and for their use in linguistics see Jaszczolt 2009 and Chilton 2014). There cannot be a mind without a brain upon which it is supervenient, but this does not mean that minds and thoughts and feelings are in a simple way 'reducible' to neurons. We might put it like this, avoiding the pitfalls of the hardware/software analogy that is sometimes used. The brain is an astonishing complex of neurons that is integrated with the rest of the body and that is constantly active. This activity, varying over time and between individuals, and capable of a degree of self-monitoring, is the 'mind'.

From a methodological point of view, it is possible to postulate three related levels of analysis. On one level, we have the self-monitoring mind, the phenomenological level; here we can become aware of events in the mind, including reasonings, emotions, sensations, and intuitions. We need this level especially for linguistic analysis of meanings as well as for non-linguistic mental phenomena. On a second level, there are theoretical cognitive sciences such as CSR, where inferences are made, hypotheses formulated, and experiments proposed—in principle this should be the in light of the currently best available scientific findings and theories, including, as we have emphasised, those developed in linguistics. At the third level, the findings from the phenomenological and theoretical levels may be mapped onto neural regions, connectivities, and biochemical transmission systems. To understand how the religious mind works, we need not only to bring in the study of religious language, we need to take into account these different levels of scientific analysis. Probably most scholars and scientists engaged in investigating human language would take something like this position.

The term 'neurotheology' has been used to designate neurological investigations of religious experience (see for example, d'Aquili and Newberg 1999; Newberg 2010; the term was first used by Aldous Huxley). Some researchers using this label regard theology and neuroscience as equally valid fields of enquiry, the one capable of contributing to the other. Others would not agree that the two fundamentally different kinds of thinking and world view are totally reconcilable and would emphasise differences. This would be so for those who accept equal but separate jurisdictions for theology and science, as is the case for the evolutionary biologist S. J. Gould's (1999) insistence on 'non-overlapping magisteria'. Others, scientists and theologians alike, would claim superiority for one or the other. The term 'neurotheology' is also problematic because it may give the impression that it refers to a kind of theology.[5] On this point we remain neutral editorially. What is important is that a broad range of research avenues are given space. It is already possible to see points of contact emerging among the three methodological and disciplinary levels evoked above—the phenomenological, the cognitive-theoretical, and the neurological. Our aim in this volume is to show how language needs to be integrated with the phenomenon under investigation; linguistics, and in particular cognitive linguistics, needs to be incorporated at all three levels.

We will not attempt a comprehensive review of neuroscientific work on religious experience, but we will select a few salient studies by way of contextualising chapters 5 and 6, as well as references in other chapters of our volume. McNamara (2006) and McNamara and Giordano in chapter 5 of the present volume provide a some-what wider overview. It is important to tread cautiously in this area and it is too early in the history of the field to be confident of findings and their interpretation. Brain imaging and lesion studies point towards the involvement of multiple neural regions and networks, though it is the case that certain physical and psychiatrically evident conditions may be particularly implicated. All sciences that have been con-cerned with religion as well as other evidence-based disciplines—cognitive science, linguistics, history, sociology, anthropology, and archaeology, for example—all point to complex involvement of brain regions involving self-awareness, metarepresenta-tion, spatial and temporal cognition, linguistic communication, stimulation and cre-ativity, and social intelligence. And very likely much more.

3.2 Neurological evidence from brain disorders

The relationship between pathologies of the brain-mind and religion has received attention from clinically oriented investigators, from research psychologists, and from neuroscientists. There are some reasonably well-established associations.

One important area of neurological research has been temporal lobe epilepsy (TLE), which has historically been associated with hyper-religiosity. The neurologist Norman Geschwind is well known for describing the symptoms of temporal lobe epilepsy, one of which, across cultures, involves intense religious ideation and emo-tions, including ecstatic states (Waxman and Geschwind 1975; Geschwind 1979, 1983). Ramachandran used semantically diverse words to test the sensitivity of TLE patients to religious stimuli (Ramachandran and Blakeslee 1998). TLE patients were significantly more emotionally responsive when they read religion-related words than when they read words with sex-related meanings or words with neither kind of meaning ('neutral'). Persinger has (controversially) reported that experimental stimulation of the temporal lobes of healthy individuals produces religious thoughts and feelings (Persinger 1983, 1987, 2003; for further case studies and summary, see McNamara 2009, pp. 82–93).

In individuals diagnosed as schizophrenic, religiousness appears to be heightened and more frequent than in the general population. Such individuals frequently expe-rience hallucinations, delusions, and what is termed 'disordered thought' with reli-gious content (for references see McNamara 2009, pp. 94–99). One widely accepted finding is increased dopamine activity, found predominantly in the left hemisphere sub-cortical structures including the amygdala, the hippocampus, and the left tem-poral lobe, as in TLE. Both conditions also show hypofunction of the prefrontal cortex, which would normally regulate dopamine activity. Dysfunction of the right hemisphere and consequent over-functioning of the left hemisphere is suggested by many studies (McGilchrist 2010; Crow 2000). Schizophrenics tend to have less asym-metry and also are vulnerable to language and discourse problems. This evidence—far from conclusive of course—strongly suggests a speculative hypothesis in which both language and religiousness have some kind of connection with the positive symptoms of schizophrenia in the human brain. Bulbulia (2009, cited in McNamara

2009, p. 97) points out that prefrontal abnormality may be the cause of source-monitoring defects (discussed by Cosmides and Tooby 2000) and suggests that if source-monitoring is not working, religious confabulation may take over. Sufferers may fail to recognise that words or thoughts are internally generated by the self and interpret them as coming from an external source.

OCD is frequently mentioned by cognitive anthropologists (Boyer 2001; Boyer and Liénard 2006, 2008; Fiske and Haslam 1997) as a human trait underlying ritualised behaviour observed in developmental stages, pathological mental conditions, and some religious practices. The question arises whether the evidence for the hyperactivity of particular brain regions and neurotransmitters in certain conditions that manifest unusually high rates of religiosity also points to the same biological processes in 'normal' religious activity, whatever that may be. Repetition is certainly a feature of both religious ritual and OCD, as also is a preoccupation with contagion, purity, danger, order, and boundary maintenance. There is a long tradition of anthropological interpretation of religious rituals and rules, for example, Mary Douglas (1966/2002), who herself was inspired by William James. Religious obsessions vary in frequency with cultural context (see Tek and Ulug 2001; noted by McNamara 2009, p. 98). The phenomenology of OCD exhibits structure that corresponds to the structures of certain kinds of religious ideation and ritual. Sufferers experience intrusive thoughts, including words and phrases that are extremely distressing for a variety of complex reasons, including cultural ones: taboo words, gods, devils, being dangerous to others (especially kin), being unclean. Extremely relevant are thoughts of being accused by a god and being 'sinful'. It is important not to overlook the fact that such thoughts can come in verbal form, including 'hearing voices', for example, the voice of God speaking direct to the subject: 'you are a bad person'.[6] Boyer and Liénard (2006) propose a general model of ritualised actions, including OCD, childhood rituals, life-stage (e.g. pregnancy) rituals, and cultural (including religious) rituals. They propose a common neurological and cognitive background, suggesting that cultural rituals are derivative from evolved structures relating to threat detection, and explain the features of ritual (iteration, etc.) as anxiety-reducing mechanisms that 'swamp' the working memory, which is generating fearsome intrusive thoughts ('I am dirty', 'I am a sinner', and so forth). In this perspective religious ritual and other cultural rituals would be exploiting, that is, adapting pre-existing neural circuitry (that can become pathological). Language is deeply involved in both the intrusive-thought phase and the compulsive ritual calming phase, in the form of strictly prescribed repeated word sequences (subvocal or spoken aloud) and in specific word avoidance.

Studies of mental conditions, such as those roughly summarised above, are highly suggestive and prompt important lines of enquiry. Studies of religious states and activities in the brains of individuals regarded as normal are also starting to emerge and are represented in the present volume. A recent example is the model of religious experience and activity developed by Patrick McNamara (2009). His model is compatible with many of the findings just summarised and is also significant for the way in which it seeks to integrate linguistic aspects. McNamara's review (McNamara 2009, pp. 214–215) of the 'ritual form' models of Whitehouse (2004), Lawson and

McCauley (1990), and McCauley and Lawson (2002), while generally positive, concludes that they do not provide answers to questions about the functions of ritual. McNamara's own approach is framed in terms of the neuropsychology of the self and social-pragmatic behaviours. The model developed in McNamara (2009; see also chapter 5 present volume) holds that religious practices derive their function and value from a mental 'decentring' process in which attention to, and even control of, self is lowered while the perceived presence of a deity is heightened. In this account the decentred self is in a 'suppositional space' (McNamara 2009, p. 50) in which it may search memory for a representation of an ideal self. It may be thought, however, that this stage occurs only in special cases,[7] and with institutional and cultural prompting. Such special cases may be manifest in mystical traditions, such as the *via negativa* in Christianity—a case examined in terms of McNamara's model by Hollingsworth (2015). A modification of McNamara's full model might be that stage 2 is followed by input from institutional agents or text, either present in the ritual or in text (ritually recited, read, or memorised in solitary meditation). Such a model is suggested by Schjoedt et al. (2013), who claim that religious states involve depletion of the frontal cortex executive control circuits, making the subject susceptible to input that is epistemically unmonitored.

McNamara's theory is correlated with convergent evidence from the brain research literature. The neurobiology of the self is taken by McNamara to be central. Collating clinical and neuroimaging findings, he proposes that self and self-agency concepts, volition, and executive function in general, are subserved predominantly by widely distributed systems in the *right* hemisphere: the orbital prefrontal cortex, anterior cingulate, insula, the anterior temporal lobes and hippocampus (McNamara 2009, pp. 60–73). These areas actually have a multiplicity of functions, and research into them varies in its conclusions. In addition to what McNamara says, we might suggest that the right hippocampus could be especially important because of its role in the self's spatial orientation, episodic memory, which underlies self-story telling, and its links with the limbic system. It is also relevant to note that the right anterior temporal lobe is homologous with the left-hemispheric language processing centres; both are recognised to be involved in semantic processing, though probably of different kinds. The right anterior temporal lobe is also reported to be involved with social knowledge and behaviours. As we have already noted, the temporal lobes are closely associated with unusual religiosity (in epileptic seizures).

McNamara surveys a wide range of neuroimaging findings, looking for convergent evidence relating to anatomical brain areas that appear to be involved in religious states of mind in religious people without medical diagnoses. His conclusion is of considerable interest: the same brain sites seem to be involved in religious states of mind, whether we are looking at 'healthy' mind/brains or at mind/brains with psychiatric disorders. Combining these three surveys (self systems, clinical religiosity, 'normal' religiosity), there seems to be strong indicative evidence for a network that includes prefrontal cortex, temporal lobe, limbic system, and the dopaminergic systems. There is a marked tendency for increases in activation to be in the right hemisphere.

From the linguistic point of view, McNamara emphasises speech acts specific to religious ritual and other forms of religious practice, because the focus on self-transformation in a social context requires some kind of mental adjustment of intentionality in relation to the external world. He also mentions politeness phenomena (Brown and Levinson 1987), and the use of pronouns (in effect the linguistic theory of deixis), and regards the use of language for certain kinds of narrative, analysed on the basis of Propp's (1928/1968) approach, as central to the way in which religious rituals create a context for decentring and recentring of the self. Religious myths are treated as linguistically mediated narratives to which are attributed explanatory power for questions about reality. In the framework outlined by McNamara and Giordano in the present volume, chapter 5, the pragmatics of speech acts remains crucial, especially in ritual. McNamara and Giordano also introduce into the 2009 theory a new emphasis on the use of metaphor and symbols,[8] which they suggest are used in ways that bind individuals to 'sacred values'. They make connections with some theologians who have discussed religious metaphor, as well as with the cognitive-semantic theory of metaphor—connections that are dealt with in detail in chapter 3 of this volume by Feyaerts and Boeve. In fact the whole phenomenon of metaphor is crucial to the theme of the present volume. Metaphor is fundamental to language and meaning; it is not just ornamental.

3.3 Brain, consciousness, and culture

Within the field of the brain sciences, the importance of metaphor for the human mind has been recognised by the psychiatrist, neuroscientist, and literary scholar Iain McGilchrist (2010, and this volume chapter 6). His view of metaphor is broadly consistent with the cognitive-linguistic approach but is set within a wider and much more detailed neurological account of human consciousness. McGilchrist (2010) amasses a very large amount of evidence from neuroscientific research, and also from philosophy and the study of cultural forms, to make the argument that the human brain is characterised by the specialisation of its two interconnected hemispheres, and the variable relationships between them in human experience and relationships. Summarising crudely, what is at issue is attention—the way one perceives and understands the world, the phenomenologically different 'perspectives' on reality that it is possible for human neural systems to give rise to. The left hemisphere[9] predominantly serves narrow manipulative focus, analytic and propositional thinking, and abstraction. The right hemisphere serves broad attention beyond the manipulative action space, and tends to be holistic, rooted in the body, connected with emotions, empathic, and relational. Language is generally thought of as a left-hemispheric system, because of the known role in language processing of Broca's and Wernicke's areas in the left temporoparietal cortex. But it is essential to bear in mind that using and understanding language communicatively, and in context, depends on massive parallel processing in the right. Any use of language, especially understanding, is innovative and creative to some degree and requires right-hemisphere processing; linguistic 'creativity' of the special kind presumably has a particular role for the right hemisphere.

McGilchrist relates metaphor processing predominantly to right-hemisphere systems (McGilchrist 2010, and this volume chapter 6), but Coulson's (2008) survey of the evidence is inconclusive. It may be that some of the unclarity comes from varying definitions of metaphor, and conceivably there are differences in hemispheric input depending on different types and complexity of metaphor, in particular the degree to which an expression is conventionalised in usage and has become opaque. In chapter 6 of the present volume, McGilchrist reviews a wide range of neuroscientific evidence that indicates that the right-hemisphere processing model for metaphor is correct, when the expressions in question are not totally conventionalised. The dividing line between so-called 'dead' and 'live' metaphors is in any case unclear. And experiments by the psycholinguist Ray Gibbs provide evidence that even apparently conventionalised expressions such as 'he grasped the idea' are not rendered wholly abstract by use, but do activate motor routines, here that of grasping with the hand (Gibbs and Matlock 2008). And as ordinary linguistic experience indicates, such supposedly 'dead' metaphors can easily be resurrected—and in such cases the likelihood would seem to be that the right hemisphere would be involved.

The broad contrasts between left and right hemisphere neuro-phenomenology may shed light on the 'modes of religiosity' strand in cognitive science of religion discussed above. The exegetic and doctrinal strands of religiosity are self-evidently ratiocinative and verbal, while 'high pageantry ritual' is likely to engage typically right-hemispheric systems, such as presencing, empathy, embodiment, and multi-sensoriality. The left-hemispheric and right-hemispheric roles in religious phenomena are indeed likely to be variable. For example, McGilchrist (2010) relates varying dominance of the left hemisphere over the right hemisphere to cultural change, cultural movements, and cultural intellectual styles. Relatively rapid historical shifts that have involved religious movements, such as the Reformation in sixteenth-century Europe, may have involved large-scale shifts to relatively stronger use of left-hemispheric systems of attention and focus; such a shift is even more likely for the Enlightenment period. Further, such an approach is fruitful for examining different types of religious behaviour, individual and collective. If one considers different types of religious ritual and different components within ritual, it is clear that some are more verbal and analytic, typically involving reading of and commentary on sacred writings, verbalised prayer, expository sermons. One might expect particular activation of left-hemisphere systems in such practices, while the right hemisphere would be expected to be more active in liturgical practices that involve more body-based, music-based, dance-based, posture- and gesture-based activities, while the language used would be integrated with these behaviours, would be more metaphorical and sense-image based.

4 LINGUISTIC COMPONENTS OF RELIGIOUS EXPERIENCE AND ACTIVITY IN A COGNITIVE AND NEUROLOGICAL PERSPECTIVE

The structures and functions of languages involve many subtle features that are recruited in religious ideation and ritual. At all levels of structure they are interwoven with many independently functioning, genetically evolved, and culturally developed modules, and at the same time serve social functions embodied in social cognition, in both cases associated with emotional circuits.

4.1 The question of evolution

In the present perspective the biggest and most general question is the relationship between religion as a human behaviour and language itself. From the evolutionary perspective, one may wonder whether religion preceded language or the other way round. We make no attempt here to give a complete review. There are some obvious possibilities, however. Language either preceded religion, providing a platform for an essentially cultural development, or the other way around, religion providing the basis for language. In the former case, one might adduce the fact that religions across cultures have historically required language for expression and dissemination. It is, however, arguable that religion, especially in its socially coordinated ritual form, relied initially on symbolic signalling, rather than the language capability of Homo sapiens. In this sense, it is possible that religion preceded language proper, especially if symbolic communication is a necessary precursor of language (Deacon 1997; see also Hurford 2012, pp. 564–566). This comes very close to a third possibility—that religion and language co-evolved. Knight (1998) argues that imagined beings emerge within ritualised symbolic signalling in mating rituals under reproductive pressures, though he does not discuss religious ritual as such (pp. 80–81). He further argues that this provides conditions of trust under which conventionalised language systems can be socially established and override 'machiavellian' behaviours. However, this argument seems to depend on assuming language to be a system for transmitting information (how can one trust the transmitter?) rather than as per se having a socially bonding function from the outset. The latter point does not rule out the possibility that ritualised behaviour developed socially coordinated forms that co-evolved with language, but ritualised behaviour need not be the source of language evolution. We cannot consider the possible evolutionary complexities here. What we do suggest, however, is that greater scientific consensus on the question of religion, ritual, and language evolution can be served by deeper investigation by researchers into the obvious involvement of language in religious systems of thought and behaviour.

Linguistic structures—grammar, lexical items, semantic schemas—make it possible for humans to communicate non-real representations for forward planning and for considering alternative cooperative actions, as well as such 'things' as possible locations (of things one wants, has lost, etc.), possible enemies and allies, and non-present realities and imaginings such as memories and dreams. Moreover, language is inherently social and collective, while at the same time the vehicle for all manner of mental representations non-present and non-instantiated things and happenings to spread in populations, as well as to mutate over time. Linguistic communication would involve mental simulacra of objects already experienced by sense perception and stored in memory. But there is more—cognitive fluidity, which comes in the various forms examined in a large part of this book, metaphor, allegory (see Unger 2012 and chapter 13 in the present volume), and conceptual integration across several modalities. These abilities are natural to biological and culturally evolved humans, and there is ample evidence that these abilities form the conceptual launch pad for mental representations, and for associated activities, that go well beyond sensory stimulation in the here and now.

4.2 Language, religious acts, and religious institutions

Taking a broad view of the human language capacity, there are two aspects that stand out: one has to do with action in and on the world, the other to do with sharing mental representations of the present world and conceived other worlds. This corresponds to Searle's (2010) distinction (pp. 15–16) between the 'conative and volitional faculties' and the 'cognitive faculties'. Searle also distinguishes a third faculty: imagination, the products of which are not expected to either match the world or change it but are recognised as fictions. While the existence of such a faculty would raise interesting questions about its possible relationship to the religious mind, we focus here on Searle's first two faculties. In this subsection we briefly consider some implications for research on the 'conative and volitional' aspects of language in the constitution of religious activity. In the next subsection we consider the representational dimension of religious activity (what Searle and others call 'cognitive', in a narrower sense than we use it in this Introduction). We should not, of course, think that these two dimensions are entirely separate.[10]

Since religions involve action, that is, ritual action (setting aside religiously motivated non-religious activity for now), we need to consider in what sense language constitutes action. What are speech acts? Every utterance, including those making statements about the world, are acts in a broad sense. But we also make utterances to create or modify social relationships and social functions. Austin (1962) distinguished locutionary acts (simply uttering words), illocutionary acts (the social force of the utterance, e.g. orders, promises), and perlocutionary effects (psychological consequences, e.g. shame, fervour . . .). Searle subsequently (1969, 1995, 2010) identified five kinds of illocutions: *assertives, directives, commissives, expressives*, and *declarations*. Declarations are always performative (a term introduced by Austin 1962), in the sense that, under the socially accepted conditions, their utterance per se actually creates social realities—for example, social relationships of membership, solidarity, authority (e.g.to nominate, to sentence, to excommunicate . . .). It is remarkable that language can and routinely does create social reality in this way, but the process is complex, since conditions have to be fulfilled (not everyone can sentence you to prison) and complex chains of prior speech acts are involved. Among philosophers of language, Searle's work in particular brings out this central role of language and focuses on the cognitive environment, especially intentionality.

The key point here is that the speech act potential of human language is fundamental to human social behaviour, particularly in the construction of social institutions of all kinds. Following the CSR line of reasoning, we have here a basic human capacity that is transferred (recruited, or exploited) in religious modes of behaviour and cognition, in two senses. First, the generation and maintenance of religious institutions in any culture depend on speech acts of declaration. Second, because speech acts have a quasi-magical power in creating social realities, they are recruited or exploited in religious acts of transformation. Speech acts are central to religious ritual: they produce and maintain as 'real' specific kinds of interpersonal relationships, including relationships with a personalised supernatural agent. Spirits and gods are addressed as speech-act understanding humans: *veni creator spiritus*. This kind of act is central to the making-present of deities and divine presences. Further, it may be hypothesised that this reality-creating function of speech acts is, in religious institutional contexts, efficacious in quasi-magical pronouncements over objects, as well as over people, in ritual acts of object transformation. Below we suggest some ways in which speech act theory applies to religion and might be further researched.

Rituals in all religions involve several sequenced parts, speech acts, and genres; these cannot be reduced to a single sentence in the Lawson-McCauley fashion (discussed above). Examples are: listening to, and recitation of, sacred texts; collective recitation of creeds (coordinated collective assertions of individual belief); listening to sermons that exploit multiple persuasive techniques; and collective prayer in the form of requests. These conceptual gadgets (Boyer's term) are marked by specific religious lexis and grammar, whose cognitive and emotional effects require detailed analysis within an appropriate linguistic-theoretical framework. In religious ritual, speech acts function under the same natural principles as they do in non-religious discourse, but in highly distinctive ways (see for example, Evans 1963; Harris 1980; Wierzbicka 2001). We consider now some examples of religious speech acts, and there is further discussion in this volume, in particular by Downes (chapter 4) and by McNamara and Giordano (chapter 5).

Assertives are generally defined as committing their utterers to the truth of the propositions they assert—a fundamental presupposition of socialised human communication (Grice 1957; Habermas 1998, 2008), extended in religious ritual into recitations of 'beliefs' assertions for which the utterer may have none of the warrants expected in non-religious assertives.

The category of *directives* includes linguistic constructions conventionally understood as intended to cause a hearer to carry out some action. In languages they may be reflected in 'imperative' verb forms ('do what I say!'), but such forms are not necessarily used to make directives. They can be performed explicitly: 'I (hereby) request (beg, plead with you to . . .) help (save, aid, deliver . . .) us'. Religious directives can work in two directions: directed by believers to deity and the reverse. In collective and personal prayer, directives are frequent and addressed by participants to a supernatural agent, in the form of what appear to be orders, commands, requests, pleas, and related speech acts. An example is Christian petitionary prayer ('give us . . .', 'save us', 'come to us . . .', 'forgive me . . .'), discussed by Downes (2011, and chapter 4 this volume). Even humble petitions ('beseeching', for example) are a form of directive, since they are acts that are conative, that is, they attempt to get a supernatural agent to act in accordance with the wishes of the speaker. Directives work in the opposite direction also, in particular in sacred text and sermons, where religious participants are recipients of directives (commandments, orders, requests, and the like) issued by authoritative written material or by religious leaders.

Commissives are speech acts conventionally understood in relevant contexts to commit the speaker, speakers, or a religious leader representing them to a course of action or emotional stance. Making (or taking) a vow is a clear-cut case of the projection of an important public speech act (e.g. marriage vows) made before, that is, 'in the presence of', a supernatural agent as a means of reinforcement or sanction, since such an agent may be projected as both a witness and as a judge. These are often simultaneously vows *to* a deity, a kind of publicly witnessed transaction, performd on the basis of normal non-religious speech act behaviour in human societies.

Expressives in human societies are used to assert feelings and attitudes in a performative way: giving thanks, making apologies are such. This type of speech act, with the addressee being a deity, is projected in ritual acts of *praising* and *thanking*. 'We praise you, O lord' seems to be ritualised as a performative; the mere saying of the words, though they look like a simple assertion, is taken as an enacting of their referential meaning. Apologies, which ordinarily occur as part of a two-sided interaction ('I apologise'–'Don't worry about it!'), are speech acts playing an important role in reducing social conflict and enhancing social cohesion. This pattern is recruited in many religions, and in various forms, a deity or surrogate religious leader being substituted for an ordinary member of society. There is also a connection with the quasi-judicial projections already noticed, and with the imposition (including self-imposition) of penances, propitiations, and sacrifices. In religious practice this type of directive pair-structure manifests as formalised confession and absolution, whether collective or individual. Both the confession and absolution are performative productions of, and transformations of, religious 'realities' based on ordinary human social realities.

In everyday social life *declarations* have the job, under the appropriate social conditions, of changing the structure of everyday social reality. They do so by asserting a new social reality which is simultaneously created in the act of utterance. Searle (2010, p. 16) makes the strong claim that 'all of non-linguistic human institutional reality is created by Declaration'. Prototypical religious ritual examples are initiations, blessings, and consecrations of people and objects, which transform the status of both people and objects. They may frequently involve ritual actions, or the instrumental use of already sacred objects, such as wands or holy water. But, crucially, instrumental actions of this type are integrated with verbal action—speech acts. It is this combination that, religiously speaking, changes inanimate objects from one state to another.(cf. Chilton and Cram on transubstantiation, chapter 16 this volume). Further, such declarative acts depend on prior religious institutions that in turn depend on declarations, and are underpinned by other conditions. Generally, such acts have to be performed by an individual, e.g. a priest or shaman, who has been authorised more or less formally by declarative acts, thereby receiving 'deontic powers' (for this term, see Searle 2010). Receiving specific powers by declarations is normal also for the nomination of individuals (e.g. car park attendants, Presidents); this human practice is simply projected in religious institutions. Specific buildings and parts of buildings and a specific moment in a ritual sequence may be required (for more on deontic powers and status functions in the context of religious institutions see Kopytowska, chapter 17 in this volume).

4.3 Language, metaphor, and religious conceptualisation
4.3.1 Metaphor and blending: The basics

Metaphor is one of a group of cognitive abilities that have to do with conceptual transfer, merging, and association. That it is a cognitive ability peculiar to humans so far is known. What must be made clear is that it is not mere optional ornamentation but part of the way our minds work in the processes of literally *making* sense, whether empirically justifiable or not, and it is not, either, simply a device confined to literary creativity. But it is plausible to think that metaphor arose from the emergence of the capacity for what Mithen (1996) calls 'cognitive fluidity' in early modern humans some 100,000 years ago.

The precise neuro-cognitive mechanisms of metaphor are not yet known in detail. The central ideas in the cognitive modelling of metaphor proposed in CMT are straightforward, however. The emphasis is on cross-domain uni-directional mappings (in the logico-mathematical sense of the term): that is, homomorphisms from elements in one cognitive domain (the source domain, e.g. physical space) to elements in another (the target, e.g. time). The 'domains' here are experiential frames learned from the cultural environment (e.g. warfare, journeys, houses) or, more fundamentally, image schemas, particular those rooted in spatial cognition, navigation, and orientation (up-down, near-far, path-goal, inside-outside, etc.; see Johnson 1987; Mandler 2004). This is why metaphor is regarded as an aspect of the 'embodied mind': abstract ideas are cognitively constructed from bodily experiences (Lakoff 2003; Feldman and Narayanan 2004). In CMT the cross-domain mappings go in one direction: from the innate or learned schemas to conceptual domains that are underspecified, that is, highly abstract or vague. Mathematics and science use such cognitive tools instinctively (Lakoff and Núñez 2000), as do concepts in everyday discourse such as time, love, and others that have been extensively commented upon in CMT literature (e.g. Lakoff and Johnson 1980; Kövecses 1990). It is strongly suggested by CMT that humans uniquely possess a specialised ability for cognitive transfers of this kind, a possibly pre-linguistic ability. While Carruthers (2006, pp. 324–327) has questioned the existence of such a specialised pre-linguistic capacity, he does not deny the importance of metaphor in human creativity, simply arguing it can be accounted for by other cognitive processes and by the creative potential of language.

It was soon found that such mappings were partial and also more complex. Conceptual domains themselves contain complex and variable frame structure, and not all the potential elements are mapped metaphorically to a target domain.

Moreover, Fauconnier and Turner found many kinds of conceptual integration that were not binary projections from one domain to another but consisted of concepts projected from whole networks of conceptual domains into a conceptually integrated 'mental space' (Fauconnier 1994; Fauconnier and Turner 2002). Their conceptual blending theory (CBT), also referred to as conceptual integration theory, is generally concerned with analysing particular examples, though blends can be conventionalised and stored long term, as well as with grammatical and other formats that yield blends. Conceptual integration is not only linguistic; it may also involve a combination of linguistic and non-linguistic input sources. Fauconnier and Turner discuss the notion of 'material anchors' in cultural space for complex conceptual integration networks whose inputs come from many domains. Rituals themselves and objects, such as the bread used in Christian eucharist rituals, are such anchors. So are religious buildings, such as churches and cathedrals (Scott 2003; Fauconnier and Turner 2002, pp. 206–210).

While CMT offers static models, CBT claims to model dynamic conceptual integration by using a 'basic diagram', as exemplified in Antović's analysis of central concepts in Eastern Orthodox Christianity (chapter 15 in this volume). The basic diagram consists minimally of four spaces: two input spaces, a generic space, and the blend space. Mental spaces are currently active conceptualisations structured by frames. The input spaces are connected by lines representing 'cross-space mappings' between elements of each space. These mappings are partial conceptual correspondences of various types—role matches, identity of elements, cause-effect, analogy, and so forth. The generic space contains elements shared by the input spaces; each element in the generic space is linked back by two lines, one into each input space. In effect, the generic space represents a conceptual abstraction process. The fourth space, the blend space, is where conceptual integration of the two input spaces is represented as emerging as the mind processes the triggering material (a text, an utterance, visual images . . .). Not all conceptual material from the two inputs gets projected, and an element may go into the blend space without having a cross-space correspondence to the other input space. Large amounts of background knowledge may be involved.

How these kinds of cognitive fluidity, whether modelled by CMT or CBT, actually work at the neural level is not fully understood at the neural level. It is likely that right-hemisphere processes play some significant role, though the evidence is equivocal. Neural binding is assumed to take place, creating dynamic neural networks, especially in the case of cognitive blends when two representations may be synchronous, or closely consecutive, without a specified propositional relation relating them explicitly in conceptual-linguistic terms.

Given what has been discovered about cognitive fluidity and its presence in both linguistic and non-linguistic cognition, we would expect metaphor and conceptual integration to occur in religious speculation, ritual, and formal theology. This is indeed the case, as is indicated throughout this volume, especially those chapters assembled in Part II, which focuses on metaphor. While both metaphor and blending seems ubiquitous in religious discourse of all types, it must be noted that metaphors are used selectively and in all likelihood inhibit certain entailments potentiated by metaphorical mappings. Among the mappings selected, spatial input appears, not surprisingly, to be extremely important, and we conclude this section by offering a neurally based account of some typical religious conceptualisations.

4.3.2 Spatial cognition in religious metaphor: Toward a neural account

Previc (2006, 2009) links mental phenomena found in religion with spatial cognition and provides evidence to identify the specific neural and biochemical processes involved. What is of particular interest from our point of view is the potential for linking Previc's analysis of religiousness with the linguistic-conceptual system as modelled independently in cognitive linguistics.

The perception, attention, and motor systems of the human mind, the most salient of which is vision, involves what is generally termed peripersonal space and extrapersonal space. Previc (1998) argues for recognising two zones concerned with extrapersonal space, the focal-extrapersonal system and the action-extrapersonal. It is the action-extrapersonal system of the brain that enables humans to orient to, and navigate in, extrapersonal space to varying relative distances. It is an intrinsic part of Previc's claim that such orienting and navigating must to a degree require 'off-line' processing, in planning and thus in imagining. The focal pathway runs from the occipital cortex to the lateral inferior temporal cortex, with projections to frontal and parietal vision fields. The action system runs from occipital cortex medially through the temporal lobe, that is, through the regions close to the centre of the brain connecting with the hippocampus, limbic system, anterior cingulate, and orbitofrontal cortex. These connections underpin the associations between episodic memory and emotions. Parts of the system are involved in thinking about the future—metaphorically 'orienting to' time that is 'distant'. Metaphorical abstraction from physical distance, though he does not state it in quite this way, is part of Previc's argument for a close association between religiousness and spatial cognition. A further part of the association is the fact that more distant regions of the visual field correlate with the upper visual field. There are empirical observations linking upward eye movements even with tasks that are not overtly spatial (e.g. reasoning tasks and visual recall). Significantly, the ventral visual attention pathways are generally localised to the *left* hemisphere, as is abstract thought and the processing of language structure (though extensively connected to the right for encyclopaedic knowledge and contextual interpretation).

In biochemical terms, Previc (1998) makes a strong argument that the neural pathways involved in attention and activity oriented to extrapersonal space, upper visual fields, and 'distant' time depend on the neurotransmitter dopamine—as do highly motivated exploratory behaviour of all types, including those that are abstract. The other spatial zones, peripersonal space, and body-centred perception and activity are linked with different neurotransmitters, notably serotonin. Previc then offers empirical evidence showing that dopamine is elevated in the extrapersonal pathways in dreams and hallucinations as well as in the clinical disorders that exhibit hyperreligiosity—the ones referred to above, namely, mania, TLE, schizophrenia, and OCD. The final move is to argue for similarities in a range of religion-related motifs, for example, the prevalence cross-culturally of the association of upper space with the divine and depths with the diabolical. There is thus a detailed evidence base for connecting certain experiences and behaviours regarded as religious with certain aspects of spatial cognition, which is itself rooted in identifiable neuroanatomy and biochemistry.

Extending somewhat Previc's examples, it is worth noting the many ways in which the fundamental distinction between distant/upper space and proximal/lower space manifests itself in human religious artifacts. Height and distance are present in the vocabulary of verbal religious narrative, prayers, and invocation: gods are 'the most high', 'super-natural', dwell on mountain tops and in the sky; holy men travel long distances and up mountains to encounter gods, visit the underworld, rise from the dead, and so forth. The same concepts are represented in religious art and in religious buildings, in architectural features connected with liturgical practices, and in liturgical postures and positions. Religious language in all its genres displays vocabulary whose conceptual structure is rooted in height/depth and remoteness/presence concepts. It is also possible that ritual practices and also private ritual exploit switches between the two systems—that is, between lower-proximal-serotonergic and upper-distal-dopaminergic systems—as in prostrating versus raising arms and eyes to heaven, or attending to holy objects in peripersonal space versus attending to abstractions in distant spaces and times.

Previc's theory meshes well with research that is independently established in cognitive linguistics, in particular cognitive semantics and CMT. The crucial step in Previc's argument in fact requires a theory of metaphor (including an account of the neural substrate of metaphor) for completeness if the close connections between religious phenomena and spatial cognition are to be fully accounted for. After all, relative distance and height are not per se meaningful in any religious sense, although it could be the case that it is the intrinsic importance of the spatial for the human mind that is actually the source of what is meaningful.

4.3.3 Applying metaphor theory to religion: The work so far

There have been some applications of cognitive metaphor theory to emotional and aesthetic effects in literary genres, and this has included a few mentions of biblical texts (Lakoff and Turner 1989). Turner (2003) has a penetrating analysis of multiple conceptual inputs that are integrated in the Christian narrative of the crucifixion. Antonio Barcelona (1997, 1999) was one of the first to apply CMT to Christian doctrine, and he develops this approach further in the present volume. There have been historical precursors, however, as noted by Jäkel (1999) and by Antović (present volume chapter 15).[11]

At the present time, extended systematic research into metaphorical expressions in religious texts and practices is only just beginning. Computer-aided studies using concordancing software comparing linguistically realised metaphors in and across religious texts are now feasible (e.g. Charteris-Black 2004; Lan 2012; see also Gao and Lan, chapter 10 in this volume; and El-Sharif 2011, and chapter 11 in this volume). Quantitative research of this type has the potential to reveal conceptualising patterns in human religiosity. However, there are a number of methodological problems to be resolved. The most basic question is: what counts as metaphor? The matter of conventionalisation has already been mentioned. Closely related is the fact that the mental processing of metaphorical expressions is dependent on context, although this does not mean that the schematic lexical-conceptual fields cannot be counted and their distribution established, if appropriate definitions and procedures can be agreed upon—as has been attempted by Steen et al. (2010) and the Pragglejaz group. Given appropriate working methods, there are two basically different approaches. One is to identify distributional patterns in the selection of source domains to represent religious concepts: taking the concept 'God', for example, which source domains are selected across belief systems to represent it? The other approach goes the other way: find metaphorical expressions and ask which religious concepts they represent. In the latter case, the question is which classification of metaphorical source domains to use—there are differing proposals in the linguistics metaphor literature. A systematic research programme is needed to achieve statistically reliable results. The work done so far is at the pioneering stage and not obviously consistent. It should be noted that large-scale quantitative investigations will always, in the nature of things, need to run parallel with the investigation of the mental processes involved in the processing of contextual instantiations. At this more fine-grained level, computer-aided studies of large corpora remain limited and unsatisfying. What constitutes religious meaning for individuals and communities will require phenomenological work within a scientific cognitive framework of the kind provided by CMT and CBT, and other emerging cognitive-linguistic techniques. Importantly, it is at this level that the cognitive science and linguistics approaches interface with empirical neural-level research and theorisation.

The investigation of metaphor and other cognitive-linguistic phenomena can raise complicated issues when seen in relation to belief systems. Does pointing out the metaphorical nature of religious concepts carry implications for the truth of religious ideas? For example, 'God is a father' may be said to be metaphorical (cf. El-Sharif, chapter 11 in this volume). For religious believers it is also 'true' in some sense. It may be asserted by some that the expression is *both* metaphorical and true (cf. Barcelona, chapter 13 in this volume). For those looking to explain the existence of religion in homo sapiens in the first place, as is the case for CSR, the accumuation of evidence showing that religious concepts emerge quite naturally as the result of both genetically evolved and culturally developed cognitive capacities (for fluid cognition, for language) may carry serious implications for religious truth-claims. There are some complicated philosophical questions (with an obvious linguistic dimension) here concerning a different sense of the English word *true*. Some of these differences may in fact have to do with different kinds of 'truth' as represented by the left and right hemispheres (cf. McGilchrist 2010, and chapter 6 in this volume). We must leave such questions to the reader. The range of information about religious concepts and emotions in the human mind-brain, and the way in which use of language produces, supports, and perpetuates religious conceptualisations and practices, continues to grow.

NOTES

1. Guthrie (1980, p. 181) makes 'analogy and metaphor' one of the three key elements of his cognitive theory of religious thought and action.
2. Daniel Dennett notes (2006, p. 318): 'Some people seem impervious to religious ritual and all other manifestations of religion, whereas others—like me—are deeply moved by the ceremonies, the music, the art—but utterly unpersuaded by the doctrines.'
3. Knight (1998) links ritual to reproductive pressures and ritualised mating communication initiated by females. But it does not seem necessary to assume one single mechanism of socially organised ritual for the whole of the human species.
4. The features of liturgical language in whichever world religion are reminiscent of the genre of poetry, and may well, as McGilchrist argues in chapter 6 of this volume, be dependent on particular regions of the human brain, primarily in the right hemisphere.
5. Some might make a similar point about the term 'theolinguistics', which occurs in our volume (see David Crystal, chapter 1 and Feyaerts and Boeve, chapter 3). It is important to give consideration to the notion in order to draw attention to the significance of language in relation to religion as a matter of wide scholarly and scientific attention.
6. 'Voices' appear to come in various strengths. The reports of some sufferers suggest clear auditory hallucinations; in other reports they seem to be in some way faint or not real. Neither linguists nor clinicians seem to have looked into this, though there are mentions of 'inner speech', which everyone engages in, and which may be the basis for pathological 'voices' too.
7. Metaphor and symbol need to be distinguished, but we will not go into theoretical definitions here.
8. Typically, in people who are right-handed; the situation is reversed for left-handers.
9. Note that speech act theory tends not to incorporate a detailed cognitive account. Note also that speech acts are not generally encoded in grammatical form but depend on a) relevance and context, and b) non-linguistic cognitive capacities, such as theory of mind.
10. Chilton (1977, chapters 5 and 6) systematically investigated the distribution of source domain ('vehicle') and target domains ('tenor') in a seventeenth-century Catholic devotional text.

REFERENCES

Andresen, J. (2001). *Religion in Mind: Cognitive Perspectives on Religious Belief, Ritual and Experience*. Cambridge: Cambridge University Press.
Atran, S. (2002). *In Gods We Trust*. New York: Oxford University Press.
Austin, J. L. (1962). *How to Do Things with Words*. Cambridge, MA: Harvard University Press.
Barcelona, A. (1997). Constitutive metaphors in the trinitarian dogma. *Linguistic Agency, University of Duisburg Series A: General and Theoretical*, 1–25.

Barcelona, A. (1999). The metaphorical and metonymic understanding of the trinitarian dogma. In Lieven Boeve, Kurt Feyaerts, and James Francis (eds.), *Metaphor and God-Talk*, pp. 187–213. Bern: Peter Lang.

Barkow, J., L. Cosmides and J. Tooby (1992). *The Adapted Mind: Evolutionary Psychology and the Generation of Culture*. Oxford: Oxford University Press.

Baron-Cohen, S. (1995). *Mindblindness: An Essay on Autism and Theory of Mind*. Cambridge, MA: MIT Press.

Barrett, J. L. (2000). Exploring the natural foundations of religion. *Trends in Cognitive Sciences* 4 (1), 29–34.

Barrett, J. L. (2004). *Why Would Anyone Believe in God?* Walnut Creek, CA: AltaMira.

Barrett, J. L. (2011). Cognitive science of religion: Looking back looking forward. *Journal for the Scientific Study of Religion* 50 (2), 229–239.

Bisschops, R. (1994). *Die Metapher als Wertsetzung*. Frankfurt: Lang.

Bisschops, R. (1999). Metaphor as the internalisation of a ritual, with a case study of Samuel Holdheim (1806–1860). In Ralph Bisschops and James Francis (eds.), *Metaphor, Canon and Community*, pp. 284–307. Bern: Peter Lang.

Bisschops, R. (2003). Are religious metaphors rooted in experience? On Ezekiel's wedding metaphors. In Kurt Feyaerts (ed.), *The Bible through Metaphor and Translation I*, pp. 113–152. Bern: Peter Lang.

Bisschops, R. and J. Francis (eds.) (1999). *Metaphor, Canon and Community: Jewish, Christian and Islamic Approaches*. Frankfurt: Lang.

Black, M. (1962). *Models and Metaphors*. Ithaca, NY: Cornell University Press.

Boeve, L. and K. Feyaerts (eds.) (1999a). *Metaphor and God-talk*. Frankfurt: Lang.

Boeve, L. and K. Feyaerts (1999b). Religious metaphors in a postmodern culture: Transverse links between apophatical theology and cognitive semantics. In L. Boeve and K. Feyaerts (eds.), *Metaphor and God-talk*, pp. 153–184. Frankfurt: Lang.

Boyer, P. (1993). Cognitive aspects of religious symbolism. In P. Boyer (ed.), *Cognitive Aspects of Religious Symbolism*. Cambridge: Cambridge University Press.

Boyer, P. (1994a). Cognitive constraints on cultural representations: Natural ontologies and religious ideas. In L. Hirschfeld and S. Gelman (eds.), *Mapping the Mind: Domain Specificity in Cognition and Culture*. Cambridge: Cambridge University Press, pp. 391–411.

Boyer, P. (1994b). *The Naturalness of Religious Ideas*. Berkeley: University of California Press.

Boyer, P. (2001). *Religion Explained*. Cambridge: Cambridge University Press.

Boyer, P. and P. Liénard (2006). Why ritualized behavior? Precaution systems and action parsing in developmental, pathological and cultural rituals. *Behavioral and Brain Sciences* 29 (6), 1–56.

Boyer, P. and P. Liénard (2008). Ritual behavior in obsessive and normal individuals: Moderating anxiety and reorganizing the flow of action. *Current Directions in Psychological Science* 17 (4), 29–24.

Brown, P. and S. C. Levinson (1987). *Politeness: Some Universals in Language Usage*. Cambridge: Cambridge University Press.

Bulbulia, J. (2009). Religiosity as mental time travel. In J. Schoss and M. Murray (eds.), *The Believing Primate: Scientific, Philosophical and Theological Perspectives on the Evolution of Religion*. Oxford: Oxford University Press.

Carruthers, P. (2006). *The Architecture of the Mind*. Oxford: Oxford University Press.

Charteris-Black, J. (2004). *Corpus Approaches to Critical Metaphor Analysis*. Basingstoke: Palgrave Macmillan.

Chilton, P. (1977). *The Poetry of Jean de La Ceppède: A Study in Text and Context*. Oxford: Oxford University Press.

Chilton, P. (2014). *Language, Space and Mind*. Cambridge: Cambridge University Press.

Cosmides, L. and J. Tooby (2000). Consider the source: The evolution of adaptations for decoupling and metarepresentations. In D. Sperber (ed.), *Metarepresentations: A Multidisciplinary Perspective*, pp. 53–115. Oxford: Oxford University Press.

Coulson, S. (2008). Metaphor comprehension and the brain. In R. W. Gibbs (ed.), *The Cambridge Handbook of Metaphor and Thought*. Cambridge: Cambridge University Press.

Crow, T. J. (2000). Schizophrenia as the price that *Homo sapiens* pays for language: A resolution of the central paradox in the origin of the species. *Brain Research Reviews* 31, 118–129.

Crystal, D. (1965). *Linguistics, Language and Religion*. London: Burns and Oates.

d'Aquili, E. and A. B. Newberg (1999). *The Mystical Mind: Probing the Biology of Religious Experience*. Minneapolis: Fortress Press.

Davidson, D. (1970). Mental events. Reprinted in *Essays on Actions and Events*. Oxford: Clarendon Press.

Dawkins, R. (1976). *The Selfish Gene*. Oxford: Oxford University Press.

Dawkins, R. (1989). *The Extended Phenotype*. Oxford: Oxford University Press.

Deacon, T. (1997). *The Symbolic Species*. London: Penguin.

Dennett, D. C. (2006). *Breaking the Spell: Religion as a Natural Phenomenon*. London: Penguin.

DesCamp, M. T. and E. Sweetser (2005). Metaphors for God: Why and how do our choices matter for humans? The application of contemporary cognitive linguistics research to the debate on God and metaphor. *Pastoral Psychology* 53 (3), 207–238.

Douglas, M. (2002 [1966]). *Purity and Danger: An Analysis of the Concepts of Pollution and Taboo*. London: Routledge.

Downes, W. (2011). *Language and Religion: A Journey into the Human Mind*. Cambridge: Cambridge University Press.

Egge, J. (2013). Theorizing embodiment: Conceptual Metaphor Theory and the comparative study of religion. In S. Pathak (ed.), *Figuring Religions: Comparing Ideas, Images, and Activities*. Albany: SUNY Press.

El-Sharif, A. (2011). *A Linguistic Study of Islamic Religious Discourse: Conceptual Metaphors in the Prophetic Tradition*. PhD Thesis. Queen Mary University of London.

Evans, D. D. (1963). *The Logic of Self Involvement*. London: SCM Press.

Fauconnier, G. (1994). *Mental Spaces: Aspects of Meaning Construction in Natural Language*. Cambridge: Cambridge University Press.

Fauconnier, G. and M. Turner (2002). *The Way We Think: Conceptual Blending and the Mind's Hidden Complexities*. New York: Basic Books.

Feldman, J. and S. Narayanan (2004). Embodiment in a neural theory of language. *Brain and Language* 89(2), 385–392.

Feyaerts, K. (ed.) (2003). *The Bible through Metaphor and Translation: A Cognitive Semantic Perspective*. New York: Peter Lang.

Fillmore, C. J. (1982). Frame semantics. In The Linguistic Society of Korea (ed.), *Linguistics in the Morning Calm*, pp. 111–137. Seoul: Hanshin Publishing Co.

Fiske, A. P. and N. Haslam (1997). Is obsessive-compulsive disorder a pathology of the human disposition to perform socially meaningful rituals? Evidence of similar content. *Journal of Nervous and Mental Disease* 185, 211–222.

Fodor, J. (1983). *The Modularity of Mind*. Cambridge, MA: MIT Press.

Fodor, J. (2000). *The Mind Doesn't Work That Way*. Cambridge, MA: MIT Press.

Geschwind, N. (1979). Behavioural changes in temporal lobe epilepsy. *Psychological Medicine* 9, 217–219.

Geschwind, N. (1983). Interictal behavioral changes in epilepsy. *Epilepsis* 24 (suppl. 1), 523–530.

Gibbs, R. W. and T. Matlock (2008). Metaphor, imagination and simulation: Psycholinguistic evidence. In R. W. Gibbs (ed.), *The Cambridge Handbook of Metaphor and Thought*, pp. 166–176. Cambridge: Cambridge University Press.

Gould, S. J. (1999). *Rocks of Ages: Science and Religion in the Fullness of Life*. New York: Ballantine.

Grice, H. P. (1957). Meaning. *The Philosophical Review* 66 (3), 377–388.

Guthrie, S. E. (1980). A cognitive theory of religion. *Current Anthropology* 21(2), 181–203.

Habermas, J. (1998). *On the Pragmatics of Communication*. Edited by M. Cook. Cambridge, UK: Polity.

Habermas, J. (2008). *Between Naturalism and Religion: Philosophical Essays*. Cambridge, UK: Polity.

Harris, J. F. (1980). Speech acts in God talk. *International Journal for Philosophy of Religion* 11(3), 167–183.

Haskell, E. (2008). Metaphor, transformation and transcendence: Toward an understanding of Kabbalistic imagery in *Sefer hazohar*. *Prooftexts: A Journal of Jewish Literary History* 28(3), 337–342.

Haskell, E. (2012). *Suckling at My Mother's Breasts: The Image of a Nursing God in Jewish Mysticism*. Albany, NY: SUNY Press.

Haskell, E. (2013). Bathed in milk: Metaphors of suckling and spiritual transmission in thirteenth-century Kabbalah. In Shubha Pathak (ed.), *Figuring Religion: Comparing Ideas, Images, and Activities*, pp. 117–145. Albany, NY: SUNY Press.

Hayes, G. A. (2003). Metaphoric worlds and yoga in the Vaiṣṇava Sahajiyā Tantric traditions. In D. Carpenter and I. Whicher (eds.), *Yoga: The Indian Tradition*, pp. 162–184. London: Routledge.

Hayes, G. A. (2005). Contemporary metaphor theory and alternative views of Krishna and Rādhā in Vaishnava Sahajiyā tantric traditions. In G. L. Beck (ed.), *Alternative Krishnas Regional and Vernacular Variations on a Hindu Deity*, pp. 19–32. Albany: SUNY Press.

Hayes, G. A. (2008). Using contemporary metaphor theory in the study of medieval Vaiṣṇava Sahajiyā texts. *Journal of the Asiatic Society* 50 (3), 75–92.

Hayes, G. A. (2012). Conceptual blending theory, 'reverse amnesia', and the study of tantra. *Oxford Journal of Hindu Studies* 5, 193–209.

Hayes, G. A. (2014). Possible selves, body schemas, and *sādhana*: Using cognitive science and neuroscience in the study of medieval Vaiṣṇava Sahajiyā Hindu tantric texts. *Religions* 5, 684–699.

Hirschfeld, L. A. and S. A. Gelman (eds.) (1994). *Mapping the Mind: Domain Specificity in Cognition and Culture*. Cambridge: Cambridge University Press.

Hollingsworth, A. (2015). The architecture of apophasis: Exploring options for a cognitive scientific interpretation of the via negativa. *Religion, Brain and Behavior*. 11 Jun 2015. DOI: 10.1080/2153599X.2015.1032998.

Howe, B. and J. B. Green (eds.) (2014). *Cognitive Linguistic Explorations in Biblical Studies*. Berlin: de Gruyter.

Hurford, J. R. (2012). *The Origins of Grammar: Language in the Light of Evolution*. Oxford: Oxford University Press.

Jäkel, O. (1999). Kant, Blumenberg, Weinrich: Some forgotten contributions to the cognitive theory of metaphor. In R. Gibbs and G. Steen, *Metaphor in Cognitive Linguistics*, pp. 9–28. Amsterdam: John Benjamins.

Jäkel, O. (2002). Hypotheses revisited: The cognitive theory of metaphor applied to religious texts. *Metaphoric.de* (2), 20–42.

Jäkel, O. (2003). How can mortal man understand the road he travels? Prospects and problems of the cognitive approach to religious metaphor. In K. Feyaerts (ed.), *The Bible through Metaphor and Translation: A Cognitive Semantic Perspective*, pp. 55–86. New York: Peter Lang.

James, W. (1982 [1902]). *The Varieties of Religious Experience*. New York: Penguin.

Jaszczolt, K. M. (2009). *Representing Time: An Essay on Temporality as Modality*. Oxford: Oxford University Press.

Johnson, M. (1987). *The Body in the Mind*. Chicago: University of Chicago Press.

Knight, C. (1998). Ritual/speech coevolution: A solution to the problem of deception. In J. R. Hurford, M. Studdert-Kennedy, and C. Knight (eds.), *Approaches to the Evolution of Language*, pp. 68–91. Cambridge: Cambridge University Press.

Kövecses, Z. (1990). *Emotion Concepts*. Berlin: Springer-Verlag.

Lakoff, G. (1987). *Women, Fire and Dangerous Things: What Categories Reveal about the Mind. Chicago*: Chicago University Press.

Lakoff, G. (2003). The embodied mind, and how to live with one. In A. J. Sanford (ed.), *The Nature and Limits of Human Understanding: The 2001 Gifford Lectures at the University of Glasgow*, pp. 47–108. New York: T&T Clark.

Lakoff, G. and M. Johnson (1980). *Metaphors We Live by*. Chicago: University of Chicago Press.

Lakoff, G. and M. Johnson (1999). *Philosophy in the Flesh*. New York: Basic Books.

Lakoff, G. and R. E. Núñez (2000). *Where Mathematics Comes From: How the Embodied Mind Brings Mathematics into Being*. New York: Basic Books.

Lakoff, G. and M. Turner (1989). *More than Cool Reason: A Field Guide to Poetic Metaphor*. Chicago: University of Chicago Press.

Lan, C. (2012). A cognitive perspective on the metaphors in the Buddhist sutra 'Bao Ji Jing'. *Metaphor and the Social World* 2 (2), 154–179.

Lawson, E. T. (2000). Towards a cognitive science of religion. *Numen* 47 (3), 338–349.

Lawson, E. T. and R. N. McCauley (1990) *Rethinking Religion: Connecting Cognition and Culture*. Cambridge: Cambridge University Press.

Mandler, J. M. (2004). *The Foundations of Mind: The Origins of Conceptual Thought*. Oxford: Oxford University Press.

McCauley, R. N. and E. T. Lawson (2002). *Bringing Ritual to Mind: Psychological Foundations of Cultural Forms*. Cambridge: Cambridge University Press.

McFague, S. (1982). *Metaphorical Theology: Models of God in Religious Language*. Philadelphia: Fortress Press.

McGilchrist, I. (2010). *The Master and his Emissary: The Divided Brain and the Making of the Western World*. New Haven: Yale University Press.

McNamara, P. (ed.) (2006). *Where God and Science Meet*. 3 volumes. Westport, CT: Praeger.

McNamara, P. (2009). *The Neuroscience of Religious Experience*. Cambridge: Cambridge University Press.

Mithen, S. (1996). *The Prehistory of the Mind: A Search for the Origins of Art, Religion and Science*. London: Thames and Hudson.

Newberg, A. B. (2010). *Principles of Neurotheology*. Burlington, VT: Ashgate.

Pathak, S. (ed.) (2013). *Figuring Religions: Comparing Ideas, Images, and Activities*. Albany: SUNY Press.

Persinger, M. (1983). Religion and mystic experiences as artifacts of temporal lone function: A general hypothesis. *Perceptual and Motor Skills* 57, 1255–1262.

Persinger, M. (1987). *Neuropsychological Bases of God Beliefs*. Westport: Praeger.

Persinger, M. (2003). The sensed presence within experimental settings: Implications for the male and female concept of self. *The Journal of Psychology: Interdisciplinary and Applied* 137 (1), 5–16.

Pinker, S. (1997). *How the Mind Works*. London: Penguin.

Previc, F. H. (1998). The neuropsychology of 3-D space. *Psychological Bulletin* 124, 123–164.

Previc, F. H. (2006). The role of extrapersonal brain systems in religious activity. *Consciousness and Cognition* 15, 500–539.

Previc, F. H. (2009). *The Dopaminergic Mind in Human Evolution and History*. Cambridge: Cambridge University Press.

Propp, V. (1968 [1928]). *Morphology of the Folktale*. Austin: University of Texas Press.

Ramachandran, V. S. and S. Blakeslee (1998). *Phantoms in the Brain: Probing the Mysteries of the Human Mind*. New York: William Morrow.

Rappaport, R. A. (1979). *Ecology, Meaning and Religion*. Berkeley, CA: North Atlantic Books.

Ray, B. (1973). Performative utterances in African rituals. *History of Religions* 13, 16–35.

Schjoedt, U., J. Sørensen, K. L. Nielbo, D. Xygalatas, P. Mitkidis and J. Bulbulia (2013). Cognitive resource depletion in religious interaction. *Religion, Brain & Behavior* 1 (3), 39–86.

Scott, R. A. (2003). *The Gothic Enterprise: A Guide to Understanding the Medieval Cathedral*. Berkeley: University of California Press.

Searle, J. (1969). *Speech Acts: An Essay in the Philosophy of Language*. Cambridge: Cambridge University Press.

Searle, J. (1995). *The Construction of Social Reality*. London: Penguin.

Searle, J. (2010). *Making the Social World: The Structure of Human Civilization*. Oxford: Oxford University Press.

Seaquist, C. (2006). Mind design and the capacity for ritual performance. In P. McNamara (ed.), *Where God and Science Meet: The Neurology of Religious Experience*, volume 2, *The Neurology of Religious Experience*, pp. 205–227. Westport: Praeger.

Slingerland, E. (2004a). Conceptions of the self in the *Zhuangzi*: Conceptual metaphor analysis and comparative thought. *Philosophy East and West* 54(3), 322–342.

Slingerland, E. (2004b). Conceptual metaphor theory as methodology for comparative religion. *Journal of the American Academy of Religion* 72 (1), 1–31.

Slingerland, E. (2011). Metaphor and meaning in early China. *Dao: A Journal of Comparative Philosophy* 10 (1), 1–30.

Slone, D. J. (ed.) (2006). *Religion and Cognition: A Reader*. London and Oakville: Equinox.

Smith, A. C. T. (2014). *Thinking about Religion: Extending the Cognitive Science of Religion*. Basingstoke: Palgrave Macmillan.

Sørensen, J. (2003). The question of ritual. *Scripta Instituti Donneriani Aboensis* 18, 207–220.

Sørensen, J. (2007). Acts that work: A cognitive approach to ritual agency. *Method and Theory in the Study of Religion* 19, 281–300.

Soskice, J. M. (1985). *Metaphor and Religious Language*. Oxford: Clarendon Press.

Sperber, D. (1975). *Rethinking Symbolism*. Translated by A. Morton. Cambridge: Cambridge University Press.

Sperber, D. (1994). The modularity of thought and the epidemiology of representations. In L. Hirschfeld and S. Gelman, *Mapping the Mind: Domain Specificity in Cognition and Culture*, pp. 39–67. Cambridge: Cambridge University Press.

Sperber, D. (1996). *Explaining Culture: A Naturalistic Approach*. Oxford: Blackwell.

Sperber, D. (2000). An objection to the memetic approach to culture. In Robert Aunger (ed.), *Darwinizing Culture: The Status of Memetics as a Science*, pp. 163–173. Oxford: Oxford University Press.

Sperber, D. (2006). The epidemiology of beliefs: A naturalistic approach. In D. J. Slone (ed.), *Religion and Cognition: A Reader*, pp. 36–53. London and Oakville: Equinox.

Sperber, D. and D. Wilson (1995). *Relevance: Communication and Cognition*, 2nd edition. Oxford: Blackwell.

Steen, G. J., A. G. Dorst, J. B. Herrmann, A. Kaal, T. Krennmayr, and T. Pasma (2010). *A Method for Linguistic Metaphor Identification*. Amsterdam: John Benjamins.

Sweetser, E. and M. T. DesCamp (2014). Motivating biblical metaphors for God: Refining the cognitive model. In B. Howe and J. B. Green (eds.), *Cognitive Linguistic Explorations in Biblical Studies*, pp. 7–24. Munich: de Gruyter.

Swinburne, R. G. (1992). *Revelation: From Metaphor to Analogy*. Oxford: Clarendon Press.

Swinburne, R. G. (1999). Analogy, metaphor, and religious language. In L. Boeve and K. Feyaerts (eds.), *Metaphor and God-Talk*, pp. 63–74. Bern: Peter Lang.

Tek, C. and B. Ulug (2001). Religiosity and religious obsessions in obsessive compulsive-disorder. *Psychiatry Research* 104 (2), 99–108.

Tomasello, M. (1999). *The Cultural Origins of Human Cognition*. Cambridge, MA: Harvard University Press.

Turner, M. (2003). Double-scope stories. In D. Herman (ed.), *Narrative Theory and the Cognitive Sciences*, pp. 117–142. Stanford, CA: CSLI.

Unger, C. (2006). *Genre, Relevance and Global Coherence: The Pragmatics of Discourse Type*. Palgrave Studies in Pragmatics, Language and Cognition. Basingstoke: Palgrave Macmillan.

Unger, C. (2012). Towards a relevance theory account of allegory. In *Selected Papers from the Interpreting for Relevance Conference Warwzaw 2012*. Cambridge: Cambridge Scholars Publishing.

van Noppen, J. P. (ed.) (1981). *Theolinguistics*. Brussels: Studiereeks Tijdschrift Vrije Universiteit Brussel, New series No 8.

van Noppen, J. P. (ed.) (1983). *Metaphor and Religion*. (Theolinguistics 2).
Brussels: Studiereeks Tijdschrift Vrije Universiteit Brussel, New series No 12.
van Noppen, J. P. (ed.) (1988). *Erinnern, um Neues zu sagen: Die Bedeutung der Metapher für die religiöse Sprache*. Frankfurt am Main: Athenäum.
van Noppen, J. P. (1999). *Transforming Words: Tthe Early Methodist Revival from a Discourse Perspective*. Frankfurt: Lang.
van Noppen, J. P. (ed.) (2011). Critical theolinguistics vs. the literalist paradigm. *Sociolinguistica* 25, 28–40.
Waxman, S. G. and N. Geschwind (1975). The interictal behavior syndrome of temporal lobe epilepsy. *Archives of General Psychiatry* 32 (12), 1580–1586.
Whitehouse, H. (1995). *Inside the Cult: Religious Innovation and Transmission in Papua New Guinea*. Oxford: Oxford University Press.
Whitehouse, H. (2000). *Arguments and Icons: Divergent Modes of Religiosity*. Oxford: Oxford University Press.
Whitehouse, H. (2004). *Modes of Religiosity: A Cognitive Theory of Religious Transmission*. Lanham, MD: Altamira Press.
Whitehouse, H. and J. Laidlaw (2007). *Religion, Anthropology and Cognitive Science*. Durham, NC: Carolina Academic Press.
Wierzbicka, A. (2001). *What Did Jesus Mean? Explaining the Sermon on the Mount and the Parables in Simple and Universal Human Concepts*. New York: Oxford University Press.

PART I
Religious Language, Mind, and Brain

It is perhaps possible to have states of mind described as religious that do not involve language, and also to perform actions regarded as religious that do not involve language. But the role of language, spoken or written, in organised religions is enormous. We have these two aspects: the mental and the linguistic. Their interdependence in religious experience and behaviour is what concerns us in this book. Part I reflects the fact that there are very many ways to go about investigating the intertwining of religion, language, and the human mind: each of the six chapters represents different approaches to language, to thoughts and emotions, and to religion itself.

In chapter 1 David Crystal represents the earliest attempts in modern linguistics to describe the distinctive characteristics of religion using methods from linguistics. His approach comes from within the Christian tradition, as does that of Anna Wierzbicka in chapter 2. Wierzbicka's descriptive framework, however, seeks to move beyond English, posing cross-cultural and cross-linguistic questions about the communication of Western Christian theological concepts. This approach makes use of her Leibnizian theory of universal semantic description, 'natural semantic metalanguage'. Chapter 3 takes us into the cognitive revolution that has taken a place not only in the social sciences, anthropology, and linguistics, but also in theology. Kurt Feyaerts and Lieven Boeve provide a survey of the ways in which linguistics, philosophy, theology, and the cognitive sciences have interacted. At the forefront is the role of metaphor and other forms of concept formation—a topic that occupies an important role in the remainder of this volume.

The remaining chapters of this first part are interlinked but range wide. William Downes in chapter 4 addresses a particular genre of religious verbal practice, prayer. Within an interdisciplinary context that includes both linguistics and cognitive science, this chapter dissects the structures of ritual prayer forms, drawing on tools from sociolinguistics and, importantly, from the field known to linguistics as pragmatics—the investigation of situational processing of linguistic and related input. Downes' way of addressing religious practice and experience is picked up, within the disciplinary framework of neuroscience, by Patrick McNamara and Magda Giordano in chapter 5, who elaborate earlier work by incorporating a neural account of the particular place held by human language in the human experience of religious states of mind and religious acts. The making of different sorts of meaning is at the heart of the attempt to understanding the nature of religious experience and behaviour. In the chapter that concludes Part I, Iain McGilchrist sets out a theory of the overall architecture of the human mind-brain: the brain's two hemispheres interact in distinct yet complementary and interactive ways. In this perspective, it is the right hemisphere, the supposedly 'silent hemisphere', that undergirds the holistic processing that is of interest in the study of certain kinds of religious experience. Furthermore, McGilchrist argues that it undergirds the processing of non-analytic language, in particular the sorts of metaphorical conceptualisation so often observed in all religious means of expression.

CHAPTER 1

Whatever Happened to Theolinguistics?

DAVID CRYSTAL

In the beginning, we are told, was the Word. So however we interpret that sentence, it is evident that language is inevitably going to be prioritised in religious enquiry. Linguistics is the science of language. We might therefore expect a branch of that subject to develop whose remit is the investigation of all aspects of religious language. And so it proved to be. It is called theolinguistics.

Or, perhaps I should say, *was* called. For the flurry of interest which accompanied the first mentions of this subject in the 1980s seems to have largely disappeared. I continue to include the term in my various writings, so that, for example, in the sixth edition of my *Dictionary of Linguistics and Phonetics* (Crystal 2008) you will see an entry as follows:

> **theolinguistics** (*n.*) A term which has been used for the study of the relationship between language and religious thought and practice, as illustrated by ritual, sacred texts, preaching, doctrinal statements and private affirmations of belief.

But note the 'has been used'. In all the other domains of applied linguistics listed in my dictionary (such as forensic linguistics, clinical linguistics, and educational linguistics) there are hundreds of professional linguists exploring the relationship between language and the associated area (law/crime, disability in spoken or written language, language teaching and learning in schools). Each domain has its courses, conferences, textbooks, academic journals, and professional bodies. Little of this has happened in the case of theolinguistics.

A word about 'professional linguist'. A distinction must be made between people who have a general interest in language, or for whom language is an important but subordinate element in their professional expertise, and linguists, in this sense, whose training places language and languages centre stage. It is a bit like the distinction between people who can cook and chefs, or people who can drive and car mechanics, except that language is far more complex and multi-faceted than cooking and driving—to my mind, the most complex behaviour known to humanity, with its dozens of sounds, thousands of grammatical constructions, millions of words, and an indefinite and probably infinite number of uses. Linguistics is the science of all of that, and linguistics is what linguists, in this sense, do.

The 'interest' group, of course, comprises everybody: I have never met anyone who was not interested in language and how it works. And certainly, when it comes to the study and practice of religion, language is a major topic in the professional lives of theologians, biblical scholars, liturgists, preachers, missionaries, and others. But there is a big difference between those whose knowledge of language forms just one element in their intellectual domain, or whose expertise is wholly in relation to a single language or set of languages (such as the Biblical languages) and those where linguistics forms the central pillar of their intellectual life, and where all of the 6000 or so languages in the world provide the subject-matter. The primary aim of linguistics is to establish general principles for the study of all languages and to determine the universal characteristics of human language as a biological phenomenon. Its remit is therefore large, covering everything from the origins of language to the way languages die, from language acquisition in babies to language senescence in the old. The detailed description of individual languages forms an important part of this task, and this includes the relating of linguistic features (of pronunciation, orthography, grammar, vocabulary, and patterns of discourse) to the temporal, regional, social, occupational, and individual situations in which language is used. Given the number of religions in the world, and the number of their language-using adherents, we would thus expect the study of religious language to form an important and burgeoning part of linguistics. This has happened with the study of the language of science; we might expect it to have happened with the study of the domain that is most often juxtaposed with science.

There is, after all, no shortage of religious subject-matter crying out for analysis using the theories and methods of linguistics. From a linguistic point of view, the study of religious language will always have two sides: within an individual language, the formal identification of those features which distinguish this variety from all other varieties in that language; and the functional identification of the contexts in which the variety is used, and which promote diversity in its use. At a more advanced level, a comparative dimension is present, in which one would compare and inter-relate the formal and functional properties of the way religious experience is treated across several languages. The aim would be to work towards a theory of religious language—to determine the universal features of linguistic expression that characterise religious discourse, to relate these to the other aspects of human behaviour explored by such fields as psychology and anthropology, and to establish fruitful connections between its findings and the other domains of religious studies. This is what people who called themselves theolinguists would be expected to do. And there was a moment in living memory when it seemed as if it was going to happen.

1 THE BIRTH OF THEOLINGUISTICS

The term *theolinguistics* was not around when I first started writing about religious language. There is no use of it in my *Linguistics, Language and Religion* (Crystal 1965).

I talk a lot about 'theophoric language' in that book, but don't use the later term. It simply wasn't the parlance of the day. None of the so-called 'hyphenated terms' that would one day identify branches of linguistics (socio-linguistics, psycho-linguistics, neuro-linguistics, etc.) had yet become established. I saw the study of religious language from a linguistic point of view as essentially a branch of stylistics, and that is how it appears in a later book (Crystal and Davy 1969). The only feature of my 1965 book which would make it mentionable in any history of linguistics is that, being written for the Roman Catholic firm of Burns and Oates, in their *Faith and Fact* series, it was given official permission, the 'Nihil Obstat' and the 'Imprimatur'—I think the only book with linguistics in its title ever to be so designated!

I was by no means the only linguist interested in religious language in the 1960s. It would have been surprising if it were otherwise, as language had become a real talking-point in that decade. The breathtaking consequences of Vatican II (1962–5) were being assimilated, including a transformation of liturgical language and a new appreciation of the role of the vernacular. John Robinson, the Bishop of Woolwich, was making headlines with his proposals about the need for a new God-language in *Honest to God* (1963). A. Q. Morton was making headlines with his stylometric investigations into the Pauline Epistles. A. J. Ayer and the logical positivists were still propounding a philosophy in which language played a central part. Recent textual discoveries, notably the Dead Sea Scrolls, were being made available. And the *Jerusalem Bible* arrived (1966).

Within linguistics, the 1960s was also a crucial decade. Linguistic theory had taken a giant leap forward in 1957, with the publication of Noam Chomsky's *Syntactic Structures*, and the 1960s proved to be a period of radical rethinking about the aims and methods of the subject. The first undergraduate degree courses in the subject appeared in Britain (1965), along with the first popular introductions to the subject, including my own (Crystal 1968, 1969). The Linguistics Association of Great Britain, founded in 1959, started to hold annual conferences. *The Journal of Linguistics* began publication in 1964. It was all happening.

Linguists evidently began thinking seriously about the way their subject could contribute to the study of religion, the evidence being the books which started to appear in the early 1970s. William J. Samarin, for example, professor of anthropology and linguistics at Toronto, and the author of books on field linguistics and African languages, published his investigation into glossolalia, *Tongues of Men and Angels* (1972). Felicitas D. Goodman brought anthropology and linguistics together in her cross-cultural approach to the same topic, *Speaking in Tongues* (1972). Samarin then organised a conference on Sociolinguistics and Religion in 1972, one of the annual linguistics meetings held at Georgetown University, Washington, the outcome being the anthology *Language in Religious Practice* (Samarin 1976). Other conferences exploring a linguistic approach were also being held early in that decade, such as the session on 'A Sociolinguistic Examination of Religious Behaviour' at the annual meeting of the Society for the Scientific Study of Religion, held in Chicago in 1971. And we must not forget those people with an earlier philological training who began to explore religious language in new ways, such as the Old Testament scholar James Barr in *The Semantics of Biblical Language* (1961), who at one point (p. 24) regrets 'the failure to relate what is said about either Hebrew or Greek to a general semantic method related to general linguistics'.

The term *theolinguistics* was introduced by the Belgian linguist Jean-Pierre van Noppen in 1981, inspired by John Robinson's earlier use of *theography*, and formed the title of a collection of papers called simply *Theolinguistics*. In his preface, van Noppen (1981) introduces the new label:

> The pluridisciplinary field of investigation offered by the linguistic articulation of religious belief and thought—a notion condensed, in a Western perspective, in the neologism *theolinguistics*—raises a number of issues that are, at least, far from being exhausted. The new term covers an area of interest with a history as old and respectable as Man's attempt to voice, with the means of conception and expression at his disposal, his understanding of the divine . . . but it is meant to refer more specifically to the interest in language whose origins can be traced back to the turn of the century, and which was to result in the church-wide debate over religious language—a debate which gained momentum on the eve of the 'Death of God' movement and which, unabated by more recent trends on the theological scene, claimed for years a priority in theological thought. (pp. 1–2)

He identifies, along with theologians and philosophers, linguists, psychologists, anthropologists, and sociologists as relevant contributors to this subject, and adds:

> A credible theolinguistics can only grow out of the various disciplines' mutual awareness of each others' methods and standards . . . the theologian should not work with obsolete conceptions of language, nor the linguist hold naive or fallacious views of theology; and neither should build his argument on unstable philosophical premisses [*sic*]. (p. 2)

The twenty-one papers in the volume were certainly interdisciplinary, with the contributors displaying backgrounds in semiotics, philosophy, theology, literary criticism, psychology, and linguistics. Apart from van Noppen himself, the linguists involved were myself, Jean Dierickx, Eugene Nida, Marie-Louise Rotsaert, and William Samarin. The theologian F. W. Dillistone concludes his opening paper to that volume with the sentence: 'Theolinguistics is one of the most urgent and yet most demanding disciplines of our time' (van Noppen 1981, p. 20).

2 LATER DEVELOPMENTS

Theolinguistics 1 was a promising start, and two years later a second volume appeared, *Metaphor and Religion (Theolinguistics 2)*, focusing on a single theme, metaphor in religious discourse (van Noppen 1983). This time the linguists were less prominent: apart from van Noppen, only two out of the fifteen contributors could be said to be card-carrying linguists, Nicole Delbecque and János Petöfi. This set the tone for the way the subject developed over the next decades. The early development of an academic subject is driven by personalities, and van Noppen's own interest in metaphor—reinforced by the new attention being paid to this topic within linguistics at the time, notably in *Metaphors We Live by* (Lakoff and Johnson 1980)— heralded one road which became quite well-trodden.

Another popular road was a focus on discourse. Discourse analysis, defined by Michael Stubbs (1983) in an influential book as 'the sociolinguistic analysis of natural language', arose when linguists became dissatisfied with approaches which concentrated solely on the analysis of single sentences. It became evident that conversations, narratives, and other forms of connected speech and writing were the norm in communicative behaviour, and this led to a fresh focus on the analysis of utterances and texts in real contexts. Analogous interests, especially by ethnographers and sociologists (such as Erving Goffman), introduced a cross-disciplinary perspective which went under various labels, such as conversation analysis and text linguistics, but the outcome for theolinguistics was a renewed exploration of the properties of religious discourse. This change of orientation is well reflected in two of my own articles. In 1964 I wrote an article called 'A liturgical language in a linguistic perspective' (Crystal 1964). Twenty-five years on, I entitled a contribution to a new anthology, 'A liturgical language in a sociolinguistic perspective' (Crystal 1990).

Probably the most important manifestation of the new orientation was the series which began to appear in the 1990s, published by the German firm of Peter Lang, called *Religions and Discourse*, with the following remit:

> *Religions and Discourse* explores religious language in the major world faiths from various viewpoints, including semiotics, pragmatics and cognitive linguistics, and reflects on how it is situated within wider intellectual and cultural contexts. In particular a key issue is the role of figurative speech. Many fascinating metaphors originate in religion e.g. revelation as a 'garment', apostasy as 'adultery', loving kindness as the 'circumcision of the heart'. Every religion rests its specific orientations upon symbols such as these, to name but a few. The series strives after the interdisciplinary approach that brings together such diverse disciplines as religious studies, theology, sociology, philosophy, linguistics and literature. . . .

The link with *Theolinguistics 2* is clear, and is reflected in the opening two titles of the series, which were a selection of the papers delivered at the 25th LAUD symposium on 'Metaphor and Religion'. (LAUD, Linguistic Agency University Duisburg, began in 1973 as an innovative collaboration between linguistics groups at the German universities of Trier, Duisburg, and Landau.) The titles of both volumes show the earlier influence: *Metaphor, Canon and Community* (Bisschops and Francis 1999) and *Metaphor and God-talk* (Boeve and Feyaerts 1999). The third volume also provided continuity with the theolinguistics initiative, being written by van Noppen (*Transforming Words*, 1999), who used a discourse perspective to investigate the early Methodist revival. The fifth, too, had a linguistics orientation, Noel Heather's *Religious Language and Critical Discourse Analysis* (2000)—the 'critical' in the title reflecting a movement in the subject which aims to reveal hidden power relations and ideological processes at work in texts. (A 'critical discourse analysis' studies the relationship between discourse events and sociopolitical and cultural factors, especially the way discourse is ideologically influenced by and can itself influence power relations in society.) And there was one other: volume 15 in the series, a conference proceedings edited by Kurt Feyaerts, *The Bible through Metaphor and Translation* (2003).

But that was it. There was never a *Theolinguistics 3*, though van Noppen did collate several of the theolinguistic articles in a German translation a few years later (1988). And gradually, work from a linguistics stable became less prominent in the *Religions and Discourse* series. There were (by early 2016) fifty-five books in the series, and only the above five come from people in whose background linguistics plays a central role. Of the others, according to the publisher's identification of books by the academic discipline of the authors, there are forty with a background in theology, ten in literature, six in gender studies, four in the history of religions, two in philosophy, and one each in psychology and cultural studies (some authors have more than one background). Moreover, given the potentially broad reach of theolinguistics as a whole, these five works explore only two themes: metaphor and discourse. And these emphases continue in later papers. Van Noppen (2011), for example, reflects on what he calls a 'critical theolinguistics'. He reminds his reader of the original subject, 'the study of the *logos* about *theos*: a science whose object is God as *word*, not as *being*', and he summarises its emphasis to date:

> In our regions the discipline has tended to focus mainly (though not exclusively) on Christian language use, whether descriptive (*about* the divine, as in sermons, creeds or 'theography' . . .) or ascriptive (addressed *to* the divine, as in hymns or prayers). . . . As a branch of linguistics, theolinguistics calls for a discourse approach inasmuch as religious language is best described and assessed within a context of belief where its utterances are regarded as meaningful.

And he goes on to talk about how 'the discourse-minded theolinguist' aims to establish a meaningful relationship between texts and their social conditions, and of course (bearing in mind the 'critical' in his title) to expose any misuses of religious discourse.

To briefly illustrate his approach: he contrasts George H. Bush's inaugural address, in which he asked God to 'make us strong to do your work'—the underlying assumption being that the nation's fate is determined by divine providence—with Rev. Gene Robinson's invocation before Barack Obama's inaugural, 'Hold him in the palm of your hand, that he might do the work we have called him to do', and points out that 'the difference in the source of the calling ("You, God" or "We the People") invests the president-elect with a very different brand of power'. Other examples of the way critical theolinguistics operates would be the analysis of how individuals select scriptural passages to support their different ideological positions, the implications of using gendered pronouns with reference to God (*he/she/it*) in a society where feminist issues are prominent, and the evaluation of the historical versus the mythological content of scriptural passages—a perspective which comes to the fore when considering the creationist/evolutionist debate. The approach draws attention to the need for two perspectives: 'we need not only the semantics of discourse (i.e. what the words and sentences mean), but also the pragmatics of discourse (what the words and sentences *do* for people)' (van Noppen 2011).

3 FRESH PERSPECTIVES

Now, I do not for one moment wish to minimise the insightful contributions that can be found in a discourse-oriented approach to religious language. I totally agree that, ultimately, all language analysis has to be discourse-related. But this must not be taken to mean that there is no role for the 'non-discourse-minded' theolinguist. After all, it is not as if the within-sentence nuts and bolts of religious language have all been described for the wide range of varieties of religious language that exist—let alone for the vast range of languages that have as yet received no exploration of their religious expression at all. Even in relation to English, there are still very few empirical studies of the detail of what actually happens—in pronunciation, orthography, grammar, and vocabulary, to take just these four areas—when people engage in religious discourse. And theolinguists need, above all, to avoid a solely Anglocentric view of religious language—or, a fortiori, an Indo-European one.

This last point needs exposition. It is a truism of comparative linguistics that the languages of the world express a mosaic of visions of what it means to be human. Although languages have a great deal in common, as evidenced by the equivalences achieved by successful translation, it is also clear that languages display varying amounts of uniqueness. We acknowledge this whenever we find it necessary to apologise for an inexact translation of one language into another, or fall back on such expressions as 'the French have a word for it'. No one has yet quantified the amount of cultural uniqueness expressed by a language. It will vary depending on the amount of linguistic and cultural distance between the speech-communities (the gap between, say, English and French is going to be much smaller than that between English and Chinese). But almost certainly religious expression will form an important part of the linguistic distinctiveness that reflects cultural identity. A sense of the scale of the challenge is provided by Section 1 of the *Concise Encyclopedia of Language and Religion* (Sawyer and Simpson 2001), where sixty-two entries summarise the role of language in many of the world's religions and religious movements (African traditional religions, Australian aboriginal religions, the Baha'i Faith, Kwanzaa, Macumba, Melanesisn religions . . .). I should be surprised if there was a substantial bibliography of descriptive linguistic studies for most of the sixty-two topics, and I suspect that in some cases no linguistic work would have been done at all. William Samarin was one who was able to comment on religious language in such 'exotic' (to Western ears) contexts as Swahili and Sango, but few of us are able to match his range. There is probably much more going on in the theolinguistic world (in Poland and Slovakia, for example) than is represented by the literature in English, and at some point any arguments about the scope and future of theolinguistics will need to take these studies into account.

Even if we stay within the familiar world of English linguistics, there is still a great deal of basic descriptive work on religious language that remains to be done. English is now a global language, used by over two billion people in every country on earth. One of the most notable developments, over the last 50 years, has been the growth of what are often called 'new Englishes'. We have long been used to the fact that British English and American English are different dialects—different in sounds, spellings, grammar, and vocabulary—and most of these differences are now well understood, and recorded in dictionaries, grammars, and manuals of style. But today, these are but two of a panoply of varieties that can be found all over the globe. Following political independence, the nations that had used English in the colonial era immediately began to adapt the language to reflect their local identity. Thousands of new words entered their usage, as can be seen today in the various dictionaries (of Jamaican English, Ghanaian English, Singaporean English, and so on) that have been compiled. These 'new Englishes' added to the 'old Englishes' that had been around for a much longer period, such as Australian, South African, and Indian English. The result is a modern language which now exists in dozens of different varieties around the English-speaking world. Several academic journals, such as *English World-Wide* and *English Today*, focus on describing the differences in form and use displayed by these varieties. Religious language is bound to have been affected by these local pressures, but so far, hardly any study of indigenous adaptations in this domain has taken place. In all the eighty-four issues to date (as of 2016) of *English World-Wide*, there is not one major study of religious expression in a 'new English'.

Diversity is one side of the coin of linguistic description; the other side is language change. Even if there had been a theolinguistic study of one of these varieties in, say, 1980, the results would need re-assessing thirty years on. Only dead languages do not change. And living languages can change at a surprising rate, especially these days as a result of the Internet. Moreover, not only do the forms of the language change (new words, pronunciations, grammatical patterns), but attitudes to those forms change. A usage that one generation hates for its novelty can become established by later generations, and receive no criticism at all. Who would now believe that the word *balcony* once had its stress on the middle syllable [bal-<u>coh</u>-nee], and that people then could not stand the newfangled pronunciation [<u>bal</u>-co-ny]? Every generation has its likes and dislikes about language. And every generation is a mixture of generations, with young and old having different likes and dislikes. Taking all these attitudes into account must be one of the biggest challenges facing those, such as translators and liturgists, having to provide texts for religious communities, or those, such as preachers and missionaries, who have to talk to them.

I say 'must be' because I do not know if many of those involved in the professional presentation of religious language are very aware of the issues, or even of the extent to which there is a problem. Take, for example, the 2012 Roman Catholic translation of the Mass, which introduced a raft of changes to the vernacular version that had been in use after Vatican II. The extent and character of the changes took everyone by surprise, and generated huge amounts of criticism and controversy. I have been able to read only a tiny part of the correspondence elicited by the translation, but my impression is that reactions to individual points of usage (both positive and negative) varied greatly from country to country—which is exactly what one would expect, in light of the above. At least in 1967, when English was about to replace Latin, the International Committee on English in the Liturgy printed booklets with alternative translations to gauge public reaction, and asked linguists to analyse the findings. I do not know of any such activities having taken place in relation to the current translation, or whether the translators were even aware of the huge diversification that had happened to English over the past 40 years. Nobody was talking about global varieties of the language in the 1960s. It is a major talking point now, and it would form an important element in any revitalised theolinguistics of English. Analogous concerns, though not on such a global scale, of course affect all internationally used languages.

4 THE ROLE OF PRAGMATICS

Another major change in the linguistic climate since the 1980s, and one which is highly relevant for theolinguistics today, is the development of the subject now known as pragmatics. This has already been mentioned in relation to the work of van Noppen and the critical discourse analysts, but it is such an important addition to the metalanguage of linguistics that it needs some further exposition. Van Noppen's definition of the pragmatics of discourse ('what the words and sentences *do* for people') emphasises one aspect of the subject. Pragmatics today actually encompasses three. I define it as the study of the *choices* we make when we use language, of the *intentions and assumptions* behind those choices, and the *effects* that the choices convey. Anyone familiar with the pragmatics literature written since the subject first achieved definition within linguistics (during the 1980s) will have encountered a diversity of treatments, because some authors focus on the choices, some on the intentions, and some on the effects. An emphasis on *doing* relates chiefly to the latter. The point loomed large in the early pragmatics literature, which paid particular attention to the notion of 'speech acts'—the actions performed by utterances, such as promising and resigning, or (in religion) christening and marrying.

Here's an example of how each of the three aspects operates. In a language like French (and, of course, in religious language in English), there is a distinction between second-person pronouns. It is not enough to learn that in French *tu* is singular and *vous* is plural. That would be to take a purely grammatical view of the contrast. From a pragmatic point of view, we need to know that, when one speaks French, one has a choice. We may address a single individual as *tu* or *vous*, and the choice is constrained by several factors. A pragmatically aware description of these pronouns would point out that adult French people use *tu* chiefly when talking to children, to animals, to intimates, and (if you are Protestant) God; *vous* is used elsewhere. That is the choice available to them. But in a real interaction, two other questions remain: what does a speaker intend by using *tu*, and what would be the effect of so doing? Pierre meets Marie. Pierre likes Marie. He decides to address her with *tu* (the French have a verb for this, *tutoyer*). His intention is clear. But what will be Marie's reaction? If she responds with *tu*, the effect is as Pierre intended. If she slaps his face, it is not. There is often a mismatch between intentions and effects.

Transferring this example to the liturgical issue above, there was clearly a considerable distance between the intentions and assumptions made by the liturgical translators and the effects their choices had on large numbers of the Mass-attending public. After the event, various newspapers and journals debated the reasons behind the choices—such as the desire to follow more closely the original Latin text (as with the response *And with your spirit* replacing *And also with you*, reflecting *Et cum spiritu tuo*). Arguments for and against alternative translations took up a great deal of column space. But by then it was too late, for none of this removed the upset that many people felt. Such debates should have been held a long time before the final decisions were made, and with due diligence, taking into account any differences of usage among the main international varieties of English. A modicum of pragmatic linguistic awareness introduced at the right time could have resulted in a more positive climate.

5 AN ILLUSTRATION

Looking back at the theolinguistic literature to date, one gets the impression that the subject is only concerned with abstract, open-ended, and theologically profound subject-matter, and with the elucidation of questions which may not be wholly answerable (Crystal 1976, 1981). But many interesting questions about religious language are much more concrete, determinate, and definitely answerable, as several case studies have illustrated.

Take, for example, the question of how far religious language permeates everyday language, generalising the question from 'metaphors we live by' to all linguistic features. To what extent does modern English, when used in non-religious contexts, display vocabulary, idiom, grammar, and style that can be traced back to a religious source, such as a particular translation of the Bible? The question was formally raised in relation to the 400th anniversary of the King James Bible in 2011. Just how much influence did this translation have? The exaggerations at the time were widespread. In an article in *The Tablet* (3 April 2010) called 'England's gift to the world', MP Frank Field (the director of the 2011 Trust established to coordinate the anniversary celebrations) quoted the novelist and media pundit Melvyn Bragg as saying that the King James Bible (KJB) is 'quite simply the DNA of the English language'. It was a striking metaphor, but a hugely misleading one. DNA is in every cell we possess; but the KJB is by no means in every word we write. A great deal of mythology about biblical language was in circulation at that time.

It was time for a linguistic analysis, and I report here the outcome of a lexical study. A search in the *Oxford English Dictionary* to identify the presence of words that have their first recorded usage in the KJB resulted in a very small total (forty-seven, according to the latest revision). A search for the idioms found in the KJB that continue to be used in present-day English produced a larger but still (to most people) surprisingly small total (257). However, neither total should surprise us. We need to recall that the aim of the translators, as they say in their Preface, was not to make a new translation, 'but to make a good one better, or out of many good ones, one principal good one'. They had little choice in the matter, as the guidelines for their work, which had been approved by the King, required them to use the Bishops' Bible (in the 1602 edition) as their first model, making as few alterations as possible; and, when this was found wanting, they could refer to earlier versions. Unlike Shakespeare, they were not great innovators, so the number of neologisms was never going to be large, as can be seen from the list of first recorded usages (the three asterisked items also appear in another 1611 publication):

abased (as an adjective), accurately, afflicting (as a noun), algum ('algum tree'), any-whither, armour-bearer, backsliding (as an adjective), battering-ram, Benjamite, catholicon, confessing (as a noun), crowning (as an adjective), dissolver, dogma-tize, epitomist, escaper, espoused (as an adjective), exactress, expansion, Galilean (as a noun), gopher, Gothic (as an adjective), grand-daughter, Hamathite, infallibil-ity*, Laodicean (as a noun), lapful*, light-minded, maneh (Hebrew unit of account), miscarrying (as an adjective), Naziriteship, needleworker, night-hawk, nose-jewel, palmchrist, panary ('pantry'), phrasing (as a noun), pruning-hook, rosebud, rose of Sharon, Sauromatian, shittah (type of tree), skewed, taloned* (as an adjective), way-mark ('traveller guide'), whosoever, withdrawing (as an adjective)

In relation to idioms, the important point to note is that most of them do not orig-inate in the King James translation at all. Rather they are to be found in one of the translations that appeared in the preceding 130 years—Wycliffe's translation (the first into English, in 1388), Tyndale's translation of the New Testament and the first six books of the Old (1526–1530), the Bishops' Bible (1568), the Geneva Bible (1560), and the Douai-Rheims (1582 New Testament, 1609–1610 Old Testament). Tyndale is especially important. Only eighteen expressions are stylistically unique to the King James Bible:

east of Eden, know for a certainty, how are the mighty fallen, a still small voice, the root of the matter, to every thing there is a season, much study is a weariness of the flesh, beat their swords into plowshares, set thine [your] house in order, be horribly afraid, lay up for yourselves treasures in heaven, get thee behind me, suffer little children, no small stir, turned the world upside down, a thorn in the flesh, unto the pure all things are pure, let us now praise famous men

Every other idiomatic expression is shared with at least one of the earlier transla-tions. In many cases, it is found in all of them—such as *milk and honey* or *salt of the earth*. The full description is given in the appendix to Crystal (2010).

Once the basic descriptive material is laid out (the 'what'), we can begin to analyse it in terms of the temporal, regional, social, occupational, and personal factors which account for its character (the 'when', 'where', and 'who'), and here of course sev-eral interesting questions arise. To take just one that came up at the time: how does Douai-Rheims stand compared to the other versions? Is there evidence in this solidly Protestant Bible of a Catholic influence on present-day idiom? The examples suggest that there is. Gordon Campbell, in his historical account of the KJB (2010), draws attention to the scholarly background of the Douai-Rheims translators, along with the kind of insights obtained from their use of the Latin Vulgate. Their Old Testament was published too late for it to have had as much influence as their New Testament, but Campbell illustrates several clear links. And there is a clear connection between Douai-Rheims and the present day with respect to idiomatic expressions.

There are twenty-seven instances where an expression appears in the KJB and one of the other translations. Of these, one is in Tyndale, five are in the Bishop's Bible, and ten are in Geneva, but eleven are in Douai-Rheims:

> white as snow (Numbers)
>
> whips . . . scorpions (1 Kings)
>
> tell it not . . . publish it not . . . (2 Samuel)
>
> woe is me (Psalms)
>
> of making many books there is no end (Ecclesiastes)
>
> sufficient unto the day is the evil thereof (Matthew)
>
> what God hath joined together, let no man put asunder (Matthew)
>
> many are called, but few are chosen (Matthew)
>
> render . . . unto Caesar the things which are Caesar's (Matthew)
>
> whited sepulchres (Matthew)
>
> see through a glass darkly (1 Corinthians).

The KJB translators must certainly have read their Douai-Rheims *Matthew*, and the scattering of other parallels suggests that they saw some of the Old Testament material too. Coincidence might account for one or two cases of identity, but hardly eleven.

Also interesting are the cases where we have a modern biblical idiom that does not appear in the KJB at all. There are just seven of these, and three of them are found in exact form in Douai-Rheims only:

> the way of all flesh [the others all have 'earth' for 'flesh']
>
> let your light shine [the others say 'let your light so shine']
>
> charity covers [covereth] a multitude of sins [Tyndale, Geneva and Bishops all have 'love' for 'charity'; Wycliffe has 'charity' but talks about 'the' multitude of sins].

I conclude that there has been a limited but definite Douai-Rheims influence on modern English idiom.

Accurate description and analysis of the linguistic features of a text and of its geographical and temporal provenance is a *sine qua non* of theolinguistic enquiry, but no linguist should stop with questions of 'what', 'when', 'where', and 'who'. They must also explore 'how' and 'why'—an explanatory phase—and this often requires an investigation of a psycholinguistic nature. In relation to the KJB, given that relatively few people in the early 1600s had the literacy skills to read it, and noting that most of a congregation would have been exposed to its language auditorily through church attendance, we have to ask if there were features of the spoken language that would have aided the transmission of the idioms into popular consciousness. Rhythm is the obvious candidate, for a great deal of research in psycholinguistics has shown that one of the important functions of rhythm is to aid auditory memory. We remember a text we have heard in short grammatical 'chunks'—and if the number of content words (i.e. meaning-carrying words, excluding the words that show the structure of the sentence) in those chunks exceeds five, most people have difficulty.

This is a regular experience when during a church service we try to repeat a response—for example, to a psalm—without reading it from a crib sheet. As long as the response is five short content words or less, we have no problem. Anything over this, and we struggle to remember it. Compare these, taken from the Mass—I underline the content words:

> The <u>Lord</u> is my <u>light</u> and my <u>help</u> (*Second Sunday of Lent, Year C*)—three content words, no problem.
>
> I will <u>walk</u> in the <u>presence</u> of the <u>Lord</u> in the <u>land</u> of the <u>living</u> (*Second Sunday of Lent, Year B*)—five content words, still no problem
>
> Your <u>ways</u>, <u>Lord</u>, are <u>faithfulness</u> and <u>love</u> for <u>those</u> who <u>keep</u> your <u>covenant</u> (*First Sunday of Lent, Year B*)—seven content words strain our ability

Most responses are, mercifully, short.

The same principle applies to biblical idioms. Virtually all the idioms that show the influence of the Bible are short: the average length of all 257 expressions is 4.3 words—within that comfortable chunking length. And when we examine individual instances, we can see the way in which usage has favoured that norm. Take *fly in the ointment*. This does not in fact turn up in any biblical translation. The KJB has

> Dead flies cause the ointment of the apothecary to send forth a stinking savour.

Compare this with the earlier versions:

> Wycliffe: flies that die, lessen the sweetness of ointment.
>
> Geneva: dead flies cause to stink, and putrefy the ointment.
>
> Bishop's: a dead fly doth corrupt sweet ointment.

What is the difference? The other translations separate the critical words, *flies* and *ointment*. King James brings them together: 'flies cause the ointment'. This puts them into the same chunk of working auditory memory: they are more likely to be retained by the listener. And it is then a relatively short step for the forces of analogy to oper-ate to adapt the phrasing to one of the commonest rhythmical patterns in English:

> flies cause the ointment > flies in the ointment > fly in the ointment

Compare *bee in the bonnet, head in the sand, stain on the character*, and hundreds more. It does not happen straight away: it took nearly a century before we find the first recorded instance of *fly in the ointment*.

The idioms total means that we must not exaggerate the influence of the KJB on English, as was repeatedly done in the lead-up to the anniversary celebrations. It is true to say, as several commentators do, that no other literary source has matched this edition for the number of influential idioms that it contains; but it is not true to say that the KJB originated all of them. Rather, what it did was popularise them. It gave the idioms a widespread public presence through the work being 'appointed to be read in Churches', and it enabled them to be retained in the auditory memory of the congregations through their rhythmically succinct character. The result was that an unprecedented number of biblical idioms captured the public imagination, so much so that it is now impossible to find an area of contemporary expression that does not from time to time use them, either literally or playfully. We find them appearing in such disparate worlds as nuclear physics, court cases, TV sitcoms, recipe books, punk rock lyrics, and video games, and being adapted in all kinds of imaginative ways to suit their new settings. A banking crisis produced 'Am I my Lehman Brothers' keeper?' A political confrontation produced 'Bush is the fly in Blair's ointment'. The KJB was never 'authorised' (despite its popular name) in any legal sense, but no other translation reached so many people over so long a period, or generated so many variations.

6 THE FUTURE OF THEOLINGUISTICS

The KJB study illustrates, from a concrete and relatively straightforward linguistic domain, the lexicon, the stages through which a theolinguistics moves. The first stage—also emphasised by van Noppen (2011, p. 29)—is to provide a corrective to misleading ideas about the nature of religious language: in the above, the exaggerated claims for KJB influence on everyday speech. This can only be done by the meticulous and time-consuming process of gathering empirical data—here, involving a reading of the whole of the KJB to identify all the relevant idioms (for no comprehensive collection had been made before), and then a re-reading to check that none had been left out. We are talking about the best part of a million words, but corpora of this size are these days a normal part of linguistic investigation. One of the things that theolinguistics can do is replace anecdotal and impressionistic accounts of a use of religious language by gathering corpora of a sufficient size to warrant valid descriptive statements.

The next stage is description (the 'what'): the data—words, idioms, grammatical patterns, sounds, and so forth—have to be given a precise description using one of the models available in linguistics. For the lexicon or the orthography of a language, this is often a simple listing of relevant usages; for grammar and pronunciation, a sophisticated descriptive apparatus may need to be employed. In cases where a language has received little or no description, the theolinguist may need to carry out basic investigative work, even to the extent of devising an alphabet to write the language down, as has often happened when missionary organisations engage in the task of Bible translation with unfamiliar languages.

The third stage is analytical: the formal patterns established by the description need to be related to the temporal (the 'when'), regional, social, occupational (the 'where'), and personal (the 'who') variables that we know condition usage. In the illustration, this involved a comparison of idiomatic expressions in texts belonging to different religious traditions. The risk, always, is premature generalisation, given the wide range of genres that comprise the repertoire of religious language—prayers, hymns, sermons, divinations, blessings, scriptural texts, ritualised events (healings, weddings, funerals . . .), and much more, all of which have to be seen within the context of differing traditions and settings. These variations are the phenomena which keep sociolinguists and stylisticians happily occupied, and sociolinguistic and stylistic perspectives have formed a major part of theolinguistic enquiries to date (see, e.g., Crystal 1976, 1998; Holt 2006; Hammond 2015).

The fourth stage is explanatory (the 'how' and 'why'), which in the illustration involved considerations of a psycholinguistic nature. It is at this stage that 'a credible theolinguistics' (as van Noppen put it above) reaches out to the other disciplines involved in the study of religious language. The further implications of the *Douai/ KJB* question, for example, go well beyond the expertise of theolinguists and must be debated by others. But the provision of empirical evidence, and the identification of relevant factors, are things that theolinguists can provide to help take that debate forward. I very much hope, therefore, that the subject has a future that lives up to the promise it displayed in the 1980s. All we need is for a few more linguist labourers to enter the theolinguistic vineyard.

REFERENCES

Barr. J. (1961). *The Semantics of Biblical Language*. Oxford: Oxford University Press.
Bisschops, R. and J. Francis. (eds.) (1999). *Metaphor, Canon and Community: Jewish, Christian and Islamic Approaches*. Frankfurt: Lang.
Boeve, L. and K. Feyaerts. (eds.) (1999). *Metaphor and God-talk*. Frankfurt: Lang.
Campbell, G. (2010). *Bible: The Story of the King James Version*. Oxford: Oxford University Press.
Crystal, D. (1964). A liturgical language in a linguistic perspective. *New Blackfriars* 46(534), 148–156.
Crystal, D. (1965). *Linguistics, Language and Religion*. London: Burns and Oates.
Crystal, D. (1968). *What Is Linguistics?* London: Edward Arnold.
Crystal, D. (1969). *Linguistics*. Harmondsworth: Penguin.
Crystal, D. (1976). The problem of language variety: An example from religious language. In G. Vesey (ed.), *Communication and Understanding*, 1975–1976 Royal Institute of Philosophy Lectures, pp. 195–207. Hassocks, UK: Harvester Press.
Crystal, D. (1981). Generating theological language. In J. P. van Noppen (ed.), *Theolinguistics*, pp. 265–281. Brussels: Studiereeks Tijdschrift Vrije Universiteit Brussel, New series No 8.
Crystal, D. (1990). A liturgical language in a sociolinguistic perspective. In D. Jasper and R. C. D. Jasper. (eds.), *Language and the Worship of the Church*, pp. 120–146. Basingstoke: Macmillan.

Crystal, D. (1998). Why did the crowd think St Peter was drunk? An exercise in applied sociolinguistics. *New Blackfriars* 79(924), 72–76.

Crystal, D. (2008). *A Dictionary of Linguistics and Phonetics*, 6th edition. Oxford: Blackwell.

Crystal, D. (2010). *Begat: The King James Bible and the English Language*. Oxford: Oxford University Press.

Crystal, D. and D. Davy (1969). *Investigating English Style*. London: Longman.

Feyaerts, K. (2003). *The Bible through Metaphor and Translation: A Cognitive Semantic Perspective*. Frankfurt: Lang.

Goodman, F. D. (1972). *Speaking in Tongues: A Cross-cultural Study of Glossolalia*. Chicago: University of Chicago Press.

Hammond, C. (2015). *The Sound of the Liturgy: How Words Work in Worship*. London: SPCK.

Heather, N. (2000). *Religious Language and Critical Discourse Analysis: Ideology and Identity in Christian Discourse Today*. Frankfurt: Lang.

Holt, R. (2006). A socio-linguistic approach to religious language. *Australian eJournal of Theology* 6, 1–14.

Lakoff, G. and M. Johnson (1980). *Metaphors We Live By*. Chicago: University of Chicago Press.

Robinson, J. A. T. (1963). *Honest to God*. London: SCM Press.

Samarin, W. J. (1972). *Tongues of Men and Angels: A Controversial and Sympathetic Analysis of Speaking in Tongues*. New York: Macmillan.

Samarin, W. J. (ed.) (1976). *Language in Religious Practice*. Rowley, MA: Newbury House.

Sawyer, J. F. A. and J. M. Y. Simpson (eds.) (2001). *Concise Encyclopedia of Language and Religion*. New York: Elsevier.

Stubbs, M. (1983). *Discourse Analysis: The Sociolinguistic Analysis of Natural Language*. Oxford: Blackwell.

van Noppen, J. P. (ed.) (1981). *Theolinguistics*. Brussels: Studiereeks Tijdschrift Vrije Universiteit Brussel, New series No 8.

van Noppen, J. P. (ed.) (1983). *Metaphor and Religion. (Theolinguistics 2)*. Brussels: Studiereeks Tijdschrift Vrije Universiteit Brussel, New series No 12.

van Noppen, J. P. (ed.) (1988). *Erinnern, um Neues zu sagen: Die Bedeutung der Metapher für die religiöse Sprache*. Frankfurt am Main: Athenäum.

van Noppen, J. P. (1999). *Transforming Words: The Early Methodist Revival from a Discourse Perspective*. Frankfurt: Lang.

van Noppen, J. P. (ed.) (2011). Critical theolinguistics vs. the literalist paradigm. *Sociolinguistica* 25, 28–40.

CHAPTER 2

Speaking about God in Universal Words, Thinking about God outside English

ANNA WIERZBICKA

1 INTRODUCTION: BASIC ASSUMPTIONS

In a rapidly changing and globalising world, there are few ideas which deserve re-thinking more than the concept of God. There are billions of people living on Earth today who say that they believe in God, and there are if not billions then many millions of people who say they don't. What exactly do people mean when they say 'I believe in God' or 'I don't believe in God'? This depends, of course, on the meaning of the word *God*. Many people, however, do not have a clear idea of what this word means, as illustrated in the following dialogue between a young daughter and her mother in an autobiographical essay in Yelizaveta Renfro's book, *Xylotheque* (2014):

> I asked my mother: 'What is God and why don't we believe in it?' 'God is something that ignorant people believe in because they are afraid of the truth', she told me. (p. 66)

Yet the word *God* and its equivalents such as *Dieu* (French), *Gott* (German) or *Dio* (Italian) have been established in European languages for many centuries, carrying a meaning shaped by the Christian tradition and the Apostles' Creed: 'Credo in unum Deum, Patrem Omnipotentem. . . .' Of course the Creed, which belongs to a shared European cultural legacy, is not a definition. Whether *God*, in the sense of the Christian Creed, means exactly the same as the *Yahweh* of Judaism or *Allah* of Islam, is a very interesting question, which however is outside the scope of the present chapter. It is certainly a word whose meaning is different from that of the ancient Greek word *theos*, which had a plural (*theoi*). *God*, as in the Creed, does not have a plural. For speakers of European languages, believers and non-believers, it is a cultural key word, which needs to be precisely explicated—for the purpose of 'cultural literacy' and intercultural understanding. (For an insightful recent study of the relationship between languages and religion, see Ostler 2016).

In the increasingly secular West and in the predominantly secular Western academic world, questions about the meaning of the word *God* are sometimes dismissed these days as unimportant and even Eurocentric. It is increasingly suggested in contemporary scholarship that questions about 'God' should be replaced by questions about something else—first of all, 'religion', and better still, 'religious experience'. For example, in their 'Postscript on Religious language—A word of caution', the authors of *Comparative Religious Ethics* write (emphasis added):

> Theravada Buddhists in ancient India refused to use the word 'God' to describe their religious experiences. Instead they spoke of 'emptiness' and 'the void' and the inadequacy of all metaphors to explain their experience, which they called 'nirvana'. The word 'God', which is so familiar to Western religious experience, is just one of a class of diverse terms used in different religions and cultures to express that which is ultimate in power, importance, and meaning. This class of terms includes not only the 'God' of Western theism but also the impersonal Brahman reality of Hinduism, the mysterious Emptiness of Buddhism, and the impersonal nameless power of harmony at work in all things, called the Tao, in Chinese religions. And some of these terms are quite paradoxical. (Fasching and deChant 2001, p. 39)

This is a laudable but, in my view, misguided attempt to avoid Eurocentrism in comparative cultural studies. To begin with, as documented in my book *Experience, Evidence and Sense* (Wierzbicka 2010), 'experience' is a modern English concept, without exact equivalents in other European languages, let alone languages of 'the rest of the world'. To talk about different cultural traditions in terms of the English concept of 'experience' would be a good example of a cultural bias called Anglocentrism (cf. Wierzbicka 2014a; Goddard and Wierzbicka 2014).

Unlike *experience*, the word *religion* does have its counterparts in other modern European languages. However, as documented in Brent Nongbri's book *Before Religion* (2013), the word *religion* didn't have a counterpart in Latin or Ancient Greek, and doesn't have counterparts in many languages outside Europe today. As Nongbri puts it (citing many references), 'in the academic field of religious studies, the claim that religion is a modern invention is not really news' (p. 3). Thus, while talking about Judaism, Buddhism or Hinduism as a 'religion' may be convenient in certain circumstances, it is really a Eurocentric and 'chronocentric' (Bromhead 2009) way of speaking. The idea that the word *God* and its equivalents in other European languages should be explained (or explained away) with references to the word *religion* or the phrase 'religious experience' may appeal to modern Western secularism, but from a cross-linguistic and cross-temporal point of view it is not sustainable.

Fasching and deChant (2001) conclude their discussion of 'religious language' with the following remark:

> Our discussion of religious language should help us to appreciate just how challenging it can be to study and compare various religious traditions. Religious communities and religious traditions from different parts of the world use different metaphors and symbols, and they also mix the way of analogy and the way of negation in varying degrees. [. . .] For example, it may seem that a Jewish theist and a Theravada Buddhist hold diametrically opposed religious beliefs, for Jews believe in a personal God and Theravada Buddhists do not. [. . .] Perhaps theistic and non-theistic religious experiences are really not that far apart. However, it is also possible that they are really talking about truly different experiences.
>
> How to resolve this type of question is a problem that has not yet been fully worked out by scholars of comparative religions. (p. 40)

The Natural Semantic Metalanguage (NSM)—the semantic theory on which the present chapter is based—proposes a solution, or at least the beginning of a solution to this problem (see section 4). This solution relies, first, on culture-specific key words, and second, on culture-independent shared concepts in terms of which those key words can be made intelligible to cultural outsiders.

According to this approach, in an 'interfaith' meeting between Christians, Buddhists and Taoists (for example) conducted through Minimal English as a lingua franca, the representatives of these different traditions should avoid the use of words and culture-specific English phrases like 'the ultimate', 'the ineffable', 'the supernatural' or 'religious experience', which play no special role in the lives of Christians, Buddhists and Taoists, but say, to begin with: 'for us, what is most important is called "God"', 'for us, what is most important is called "nirvana"', and 'for us, what is most important is called "Tao"'. Having introduced those key words that millions of people in certain cultural traditions actually live by, some representative of these traditions can attempt to explain those concepts (as embedded in their languages) through shared, culture-independent human concepts such as 'someone', 'something', 'know', 'want', and the like, used in carefully crafted configurations (see section 4).

To sum up thus far, the concept of 'God' is not universal, and neither are concepts like 'Tao' or 'nirvana'. All these concepts, however, are very important to large parts of humanity, and in the interest of global understanding should be explained, as best as possible, to cultural outsiders. Such global understanding cannot be achieved through words of academic English, which are not cross-translatable into other languages of the world and which play no special role in the lives of the insiders. This chapter attempts, *inter alia*, to articulate the concept of 'God', as embedded in the lexicons of European languages, shaped by the historically dominant cultural tradition of Christianity.

To choose this particular topic for a detailed treatment should not be misconstrued as privileging the Christian concept of 'God' over, for example, 'Tao' or 'Jukurrpa' (a key religious concept of Australian Aboriginal culture). The chapter continues a long tradition of analysing important culture-specific concepts embedded in diverse languages through shared human concepts which have emerged from empirical cross-linguistic investigations, a tradition initiated by my (Wierzbicka) 1992 book *Semantics, Culture and Cognition* and 1997 book *Understanding Cultures through Their Key Words*. For a more recent example of this tradition, the reader is referred to the paper by Goddard and Wierzbicka (2015), 'What does Jukurrpa ("Dreamtime", "the Dreaming") mean?', analysing the key religious concept of Australian Aboriginal culture through universal human concepts—the same concepts in terms of which 'God' is analysed here.

2 TALKING ABOUT GOD IN A NEW CONCEPTUAL LANGUAGE

In this chapter, I will try to show that it is possible to articulate Christian beliefs, including the concept of 'God', in a new conceptual language which can be called 'Basic Human' (Wierzbicka 2014a). This 'Basic Human' is a minimal language which corresponds by and large to the shared lexical, grammatical and conceptual core of all (or nearly all) languages. This mini-language has as many versions as there are languages, so there is 'Minimal English', 'Minimal Polish', 'Minimal Japanese', and so on.

For practical reasons, the version of this 'Basic Human' used in this chapter will be English (rather than, say, my native Polish, or Latin). But this will not be the usual English, with all its historically shaped cultural baggage. Rather, it will be 'Minimal English', whose lexicon includes with few exceptions words which, evidence suggests, have their counterparts in all languages of the world and thus can be regarded as 'universal words' (Wierzbicka 2011). The chapter will illustrate the use of such 'universal words' for exploring some concepts, ideas, and stories essential to Christianity, with a view to facilitating effective communication between adherents of different religions, as well as between believers, agnostics, and atheists. In this context, special attention will be given to the Christian concept of 'God'.

In his book *Science and Soul*, Australian biologist and theologian Charles Birch (2008, p. 159) writes: 'The word "God" is fraught with many meanings, some of which are erroneous and simplistic (. . .). So confusing is the diversity of meanings of the word God that some theologians have called for a moratorium on the word'. Birch has in mind here, in particular, the Protestant theologian Paul Tillich, of whom he says elsewhere in his book that 'Tillich would have liked to have called for a moratorium on the word "God" because of the variety of meanings given to it, and replaced it with "ultimate concern"' (pp. 89–90).

But what does this phrase 'ultimate concern' really mean, we may ask. Birch, drawing on Tillich, explains it with reference to the biblical story of Mary and Martha.

> Like biblical Martha we are concerned about many things, but miss the one that matters. That is the concern that is ultimate in the sense of fulfilling human life. This is the pearl of great price. The only appropriate response to ultimate concern is with infinite passion: with all our mind and soul and strength. This was Mary's concern when Jesus visited the home of Mary and Martha. (Birch 2008, p. 89)

Both Tillich's and Birch's writing can be very appealing, and most Christians would not want to argue with the story of Mary and Martha or with the parable of the pearl of great price. Still, if an animist in Papua New Guinea or Africa or someone raised in a secular milieu in the West were to ask about the Christian 'God', an answer framed in terms of 'ultimate concern' would not be very helpful. Nor would be Birch's further explanation: 'Ultimate concern has the subjective side that is our being ultimately concerned. The objective side is the *object* of our ultimate concern. The object is called God' (2008, p. 89).

With all due respect to both Tillich and Birch, as a semanticist, I would prefer to call for a moratorium on words like 'subjective, 'objective', and 'ultimate', and keep the word 'God'—explaining it not via technical philosophical and theological vocabulary but in simple words independent of the European philosophical tradition and cross-translatable into all languages of the world, including those into which Christianity and the Bible are being introduced for the first time. My point here is not to create an opposition between, on the one hand, theoretical pursuits of philosophy and theology, and on the other, practical tasks of intercultural understanding, for example, in a missionary context. Rather, the question is how genuine understanding can be achieved in any domain, be it philosophy, theology, 'religious studies', international relations, and so on.

There is a persistent line of thought in the humanities, including philosophy, that to explain concepts and ideas in a scientifically valid way we need to avoid simple words of ordinary language and have to reach for words that only experts, or at least highly educated people, are familiar with. There is also an opposite tradition, going back to Leibniz, which holds that complex and unfamiliar concepts (including philosophical and scientific ones) can only be truly understood via simple and familiar ones—down to those which are intuitively self-explanatory. It is the latter tradition which inspires NSM research, so at least one quote from Leibniz (1903) will be in order here:

> If nothing could be understood in itself nothing at all could ever be understood. Because what can only be understood via something else can be understood only to the extent to which that other thing can be understood, and so on; accordingly, we can say that we have understood something only when we have broken it down into parts which can be understood in themselves. (*Opuscules et fragments inédits de Leibniz*, p. 430)

The contrast between these two traditions (one, seeking to explain the complex in terms of the simple, and the other, explaining the complex in terms of the more complex) should not be seen as one between a more practical orientation and a more theoretical one. The practical value of explanations couched in simple and intelligible words and phrases is presumably beyond doubt, but in the Leibnizian tradition, the direction from complex to simple (rather than the other way around) is seen as, above all, *theoretically* more justified. Hence Leibniz's insistence on the need to identify 'the alphabet of human thought', which is also the cornerstone of the NSM theory (see section 4).

In cross-cultural studies, there is an additional reason to aim at analyses framed in simple rather than complex terms: virtually always, it is simple rather than complex concepts that are cross-translatable and that allow us to capture what anthropologists call 'the insider perspective'. As Goddard (2017a, pp. 55–56) notes in relation to cross-cultural studies of social interaction, 'Some approaches . . . make no real attempt to capture, represent or understand what is happening from the point of view of the participants themselves. [. . .] Though such approaches may yield interesting and potentially valuable results, they can be fairly characterised as adopting an "outsider perspective"'. The same applies to cross-cultural studies of 'religion'.

But opting for the 'insider perspective' doesn't by itself ensure that an authentic insider perspective is reached. The key problem, 'in which issues of terminology, methodology and epistemology are intertwined' (p. 56), is formulated by Goddard as follows:

> How can the insiders' perspectives (. . .) be faithfully and authentically depicted if the descriptive terms and categories employed by the analyst are far removed from the insiders' own ways of speaking? If the local categories and ways of speaking of a given linguaculture are highly language-specific, i.e. resistant to translation, how can their meanings be described so as to be accessible to people from other languages and cultures? Given that English is increasingly the global lingua franca of science, what can be done to ensure that English-specific terms and categories are not reified, naturalised, and treated as culture-neutral? (2017a, p. 56)

Again, these questions apply to 'religion' as much as to any other area of cross-cultural studies, and they underlie the ideas developed in the present chapter.

3 TALKING ABOUT 'GOD' IN SUDAN AND AMAZONIA

The concept of 'God' is central to Christianity. It is also an important semantic molecule of English and other European languages, which shows up in the meaning of a great many other words, such as (in English) *church, priest, altar, nun, Bible, psalm, chapel, theology, religion*, and so on. Explaining the meaning of the word *God* to speakers of languages which don't have a lexical equivalent of it is a challenge—as Christian missionaries in many parts of the world have often found, and commented on.

While words and phrases of academic theology and 'religious studies' have seldom been found to be very helpful in meeting this challenge, the experience of missionaries could be very instructive to the experts, if they chose to pay attention to it. As anthropologist Wendy James notes in relation to the Nilotic language Uduk in Sudan, 'central to the mission's translation project was the invention of a name for God'. James refers in this context to her 1988 book about the Uduk people and to an earlier book by a Christian missionary Michael Forsberg. Forsberg was working together with his wife Enid on a project of translating the Bible into Uduk, and they were consulting with another missionary, Nick Simponis, who was in Sudan.

> Every tribe on earth had a name for God, we thought, yet we had found no such name in the Uduk language.

'In your notes you have *arum* as meaning "god", I said to Nick one day. 'The way the Uduks use it, it seems to mean "spirit", especially the spirits of the dead'.

'God is a spirit, isn't He?' Nick rejoined.

'Yes, but His name isn't *spirit*. According to Uduk ideas when we call God *arum* we are saying that He is the spirit of a person who once died, a ghost. I don't think they believe in any one spirit who has only had spirit existence from the beginning'. (Forsberg 1958, p. 156)

Thus both Michael and Enid Forsberg felt that it was not satisfactory to introduce 'God' as simply an '*arum*' ('spirit'), given that *arum* had a very wide range of use in Uduk and didn't point to what they understood to be the most important part of the 'God' concept.

Many breakfast, dinner, and supper conversations later, we decided that it was misleading to call God *arum*.

'I studied phonetics in Bible school,' Nick said one day, 'and we were told that if there is no adequate name for God in a language, we should just use the English name. After all, no matter what word we use, we'll have to describe Him to the people, and tell them who He is.'

We did not feel qualified to argue, so we started to tell the people about *God*. Our first attempt at a hymn, set to the music of 'We Praise Thee, O God, for the Son of Thy Love' (but not a translation of the hymn), looked like this:

> God diid imis
> God diid imis
> Akim bidi yuka Yesus

We taught the people to sing it but it did not sound quite right. (Forsberg 1958, p. 156)

The intuition that the Forsbergs had was that 'God' was not just a name (like 'Jesus'), but a complex concept with some ingredients that could be pinpointed in intelligible words. Above all, it seemed clear that 'God' was someone not like people, and someone 'above' people.

'That English word "God" sounds terribly out of place in the Uduk hymn,' Enid observed one day.

'I don't like it either,' I admitted.

'Nick is right in saying that we'll have to tell the people what God is like regardless of the name we use for Him,' she continued, 'and since that is so, I'd rather adapt a word of theirs that fits into the language and then tell them who He is'. Nick, too, had begun to feel that the word 'God' fitted rather awkwardly into the Uduk vocabulary. So we began new discussions. 'Perhaps we would doctor up their word for spirit,' Nick suggested.

'Why don't we just call him "*wadhi gi mis*, the one above"?' Enid added.

Nick and I agreed. We had not dreamed that one day we would be giving God a name. But that was not the end.

Later, when our first Christians began to think for themselves, they said, 'Wadhi means a person with a human body. You say God is a spirit. We should call Him "the Spirit above".'

So God's name was revised for the last time. He became 'Arum gi mis'. (Forsberg 1958, p. 157)

The language in which Forsberg writes about the Uduk converts to Christianity is dated and in some instances very patronising, but I think his impulse was to search for genuine intercultural understanding. As James (1988, p. 225) notes, the phrase 'Arum gi mis' ('the spirit above') was later represented as one word *Arumgimis*. According to James, the word specifies 'the Arum which is the Sky', an exclusive being, distinct by implication from other *arum*. Zeroing in on the phrase 'Arum gi mis', soon contracted to one word, *Arumgimis*, may have been an inspired choice, but it did not, by itself, solve the challenge of creating a new meaning, corresponding to the concept used in sentences like 'In the beginning God created the heaven and the earth' (Genesis 1:1), 'God knoweth your hearts' (Luke 16:15), and 'The things which are impossible with man are possible with God' (Luke 18:27).

James (2013, p. 341) comments that 'putting the scriptures into a local African language . . . is not merely a matter of "translation" but of creating new registers which enshrine these things along with a new respect for writing—not just as something deployed by outsiders, but now entrenched among themselves as the Word of God'. It needs to be emphasised, however, that it is not only a matter of creating new registers but also of creating new ways of thinking, enshrined either in loan words or in new meanings of indigenous words. To ensure a clear understanding of such new meanings it is important to be able to explain them, at some point, in simple words of the local language. For example, to translate into Uduk the first sentence of the Bible—'In the beginning God created the heaven and the Earth' (the 1611 translation known as the King James Version, hereafter KJV)—one would no doubt need to find, or to forge, a suitable Uduk word, but one would also need to link it with desired meaning. This could be done (only) through a commentary couched in simple words available, with exactly the same meanings, in both Uduk and the language of the translator him- or herself.

From a Judeo-Christian point of view, the first step in such a commentary would be to locate the local word for 'someone': whatever else 'God' means, from a Judeo-Christian point of view *God* is not an abstract noun like *concern*, but a 'personal' noun meaning 'someone'. Having located the local word for 'someone', one would need to locate some other words essential for talking about that 'someone' who, according to the Judeo-Christian tradition, 'created heaven and earth'.

Once we step away from technical words of European philosophy and theology and try to think, instead, in simple, intelligible, and cross-translatable words of 'ordinary language', we realise that to talk meaningfully about 'God' we will also need the word 'good' (as in 'someone good'), and a certain number of other words, such as *can, want, say,* and *do*. Using this approach consistently, we will be following the methodology already referred to, that of the Natural Semantic Metalanguage.

In a recent book co-authored by Yanomami Indian Davi Kopenawa and French anthropologist Bruce Albert, the former is reported as saying (in Yanomami) to the latter (2013, p. 206):

> When I was a child, the missionaries really wanted me to know *Teosi* ['God', from Portuguese *Deus*]. (. . .) *Teosi*'s words belong to white people. They used to be unknown in the forest. They appeared among us not very long ago. (. . .) This is why we do not really understand them. We barely know their upstream meaning [i.e. superficial, as opposed to full meaning]. Our thought cannot open them out (. . .).

It is difficult to see how the 'downstream' meaning of any culturally important messages formulated in culturally shaped Portuguese words could ever be understood by speakers of a language as culturally and conceptually distant from Portuguese as Yanomami (and of course vice versa) without cross-translatable words. This is what the NSM approach is, essentially, all about: showing how clear understanding—including cross-cultural understanding—can be achieved through intelligible, cross-translatable words, and how simple, intelligible words can help 'open out' the meanings of complex and incomprehensible words, phrases, and messages.

4 NATURAL SEMANTIC METALANGUAGE

What I have called, informally, 'Basic Human' is generally known in linguistics as 'Natural Semantic Metalanguage' (cf. e.g. Wierzbicka 1996; Goddard 2011; Goddard and Wierzbicka 2002, 2014). Both terms refer, essentially, to the common core of all languages, but they look at it from two different perspectives. When we talk about 'Basic Human' we are thinking of that shared core of all languages as a mini-language available to all people for talking to others on a basic human level, when a hundred or so words are sufficient for saying what one wants to say.

The idea that, despite their great diversity, human languages have a shared core goes back to Leibniz, who was the first European thinker to propose a comparative study of the languages of the world. In Leibniz's conception, the shared core of human languages corresponds to the shared core of human thought—not in the sense of a shared body of ideas but in the sense of an innate conceptual 'equipment' shared by all people. At the heart of that innate conceptual equipment lies, according to Leibniz (Couturat 1903), 'an alphabet of human thoughts' (or, in Leibniz's original Latin, *alphabetum cogitationum humanarum*). His key insight was that all human thoughts can be resolved into a small number of 'primitive concepts'.

When the same mini-language is used for talking about the meaning of words (or other linguistic expressions), it is referred to as 'natural semantic metalanguage', to emphasise that it is a language used for talking about language (hence 'meta'), that it is used for talking about meanings (hence, 'semantic'), and that it is part of ordinary natural language (hence, 'natural').

NSM includes a mini-lexicon of sixty-five simple words (with matching equivalents in all sampled languages) and thirty to forty other words which are not simple (elementary) but which also appear to be universal. These are called 'universal semantic molecules'. The words *men, women, children, give birth, day, night* and *(living) creatures* are good (and relevant) examples here. The full set of universal semantic primes expressed through their English exponents is presented in Table 1. Equivalent tables for twenty-three other languages can be found on the NSM homepage (see NSM Homepage Downloads).

For reasons of space, it is impossible to fully explain here how exactly this set has been arrived at, but the main method was that envisaged by Leibniz: trial and error, applied, by many scholars and over many years, both intralinguistically (within selected languages) and cross-linguistically. (The interested reader can consult readily available recent accounts in publications such as Wierzbicka 2015b and Goddard and Wierzbicka 2014, and follow the references cited there.) The main fact which needs to be emphasised here is that the set of sixty-five panhuman conceptual primitives identified through NSM research has been extensively tested both in intralinguistic and in cross-linguistic research. Philosopher David Chalmers (2012) comments, referring to NSM, that it has been 'used to analyse an extraordinary range of expressions in many different languages' (p. 9).

In addition to the mini-lexicon of primes and molecules, NSM has its own mini-grammar which matches the shared grammatical core of all (or nearly all) languages. Together, the mini-lexicon and the mini-grammar form a mini-language, which in

---

Table 1. UNIVERSAL SEMANTIC PRIMES EXPRESSED THROUGH
THEIR ENGLISH EXPONENTS

I, YOU, SOMEONE, SOMETHING~THING, PEOPLE, BODY	substantives
KINDS, PARTS~HAVE PARTS	relational substantives
THIS, THE SAME, OTHER~ELSE	Determiners
ONE, TWO, SOME, ALL, MUCH~MANY, LITTLE~FEW	Quantifiers
GOOD, BAD	Evaluators
BIG, SMALL	Descriptors
KNOW, THINK, WANT, DON'T WANT, FEEL, SEE, HEAR	mental predicates
SAY, WORDS, TRUE	Speech
DO, HAPPEN, MOVE	actions, events, movement
BE (SOMEWHERE), THERE IS, BE (SOMEONE/SOMETHING)	location, existence, specification
(IS) MINE	Possession
LIVE, DIE	life and death
TIME~WHEN, NOW, BEFORE, AFTER, A LONG TIME, A SHORT TIME, FOR SOME TIME, MOMENT	Time
PLACE~WHERE, HERE, ABOVE, BELOW, FAR, NEAR, SIDE, INSIDE, TOUCH	Place
NOT, MAYBE, CAN, BECAUSE, IF	logical concepts
VERY, MORE	intensifier, augmentor
LIKE~AS~WAY	Similarity

different contexts can be thought of as either 'a natural semantic metalanguage' (NSM) or as 'Basic Human'. When this mini-language is used in its English version, it can be referred to as 'Minimal English' (cf. Wierzbicka 2014a). More recently the term Minimal English has tended to be used for minimal versions of English resting on the bedrock of NSM but somewhat enlarged in relation to 'pure' NSM (Goddard 2017b). It can be said, then, that all the semantic texts presented in this chapter are formulated in Minimal English.

Well-known typologist Nicholas Evans, who is not an NSM practitioner and who has expressed doubts about a few NSM primes as proposed lexical universals, acknowledges the status of NSM as a most highly developed system for cross-linguistic identification of meaning:

> NSM practitioners have produced a vast body of semantic analyses across dozens of languages, and at present can lay claim to having developed the approach that has gone deepest into the possibilities of setting up a cross-linguistically valid set of basic semantic categories in which all meanings can be stated. (Evans 2010, pp. 516–517)

Ultimately, the point is not whether the set of universal semantic primes posited by NSM is correct in every respect, but to what extent it can serve the cause of 'human understanding' and cross-cultural communication. On this point, I will allow myself to quote another scholar who is neither an NSM practitioner nor a firm believer in the set of semantic primes posited by NSM, but who is well aware of the dangers of Anglocentrism and Eurocentrism in the humanities and social sciences: philosopher and historian of science Oren Harman (2016, pp. 422–425):

> Fundamental and unique to NSM is the principle that one should only say something about another culture with words that could be used by that same culture. Whether or not one believes in innate semantic primes, it is difficult not to see how such a principle may help rid cultural translations of cultural biases.

It may not be immediately obvious that what Harman says here applies not only to anthropology but also to philosophy and theology. To say in English something authentic about how Uduk (or Yanomami) speakers think, we need to try to stick to English words which have Uduk (or Yanomami) equivalents, and avoid words like 'ultimate', 'subjective', 'objective' or 'experience'. Similarly, to say in English something authentic about how *humans* think, we need to try to stick to English words which have their equivalents in most, if not all, human languages. This too, means avoiding words like 'ultimate', 'subjective', 'objective', and 'experience', and trying to stick to cross-translatable words like 'someone', 'want', 'know', 'live, 'die', and 'people', that is, to well-tested candidates for membership in the 'alphabet of human thought'. Or such is the guiding principle of the NSM approach.

5 TRANSLATING THE 'APOSTLES' CREED' INTO NSM
5.1 'God'

Using the above approach systematically, in my book *What Christians Believe* (Wierzbicka 2017; see also Wierzbicka, To appear) I have developed the following 'definition' (explication) of the Christian concept of 'God':

> *God*
> There is someone not like people.
> This someone is someone above people.
> This someone is above everything.
> This someone is now, always was, always will be.
> This someone is everywhere.
> There is no one else like this someone.
> God is this someone.
>
> People can't see God.
> At the same time, people can know some things about God.
> They can know these things because God wants it.
> People can know that it is like this:
> > God is good.
> > If God wants something, it is something good.
> > If God does something, it is something good.
> > If God wants something to happen, it can happen because of this.
> > If God says about something: 'I want it to happen', it happens.
> > If God says about something: 'It is like this', it is true.
> > God knows everything.

At the same time, people can know that it is like this:

> God knows all people.
> God feels something very good towards all people.
> God wants to do good things for all people.
> God wants to speak to all people.
> All people can know God, God wants it.
> All people can live with God, God wants it.

Essentially, the concept of 'God' was chosen for a detailed treatment here for the same reason for which the concept 'Jukurrpa' embedded in Warlpiri and many other Australian languages was chosen in Goddard and Wierzbicka's 2015 paper 'What does *Jukurrpa* ("Dreamtime", "the Dreaming") mean?' The concept of 'Jukurrpa' is of great significance in Australian Aboriginal culture, and in Australia, it is very important for intercultural communication and education that this cultural concept should be well understood. In European languages and cultures (strongly influenced, historically, by Christianity), the concept of 'God' occupies an important place and also needs to be well understood. (Apart from 'religion', the significance of the concept of 'God' for European literatures, painting, music, architecture, etc. hardly needs to be justified.)

The choice of particular components included in the explication above does not seem particularly controversial from the point of view of New Testament studies or Christian theology, although it could of course be the subject of a lengthy discussion. Such discussion, however, would be outside the scope of the present chapter, whose aim is not theological but semantic: the main point is that the language of traditional theology, which is often opaque and seldom cross-translatable, can be replaced with simple, clear, and intelligible words and phrases whose cross-translatability has been tested through extensive empirical studies. At the same time, the semantic text above offers a model for how alternative explications of 'God' could be developed, without any words and phrases which are not cross-translatable into the languages of 'the rest of the world'.

Commenting on the translation of religious meanings between cultures, anthropologist Wendy James (2013) writes: 'we live in distinct communities. But at the same time *translation* is one of the distinctly human gifts (. . .). The moral sphere of our common humanity must extend beyond one language or local cultural form. (. . .) A potential for translation is a capacity of "intellectual agency" we all share'. But to what extent, exactly, can concepts such as 'God' be translated, and understood, through words spoken in distinct linguistic and cultural communities? A phrase which means, literally, 'Spirit in the sky' may be the best possible rendering of the Christian concept of 'God' in a language like Uduk, but in order for this phrase to 'work' to convey the intended concept, a new meaning must, over time, emerge from it. This new meaning can be created through new contexts of use, but also, through explanations couched in words that are cross-translatable between the source language and the target language. Only an explication couched in cross-translatable words can be understood in the same way in both languages and thus be a guarantor of genuine mutual understanding between the speakers of distinct linguistic and cultural communities. This is what the explication of 'God' presented here hopes to achieve.

Once again, to avoid possible misunderstandings it needs to be emphasised that exactly the same approach is taken in NSM research in relation to key 'religious' concepts in other traditions, for example, the key Buddhist concept 'dukkha' in Wierzbicka (2014b) (based on Obeyesekere 1985), the Japanese Buddhist 'jihi' in Hasada (2008), the Melanesian concept 'mana' in Wierzbicka (2014a), and the Australian Aboriginal concept 'Jukurrpa' in Goddard and Wierzbicka (2015).

5.2 God, creator of the world

The opening line of the Apostles' Creed reads: 'I believe in God, the Father almighty, creator of heaven and earth'. According to the explication of 'God' presented here, some components corresponding, loosely, to 'Father' and to 'almighty' are included in the concept of 'God' itself. On this interpretation, the phrase 'the Father almighty' doesn't add anything to 'God', but rather, makes some of its components semi-explicit. As for 'creating heaven and earth', however, this can be seen as an amplification, rather than part of the explication, of the core Christian concept of God.

The *Compendium of the Catechism of the Catholic Church* (2005) in its series of questions and answers asks (p. 40): 'Who created the world?' The answer reads: 'The Father, the Son, and the Holy Spirit as the one and indivisible principle of creation even though the work of creating the world is particularly attributed to God the Father'. Unfortunately, this is a good example of the impenetrable and untranslatable language of much of the traditional European theology. The further statements on the topic of creation are not any clearer (or more translatable):

> The world is not the result of any necessity nor blind fate, nor of chance. God created 'out of nothing' (*ex nihilo*) (2 Maccabees 7:28): a world which is ordered and good and which he infinitely transcends. God preserves his creation in being and sustains it, giving it the capacity to act and leading it towards its fulfilment through his Son and the Holy Spirit. (p. 41)

For readers alienated by the difficult and untranslatable language of the *Compendium*, it is good to know that a more reader-friendly version of essentially the same series of questions and answers can be found in YOUCAT: *Youth Catechism of the Catholic Church* (2011)—a version of the catechism aiming 'to translate the Catechism of the Catholic Church into the language of young people' (from the Foreword by Pope Benedict XVI, p. 9). In YOUCAT's section on the creation we read, for example:

> God willed the world; he sustains it and will perfect it. *Being created* is a lasting quality *in* things and a fundamental truth *about* them. (. . .) God alone, who is beyond time and space, created the world out of nothing and called all things into being. Everything that exists depends on God and continues in being only because God wills it be. (pp. 37–38)

The absence of phrases like 'principle of creation' and 'infinitely transcends' in the youth version of the catechism is noteworthy and praiseworthy, and it is in keeping with the vision of 'unity in diversity' set out in Pope Benedict XVI's Foreword:

> We realized at the time we were working on the book that not only are the continents and cultures diverse, but that even within individual communities there are again diverse 'continents': The worker thinks differently from the farmer; a physicist differently from a philologist; an executive differently from a journalist; a young man differently from an old man. So we had to find a way of thinking and speaking that was in some way above all these differences, a common space, so to speak, between different worlds of thought. (pp. 8–9)

This is the key question: how to find a way of thinking that is 'above' all the different cultural worlds of thought and provides a common space for all people living in all these worlds. As decades of cross-linguistic investigations in the NSM framework have shown, such a common space can be found in the shared core of all languages which has come to light through decades of empirical cross-linguistic investigations (see, in particular, Goddard and Wierzbicka 1994, 2002; Goddard 2008; Peeters 2006; Goddard and Wierzbicka 2014; NSM Homepage). Trying to speak about the idea of 'creation' and about God as 'Creator' from within that common space, in *What Christians Believe* (2017) I have proposed the following semantic text (presented here in an abbreviated form):

The world exists because God wants it to exist

There are people on earth, there are many things on earth,
    many things are happening on earth.
  There is the sky above the earth, there is light, there is the sun, there is the moon,
    there are stars.
It is like this because God wants it to be like this.
It wasn't always like this. A very very long time ago, it was like this:
  There was no earth, there was no sky, there was no light; there were no places
    as there are now,
  there were no people, there was nothing anywhere, nothing was happening
    anywhere.
  There was God.

Before there was anything anywhere, God said something. God said:
"I want there to be places of some kinds, I want some things to be happening in
    these places."
When God said this, something happened, it happened as God wanted.
God said: "I want there to be light". When God said this, there was light.
God said: "This is very good."
After this, many other things were happening for a very long time, as God wanted.
After some time, it was like this:
  There were places of many kinds, many things were happening in these places.
  There was the earth, there was the sky, there was the sun, there was the moon,
    there were stars.
  It was like this because God wanted it to be like this. God said: "This is very good."

For a very long time many things were happening to the earth,
  they were happening because God wanted it.
For a long time, it was like this: no things were growing on earth,
  no living creatures were living on earth.
After this, it was not like this anymore, it was like this:
  things of many kinds were growing on earth
  living creatures of many kinds were living on earth.
All this was as God wanted. God said: "This is very good."
When it was like this, for a long time there were no people on earth.

After this, there were people living on earth.

It was like this because God wanted it. God said: "This is very good."

The main difference between this 'brief history of creation' and those offered in works such as the *Compendium of the Catechism of the Catholic Church* or even YOUCAT is its language: it is a story told almost exclusively in 'Basic Human', and for the most part , in universal semantic primes. Those which are not primes include 'creature', 'grow', 'Earth', 'sky', 'light', 'sun', 'moon', 'stars', which are, evidence suggests, universal, or near-universal, semantic molecules (cf. Goddard and Wierzbicka 2014).

It is not my purpose here to justify the content of the above semantic texts from a theological point of view, but rather to show that the traditional Christian doctrine can be expressed in simple and cross-translatable words and phrases. Some aspects of these texts are of course open to debate. The main point here is to ensure clarity, precision, and cross-translatability.

6 'SIN' AND 'LOVE' RENDERED IN NSM
6.1 'Sin'

In the same passage in which he recounts Tillich's rejection of the word *God*, Birch (2008, p. 90) writes: 'Likewise he avoided the word "sin". It had become distorted to mean acts that contradict conventional morality, especially in relation to sex. His alternative word for "sin" is "estrangement"'.

Tillich's distrust of the word *sin* is understandable and his proposed alternative is attractive, as far as it goes, but it is clearly not sufficient. The fact is that the word *sin* (in the New Testament Greek, *hamartia*) is common in Jesus' sayings. To focus on a few examples (from the KJV), Jesus said:

> He that is without sin among you, let him first cast a stone at her. (John 8:8)
>
> Her sins, which are many, are forgiven, for she loved much. (Luke 7:47)
>
> Son, be of good cheer; thy sins be forgiven thee. (Matthew. 9:2)
>
> Whoever committeth sin, is the servant of sin. (John 8:34)
>
> Neither do I condemn thee: Go, and sin no more. (John 8:11)
>
> . . . for sinners also love those that love them. (Luke 6:32)
>
> I came not to call the righteous, but sinners to repentance. (Mark 2:17)

For anyone who wants to understand Jesus' teaching, his concept of 'sin', 'hamartia' needs to be explained in words that are simple and intelligible (as well as cross-translatable), and not (or not only) replaced with philosophical terms such as 'estrangement'.

How can one talk about 'sin', then, in simple and intelligible words? The best first approximation seems clear: when Jesus said to the elders 'he that is without sin among you' he meant 'he who has never done anything (very) bad'. The second best approximation will need to expand a little on the first one, linking it, as Jesus often did, and as Tillich implicitly does too, with a person's relation to God (obviously, when Tillich says 'estrangement' he means 'estrangement from God').

Trying to articulate this link between the New Testament concepts of 'sin' and 'God' in simple and cross-translatable words, one comes inevitably (in my view) to the phrase 'to live with God' anchored in the biblical expressions 'dwelling with God', 'abiding with God', 'The house of the Lord', and so on (cf. Wierzbicka 2001, chapter 4).

> Lord, who shall abide in thy tabernacle? (Psalm 15:1)
>
> One thing have I desired of the Lord, that I will seek after; that I may dwell in the house of the Lord all the days of my life; (Psalm 27:4)
>
> if a man loves me, he will keep my words; and my Father will love him, and we will come unto him, and make our abode with him. (John 14:23)

As the examples quoted earlier illustrate, in the Gospels, Jesus talks about 'sins' (*hamartia*), 'sinning' (*hamartano*), and 'sinners' (*hamartoloi*). Presumably, all these examples refer, in different ways, to 'doing something very bad' and 'not living with God'. What Tillich appears to be doing, in effect, is deemphasising the first of these two aspects and highlighting the second. To explain Jesus' teaching clearly, however, we need to refer to both, and also, to the causal link between the two. Tentatively, I would propose the following:

People don't live as God wants them to live

Often people don't live like God wants people to live.
Often people live like this:

> They feel something bad towards other people.
> They want to do bad things to other people.
> They don't want to do good things for other people.

When someone lives like this, this someone can't live with God.
Because many people often live like this, many people don't live with God.
This is very bad for these people.

As Tillich himself states in another book (*The Protestant Era*, 1951), 'the basis of Christian ethics (. . .) [is] the principle of love, in the sense of the Greek word *agape*' (p. 172). If 'God is love' (as, e.g., we read in St. John's first letter), then living with God must somehow involve 'living with love'. But what is 'love', in the New Testament sense? Tillich's explanation of 'love' as 'agape' begs the question: what exactly is the meaning of *agape*, as this word is used in New Testament Greek?

A great deal has of course been written on this subject in English and in some other European languages, in particular, in various Bible dictionaries and encyclopedias. The explanations offered in this literature, however, are usually very complex and couched in words which have no equivalents in most languages of the world (cf. e.g. entries on 'love' in *The Anchor Bible Dictionary*, 1992; *Dictionary of the Bible*, Hastings 1958; *Dictionary of the Bible*, McKenzie 1965; or the *New Catholic Encyclopedia*, Catholic University of America 1967–1996).

6.2 'Love'

In her book *Sister Wendy's Bible Treasury: Stories and Wisdom through the Eyes of the Great Painters* (2012, p. 159), art historian and Bible commentator Sister Wendy Beckett writes:

> One of the Scriptural definitions of God is that God himself is love; it is a quality so essential to his very being that without it God would not be God. Everything Jesus did and said had love for its impulse, love for its meaning. For these 30-odd years human beings could actually see for themselves, in flesh and blood, what love was. Seeing, of course, is only part of the message. Love is not an intellectual understanding, though it is that as well, and it is certainly not an emotional response: Love is action. Jesus never spoke about 'feeling' love, but about responding to the needs of other people. (. . .)
>
> Since in our language the word 'love' often—in fact usually—does have emotional connotations, it is frequently better, I think, to replace it by 'reverence'.

In reading this proposal to replace the word 'love' with the word 'reverence' we can recognise the same impulse which led Tillich to propose replacing the word 'God' with the phrase 'ultimate concern', and the word 'sin' with the word 'estrangement'. What we recognise here is the distrust of traditional Christian language, which for some people today can be misleading, off-putting, and worn out. This impulse is understandable, but the solution hardly seems adequate. From the perspective adopted in this chapter and in the author's earlier attempts to address the question 'What did Jesus mean?' (cf. Wierzbicka 2001), here as elsewhere, the best solution lies in looking for a semantic invariant (a common core of different uses) expressible in simple and cross-translatable words.

'"Love" is not an emotional response', says Sister Wendy Beckett, who wants to argue against reducing 'love' to feelings, and wants to link love with 'doing'. This move is understandable, but there is no reason why 'doing' should be **opposed** to 'feeling' rather than combined with it.

In St. Paul's first letter to the Corinthians, which is the paramount Christian commentary on Jesus's meaning of 'love', we read:

> And though I bestow all my goods to feed the poor, and though I give my body to be burned but have no love, it profits me nothing. (1 Corinthians 13:3)

Surely the person who bestows all his or her goods to feed the poor is **doing** a great deal. Evidently, however, in St. Paul's view **doing** is not enough—apparently, feeling is needed as well. This leads us to the following (provisional) explication of the New

Testament concept expressed by the Greek verb *agapan*, which with time became absorbed into the conceptual lexicon of all European languages in words like the English verb 'to love' or the noun 'love' (at least in one of its meanings):

Someone X loves someone Y

someone X feels something very good towards someone Y
X does many things because of this

If we test this short explication against narrative definitions of 'love' in the Gospels such as the parables of the lost sheep and the prodigal son, it appears to work quite well. The shepherd feels something very good towards his sheep and he does many things because of this (e.g., searches for them, tirelessly, when they get lost). Similarly, the father of the prodigal son feels something very good towards his foolish younger son, and does many things because of this (such as allowing him to follow his fantasy, and then running to meet him when he returns).

However, when we test this provisional explication against the exchange between Jesus and Simon Peter (John 21:16, KJV)

—Simon, son of Jona, lovest thou me?

—Yea, Lord, thou knowest that I love thee,

it becomes apparent that the provisional explication requires a certain modification. Here, Jesus appears to be asking Simon Peter: 'do you feel something very good towards me? and are you willing to do many things because of this?' rather than 'do you feel something very good towards me? and are you doing many things because of this?' This suggests that in order to fit this example (as well as various other ones) the provisional two-component explication needs to be modified as follows:

Someone X loves someone Y

someone X feels something very good towards someone Y
X wants to do many things because of this

But this version, too, is only provisional, because it doesn't seem to tell the whole story.

In my earlier work on this meaning of 'love' in Jesus's words and images (cf. Wierzbicka 2001), I concentrated on the idea that 'loving' people (in the New Testament sense of the word) involves 'wanting to do good things for them'. If we test this hypothetical semantic component against the evidence of the two key parables that we have just considered, it seems clearly applicable, too: the shepherd wants to take care of his lost sheep, and the father wants to put the best robe on his son, a ring on his finger, and shoes on his feet, so the component of 'wanting to do good things for someone' (the one whom one loves) applies here too. At the same time, an explication which focuses too narrowly on wanting to do good things for the loved person does not allow for all the seemingly foolish or 'pointless' things that a loving person may do (such as risking the security of the other sheep, or waiting for years at the window for the return of a prodigal son). And when the old father runs to meet his son, and embraces him, and kisses him, is he doing (or wanting to do) something good for the son, or simply 'doing' something, overcome by feeling?

Considering a broader range of examples, I have come to the conclusion that an exclusive emphasis on 'wanting to do good things for the loved person' was one-sided, and that 'feeling something very good towards this person' and 'wanting to do many things because of this' also needs to be included.

When we look at the New Testament concept of 'love' (*agape*) from a broad cross-linguistic and cross-cultural perspective, one of its most striking aspects is its applicability to very different kinds of relationships: God loves people, people can love God, people can love other people, God the Father loves Jesus, Jesus loves his disciples, Jesus wants his disciples to love one another, Peter says that he loves Jesus, St. Paul tells husbands to love their wives. . . . If we want to posit a unitary meaning for all these different uses, the best explication appears to be one including three semantic components rather than only two, as follows:

Someone X loves (agapan) someone Y

X feels something very good towards Y
X wants to do many things because of this
X wants to do good things for Y.

This is not to say that there are no differences between different 'loving' relationships, and that, for example, 'mother love' is exactly the same as 'brother love', or that God's love for people is exactly the same as human love. My point here is not that speakers of English do not, and cannot, differentiate between different kinds of 'love', but that 'wanting to do good things for someone' is part of the semantic invariant of the English verb *love* (and of the New Testament *agapan*), whereas 'wanting bad things not to happen to someone' is not.

At this point, it will be in order to take at least a quick look at the English word *charity*, and its relation to *love* (noun and verb). As noted by the *Oxford English Dictionary,* a distinction between Latin *diligere* ('to love', for the Greek verb *agapan*) and Latin *caritas* ('love', for the Greek noun *agape*) was introduced by the Vulgate, the fourth century Latin translation of the Bible. The KJV followed suit and rendered the verb *agapan* as 'to love' and the noun *agape* as 'charity'. It is important to note here that over the centuries *charity* has moved a long way away from *love*, to which it was once quite close, as the following examples also from the *Oxford English Dictionary* indicate:

1430. The King, the queen of Corinth, the country, has the child in so great charity.
1667. Relations dear, and all the charities of father, son, and brother. (Milton, *Paradise Lost*)
1758. Charity, or tenderness for the poor . . . is, I think, known only to those who enjoy . . . the light of Revelation.

But the phrase 'cold as charity' also goes quite far back in the history of the English language, as these two examples illustrate:

1785. Cold is thy heart and as frozen as charity!
1864. The wind is as cold as charity.

In contemporary English, *charity* clearly does not imply 'very good feelings' toward the people for whom someone wants to do good things. From this point of view, lovers of the KJV must regret the fact that its translators chose to render the noun *agape* in English as *charity* rather than *love*, especially in relation to St. Paul's hymn to love (*agape*) in the first letter to the Corinthians, which is often read at weddings, even in the 21st century. They must also applaud the decision of the editors of the Revised Version of the Bible (the New Testament first appeared in 1881) to substitute *love* everywhere for *charity*.

What is most relevant here is that in its contemporary meaning, *charity* implies 'wanting to do good things for other people' but not 'feeling something very good towards these people', whereas both the verb 'to love' and the noun *love* carry each of those components, and also, as I have suggested, a component of 'wanting to do many things' (because of feeling something very good towards someone). All these three components appear to continue the legacy of the New Testament 'love' as 'defined', for example, in St. John's first letter (4:4–16):

7 Beloved, let us love one another: for love is of God; and every one that loveth is born of God, and knoweth God.

8 He that loveth not knoweth no God; for God is love.

9 In this was manifested the love of God toward us, because that God sent his only begotten Son into the world, that we might live through him.

10 Herein is love, not that we loved God, but that he loved us, and sent his Son *to be* the propitiation for our sins.

11 Beloved, if God so loved us, we ought also to love one another.

12 No man hath seen God at any time. If we love one another, God dwelleth in us, and his love is perfected in us. (. . .)

14 And we have seen and do testify that the Father sent the Son *to be* the Saviour of the world. (. . .)

16 And we have known and believed the love that God hath to us. God is love; and he that dwelleth in love dwelleth in God, and God in him.

7 TRANSLATING GOSPEL NARRATIVES INTO NSM
7.1 What did Mary say to God?

The *Compendium of the Catechism of the Catholic Church* (2005) includes a section (No. 97) entitled 'How does Mary cooperate in the divine plan of salvation?'. The exact meaning of this question would be difficult to explain to speakers of most languages of the world, because they don't have exact equivalents for the English words *cooperate, plan,* or *salvation.* The meaning of *cooperate* is peculiar to the semantic universe of English (see Wierzbicka 2014a, chapter 9), that of *plan* has equivalents in many European languages but not in many others, whereas *salvation* is a Christian concept shared by languages with a strong Christian tradition but not by others.

Arguably, if the *Compendium* tried to connect with 'ordinary people', including children and cultural outsiders, it would start with a different question, such as, I would suggest, 'What did Mary say to God?' This could be then expanded by other questions that would be both easy to understand, and free of unnecessary cultural baggage, such as 'Why did Mary say this?', What happened because of this?', 'What did Mary say about it later (to Elizabeth)?

But if the question in the title of section No. 97 is neither clear nor precise, nor is the answer, which reads, 'When the angel announced to her that she would give birth to 'the Son of the Most High' (Luke 1:32), she freely gave her consent with 'the obedience of faith' (Romans 1:5). Again, this formulation could not be translated into most languages of the world, because they would not have phrases matching 'freely gave her consent', or words matching *obedience.* Using simple and cross-translatable words of Minimal English in *What Christians believe* (Wierzbicka 2017) I have formulated the content of what Mary said to God as follows:

A woman called Mary says 'Yes.' to God (abbreviated version)

Jesus's mother was called Mary, she lived in a town called Nazareth in Galilee.
(In Aramaic Mary's name was Mariam, people spoke Aramaic in Galilee at that time.)

Mary didn't have a husband, she knew that a man called Joseph would be her husband
    in a short time.
Joseph lived in Nazareth, people in Nazareth knew that in a short time
    Joseph would be Mary's husband.
Sometime before Jesus was born, something happened to Mary.

Before it happened, she didn't know that something like this could happen to her.

It happened like this:
    One day Mary saw someone not like people, she thought:
        "this is an angel" (in Aramaic, "mal'ak").
    Then this angel spoke to her, Mary knew at that moment that God wanted
        to say something to her.

The angel said to Mary:
    "I want to say something very good to you, Mariam.
    God is with you, God feels something very good towards you."
Mary didn't know why this was happening to her,
    she didn't know what she could think about it.

Then the angel said to her:
    "Don't think like this, Mariam: 'something bad can happen to me now'.
    Think like this: 'something very good is now happening to me.'

In a very short time, something will happen to you, it will happen
    because God wants it to happen.
Because of this, after some time you will give birth to a child (a son),
    you will call him Jesus.
He will not be someone like other people, people will call him the Son of God.
He will be the king of the people of Israel, like David,
    sometimes people will call him: "Son of David".
He will be king forever."

Mary said to the angel: "How can this happen to me? I don't have a husband."

The angel said to Mary:
"If God wants something to happen, it can happen.
It will happen to you because God wants it to happen.
This child will be called the Son of God."

Mary knew that she could say at that moment: "I don't want it to happen to me."

She didn't say this. She said:
"I want it to happen to me as you say.
I want it to happen to me because God wants it."

Most of the words used in this semantic text stand for universal semantic primes. A few are not primes but universal semantic molecules: 'be born/give birth', 'woman', 'husband', 'child'. 'Son' is a near-universal molecule: most languages appear to have a word for 'son', but some distinguish lexically between a 'mother's son' and a 'father's son'. In the case of the phrase 'He is the Son of God', however, such distinctions would not cause any problems for translatability, because given the Bible's cultural context, clearly the word to choose for 'son' would need to be a 'father's son' rather than a 'mother's son'. The concept of someone being 'called' something (as in 'this woman was called Mary') also appears to have equivalents in most languages (although there is some variation here which requires further investigation).

Finally, there are two 'Christian' words in the story of 'Mary saying 'yes' to God': *God* and *angel*. 'God' is an important semantic molecule in all European languages, and of course many non-European ones, but, as we have already seen, it can be explicated through universal semantic primes. The word *angel* is not a productive semantic molecule but is also translatable across the languages which have a word for 'God' (in the Judeo-Christian sense of the word). (For in-depth analysis of this concept in a comparative perspective, see Habib 2011.)

7.2 What did Jesus say to his Father before he died?

To a large extent, what applies to Mary's response to God during the 'Annunciation' applies also to Jesus' response to God on the night before he died. In the *Compendium to the Catechism of the Catholic Church* (2005), the relevant section (No. 121) is entitled 'What happened in the Agony in the Garden of Gethsemane?' The answer to this question looks as follows:

> Despite the horror which death represented for the sacred humanity of Jesus 'who is the Author of Life' (Acts 3:15), the human **will** of the Son of God remained **faithful** to the **will** of the Father for our salvation. Jesus accepted the **duty** to carry our sins in his Body 'becoming **obedient** unto death' (Philippians 2:8). (*Compendium*, p. 54)

Arguably, this explanation, too, is far less clear, and less accessible, than it could be. The word *duty* is highly language-specific, and its meaning is saturated with Anglo history and culture (cf. Wierzbicka 2015a). It is also a word which does not have the same resonance in present-day English that it had a hundred, or a hundred and fifty, years ago, and these days many younger speakers of English might find it positively off-putting. The word *obedient* is not equally English-specific, but it is likely to be even more off-putting to many speakers of English today. The English word *faithful* is also culturally shaped, and consequently unhelpful as a tool for explaining Jesus' way of thinking (because there was no such concept in Jesus's language). It is also anything but cross-translatable into most languages of the world outside Europe. The word *will* (as in *the will*) is perhaps more helpful here than *duty, obedient,* or *faithful,* but it is not nearly as helpful as the simpler, more intelligible, and universally cross-translatable word *want* would be. It is refreshing, therefore, to see the simple word *want* appear, instead of the more conventional *will,* in Sister Wendy Beckett's brief meditation on Gethsemane, in her *Spiritual Letters* (2013, p. 305):

> We often think that love and holiness mean no bad thoughts, no struggle. But these things are the very strife in which love is shown. Never did Jesus love more than in the Garden when he didn't 'want to' but yet chose pure surrender. And the choosing and the turmoil lasted hours. So if ours lasts days . . . weeks . . . years: Fiat! It all redeems both us and the world.

But to get the meaning of the Gethsemane scene 'right' using simple words like *want,* and simple phrases like *good thoughts,* is not a simple matter, and it is of course no accident that the word *want* appears in the extract above in inverted commas or that it is accompanied by more complex and less self-explanatory words such as *surrender* and *fiat.* The word *fiat* is particularly misleading in the passage above, because Sister Wendy is evidently using it in the original Latin sense of 'let it be so', whereas in English, this loan from Latin has acquired a different meaning. The *Collins Cobuild English Language Dictionary* (1991) explains this new, specifically English, meaning as follows: 'A *fiat* is an official order given by someone in authority; a formal word'. Clearly, Jesus' attitude to his Father, whom he addressed as 'Abba' (a child's loving word for his or her father), was nothing like that implied by the English word *fiat.* Furthermore, to a Christian (and especially Catholic) reader, the word *fiat* evokes Mary's answer to the angel in the Latin version of the New Testament:

> Ecce ancilla Domini; fiat mihi secundum verbum tuum. (Luke 1:38)

> 'Behold the handmaid of the Lord; be it unto me according to thy word'. (KJV)

Thus, the 'fiat' attitude attributed here to Jesus is that of a person who has been **asked** to do something, and who freely chooses to do what someone else wants (because this person **wants** to do what this someone else wants them to do).

The insistence on doing God's will is clearly one of the key motifs in Jesus' teaching, expressed, for example, in such undisputedly authentic sayings as Matthew 12:50: 'For whoever does the will of my Father in heaven is my brother, and sister, and mother'. This motif is sometimes misrepresented in the secondary literature on the Gospels, with its frequent insistence on the word *obedience*. For example, Barclay (1975/1993, pp. 289–290) in commenting on Matthew 7:21, writes, 'Fine words can never be a substitute for fine deeds. There is only one proof of love, and that proof is obedience . . . Faith without practice is a contradiction in terms, and love without obedience is an impossibility'.

But Jesus didn't teach blind obedience, and it is a misrepresentation to interpret his reference to the will of the Father as 'obedience'. *Obedience* suggests an attitude that can be represented as follows:

someone (A) thinks about someone else (B):
'if this person (B) wants me to do something, I have to do it.'

This is not Jesus' attitude to his Father as portrayed in the Gospels

The idea of *wanting* to do God's will is pervasive in the New Testament. For example, in John's Gospel Jesus says about God, 'If anyone wants to do his will, he shall know . . .' (Matthew 7:17). Elsewhere, this willingness is indicated even more strongly, by the use of the verb 'to seek' (Greek *zēteō*): 'I do not seek my own will but the will of the Father who sent me' (John 5:30). Jesus as represented in John's Gospel also makes it clear that he has voluntarily 'come down from heaven' because he *wants* to do 'the will of him who sent me', and that 'the will of him who sent me' is that people should have 'everlasting life' (John 6:38–40). Jesus' references to doing the will of the Father need to be seen in the context of these implications of willingness and freedom. The main idea is not 'I have to do it because God wants me to do it', but rather, 'I want to do it because God wants me to do it'.

This is indeed closer to *surrender* (another English word called upon in Sister Wendy's account of Jesus' prayer in Gethsemane) than to *obedience*: closer—but not identical. I contend, however, that using simple and cross-translatable words we can make the intended meaning both much clearer and much more universally accessible, and in *What Christians Believe* (Wierzbicka 2017) I have proposed the following (partial) account:

Gethsemane

When Jesus was with the Apostles in the Garden of Olives that night, he said to them:
   "The Bible says: 'if something very bad happens to the shepherd,
      the sheep run away.'
   I want you to know that it will be like this tonight.

I want you to know that very soon I will die.
At the same time, I want you to know that not long after I die, I will live,
    you will see me in Galilee."
Then he went away a little from the place where they all were.
He wanted three of them to be with him
    (one was Peter, one was John, one was James, John's brother),
        he wanted them to be awake.
He thought like this:
    "I knew before that very bad things would happen to me,
        now I know: this will happen now."
He said to these three Apostles then:
    "It is like this in my soul now: I feel something very very bad;
        someone can feel like this when they are dying."
    I want you to be with me now, I want you not to be asleep
        when it is like this in my soul".
Then he went away a little from the place where they were
    because he wanted to speak to God.
He fell to the ground, his face was touching the ground.
He spoke to God like this then:
    "Abba [Father], if this can not-happen to me, I want it not to happen.
    At the same time I want everything to happen as you want, not as I want."

8 TRANSLATING CHRISTIAN ESCHATOLOGY INTO NSM

Of the 'last' or 'final' judgement, the *Compendium of the Catechism of the Catholic Church* (p. 72) writes:

214. In what does the final judgment consist?
The final or universal judgment consists in a sentence of happiness or eternal con-demnation, which the Lord Jesus will issue in regard to the 'just and the unjust' (*Acts* 24:15) when he returns as the Judge of the living and the dead. After the last judgment, the resurrected body will share in the retribution which the soul received at the particular judgment.

This short text bristles with complex, untranslatable, and far from reader-friendly words like *sentence, condemnation,* and *retribution,* and with somewhat internally conflicted phrases such as 'a sentence of happiness' or 'share in the retribution'.

It is also a text relying in its phrasing on the traditional language of Christian eschatology and not taking into account interpretations arising from new cross-culturally informed hermeneutics such as that represented by Polish Catholic theologian Wacław Hryniewicz's (2012) book *God's Spirit in the World: Ecumenical and Cultural Essays.* The main point emphasised in this book is that to discuss the intended meaning of Jesus' eschatological sayings we need cross-cultural aware-ness, because these sayings continue the traditions of the Jewish prophetic speech genre known in biblical studies as 'Drohrede' (German for 'threat speech'), that is, a language of warnings and admonitions presented as predictions. As Hryniewicz tirelessly documents in his books, this true purpose of dire apocalyptic images was well understood by early Church Fathers such as Clement of Alexandria, Origen, and St. Gregory of Nyssa. Speaking of such prophetic Jewish forms of speech, Hryniewicz comments:

> It is precisely this illocutionary force that is different from what the surface form of some utterances might suggest. Jesus' often repeated call for trust in merciful God should not be misinterpreted as a threat or prediction of an irrevocable and unhappy future, which can only cause fear and despair. Such misinterpretations would contradict the convention of the Jewish prophetic speech.

As Hryniewicz (2012) further points out, in the Apostles' Creed 'the forgiveness of sins constitutes an essential part of the Christian faith: "I believe in the forgiveness of sins". There is no mention of an unforgiving God and hell in the Christian Creed' (p. 82). Commenting on the widespread failure to understand the cultural scripts of Jewish prophetic speech, Hryniewicz draws on the work of the French historian Jean Delumeau:

> The doctrine of God's non-forgiveness and everlasting hell has for centuries domi-nated the Church's traditional preaching. It may be considered as one of the main causes of the de-christianisation of the West in modern times. The French historian Jean Delumeau shows in his well-documented monograph that starting with the sixteenth century there emerged a movement rejecting [the kind of] Christianity which preached the unforgiving and punishing God and threatened the sin-ful humankind with an eternity of hell. This movement, intensified in the post-Enlightenment period, led in consequence to the denial of all transcendent reality. Such was the result of the misinterpretation of the apocalyptic images and warn-ings of the Bible. (p. 84)

In relation to the New Testament teachings of 'the Last Judgment', the key point here is that the 'punishment' envisaged for those people who lived their lives away from God and 'against God' can be seen as 'therapeutic' and (Hryniewicz's word) 'soul-changing' rather than 'everlasting' in a literal sense.

In keeping with such insights from a biblical hermeneutics informed by cross-linguistic pragmatics, in *What Christians Believe* I have interpreted the 'Last Judgment' as follows:

What will happen to all people—what God wants (partial rendering)

When Jesus didn't live on earth anymore, the Apostles knew that he was with God, as he was before he was born.

They knew that after some time all people will see him, that when they see him, they will know who he was.

All people will know then how he died, why he died like this; they will know that
he lives, that he will live forever.

At the same time, the Apostles knew that it will be like this:
People will know then that when they see Jesus, he sees *them*,
that he knows what they are like inside.
They will know that he knows how they lived,
at the same time *they* will know how they lived.
They will know when they did something good for other people,
at the same time they will know that they were doing
something good for God then.
They will know when they didn't want to do something good for other people,
at the same time they will know that they didn't want to do
something good for God then.
They will then think about some things like this:
"When I did this, I did something very bad".
They will think about some other things like this:
"When I did this, I did something good."
Jesus will say to some people then: "You can live with God now as you are now";
if he says this to someone, this someone will feel something very very good.
He will say to some other people: "You can't live with God now as you are now";
if he says this to someone, this someone can feel something very very bad.

At the same time, the Apostles thought like this: Jesus will not say to anyone:
"You can never live with God".
They could think like this because they knew what Jesus wanted to say about God
when he said this:
A shepherd had a lot of sheep. One sheep didn't want to be with him,
with the other sheep. It went away.
It was far from the shepherd for a long time,
many bad things happened to it because of this.
The shepherd went to many places
because he wanted to bring that sheep back to the other sheep.
Because he did this, after some time, that sheep was with him,
with all the other sheep.
The shepherd felt something very very good because of this.
God is like this shepherd.

In terms of content, two aspects of this mini-text require some comment: first,
the idea that the judgement will be, in a sense, self-judgement, and second, the
open-endedness and temporal indeterminacy of the 'verdict'. The first idea builds
on Jesus' teaching embodied in the parable of the prodigal son: just as the son who
has squandered all his money finally comes to his senses and sees his life in the light
in which his father must have seen it, so, we are to understand, it will happen at
the Last Judgment. To quote Swiss Catholic theologian Josef Imbach (1987, p. 37):

This means: he recognizes his wrong. It is not the father who judges him, but he himself pronounces the judgment: 'Father, I have sinned against heaven and before you, and I am no longer worthy to be called your son.' Precisely this parable has the power of protecting the image of the 'Last Judgment' from a false interpretation, which forces God into the role of a vengeful judge. (1987, p. 37)

Likewise, another Swiss theologian, Hans Urs von Balthasar (1983, p. 293) quotes, with admiration, the 'bold statement' by the fourth-century Father of the Church Ambrose: 'Idem homo et salvatur ex parte, et condemnatur ex parte', ('the same human being is both partially saved and partially condemned'). (For further discussion see my *What Did Jesus Mean*, chapter 15.)

It is important to note at this point that according to the Gospels the self-judgement that will be passed on oneself in the light of Jesus' presence will extend not only to things that one did but also, to things that one did not do, and that the *good things* that one did or didn't do are those that one wanted or didn't want to do for other people. Thus, in the great scene of the 'Last Judgment' in St. Matthew's Gospel, 'the Son of Man' explicitly identifies himself with 'the least of these my brethren' and says to those 'on his right hand' (Matthew 25:35–36, Revised Standard Version):

> For I was hungry and you gave me food, I was thirsty and you gave me drink, I was a stranger and you welcomed me, naked and you clothed me, I was sick and you visited me, I was in prison and you came to me.

And to those 'on the left hand', the 'Son of Man' says (Matthew 25:42–43):

> For I was hungry and you gave me no food, I was thirsty and you gave me no drink, I was a stranger and you did not welcome me, naked and you did not clothe me, sick and in prison and you did not visit me.

The second aspect of the explication of the 'Judgment' scene presented here which requires comment concerns the open-ended character of the 'final judgment': the 'now' in the verdict 'you can live with God now' or 'you can't live with God now'. On this interpretation, words like 'everlasting', 'eternal', and 'never' are instances of the Biblical hyperbole characteristic of Jewish 'cultural scripts' of the time, and of the prophetic 'warning discourse' in particular. The Russian Orthodox theologian Sergius Bulgakov has written about this as follows:

> In Christian eschatology the question is always present of the eternity of the pains of hell and the final reprobation of those sent into 'the everlasting fire, prepared for the devil and his angels.' From earliest times doubts have been expressed as to the eternal duration of these torments. . . . From the earliest times there have been two tendencies in eschatology: the rigorists affirm the suffering is eternal, final, and without end, the others, whom Augustine ironically calls . . . *misericordes* ('merciful'), deny the eternity of punishment and the persistence of evil in creation and acknowledge the

final victory of the Kingdom of God, when 'God shall be all in all' [Paul I Corinthians 15:28]. The doctrine of *apokatastasis* is not only that of Origen, whose orthodoxy has been questioned because of certain of his opinions, but also of St. Gregory of Nyssa, glorified by the Church as Doctor, and his disciples. (1976, pp. 134–135) (For further discussion, see *What Did Jesus Mean?*, Wierzbicka 2001, chapter 15.)

As for the words used in the 'Last Judgment' text, with three exceptions, all of them stand for universal semantic primes, and so do not require explanations and are readily cross-translatable. The exceptions are 'God', 'Earth', and 'Apostles'. (For the latter two, see *What Christians Believe*.)

9 CONCLUDING REMARKS

As we have seen, in talking about God it is common to rely on complex European or Anglo English concepts embodied in words such as *estrangement, reverence, obedience, transcendence, surrender,* and *retribution*. Furthermore, many people rely on such complex and often obscure concepts in their thinking about their own or other people's faith without even asking themselves what exactly these words mean. In this chapter, I have tried to show that it is quite possible to speak, and to think, about God without relying on such complex and culturally shaped concepts, and to think about God and faith afresh, in a new conceptual language.

To quote Sister Wendy Beckett once more, commenting on God's 'revelation of Himself in the Scriptures' (2014, pp. 60–61):

> The essential reading will always be the Bible. Let me add immediately that we need the Bible with commentaries. Of itself the Word of God can be perplexing. Scholars can explain to us the thought patterns of the past, the true meanings of the words that have changed over the centuries. (. . .)
>
> In one sense Scripture is all-important. In another sense it is dangerous by itself, because these are very ancient texts and no amount of good will can ensure that we truly understand them.

Providing commentaries on the Scriptures is an ongoing task for generations of Christians and students of Christianity. It is also a task for many disciplines. As I hope to have shown in this chapter, these disciplines need to include cross-linguistic semantics—especially of a kind that can provide strong safeguards against Anglocentrism, Eurocentrism, and 'chronocentrism'. But of course it is not only a question of providing helpful commentaries on the Scriptures, but of opening up new perspectives on talking, and thinking, about God. More generally, it is a question of being able to talk to other people, wherever they live or come from, and to achieve at least a measure of genuine mutual understanding.

The manifest existence of thousands of very different languages (different not just in sounds and forms but in meanings and perspectives on the world) is an astonishing fact about humanity, a cause for wonder and celebration. But so is the existence of one shared human language (mini-language) hidden within them all.

What is more, it is hard not to think that the diversity and the unity are in fact two inseparable facets of what French visionary scientist and thinker Pierre Teilhard de Chardin (1955) called 'le phénomène humain' ('the human phenomenon'). As humans we can take pride and delight in being so diverse in our ways of living, thinking, and knowing, but we also need to have a measure of mutual understanding. This is especially so where humanity's 'big questions' are concerned, such as Who are we? Why are we on Earth? How are we to live? How can we live well with other people? Who is God? The shared mini-language hidden within all human languages makes human dialogue about such questions not only desirable but also possible.

REFERENCES

Balthasar, Hans Urs von (1983). *Theodramatik*, Band IV. Einsiedeln, Switzerland: Johannes Verlag.

Barclay, William (1993 [1975]). *The Gospel of Matthew*, vol. 1. Edinburgh: Saint Andrew Press.

Beckett, Sister Wendy (2012). *Sister Wendy's Bible Treasury: Stories and Wisdom through the Eyes of the Great Painters*. Maryknoll, NY: Orbis Books.

Beckett, Sister Wendy (2013). *Spiritual Letters*. Maryknoll, NY: Orbis Books.

Beckett, Sister Wendy (2014). *Sister Wendy on Prayer*. London: Bloomsbury.

Birch, Charles (2008). *Science and Soul*. Sydney: University of New South Wales Press.

Bromhead, Helen (2009). *The Reign of Truth and Faith: Epistemic Expressions in 16th and 17th Century English*. Berlin: de Gruyter.

Bulgakov, Sergius (1976). *A Bulgakov Anthology*. Edited by James Pain and Nicolas Zernov. Philadelphia: Winchester Press.

Catholic University of America (1967–1996). *New Catholic Encyclopedia*, 10 vols. New York: McGraw-Hill.

Chalmers, David (2012). *Constructing the World*. Oxford: Oxford University Press.

Collins Cobuild English Language Dictionary (1991). London: Harper Collins.

Compendium of the Catechism of the Catholic Church (2005). San Francisco, CA: Ignatius Press.

Couturat, Louis (1903). *Opuscules et Fragments Inédits de Leibniz*.

Evans, Nicholas (2010). Semantic typology. In Jae Jung Song (ed.), *The Oxford Handbook of Linguistic Typology*, pp. 504–533. Oxford/ New York: Oxford University Press.

Fasching, Darrell J. and Dell deChant (2001). *Comparative Religious Ethics: A Narrative Approach*. Oxford: Blackwell.

Forsberg, Michael (1958). *Land beyond the Nile*. New York: Harper.

Freedman, David Noel (ed.) (1992). *The Anchor Bible Dictionary*, 6 vols. New York: Doubleday.

Goddard, Cliff (ed.) (2008). *Cross-Linguistic Semantics*. Amsterdam: John Benjamins.

Goddard, Cliff (2011). *Semantic Analysis: A Practical Introduction*, revised 2nd ed. Oxford: Oxford University Press.

Goddard, Cliff (2017a). Ethnopragmatic perspectives on conversational humour, with special reference to Australian English. *Language and Communication* 55, 55–68. Special Issue 'Conversational humour: Spotlight on languages and cultures', edited by Marta Dynel and Valeria Sinkeviciute.

Goddard, Cliff (ed.) (2017b). *Minimal English for a Global World: Improved Communication Using Fewer Words*. London: Palgrave.

Goddard, Cliff and Anna Wierzbicka (eds.) (1994). *Semantic and Lexical Universals*. Amsterdam: John Benjamins.

Goddard, Cliff and Anna Wierzbicka (eds.) (2002). *Meaning and Universal Grammar: Theory and Empirical Findings*, 2 vols. Amsterdam: John Benjamins.

Goddard, Cliff and Anna Wierzbicka (2014). *Words and Meanings: Lexical Semantics Across Domains, Languages, and Cultures*. Oxford: Oxford University Press.

Goddard, Cliff and Anna Wierzbicka (2015). What does *Jukurrpa* ('Dreamtime', 'the Dreaming') mean? A semantic and conceptual journey of discovery. *Australian Aboriginal Studies* 1, 43–65.

Habib, Sandy (2011). Angels can cross cultural boundaries. *RASK, International Journal of Language and Communication* 34, 49–75.

Harman, Oren (2016). Avoiding weird parents: A comment on Anna Wierzbicka's 'Back to mother and father'. *Current Anthropology* 57(4), 422–425.

Hasada, Rie (2008). Two 'virtuous emotions' in Japanese: *Nasake/joo* and *jihi*. In Cliff Goddard (ed.), *Cross-Linguistic Semantics*, pp. 331–347. Philadelphia: John Benjamins.

Hastings, James (1958). *Dictionary of the Bible*. Edinburgh: T. & T. Clark.

Hryniewicz, Wacław (2012). *God's Spirit in the World: Ecumenical and Cultural Essays*. Washington, DC: Council for Research in Values and Philosophy.

Imbach, Josef (1987). *Himmel-Glaube und Höllen-Angst. Was wissen wir vom Leben nach dem Tod?* München: Kösel.

James, Wendy (1988). *The Listening Ebony: Moral Knowledge, Religion, and Power among the Uduk of Sudan*. Oxford: Oxford University Press.

James, Wendy (2013). Translating God's words. In Janice Boddy and Michael Lambek (eds.), *A Companion to the Anthropology of Religion*, pp. 329–343. Chichester, U.K.: Wiley Blackwell.

Kopenawa, Davi and Bruce Albert (2013). *The Falling Sky: Words of a Yanomami Shaman*. Cambridge, MA: Belknap Press.

Leibniz, Gottfried Wilhelm (1903). *Opuscules et fragments inédits de Leibniz*. Extraits des manuscrits de la Bibliothèque royale de Hanovre par Louis Couturat. Paris: Presses universitaires de France.

McKenzie, John L. (1965). *Dictionary of the Bible*. London: G. Chapman.

Nongbri, Brent (2013). *Before Religion: A History of a Modern Concept*. New Haven, CT: Yale University Press.

NSM Homepage. https://www.griffith.edu.au/humanities-languages/school-humanities-languages-social-science/research/natural-semantic-metalanguage-homepage

NSM Homepage Downloads. https://www.griffith.edu.au/humanities-languages/school-humanities-languages-social-science/research/natural-semantic-metalanguage-homepage/downloads

Obeyesekere, Gananath (1985). Depression, Buddhism, and the work of culture in Sri Lanka. In A. Kleinman and B. Good (eds.), *Culture and Depression: Studies in the Anthropology and Cross-cultural Psychiatry of Affect and Disorder*, pp. 134–152. Berkeley: University of California Press.

Ostler, Nicholas (2016). *Passwords to Paradise: How Languages have Re-invented the World's Religions*. London: Bloomsbury.

Oxford English Dictionary. http://www.oed.com/

Peeters, Bert (ed.) (2006). *Semantic Primes and Universal Grammar: Empirical Findings from the Romance Languages*. Amsterdam: John Benjamins.

Renfro, Yelizaveta P. (2014). *Xylotheque: Essays*. Albuquerque, NM: University of New Mexico Press.

Teilhard de Chardin, Pierre (1955). *Le phénomène humain*. Paris: Editions du Seuil.

Tillich, Paul (1951). *The Protestant Era*. London: Nisbet.

Wierzbicka, Anna (1992). *Semantics, Culture and Cognition: Universal Human Concepts in Culture-specific Configurations*. New York: Oxford University Press.

Wierzbicka, Anna (1996). *Semantics: Primes and Universals*. New York: Oxford University Press.

Wierzbicka, Anna (1997). *Understanding Cultures Through Their Key Words: English, Russian, Polish, German and Japanese*. New York: Oxford University Press.

Wierzbicka, Anna (2001). *What Did Jesus Mean? Explaining the Sermon on the Mount and the Parables in Simple and Universal Human Concepts*. New York: Oxford University Press.

Wierzbicka, Anna (2010). *Experience, Evidence and Sense: The Hidden Cultural Legacy of English*. New York: Oxford University Press.

Wierzbicka, Anna (2011). The common language of all people: The innate language of thought. *Problems of Information Transmission* 47 (4), 380–399.

Wierzbicka, Anna (2014a). *Imprisoned in English: The Hazards of English as a Default Language*. New York: Oxford University Press.

Wierzbicka, Anna (2014b). 'Pain' and 'suffering' in cross-linguistic perspective. *International Journal of Language and Culture* 1 (2), 149–173.

Wierzbicka, Anna (2015a). Can there be common knowledge without a common language? German *Pflicht* versus English *duty*. *Common Knowledge* 21 (1), 141–171.

Wierzbicka, Anna (2015b). Natural Semantic Metalanguage. In *The International Encyclopedia of Language and Social Interaction*, pp. 1076–1092. Wiley. DOI: 10.1002/9781118611463.wbielsi150

Wierzbicka, Anna (2017). *What Christians Believe: The Story of God and People* [in Polish]. Kraków: Znak.

Wierzbicka, Anna (To appear). *What Christians Believe: The Story of God and People in Minimal English*. New York: Oxford University Press.

YOUCAT: Youth Catechism of the Catholic Church (2011). San Francisco, CA: Ignatius Press.

CHAPTER 3

Religious Metaphors at the Crossroads between Apophatical Theology and Cognitive Linguistics

An Interdisciplinary Study

KURT FEYAERTS AND LIEVEN BOEVE

This chapter represents a thoroughly revised and updated version of the authors' (Boeve and Feyaerts) 1999 article *Religious Metaphors in a Postmodern Culture: Transverse Links between Apophatical Theology and Cognitive Semantics*, which was (one of) the first attempts to compare and make use of expertise from both theology and cognitive linguistics in analysing religious discourse. From a theological point of view, the 1999 article turned out to be a highly programmatic one: most of Boeve's future publications can be traced back to it as elaborations of its core ideas, partially formulated as intuitions at the time, thus revealing a fundamental ideological continuity from 1999 to the present. Also, recent theological publications on the matter of a cognitive (linguistic)-inspired view of religious metaphors (e.g. Masson 2014) are very much in line with the analysis in the 1999 article. Apart from a bibliographical update, no essential changes have been made to the theological argumentation of the early version of this article. From the perspective of cognitive linguistics and Conceptual Metaphor Theory in particular, a more nuanced and elaborate view, in which aspects of intersubjective, cultural, and discursive organisation play a more prominent role, has developed over the years. Here also, the major upgrades and extensions of this theoretical model have been integrated in the text. Yet, similar to the theological perspective, the basic lines of the cognitive linguistic argumentation of the 1999 paper, as well as the convergence with the rediscovery of negative theology in a postmodern context, appear to have maintained—and maybe even strengthened—their analytic relevance.

The interdisciplinary approach in the present chapter is inspired by the observation that the rediscovery of the tradition of negative theology by postmodern philosophy and theology seems to share major points of interest with the cognitive linguistic theory of language. Although specific religious metaphors do appear throughout the text, our presentation does not deal in the first place with their analysis. Its primary goal is situated on a more theoretical level, that is, an attempt to compare two epistemological systems in a fruitful and promising way. There are three major parts. The first two give an overview of the disciplines involved in this project. Each of these parts is conceived as some kind of introduction for scholars from other disciplines. The first part deals with aspects of apophatical (or negative) theology and presents its rediscovery by postmodern theology. The second part describes central aspects of cognitive semantics with special attention to the theory of conceptual metaphor. In the third part we bring the two theories together in search of both similarities and differences between them. It will be shown that there surely are common points of interest and methodology, and that each approach can benefit from the other. To conclude this third part we illustrate this possible benefit for theology.

Leaving the safe haven of one's own discipline may open new perspectives and offer additional background for one's own research. What we present in this article is to be considered a first attempt to overcome theoretical and terminological difficulties in order to pave the way for further analysis of the complex issue of religious discourse from an interdisciplinary perspective.

1 THE REDISCOVERY OF APOPHATICAL THEOLOGY AS ULTIMATE EXPRESSION OF THEOLOGICAL CRITICAL CONSCIOUSNESS

1.1 The history of theology: A continual recontextualisation of the 'fides quaerens intellectum'

The history of doing theology teaches the close observer that the vocabulary particular to theology as well as the schemes of argumentation are most often borrowed from the cultural environment in which they were developed. Moreover, even the coming into being of theology itself, in line with the Anselmian adage *fides quaerens intellectum*, defined as the attempt to reflexively elucidate the Christian faith, is due to the Hellenistic context in which early Christianity took shape (cf. e.g. Allen 1985). Throughout the history of theology, contemporary philosophy always received special attention. Theologians turned first to (neo)-Platonism, and later on also to Aristotelianism. Both of these provided concepts and patterns of reasoning supposed to facilitate the reflective disclosure of what and how Christians of their epoch and context believed. From modern times on, theologians also related their discourse to the increasingly diverse natural sciences and humanities. This is the case, for instance, in 19th-century apologetics which accredited to 'supernatural experience', such as miracles and special revelations, evidential value for supernatural, religious truth claims, in a manner analogous to the procedures of empirical inquiry in positive sciences. In the same way, political theologies and theologies of liberation during the 1970s and 1980s used socio-analytical frames of interpretation in order to establish the social relevance of their theologising. What concerns theology also concerns faith and the praxis of faith: these, too, were shaped in continual relation to the context wherein they were handed down. Creed, ritual and sacramental praxis, moral code and formation of community are engaged in a dynamic process of tradition handed over and context-related formation of new tradition.

We elaborate this in two moments, especially concerning religious language (that is to say, the evocation and interpretation of religious experiences). (1) Religious language is not shaped *ex nihilo*; religious experiences are not independent events, taking human beings by surprise, and interpreted religiously only afterwards. Human beings have religious experiences, only because they are embedded in a religious framework. (2) At the same time, only such religious experiences enable the religious framework to survive. A living religion consists of the continuing dialectical interaction between interpretation and experience. New experiences always occur within an interpretative frame, called tradition, which at the same time (partially) forms the context of both the new experience and the interpretation of this experience. This does not mean that the new experience does not add anything to the interpretative framework, but it does mean that it is not independent of this framework. Experience is always interpreted experience; interpretation is always experience-related interpretation. But, again, the fact that the new, always contextually embedded experience is not independent from the religious interpretative framework does not mean that it does not add anything to the existing interpretation schemes. Experience can press upon the existing traditional interpretation schemes in a way that a new interpretation, coming from the given interpretation schemes and grafted onto the experience, which presses upon these schemes, involves a shift with regard to these existing schemes. This can happen when, for example, an experience, because of a change in context, can no longer be expressed by traditional words which expressed this experience in the older context. The military language used in the naming of God in the Hebrew Bible, for instance, no longer seems to be appropriate to a lot of contemporary believers. Retrospectively, tradition and, more specifically, the religious language which developed through history, can be perceived as a series of transfers of meaning—meaning which can be accessed only by means of concrete words, sentences, and texts, always specifically embedded in a particular historical context. In the interaction of contextual experience and traditional interpretation, religious language re-contextualises itself and shifts (cf. Schillebeeckx 1989; see also Boeve 2003, 2007, and 2009).

The fact that religious language is intrinsically bound to the context in which it arises is due to the hermeneutical-critical consciousness which is proper to religion: it is the consciousness that the 'reality' at which religious language aims, and refers to, in the end cannot be put into words, cannot be signified, without misjudging it: the *deus semper major*. Certainly, from the sixth century on this consciousness has been made explicit in negative, or apophatical, theology.

1.2 Apophatical theology and knowledge about the *'deus semper major'*

A Syrian monk living at the end of the fifth and the beginning of the sixth century wrote five booklets (and some letters) which have been of major influence for the further development of theology, this partially due to the fact that he hides behind the pseudonym and authority of Dionysius the Areopagite, also known as Pseudo-Dionysius, the Athenian disciple of Paul (Acts 7:34). We know four tracts and some letters from Pseudo-Dionysius. In his reflection on the naming of (and being related to) God, Pseudo-Dionysius links the speculative Neo-Platonism of late antiquity (Proclus)—and its intensive concern for the way in which philosophical language meets its limits in addressing the absolute, the one, the good, the cause of everything—with traces of apophasis from the Jewish-Christian belief in God (as was reflected upon by some of the Patristic Fathers, including Gregory of Nyssa; cf. Carabine 1995, pp. 279–300; see also Hochstaffl 1976; and Mortley 1986).

For Pseudo-Dionysius, God cannot be known in essence, but only in creative, causal, divine activity—just as it is the sun's rays which we perceive and not the sun itself. Creation, coming from God, refers to God, but without determining God. Creation, as a *sign* of the invisible, is a trace of God. Knowledge about creation leads necessarily to knowledge about God, although, because of its being bound to creation, this will always be secondary knowledge. Pseudo-Dionysius calls this the level of "cataphatic" or affirmative theology. Names and titles which are predicated of God, theological names such as Trinity, Father, Son, Spirit, and intelligible or conceptual names such as the good, one, beauty, truth, life, love, and representations of the experiential world such as sun, rock, water, wind—all these have a strictly *symbolic* nature: they stand for what we predicate of God, but they do not touch God (Dionysius the Areopagite, Migne PG 3 (1857), 1032D–1033C; Luibheid translation [1987] pp.138–139). In the end, this is also true for divine names such as Trinity, and even for the name 'the One'. Not even these names exhaust the divine essence, or make God knowable. They are names referring to what is beyond all names, beyond all naming. Only through the negation of these names can one create a space for God. Not a single name can be spared: neither titles borrowed from everyday experience, nor abstract concepts. In the end, only negations can be true, according to Pseudo-Dionysius; affirmations cannot possibly come up to the mark. At stake in this never-ending process of negating—starting with the sensible names and ending with the abstract conceptual names—is not the negating of God, but the affirmation of the impossibility of naming and conceiving God. In the negation and in the negation of the negation, Pseudo-Dionysius attempts to evoke what does not permit evocation through language.

We add two more remarks. First, for Pseudo-Dionysius apophasis is not only a theological method enabling us to speak of God as the unspeakable, to name God as the unnameable, and to know God as the unknowable, but also a specific way of looking for and dealing with God—namely, mysticism. Secondly, the incorporation of Neo-Platonic ideas and thinking patterns founded apophasis, as it were, cosmologically, or ontologically. In this regard, affirmative theology is grafted onto what comes forth from God in creation, onto 'the outgoing (*proodos*) from God who always remains in himself (*monè*), while apophatical theology signifies the return (*epistrophè*) of all things to their source'.[1] Ontologically as well as (or: because of this) logically, God is beyond the One. Precisely because of God's transcendence in relation to creation, human language does not reach unto God.[2] 'We make assertions and denials of what is next to it, but never of it, for it is both beyond every assertion, being the perfect and unique cause of all things, and by virtue of its preeminently simple and absolute nature, free of every limitation, beyond every limitation; it is also beyond every denial'.[3]

Negative theology received its classical expression in the work of Thomas Aquinas (1225–1274). In his theological methodology Aquinas reserved a central place for apophatical critical consciousness: it functions as methodical presupposition for all naming and knowing of God. Who/what God is cannot be conceived or expressed in language by humans. This claim does not prevent Thomas from talking about God and investigating the cognitive value of this God-talk. 'Analogy' consists in a way of speaking (and knowing) which is not literal but at the same time goes beyond so-called metaphorical language. Although Aquinas asserts that God cannot be expressed in words and known in God's essence, in Godself, and can only be reached through creation—as Pseudo-Dionysius already stated—he nevertheless stresses that creation can teach us something essential about God (though not the divine essence). Moreover, simple perfections possessed by creatures—being good, wise, etc.—belong more to God than to creatures. We predicate them more appropriately of God, because God possesses these simple perfections in a more proper manner, not in the way of creatures, but by excellence: if one predicates of God that God is good, then it is affirmed that God is not good as creatures are good, but exceedingly good. This does not mean that this goodness is of a totally different kind than human goodness, as if the word would be plurivocal. It is only analogically that one can at the same time say of God and creatures that they are good. 'Whatever is said of God and creatures is said according as there is some relation of the creature to God as to its principle and cause, wherein all the perfections of things pre-exist excellently'.[4] Consequently, whatever is predicated analogically of God, in fact is predicated more truly of God than of creatures: a creature possesses a perfection only because this perfection pre-existed in an eminent way in God and flows from God on to creation. Still, it remains true that we know this perfection only through creation and that we can predicate it of God only from there.[5]

In Aquinas the logical, cognitive order ultimately leans upon the ontological order. It is only because of the fact that God is eminently good that creatures can be good. In the end, Thomas Aquinas modifies Pseudo-Dionysius' apophatical theology: when he affirms that God is unknowable, he does not mean that God is in no way knowable, but that ultimately no knowledge of God is adequate. In this perspective, negative theology remains methodologically important, but begins to function as a background for affirmation. Nevertheless, one commentator has stated that, in the end, for Thomas Aquinas as for Pseudo-Dionysius, negative theology 'is not merely *apophasis* but *aphasia*, a devout and learned silence' (O'Rourke 1992, p. 61).

In the history of theology, the critical consciousness which was expressed in apophatical theology took on a narrowed, standardised place in the so-called *tres viae* of scholastic theology; the *via affirmativa*, the *via negativa*, and the *via eminentiae.* Through affirmation something is predicated of God, which afterwards—in the second way—is negated, and finally again is affirmed, but this time in an eminent way, by excellence: God is good; God is not good in the way we humans are good; God is the excellence of goodness. In this threefold theological method, negative theology increasingly becomes in the course of history de facto a mere qualification of the positive naming of God, a rather harmless supplement which, as such, does not thoroughly affect the naming of God.

1.3 The rediscovery of negative theology in the postmodern context

The fact that apophatical theology has regained the attention of theologians today is certainly due especially to those philosophers who are commonly referred to as 'postmodern' or as 'thinkers of difference', including Jean-François Lyotard and Jacques Derrida. The latter explicitly acknowledges the link between deconstructionism and the tradition of apophatical theology,[6] a remark which attracted a lot of attention especially from American theologians, often rooted in the tradition of the 'Death of God' theology.[7] Derrida notes that, when theologians negate 'God', they are also negating, in the very act of negation, the negation of God: this is what Derrida calls 'de-negation'—which is certainly not identical with mere 'affirmation'. In fact, 'the most negative discourse [. . .] preserves a trace of the other' (Derrida 1992, p. 97). The negation cannot conceal—but on the contrary, reveals—that there is always already 'otherness' which precedes discourse and makes it possible. We do not stand at the origin, we do not possess this origin, and are not the masters of it. In this connection, Jean-François Lyotard wrestles in his various writings with the task of representing the unrepresentable in its unrepresentability, of naming what is unnameable in its 'unnameability'.[8] For Lyotard, postmodern sensibility consists in the consciousness that all naming—all representation—is accompanied and surrounded by that which cannot be named, with that which is not representable. This unnameability, unrepresentability, not only conditions the naming and representing, but also criticises it in the most fundamental way possible: it calls into question every claim at exhaustivity, at foundation in reality and absolute legitimation, at determining and mastering what is at stake. As 'event' or 'interruption' the unnameable breaks into every discourse. The so-called master narratives wanted to forget precisely this, and for this reason—this forgetfulness—became hegemonic. In contrast, Lyotard attempts to construct a discourse, which highlights or evokes this 'event' or 'interruption' in all speech, without mastering it hegemonically. More specifically he calls us not to forget the forgetting of the 'event'. Taking this warning into account, only the narratives which respect the unnameable—that which cannot be appropriated without negating its specificity—can legitimately be called postmodern. In contrast with the so-called 'master narratives', we propose to call them 'open narratives'.[9]

To understand this correctly, one must observe that in the discourses of Derrida, and by extension Lyotard, negative theology appears as a philosophical category, and refers to a postmodern sensibility of the irreducible otherness accompanying discourse and to the consciousness of its ungraspability, its undeterminability (cf. Boeve 2012). In the terminology of Lyotard, whoever wishes to grasp or to master the 'event', the 'heterogeneity', falls into the seduction of a hegemonic narrative and ends up in metaphysics. If negative theology comes to the fore in postmodern philosophy, it is because of the supposed familiarity of postmodern sensibility with what is at stake in apophasis: an openness for irreducible otherness, which prevents narratives, discourses, from attempting to become master of that which enables, challenges, and critiques all narration and discourse. In this perspective, apophatical theology functions as a philosophical presupposition of a philosophical discourse, which intends to create for itself the profile of an 'open narrative'. Theologically speaking, apophatical theology cannot be limited to a methodological issue, but is immediately embedded in a striving for God, in mysticism. For the purpose of this contribution, however, the accentuation of the methodological perspective can suffice.

Evidently, theologians should be interested in the kind of postmodern thinking referred to as philosophy of difference. As in the past, theology must let itself be challenged by contemporary philosophy in order to find appropriate patterns to recontextualise itself and build up a renewed plausibility. Doing this, theology should not only apply the postmodern criticism of the master narratives and the metaphysical foundations behind them, but it should at the same time seek chances to conceive in a new, contextually plausible way the dialectical relation between transcendence and immanence in reference to the thinking patterns stemming from the reflection on the contemporary sensibility for irreducible otherness. Indeed, theology has a future only as an 'open narrative', and in this regard it can learn from the philosophers of difference what theology's old tradition of apophasis can contribute. Kevin Hart (1989/1991), for instance, has applied the deconstructionist method and vocabulary offered by Derrida to discuss what theology is about, and how theology can survive in a postmodern context.[10] For, according to Hart, theology as such is not threatened in the anti-metaphysical postmodern condition: 'What Derrida offers us, in short, is a way to trace and circumscribe the metaphysics within theology. So deconstruction is not an attack against theology but an answer to the theological demand for a "non-metaphysical theology"' (Hart 1989/1991, p. xi). Regarding the work of Pseudo-Dionysius, Hart concludes that negative theology after (and with) Derrida methodologically functions as a 'supplement' of affirmative theology. As supplement, however, negative theology functions as 'origin' and 'ground' of theologising because it makes clear 'that origin and ground are themselves supplements. Negative theology is a supplement which is, strictly speaking, prior to all the statements of positive theology. [. . .] [N]egative theology performs the deconstruction of positive theology. In doing so, negative theology reveals a non-metaphysical theology at work within positive theology. But it is [. . .] incapable of isolating non-metaphysical from positive theology' (Hart 1989/1991, p. 104).[11]

1.4 The interest of theological methodology in cognitive linguistics

Postmodern philosophy rejects the (epistemological) intuition that the logical order represents the ontological order. No discourse can pretend to be grounded in reality; metaphysical legitimation has become suspect. From this perspective, negative theology stands for the refusal to perceive one's own discourse as expressing the ontological order, and to legitimate one's own narrative (and its claims) by referring to God as grounding origin. A theology which attempts to recontextualise itself, and therefore takes the postmodern criticism seriously, can no longer simply found its discourse on 'God' and put forward claims of objectivity, universality, and cognitivity as it did before. As an open narrative, theology has to learn to perceive its radical contextual dependency, its own particularity and contingency, precisely from the commitment it has to the divine otherness which itself cannot be expressed in the theological discourse and, moreover criticises every theological discourse because of this inexpressibility. Postmodern recontextualised theology starts from a contemplative openness to this otherness, to which it bears witness without claiming to represent it. Moreover, naming God immediately urges the witnessing of this unrepresentability.[12] Behind all theological discourse a negative theological presumption is present.[13]

Nevertheless, bearing witness to God with respect to God's irreducible otherness implies a discourse, implies language. And, as Thomas Aquinas argued, the consciousness of God's incomprehensibility does not prevent us from naming God and, by doing so, saying something about God. Aquinas himself sought to resolve this ambiguity by analogy, an attempt to condition our God-talk in a way that would respect God's incomprehensibility. But, as we have seen, in analogy the logical order also presupposes the ontological order, and precisely this link is firmly criticised by 'postmodern' negative theology. Given the negative theological presumption, how can God-talk and, more generally, religious language really say something about God and the reality of religious life? And what sort of cognitivity is implied in this sort of discourse?

In the last decades, many authors have attempted to figure out how we can name and know God in spite of God's otherness. This often leads them to use the category of 'metaphor'.[14] Almost always, the question arises how to evaluate the specific cognitive value of religious 'metaphors'.[15] On this question, cognitive semantics can offer some interesting ideas and thought patterns to theology. In this linguistic approach, special attention is given to the relation between metaphor and cognitivity. More specifically, the metaphorical structure of a large part of our knowledge is also acknowledged there. Perhaps cognitive semantics can provide excellent chances for theology to recontextualise its hermeneutical critical consciousness in the present postmodern context. More particularly, theologians can learn something from it about this context and the place it gives to cognitivity. They then can discover some transverse links between cognitive semantics and their own discipline, and perhaps, by using these links creatively, give renewed expression to the theological sensibility for the *deus semper major*.[16]

2 COGNITIVE LINGUISTICS AS A USAGE-BASED ACCOUNT FOR DESCRIBING LINGUISTIC MEANING

This contribution is rooted in cognitive linguistics (henceforth CL), whose emergence in the early 1980s of the previous century meant a breakaway from structuralism-inspired mainstream linguistics. It was developed in the works of several linguists, with George Lakoff, Charles Fillmore, Leonard Talmy, and Ronald Langacker as its most prominent first-hour exponents. The following sections will deal with some important claims made by CL that may be of specific interest for the topic of this contribution.[17]

One of the basic tenets of CL is that language as a semantic system[18] does not represent an autonomous system with a separate cognitive status. Instead language is considered one cognitive ability among and interacting with many other cognitive abilities like imagination, understanding, perception, reasoning, etc. CL also profiles itself as a *usage-based* account of linguistic analysis, according to which a speaker's linguistic system and therefore also meaning emerges on the basis of recurrent patterns in fully contextualised instances of language use. Hence, meaning no longer qualifies as an exclusively semantic phenomenon without any interference from outside the linguistic system.

2.1 The structuralist-objectivist tradition

The cognitive linguistic view opposes, among others, the classical structuralist approach, where meaning is characterised as an inherent property of a lexical item.[19] Structuralists consider meaning as the fixed value an expression (morpheme, word, idiom, sentence) carries with it and which can be retrieved or 'unpacked' in the interpretation process by any member of the speech community.

Behind this structuralist approach hides an objectivist view on reality, which accepts that the world is made up of objects with inherent properties, existing independently of any human interaction with or understanding of the world. Accordingly, we can say things about reality, which can be judged as being objectively true or false. As human beings, however, we can make mistakes or be misled by perceptions, emotions, cultural bias, etc. Therefore, in consequence, structuralist semanticists cannot possibly rely upon subjective impressions of and judgements about truth. 'To describe reality correctly', they look for 'words whose meanings are clear and precise, words that fit reality' (Lakoff and Johnson 1980, p. 187).

On a purely linguistic level, structuralists determine the exact value of a meaning, for instance, by describing the different semantic relationships (synonymy, antonymy, hyponymy, hyperonymy) in which a particular meaning is involved with other elements of the system.[20] Knowledge structures that do not have the status of a semantic feature, that is, elements which are not an essential part of the definition constituting the meaning(s) of an item as a unified classical category, are not the concern of semantics but of pragmatics.

In this view, for example, a biological dimension like sex is considered a semantic feature because it is commonly reflected in different linguistic forms (compare the differentiation of *horse* in *mare* vs. *stallion*). Encyclopaedic features like colour, smell, coat of hair, etc. are normally not expressed linguistically, and therefore they are functionally less important for the distinction between different words in a semantic field.

2.2 Meaning is conceptualisation

In CL, any linguistic unit counts as a symbolic structure defined as the pairing of a phonological with a semantic pole.[21] Although this may evoke memories of Saussurean linguistics, CL defines itself as a usage-based model of linguistic analysis, thus locating meaningful structure entirely within the contextual and situational specifics of a usage event, the nature of which is basically dialogic. In CL, meaning is generally identified as the conceptualisation associated with linguistic expressions. Since any utterance is embedded in a broadly defined *interactional context*, elements pertaining to bodily, mental, social, and cultural circumstances may all be conceptualised as aspects of meaning (Langacker 2001, p. 145). Apart from linguistic features, meaning thus includes all kinds of encyclopaedic knowledge as well as emotional, attitudinal, or other experiences that somehow relate to the usage event. Or to put it another way, meaning is a cognitive structure, which is always embedded in a larger context of knowledge, understanding, and beliefs.[22]

This conceptual view on meaning implies a rejection of objectivism together with the idea of absolute truth. In CL, truth becomes a relative notion, depending on the way we *understand* reality in our conceptual system. It does *not* imply however, that the concept of truth is abandoned in favour of a radical subjective autonomy (see below).

Due to factors that pertain to the context and situation of an interaction, some conceptual structures are more highlighted than others as parts of an utterance's meaning. In successful communication, interlocutors are joined in their common focus on the conceptual entity that is designated by a linguistic unit, and which is referred to as the unit's *profile*. In its most basic representation, then, meaning resides in the tension between the profile and the so-called *base*, which represents the profile's background, in which all kinds of conceptual structures are activated with different degrees of salience. The broader knowledge structures, which function as the conceptual background for a meaning, are called *domains*. It is in the interaction between profile and base that the meaning of a linguistic item resides. To illustrate this, Taylor (1989, p. 86) compares the meaning of *salt* and *sodium chloride*. Both expressions have the same referent, but yet their meaning is different because they each profile another concept on a different base. While *salt* profiles the spice in the domain FOOD, *sodium chloride* highlights the molecular composition of this substance in the domain CHEMICAL SUBSTANCE. This difference does not mean, however, that the domain of food is absent from the conceptual background of *sodium chloride*. Nor is the domain of chemical substance absent from the conceptual structure of *salt*. The difference lies in the fact that in each of these cases the domains in question represent a less prominent context for the respective profiles.

2.3 Socio-cognitive aspects of meaning

Meaning does not just reside in some static tension between a profile and its base. Also the interactional dynamics as well as the multimodal aspects of any usage event (for instance, prosody, facial expression, gesture, and gaze behaviour) that accompany an utterance are integral parts of its meaning.[23]

As a matter of fact, we adopt a socio-cognitive model of linguistic analysis, according to which the essence of meaning, as opposed to the claims of traditional cognitive accounts of meaning, does not reside in the active cognitive involvement of a single participant (the speaker *or* the hearer) in the process of conceptualisation. We claim, instead, that an adequate description of meaning also involves analysing the constant process of meaning coordination among *interlocutors* as members of the 'ground' (Brône 2010, p. 399ff). Speakers who engage in interaction do not produce their utterances in a social-interactional vacuum, but design them for an addressee. This is obvious in face-to-face conversation, but equally holds for less directly interactional activities where the interlocutors must be imagined, such as composing a song, writing a newspaper article, or reasoning about God.

Although this socio-cognitive view on language may seem rather uncontroversial to cognitive-functional paradigms of linguistic analysis, the social dimension of interaction is traditionally relegated to the periphery in cognitive research (Barlow and Kemmer 2000, p. ix). Only recently, a number of studies in cognitive and interactional linguistics have started to explore both the cognitive structure and the interpersonal dynamics of interactional discourse.[24]

This aspect of meaning is commonly referred to in terms of *intersubjectivity* (Trevarthen 1999; Langacker 2001; Verhagen 2005, 2008, among others), which we define as our cognitive ability to take other people's perspective and to model the mental states of our interlocutors. This view is very much in line with the *theory of mind* (Whiten 1991; Tomasello 1999; Givón 2005), which revolves around our ability to identify and differentiate the mental from the physical world and, more specifically, the ability to conceptualise thoughts, ideas, emotions, attitudes, beliefs, etc. in other people's minds (Brône 2010, pp. 91–92):[25]

> Linguistic expressions are cues for making inferences, and understanding thus consists not primarily in decoding the precise content of the expression, but in making inferences that lead to adequate next (cognitive, conversational, behavioral) moves. (Verhagen 2005, p. 22)

2.4 Prototype effects in category structure

Before we elaborate the importance of metaphor in our conceptual system, we want to draw attention to the *prototype-based view on category structure* which is one of the fundamental principles of CL.[26] It offers a methodological response to the question why cognitive linguists show so much interest in metaphor.

As opposed to structuralists, who typically consider an expression with its meaning(s) a closed category with sharp internal and external boundaries, cognitive semantics adopts the view, developed in psychology, which claims that (a) not all categories can be defined by a fixed set of necessary and sufficient conditions applying to *all* the members of a category, and (b) not all category members have the same prominence (see Rosch 1978; Rosch and Mervis 1975). According to this last feature, internal category structure may consist of a prominent (salient) centre called the *prototype* and a less prominent periphery. The first characteristic indicates that the boundaries of a category may be vague and/or flexible.

What interests us most here are the principles of categorisation that are inherent in this prototype theory. Instead of the fulfilment of a set of definitional criteria which turns categorisation into a digital all-or-none matter, the important principle underlying category membership is *analogy*.[27] In this view there is no need for *all* category members to share one or more properties with each other. All that it takes for a new element (like a new meaning of an expression) to be categorised as a member of a particular category is that there should be some kind of correspondence (similarity) with an already existing member of the category. It thus appears that conventional categories[28] function as *flexible interpretation frames* for new, unconventional experiences. Consequently, a lexical category consisting of the different meanings of an expression is structured basically as a set of clustering, overlapping elements, chained to each other by family resemblances. Cognitive semantics distinguishes two major principles of categorisation: (1) extension from a prototype (through metaphor, metonymy, specialisation, or generalisation) and (2) schematisation, which is the ability to capture the commonality of two experiences in a higher abstract structure (schema).

This dynamic view on categorisation led cognitive linguists to one of their major themes of interest: the study of semantic change, which is reflected on a synchronic level in the study of polysemy.[29] It is also in this general context that cognitivist metaphor research must be situated.

3 CONCEPTUAL METAPHOR THEORY

CL has always shown great interest in the analysis of metaphor as a ubiquitous verbal and cognitive phenomenon.[30] In their pioneering work on this topic, some thirty years ago, Andrew Ortony, George Lakoff, Mark Johnson, and Mark Turner,[31] and dozens of scholars following them, have firmly established Conceptual Metaphor Theory (henceforth CMT) as a powerful, hence also often criticised, paradigm for analysing the complex interplay of linguistic, social, and cognitive dynamics. Over the last thirty years, CMT has clearly evolved from a first-generation cognitive-linguistic account for deriving pre-linguistic experiential structures from readily accessible linguistic utterances (language as a direct gateway to the mind) to one of the empirically and interdisciplinarly grounded methods currently applied to obtain a better insight in the complexity of meaning and cognition (Fusaroli and Morgagni 2013, pp. 1–3).

CMT advanced the basic claim that fundamentally our knowledge system is metaphorically organised. Abstract domains of experience appear to be systematically organised through metaphoric mappings from concrete, sensorimotor domains of experience. A conceptual metaphor like for example, MIND IS A CONTAINER, MORE IS UP etc. is then defined as 'the projection of basic experiential structure from concrete domains of experience such as objects, movements, and spatial orientation to abstract domains of experience such as mathematics and morality' (Fusaroli and Morgagni 2013, p. 1).

In line with this basic claim, many CMT studies have drawn attention to the fact that metaphorical patterns play a major role not only in typical figurative speech, but also and more importantly in our everyday language use, which we commonly experience as being literal. We are all well aware of the figurative, imagistic language we use when we are talking about emotions, aesthetic impressions etc., but it is far less obvious to accept that also our daily ordinary language use abounds with metaphor. Compare, for instance, expressions like *I have troubles* and *I lost my self-confidence*, in which an abstract concept (a property) is metaphorically understood as a concrete possessible object (reification metaphor), or also frequently occurring expressions like *I am in trouble/in love* and *he is running out of luck*, in which an abstract state is metaphorically construed as a location in space. Although expressions like these are well established (*conventionalised*) and considered to be literal, they are still essentially metaphoric in nature as they systematically structure an abstract concept or domain (a state, a feeling, etc.) in terms of the elements and physical and logical relations that make up the internal structure of a concrete domain (the possession of an object, a location).

CMT explains the systematicity of these mappings by the embodied nature of our knowledge system: our inherent situatedness in the physical space provides generally shared bodily experience, which seemed to justify the identification of prelinguistic, universally valid structures of our conceptual world. Already in its early years, CMT experienced a big and rapidly growing success.[32] It served as the theoretical background and methodological guideline for dozens of CL studies exploring the conceptual structure of the most diverse domains of human experience, including mathematics (Lakoff and Núñez 2000), political discourse (Lakoff 2002, 2006), literature (Lakoff and Turner 1989), pictorial representations and comics (Forceville 1998, 2005, 2006; Shinohara and Matsunaka 2009), emotions (Kövecses 1990, 1995, 2000; Sauciuc 2013), co-speech gestures (Cienki and Müller 2008a, 2008b; Cienki 2013), sign languages for the deaf (Taub 2001), and cultural knowledge encoded as body *habitus* or action structure (Casasanto 2009a; Kimmel 2005).

3.1 Thirty years on: A critical evaluation of CMT

In the course of the past thirty years, disclosing the conceptual organisation of abstract knowledge domains was not CMT's only merit. In his overview article of thirty years of CMT, Gibbs (2013, pp. 15–16) identifies four major concerns in the broad domain of humanities and cognitive sciences in which CMT has achieved a major impact. First, CMT has boosted the popularity of CL, offering valuable insights into 'the overall unity of human conceptual structures, bodily experience and the communicative functions of language' (2013, p. 15). Second, CMT has offered both a theoretical model and an empirical method to demonstrate the pervasiveness of metaphor in language and thought across various knowledge domains, cultures, and contextual discourses. Third, on a philosophical level, CMT has induced a new, systematic (re-)consideration of the relationship between language and thought, and of the architecture of abstract knowledge domains in particular. Fourth, and finally, Gibbs attributes to CMT the leading role in the realisation of the 'second revolution' (Lakoff and Johnson 1999) in cognitive science, which concerns the investigation of embodied cognition: 'CMT has significantly enhanced understanding of the dynamic links between bodily experience, pervasive patterns of thought, culture, and linguistic structure and behaviour' (Gibbs 2013, p. 16).

Fusaroli and Morgagni (2013) have pointed out that over the years, CMT has been criticised and nuanced in three areas. By far the most elaborated nuance of CMT, first, concerns the inclusion of the cultural and social dimension as relevant elements of the pre-linguistic experiential structures that provide the ultimate grounding of conceptual metaphors. Although already formulated at an early stage (compare, for instance, Geeraerts and Grondelaers 1995), this criticism has become very prominent and widely accepted in recent years (see Evans 2013; Fusaroli et al. 2011; Ziemke et al. 2007; among many others). In line with the intersubjective turn in cognitive (linguistic) research, Leezenberg (2013) dismisses the reductionist view, by which grounding experience and cognitive processes are confined to individuals. These are located, instead, in the intersubjective interaction of largely distributed social and linguistic practices.

At this point, where multiple types of knowledge are taken into account as feeding into the metaphoric structure, we briefly refer to Conceptual Integration Theory (CIT) or 'blending theory', elaborated by Gilles Fauconnier and Mark Turner (2002, 2008).[33] This model, which also serves the analysis of both semiotic expression and conceptual structure, takes into account the possibility of multiple input spaces with different types of relationships holding between them, as well as conceptual structures which only emerge in the blended space. As such, CIT and CMT provide partially overlapping yet essentially complementary analytic perspectives onto the complexity of (non-)verbally expressed and conceptual knowledge structures.

A second point of criticism inserts an aspect of flexibility and dynamism into the concept of conceptual metaphor, which originally tended to be perceived as a stable and universal cognitive structure. Diachronic metaphor research, for instance by Allan (2013), has demonstrated the dynamic character of conceptual metaphors and their linguistic expressions: over time, they appear, get modified, and then disappear again. As Fusaroli and Morgagni (2013, p. 4) put it, 'these findings fully bring CMT into a dynamic perspective on cognition, where experiential patterns constitute slowly evolving constraints for fast evolving, ongoing, context-sensitive cognitive processes' (see also: Spivey 2007; Dale et al. 2013).

Finally, and third, CMT is believed to benefit from more large-scale empirical research, as demonstrated by the Pragglejaz Group method (2007) for establishing explicit criteria for identifying metaphors in the context of discourse analysis.[34] Also, experimental studies have come up with empirical evidence for some of the intuitively plausible principles of CMT, among them the basic assumption that some abstract domains are disclosed and internally organised by metaphoric mappings from other domains, not just in terms of linguistic expressions, but also on the underlying level of cognitive structures. Taking this one step further, recent experimental studies strongly indicate an interesting 'backward' influence of the specific linguistic profiling of a metaphor (for instance, the expression of time in terms of a linear vs. a three-dimensional space) on the way people actually think about a target concept such as time (Casasanto 2009b).

3.2 Metaphor as a conceptual phenomenon

A major claim of CMT is that metaphor is a pervasive *conceptual phenomenon*, which reveals itself in numerous expressions on verbal as well as non-verbal (gestural, postural, pictorial, behavioural, etc.) levels of expressions. Crucially, some concepts are not just *represented* as metaphoric, but their internal structure is essentially made up of coherent logical structures imported from other knowledge domains or concepts. If metaphor were merely a matter of linguistic representation, 'we would expect different linguistic expressions to be different metaphors' (Lakoff 1993, p. 209). Apparently, this is not the case. Compare for instance the examples under (1) below. They all represent different linguistic instantiations of a single generalised metaphor structuring the mind as a machine.

(1)   He has a *screw loose*.
       I am a little *rusty* today.
       My *computer* cannot handle so much information at the same time!
       My mind just isn't *operating* today.
       She had a nervous *breakdown* again.

We can now define metaphor as the *mapping of two concepts belonging to different knowledge domains*. As a result of this mapping, one concept which is typically abstract (the *target*) is expressed and understood in terms of another, experientially accessible concept (the *source*).[35] This structural projection from source to target domain consists of a correspondence between entities[36] in both domains. On a very abstract level, this mapping takes the form of a *topological* (image-schematic) projection whereby the image schematic structure from the source is mapped onto the target. Image schemata are very abstract structures (concepts), which according to Johnson (1987) emerge directly at the level of our bodily interaction with the world. They are relatively simple structures, which play an important role in the structuring of our experience and our conceptual system.[37] Examples of image schemata are structures like CONTAINER, BALANCE, BLOCKAGE, PART-WHOLE, PATH, etc., but also spatial orientations like UP-DOWN, CLOSE-FAR, etc. A good illustration of how image schematic structure can be mapped onto a target is the conceptualisation of the mind as a container in expressions like *what do you have* in *mind?; it slipped* out of *my mind*.

3.3 Metaphor as imagistic reasoning

Through systematic (topological) mappings of *logical* knowledge structures from a source to a target domain, the latter obtains its internal conceptual design mainly through the rationality that comes with the inference patterns and logical entailments in the source domain.[38] As Lakoff and Johnson (1980, p. 193) put it: 'Metaphor is one of our most important tools for trying to comprehend partially what cannot be comprehended totally: our feelings, aesthetic experiences, moral practices, and spiritual awareness'. The crucial point here is that many concepts, mostly abstract ones like LOVE, ANGER, LUCK but also GOD, are *essentially* metaphorically structured. This is not a matter of choice of representation, since there does not seem to be any alternative.

A classic example of a generalised metaphor is LIFE IS A JOURNEY, which shows up in expressions like those under (2) below (most examples from Lakoff 1993):

(2)   We are at a *crossroads* in our life.
      His life got *off the track*.
      There is no *way back*!
      Our relationship hit a *dead-end street*.
      We may have to *go our separate ways*.
      She gave her life a *new direction*.

More than just describing aspects of life in terms of a journey, these examples project our knowledge about travelling onto different aspects of life. The mapping consists more specifically of the structuring of LIFE according to the image schema PATH. This schema implies that life is generally conceived as a movement from a starting-point (SOURCE) in a specific direction towards a specific destination (GOAL). Apart from this global structural mapping between life and a journey, there are also more specific ontological correspondences occurring between both domains. A traveller corresponds with a living person, travelling destinations structure goals in life, decisive moments in life are understood in terms of crossroads, the road already covered corresponds to past periods of our life, etc. However, the mapping does not consist of these static correspondences alone. Its conceptual strength lies in the entire logic of journeys that is being implemented in the domain of life. Consequently, it is no problem to infer from these basic correspondences what concepts are profiled in the target domain when we use source domain images like a train getting off the track, hitting a long and bumpy road, choosing a wrong direction, a car that goes too fast and then breaks down, etc.

Another example of a conceptual metaphor is the spatial representation of abstract concepts like MORE (QUANTITY), HAPPY, GOOD (QUALITY), UNKNOWN on a vertical scale as UP. This kind of mapping has the status of an 'orientational metaphor' and it concerns mainly the topological projection of the image schema UP-DOWN together with its logic of verticality onto the target. This mapping shows up in the examples in (3):

(3) Prices were already *high* and now they are *rising* again.
   She had her *ups and downs*.
   These drugs make you feel *high* for a few hours but in the end they ruin
      your health!
   This CD-player proves to be of *top-level* quality.

It appears that certain complex concepts, like for example LIFE, DEATH, LOVE, but also GOD may be structured metaphorically in terms of more than one single source domain. Lakoff and Turner (1989, p. 52) point to the different metaphors for life as in LIFE IS A JOURNEY/A GAME/A BURDEN/A FIRE, etc. These different source domains impose different perspectives on the target structure. With each metaphor, other aspects of the target concept are highlighted. Each of these metaphors reflects a different experience and interpretation of life.

3.4 Examples from religious speech

We find similar examples in religious speech, where God is characterised metaphorically in many ways. As an illustration we cite the following four metaphoric extensions:

(4) GOD IS SHEPHERD
    GOD IS KING
    GOD IS LORD OF HOSTS
    GOD IS FATHER

Superficially these metaphors appear as four different ways of conceptualising God.[39] On a more schematic level, however, these generalised metaphors have the notion LEADERSHIP in common. It should be clear that this schema as well represents a metaphoric mapping, allowing us to look upon the more specific metaphors in (4) as related members of a category, each highlighting different aspects or kinds of leadership:

• SHEPHERD focuses on non-violent, peaceful leadership over a helpless group;
• KING focuses on powerful large-scale leadership over a whole people;
• LORD OF HOSTS focuses on powerful military leadership against an evil enemy;
• FATHER focuses on caring family leadership over ones children (pater familias).

Behind these four mappings hide four different understandings of God in four different conceptual frameworks, each of which is grounded in different experiences and socio-cultural contexts. In each of these metaphors the concept GOD is structured by the logic of the source domain, thus leading to several metaphorical entailments.

Take for example the metaphor GOD IS SHEPHERD,[40] which entails that the people belonging to God is understood as a helpless *flock of sheep* which needs to be *guided* and *brought back home* by the *shepherd*. A good shepherd tries to bring home all of his sheep and therefore even when one sheep *gets lost*, he starts *looking for it* because all sheep are equally important to him. A good shepherd also *takes care* of his sheep, he *feeds* them by *showing the way* to *green pastures*, he *protects* them against the attacks of *wild animals*, etc.[41] All these entailments in the source domain are mapped onto the target, which is consequently extended to the relationship between God and humankind. The many entailments constituting a coherent system illustrate that metaphor is not just a superficial, arbitrary matter of putting or phrasing God in terms of a shepherd. These multiple mappings reveal an internally coherent logical system, which in the metaphor is made available for structuring the abstract target domain.

Notice however that the projection from source to target is selective and that not every element of the source domain automatically participates in the metaphoric mapping. Take for example the sheepdog, which appears in the source domain as the shepherd's reliable servant and friend. However, there is no mapping of the concept SHEEPDOG onto an element of the religious target domain. A plausible explanation for this blocking can be found along the lines of the *invariance principle*,[42] which states that metaphorical mappings preserve a conceptual structure which is common to both the source and the target domain (see below). In this case, a conflicting constellation arises between the position of the sheepdog as a controller over sheep in the source domain and the position of the generic category of dogs relative to human beings in the cosmological hierarchy of things and beings.[43] In this hierarchy, all animals are ranked lower than humans. This culturally anchored hierarchy, in which the relationship between all kinds of classes and entities is metaphorically structured in terms of relative vertical positions on a scale (POWER/CONTROL IS UP), is a part of the conceptual structure of the target concept GOD in the GOD IS SHEPHERD metaphor. Applying the logic of this metaphor, the dog would have to be mapped on some entity ranked between God and human beings, for example an angel.[44] However, this mapping never occurs because of the conflicting values the concept DOG bears in source and target domain.

In the framework of this interdisciplinary contribution, it is not our purpose to provide a detailed analysis of specific metaphoric mappings onto the concept GOD, but with this somewhat elaborated example we hope to have demonstrated the structural strength of metaphor as a structuring mechanism of both verbal expression and thought. The metaphors listed under (4) are meant as illustrations of the fact that abstract religious concepts to a large extent require metaphoric mappings and that they can be understood in many ways. According to CMT, each of these different metaphors asks us to *give up GOD as an objective reality that exists with its inherent properties independently of any human understanding, transcendently waiting to be discovered in its essence.* However, it would also be erroneous to alternatively define GOD as the sum of all the different metaphors we can think of, as doing so again would be an attempt to reduce God to a conglomerated essence.

We are well aware of the fact that in a diachronic perspective the different metaphors in (4) reveal something about the socio-cultural conditions under which these specific metaphors came into existence. Through the course of time, most of the lexical categories (words) used for understanding GOD have not changed that much[45] so that on the level of (non-)verbal expression the formal side of these images (the word *form* that is) remains rather stable: as conventionalised metaphors they are always available. The conceptual content of these metaphors, as well as the meaning of the corresponding linguistic expressions, however, is not inherently stable. Instead, it constantly evolves along with the changing external circumstances (cultural and scientific evolution, Zeitgeist, personal experiences, etc.). Compare, for instance, the metaphoric structure of God as FATHER in present day western culture on the one hand, with its interpretation in ancient patriarchal cultures, where the leadership role of the father is strongly emphasised, on the other. Although the lexical category (the word) has remained the same, the interpretation of the word along with the rich underlying concept is quite different. As apparent from the example GOD IS LORD OF HOSTS, some metaphors may become opaque (idiomatised) because of the disappearance of external circumstances, which might provide motivation for a particular image.

For a detailed diachronic analysis of some religious metaphors from a cognitive semantic point of view, we refer to Yri (1998), who demonstrates that just like any other abstract concept in other domains of knowledge, religious concepts like SALVATION or PERDITION originate in everyday language use, thus giving rise to metaphoric structures. More specifically, this study deals with the issue of metaphoric structures in a diachronic translation perspective. It shows that a single target concept may be structured in different source domains in the different languages texts are translated into. For example, in Hebrew the concept of SALVATION is structured in the domain MILITARY, whereas in Greek and in Latin it is the domain HEALTH that functions as the source structure (see below).

3.5 Embodied grounding of conceptual metaphors

Observing that abstract concepts are conceptualised in terms of other, more easily accessible concepts is one thing. The question, however, of *why* a particular concept serves as the source for a particular target concept is another. What determines the pairing of these concepts? Are there any constraints? Why do these metaphoric expressions make sense to us at all?

Questions like these ask for the grounding of metaphoric mappings, and they bring us to the central tenet of CL as an *experience-based* account of language *and* thought. Apparently, conceptual metaphors do not occur arbitrarily, nor are they generated by a radical subjectivism according to which an autonomous subject 'sich von niemandem, auch nicht von der Welt, etwas diktieren läßt und selber derjenige ist, der Sinn stiftet' (de Pater 1996, p. 1501).[46] In this respect, Lakoff (1987, p. 266) warns against a Romantically inspired interpretation of 'experience' in terms of individual ad hoc experience:

> 'Experience' is [. . .] not taken in the narrow sense of the things that have 'happened to happen' to a single individual. Experience is instead construed in the broad

sense: the totality of human experience and everything that plays a role in it—the nature of our bodies, our genetically inherited capacities, our modes of physical functioning in the world, our social organisation etc.

Compare, for example, the orientational metaphor MORE IS UP already mentioned. It is through our experience that we know that when we add more of a substance to a pile, that pile goes up; when we pour water into a glass, the level of water in the glass rises; etc. The opposite correlation, where more corresponds to down, has no such experiential basis and, not surprisingly, is not expressed in language. In our Western culture, we also value the experience of having more of something more positively than having less or not enough of something (GOOD IS UP). And when we feel happy, like when our favourite soccer team scores a decisive goal or when we win the lottery, we jump up spontaneously, stretch our arms in the air, make ourselves as tall as possible, etc., instead of falling to the ground and making ourselves as small as possible (HAPPY IS UP). These bodily and sensory determined experiences represent 'natural' or embodied restrictions for possible metaphorical projections. A similar experiential basis underlies the pairing UNKNOWN IS UP. The sky is the sphere on earth that longest resisted human control. Until modern times, humans could only dream of conquering the skies and from there looking down on the earth. It may be not too surprising, then, that already in the prehistoric age, spiritual powers and gods were conceptualised as situated above them in the unknown skies. Furthermore, powerful and mysterious natural phenomena like thunder and lightning, wind and rain, but also the sun, the moon, and the stars, can be observed in the sky. These experiences may function as an original sensory-based motivation for metaphors such as UNKNOWN/POWER IS UP and by extension also for the ancient-Christian metaphor GOD IS UP.

As apparent in the examples in (4), identifying schematic motivating metaphors like GOOD IS UP or UNKNOWN IS UP does not suffice to adequately grasp an utterance's metaphoric meaning along with the underlying, conceptually rich image that motivates it.

3.6 Grounding in cultural models

In the course of time many basic human experiences have lost their value as a motivational structure and have become established primarily as fixed social-cultural models. A good example of this is what Lakoff and Turner (1989, p. 166) categorise as the 'Great Chain of Being', which they define as 'a cultural model that concerns kinds of beings and their properties and places them on a vertical scale with "higher" beings and properties above "lower" beings and properties'. The Great Chain is a schematic version of the many specific models that have been developed in Western ancient-Christian tradition for more than two thousand years and which still exists 'as a contemporary unconscious cultural model indispensable to our understanding of ourselves, our world, and our language' (Lakoff and Turner 1989, p. 167). Typically, in this hierarchic model God always occupies the highest position *above* all other creatures. The Great Chain is a model that shows up in the works of Plato and Aristotle, of almost every medieval author, in the works of Dante, but also of Shakespeare and many others. When the Russian astronaut Yuri Gagarin, after having completed the first flight of man in space, declared that he could not find any trace of God in space, he demonstrated in a naive way the actual presence of this ancient cultural model.[47]

Another good example of a powerful cultural model is presented in Geeraerts and Grondelaers (1995), with an analysis of the metaphor ANGER IS HEAT. They show that our present-day vocabulary used for expressing feelings of anger is to a large extent culturally determined by the medieval humoral doctrine.[48]

3.7 Experientialism between objectivism and subjectivism

To conclude this part on CL, and at the same time as a window on an interdisciplinary approach to our topic, we would like to locate more precisely CL's epistemological background.[49] In the course of this section, we distanced cognitive semantic experientialism from objectivism as well as from subjectivism.[50] Lakoff and Johnson (1980, p. 192ff) present experientialism as a possible third choice, a synthesis of these two poles. It seems that, in experientialism, neither of these approaches is fully rejected or fully accepted (Lakoff and Johnson 1980, p. 226ff).

What experientialism preserves from objectivism is the acceptance of a reality consisting of real things, which exists independently from any subjective interpretation, as well as the view that truth exists. However, it rejects the idea of an absolute truth about an absolute ontological order, just as it rejects the view of a stable, inherent meaning, which independently of context, interaction, and situation would remain attached to a (non-)verbal form. Meaning, conceptual understanding, and truth are always relative to a specific usage event.

What experientialism preserves from subjectivism is the view that meaning is not an object-inherent, subject-independent value, but always meaning *to* an intersubjectively and culturally determined individual in their participation in a communicative usage event. In taking on an intersubjective dimension, the CL account of meaning abandons the idea that the construction of a coherent conceptual system (as through metaphoric imagination) is an unconstrained personal (subjective) matter.

In conclusion, cognitive linguistic research into the structural importance of metaphor boils down to the observation that our conceptual system is determined by our *embodied and culturally determined understanding of* and *interaction with* the world. As a consequence, no claim whatsoever can be made towards objective truth.[51] In the light of this diversified experiential basis, our conceptual system turns out to be *basically metaphorically* structured. With regard to the possibilities this radically conceptual approach of metaphor may offer, not only to linguistics but also—and this is what especially interests us here—to other disciplines, we close this second part with the following tentative claim made by George Lakoff, which immediately orients us towards the third part: 'The contemporary theory of metaphor is [. . .] not only interesting for its own sake. It is especially interesting for the challenge it presents to other disciplines. If the results of the contemporary theory are accepted, the defining assumptions of whole disciplines are brought into question' (Lakoff 1993, p. 249).

4 COGNITIVE LINGUISTICS AND POSTMODERN THEOLOGY AFTER THE REDISCOVERY OF THE APOPHATICAL THEOLOGICAL TRADITION

In this concluding section we wish to highlight some possible transverse links between a postmodern, apophaticly structured theology and cognitive semantics. We therefore pay special attention to the mutual interest they have in each other, to schematic resemblances between the two, and we conclude by offering a possible recontextualisation of theology by incorporating some features of cognitive semantics.

4.1 Cognitive linguistics and postmodern theology: A mutual interest?

At the end of the first section, we mentioned that in the given circumstances cognitive semantics could be of major importance for a theology which rediscovered—via postmodern philosophy—the tradition of the apophatical theology as the sharpest expression of a properly theological, critical hermeneutical consciousness. Theology can no longer claim that it expresses (and is legitimated by) the ontological order. The apophatical theological consciousness questions each metaphysical reappropriation of God in theology. Apophatic theology, as Kevin Hart has stated (1989/1991, p. 104), 'reveals a non-metaphysical theology at work within positive theology'. It warns theologians that God is not a known factor in theology, ontologically secured, with a specific place in the theological language game, playing its role as other factors do; God withdraws from theology in theology. Especially in a postmodern context, the theology which reckons with its apophatic basis refuses the illusion of a link between the (theo)logical and onto(theo)logical orders. But we must not forget that God is indeed mentioned in theological discourse. This discourse actually discovered its radical contextual dependency, its particularity and contingency, from the confrontation with the divine otherness to which it bears witness, and by which every claim of objectivity and universality will be criticised (cf. Boeve 2014). To clarify to what extent theology can still be cognitive—and how this cognitivity can be characterised—theologians can learn from cognitive semantics, first and especially from its refusal to define cognitivity in terms of an objectivism legitimating it with reference to an ontological structure, and secondly from its awareness of the experiential and cultural grounding of our knowledge, large parts of which turn out to be metaphorically structured.

Under the intriguing title *Without Metaphor, No Saving God*, theologian Robert Masson (2014) makes an admirable attempt at mutually aligning both cognitive (linguistic) science and theology to one another. The book presents a well-documented interdisciplinary analysis of the interacting ('tectonic') character of the different conceptual layers in religious discourse. In an attempt to 'offer a nuanced framework in terms of both cognitive science and theology for explaining how we conceptualize God' (Masson 2014, p. 4), Masson investigates the explanatory power of adopting an integrated cognitive perspective, in which CMT is embedded in an overarching approach of CIT,[52] for the analysis of religious discourse.

As a general hypothesis, Masson defends the position that 'the cognitive linguist's understanding of the embodied mind and of the role played by figurative conceptualization and inference (. . .) augur a fundamental change in our understanding of the religious and theological landscape' (Masson 2014, p. 16). In line with this hypothesis, he admits that cognitive (linguistic) analyses[53] pose a challenge to the theologian to explain how meaningful conceptualisations of a transcendent God—along with the many corresponding inferences relating to this concept—can emerge from our embodied historical, social, and cultural existence (58). In facing this challenge, Masson (35) clarifies that the notion of the embodied mind does not presuppose or require religious discourse to be merely a product of mind and culture. Accordingly, knowledge of God isn't 'merely metaphorical' in the conventional sense of being only of secondary or derived nature:

> God is not a metaphor. My hypothesis that there is no saving God without metaphor does not deny God's existence. (. . .) Knowledge of God is genuinely human knowledge. The Christian conception of God is human all the way down. (. . .) What is known is not the same as how it is known. The divine can be mediated in the human without being derived from humanity, or conflated and confused with the human. (Masson 2014, p. 189)

From a linguistic point of view, the fundamental question which concerns us in this context is how CL or, for that matter, CMT deals with religious concepts like GOD. Yri observes that, for a linguist at least, this kind of concept does not require any special kind of treatment vis-à-vis other concepts:

> The inaccessible part of the religious world presents no problem for linguistic semantics [. . .], granted that religion is seen as one of many domains in semantic structure. Religious concepts will belong to basic and abstract domains entirely on a par with all other concepts in a language. (Yri 1998, p. 17)

Consequently, within this linguistic theory there is—contrary to the position of the fundamental theologian—no transcendental gap separating the observer from his or her object of research: 'But what might be termed a transcendental barrier in the philosophy of religion, the area beyond which is unknown unless communication takes place from the other side, will be treated as language users' ability to impose structures on abstract domains in cognitive semantics' (Yri 1998, p. 17). This does not mean, however, as already pointed out by Masson (cf. supra), that this view attempts to reduce the reality of God to merely an idea created by humans. A conclusion like this would be trivial in the sense that it ignores the important distinction between the world and its conceptualisation. Analysing the concept of God from a CL perspective does not deny in any way the existence of God, but it also does not provide proof of his objective existence. As such, utterances like *God exists* or *God is truly good* present no problem for a cognitive linguistic analysis. They can be valued 'true' or 'false' but always—and that is the crucial point—within a relative knowledge system of experience, understanding, and belief. Paraphrasing Lakoff, we can thus claim that there can be no objectively correct description *of* the God's eye point of view.[54]

The interest of CL in postmodern apophatic theology concerns the emphasis of the divine otherness which transcendently escapes every possible representation. On the methodological level of CL, this radical awareness of our religious narratives falling short of a full understanding of a concept like GOD can be projected onto the relationship between semantic and conceptual structure. Within a cognitive linguistic framework, this relationship draws attention to the inherent *symbolic* nature of meaning as a selective, underspecified, and conventionalised representation of rich, boundless conceptual structures. Hence this postmodern awareness of non-representability also confirms indirectly the importance of the linguistic notion 'construal' according to which a particular scene can be represented in multiple ways,[55] thus implying that every single construal, i.e. every linguistic expression, falls short of the individually determined conceptual content.

4.2 Schematic resemblance between CL and postmodern theology

In the rejection of extreme objectivism, CL finds a partner in theology, which has rediscovered in the present postmodern context the ancient tradition of negative theology. Comparable to what CL currently emphasises as the embodied, inter-subjective, and cultural ('experiential') grounding of our knowledge structures, postmodern-inspired negative theology emphasises radical contextual dependency as the basic characteristic of living religion.

On a lower level, this schematic resemblance between both theories is reflected in similar dynamic views on categorisation (interpretation). In CL the categorisation of new interpretations is governed by a prototype-based view on meaning structure and category extension, according to which conventional meanings function as flexible interpretation frames for new meanings. Basically the same interaction between structural stability and adaptability underlies the postmodern view on theological discourse. New religious experiences are necessarily interpreted on the base of tradition while at the same time religious tradition is constantly being changed (recontextualised) by every new experience.

Despite these schematic resemblances, CL and postmodern theology still represent two epistemological paradigms, each of which has its own specific properties. It appears that in both approaches the feature of flexibility and openness towards new experiences is motivated and interpreted in a different way.

In CL structural flexibility is highlighted as an essential feature of a prototype-based categorial system. Special emphasis thus lies on the *adaptability of the semantic categories* (the semantic range of a word) vis-à-vis the richness and novelty of new experiences. Theology in a postmodern context, on the other hand, centres primarily on God's non-representable, unspeakable otherness, by which every theological discourse is determined. It is the awareness of this otherness which grounds the dialectic interaction between tradition (system) and new experience resulting in the extension of the tradition. More than the adaptability of the system itself, however, it is the *elusiveness of the Other* which highlights the inherent necessity of this flexibility. Because of the irreducible otherness of the Other, which accompanies every formation of tradition, and because of the dependency of this formation process on the context, tradition cannot possibly remain sacrosanctly stable—that is, if it intends to bear witness to this Other in various diachronic and synchronic contexts.

Alternatively, one could state that in CL the principle of *family resemblance* is put into profile, whereas postmodern negative theology shows a particular interest in the philosophical notion of *différence* according to which there is always an aspect escaping every attempt at categorisation (conceptualisation). It must be clear, however, that these apparent differences are not mutually exclusive. Instead, they represent different but complementary perspectives: CL points at the 'positive' possibilities in categorising experiences. The act of categorising an entity is always motivated by some kind of resemblance with existing conventional knowledge structures, though at the same time resemblance implies non-identity and otherness: new experiences always contain new and unknown aspects which are not caught by the conventional system.[56] Negative theology focuses on the radicality of this newness, of this otherness, accompanying every attempt at categorisation; and in this way it questions categorisation as such. The 'negation' implied in apophatical theology thus theologically functions as a frame for 'positive' categorising.

As becomes apparent in the two approaches, these different perspectives may be carefully explained by noticing the unbridgeable gap which separates theology from God but which turns out to be of no particular methodological importance to CL. Despite the different angles from which the conceptualisation of God is looked at, both theories, belonging to two different disciplines, have a major general characteristic in common: the rejection of a reality absolutely describable in fixed categories or narratives in favour of multiple contextually embedded and metaphorically structured understandings of what is (or was) conceived as 'reality'.

4.3 Theology challenged by CL: An attempt at recontextualisation

Rather than elaborate a complete recontextualisation of theological methodology concerning the naming of God and the concepts of tradition, tradition-formation, and the handing over of tradition, we shall here sketch some perspectives which cognitive semantics can open for fundamental theology, its self-consciousness, its epistemology, and its method.

In fact, for theologians who take seriously their task of a contextually embedded *fides quaerens intellectum*, the patterns of thought present in cognitive semantics form an element of the context. A new context, affecting (and affected by) religious experience and praxis, urges them to recontextualise theological (traditional) concepts, and, if necessary, their insights into theological methodology concerning theological conceptualisation (and tradition formation) itself.

The translation of the apophatic hermeneutical critical consciousness of postmodern theology into the language of CL, for instance, implies an emphasis that the concept GOD is *semantically non-autonomous*—and this in the most radical way. In this respect, Masson (2014, p. 55) openly advocates the position that 'there is no theology without metaphor'. As mentioned earlier, this attribute is ascribed to concepts (or aspects of concepts) which cannot be structured (understood) in terms of their own domain of knowledge without interference from other unrelated domains. As a contrasting example, compare a semantically autonomous concept like CHAIR, which is understood in terms of inherent domains like FURNITURE, MATERIAL, SHAPE, etc. 'God', on the contrary, does not evoke knowledge patterns of itself, without interference from other domains. Therefore all knowledge about God is necessarily metaphorical. Hence the conceptual structures and the logic of the domain GOD are borrowed from other, more concrete domains. Furthermore, the apophatic presumption of theology radicalises this non-autonomy, and criticises all attempts to hold as literal any conception of God. Because of this unrepresentability, theology has to cope with the constant withdrawal of the target in the act of metaphorical mapping.[57] With regard to God-knowledge, theologians have to be aware of the diverse metaphorical mappings, the different source domains, and the relation they bear to the target domain, in order to acknowledge the specific nature of knowledge about God. In this way, CL provides an epistemological model for a theology framed as 'open narrative'. The striving for cognitivity in theology no longer regards the foundation or legitimation of Christian truth claims, but intends to establish plausibility and insight, by revealing the conceptual structures (*fides quaerens intellectum*). In this regard, theology shares with CL one of its basic presuppositions, namely, that one is always striving for motivated language—even where at first sight there is no adequate interpretation apparent or where formerly established meaning has weakened, one is eager to discover conceptual links providing interpretation (i.e. taking part in ongoing processes of reinterpretation and re-motivation). The observation, for example, that some metaphors of God—GOD IS SHEPHERD, FATHER, LORD OF HOSTS, KING—can still be generalised (GOD IS LEADER), does not imply that the latter is more appropriate than those first metaphors: in fact, it only gives a deeper account of our (diachronic and synchronic) conceptualisation of God.[58]

This leads us to the following observation: the theoretical framework of CL provides theologians with some insight into particular processes of 'literalisation' in the course of religious and theological history. Because of the experiential grounding of our knowledge system (its primary source domains are all bound in one way or another to human interaction with physical reality), it can be made plausible that one of the main religious and theological temptations is to forget the metaphorical mapping implied in each statement about God.[59] The spatialisation and

temporalisation at work for centuries (and which in a sense still continues) in eschatology (the doctrine concerning resurrection, life-after-death, heaven, purgatory,
hell) illustrate this. The metaphors GOOD IS UP and EVIL IS DOWN explain the spatialisation of heaven and hell, and of the localisation of God (see the Great Chain
of Being). The imagery of the angels, located in heaven, as personifications of the
causes of good things, is due to metaphors like GOOD IS UP and EVENTS ARE ACTIONS.
Other examples could be found with regard to GOD IS FATHER, or GOD IS PERSON, and
so on. One is likely to neglect the metaphorical mapping of conceptual structures of
a source domain (biological and culturally embedded FATHERHOOD, and human PER-
SONHOOD) onto the target domain GOD in religious and doctrinal statements which
express these conceptual patterns: when doing so, the semantic non-autonomy of
the domain GOD is ignored.

As mentioned before, the living Christian tradition can be identified with the
ongoing process of meaning formation during history and its transfer from the past
to the present. We have already acknowledged that in this formation and transferring process the historical context is of major importance. In view of the metaphorical mappings implied in religious knowledge, it is indeed relevant to perceive *how*
the source domains were and are situated within a specific context, and how these
domains have been affected by changes in the context (these changes can be due
to historical events and internal cultural shifts, but are also provoked by the mere
translation of texts, as when concepts in the original language and their translations
are not structured in terms of the same source domain). In this respect CL refers to
the principle of economy which presupposes a certain flexibility of categories: many
meanings have been expressed by means of the same vocabulary throughout history.
We do not invent a completely new vocabulary for each new concept. As a matter
of fact, this sheds new light on the problematic issue of the stability of the tradition, or rather, on the family resemblances between different diachronic as well as
synchronic instantiations of what is called the Christian tradition—with the various
questions this implies for the identity of Christianity throughout history and in our
pluralistic culture.

But we must ask not only how source domains and contextual changes influence
the conception of the religious domain, but also *why* a specific source domain has
been used to map its conceptual structure metaphorically onto the religious target
domain. In general, a dynamic, contextually embedded interrelation between an
established interpretation frame (tradition) and new experiences can be discovered as responsible for shifts in the religious tradition. CL can then provide the
means to elucidate the changes which have taken place. We illustrate this with the
example of the shift in Third World theologies of liberation, which originated in
Latin America in the late 1960s, from the metaphor GOD/JESUS IS SAVIOUR to GOD/
JESUS IS LIBERATOR.[60] As metaphor is a mapping from one conceptual frame to
another, the exploitation of a conceptual frame (POLITICAL LIBERATION), which is
usually *not* taken to apply to the traditional religious conceptualisation of 'saving'
or 'redeeming', is a clear case of metaphorical mapping. Because of the experience
of massive poverty and the growing religiously motivated consciousness that, in
order to regain its evangelical authenticity, religion had to deal with it—including

in a liberative social praxis—the metaphor GOD/JESUS IS SAVIOUR as such was no longer deemed adequate. In fact, the conceptualisation of GOD in terms of SAVIOUR/ SALVATION, is essentially metaphorical as one is mapping conceptual schemes and expressions from a source domain of PRESERVING IN GOOD CONDITION onto the religious domain (the verb in Greek is *soizein*, in Latin: *salvare*).[61] More specifically, this PRESERVING IN GOOD CONDITION is also interpreted in a 'medical' way as PRE-SERVING OR RESTORING HEALTH, LIFE.[62] For contextual reasons, liberation theologians wanted to highlight the social impact of the salvific action of God in history, and to criticise more exclusively spiritual conceptions of salvation such as spiritual health and eternal life seemingly without (practical) consequences for personal and social welfare here and now. Instead, liberation theologians preferred to name God/ Christ liberator, and to identify salvation with liberation. By this, they perceived God's salvific action in history and the world along the conceptual lines developed in the domain of LIBERATION from prison, slavery, poverty, political oppression, and so on, involving the notions of social liberative praxis, conflict, etc. In order to perform this conceptual shift, liberation theologians found inspiration in the Old Testament, more specifically in the Exodus-narrative, the liberation of the Jewish people from the oppression of Egypt. In this context, the Hebrew concept/ expression YASA/*yasa* is used, with Jahweh as subject (and usually translated in the Septuagint as *soizein*), which prototypically means 'to help, to intervene in an armed conflict with victory over the enemy as a result' (Yri 1998, p. 45ff.[63]) Doing so, liberation theologians no longer mapped conceptual patterns metaphorically from a foremost medical source domain of LIFE PRESERVATION AND HEALTH, but from a source which is originally military, and has strong links with social conflicts and the removal of persons or communities from a situation of oppression. In a similar way, one could investigate to what extent the imagery of GOD IS FATHER has been affected by changes in the cultural and social perspectives on being a father and by the feminist criticism of patriarchy.[64] In this respect, Sally McFague's new metaphors for naming God, GOD IS MOTHER, GOD IS LOVER, and GOD IS FRIEND, illustrate the impact of the changes in human relationships on the conceptual struc-tures in the religious domain (McFague 1988).

Nevertheless, for the purpose of our contribution it is useful to quote McFague's account of one of the theologian's most deceptive temptations (1988, p. 181): 'Even a metaphorical, heuristic theology that believes itself to be sceptical, open-ended, and pluralistic [in casu her own theologising] can become enamoured of its experi-ment, finding its new models a sufficient improvement on alternatives that they become subtly elevated to a new trinity with a position of authority'. On the lines of this reflection we conclude this essay.[65]

NOTES

1. cf. Carabine (1995, p. 3): 'In the Pseudo-Dionysius, the way down from the original darkness of God to the light of creatures is a way of knowing, a continual theophany of being. The way up, on the other hand, is an assent from the light of creatures to the darkness of God and is a process of leaving creatures behind'.

2. 'The divine transcendence is [. . .] the transcendence even of difference between God and creation. Since there is no knowable "distance" between God and creation, there is no language in which it is possible to state one. For all our terms of contrast state differentiations between creatures' (Turner 1995, p. 45).
3. Migne PG 3, col. 1048B; Luibheid translation (1987), p.141.
4. Thomas Aquinas, *Summa theologiae*, Ia, Q. 13, art. 5; Pegis (1945, p. 120).
5. cf. Thomas Aquinas, *Summa theologiae*, Ia, Q. 13, art. 3; Pegis (1945, pp. 116–117): 'Our knowledge of God is derived from the perfections which flow from Him to creatures; which perfections are in God in a more eminent way than in creatures. Now our intellect apprehends them as they are in creatures, and as it apprehends them thus it signifies them by names. Therefore, as to the names applied to God, there are two things to be considered—viz. the perfections themselves which they signify, such as goodness, life, and the like, and their mode of signification. As regards what is signified by these names, they belong properly to God, and more properly than they belong to creatures, and are applied primarily to Him. But as regards their mode of signification, they do not properly and strictly apply to God; for their mode of signification befits creatures'.
6. cf. Derrida (1992). An introduction of the relationship between deconstructionism and the negative theology of Pseudo-Dionysius is offered by Blans (1996); see also Boeve (2002).
7. cf., e.g., Coward and Foshay (1992), and Scharleman (1992).
8. See Lyotard (1988a, 1988b, 1991, and 1993).
9. cf. Boeve (2011) and (2014), in which the relation between 'open' and 'narrative' is further elaborated on, in dialogue with Lyotard's criticism of the hegemonic nature of (modern) master narratives.
10. For a summary and evaluation of this study, see Gleeson (1992).
11. See also Mortley (1986, p. 277) on the role of the *via negativa* for present theologising: 'The *via negativa* establishes the contradiction of revelation, but rather than bearing destruction within itself, it has an enhancing and expanding capacity. Like the breaking of icons, it destroys the narrow focus, and puts an end to theological pharisaism'.
12. cf. Boeve (2014).
13. cf. Boeve (1997, 2012).
14. See, e.g., Soskice (1985, p. 140): '[The] separation of referring and defining is at the very heart of metaphorical speaking and is what makes it not only possible but necessary that in our stammering after a transcendent God we must speak, for the most part, metaphorically or not at all'.
15. On this, cf. Soskice (1985, p. 141): 'The theist can reasonably take his talk of God, bound as it is within a wheel of images, as being reality depicting, while at the same time acknowledging its inadequacy as description'.
16. Moreover, this will allow them to place the theological incorporation of more classical theories of 'metaphor' (cf. note 20) in a broader perspective.
17. We wish to thank Dirk Geeraerts for valuable comments on this section.
18. According to Langacker (1987, p. 5), meaning is to be considered 'the most fundamental issue of linguistic theory'.
19. By *lexical item* we mean any formal linguistic unit (morpheme, word, sentence, . . .) paired to a single meaning.
20. Compare in this respect structuralist lexical field research (J. Trier, H. Geckeler, E. Coseriu and others) which aims at describing the full meaning of words on the basis of their exact position with respect to other words in a semantic field.
21. Cognitive (Construction) Grammar defines an expression as a bipolar symbolic unit: it consists of the association of a phonological representation with a semantic representation; see also, among others Goldberg (2006).
22. See also Taylor (1989, p. 83ff).
23. Discussing each of these dimensions would lead us too far away from the present topic. Only one crucial dimension of meaning, the *ground*, may require our specific

attention. As the central element of the context of speech, the *ground* consists of the communicative event itself, the speaker and hearer, their interaction, and the specific circumstances (time and place) of the utterance (Langacker 2008, p. 259).

24. An interesting overview with regard to the introduction of the interactional dimension in metaphor and conceptual integration (blending) studies is provided by Brandt (2013).

25. See also Feyaerts (2013), Feyaerts and Oben (2014), Veale et al. (2013). This rather recent view of language as fundamentally dialogic and socially determined is, as noticed by Brandt (2009, p. 38), very much in line with similar social reorientations of other disciplines like psychology and (social) neuroscience (Gallese 2005, 2007; Gallagher 2009).

26. For a detailed account of the influence of prototype theory in linguistics, see for example, Geeraerts (1989), but also Geeraerts et al. (1994) for a profound analysis of prototype effects with respect to lexical variation.

27. This principle reflects the notion of 'family resemblance' used by Wittgenstein.

28. For the most part, it is the prototypical meaning of an expression which functions as the base for meaning extension, but this process can also occur with peripheral members of a category.

29. Compare Geeraerts (1997), chapter 1.

30. We also refer to the huge amount of studies on the role of *metonymy* as a conceptual principle structuring our knowledge system; see for instance, among others, Dirven (1993); Radden and Kövecses (1999); Feyaerts (2000); Panther and Thornburg (2007). In this context, however, we will not go any further into this matter.

31. See especially Ortony (1979, second edition 1993), Lakoff and Johnson (1980), Lakoff (1987), Lakoff and Turner (1989), and Lakoff (1993).

32. Gibbs (2013, p. 14) notes: 'The vast interdisciplinary literature suggests that CMT has become the dominant perspective on metaphor. It has touched dozens of academic fields and topics'.

33. For practical reasons we cannot further elaborate into blending theory here.

34. Compare, in this respect, also pioneering work by Gibbs (2006); Gibbs and Colston (1995); Gibbs and Matlock (1999); Gibbs and Tendahl (2006); Boroditsky (2001); and Casasanto (2009a/b), among others.

35. As a matter of convention, conceptual metaphors are represented with the form TARGET CONCEPT IS SOURCE CONCEPT.

36. Lakoff describes these mappings in terms of the correspondence between *ontological* structures (Lakoff and Johnson 1980, pp. 25–32). Although 'ontology' is referring to an experienced reality that is always embedded in a conceptual framework, the use of this terminology might be confusing with regard to the traditional philosophical use of 'ontology'.

37. Johnson (1987, p. 29) defines an image schema as 'a recurrent pattern, shape, and regularity in, or of, [our] ongoing ordering activities. These patterns emerge as meaningful structures for us chiefly at the level of our bodily movements through space, our manipulation of objects, and our perceptual interactions. [. . .] I conceive of them as structures for organising our experience and comprehension'.

38. Lakoff and Johnson (1980, p. 193) speak of *imagistic reasoning*.

39. In his Gifford lectures, George Lakoff (2003) identifies three major metaphors for the divine: 1. GOD AS PARENT (King, Lord, Lover, Creator, Shepherd, etc.); 2. GOD AS THE INFINITE (All-Seeing, All-Knowing, All-Powerful, All-Good, First Cause), and 3. GOD AS IMMANENT.

40. Especially Psalm 23 ('The Lord is my shepherd; I shall not want. In verdant pastures he gives me repose; beside restful waters he leads me . . .') as well as John 10:1–18 ('I am the good shepherd; the good shepherd lays down his life for the sheep . . .') (*The New American Bible* 1971).

41. While characterising the bucolic domain, we noticed a 'temptation' to describe some aspects of it from a religious perspective. This interesting observation might indicate

an opposite projection according to which the abstract religious domain serves as the source for a concrete domain. For similar observations we refer to Yri (1998, p. 163). In this respect, we subscribe to the conclusion drawn by Rudzka-Ostyn (1994, p. 443): 'it is not always obvious which of the domains that participate in semantic extension is to be regarded as source and which as target. They depend vitally, though not exclusively, on the perspective adopted'.

42. Although this principle is heavily debated, Brandt (2009, p. 51) states that 'some version of CMT's Invariance Principle—asserting that mappings preserve the image-schematic structure of the source domain consistent with the inherent structure of the target domain—may still apply (. . .)'.

43. Lakoff and Turner (1989, pp. 170–181) speak of this hierarchy in terms of the 'Great Chain of Being'.

44. In this respect we refer to mappings like GOD IS LORD OF HOSTS/KING, in which angels are conceptualised in terms of soldiers or officers serving in God's army (as in the Jesuits' 'miles Christi' ideal).

45. For reasons of economy, we do not use a new word for every new experience. It appears that our cognitive ability of categorisation combines structural stability with flexible adaptability.

46. An autonomous subject 'does not allow anybody, not even the world, to dictate it; it is the subject itself that 'makes' (generates) sense'. Lakoff and Johnson (1980, p. 185) paraphrase this subjectivist view as the 'Humpty-Dumpty notion that something means "just what I choose it to mean—neither more nor less"'.

47. A variant of this verticality metaphor, already present in Platonic-Aristotelic philosophy, may be the interior-exterior model, according to which more spiritual and individually religious experiences are situated more inside ourselves, in the soul, whereas non-religious experiences are experienced and therefore also located (on the) outside (part of) our body.

48. Another question to be raised here, as Kövecses (1995) aptly puts it, is whether such cultural models cannot themselves be reduced to bodily based experiences.

49. For an elaborate description of the location of CL in a broader philosophical context we refer to Geeraerts (1993).

50. We are aware of the fact that both approaches can hardly be presented as well-delineated scientific models and that this invoked dualism—with experientialism somewhere in the middle—is an oversimplification of a complex philosophical debate, which cannot possibly be explored any further here.

51. As Lakoff (1987, p. 259) puts it: 'There can be no objectively correct *description* of reality from a God's eye point of view'.

52. Through the integration of both disciplines, he aims to advance the discussion of a series of significant theological and religious controversies.

53. Masson also takes research by the recently emerged cognitive science of religion (CSR) into account.

54. Also compare Masson (2014, p. 27): 'There is no "stepping outside" our bodily, socially, and culturally constituted conceptual frameworks to gain a God's-eye view of reality independent from metaphorical and figurative conceptualizations. There is no escaping the constitutive role of embodied mind.'

55. Compare the title of Casad's article (1995), 'Seeing it in more than one way'.

56. See in this respect also Geeraerts (1993, p. 72f).

57. This critique also deconstructs Thomas Aquinas' attempt to guarantee some privileged knowledge about God by distinguishing between metaphor and analogy—and especially in the case of analogy, by settling the logical order upon the ontological order.

58. Another example: from an apophaticly framed theology on, even GOD IS GOOD (from Thomas Aquinas, theologians have learned that this being good is not just a property of God, but constitutes God's essence) should be considered to be metaphorical (although linguists might perceive this as a metonymic pattern): not only is the

conceptual structure of the GOOD domain mapped onto the target GOD; but, at the same time, the abstract concept GOOD itself is metaphorically structured in several mappings (e.g. GOOD IS UP, where structures from the domain of vertical scale [up and down] are projected onto the concept GOOD).

59. The 'forgetting' of the metaphorical mapping implied in God-knowledge can have various causes, including a lack of sensitivity for the specificity of religious language, the attempt to secure or legitimate religious knowledge claims (in a master narrative without openness), and so on.

60. For more historical and theological background, see Ellacuría and Sobrino (1993).

61. Our argument does not imply that we equate meaning with etymology. Rather, it demonstrates that (relations among) current meanings may very well result from a diachronic process of metaphorical meaning extension. Yri (1998, p. 57ff.) presents an elaborate study of the polysemy structure of SAVIOUR in classical Greek, in the Septuagint, and in the New Testament.

62. In the German and Dutch translation the 'medical' element is even stronger: *Heil/heil* 'salvation' is, for instance, related to *heilen/helen* (to heal) as well as to Dutch. *heelmeester* 'surgeon'.

63. Yri's study especially investigates the changes in meaning because of translations which imply shifts in source domains.

64. cf. e.g. McFague (1982, p. 145ff).

65. We wish to thank Jeffrey Bloechl and Sabien Van Oost for proofreading major parts of this article and René Dirven and Jean-Pierre van Noppen for their comments on earlier versions of this essay.

REFERENCES

Allan, Kathryn (2013). An inquest into metaphor death: Exploring the loss of literal senses of conceptual metaphors. *Journal of Cognitive Semiotics* 5(1–2), 291–311.

Allen, Diogenes (1985). *Philosophy for Understanding Theology*. Atlanta: John Knox Press.

Barlow, Michael and Suzanne Kemmer (2000). *Usage-based Models of Language*. Stanford, CA: CSLI Publications.

Blans, Bert (1996). Negatieve theologie en deconstructie. *Bijdragen. Tijdschrift voor filosofie en theologie* 57, 2–19.

Boeve, Lieven (1997). Postmodernism and negative theology: The A/theology of the 'open narrative'. *Bijdragen. Tijdschrift voor filosofie en theologie* 58, 407–425.

Boeve, Lieven (2002). The rediscovery of negative theology today: The narrow gulf between theology and philosophy. In Marco Olivetti (ed.), *Théologie negative*, pp. 443–459. CEDAM Rome.

Boeve, Lieven (2003). *Interrupting Tradition: An Essay on Christian Faith in a Postmodern Context*. Louvain Theological and Pastoral Monographs 30. Leuven, Belgium: Peeters Press.

Boeve, Lieven (2007). *God Interrupts History: Theology in a Time of Upheaval*. New York: Continuum.

Boeve, Lieven (2009). Systematic theology, truth and history: Recontextualisation. In Mathijs Lamberigts, Lieven Boeve, and Terrence Merrigan (eds.), *Orthodoxy: Process and Product*, pp. 27–44. Leuven, Belgium: Peeters Press.

Boeve, Lieven (2011). Naming God in open narratives: Theology between deconstruction and hermeneutics. In Joseph Verheyden, Theo L. Hettema, and Pieter Vandecasteele (eds.), *Paul Ricoeur: Poetics and Religion*, pp. 81–100. Leuven, Belgium: Peeters Press.

Boeve, Lieven (2012). Theological truth in the context of contemporary continental thought: The turn to religion and the contamination of language. In Frederiek Depoortere and Magdalen Lambkin (eds.), *The Question of Theological Truth: Philosophical and Interreligious Perspectives*, pp. 77–100. Amsterdam: Rodopi.

Boeve, Lieven (2014). *Lyotard and Theology: Beyond the Christian Master Narrative of Love.* London/New York: Bloomsbury T&T Clark.

Boeve, Lieven and Kurt Feyaerts (1999). Religious metaphors in a postmodern culture: Transverse links between apophatical theology and cognitive semantics. In Lieven Boeve and Kurt Feyaerts (eds.), *Metaphor and God-talk*, pp. 152–184. Bern: Lang.

Boroditsky, Lera (2001). Does language shape thought? Mandarin and English speakers' conceptions of time. *Cognitive Psychology* 43(1), 1–22.

Brandt, Line (2009). Metaphor and the communicative mind. *Cognitive Semiotics* 5(1–2), 37–107.

Brandt, Line (2013). *The Communicative Mind: A Linguistic Exploration of Conceptual Integration and Meaning Construction.* Newcastle upon Tyne: Cambridge Scholars Publishing.

Brône, Geert (2010). *Bedeutungskonstitution in verbalem Humor: Ein kognitivlinguistischer und diskurssemantischer Ansatz.* Frankfurt/Main: Lang.

Carabine, Deidre (1995). *The Unknown God: Negative Theology in the Platonic Tradition: Plato to Eriugena.* Louvain Theological and Pastoral Monographies. Leuven, Belgium: Peeters Press.

Casad, Eugene H. (1995). Seeing it in more than one way. In John Taylor and Robert E. MacLaury (eds.), *Language and the Cognitive Construal of the World*, pp. 23–49. Berlin: de Gruyter.

Casasanto, Daniel (2009a). Embodiment of abstract concepts: Good and bad in right- and left-handers. *Journal of Experimental Psychology: General* 138(3), 351–367.

Casasanto, Daniel (2009b). When is a linguistic metaphor a conceptual metaphor. In Vyvyan Evans and Stéphanie Pourcel (eds.), *New Directions in Cognitive Linguistics*, pp. 127–145. Amsterdam: John Benjamins.

Cienki, Alan (2013). Conceptual Metaphor Theory in light of research on speakers' gestures. *Journal of Cognitive Semiotics* 5(1–2), 349–366.

Cienki, Alan and Cornelia Müller (eds.) (2008a). *Metaphor and Gesture.* Amsterdam: John Benjamins.

Cienki, Alan and Cornelia Müller (2008b). Metaphor, gesture and thought. In Raymond W. Gibbs (ed.), *Cambridge Handbook of Metaphor and Thought*, pp. 483–501. Cambridge: Cambridge University Press.

Coward, Harold and Toby Foshay (eds.) (1992). *Derrida and Negative Theology.* Albany: State University of New York.

Dale, Rick, Riccardo Fusaroli, Nicholas Duran, and Daniel C. Richardson (2013). The self-organization of human interaction. *Psychology of Learning and Motivation* 59, 43–95.

de Pater, Wim A. (1996). Sprachphilosophie in der Theologie. In Marcelo Dascal, Dietfried Gerhardus, Kuno Lorenz, and Georg Meggle (eds.), *Sprachphilosophie: Ein internationales Handbuch zeitgenössischer Forschung*, volume 2, pp. 1489–1505. Berlin and New York: de Gruyter.

Derrida, Jacques (1992). How to avoid speaking: Denials (English translation of *Comment ne pas parler. Dénégations*, 1987). In Harold Coward and Toby Foshay (eds.), *Derrida and Negative Theology*, pp. 73–142. Albany: State University of New York.

Dionysius the Areopagite (1857). *S. Dionysii Areopagitae opera omnia quae exstant*, Patrologia Graeca 3, edited by J.-P. Migne. Paris: Imprimerie Catholique.

Dionysius the Areopagite (1987). *Pseudo-Dionysius: The Complete Works*, translated by C. Luibheid. New York: Paulist Press.

Dirven, René (1993). Metonymy and metaphor: Different mental strategies of conceptualisation. *Leuvense Bijdragen* 82, 1–28.

Ellacuría, Ignacio and Jon Sobrino (eds.) (1993). *Mysterium liberationis: Fundamental Concepts of Liberation Theology.* Maryknoll, NY: Orbis.

Evans, Vyvyan (2013). Metaphor, lexical concepts, and figurative meaning construction. *Journal of Cognitive Semiotics* 5(1–2), 73–107.

Fauconnier, Gilles and Mark Turner (2002). *The Way We Think: Conceptual Blending and the Mind's Hidden Complexities*. New York: Basic Books.

Fauconnier, Gilles and Mark Turner (2008). Rethinking metaphor. In Ray Gibbs (ed.), *Cambridge Handbook of Metaphor and Thought*, pp. 53–66. New York: Cambridge University Press.

Feyaerts, Kurt (2000). Refining the inheritance hypothesis: Interaction between metaphoric and metonymic hierarchies. In Antonio Barcelona (ed.), *Metaphor and Metonymy at the Crossroads: A Cognitive Linguistic Perspective*, pp. 59–78. Berlin and New York: de Gruyter.

Feyaerts, Kurt (2013). A cognitive grammar of creativity. In Tony Veale, Kurt Feyaerts, and Charles Forceville (eds.), *Creativity and the Agile Mind: A Multi-disciplinary Study of a Multi-faceted Phenomenon*, pp. 205–227. Berlin: de Gruyter.

Feyaerts, Kurt and Bert Oben (2014). Tracing down schadenfreude in spontaneous interaction: Evidence from corpus linguistics. In Wilco van Dijk and Jaap Ouwerkerk (eds.), *Schadenfreude: Understanding Pleasure at the Misfortune of Others*, pp. 275–291. Cambridge: Cambridge University Press.

Forceville, Charles (1998). *Pictorial Metaphor in Advertising*. London: Routledge.

Forceville, Charles (2005). Visual representations of the idealized cognitive model of *anger* in the Asterix album *La Zizanie*. *Journal of Pragmatics* 37(1), 69–88.

Forceville, Charles (2006). The SOURCE-PATH-GOAL schema in the autobiographical journey documentary. *New Review of Film and Television Studies* 4(3), 241–261.

Fusaroli, Riccardo, Tommaso Granelli, and Claudio Paolucci (eds.) (2011). *Versus* 112–113. (Special issue: The External Mind).

Fusaroli, Riccardo and Simone Morgagni (2013). Conceptual Metaphor Theory: Thirty years after. *Journal of Cognitive Semiotics* 5 (1–2), 1–13.

Gallagher, Shaun (2009). Philosophical antecedents to situated cognition. In Philip Robbins and Murat Aydede (eds.), *Cambridge Handbook of Situated Cognition*, pp. 35–51. Cambridge: Cambridge University Press.

Gallese, Vittorio (2005). Embodied simulation: From neurons to phenomenal experience. *Phenomenology and the Cognitive Sciences* 4, 23–48.

Gallese, Vittorio (2007). Mirror neurons and the social nature of language: The neural exploitation hypothesis. *Social Neuroscience* 3(3), 317–333.

Geeraerts, Dirk (1989). Prospects and problems of prototype theory. *Linguistics* 27, 587–612.

Geeraerts, Dirk (1993). Cognitive semantics and the history of philosophical epistemology. In Richard A. Geiger and Brygida Rudzka-Ostyn (eds.), *Conceptualizations and Mental Processing in Language*, pp. 53–79. Berlin and New York: de Gruyter.

Geeraerts, Dirk (1997). *Diachronic Prototype Semantics: A Contribution to Historical Lexicology*. Oxford: Oxford University Press.

Geeraerts, Dirk, Stefan Grondelaers and Peter Bakema (1994). *The Structure of Lexical Variation: Meaning, Naming, and Context*. Berlin: de Gruyter.

Geeraerts, Dirk and Stefan Grondelaers (1995). Looking back at anger: Cultural traditions and metaphorical patterns. In John Taylor and Robert E. MacLaury (eds.), *Language and the Cognitive Construal of the World*, pp. 153–179. Berlin: de Gruyter.

Gibbs, Raymond W. (2006). *Embodiment and Cognitive Science*. Cambridge, UK: Cambridge University Press.

Gibbs, Raymond W. (2013). Why do some people dislike Conceptual Metaphor Theory? *Cognitive Semiotics* 5(1–2), 14–36.

Gibbs, Raymond W. and Herbert L. Colston (1995). The cognitive psychological reality of image schemas and their transformations. *Cognitive Linguistics* 6(4), 347–378.

Gibbs, Raymond W. and Teenie Matlock (1999). Psycholinguistics and mental representations: A comment. *Cognitive Linguistics* 10(3), 263–269.

Gibbs, Raymond W. and Markus Tendahl (2006). Cognitive effort and effects in metaphor comprehension: Relevance theory and psycholinguistics. *Mind and Language* 21(3), 379–403.

Givón, Talmy (2005). *Context as Other Minds: The Pragmatics of Sociality, Cognition and Communication*. Amsterdam/Philadelphia: John Benjamins.

Gleeson, Gerald P. (1992). Deconstructing the concept of God. *Pacifica* 5, 59–66.

Goldberg, Adele (2006). *Constructions at Work: The Nature of Generalization in Language*. Oxford: Oxford University Press.

Hart, Kevin (1989/1991). *The Trespass of the Sign: Deconstruction, Theology and Philosophy*. Cambridge: Cambridge University Press.

Hochstaffl, Josef (1976). *Negative Theologie: Ein Versuch zur Vermittlung des patristischen Begriffes*. München, Germany: Kösel.

Johnson, Mark (1987). *The Body in the Mind: The Bodily Basis of Meaning, Imagination, and Reason*. Chicago: University of Chicago Press.

Kimmel, Michael (2005). Culture regained: Situated and compound image schemas. In Beate Hampe (ed.), *From Perception to Meaning: Image Schemas in Cognitive Linguistics*, pp. 285–311. Berlin: de Gruyter.

Kövecses, Zoltán (1990). *Emotion Concepts*. Berlin/New York: Springer Verlag.

Kövecses, Zoltán (1995). Anger: Its language, conceptualization, and physiology in the light of cross-cultural evidence. In John Taylor and Robert E. MacLaury (eds.), *Language and the Cognitive Construal of the World*, pp. 181–196. Berlin: de Gruyter.

Kövecses, Zoltán (2000). *Metaphor and Emotion*. Cambridge: Cambridge University Press.

Lakoff, George (1987). *Women, Fire, and Dangerous Things: What Categories Reveal about the Mind*. Chicago: University of Chicago Press.

Lakoff, George (1993). The contemporary theory of metaphor. In Andrew Ortony (ed.), *Metaphor and Thought* (2nd ed.), pp. 202–251. Cambridge: Cambridge University Press.

Lakoff, George (2002). *Moral Politics: How Liberals and Conservatives Think*. Chicago: University of Chicago Press.

Lakoff, George (2003). The embodied mind, and how to live with one. In Anthony J. Sanford (ed.), *The Nature and Limits of Human Understanding: The 2001 Gifford Lectures at the University of Glasgow*, pp. 47–108. New York: T&T Clark.

Lakoff, George (2006). *Whose Freedom? The Battle Over America's Most Important Idea*. London: Macmillan.

Lakoff, George and Mark Johnson (1980). *Metaphors We Live By*. Chicago: University of Chicago Press.

Lakoff, George and Mark Johnson (1999). *Philosophy in the Flesh: The Embodied Mind and its Challenge to Western Thought*. New York: Basic Books.

Lakoff, George and Rafael Núñez (2000). *Where Mathematics Comes From: How the Embodied Mind Brings Mathematics into Being*. New York: Basic Books.

Lakoff, George and Mark Turner (1989) *More than Cool Reason: A Field Guide to Poetic Metaphor*. Chicago: University of Chicago Press.

Langacker, Ronald W. (1987). *Foundations of Cognitive Grammar. Vol. I. Theoretical Prerequisites*. Stanford, CA: Stanford University Press.

Langacker, Ronald W. (2001). Discourse in cognitive grammar. *Cognitive Linguistics* 12(2), 143–188.

Langacker, Ronald W. 2008. *Cognitive Grammar: A Basic Introduction*. Oxford: Oxford University Press.

Leezenberg, Michiel (2013). From cognitive linguistics to social science: Thirty years after *Metaphors We Live by. Journal of Cognitive Semiotics* 5(1–2), 140–152.

Lyotard, Jean-François (1988a). *The Differend: Phrases in Dispute*. Manchester: University Press (English translation of *Le différend*, 1983).

Lyotard, Jean-François (1988b). *Peregrinations: Law, Form, Event*. New York: Columbia University Press.

Lyotard, Jean-François (1991). *The Inhuman: Reflections on Time*. Cambridge: Polity Press (English translation of *L'inhumain: Causeries sur le temps*, 1988).

Lyotard, Jean-François (1993). *The Postmodern Explained: Correspondence 1982–1985*. Minneapolis: University of Minnesota Press (English translation of *Le postmoderne expliqué aux enfants: Correspondance 1982–1985*, 1986).

Masson, Robert (2014). *Without Metaphor, No Saving God: Theology after Cognitive Linguistics*. Leuven, Belgium: Uitgeverij Peeters.

McFague, Sally (1982). *Metaphorical Theology: Models of God in Religious Language*. Philadelphia: Fortress Press.

McFague, Sally (1988). *Models of God: Theology for an Ecological, Nuclear Age*. Philadelphia: Fortress Press.

Mortley, Raoul (1986). *From Word to Silence II: The Way of Negation, Christian and Greek*. Theophaneia. Beiträge zur Religions- und Kirchengeschichte des Altertums. Bonn: Hanstein.

New American Bible (1971). Chicago: Good Counsel Publishers.

Ortony, Andrew (1979, second edition 1993). *Metaphor and Thought*. Cambridge: Cambridge University Press.

O'Rourke, Fran (1992). *Pseudo-Dionysius and the Methaphysics of Aquinas*. Studien und Texte zur Geistesgeschichte des Mittelalters 32. Leiden: Brill.

Panther, Klaus-Uwe and Linda Thornburg (2007). Metonymy. In Dirk Geeraerts, and Hubert Cuyckens (eds.), *The Oxford Handbook of Cognitive Linguistics*, pp. 236–263. Oxford: Oxford University Press.

Pegis, Anton C. (ed.) (1945). *Basic Writings of Saint Thomas Aquinas*. New York: Random House.

Pragglejaz Group (2007). MIP: A method for identifying metaphorically used words in discourse. *Metaphor and Symbol* 22(1), 1–39.

Radden, Günter and Zoltan Kövecses (1999). Towards a theory of metonymy. In Günter Radden and Klaus-Uwe Panther (eds.), *Metonymy in Language and Thought*, pp. 17–59. Amsterdam and Philadelphia: John Benjamins.

Rosch, Eleanor (1978). Principles of categorization. In Eleanor Rosch and Barbara B. Lloyd (eds.), *Cognition and Categorization*, pp. 27–48. Hillsdale, NJ: Lawrence Erlbaum.

Rosch, Eleanor and Carolyn B. Mervis (1975). Family resemblances: Studies in the internal structure of categories. *Cognitive Psychology* 7, 573–605.

Rudzka-Ostyn, Brygida (1994). Metaphor, schema, invariance: The case of verbs of answering. In Keith Carlon, Kristin Davidse, and Brygida Rudzka-Ostyn (eds.), *Perspectives on English: Studies in Honour of Professor Emma Vorlat*, pp. 408–447. Leuven, Belgium: Peeters.

Sauciuc, Gabriela-Alina (2013). The role of metaphor in the structuring of emotion concepts. *Journal of Cognitive Semiotics* 5(1–2), 244–267.

Scharleman, Robert P. (ed.) (1992). *Negation and Theology*. Charlottesville: University Press of Virginia.

Schillebeeckx, Edward (1989). *Mensen als verhaal van God*. Baarn, Netherlands: Nelissen.

Shinohara, Kazuko and Yoshihiro Matsunaka (2009). Pictorial metaphors of emotion in Japanese comics. In Charles Forceville and Eduardo Urios-Aparisi (eds.), *Multimodal Metaphor*, pp. 265–293. Berlin: de Gruyter.

Soskice, Janet M. (1985). *Metaphor and Religious Language*. Oxford: Clarendon Press.

Spivey, Michael J. (2007). *The Continuity of Mind*. Oxford: Oxford University Press.

Taub, Sarah F. (2001). *Language from the Body: Iconicity and Metaphor in American Sign Language*. Cambridge: Cambridge University Press.

Taylor, John R. (1989). *Linguistic Categorization: Prototypes in Linguistic Theory*. Oxford: Clarendon Press.

Tomasello, Michael (1999). *The Cultural Origins of Human Cognition*. Cambridge: Harvard University Press.

Trevarthen, Colwyn (1999). Intersubjectivity. In R. Wilson and F. Keil (eds.), *The MIT Encyclopedia of Cognitive Sciences*, pp. 413–416. Cambridge, MA: MIT Press.

Turner, David (1995). *The Darkness of God: Negativity in Christian Mysticism*. Cambridge: Cambridge University Press.

Veale, Tony, Kurt Feyaerts, and Charles Forceville (2013). E unis pluribum: Using mental agility to achieve creative duality in word, image and sound. In Tony Veale, Kurt Feyaerts, and Charles Forceville (eds.), *Creativity and the Agile Mind: A Multidisciplinary Study of a Multi-faceted Phenomenon*, pp. 37–57. Berlin: de Gruyter.

Verhagen, Arie (2005). *Constructions of Intersubjectivity: Discourse, Syntax and Cognition.* Oxford: Oxford University Press.

Verhagen, Arie (2008). Intersubjectivity and the architecture of the language system. In Jordan Zlatev, Timothy P. Racine, Chris Sinha, and Esa Itkonen (eds.), *The Shared Mind: Perspectives on Intersubjectivity*, pp. 307–331. Amsterdam: John Benjamins.

Whiten, Andrew (1991). *Natural Theories of Mind: Evolution, Development and Simulation of Everyday Mindreading.* Oxford: Blackwell.

Yri, Kjell Magne (1998). *My Father Taught Me How to Cry, but Now I Have Forgotten: The Semantics of Religious Concepts with an Emphasis on Meaning, Interpretation, and Translatability.* Acta humaniora 29. Oslo: Scandinavian University Press.

Ziemke, Tom, Jordan Zlatev and Roslyn M. Frank (2007). *Body, Language, and Mind.* Berlin: de Gruyter.

CHAPTER 4

Linguistics and the Scientific Study of Religion

Prayer as a Cognitive Register

WILLIAM DOWNES

This chapter is a part of a larger research programme in the study of religious language, thought, and experience. The aim is to use linguistics as a methodology for the analytical investigation of culture. Linguistics provides the theory, and how texts are comprehended, the empirical basis. The linguistics I deploy is eclectic, suiting the purposes at hand. Particularly useful has been cognitive pragmatics, Sperber and Wilson's (1995) relevance theory and Sperber's (1996) epidemiology of representations and 'London School' socio-functional linguistics, especially the notion of register (Firth 1957/1968, pp. 175–179; Halliday et. al. 1964, pp. 75–110; Halliday 1978, pp. 31–35, 122–125). Of the two approaches, I used cognitive pragmatics to study language and religion (Downes 2011) and register to analyse a prayer (Downes 1998, pp. 308–322).

1 COGNITIVE REGISTER

Combining the two approaches, I term the current study an inquiry into *cognitive register*. This interprets language use in contexts of situation and culture which constitute ways of thinking, feeling, and motivation which are otherwise impossible. My working hypothesis is that multi-dimensional cognitive complexes like religion socially emerge into culture from innate capacities through these linguistically enabled modes of cognition. Cultural complexes are acquired through learning their cognitive registers, and therefore the particular thoughts, feelings, and motivations that they enable. What is acquired is not only concepts, but a total felt experience (Downes 2000). Cognitive register, to the degree it deals with meaning, is a linguistic relative of Wittgenstein's philosophical 'deep grammar' and 'language games'. In this respect, I will utilize D. Z. Phillips' *The Concept of Prayer* (1981). Firth himself (1957/ 1968, p. 179) makes this connection with Wittgenstein, which I will explicate in section 6.1. Related to this and true to Firthian origins, linguistically enabled styles of cognition are normally also susceptible to socio-functional interpretation.

I begin by attempting to characterize religion as an emergent cultural complex which consists of mental representations with four key properties: first, reference to supernatural entities, more or less abstract or personalized, which transcend the everyday, natural world; second, rationalization of this realm; third, with respect to propositional attitudes, the affective-motivational; and fourth, normative 'oughtness', what to do and how to be (Downes 2011, pp. 14–52). This cultural complex is made manifest in both language and other behaviours by a family of semiotic techniques, of which cognitive registers are the mental and linguistic form. These are used in contexts for disseminating, mentally interiorizing, practically applying, and evolving religious representations within a social world. Religion forms part of civil society, with an especially normative, ethical-educative, ideological function. It can have multiple, diverse, often conflicting relationships with both state and economy.

Representations and the cognitive registers through which they are made manifest, when widely diffused, become each person's changing cultural and social identity. When these are religious, they are within a context of human suffering and mystery, which is ultimately baffling. Because this context, indeed the whole world of experience, does not entail a unique interpretation, it cannot determine any one certain cultural response. It is this uncertainty about reality, and hence the correct relationship to it, that is the ultimate context of religion.

Representations and their registers create a *normative* social group with more or less rationalized common concepts, affects, and motivations. This consists of persons who share 'oughtness' with respect to how they ought to feel, evaluate, and comprehend the world. They try to believe and behave as they ought according to the identity of their religiously defined community (Downes 2011, pp. 42–44, 232–235). Since norms don't refer to what people actually do, but what they ought to do, these are purely a mental and language phenomenon, and cannot be discovered from an empirical description of behaviour. Normative values are at least tacitly involved in all human action, so understanding how norms are internalized and applied is urgent. Prayer is perhaps the most important way, certainly the main conscious, personal way, in which religious norms can be deeply internalized, innovatively applied, and hence widely disseminated.

2 PRAYER AS A THEOLOGICAL PROBLEM

This essay will concentrate on Christian prayer, mainly because that is the tradition with which I am most familiar. What do we mean by 'prayer'? Like all religious terminology, the sense of the word isn't precise. There are two basic aspects: first and most generally, contact with a more or less personal supernatural entity and second, and more specifically, 'talking' to a more or less personal supernatural entity. In sociolinguistic terms, the former conception is an *encounter*, focused co-presence, non-verbal or verbal; and the latter is verbal, a subset of the first (Goffman 1963). An important type of non-verbal prayer encounter is *contemplative prayer*, or *meditation*, paths to mystical religious experience.

In this essay we are concerned only with communicative encounters. It is worth noting that communication is not co-extensive with language. Any non-verbal encounter is communicative if it involves a behaviour which intends to convey a message (Grice 1957; Sperber and Wilson 1995). Therefore, any act, verbal or non-verbal, performed with the intention of communicating with God, can be treated as prayer. But we will analyse only verbal prayer.

There are further distinctions which can be drawn about the relation of prayer to its verbal medium on various simultaneous dimensions. A linguistic prayer can be silent, inner speech, or spoken aloud, either in private or in public. If in a public religious situation, prayer can be part of a collective liturgical activity. That activity can either be vocalized by every individual in a group, or by a prayer leader, in which case verbal prayer is a special kind of attentive listening (Downes 1998, pp. 319–320). On another dimension, prayer can be spontaneous, or the recitation or reading of, respectively, a memorized or written text. Spoken liturgical prayer has distinctive sound properties, melding into chant, sung prayer, and hymn. In literate traditions, prayers have been composed, written down, collected, and translated, forming part of scripture and having special authority. On another dimension, prayer can be accompanied by non-verbal signs, outstretched arms, kneeling posture, etc. On yet another dimension, that of dialogue, there is the question of 'listening to God' and the theological problem of 'answers'.

As Phillips points out, to make sense of prayer is to come to understand the way that the language is used by religious believers. He claims that knowing how to use that language is to 'know God'. This is by virtue of the way that the concept, God, is relevant to prayer. Prayer presupposes a purported 'knowledge of God' in the believer's conception of God. As opposed to contemplation and meditation, verbal prayer is talking to God—it is by definition oriented to the interpersonal function of language (Halliday 1978, pp. 21–22, 116–117, 144). Intended as verbal communication, it presupposes that God can be treated as a *pragmatic person* (Downes 2011, p. 38). Since the term 'pragmatic' refers to the use of language in context, especially communication, it enumerates just the necessary and sufficient properties of communicative competence. This is a defining property of 'persons'. It follows that prayer presupposes a personal God (is theistic) who must have the properties of one with whom, somehow, however mysteriously, it must make sense to communicate. Pragmatic personhood also opens the door to dialogue. Given this possibility, not only 'revealed' scriptures, but private thoughts that emerge into consciousness or even patterns within events, are often interpreted as communications from God, replies to prayer. This inner voice is not the same as 'hearing voices' in psychiatric contexts. If God is a pragmatic person, it makes sense both to 'talk to God' and 'listen to God'. These phrases are often used in books on prayer, and one needs to understand what is meant in these contexts.

It is the mismatch between God as a pragmatic person and other properties of God that creates the theological problem of prayer. If one takes God as a pragmatic person *literally*, then there is no problem. But this concept of God becomes almost unrecognizably humanized; simply a super-version of you or me. This might be the case in folk or popular religion. This God could come and go, learn new things and be surprised by them, change their mind in the face of arguments, pleading, or promises, do special favours for me and not for you because I am God's favourite, and so on. For sophisticated theology, this is all idolatry. Therefore, the presupposition that God is a pragmatic person in the human sense must be merely an analogy. If this is accepted, then rationally working out the analogy is to grapple with a theological problem in its specialized context of situation and culture. There may be many different degrees of awareness of these problems, more or less relevant to actual people in the contexts in which they pray. Phillips talks about 'deep religious believers', who have a more sophisticated grasp of prayer, a group which must contrast with more naïve believers who verge on 'the realm of superstition' with respect to their petitions (Philips 1981, pp. 122–123). There are also modernist concepts of God which many theologians today would reject because of the humanization of the concept (Hyman 2010).

Phillips points out that the very possibility of the act of praying for the believer is definitive of understanding what the language game 'talking to God' means (Phillips 1981, p. 37f.). However, as linguists, we approach believers' understanding by 'bracketing' the objective felicity of their theological commitments, while still including them, when necessary, in our account of prayer. It is irrelevant whether the referent of 'God'—or any other supernatural entity—is real or exists. *Qua* linguists, we neither say that they exist or don't exist. We represent only what believers do, how they claim to understand it, and how that relates to our theory of language, how it could have meaning in context. Bracketing the issue in this way is not the same as taking an atheist stance. Methodologically, we suspend judgement about the concepts, commitments, and attitudes of those who pray, while grasping these through the process of *verstehen*, the intuitive understanding of human behaviour (Abel 1960, p. 158). This is the scientist's application of their own mind-reading and empathetic capacities and distinguishes our scientific approach from Phillips' philosophical theology, which, sharing commitments with its subjects, tries to find the best theological solution to the problem of prayer.

3 FUNCTIONS AND GENRES OF PRAYER

Prayer has a number of traditional communicative functions. These include invocation, praise, devotion/worship/adoration, thanksgiving, benediction or blessing, penitence, petition, remonstrative prayer of complaint, dedication, intercession, and contemplative and meditative prayer—more properly mysticism—mentioned above.

Except for the last, these should be thought of as types of communicative functions, to be distinguished from the way they are linguistically realized. A given prayer tends to weave more than one of these together in the same text. Even an estranging intonation can manifest an attitude of sacred separateness and awe in the function of worship. Realization takes the form of *generic templates*. These are ideal structures projected from culture which pre-code how to perform the situation type of prayer. It is by internalizing these genres that a believer learns how to pray, enacting the actual situations that make up their prayer life (Halliday 1978, pp. 133–134).

Petitionary prayer, often considered the most basic form of prayer, is the subject of this essay. In Figure 1, I set out its generic template. There is an invocation, a petition and its content which I claim are obligatory, with the caveat that there are cases, especially in inner and/or spontaneous speech, where the invocation can be structurally conflated with the petition, as the understood subject of an imperative, or the implicit or explicit indirect object of a performative verb which enacts the petition. (A performative verb is one whose sincere utterance can actually perform the action named by the verb; e.g. *I beg* you to do it today.) The relation of invocation and petition is a structure which is not a sequence. Although the invocation most often precedes the petition, it can be placed elsewhere, for example, interrupting petition and content. The condition, coda, and amen are optional elaborations, characteristic of more formal written, liturgical prayer. Each structural part of a prayer can be iterated, repeated any number of times. (The technical term for this phenomenon is 'recursion'.)

3.1 Invocation

I outline the invocation function and its structure in Figure 2. The addressee, treated as a pragmatic person, can be either summoned or addressed, or the two can be combined recursively: for example, 'O God! Thou art my rock, I seek thee . . .' (Psalm 63:1). If summoned, this is usually achieved, not by nominal address, and never with summoning intonation, but by a clause, most commonly an imperative: 'Lord, hear my voice! Let thy ears be attentive to the voice of my supplication' (Psalm 130:2); 'Come, O Holy Spirit' (Prayer to the Holy Spirit; *A Simple Prayer Book* 1997, p. 10). But sometimes it is achieved by a performative: 'Out of the depths, I cry to thee, O Lord' (Psalm 130:1); 'I cry aloud to God, aloud to God, that he may hear me' (Psalm 77:1). The performative is rare in contemporary Christian prayer, but appears in both the psalms and the mystery religions of antiquity.

More common is the complex nominal structure of invocation in Figure 3. This constitutes an interpersonal relationship by directly addressing the transcendent pragmatic person, who is treated as already conversationally present and doesn't need to be explicitly summoned. Consider the Invocation in the *Hail Mary*, a prayer which itself is performed over and over again in the Rosary, a specialized member of the register of prayer. The effect of repetition in inducing altered cognitive states is well known. In this prayer, the invocation is iterated repeatedly. The iterated structures are italicized and tone group boundaries indicated:

> *Hail // Mary // full of grace // the Lord is with thee // blessed art thou amongst women //*
> *and blessed is the fruit of thy womb // Jesus // Holy Mary // Mother of*
> *God //* pray for us sinners // now // and at the hour of our death // Amen.

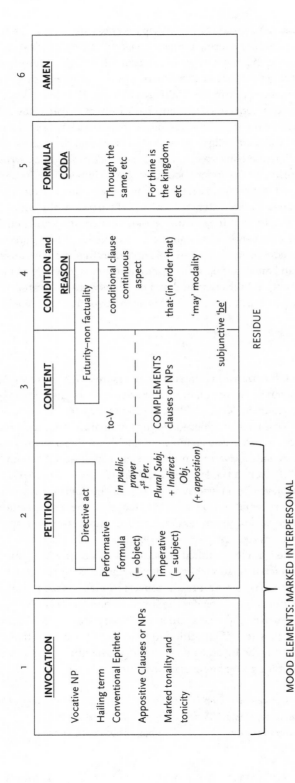

Figure 1 Generic form of English petitionary prayer

	1	2	3	4	5	6
	INVOCATION	**PETITION**	**CONTENT**	**CONDITION and REASON**	**FORMULA** **CODA**	**AMEN**
	Vocative NP	Directive act	Futurity–non factuality	conditional clause	Through the same, etc	
	Hailing term	Performative formula (= object) →	to-V	continuous aspect	For thine is the kingdom, etc	
	Conventional Epithet	*in public prayer* *1st Per.* *Plural Subj.* *+ Indirect Obj.* *(+ apposition)*	COMPLEMENTS clauses or NPs	that-(in order that)		
	Appositive Clauses or NPs	Imperative (= subject) ↓		'may' modality		
	Marked tonality and tonicity		subjunctive '**be**'			

RESIDUE

MOOD ELEMENTS: MARKED INTERPERSONAL
(1) RECURSION POSSIBLE WITHIN ANY SECTION
(2) OPTIONAL EXCEPT 1 + 2.

Figure 2 Invocation: Function and structure

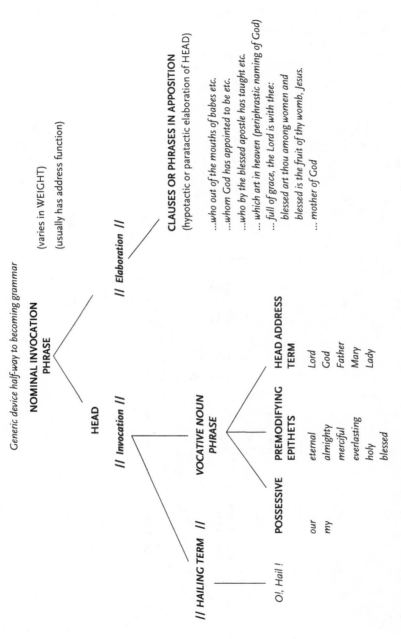

Figure 3 Grammar of nominal invocation

There are two separate nominal invocations in this prayer with 'Mary' the head of both, the second expanded by the premodifying epithet, 'Holy'. These are vocative noun phrases which make explicit through a situated act of reference to the supernatural addressee of the prayer, who is treated as conversationally present. They presuppose an ontological commitment to the entity 'Mary', which varies with the believer's explicit or tacit theology. Both invocations are elaborated. The elaboration of the first is extensive, consisting of one phrase—analysable as a reduced non-restrictive relative clause—plus three further clauses in apposition. In the second invocation, there is one phrase in apposition, another reduced relative, 'Mother of God', parallel to the first.

Address always involves recognizing the relative status of the addressee (Brown and Gilman 1960). Invocations can be so elaborate and excessive that this is itself meaningful. They are said to 'conversationally implicate' an extra function, that of praise. (A 'conversational implicature' is something that a speaker implies and a hearer can infer that crucially depends on the context of the conversation. In this case, the hearer is explaining to themselves why the invocation is so elaborate and concludes that it is to honour the addressee, the mother of God, hence is an act of praise.) Praise expresses obeisance to supernatural power by analogy with addressing a sovereign. We learn from this both how the possibility of recursion can itself be used to achieve a cognitive effect and how the same structure can be relevant in two ways, fulfilling two functions, address and praise. At least three different social models or analogies for the addressee relationship are available; monarchical, familial, and personal fellowship. The monarchical is the most power-oriented. By contrast, in the *Hail Mary*, the relation is both familial and personal, seeking Mary's nurturance through her intercession with her son. It is a gendered relationship. Elsewhere, she is the monarchical 'Queen of Heaven', the glorified Christ's royal consort.

Authoritative written prayers of a tradition, such as the *Shema*, the *Kaddish*, the *Lord's Prayer*, and the *Hail Mary*, have histories. In the case of the last, it was 'Originally purely an Invocation praising Mary based on Luke 1.28 and 42 . . . the Petition . . . *Pray for us sinners* . . . was appended by the Carthusians about . . . 1350 . . . receiving its definitive form along with the complete text of the *Hail Mary* in 1568 in the breviary of Pius V' (Jungmann 1978, p. 109).

3.2 Petition and the imperative

Petitionary prayer normally has an overt Invocation. Petition is often said to be the primitive form of prayer and why this could be so will become clear. Petitions are realized in two ways, by the use of the imperative sentence type or by a performative formula containing one of a set of verbs of supplication: *beg, beseech, implore*, etc. The two ways can appear together, as in *Grant, we beseech thee. . . .*

Both linguistic forms have traditionally been considered humble requests, *directives*, which literally convey the force of that specific class of illocutionary acts. According to Searle and Vanderveken (1985, pp. 37–62, 179–216) there are five essential illocutionary points. In directives, the speaker attempts to get the hearer to carry out a future course of action. The primitive directive verb is 'to direct'. All the above performatives are included in this class. In terms of intentionality, this representation projects words onto the world, essentially using language to try to bring about a future state of affairs. Applied to petitionary prayer, this means that the prayer *literally* counts as an attempt to cause God to do something that he wouldn't otherwise do, by virtue of the recognition that the speaker intends to produce this effect. To be a genuine directive petition, the prayer must be intended to be the *reason* that God does the act in question. In summary, it is an attempt to get God to conform to the speaker's will.

I claim that this directive interpretation is the folk view of prayer. It is the relation that would be appropriate for a humble supplicant petitioning a prince, in order to obtain a favour in their gift. But, as we shall see, there are theological problems with this applied to prayer. Here also is the implicit relation of petitionary prayer to *spells*, formulaic texts which, when enacted felicitously, are words which have the power to control the supernatural, to conform it to the magician's intentions. The perlocutionary uptake of the directive for the supernatural is obligatory; that is the power of the utterance.

One of the reasons that petitionary prayer has been 'folk-interpreted' in these ways is that it seems natural to think that the imperative grammar *must* always enact some sort of directive, like a request or command. If this were so, then every sentence in the imperative could be literally paraphrased by a corresponding performative verb, like 'request' or 'command'. This is called the 'performative analysis' (Ross 1970). It means that to utter an imperative sentence would necessarily and automatically be understood as trying to get the hearer to do something. As long as the conditions for the underlying performative are satisfied in the context, it necessarily conveys that speaker intention—*Do A*. But this means that many common uses of the imperative, like granting permission or expressing a wish or a preference, have to be some sort of non-literal, indirectly inferred use of the grammatical form. The philosopher John Searle calls these 'indirect speech acts', a case where the speaker says one thing but actually intends another (Searle 1975).

However, alternative pragmatic analyses are now available that don't assume that the imperative *must* always be a directive. Instead, the sentence types encode much less, and communicative intents are conveyed uniquely in each context. In other words, the imperative is not equivalent to a performative. In Downes (1977) I argued that the semantic content of the grammatical imperative was exhausted by the representation of a hypothetical state of affairs which the hearer could make true. This semantic structure can then be used to implicate any proposition consistent with it, depending on the context. For example, it could be used to express a wish about a past state of affairs of which the speaker is ignorant: the speaker could have heard a loud bang from somewhere they can't see and say, 'Don't have fallen again, please'. This *can't* be a directive, yet it is well formed. Whether the directive was the usual use of imperatives would depend on culture, not on grammar.

In a similar vein, Sperber and Wilson (1995) develop a relevance theory account of the sentence types. In relevance theory, the speaker's informative intentions are inferred in each unique context according to the principle of relevance. This principle guarantees that in a communicative context what is said will be optimally relevant. It follows that by processing for relevance, the hearer automatically determines what the speaker intended to convey. From the point of view of utterance as action, Sperber and Wilson (1995, p. 246) recognize three basic acts—saying, asking, and telling—associated with a wide range of different syntactic devices. The declarative, interrogative, and imperative sentence types are only one such device. What is intended by an utterance, beyond the bare fact of saying, asking, or telling, must be inferred. Thus, in their analysis of sentence types, the imperative only conveys, 'the speaker is telling the hearer to p' (Sperber and Wilson 1995, p. 251). They gloss such imperative 'telling' as: the thought 'that p' represents a desirable state of affairs.

All other intentions are inferred following the principle of relevance. This new analysis suggests that we interpret the supplicatory, or 'humble', set of performatives used in prayer—*beg, beseech, implore*, etc.—not necessarily as directives, but as representations only of what is *desirable*. What happens with respect to the speaker's desire depends solely on the will of the overwhelmingly powerful addressee. There is no necessary intention to get this addressee to conform to the speaker's will; that would be presumptuous, not humble.

These alternative analyses are significant for petitionary prayer. They detach it from any necessarily literal connection with directives. Instead, the utterance is most intimately connected with desire, an affective-motivational attitude to a proposition. This is interestingly convergent with Phillip's (1981, p. 121) claim that petitionary prayer is *really* only the expression of speaker's desires, without directive intent. However, Phillips restricts this interpretation to theologically sophisticated believers. He writes, 'When *deep religious believers* pray *for* something, they are not so much asking God to bring this about, but in a way *telling* Him of the strength of their desires' (my italics). He goes on to say that they do this so that their desires, which may not be fulfilled, would not nevertheless destroy their lives. They are 'asking to be able to go on living'. This is presented as a solution to the theological problem of petitioning God as if he were a pragmatic person. So now we have two contrasting cognitive procedures with respect to petitionary prayer: the folk directive interpretation and the deep believers' desire interpretation. One cognitive register has two interpretations.

These new analyses of the imperative when applied to prayer raise the issue of how desire, when it has as its object hypothetical states of affairs, relates to the other dimensions of religion listed above: the supernatural, normativity, and rationalization. We now turn to this issue.

4 THE IMPERATIVE AND THE MIND-BRAIN'S SEEKING SYSTEM

Prayer is a cognitive register. But cognition is the operation of the whole mind-brain. It therefore encompasses not only thinking but also emotions, and not only the mind, studied by philosophy and cognitive psychology, but the brain, studied by neuroscience and other brain sciences. In fact, these studies are inseparable because methodologically, the functional identification and interpretation of brain physiology depends on psychology. Conversely, psychology itself changes as it confronts and integrates new possibilities arising from better understanding the brain.

The new analyses of the imperative claim that it makes manifest desire. What is desired is made explicit either by, or inferable from, the propositional content of the imperative. My hypothesis now is that implementing desire through behaviour involves one of the mind-brain's most basic complexes: the SEEKING system, as described by *affective neuroscience* in Jaak Panksepp's 1998 book of that name. (I will follow Panksepp in employing caps to highlight his basic, well-established, emotional systems.) The imperative is the linguistic realization of this system.

In the study of our emotional life, the distinction has long been made between *basic* and *secondary* emotions. Basic emotions are universal and innate, and they are often related to the facial expressions by which all humans express them; a universal bodily semiotic. There are a number of inventories. Damasio (1996) lists 'happiness, sadness, anger, fear and disgust'; and Carruthers (2006) adds 'surprise' and replaces 'happiness' with 'joy' (Downes 2000). Contrasted with these are the secondary emotions, in which the basic emotions have been conceptually shaped and interpreted according to context, and which are made manifest in our rich affective vocabulary. With respect to the phenomenology of emotion or 'felt experience', I previously wrote that 'emotions are construals of bodily states of arousal in contexts of situation and culture' (Downes 2000, p. 101). This refers to the secondary emotions, to the rich, unlimited way that the output of the basic systems is interpreted in context, made public to consciousness and disseminated, all requiring language. Only in this secondary sense can emotions be said to be sociolinguistically constructed. Very subtle feeling states can be made manifest, represented, interpreted, and aroused in personal relationships, culture, and politics. Although separate systems, emotions are connected to both empathy and mind-reading.

In his study of the affective structures of the mammalian brain, based on research into animals, Panksepp (1998) describes those systems which have been empirically well established in the literature: FEAR (alarm at threat), RAGE (frustration at restraint), SEEKING (motivation/ behavioural activation), the social emotions of CARE (nurturance), LUST (sex), PANIC (need for alleviation of threatened social loss, crucial for social attachment), PLAY (decoupled modelling behaviour), and REM (decoupled dreaming). He suggests that there are others: for example, DOMINANCE–SUBMISSION. The literature portrays others such as 'ALTRUISM' and 'EMPATHY', etc. Neuroscience must be integrated with the other cognitive sciences, in this instance not least with the concept of modules. In Panksepp's analysis, affectivity is clearly modular. This also raises the possibility of the experience of mixtures of inputs and of secondary emotions which are inter-modular combinations of primary emotions, for example, the combination of RAGE, FEAR, and PANIC or CARE with or without LUST.

Panksepp (1998, p. 48) defines neurally based systems which 'can be used equally well in brain research and in . . . psychological studies' as well as 'being capable of elaborating subjective feeling states that are affectively valenced', although it remains unknown how subjectivity is neurologically accomplished. These are some of the properties of basic emotions. (1) They are genetic and automatically respond to life-challenging situations—unconditional responses to sensory stimuli which they then modulate. I would add that these genetic universal systems are *representations*, because they give the organism new *information* about the stimuli that elicit them. Similarly, in Downes (2000), I called emotions 'signs' of those situations they represent—our emotions as a semiotic system. (2) They generate instinctual motor outputs, for example, facial expressions, fight or flight, expressions of sexual interest, etc. (3) They have positive feedback loops that give them a life independent of immediate stimuli. (4) They are modulated by higher level cognition. (5) They modify that same higher level cognition. And (6) They generate conscious feelings.

Although independent, all the systems are complexes that have high degrees of connectivity with each other and other systems; (4), (5), and (6) are the linguistically constituted secondary emotions of conscious experience, to the degree they are not ineffable. We struggle to articulate much emotional complexity and unstable intermodular feelings where there is no obvious lexicalization of the purely emotional mental representation. But the available linguistic re-representations construe basic emotional representations by relating them in the maximally relevant way to context. For example, the FEAR system situated in the context of an examination is named 'exam anxiety', and so on.

Let us now consider SEEKING. First, this names a distinct neuro-physiological system which is concentrated in the *lateral hypothalamic* or LH corridor and corresponds to one of the neuro-chemical DA (dopamine) circuits. It responds to regulatory imbalances in general. Its stimulation 'provokes the most energized exploratory and search behaviour an animal is capable of exhibiting' (Panksepp 1998, p. 145). The system is described in detail in Panksepp (chapter 8). Second, the system is like a column which extends across two of the three levels of the mammalian brain, the old mammalian mid-brain and the new mammalian *neo-cortex*, affect-motivation and conceptualization, respectively. This is a neurological parallel with the basic-secondary emotion distinction. Third, the system responds to specific goals, such as a *homeostatic imbalance* or input from systems such as FEAR or PANIC, but it also functions independently of any specific goal, in pure exploration.

SEEKING is interpreted cognitively by Panksepp (1998, p. 52) as an 'appetitive-motivation . . . system, which helps elaborate energetic search and goal-directed behaviors in behalf of any of a variety of distinct goal objects'. It mediates 'wanting', as opposed to 'liking'. He writes, 'the SEEKING system appears to control appetitive activation—the search, foraging, and investigatory activities—that all animals must exhibit before they are in a position to emit consummatory behaviours' (Panksepp 1998, p. 146). The system itself is so subjectively rewarding, *more so than any actual consummation,* that animals will self-stimulate it until they are exhausted, this in the absence of any specific desire, any goal. Finally, with respect to humans, Panksepp (1998, p. 145) proposes that 'This harmoniously operating neuroemotional system *drives* and *energizes* many mental complexities that humans experience as persistent feelings of interest, curiosity, sensation seeking and, in the presence of a sufficiently complex cortex, the search for higher meaning'. Translated into specifically human intellectual culture, this autonomous exploratory instinct leads the species-mind to inquiry of all kinds.

4.1 The emergence of petitionary prayer

How then does SEEKING relate to petitionary prayer? I suggest that two kinds of SEEKING are involved. First, by *telling a desire* a specific goal is articulated, opening up all its possible implications in context of culture. But second, the principle behind prayer is the pure activation of SEEKING a transcendental God, who is the ideal end of all inquiry. Of course, because transcendental, this consummation is impossible. Concepts like God are relevant mysteries which can be re-interpreted and applied in new contexts without limit (Downes 2011).

Furthermore, there is a natural connection between the SEEKING system and the emergence of the supernatural. In Downes (2011, pp. 78–82), I show that the inferential path necessary to achieve any given goal, because it is maximally relevant, generates a possible inference that the world is 'intentional' in the sense that it 'represents', is 'about', goals that humans want. This is because, if the desired goal is achievable, there in fact *must* be an inferential path which is maximally relevant with respect to its achievement. Therefore, it must appear to the mind/brain that the input from the world represents human beings in such a way that they can, or in some cases cannot, achieve their desires. To be successful the inferential path must contain truths. It follows that the mind/brain would SEEK to discover whatever unseen intentional power lies behind these truths that enable it to achieve what it desires.

This gives us an account of the emergence of both prayer in general and its petitionary form. They emerge in cultural evolution when it becomes possible to grasp the apparent abstract intentionality of the world with respect to goals. The mind-brain SEEKS the mind-like supernatural entity behind this 'aboutness'—this mystery that appears to represent it—that both enables and frustrates. Within that overall SEEKING, the most urgently specific goals to be sought are the objects of those desires most relevant to the speaker or the group, that most deeply motivate them in context, or in general. These provide the semantic content of petitionary prayers.

But the transcendent intentionality also relates to *all* the basic emotions in complicated ways. This leads to the various functions of prayer. It is itself the deepest alleviation of PANIC—metaphysical loneliness—and postulates CARE, nurturance, by the supernatural. This leads to prayers of intimate devotion and thanksgiving. FEAR manifesting itself as metaphysical awe and terror at an unknowable power governing all reality—Otto's *mysterium tremendum*—that enables or frustrates all goals, motivates attempts to placate and submit (Otto 1958 [1923], p. 12–24). FEAR may manifest itself as prayers of adoration, praise, and submission. RAGE might lead to prayers of complaint and accusation, SEX for passionate, orgiastic union with the supernatural other, guaranteeing fertility, as well as physical intimacy. Functions and genres of prayer can thus be correlated with the various affective systems. Taken together, these emotionally constitute prayer, or worship, with respect to language as a class of secondary emotions. Religion is about feeling. These create a context for petitionary prayer in terms of a developed affective attitude to the concept, God.

It follows that prayer naturally originates as a 'hegemonic' register within culture (Fowler 1996, pp. 191–196). I use this term in Gramsci's sense (Forgacs 1988, pp. 189–222). Therefore, it means that prayer's claim to efficacy is accepted consensually within the dominant cultural grouping. This makes it indisputably normative. However, I further suggest that, in Western modernity, prayer no longer has that hegemonic status. It has become a *subaltern register* in an overwhelmingly secular context of culture (Taylor 2007). To pray now conveys only subcultural identity.

Fowler's more purely 'linguistic' diagnostic is when hegemonic, a register is not mixed with other registers within 'plural texts', but has a clarity which aims at absolute authority over the addressee. He uses prayer as an example. I would dispute this. (I would propose that the 'plain style' of Standard English prose is an example of hegemonic register.) *Contra* Fowler, I suggest that evidence that religious language is a subaltern register is the incomprehension it provokes. Phillips notes that for many secular intellectuals 'one is at a loss what to make of prayer' in a context where 'religion *means* nothing to one' (Phillips 1981, p. 19, my italics). The diagnostic of whether a register is hegemonic or subaltern is not textual but cognitive clarity, believing one really can achieve relevance using that genre, knowing what one sincerely—not just playfully—ought to do in context.

4.2 Problems with interpreting the directive analysis

As noted in section 2, there are theological problems taking prayer as a sincere directive, a literal attempt to change God's will with words. God must be the sort of pragmatic person who is a language user, who can be informed of new information because there are things he doesn't know, to whom one can issue a felicitous directive and who sometimes can 'change his mind' because of this, intervening to produce an outcome that would not have occurred unless believers requested it.

These divine attributes would naturalize or humanize the concept, God, in a way that is theologically inconsistent (Phillips 1981, especially pp. 81–130; Hyman 2010). Not only does this interpretation make a prayer very close to a 'spell', words that magically control events, and hence mere superstition, but it has morally disreputable and dangerous consequences. This is because God's uptakes would then appear arbitrary; for example, when he saves one life and takes another. Why did the prayer fail in the one case and not the other? Gavin Hyman, in his 2010 book on atheism (referred to also above), claims that this naturalized God is a quite recent historical product, the result of accommodating theology to scientific modernity. Compared to the more transcendent earlier concept of God, analogy in theological language in Aquinas' sense is almost lost. Consequently, if an imperative is taken as a directive, it must be either literally efficacious in changing the world, as in Brümmer (1984), or merely therapeutic, as in Kant (1960 [1793], pp. 182–185). But because of the pragmatic analysis of the imperative, we are in a different linguistic position in which to view the speech act semantics of the utterance. It is not *necessary* to think of it as a directive at all. It becomes natural to view an utterance of an imperative simply as the SEEKING system making manifest in language the desirability of the hypothetical goal represented by the content of the imperative. Prayer is simply a manifestation of this 'wanting', in Panksepp's words. But must this also necessarily be an attempt to change the world? What is the relation of SEEKING to the directive interpretation? What is the input to understanding the relevance of the imperative to the speaker and their intended addressee (their concept of God)?

In the pragmatic analysis, to take an imperative as a directive becomes less relevant than to construe it as 'telling desire'. To intend the utterance of a prayer as a directive not only requires more cognitive work to achieve relevance, but leads to the inconsistencies just mentioned for the theological concept, God. Therefore, with respect to prayer, a 'telling desire' interpretation is preferred on contextual grounds. If directive intent is also present, it is 'added on'.

However, I claimed above that a directive intention is the folk way of prayer. So why would a naïve believer do the extra inferential work? On the face of it, only if the believer thought either that the supernatural can be persuaded, or, worse, magically compelled to do something they otherwise wouldn't by the prayer, would it be inferentially worthwhile to intend it as a directive. This may indeed be the intention behind much naïve petitionary prayer. But in fact, if a believer regularly intends directives whose results are largely a matter of chance, the likely outcome over time would be either to blame either God or oneself for the failures or come to realize that petitioning is pointless.

So we need another reason for the folk interpretation. The SEEKING system energizes motivation with respect to desires. It generates exploratory action with respect to goals. This might be termed 'will'. So we need to distinguish the affective state of desire, wanting, from actual motivation, the will. When the imperative makes manifest SEEKING, it tells desire, but it can also manifest the *will* that the desired state become true. If it is believed that this can be accomplished through words, it can lead to directive intention, using the words to try to achieve the goal. But this is not necessary. It can just make manifest what the SEEKING system wills as a corollary of its desired goal, without attempting to actually achieve it, in that context. It tells what is desired, therefore would be willed, but doesn't necessarily act wilfully by expecting the hearer to bring it about. Alternatively, it could wilfully intend the directive.

The difference between desire and will is a transition from affect to motivation within SEEKING. It is the *logical* separation of the two aspects of SEEKING: affectivity, the *desire*, and the energized motivation to achieve it, the *will,* that allows normative *inhibition* to intervene in behaviour (Downes 2011, pp. 28–30, 42–44, 91–95). This enacts the censorship function of normativity, unconsciously or consciously—if the potential violation is especially problematic. The mind doesn't inhibit spontaneous desires, but motivated by norms, it wills that an energized SEEKING system not act out unwanted desires. This is sometimes called 'cortical or impulse control'.

Manifesting will by trying, however futile, to get what is willed, is stronger than merely telling the desire behind it. If a desired goal is *so relevant* to the believer that they intend to will it by using the imperative as a directive aimed at God, theological inconsistency just doesn't figure. The imperative can be intended as a directive. It spontaneously expresses the force of the believer's will. The will to achieve the object of desire testifies to the strength of the desire. So the directive folk interpretation makes manifest an unruly will in a way that the deep believers' mere telling of desire doesn't. The directive intention spontaneously expresses the power of desire and the wilfulness of the believer. The longer-term process of a prayer life is to effect a change in that wilfulness.

In the next section, I will try to show that even so, petitionary prayer never functions in terms of God conforming to the speaker's will, but that it pragmatically functions, automatically, to achieve the psychological opposite: to conform the believer to their concept of God's will, transforming their wilfulness. Theologically, in petitionary prayer they come to understand God's will. It follows that Phillips' deep believers conceive of prayer differently, not because they are more theologically sophisticated, but because their wills are already more 'broken' by religious norms.

5 PETITIONARY PRAYER AND SEEKING

The next step is to apply our analysis to petitionary prayer. As we said, an utterance is always performed in a context of situation. In Figure 1 the invocation phase of prayer, combined with other semiotics, for example, posture, provides a discourse marker which initiates the register constituting the situation. Simultaneously, frames of religious assumptions, canonical texts, and previous explications and prayer contexts become the mental encyclopaedia's most accessible information. (In public prayer, the beliefs and observable behaviour of the religious community also become very accessible.)

There is also an *affective context of situation*. First, the SEEKING system is aroused in the context of attitudes towards the concept, God, the hearer. In the theology of prayer, these attitudes are the gift of grace, which enables prayer. Before SEEKING the specific content of any petition, the SEEKING system is first fundamentally oriented to 'SEEKING God'—depending on how the concept is understood. So in addition to its earlier mentioned roles, the Invocation provides a device for mobilizing appropriate attitudes lexicalized as 'awe' and 'respect', 'devoted love', 'confident intimacy', and 'friendship'. These are the linguistically interpreted outputs of social emotions, originating in the PANIC and NURTURANCE systems. In social terms, they motivate solidarity with power. These attitudes are expressed either minimally through the address term or much more fully. Compare the Hail Mary to the simple Lord's Prayer's 'Father in heaven'. In addition to this function, the Elaboration phase of the Invocation also affords a slot where context for the petition can be explicitly pre-accessed, becoming already accessible for calculating the relevance of the following petition. Next comes the petition itself. It makes manifest a second level of SEEKING. This is the desirability of the content, which the speaker SEEKS and would will to become true if that was possible.

But the minimal context of the petition is not complete. We can ask, what other factor *must* be assessed in every utterance of an imperative, where we *tell* the hearer p? This factor is the will of the addressee regarding p, which determines the relevance of the utterance for them. For example, if the speaker makes manifest a desire they believe is inappropriate to a hearer, the intended message is affected. Petitionary prayer does not merely make manifest the speaker's desire and will. It co-ordinates *two* loci of desire and will, the speaker's and God's as they conceive the latter. These differ in that God's desire and will is not only *not* the same as the believer's but is assumed to *always* take precedence over the latter. (This is true even if—within the bracketing convention—both are solely part of the believer's mental life because there is no God.) The *affective* context unconsciously *motivates* the speaker to conform their will to their concept of God's will and therefore to discover what this is, what God desires, with respect to what they themselves desire in each unique context. On the conceptual level, the theological context interacts with the speaker's affective motivational context. Prayer is a device for conforming of wills. Or rather for enforcing their concept of God's will on the believer's own will. There are two levels of SEEKING: first, the believer SEEKS God's sovereign will with respect to what they desire because they love God above all; and second, the believer SEEKS what they specifically desire. In petitionary prayer these two are mediated and conformed. This may require the frustration or inhibition of desire that the believer would otherwise will.

5.1 The workings of the cognitive register: General principle

The hypothesis is that prayer is a device for conforming the speaker's will to God's will. This happens if one prays sincerely, *irrespective* of whatever else one thinks one is doing (see below for a caveat). That is the socio-cultural function of the cognitive register. This happens whether or not the speaker is conscious of it, as long as the speaker is a sincere SEEKER after God as they conceive that transcendental goal—on an affective-motivational quest for God—in the context of their other desires. There is no difference in this respect between Phillips' deep believer and the superstitious believer. If you are fully involved with prayer, these psychological processes will occur at least partially below the level of consciousness. That is what is meant by the claim that prayer is always answered.

Now we will examine four cases where the speaker's assumptions with respect to the generic input vary in the context. Any division into types is of course very artificial, because distinctions can be drawn on many dimensions. First, however, we can state a general principle of petitionary prayer. This is that the believer is prohibited from SEEKING—manifesting a desire and the will that it be accomplished—that they believe contravenes their religious norms. This has the effect of submitting problematic desires to normative evaluation, sorting passions into those that can and can't be told in the petition. This is a powerful norm enforcement device, even before a petition is formulated.

5.2 Four cases

5.2.1 First case: The self-enacting dimension

Very often the act of praying itself brings about the object of the petition. The form and content of the prayer are such that to sincerely make manifest the desirability of *p* achieves it (Phillips 1981, pp. 124–128). The simplest case would be to make explicit the content of the desire, for example, 'Lord, strengthen my love for you'. If this is sincerely uttered, it makes manifest that the speaker desires the very outcome that is produced by the act itself. The speaker's love strengthens, becomes more available as a motive. More complicated cases occur where an outcome which is only inferable from the content is accomplished in this self-constituting way. Because self-constituting, these prayers are performative utterances.

Of the traditional seven petitions in *The Lord's Prayer*, at least three, arguably, have aspects of self-enactment. These are 'hallowed be thy name'; 'thy will be done on earth as it is in heaven'; 'And forgive us our trespasses, as we forgive those who trespass against us' (*Common Worship: Daily Prayer*, p. 816). These make manifest three related desires: first, that God's name be treated as holy; second, that God's will—his kingdom—be conformed to here and now; and, third, as part of this kingdom, to forgive our moral debtors, just as God forgives us for our moral debts, admitting us to his kingdom. These petitions self-enact what the speaker believes is God's will on earth through 'hallowing' and 'forgiving'. Sincerely uttered, they manifest the will to conform to God's will. Therefore, God's kingdom, as conceived in the prayer, is partially brought into being through its utterance.

Self-enactment also requires that the content be conceived of as God's will. Thus, if the believer prays for something irrelevant to God's will, 'Lord, let me win the lottery', or where God's will is unknown, 'Lord, let me recover from this illness', these do not achieve what they desire.

5.2.2 *Second case: Inferential self-enactment*

Consider two wills: that of the speaker and that of God. There are many cases of prayer where God's will with respect to what the speaker desires is known. Since a believer desires what they already know is God's will, such prayers could *never* be intended as directives aimed at God. To freely make manifest a desire for what you know the hearer wants you to ask for, is an act of assent or active conforming. For believers, God's will is known through scripture and traditional teaching.

In these cases, God's known will is the first premise in a deduction. The second premise is a desire for the first premise. The conclusion is the fulfilment of the desire, therefore God's will. The first premise can be stated as a conditional, the second as the desire, the conclusion being the consequent of the conditional. A simple example of this structure might involve the teaching that God wants his people to ask for his forgiveness, to which he will always respond. The form of argument would be

Premise 1. Conditional which states God's known will.
If anyone sincerely fulfils such and such condition X, God will Y.

Premise 2. The speaker's alignment with God's will.
The expression of a sincere desire for X.

Conclusion. Inference that God's will is achieved by 2.
Thereby Y.

The genre of the *Collect* commonly utilizes this type of underlying argument. Consider the Collect for Ash Wednesday (*Common Worship: Daily Prayer*, p. 371):

> Almighty and everlasting God, you hate nothing that you have made and forgive the sins of all those who are penitent: create and make in us new and contrite hearts, that we, worthily lamenting our sins, and acknowledging our wretchedness, may obtain of thee, the God of all mercy, perfect remission and forgiveness . . .

This prayer asks for what is God's known will. The appositive expansion of the Invocation creates a context for the petition. This presupposes God's known will, which can be recast as a conditional. The imperative manifests the speaker's desire that God make the speaker's heart contrite, a synonym of 'penitent', which satisfies the known condition for forgiveness. If the imperative is to be sincere, the believer must be, or become, genuinely contrite or penitent. Theologically, although God hates *our* sin but nothing *he* has made, it is God's known will that the believer be contrite and so forgiven. Thus, if God is asked for this he will not refuse. It follows that the believer is forgiven. This prayer is a type of self-enactment—to sincerely make manifest the desire for God to create contrition ought to be sufficient to induce it as a secondary emotion. This self-inducing is again a kind of performative utterance. In addition, the conclusion expresses feelings of reconciliation, satisfying the needs of the PANIC system.

If a believer's sincere desire for a state of affairs which is God's known will is sufficient to bring it into being, then all petitions asking for it have the potential to be at least partially self-enacting. Even though 'Thy Kingdom Come' does not bring about the kingdom wholly, it partially constitutes it by here and now aligning the believer's will with God's.

5.2.3 *Third case: God's will is inferred in context of the speaker's desire*

This is the case where the speaker believes that they don't know what God wills with respect to the context of the petition. Psychologically, it is perhaps the most important form of the cognitive register. The believer may or may not be sophisticated with respect to their faith, but since in prayer we deal with pragmatics, the problem is always the context and its relation to thought and feeling. In the case of petition, the feeling relevant to the context is the speaker's SEEKING in the context of a relevant lack. SEEKING where lack is irrelevant is more likely in cases of praise or thanksgiving.

My analysis is that the affective dynamic of this type of petitionary prayer over time leads to the contextual exploration of God's will and conformity to it. The cognitive mechanism for this is through the formation of hypotheses drawn or inferred from God's known will, accessible in the believer's encyclopaedia and publicly available in scripture, tradition, and discussion. This information, conjoined with the petition and what actually happens, warrants the new conclusions about God's will in the context of situation.

Consider that one is unemployed. In petitionary prayers the believer manifests their desire for employment now. They do all they can to find a job, but their efforts remain unsuccessful. God's will for them in this situation is genuinely unknown. If they then find a job, then all is well and good. They may conclude God has 'answered their prayer'. Indeed, the prayer may have energized personal confidence as a factor in the positive outcome, indirect self-enactment. Apart from such cases, let us assume there is no causal correlation between the desire made manifest in petitionary prayer and what subsequently happens. So when no job is found, the believer is emotionally in a quandary. Their prayer is unanswered. But why? Whose fault is this? As noted above, this is a problem with the interpretation of the prayer as a directive.

The believer may make this quandary manifest in a prayer of complaint, as in Psalm 22, 'Why have you forsaken me?'. However, religious concepts include the norm that although one might accuse God, one *ought not* to do so, even in extreme distress, but trust him in spite of this failure, unconditionally. There are the examples of Job, Christian saints, Jesus himself in Gethsemane. The norm is that trust in God ought not to be affected by evil in the world. Like reality itself, the individual is utterly dependent on God's good will. Therefore, in order to be able to perform petitionary prayer which doesn't end in accusing God—or themselves—the believer must trust that ultimately, irrespective of what happens with respect to what they want, God is always actively SEEKING them and their ultimate good. They have 'faith', therefore, whatever happens, all will be well.

This trust is the standard against which the believer SEEKS to interpret in their continuing prayer the inability to find work. They may be able to deduce their experience from the hypothesis that God permits their suffering as a 'cross', learning about their relationship with him in context and developing both patience and empathetic understanding of the suffering of others. They may suspect that it is simply just retribution for their past sins. They may confront the theological problem of evil. They may come to understand the situation in political terms, as a result of human social arrangements which are contrary to God's will—the poor, the orphan, and the widow of the Bible. They may be motivated to change the world so that it accords with the justice of God's kingdom. They may understand the situation in a theologically sophisticated way. For example, they may read D. Z. Phillips and conclude that God is bracketed from '*how* things go'. Instead, their petition serves merely to make manifest those desires that might destroy them—their love of God—in the face of a failed petition (Phillips 1981, p. 121). They may consider Simone Weil's argument, cited by Phillips, that suffering is built into the world to make people realize that they are 'nothing'. In terms of relevance theory, these are the sort of implicatures that might be contextually available to achieve relevance and thus be interpreted as answers to prayer. It is obvious that the actual possibilities are without limit. These propositional forms also structure secondary emotions as attitudes to them: for example, contextual feelings of indignation, acceptance, determination, or confidence with respect to this limitless semantic content.

Petitionary prayer in this way integrates religious assumptions into a personal situation with respect to both desire and the affective relation with the concept of God, where these are not the same. This holds irrespective of whether, theologically,

God is active in how things go in the world. *Most important, prayer becomes a mode of inquiry.* It serves SEEKING through inquiry which aligns personal desire and the overarching desire for God, in contexts which intersect personal lack and religious teachings. Psychologically, the individual will becomes aligned with God's will, as the believer comes to interpret it, in the most important contexts of situation in their cultural lives.

5.2.4 Fourth case: The community of prayer

So far we have analysed the cognitive effects of prayer on individuals, without considering the role of other believers. But religion is always social. In the fourth case, we examine prayer where others are part of the context of situation.

Prayer is often public, not least when integral to liturgy. These prayers are also central to a believer's prayer life. In public contexts, petitions are unlikely to achieve relevance through long, remembered and revisited, chains of inference involving private information and desire. Liturgy is repetition. A prayer within a liturgy repeats what has been uttered many times before; for example, psalms, canticles, litanies, the Lord's Prayer. It is entrenched in the collective encyclopaedia. I propose that collective prayers in liturgies achieve relevance mainly by virtue of the input of witnessing other believers uttering the same thing. It is like singing in a choir or marching in step. Each individual simultaneously makes manifest to each other the same epistemic, ontological, and normative commitments, and does so repeatedly. With each repetition, this strengthens just those representations which are definitive of the religious group. If the prayers are also self-enacting, as many liturgical prayers are, both the expression and the achievement of the desires is done collectively. Most importantly, in affective-motivational terms, believers co-ordinate desires and wills. In this case, we find the self-enactment of an 'imagined community'. (But does this public co-ordination also make group beliefs appear more uniform than they are?)

Intercession is another petitionary prayer which necessarily involves others. We can distinguish two types, analysed by Phillips (1981, pp. 126–128). In the first type, the believer utters a prayer of petition for some state of affairs most relevant to a beneficiary who is a member of the community. The beneficiary may or may not know that they are being 'remembered', and if the latter, may have either asked for this or not. Imagine the case where someone is about to undergo surgery and the believer says, 'I'll be praying for you'. In this case, the prayer makes manifest that two wills are identical with respect to a shared desire. This knowledge strengthens the community, the beliefs involved in the petition, and may psychologically—a kind of self-enactment—increase the chances of a successful outcome. If the beneficiary doesn't know that they are being remembered, the effect is confined to the believer and any other participants in the petition. In practice, an absent member of an imagined community may know, without being told, that they are being remembered.

Finally, we have the case of intercessions on behalf of those who are *not* members of the community. Phillips (1981, p. 128) cites Christian prayers 'for the conversion of the world'. The Anglican 'cycle of intercessions' (*Common Worship: Daily Prayer*, pp. 328–329) includes those for 'Those in authority, for the right use of power'; 'That humankind will care for creation'; 'Victims and perpetrators of violence, for healing and repentance'; and so on. In public prayer, these manifest the imagined community's collective desire and will. If sincerely uttered, if not hypocritical, the intercession co-ordinates and strengthens shared norms. It creates a context for thinking how specific outcomes might be enabled, motivating social action, political or economic. Collective epistemological and attitudinal self-enactment creates the potential for action. Such prayer is perhaps a weak version of the vow within the Gandhian tactic of *Satyagraha*—commitment to truth, energized by love—constituting the non-violent resister. This is a refusal in contexts of situation and culture to do what is repugnant to conscience and effect change through redemptive suffering (Caygill 2013, pp. 74, 110–115).

6 LINGUISTICS VS. INTERPRETATION IN PHILOSOPHICAL THEOLOGY

Linguistics confines itself to the analysis of the patterns of language, including possible ways that language functions in contexts of situation, while bracketing or remaining indifferent to the philosophical problems, the consistency or inconsistency, the truth or falsity, of how the text is interpreted by participants. The range of socially available interpretations and their philosophical problems are part of Firth's 'context of culture'. This clarifies the distinction between cognitive register and Wittgenstein's idea of a 'language game'. Philosophy describes and clarifies the context of culture with respect to conceptual confusion. By contrast, linguistics accounts for the social, psychological, and semantic/grammatical aspects of the language in which the interpretative problems present themselves to consciousness.

6.1 'Language games'

The philosophical description of a language game such as prayer explores how the linguistic patterning can be strictly interpreted 'in its own terms'—that is, theologically, to clarify its meaning within its context of culture.

Consider Kierkegaard's (1989 [1849], p. 71) description of the presuppositions of prayer:

> In order to pray there has to be a God, a self—and possibility, or a self and possibility in the cogent sense, for God is the fact that everything is possible, or that everything is possible is God. And only the person whose being was so shaken that he became spirit by grasping that everything is possible, only he has dealings with God. The fact that God's will is the possible means I can pray; if God's will is only the necessary, then man is essentially as dumb as the beast.

Kierkegaard argues that to overcome despair and become truly themselves, Christians have to become conscious that it is possible for them to conform their will to God's, absurd as this seems to reason. Only then—'before God'—can they become authentically themselves. And thus, 'The *believer* sees and understands his undoing . . . in human terms, but he has faith. . . . The manner in which he is to be helped he leaves wholly to God, but he believes that everything is possible. . . . Then too, God helps him, perhaps by letting him avoid the horror, perhaps through the horror itself; that help unexpectedly, miraculously, divinely turns up'. With respect to the concept of the miraculous, that 'depends on with what passion of mind he has grasped that help is impossible, and . . . how honest he is towards the power which nevertheless helped him' (Kierkegaard 1989 [1849], pp. 69–70).

Alternative theological interpretations of the meaning of the cognitive register of prayer are different language games. We have alluded to three: the 'folk' or directive interpretation; Phillips's argument that prayer makes manifest the speaker's desires with respect to a world in which God does not regularly intervene; and Kierkegaard's view that, in the light of the leap of faith, prayer presupposes that everything is possible for God. These alternative interpretations of prayer are alternative language games played within the cognitive register—the problems it presents for philosophical theology. By contrast, cognitive register itself is an analysis of language use from outside 'faith', using the linguistic and cognitive sciences. It describes the empirical linguistic conditions which are input to these interpretative problems. This is the role of 'bracketing' and prevents linguistics becoming theology. We can talk about a 'Wittgensteinian theology', such as that of Phillips', but not a 'scientific' linguistic theology.

6.2 Language functions irrespective of theology

We said above that prayer as 'talking to God' presupposes that God is a pragmatic person. The issue then arises of the consistency of the concept, God, also being a language user with respect to human beings. This is a matter of theology, not for linguistics. In polytheisms and aboriginal theistic religions the same problem would present itself in different contexts of culture.

If the God of theism is treated as having *all* the properties of a human communicator, then the concept becomes fully naturalized, and in this respect God is like a human person. Therefore, given the properties standardly attributed to God, this results in inconsistencies. Therefore, the theology of prayer consists of attempts to reconcile the two concepts within a single language game. Since the concept of God is a relevant mystery, and hence is constantly being re-thought in differing ways, there is an unlimited number of possibilities. In any case, rationalizations in religion remain un-decidable. The theology of prayer that best reconciles the two sides of the analogy, relative to a historical cultural context, will best enable believers to pray. It is not our job to consider theological approaches.

My core hypothesis was that the cognitive effects of prayer with respect to norms are achieved irrespective of theology. I need now to enter a caveat. For this to be accomplished, believers must unconditionally SEEK a supernatural entity that they believe is not malevolent and that reciprocally SEEKS them and their well-being with respect to religious norms. (Their concept of God must have at least these properties.) This relationship is the essential context determining the relevance of all their other desires. In conforming to God's will, persons model their lives on this mutual SEEKING. If these assumptions are sincere, prayer achieves its normative effect irrespective of how else God is conceived.

7 CONCLUSION

Petitionary prayer is a cognitive register, a variety of language used in context which has cognitive outcomes with respect to thought, feeling, and action. Processing the genre of prayer manipulates the mind-brain so that it conforms the speaker's will to what they believe is God's will, depending on how they conceive God. The religious mind-brain becomes motivated by culturally shaped emotions and motives to desire and will, and therefore behave, according to the religious norms which constitute a form of life. The cognitive register organizes motivation, manages and interprets unruly personal desires and wilfulness, in the light of religious norms. It may be thought of as a *technology* which employs language.

Prayer as a cognitive register has a number of integrative functions. It integrates the four dimensions of religion—the supernatural, the normative, the affective-motivational, and rationalization—and, using inference, applies them with respect to action in specific contexts. With respect to affect, it integrates and manages the diverse complexity of emotions and mobilizes them for action. Since each dimension of religion derives from a different module of mind, prayer serves inter-modularity, creating connections that 'tie together' the mind-brain. This integration is achieved by culturally introducing into the individual mind-brain *a variety of language as a device from outside*—a register which enables this is 'taken into the mind' from the wider culture, 'ready-made'. It doesn't have to be re-invented by each individual. This 'taking in' also serves to integrate the individual within the religious group. Lodged in individual mind-brains, it co-ordinates individuals' practical actions within a society according to religious norms. On a personal level, it integrates the phenomenal self of conscious 'felt experience' with the public person, a member of a co-operating group sharing the practice of prayer and hence enacting the same religious identity.

REFERENCES

Abel, T. (1960). The operation called *Verstehen*. In E. Madden (ed.), *The Structure of Scientific Thought*, pp. 158–166. Boston: Houghton Mifflin.
Brown, R. and A. Gilman (1960). The pronouns of power and solidarity. In T. A. Sebeok (ed.), *Style in Language*, pp. 253–276. Cambridge, MA: MIT Press.
Brümmer, V. (1984). *What Are We Doing When We Pray?* London: SCM Press.
Carruthers, P. (2006). *The Architecture of the Mind*. Oxford: Oxford University Press.
Caygill, H. (2013). *On Resistance*. London: Bloomsbury.

Common Worship: Daily Prayer: Services and Prayers for the Church of England (2002). London: Church House Publishing.

Damasio, A. (1996). *Descartes' Error: Emotion, Reason and the Human Brain.* London: Papermac/MacMillan.

Downes, W. (1977). The imperative and pragmatics. *Journal of Linguistics* 13 (1), 77–97.

Downes, W. (1998). *Language and Society.* Second edition. Cambridge: Cambridge University Press.

Downes, W. (2000). The language of felt experience. *Language and Literature* 9(2), 99–121.

Downes, W. (2011). *Language and Religion.* Cambridge: Cambridge University Press.

Firth, J. R. (1957). Synopsis of linguistic theory 1930–1955. In *Studies in Linguistic Analysis*, pp. 1–32. Oxford: Philological Society. Page reference are to the reprint in F. L. Palmer (ed.) (1968), *Selected Papers of J. R. Firth 1952–1959*, pp. 168–205. London: Longmans.

Forgacs, D. (ed.) (1988). *The Antonio Gramsci Reader.* London: Lawrence and Wishart.

Fowler, R. (ed.) (1996). *Linguistic Criticism.* Secondi edition. Oxford: Oxford University Press.

Goffman, E. (1963). *Behaviour in Public Places.* New York: The Free Press.

Grice, H. P. (1957). Meaning. *Philosophical Review* LXVI, 377–388.

Halliday, M. A. McIntosh, and P. Strevens (1964). *The Linguistic Sciences and Language Teaching.* London: Longmans.

Halliday, M. (1978). *Language as Social Semiotic.* London: Edward Arnold.

Hyman, G. (2010). *A Short History of Atheism.* London: I. B. Tauris.

Jungmann, J. (1978). *Christian Prayer through the Centuries.* New York: Paulist Press.

Kant, I. (1960 [1793]). *Religion within the Limits of Reason Alone.* Translated by T. Greene and H. Hudson. New York: Harper Torchbooks.

Kierkegaard, S. (1989 [1849]). *The Sickness unto Death.* Translated by A. Hannay. London: Penguin Books.

Otto, R. (1958 [1923]). *The Idea of the Holy.* Translated by J. Harvey. Oxford: Oxford University Press.

Panksepp, J. (1998). *Affective Neuroscience.* New York: Oxford University Press.

Phillips, D. Z. (1981). *The Concept of Prayer.* Oxford: Blackwell.

Ross, J. R. (1970). On declarative sentences. In R. Jacobs and P. Rosenbaum (eds.), *Readings in English Transformational Grammar*, pp. 222–277. Waltham, MA: Ginn and Company.

Searle, J. (1975). Indirect speech acts. In P. Cole and P. Morgan (eds.), *Syntax and Semantics* 3, *Speech Acts*, pp. 59–82. New York: Academic Press.

Searle, J. and D. Vanderveken (1985). *Foundations of Illocutionary Logic.* Cambridge: Cambridge University Press.

A Simple Prayer Book (1997). London: Catholic Truth Society.

Sperber, D. (1996). *Explaining Culture: A Naturalistic Approach.* Oxford: Blackwell.

Sperber, D. and D. Wilson (1995). *Relevance.* Second edition. Oxford: Blackwell.

Taylor, C. (2007). *A Secular Age.* Cambridge, MA: Belknap Press.

CHAPTER 5

Cognitive Neuroscience and Religious Language

A Working Hypothesis

PATRICK MCNAMARA AND MAGDA GIORDANO

Use of language in religious contexts is unlike any other domain of language use. We present in this chapter several lines of converging evidence, including neuro-science evidence, in support of the aforementioned claim concerning the distinctive-ness of religious language. We review current theories of the nature and functions of religious language and then present a theory of our own which we believes accounts for existing data on religious language and generates novel predictions concerning neurocognitive systems that should be implicated in religious language processes.

1 RELIGIOUS LANGUAGE IS NOT USED PRIMARILY FOR COMMUNICATION

While religious language is certainly used for communication with supernatural agents (SAs) or other human beings, it can also be used for the free expression of thought. It can be used, for example, to formulate and conceptualize phenomena that lie at the borderland of the knowable and the unknowable, as well as the think-able and the unthinkable. It can attempt, via the use of symbolic reference, meta-phor, narratives, and speech acts, to cognize ultimate reality and ultimate values and to commit to those ultimate values. While philosophical language also attempts to grasp ultimate realities, it eschews absolute commitment to these ultimate realities. Its stance is one of wonder, distance, understanding, and study rather than awe, rev-erence, and commitment as is the case with religion. Because religion is equally inter-ested in ultimate realities as well as ultimate values, it necessarily elicits absolute commitment from the inquirer. When philosophy elicits emotional commitment from its practitioners, it shades into religious philosophy in our view, especially if that commitment (e.g. to 'truth') becomes absolute such that one is willing to spend years building the commitment or is even willing to give one's life rather than betray the commitment. When ultimate values are even partially intuited by the mind, religious language provides commitment devices, in the form of speech acts and other linguistic devices, that help to bind the individual to those ultimate values, thus facilitating the realization of these ultimate values in daily life. Religious language builds toward absolute commitment in the sense that the commitment to a given value or SA is sustained over long periods of time. In short, the distinctiveness of religious language derives from its paradoxical orientation to a partially unknowable but always intuited reality: an ultimate reality that is the ultimate value and thus commands absolute commitment.

1.1 How to express the ineffable and how to possess ultimate value

Philosophers have designated the realms of the 'knowable unknown' (the things we know that we don't know and could know) and the 'unknown unknowns' (the things that we don't know that we don't know but that we could know if we were aware of our unawareness) as the realm of ultimate realities. Ultimate reality and value refers to the object of religious concern (Neville 2013; Tillich 2012). It answers to questions such as What really exists?, What really should we value?, Why is there something rather than nothing?, and so forth.

In his recent (2011) *Language and Religion: A Journey into the Human Mind*, William Downes treats religious language as an instance in a larger system of cognitive pragmatics of culture. The human mind is designed to produce cognitive niches and cultures. Religion is conceived as a cultural complex by way of which people attempt to think about the conceptually ultimate, to think about previously unthinkable things. Religion provides language and a communication platform that promotes conceptual innovation in so far as it addresses cultural mysteries—those things that we know that we don't know and those things we aren't even aware of not knowing.

Downes (2011) proposes that religious cognition can be viewed as an ensemble of modules, each with different functions: the mind-reading system; the meta-representational and language systems; normativity system; and affective-motivational systems. The products, roughly speaking, of these four central contents of religious representations and their relation to modular capacities are: the supernatural, rationalized contents, religious normativity, and religious experiences. Presumably, all four systems participate in the attempt to grasp ultimate realities and to construct cultural and social systems that facilitate living in accord with ultimate reality.

While we find Downes' proposal intriguing and incredibly rich, it is not clear how the interaction of these four systems produces distinctively religious language. Presumably the interaction of these four systems would also produce cognitions around secular rituals or daily moral obligations and the like. It is also not clear to us that the mind-reading system or the interaction of the mind-reading system with any of the other three systems produces the kinds of supernatural agents that most populate religious ideologies or traditions. These latter agents are at a minimum 'full strategic access agents' (FSAA; see Purzycki et al. 2012) in that many gods are not merely conceptualized as other minds or persons, but they in addition know the true contents of the believer's minds. If we, as Robin Dunbar recommends (Dunbar 2003), combine the output of the mind-reading system with the meta-representational system and suppose that gods are products of third and fourth order Theory of Mind (ToM) representations ('I am thinking about what she is thinking about what he is thinking about me, etc.'), we still do not get gods as traditionally understood in religious systems. It is not clear how hierarchical meta-representations or processes like these yield an FSAA who knows us personally inside and out. If we create an FSAA the task must involve something more than mind-reading capacities, no matter how complex. To create an FSAA, I must first, model the FSAA as a mind (first order ToM); second, I must further model/postulate that *I know that they know my mind* (second order ToM); third, I then must model that *they know that I know that they know me* and that I behave accordingly (third order ToM); and fourth, I must then model their minds in awareness of the third postulate (fourth order ToM). But even then that is not enough because something has to be said about the content of the minds we are modeling—not just the awareness or meta-awareness of one another's mental states. If gods represent ultimate realities and ultimate values, then there is a crucial next step of my evaluation of the value of their knowing me, and my awareness of their awareness of that fact, etc. Once I make a decision about the value of the SA, I then attempt to bind myself to the 'thing' of ultimate value. A human being cannot be in the presence of a thing of immense value without some sort of emotional response like reverence, devotion, or commitment.

It is this latter stance of commitment that is missing from ToM and related accounts of religious cognition and religious language. We not only attempt to know and be known by a god. We attempt to unite ourselves to them, or in the case of demonic SAs we attempt to flee/avoid them. There is an emotional response because matters of ultimate concern are involved. In Downes' model, the evaluative response would presumably be modeled by the normativity system, but it is not clear how this would happen in his account. In what follows we provide one possible account of religious language as a series of commitment devices that facilitate apprehension of ultimate values and then commitment to those ultimate values.

1.2 Distinctiveness of religious language

The distinctiveness of religious language we propose lies in its abundant use of commitment devices. These include the marked voice quality to indicate solemnity or reverential formal tone, stylized and restricted into national contours again to indicate the presence of things of ultimate value, personal volition disclaimer (to indicate that value is received from another agent or source) which is instantiated via avoidance of first person pronouns, and the abundance of speech acts, especially assertives and commissives (such as *I promise to, I intend to, I commit to, I believe that*) (Du Bois 1986; Keane 1997; McNamara 2009). Other language characteristics designed to indicate the presence of things of ultimate value include the use of archaic forms in words and grammar to heighten the sense of ineffability and the formal tone, elements borrowed from another language, solemn use of repetitive chants, declamations, and petitions.

Public religious language takes place usually in the context of rituals, a communal affair that facilitates communication with a god. As is the case with private rituals, public religious rituals are characterized by the use of a formal style, serious tone and register, and deferential language. All of these linguistic devices tend to place the participant into a 'sacred space' where it is felt that things of ultimate value have become present. Once ultimate values are cognized the next step is to secure commitment to them. To accomplish commitment, new linguistic devices are recruited— most especially the use of a variety of speech acts in both formulaic and spontaneous forms of religious language.

2 SPEECH ACTS AND RELIGIOUS LANGUAGE

A speech act is often defined as a linguistic utterance that accomplishes some action; the utterance or language itself instantiates an action. If I am a religiously certified specialist like a minister or priest or rabbi and I say 'I now pronounce you man and wife,' that utterance is an action that creates a social reality. Speech acts exhibit special formal cognitive properties and rules and they are ubiquitous in religious contexts. Searle (2007) said that the speech act is more than just the expression of an intention or the expression of a belief, it is a public performance, referring to something about the world represented by those beliefs and intentions. 'When I make a statement I not only express a belief but I commit myself to its truth' and 'intentional acts of meaning [. . .] necessarily involve a deontology' (Searle 2007, p. 40). Once deontology is collectively created, it can be extended to social reality, and a reality can be created that consists in part of representations. Thus, 'We create private property: money, property, government, marriage, and a thousand other such phenomena by representing these phenomena as existing' (Searle 2007, p. 41). Furthermore, . . . 'A person who can get other people to accept this declaration will succeed in creating an institutional reality that did not exist prior to that declaration' (Searle 2007, p. 40). It follows that the normativity module, as described by Downes, with its language of norms, and commandments helps to create a reality for the group of believers, and thus guides behavior.

Speech acts used in religious rituals include confessions of faith, praying, petitioning, promising, asserting beliefs, praising, and blessing. Speech acts include language devices by which people commit themselves to certain things: '. . . by words and symbolic actions believers bind themselves to God—and believe that he, too, binds himself to them in return through entering into the conventions of human language—with words providing the medium for divine-human interaction' (Donovan 1976, p. 84). For Downes (this volume), collective prayer during liturgy, by witnessing others say the same thing, believers co-ordinate desires and wills.

There are four main types of performative speech acts (where speaking the phrase accomplishes the action): declarations, directives, commissives, and expressives. While all four forms are found in religious language and all four can facilitate binding or commitment to truth content and value, we are most interested in commissives here, as they most obviously facilitate binding/commitment. Commissives include promises, guarantees, offers, and other language elements that accomplish the binding of the speaker to a certain standard of behavior or future course of action and so forth. The linguistic structure of commissives facilitate the binding of the agent to the object as specified in the commissive verb phrase (e.g., I promise to . . .). In present-day English, for example, the coreference of the subject (I) and the object of the verb are more tightly controlled in the case of commissives than in other subject-verb-object sentences.

Searle and Vanderveken (1985) define illocutionary force (the force associated with the use of speech acts like performatives when uttered in a specific context) in terms of seven features, claiming that every possible illocutionary force, such as the intention to commit to something that is behind a commissive speech act, may be identified with a combination of these seven features. It is worth summarizing here how commissives exhibit illocutionary force in terms of these features: 1. *Illocutionary point*: The characteristic point of a commissive like a promise is to commit oneself to something by committing oneself to a future course of action. 2. *Degree of strength of the illocutionary point*: Commissives can vary in strength. Promising to do something is one thing, but guaranteeing to do it is stronger. Giving your life for a truth or value is still another. 3. *Mode of achievement*: Commitments can be realized in multiple ways, and it makes a difference when and how commitment is realized. When one commits to a series of beliefs and rules in a religious context, they change/transform the person's character and structure by influencing much of that individual's behaviors, choices, actions, and goals. One would not expect such far-reaching behavioral consequences for commitment outside of religious contexts. 4. *Propositional content conditions*: Commissives typically require certain content conditions to be true before they can be taken seriously. I can only promise what is within my capacity to deliver. 5. *Preparatory conditions*: These are context conditions that make a commissive realistically possible. 6. *Sincerity conditions*: Promises are worthless unless the individual really intends to keep the promise. Religious contexts often require, from the individual, a display of sacrifice or costly behaviors or signals to underline seriousness of commitment to the beliefs of the group or the religion. 7. *Degree of strength of the sincerity conditions*: If I promise something at a high cost to myself (i.e. display of costly behaviors), then the strength of the promise is higher than when I promise something that exacts no costs from me (Searle and Vanderveken 1985).

Religious language elements, especially insofar as they involve commissives and related speech acts to facilitate commitments to ultimate values, will be characterized by *Illocutionary points* that enact commitment with a very high *Degree of strength of the illocutionary point* in a variety of *Modes of achievement* that are nevertheless constrained by realistic *Propositional content conditions* and *Preparatory conditions*: and that involve strict *Sincerity conditions* with a very high *Degree of strength of the sincerity conditions*.

To the extent then that religious language is specialized to grapple with questions of ultimate reality and ultimate value, it will use these sorts of linguistic devices that enable higher degrees of commitment from participants.

2.1 The self and religious language: McNamara's (2009) model of religious language

McNamara (2009) argued for a model of religious language that involved linguistically mediated cognitive processes that accomplished the elevation of a deity or value and a corresponding diminution of the Self in the presence of sacred values or the deity. The diminution of the Self was a way to mark the presence of sacred values that elicited commitment from the agent. McNamara called this process 'decentering.' Decentering is conceived as temporarily decoupling the executive Self from its position of control over executive cognitive and motor functions and placing the sense of Self in abeyance or in a 'possible world' space where a search for a new, more complex, and value-enriched Self can ensue in lieu of the old Self (McNamara 2009, p. 45). Once a higher Self is identified (with help of religious symbols), the old Self is linked up with the higher Self, thus accomplishing commitment of the old Self to a new set of values embodied in the new higher Self. McNamara (2009) proposed that religious language elements such as decline in use of first person pronouns, and increase in use of formal registers, among other things, facilitated decentering. The individual sets aside his or her own identity to interact or participate in the identity of the spirit or god; this process of reduction in Self and enhancement of an alternative identity results in integration of new values if that new identity is a positive one. It results in loss of values if identification with the new Self is a negative one (as happens in cults or cases of demonic possession). The cognitive mechanism of decentering occurs in stages: first the sense of agency or volition is inhibited, then the Self structure is placed into a suppositional logical space, and a search for a more integral version of the Self is implemented via semantic memory, i.e. that form of memory where abstract information structures are stored including everything from word meanings to cultural schemas. Finally, the old Self is bound to and integrated into the new identity, closer to the ideal Self as represented by the deity, chosen by the search process (McNamara 2009, p. 47). The decreased use of first person pronouns, along with increased use of formal, elevated tone and third person reference, mark the onset of the first stage. Speech acts such as commissives facilitate the final stage in the decentering model, wherein the old Self is bound to the newer higher Self, thus accomplishing commitment to that higher Self that embodies ultimate values for the individual. Similarly, for Downes (this volume), through petitionary prayer the speaker's will is aligned to what they believe is God's will. He proposes that petitionary prayer can be understood as a performative utterance that brings about 'the very outcome that is produced by the act itself.' The second and third stages are facilitated by other elements of religious language, such as sacred symbols, metaphors, and narratives (see Figure 1).

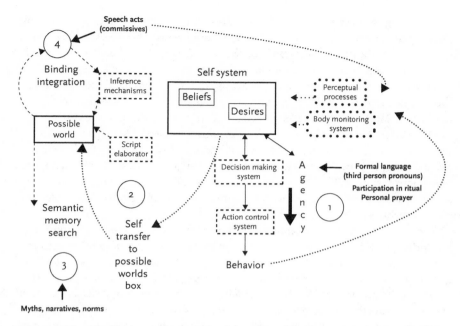

Figure 1 The role of religious language in the decentering process, based on and modified from (McNamara 2009).

Figure 1 represents the hypothetical modules involved in the decentering process as described in McNamara (2009) and the proposed role of religious language in this process, which are

1. Inhibition of Self-agency that could be brought about by the ritualized language employed in public and personal prayer.
2. Self-construct placed in possible world box in the search process for a better Self.
3. Search for 'higher' Self to integrate with support from information stored in semantic memory in the form of norms, symbols, myths, and narratives.
4. Integration of old into new Self promoted by the use of speech acts, especially commissives.

2.2 Other elements of religious language that facilitate commitment

Religious language contains an array of further elements that enable articulation of ultimate realities as well as commitment to ultimate values. These other elements include religious symbols that are references in religious myths and narratives as well as metaphors that elucidate those symbols and that operate within the myths as well. These language elements facilitate commitment because they in various ways engage emotions of participants and then translate those emotions into reverence and loyalty to values as cognitively apprehended or as embodied in higher selves.

According to Downes (2011), adherents respond to religious language, for example, prophetic texts, as they respond to poetry, not necessarily because of their structure or metric, but perhaps because of the use of metaphor. For McFague (1982), metaphor is used when we use *this* so we can use *that* as a way of saying something about *this*, which we do not adequately cognize or know. This chapter will not discuss the complexities of symbolizing, but for the sake of argument suffice it to say that in symbolic language one thinks of *this* as part of *that*, and in that loose sense they likely facilitate binding of the individual to sacred values. In McFague's view, good metaphors shock, bring 'unlikes' together, and upset convention, involve tension, and are implicitly revolutionary. Thus, one could suggest that successful metaphors in religious scripture should challenge continually and not lead to dogmatism. In this sense, a metaphorical rather than literal interpretation of scripture would yield the greatest richness.

The two subjects of a metaphor are named 'vehicle' and 'tenor,' or 'subsidiary' and 'principle' (McFague 1982). Both change by being thought of in relation to each other. In religious models, the human images that are chosen as metaphors for a god gain in stature and take on divine qualities by being place in an interactive relationship with the divine. For McFague, metaphor is part of semantics; similarly, Lakoff (1992) suggests that metaphor can be understood as a linking-up or mapping from a source domain to a target domain, and that metaphor is fundamentally conceptual, not linguistic, in nature. For him, metaphor is the main mechanism through which we comprehend abstract concepts and perform abstract reasoning (Lakoff 1992). Barbour (1974) also defines a metaphor as characterized by a novel configuration produced by the juxtaposition of two frames of reference of which the cognizer must be simultaneously aware. Frequently, there is novelty and surprise in the combinations and the fresh images that they evoke. According to him, a metaphor cannot be replaced by a set of equivalent literal statements because it is open-ended, it has an unspecifiable number of potentialities for articulation, and it is a suggestive invitation to the discovery of fresher similarities (Barbour 1974).

In the Judeo-Christian tradition, McFague finds that language in the Old Testament can be considered as a metaphor, in terms of the varied and personal imagery used to represent God (McFague 1982). In the New Testament, she finds the use of metaphor in Jesus' parables of personal relations; she supports this argument by pointing out that parables are characterized by indirect, extravagant, and mundane language (McFague 1982). Parables are judgments or assertion of similarity and difference between two thoughts in permanent tension with each other, where one way is the conventional way of being in the world, and the other is the way of the kingdom, the extraordinary way; thus they challenge conventional context, reality is redescribed through the tension generated by two perspectives on reality (McFague 1982). Echoing perhaps McNamara's decentering process (McNamara 2009), and building on Ricoeur's work (Ricoeur and Crossan 1975), she suggests that the parables work on a pattern of orientation, disorientation, and reorientation: the old Self initially oriented towards one goal gets decentered after religious experience and then begins a search for a higher reorientation; this search is facilitated by religious metaphors and narratives. In the case of parables, a parable begins in the ordinary world with its conventional standards and expectations, but in the course of the story a radically different perspective is introduced that disorients the listener; and finally, through the interaction of the two competing viewpoints, tension is created that results in a redescription of life in the world (McFague, 1982, p. 47).

2.3 Religious symbols and religious language

A brief discussion of symbols needs to be included at this point, with the caveat noted above, that symbolizing is not the focus of this paper, since it would require a much deeper and thorough examination (e.g., Neville 1996). Symbols are part of the language of a religious community present in scripture and liturgy (Barbour 1974). Many religious symbols can be understood as metaphors based on analogies with man's experience, for example, light as a symbol of knowledge, being illuminated, enlightened. Symbols may have many meanings depending on the context in which they are encountered; for instance, water may signify chaos, destruction as in the Biblical account of the deluge, but also regeneration and purification in the context of Baptism in the Christian tradition. For Barbour (1974), religious symbols are expressive of man's emotions and feelings and are powerful in calling forth his response and commitment, since they are rooted in man's experience as an active subject. In this sense, symbols likely emerge from Downes' (2011) affective and motivational module, allowing for the transformation of abstract concepts into action. We noted above that sacred symbols might also facilitate a linking up or commitment of an individual to an ultimate value by constraining the search (for a 'higher self') process as described in the decentering model above.

Religious symbols and metaphors derive their significance and meaning from religious narratives and 'myths' that 'explain' or interpret their meaning. A narrative is typically a temporal ordering of a series of events involving a challenge, climax, and ending with a resolution. The plot includes goals, and an agent who strives to achieve these goals and experiences trials and tribulations in the process. The Christian cross is a symbol that can denote a complex meaning such as 'victory even in apparent defeat' given the narrative context in which it is embedded. That narrative context is the Christians' claim/story of Jesus' crucifixion as leading to the atonement and redemption of mankind. Once valorized by the religious meta-narrative, the symbol can then serve as potent aid in the individual Christian journey through life. In McNamara's (2009) model of religious cognition, for example, the trials that an individual agent undergoes lead to the decentering process of the Self as executive agent. The sense of loss of agency that suffering entails is analogous to a crucifixion of the Self and its goals and desires. Once agency is diminished, religious individuals can use the symbols afforded to them by their religious tradition (in this case the cross) to assist in the process of building an enriched sense of agency and a more complex sense of Self oriented towards 'redemption'—another potent Christian symbol. Thus, religious narratives give the individual access to the rich store of power-infused symbols that a religious tradition offers its adherents. If the religious adherents use these symbols to live their lives in life-enhancing ways, then those symbols can be considered living symbols that shape people's lives and communities.

While it is clear that religious language, in the form of religious narratives and symbols, can be used as powerful tools by individuals in their quests for commitment to ultimate values and richer lives, elements of religious language can also be used to understand the great unknowns, both the known unknowns and even the unknown unknowns[1] (Downes 2011). Religious myths are a prime mode of religious language used to comprehend what is finally incomprehensible. For Barbour (1974), myths are narratives that manifest some aspect of the cosmic order that is highly significant in personal and corporate life, unlike a fairy tale, and it endorses particular ways of ordering experience and acting in daily life in the following ways. First, they provide a vision of the structure of reality set at the time of creation or of historical events; the present is interpreted in terms of the normative events narrated in the myth. It is relevant to daily life because it deals with perennial problems and the enduring order of the world in which man lives. Second, myths inform man about himself, he understands himself in the light of his ancestry, the community is constituted by big events in which its members participate, myth brings man into accord with a group and an ordained order, and myths inform about human nature and destiny. Third, myths express a saving power in human life. A myth has a tripartite structure: ideal state, the actual state separated from the ideal by some flaw, and saving power that can cover the flaw and establish the ideal. Myths convey a power to transform man's life. Fourth, they provide patterns for human actions; they give the examples to be followed in ritual, moral, or practical behavior, in all significant activities like eating, sexuality, work, education, etc. They are vivid and impressive, inspiring their adherents to emotional response and concrete action. Fifth, myths are enacted in rituals, not only in words but in symbolic acts, dance, gesture, drama, etc., transmitted and providing a way to participate in them. These acts create anew the forms for ordering experience and action based on the creative power and historical time.

Functions of myth according to Barbour (1974) include reduction of anxiety in the face of illness, natural disaster, and death; a source of security; and a symbolic resolution of conflicts. They serve a social function, for they promote integration of society, binding a community together, and cultural stability; they sanction the existing order and justify its status system. They provide attitudes and behavior recommendations. Myths could be understood as symbols of man's inner life, valid in so far as they 'authentically expressed man's feelings, hopes and fears, or his experiences of guilt, reconciliation and liberation from anxiety' (Barbour 1974).

Commitment is expressed importantly in the form of active participation in ritual. Ritual for Rappaport (1999) is defined as 'the performance of more or less invariant sequences of formal acts and utterances not entirely encoded by the performers' (p. 24); he considers ritual the basic social act through which the existence, acceptance, and morality of conventions are joined indissolubly (Rappaport, 1999). In religious rituals, public prayer and formal religious language is used, ritual meanings are expressed, and effects are achieved, particularly through the use of performatives or speech acts, as discussed above. For Rappaport (1999), 'the naming . . . actually brings into being the state of affairs with which it is concerned' (p. 115). In addition to the use of utterances, during ritual more or less invariant sequences of actions take place as part of the liturgy, which, importantly, are not entirely encoded by the performers. Thus, by immersing themselves in the ritual and by performing the actions and uttering the words, the participants in the ritual suspend their individual intentions, allowing the deity to express his intentions and facilitating the perception of the supernatural and of ultimate values.

Closely tied to the narratives are the norms that are encoded in each particular religion. Through their participation in rituals, adherents commit themselves, accept the rules and conventions of their belief system. For Rappaport (1999) it is the visible, explicit, public act of acceptance and not the invisible, ambiguous, private sentiment, which is socially binding (p. 122). So Downes' normativity module must be realized, at least in part, via ritual. Emotion and affect are present during ritual; emotions are part of ritual, a source of its power (Rappaport 1999). It is important to note that the term *emotion* does not only include primary emotions such as happiness or fear but moral emotions as well, including guilt, compassion, embarrassment, shame, pride, contempt, and gratitude (Moll et al. 2005). Moral emotions result when commitment to value is realized or broken (Moll et al. 2005). Given the fact that ritual can be conceived as the basic social act, primary as well as moral emotions provide the necessary cohesiveness that can sustain the permanence of the social group.

Having concluded our discussion of basic elements of religious language, we turn now to our predictions regarding potential neurologic models that might plausibly mediate these elements of religious language. We note that direct observations of neurologic changes in relation to changes in religious language use are scarce or non-existent. What follows therefore are merely suggestions, based on existing data, of how particular brain systems might support some of the elements of religious language we have discussed above. We nevertheless see these suggestions as novel predictions based on our analyses of the distinctiveness of the core elements of religious language noted above. We will necessarily have to discuss neurologic systems that have been linked to cognitive functions that in turn can plausibly be argued to support the language processes we are interested in. Therefore our discussion must necessarily be indirect, but we nevertheless feel that the exercise is valuable, as identifying neurologic systems that mediate these language processes will tell us more about these processes that can then inform our knowledge of religious language itself.

3 PREDICTIONS CONCERNING NEUROCOGNITIVE SYSTEMS IMPLICATED IN RELIGIOUS LANGUAGE AND A REVIEW OF THE SUPPORTING EVIDENCE

Before summarizing the description of the neural networks involved in cognitive functions linked to the language elements discussed above, a brief description of the methods used in the literature, and of the organization of the primate cortex, is necessary. The great majority of the experimental evidence that will be presented has to do with data obtained from neuroimaging studies that use functional magnetic resonance (fMRI), positron emission tomography (PET) or single-photon emission computed tomography (SPECT). In the case of fMRI, functional brain mapping involves quantification of blood flow changes as indicated by fluctuating deoxyhemoglobin activity in the blood (Kourtzi 2005; Raichle 2010). This blood-oxygenation-level-dependent (BOLD) signal primarily reflects the input of neuronal information and its processing at a given area rather than the output signals to other parts of the brain (Kourtzi 2005). In the case of PET studies, brain glucose metabolism is measured by using the tracer [18F]-2-fluoro-2-deoxy-D-glucose (FDG), or 6-[18F]-fluoro-L-dopa (FD) uptake in the region of interest (Raichle, 2009). FD is a marker that allows monitoring of the uptake and decarboxylation of FD to fluorodopamine (FDA), and the subsequent storage of FDA in synaptic vesicles, thus giving an indication of pre-synaptic DA function (Au et al. 2005; Farrer et al. 2003). SPECT also uses radioisotopes to evaluate regional cerebral blood flow and to measure metabolic activity indirectly (Amen et al. 2011). Hexamethylpropyleneamine oximine (HMPAO) and ethylcysteinate dimer (ECD) are two commonly available FDA-approved radiopharmaceuticals (Amen et al. 2011). Currently, the integrity of dopaminergic terminals is being evaluated by using a dopamine transporter ligand labeled with a radioisotope (Tatsch and Poepperl 2013).

Most of the imaging studies described in this chapter will refer to the cerebral cortex, the neocortex of the brain, an organ with two hemispheres, each divided into four lobes: frontal, temporal, parietal, and occipital. In each lobe, areas have been defined as primary, secondary, or associative depending on the type of information that they process; the total number of areas may exceed 100 in the human brain (Van Essen 2005). Subcortical regions such as the thalamus, the striatum, which includes the caudate nucleus the putamen and nucleus accumbens, and structures located in the midbrain such as the substantia nigra and ventral tegmental area, will be mentioned as well because of their relevance in the processing of information and motor behavior, reward and cognition.

3.1 The neurology of speech acts

Empirical studies with patients suffering from Parkinson's and Huntington's diseases support the role of basal ganglia in language, in particular in the comprehension of implicit speech acts and grammatical rules (e.g., Holtgraves and McNamara 2010; Holtgraves et al. 2010; Papagno et al. 2014; Teichmann et al. 2006). In both these disorders, the areas that are initially affected by the disease are the basal ganglia. In the case of Parkinson's disease, the dopaminergic cells that innervate the caudate-putamen, and the prefrontal cortex, die off; in the case of Huntington's disease, the intrinsic neurons of the caudate-putamen that control other subcortical areas and the cerebral cortex through various feedback loops are the ones that are lost. These areas have been shown to play an important role in the learning of habits, but few studies have considered their role in language before.

In particular, Holtgraves and McNamara (2010) showed that Parkinson's patients evidence significant deficits in recognition of speech act verbs. Briefly, in this study the participants read different scenarios presenting a conversation, followed by a lexical decision task requiring them to determine if a string of letters was a word. Importantly, the speech act types used in these studies consisted mostly of assertives and commissives—those speech acts we identified above as particularly important for religious language. Participants suffering from Parkinson's disease (PD) were slower at recognizing the word that reflected the speech act implicit in the scenario. In a second task, the participants were asked to identify the speech act performed with the utterance, and PD patients recognized a lower number of them. The authors concluded that in PD there is a language disorder that involves a selective deficit in implicit speech act comprehension, and that 'this deficit may contribute to difficulties that PD patients display during social interaction' because they are unable to understand what actions are being performed by the words used by others. The speech acts included in this study included assertives (e.g., agree), expressives (e.g., thank), directives (e.g., warn), and commissives (e.g., promise). Similar deficits in PD patients have been found in the interpretation of indirect speech (e.g., McNamara et al. 2010; Papagno et al. 2014). Taken together, these studies indicate a deficit in pragmatic communication skills in PD; speech acts are particularly important in terms of religious language because they help recognize a speaker's intentions, and represent language that is used for performing various actions, both of which are important elements when relating to supernatural agents. Interestingly, discussed below, McNamara and colleagues (Butler et al. 2009; Butler et al. 2011) have independently demonstrated that a subset of PD patients evidence significant difficulties in accessing religious concepts.

A skill related to speech act comprehension is the interpretation of instructions defined as the 'transformation of abstract mental representations of a task into actual behavior' (Stocco et al. 2012). Neuroimaging studies indicate that the lateral prefrontal cortex, the left and right parietal cortices, and the striatum participate in the different phases of encoding and executing instruction-based tasks (Abu-Akel and Shamay-Tsoory 2011; Stocco et al. 2012). The prefrontal cortex and striatum appear to code the relationship between stimuli-actions-consequences that are currently relevant, while the premotor cortex is involved in encoding more durable associations without reference to current relevance (Stocco et al. 2012; Wolfensteller and Ruge 2012). From a review of lesion studies, Gläscher et al. (2012) suggest that the anterior cingulate cortex may have a role in shifting between cognitive tasks and response states, while lateral structures of the prefrontal cortex may be involved when competing responses need to be inhibited. These regions then may contribute to a control network that maintains goals by flexibly adjusting attentional and working memory resources to changing environments and tasks demands, whereas the left VMPFC (ventromedial prefrontal cortex) may be part of a valuation and reward-learning network (Gläsher et al. 2012; Molnar-Szakacs and Uddin 2013).

Religious language in the form of norms, instructions, and commissive speech acts could be defined as implicit, habitual, or procedural knowledge and have some of the characteristics of this type of learning. It should be acquired gradually, be dependent on the valuation and reward-learning network, proceed often without conscious awareness, involve trial-by-trial learning, be driven by error correction, and learn from reward feedback. Habits form inflexible representations that do not easily generalize to new choices, so this type of learning is considered rigid, faithful, and long-lasting (Foerde and Shohamy 2011; Morgado 2005; Reber 2013; Squire 2004). Habits refer not only to overt motor behavior but also to cognitive activity, for example, to the repetitive thoughts present in human disorders such as Tourette's syndrome (Graybiel 2008). Repetitive behavior such as habits are considered to be the result of experience-dependent plasticity in the basal ganglia (Graybiel 2008).

Long-term value commitments transform the individual so that these commitments become habits and part of the person's character. Given the role of the basal ganglia in habit acquisition, procedural learning, and in understanding speech acts (Holtgraves et al. 2010; Holtgraves and McNamara 2010), it would be expected that damage to these brain structures would alter religious language. Indeed, studies have found that PD patients show delayed access to religious concepts in semantic memory (Butler. et al. 2009; Butler et al. 2011). Briefly, in these studies a word (prime) was presented before a target phrase; the word and the phrase were matched or not in terms of the category of word, civic, religious, or nonsensical. The participant had to decide if the phrase represented an activity that could be performed. In contrast to control participants, participants with PD showed slower response to religious actions than to civic actions, in fact, there was no difference in response speed between the phrases representing a nonsensical activity (e.g., push waterfall) and the phrases representing a religious activity (e.g., pray quietly). The lack of effect of the religious prime correlated with the Self report of religiousness; participants with PD reported less private spiritual practices and less positive spiritual experience in a standard measure of religiousness and spirituality (Butler et al. 2011). Thus, basal ganglia function appears to be necessary for understanding religious concepts, and possibly for meaningful religious experience.

Speech acts and over-learned language sequences that can be described as habits occur in all kinds of religious language, especially prayer. Two neuroimaging studies have addressed the issue of prayer and the neural structures associated with it (Schjødt et al. 2008; 2009). In the later study, the authors described activation of brain areas during formal prayer, defined as abstracted recitations with little personal content, versus personal prayer that involves a conversation with a personal god, and a nursery rhyme versus expressing their personal wishes, using fMRI. During personal prayer, they found activation of areas related to ToM: the temporopolar region, the medial prefrontal cortex, the temporoparietal junction, and the precuneus. The finding of activation of regions involved in ToM, the interpretation of others' emotions and beliefs, is interesting considering Downes' hypothesis (this volume) that through personal prayer the speaker is interpreting God's will and conforming his/her will to God's will. The recitation of a formal prayer activated areas involved in rehearsal and retrieval just as a nursery rhyme did. The comparison of formal prayer versus personal prayer, presented in the earlier paper (Schjødt et al. 2008), showed activation of the dorsal striatum during formal prayer. Based on these results, the authors suggested that the motivational system of the dorsal striatum plays a role in frequently repeated religious behavior; remarkably, they did not find this effect when scanning people that do not pray frequently.

3.2 The neural substrate of doctrine and experience

As described previously, during the decentering process the old Self begins a search for a higher re-orientation towards newer higher values and a commitment to those higher values. This process is facilitated by religious narratives and myths that are stored in the form of semantic memory, and that need to be consciously accessible. The neuroscientific literature points to the importance of the medial temporal lobe, and in particular to the hippocampus together with perirhinal and entorhinal cortices, as the neural substrate for semantic learning. The study of patient H. M. dramatically underscores the importance of the hippocampus in storing consciously accessible, semantic memory (Corkin et al. 1997). Recent studies indicate that regions beyond the hippocampus proper may support the acquisition of semantic knowledge (O'Kane et al. 2004; Binder et al. 2009), widening the network of areas involved in the acquisition of knowledge about the world, and including autobiographical information.

Based on a review of the literature, Aggleton (2012) proposes the existence of four systems in the medial temporal lobe relevant for the formation of declarative, consciously accessible, memories. These systems would be involved in episodic memory, affective and social learning, sensory information and integration, familiarity-based recognition, and memory retrieval; and would involve also the prefrontal cortex and subcortical areas (Aggleton 2012).

Interestingly, recent neuroimaging studies found activation of brain regions and pathways implicated in the semantic processing network with the appraisal of a statement as doctrinal/semantic versus experiential knowledge (Kapogiannis et al. 2009; Kapogiannis, Deshpande, Krueger, Thornburg, and Grafman 2014). Specifically, the results of these studies suggest that statements reflecting doctrine implicate temporal lobe regions involved in decoding metaphorical (right inferior temporal gyrus) and abstract linguistic content (left superior temporal gyrus; Kapogiannis et al. 2009). Statements reflecting experiential religion activated a network that mediates visual and motor imagery of the Self in action, based on episodic memory retrieval that included the bilateral occipital lobes (including the left precuneus), the left precentral gyrus, and the left inferior frontal gyrus (Kapogiannis et al., 2009). In their more recent study (Kapogiannis et al. 2014), the authors analyzed the connectivity of their fMRI data and found that processing of doctrinal knowledge was associated with activation in classical language areas of the brain (including Broca's region and the left superior temporal gyrus) as well as the left precuneus and inferior frontal lobes both of which have been associated with self-consciousness (Kapogiannis et al. 2014). Additional areas associated with semantic rule retrieval, the left temporoparietal junction and ventrolateral prefrontal cortex, appear to be involved in the neural representation of sacred values as deontological rules and not utilitarian values (Berns et al. 2012). In this study, the neural responses to statements of personal values ranging from the mundane to the sacred were measured using fMRI. The participants engaged in various tasks, including an auction phase when they could sell their chosen answers; those values that people refused to sell were considered sacred.

Fundamental to the analysis of the neurocognitive effects of myths, narratives, metaphor, and symbols in religious language is the analysis of emotional effects on behavior. A few studies have evaluated the brain areas activated during a religious experience specifically in religious groups. One of them evaluated religious cognition and experience in German-speaking adults from an Evangelical fundamentalist community. Participants were asked to attain a religious state during recitation or reading, while undergoing PET to evaluate regional cerebral blood flow (Azari et al., 2001). Another study with Franciscan nuns using centering prayer, reported on regional cerebral blood flow using SPECT (Newberg, Pourdehnad, Alavi, and D'Aquili 2003) and Beauregard and Paquette (2006) using fMRI, studied contemplative Carmelite nuns who were asked to relive their most intense mystical experience. In this last study, mystical experience was defined as a sense of union with God, a sense of having touched the ultimate ground of reality, an experience of timelessness and spacelessness, and positive affect including peace, joy, and unconditional love. Although among these studies there was not a perfect coincidence of areas of activation, prefrontal, frontal, parietal, and cingulate cortices were activated when the participants experienced the various religious states.

The creation of an emotional experience is best understood as resulting from the interaction of various neural networks as proposed by Lindquist and Barrett (2012). Based on the analysis of a large set of empirical literature, Lindquist and Barrett suggest that emotional experiences (and other mental states as well) are constructed from the sensations within the body associated with limbic and paralimbic brain regions (temporal, cingulate, and prefrontal cortices; hippocampus; and other areas like the amygdala, ventral striatum, and midbrain) within a *salience network* and sensations from the world, associated with sensory cortices. These sensations are interpreted 'using associations from past experience organized as emotion category knowledge that' the authors 'believe is associated with the midline cortical, lateral prefrontal and temporal regions within the "default network", as well as language-relevant brain regions' (Linquist and Barrett 2012, p. 535). The same authors hypothesize that this process would be orchestrated and regulated by a frontoparietal network, an *executive network* (Lindquist and Barrett 2012, p. 535).

4 CONCLUDING REMARKS

The distinctiveness of religious language, then, rests on its orientation to an ultimate reality, that is unknown but intuited, and that requires absolute commitment. Commitment is expressed in speech acts, especially commissives that, together with a formal linguistic style, allow the Self to suspend the sense of executive control in search of a value-enriched Self. The definition of this value-enriched Self would rest on the particular belief system represented in narratives and myths, and expressed through rituals, and through the commitment to the norms of that system. Commitment favors Self-regulation, which is associated with the positively rewarding experiences and emotions intrinsic to religious activities, thus reinforcing the process.

In terms of the neural substrate, our working hypothesis is that the repetitive nature of religious practices, and the use of speech acts involves the basal ganglia; the altered sense of Self and the intuition of the ultimate would involve brain areas related to ToM, while semantic knowledge in the form of narratives would include areas dedicated to language processing, and memory in the medial temporal lobe. The religious experience is expected to involve several brain areas, from sensory cortices to limbic and paralimbic brain regions subserving emotional responses, and several networks including an executive network.

Religious language with its distinctive characteristics and the coordinated activity of a number of neural networks is the vehicle we have to approach and bind ourselves to ultimate values—the object or 'person' of religious concern. Together, these characteristics would give religious language its distinctiveness and its long-lasting strength in guiding behavior, and could explain in part the emergence of less desirable outcomes, like religious dogmatism and sectarian violence.

NOTE

1. These are semi-propositional forms that cannot be evaluated to be completely true, the 'unknowable or mysteries' that in spite of being only partially grasped, have 'sufficient logical character to warrant' inferences (Downes 2011).

REFERENCES

Abu-Akel, A., and S. Shamay-Tsoory (2011). Neuroanatomical and neurochemical bases of theory of mind. *Neuropsychologia* 49(11), 2971–2984. doi: 10.1016/j.neuropsychologia.2011.07.012

Aggleton, J. P. (2012). Multiple anatomical systems embedded within the primate medial temporal lobe: Implications for hippocampal function. *Neuroscience and Biobehavioral Reviews* 36(7), 1579–1596. doi: 10.1016/j.neubiorev.2011.09.005

Amen, D. G., M. Trujillo, A. Newberg, K. Willeumier, R. Tarzwell, J. C. Wu, and B. Chaitin (2011). Brain SPECT imaging in complex psychiatric cases. *The Open Neuroimaging Journal* 5, 40–48.

Au, W. L., J. R. Adams, A. R. Troiano, and A. J. Stoessl (2005). Parkinson's disease: In vivo assessment of disease progression using positron emission tomography. *Molecular Brain Research* 134, 24–33. doi: 10.1016/j.molbrainres.2004.09.028

Azari, N. P., J. Nickel, G. Wunderlich, M. Niedeggen, H. Hefter, L. Tellmann, et al. (2001). Neural correlates of religious experience. *European Journal of Neuroscience* 13, 1649–1653.

Barbour, I. G. (1974). *Myths, Models and Paradigms: The Nature of Scientific and Religious Language*. London: S.C.M. Press Ltd.

Beauregard, M. and V. Paquette (2006). Neural correlates of a mystical experience in Carmelite nuns. *Neuroscience Letters* 405, 186–190.

Berns, G. S., E. Bell, C. M. Capra, M. J. Prietula, S. Moore, B. Anderson, et al. (2012). The price of your soul: Neural evidence for the non-utilitarian representation of sacred values. *Philosophical Transactions of the Royal Society B: Biological Sciences* 367(1589), 754–762. doi: 10.1016/j.neuroimage.2007.10.028

Binder, J. R., R. H. Desai, W. W. Graves, and L. L. Conant (2009). Where is the semantic system? A critical review and meta-analysis of 120 functional neuroimaging studies. *Cerebral Cortex* 19(12), 2767–2796. doi: 10.1093/cercor/bhp055

Butler, P. M., P. McNamara, and R. Durso (2009). Deficits in the automatic activation of religious concepts in patients with Parkinson's disease. *Journal of the International Neuropsychological Society* 16(02), 252–261. doi: 10.1017/S1355617709991202

Butler, P. M., P. McNamara, J. Ghofrani, and R. Durso (2011). Disease-associated differences in religious cognition in patients with Parkinson's disease. *Journal of Clinical and Experimental Neuropsychology* 33(8), 917–928. doi: 10.1080/13803395.2011.575768

Corkin, S., D. G. Amaral, G. R. González, K. A. Johnson, and B. T. Hyman (1997). H. M.'s medial temporal lobe lesion: Findings from Magnetic Resonance Imaging. *The Journal of Neuroscience* 17(10), 3964–3979.

Donovan, P. (1976). *Religious Language*. London: Sheldon Press.

Downes, W. (2011). *Language and Religion*. Cambridge: Cambridge University Press.

Du Bois, J. W. (1986). Self-evidence and ritual speech. In W. Chafe and J. Nichols (eds.), *Evidentiality: The Linguistic Coding of Epistemology*, pp. 313–336. Norwood, NJ: Ablex.

Dunbar, R. I. M. (2003). The social brain: Mind, language, and society in evolutionary perspective. *Annual Review of Anthropology* 32(1), 163–181. doi: 10.1146/annurev.anthro.32.061002.093158

Farrer, C., N. Franck, N. Georgieff, C. D. Frith, J. Decety, and M. Jeannerod (2003). Modulating the experience of agency: A positron emission tomography study. *NeuroImage* 18(2), 324–333. doi: 10.1016/S1053-8119(02)00041-1

Foerde, K., and D. Shohamy (2011). The role of the basal ganglia in learning and memory: Insight from Parkinson's disease. *Neurobiology of Learning and Memory* 96(4), 624–636. doi: 10.1016/j.nlm.2011.08.006

Gläsher, J., R. Adolphs, H. Damasio, A. Bechara, D. Rudrauf, M. Calamia, L. K. Paul, et al. (2012). Lesion mapping of cognitive control and value-based decision making in the prefrontal cortex. *Proceedings of the National Academy of Sciences* 109(36), 14681–14686. doi: 10.1073/pnas.1206608109/-/DCSupplemental

Graybiel, A. M. (2008). Habits, rituals, and the evaluative brain. *Annual Review of Neuroscience* 31(1), 359–387. doi: 10.1146/annurev.neuro.29.051605.112851

Holtgraves, T. and P. McNamara (2010). Pragmatic comprehension deficit in Parkinson's disease. *Journal of Clinical and Experimental Neuropsychology* 32(4), 388–397. doi: 10.1080/13803390903130729

Holtgraves, T., P. McNamara, K. Cappaert, and R. Durso (2010). Linguistic correlates of asymmetric motor symptom severity in Parkinson's Disease. *Brain and Cognition* 72(2), 189–196. doi: 10.1016/j.bandc.2009.08.004

Kapogiannis, D., A. K. Barbey, M. Su, G. Zamboni, F. Krueger, and J. H. Grafman (2009). Cognitive and neural foundations of religious belief. *Proceedings of the National Academy of Sciences* 106(12), 4876–4881. doi: 10.1073/pnas.0811717106

Kapogiannis, D., G. Deshpande, F. Krueger, M. P. Thornburg, and J. H. Grafman (2014). Brain networks shaping religious belief. *Brain Connectivity* 4(1), 70–79. doi: 10.1089/brain.2013.0172

Keane, W. (1997). Religious language. *Annual Review of Anthropology* 26, 47–71.

Kourtzi, Z. (2005). Combined human and monkey fMRI methods for the study of large-scale neuronal networks in the primate brain. In S. Dehaene, J.-R. Duhamel, M. D. Hauser, and G. Rizzolatti (eds.), *From Monkey Brain to Human Brain*, pp. 21–40. Cambridge: MIT Press.

Lakoff, G. (1992). *The contemporary theory of metaphor*. In A. Ortony (ed.), *Metaphor and Thought* (Second edition), pp. 202–251. Cambridge: Cambridge University Press.

Lindquist, K. A., and L. F. Barrett (2012). A functional architecture of the human brain: Emerging insights from the science of emotion. *Trends in Cognitive Sciences* 16(11), 533–540. doi: 10.1016/j.tics.2012.09.005

McFague, S. (1982). *Metaphorical Theology*. Philadelphia: Fortress Press.

McNamara, P. (2009). *The Neuroscience of Religious Experience*. Cambridge: Cambridge University Press.

McNamara, P., T. Holtgraves, R. Durso, and E. Harris (2010). Social cognition of indirect speech: Evidence from Parkinson's disease. *Journal of Neurolinguistics* 23(2), 162–171. doi: 10.1016/j.jneuroling.2009.12.003

Moll, J., R. Zahn, R. de Oliveira-Souza, F. Krueger, and J. H. Grafman (2005). The neural basis of human moral cognition. *Nature Reviews Neuroscience* 6, 799–809.

Molnar-Szakacs, I., and L. Q. Uddin (2013). Self-processing and the default mode network: Interactions with the mirror neuron system. *Frontiers in Human Neuroscience* 7, 1–11. doi: 10.3389/fnhum.2013.00571/abstract

Morgado, I. (2005). Psicobiología del aprendizaje y la memoria: Fundamentos y avances recientes. *Revista de Neurología* 40(5), 289–297.

Neville, R. C. (1996). *The Truth of Broken Symbols*. Albany, NY: SUNY Press.

Neville, R. C. (2013). *Ultimates*. Albany, NY: SUNY Press.

Newberg, A. B., M. Pourdehnad, A. Alavi, and E. G. D'Aquili (2003). Cerebral blood flow during meditative prayer: Preliminary findings and methodological issues. *Perceptual and Motor Skills* 97, 625–630.

O'Kane, G., E. A. Kensinger, and S. Corkin (2004). Evidence for semantic learning in profound amnesia: An investigation with patient H. M. *Hippocampus* 14(4), 417–425. doi: 10.1002/hipo.20005

Papagno, C., G. Mattavelli, Z. Cattaneo, L. Romito, and A. Albanese (2014). Ambiguous idiom processing in Parkinson's disease patients. *Cognitive Neuropsychology* 30(7–8), 495–506. Retrieved from http://www.ncbi.nlm.nih.gov/pubmed/24479736

Purzycki, B. G., D. N. Finkel, J. Shaver, N. Wales, A. B. Cohen, and R. Sosis (2012). What does God know? Supernatural agents' access to socially strategic and non-strategic information. *Cognitive Science* 36(5), 846–869. doi: 10.1111/j.1551-6709.2012.01242.x

Raichle, M. E. (2009). A brief history of human brain mapping. *Trends in Neurosciences* 32(2), 118–126. doi: 10.1016/j.tins.2008.11.001

Raichle, M. E. (2010). Two views of brain function. *Trends in Cognitive Sciences* 14(4), 180–190. doi: 10.1016/j.tics.2010.01.008

Rappaport, R. (1999). *Ritual and Religion in the Making of Humanity*. Cambridge: Cambridge University Press.

Reber, P. J. (2013). The neural basis of implicit learning and memory: A review of neuropsychological and neuroimaging research. *Neuropsychologia* 51(10), 2026–2042. doi: 10.1016/j.neuropsychologia.2013.06.019

Ricoeur, P., and J. D. Crossan (1975). *Paul Ricoeur on Biblical Hermeneutics*. Missoula, MT: Society of Biblical Literature.

Schjødt, U., H. Stødkilde-Jørgensen, A. W. Geertz, and A. Roepstorff (2008). Rewarding prayers. *Neuroscience Letters* 443(3), 165–168. doi: 10.1016/j.neulet.2008.07.068

Schjødt, U., H. Stødkilde-Jørgensen, A. W. Geertz, and A. Roepstorff (2009). Highly religious participants recruit areas of social cognition in personal prayer. *Social Cognitive and Affective Neuroscience* 4(2), 199–207. doi: 10.1093/scan/nsn050

Searle, J. R. (2007). What is language: Some preliminary remarks. In S. L. Tsohatzidis (ed.), *John Searle's Philosophy of Language: Force, Meaning and Mind*, pp. 15–48. Cambridge: Cambridge University Press.

Searle, J. R., and D. Vanderveken (1985). *Foundations of Illocutionary Logic*. Cambridge: Cambridge University Press.

Squire, L. R. (2004). Memory systems of the brain: A brief history and current perspective. *Neurobiology of Learning and Memory* 82(3), 171–177. doi: 10.1016/j.nlm.2004.06.005

Stocco, A., C. Lebiere, R. C. O'Reilly, and J. R. Anderson (2012). Distinct contributions of the caudate nucleus, rostral prefrontal cortex, and parietal cortex to the execution of instructed tasks. *Cognitive, Affective, and Behavioral Neuroscience* 12(4), 611–628. doi: 10.3758/s13415-012-0117-7

Tatsch, K., and G. Poepperl (2013). Nigrostriatal dopamine terminal imaging with dopamine transporter SPECT: An update. *Journal of Nuclear Medicine* 54(8), 1331–1338. doi: 10.2967/jnumed.112.105379

Teichmann, M., E. Dupoux, S. Kouider, and A.-C. Bachoud-Lévi (2006). The role of the striatum in processing language rules: Evidence from word perception in Huntington's Disease. *Journal of Cognitive Neuroscience* 18(9), 1555–1569.

Tillich, P. (2012). *Systematic Theology*. Chicago: University of Chicago Press.

Van Essen, D. C. (2005). Surface-based comparisons of macaque and human cortical organization. In S. Dehaene, J.-R. Duhamel, M. D. Hauser, and G. Rizzolatti (eds.), *From Monkey Brain to Human Brain*, pp. 3–20. Cambridge, MA: MIT Press.

Wolfensteller, U., and H. Ruge (2012). Frontostriatal mechanisms in instruction-based learning as a hallmark of flexible goal-directed behavior. *Frontiers in Psychology* 3, 192. doi: 10.3389/fpsyg.2012.00192/abstract

CHAPTER 6

God, Metaphor, and the Language of the Hemispheres

IAIN MCGILCHRIST

How does one know, or at any rate become aware of, what it is that one does not know? This is, of course, a fundamental epistemological problem, since the openness required to embrace propositions that cannot be demonstrated to follow necessarily from commonly held truths leaves one open to the possibility of self-deceit. And yet not to be aware of what it is one does not know is also, inevitably, to deceive oneself.

Not all knowledge is, however, propositional in nature. Ultimately, in fact, all knowledge derives from experience, for which there are no propositions, and many languages express at least some aspect of this difference by distinct words for the ways in which one can be said 'to know'. *Sapere* bows to *cognoscere, savoir* to *connaître, wissen* to *kennen*. When we say we know something, what we mean is that we see that it is like something else that we reckon we already know better. And those 'somethings else', followed far enough, return us in every case to embodied experience. Additionally, both the first propositions, or axioms, from which we reason, and even the value of reason itself as a tool for the discovery of truth, have to be intuited. We cannot reason our way to either.

Since language embodies thought, it follows the same path. Words are like money. In any (apparently) enclosed financial system, any number of 'virtual' transactions can be carried out, but in the end all such transactions depend on money taking its value from somebody's cows or chickens somewhere, and being translated back into real goods or services—food, clothes, car repairs—in the realm of daily life somewhere else. So it is with words. Webs of thought can be spun with them, but ultimately language represents something valuable elsewhere: its value lies only in what it represents in the world of embodied experience.

For this reason, language is essentially, not accidentally, metaphorical in nature. Metaphor embodies thought and places it, where it belongs, in a living context. In this, it bridges the gap between language and the world, a gap entailed on us by the very nature of language. The languages of science and philosophy are not only no exception to this, but particularly obvious examples of it.

Thus both the process of reason and its axioms, and the business of linguistic discourse and its terms, ultimately depend on and cannot transcend intuitive knowledge and embodied experience. Following intuition may lead us astray, right enough, but so may not attending to it: there is a wealth of evidence that those who rely on ratiocination alone make poorer judgements than those who combine reason with intuition, and often they can barely function in the world at all.

1 THE DIVIDED BRAIN

What does all this have to do with the brain? In humans, as in other mammals, as well as in birds, reptiles, and even fish, the brain is divided. This is odd, because the brain exists to make connections and is only as powerful as its connections. Odder still, the band of fibres that connects the hemispheres, the corpus callosum, which came into being only with the advent of mammals, has grown proportionally smaller (in relation to hemispheric volume) with evolution (Jäncke and Steinmetz 2003; Hopkins and Marino 2000; Aboitiz, Scheibel, and Zaidel 1992), and much of its activity in any case involves functional inhibition of the contralateral hemisphere. The corpus callosum contains an estimated 300–800 million fibres connecting topologically similar areas in either hemisphere. Yet only 2 per cent of cortical neurones are connected by this tract (Jäncke and Steinmetz 2003; Banich 2003). What is more, the main purpose of a large number of these connections is actually to inhibit—in other words to stop the other hemisphere interfering. Neurones can have an excitatory or inhibitory action, excitatory neurones causing further neuronal activity downstream, while inhibitory neurones suppress it. Although the majority of cells projecting to the corpus callosum use the facilitatory neurotransmitter glutamate, and are excitatory, there are significant populations of nerve cells (those that use the neurotransmitter gamma-amino butyric acid, GABA) whose function is inhibitory. Even the excitatory fibres often terminate on intermediary neurones, or interneurones, whose function is inhibitory (Conti and Manzoni 1994; Saron et al. 2002). Inhibition is, of course, not a straightforward concept. Inhibition at the neurophysiological level does not necessarily equate with inhibition at the functional level, any more than letting your foot off the brake pedal causes the car to halt: neural inhibition may set in train a sequence of activity, so that the net result is functionally permissive. But the evidence is that the primary effect of callosal transmission is to produce *functional* inhibition (Meyer et al. 1995; Röricht et al. 1997; Höppner et al. 1999). So much is this the case that a number of neuroscientists have proposed that the whole purpose of the corpus callosum is to allow one hemisphere to inhibit the other (Cook 1984; Hoptman and Davidson 1994; Chiarello and Maxfield 1996). Stimulation of neurones in one hemisphere commonly results in an initial brief excitatory response, followed by a prolonged inhibitory arousal in the contralateral hemisphere. Such inhibition can be widespread, and can be seen on imaging (Saron et al. 2003; Allison et al. 2000; Tootell et al. 1998).

There would appear to be an evolutionary adaptation here that connects, but also importantly separates, two spheres of cerebral activity. Why?

Birds and other animals have to solve a conundrum on which their survival depends, namely, how to eat and to stay alive at the same time. Each must pay attention to something that is already prioritised—a seed, one's prey—at the same time as being open to whatever it is that might come along during the process—be it predator or conspecific. For the first of these, one needs narrow-beam, sharply focussed attention to something that is already prioritised; for the latter, one needs precisely the opposite, namely, a broad, open, vigilant, sustained attention without commitment as to what may be found. Paying two kinds of attention in one consciousness at the same time is an almost intractable problem. The solution appears to have been the bihemispheric brain. The left hemisphere in birds and other animals provides narrow attention in order to get food, to pick up a twig to build a nest, and in general to *manipulate* the world; the right hemisphere provides a broad picture that makes it possible to watch out for predators and bond with mates, and more generally to *understand*, and to find oneself standing in relation to, the world at large. Unsurprisingly, therefore, chicks that are properly lateralised (whose hemispheres are appropriately differentiated) are more able to use these two types of attention effectively than are those in whom, experimentally, lateralisation has not been permitted to develop (Rogers 2000). Many types of bird show more alarm behaviour when viewing a predator with the left eye, thus using their right hemisphere (Hoffman et al. 2006), are better at detecting predators with the left eye (Rogers and Kaplan 2006; Rogers 2000), and will choose to examine predators with their left eye (Rogers et al. 2004), to the extent that if they have detected a predator with their right eye, they will actually turn their head so as to examine it further with the left (Dharmaretnam and Rogers 2005). Hand-raised ravens will even follow the direction of gaze of a human experimenter looking upwards, using their left eye (Bugnyar et al. 2004). For many animals, there are biases at the population level towards, again, watching out for predators with the left eye (Evans et al. 1993; Rogers 2000; Lippolis et al. 2002, 2005). In marmosets, individual animals with more strongly lateralised brains are better able, because of hemisphere specialisation, to forage and remain aware of predators (Rogers 2005). There are shorter reaction times in cats that have a lateralised paw preference (Fabre-Thorpe et al. 1993). Lateralised chimps are more efficient at fishing for termites than unlateralised chimps (McGrew and Marchant 1999). Even individual human brains that are, for one reason or another, less lateralised than the norm appear to show global deficits (Crow et al. 1998). In a word, lateralisation brings evolutionary advantages, particularly in carrying out dual-attention tasks (Rogers et al. 2004). As one group of researchers has put it succinctly: asymmetry pays (Güntürkün et al. 2000).

In predatory birds and animals, it is the left hemisphere that latches on, through the right eye and the right foot, to the prey (Csermely 2004). It is certainly true of familiar prey: in toads, a novel or unusual choice of prey may activate the right hemisphere, until it becomes familiar as an object of prey, when it once again activates the left (Robins and Rogers 2006). In general, toads attend to their prey with the left hemisphere, but interact with their fellow toads using the right hemisphere (Vallortigara et al. 1998).

The advantages accrue not only to the individual: being a more lateralised species at the population level carries advantages in social cohesion (Bisazza et al. 2000; Rogers and Workman 1989; Halpern et al. 2005). That may be because the right hemisphere appears to be deeply involved in social functioning, not just in primates, where it is specialised in the expression of social feelings, but in lower animals and birds as well (Fernández-Carriba et al. 2002; Ventolini et al. 2005). For example, chicks preferentially use the left eye (right hemisphere) for differentiating familiar members of the species from one another, and from those who are not familiar, and in general for gathering social information (Rogers 2000; Vallortigara 1992). Chicks approach their parents or an object on which they have imprinted using their left eye (Dharmaretnam and Andrew 1994), as do Australian magpies (Hoffman et al. 2006). Though black-winged stilts peck more, and more successfully, at prey using the right eye (left hemisphere), males are more likely to direct courtship displays to females that are seen with their left eye (right hemisphere) (Ventolini et al. 2005). The right hemisphere is the main locus of early social experience in rats (Denenberg et al. 1978). In most animal species, intense emotional responses are related to the right hemisphere and inhibited by the left (Andrew and Rogers 2002).

In humans, too, the hemispheres attend to the world differently. Since attention is involved in the genesis of our experiential world, so that the quality of attention we pay affects what it is that we find, this has important consequences for the type of world each hemisphere helps to mediate for us.

Attention is not just another 'function' alongside other cognitive functions. Its ontological status is of something prior to functions and even to things. The kind of attention we bring to bear on the world changes the nature of the world we attend to, the very nature of the world in which those 'functions' would be carried out, and in which those 'things' would exist. Attention changes *what kind of* a thing comes into being for us: in that way, it changes the world. If you are my friend, the way in which I attend to you will be different from the way in which I would attend to you if you were my employer, my patient, the suspect in a crime I am investigating, my lover, my aunt, a body waiting to be dissected. In all these circumstances, except the last, you will also have a quite different experience not just of me, but of yourself: you would feel changed if I changed the type of my attention. And yet nothing *objectively* has changed.

So it is, not just with the human world, but with everything with which we come into contact. A mountain that is a landmark to a navigator, a source of wealth to the prospector, a many-textured form to a painter, or to another the dwelling place of the gods, is changed by the attention given to it. There is no 'real' mountain which can be distinguished from these, no one way of thinking which reveals the true mountain.

It is often wrongly thought, however, that science uncovers such a reality. Its apparently value-free descriptions are assumed to deliver *the* truth about the object, onto which our feelings and desires are later painted. Yet this highly objective stance, this 'view from nowhere', to use Nagel's phrase, is itself value-laden (Nagel 1986). It is just one particular way of looking at things, a way which privileges detachment, a lack of commitment of the viewer to the object viewed. For some purposes this can be undeniably useful. But its use in such causes does not make it truer or more real, closer to the nature of things.

Attention also changes who *we* are, we who are doing the attending. Our knowledge of mirror neurons (Rizzolatti et al. 2001) and their function and of the effects of association-priming (Dijksterhuis et al. 2000) shows that by attending to someone else performing an action, and even by thinking about them doing so—even, in fact, by thinking about certain sorts of people at all—we become objectively, measurably, more *like* them, in how we behave, think, and feel. Through the direction and nature of our attention, we prove ourselves to be partners in creation, both of the world and of ourselves. In keeping with this, attention is inescapably bound up with value—unlike what we conceive as 'cognitive functions', which are neutral in this respect. Values enter only through *the way in which* such functions are exercised: they can be used in different ways for different purposes to different ends. Attention, however, intrinsically is a *way in which*, not a thing: it is intrinsically a relationship, not a brute fact. It is a 'howness', a something between, an aspect of consciousness itself, not a 'whatness', a thing in itself, an object of consciousness. It brings into being a world and, with it, depending on its nature, a set of values.

In experience, these two versions of the world, that of the right hemisphere and of the left, are merged or rapidly alternated in such a way that the subject is not aware of the fact. Hence the significance of what we can learn from studying the brain hemispheres: it draws attention to an aspect of the structure of the phenomenal world that otherwise might elude us. The differences that emerge between the two hemispheres in their mode of attending to the world help us to understand better not only the experiential world, but understanding itself.

I should enter some important caveats at this point. First, it should be clear that these differences are not absolute, but relative, and there is overlap between hemispheres in most respects. Nonetheless, the differences remain consistent and significant. Innate differences are subsequently amplified through experience, since expediency dictates that even a small advantage for one hemisphere in dealing with a certain kind of experience results in its being preferentially used to deal with similar experiences in the future. In this way, the hemispheres become further differentiated during development. Second, although general truths are approximate and cannot be taken for rules, they are necessary for understanding. Contrary findings will inevitably exist to any such generalities. However, general truths are no less important for that. The average temperatures in Iceland and Indonesia are clearly very different, which goes a long way to explain the wholly different characteristics of the vegetation, animal life, landscape, culture, and economy of these two regions, as well as no doubt much else that differentiates their 'feel' and the ways of life there. But it is still true that the lowest average annual temperature in Indonesia is *lower* than the highest average annual temperature in Iceland—and of course the average temperature varies considerably from month to month, as well as, less predictably, from day to day, and indeed from place to place within each region. Which leads to a third caveat: there are inter-individual differences, and individuals vary from occasion to occasion.

I should also say that I am aware that a left hemisphere or right hemisphere on its own cannot be said to do what only a person can do: 'believe', 'intend', 'decide', 'prefer', and so on. These and similar formulations should be understood as avoiding the repetition of such cumbersome locutions as 'a subject relying on the cognitive faculties of the left [or right] hemisphere believes', etc.

For a full account of the nature of the differences between the hemispheres, the reader is referred to *The Master and His Emissary: The Divided Brain and the Making of the Western World* (McGilchrist 2009). However, some broad, 'headline' distinctions could be made here. It should be understood, nonetheless, that these are very general distinctions, distinctions that ask for qualification at a length that is prohibited here.

The left hemisphere's world requires precision rather than breadth, and aims to close things down as much as possible to a certainty, whereas the right hemisphere views the broad picture and opens things up to possibility (Ivry and Robertson, 1998; Kitterle et al. 1990; Sergent 1982; Robertson et al. 1988; Robertson and Lamb 1991; van Kleeck 1989). In focussing on its object, the left hemisphere renders it explicit, and abstracts it from its context (Kinsbourne 1988; Federmeier and Kutas 1999): the right hemisphere is aware of, and able to deal appropriately with, all those things that are required to remain implicit, and are denatured once removed from their context (Alexander et al. 1989; Heilman et al. 1975). The left hemisphere conceives of its object as static, fixed, and atomistic, rather than, as the right hemisphere does, fluid, evolving, and interconnected with the rest of the world (Cummings 1997; Bender et al. 1968; Michel and Troost 1980; Müller et al. 1995; Corballis 1996; Corballis et al. 1998). Where the left hemisphere sees disconnected fragments from which the whole picture might be constructed, the right hemisphere sees the whole, the Gestalt, which is more than the sum of the parts, and from which the 'parts' have artificially to be determined (Yoshida et al. 2007; Evert and Kmen 2003; Fink et al. 1999; van Kleeck 1989). The right hemisphere is alive to what 'presences' to us (to use a Heideggerian term) pre-conceptually; the left hemisphere deals with what is already familiar as a 're-presentation', literally present after the fact (Goldberg 1990; Goldberg and Costa 1981). Where the left hemisphere sees things as general, and disembodied or abstract, the right hemisphere sees them as unique, incarnate, and concrete (Cutting 1997; Kosslyn 1987; Goldberg 1990; Hécaen and Albert 1978). If the left hemisphere is concerned with what can be counted, the quantitative and measurable aspect of experience, the right hemisphere is concerned with the qualitative (Marsolek 1995; Brown and Kosslyn 1993; Kosslyn 1987; Grossman 1988; Cutting 1997; Warrington and McCarthy 1987; Gardner 1974; Bornstein et al. 1969; Bornstein and Kidron 1959; Landis et al. 1986; Bourgeois et al. 1998). One could say that the right hemisphere's world is living, where the left hemisphere's world is mechanical and inanimate (Corballis 1998)—for example, only the left hemisphere codes for tools and machines (Gainotti 2002; Perani et al. 1995; Martin et al. 1996; Price and Friston 2002; Mummery et al. 1996; Damasio et al. 1996; Cutting 1997).

One might expect, on the basis of the above, that the ways in which the two hemispheres communicated their experience of the world would also differ. It is well known that the left hemisphere alone, in the vast majority of right-handers, is capable of speech in language, but less well known that both hemispheres are intimately involved with language reception—the right hemisphere being especially important for the understanding of an utterance as a whole, in context, with all its non-literal, implicit meaning (Foldi et al. 1983; Kaplan et al. 1990; Heilman et al. 1975). The right hemisphere therefore plays an important part in the understanding of linguistic utterance, but does not favour language as a way of expressing its perceptions of the world.

By contrast, music is the natural form of expression in the right hemisphere, and the musical aspects of language (its 'prosody'), including pitch, volume, intonation, rhythm, and phrasing, along with facial expression and body language, are all underwritten by the right hemisphere (Blonder et al. 1991; Borod 1993; Breitenstein et al. 1998; Ross et al. 1977; Haggard and Parkinson 1971; Carmon and Nachshon 1973; Wymer et al. 2002; Cutting 1997; Blakeslee 1980). The term 'phrase' is of interest because it can refer both to a musical unit, based on the breathing cycle and breath control in song, or to the abstract structure of a grammatical unit. It is indeed conceivable that the structurally more complex grammatical phrase of human language(s) evolved from some form of song used in early hominid communication. While grammatical structure is a predominantly left-hemisphere process, the right hemisphere is capable of fairly sophisticated semantics and basic syntax, if not inhibited by the left hemisphere (Querné et al. 2000; Hutner and Liederman 1991; Querné and Faure 1996; Landis and Regard 1998), and these are also not disembodied: indeed, even the deep structure of syntax is thought to be founded on the fixed sequences of limb movement in running creatures (Vowles 1970). Meaning is tightly interwoven with prosody, which is served by the right hemisphere; the left-hemisphere specialised linguistic areas are, moreover, homologues of right-hemisphere areas specialised in music and song (McGilchrist 2009, pp. 100–105; cf. also Hurford 2007, pp. 281–283, and 2012, pp. 19–97). Vocalisations are not only reactions to experience, but also communications of emotional responses, which ultimately become associated with *concepts* of emotions, as well as with objects and concepts of objects, by association (i.e. by metonymy, a frequent feature of linguistic meaning). What music does not do directly is encode referential and propositional meaning.

Darwin thought that music was the origin of human language, and the same view was held by thinkers such as Rousseau, Herder, Humboldt, and the linguist Otto Jespersen. Many contemporary anthropologists bring additional evidence to support the view that music was the primary mode of human expression, and that language as we now understand it emerged from music relatively late in human social evolution, between 80,000 and 40,000 years BC, possibly as a response to the need to communicate explicitly once societies grow beyond a certain point, and have instrumental needs that require referring to things, places, and people not present to the speakers (Milo and Quiatt 1993; Mithen 1996, 1998, 2005).

The musical aspects of language are particularly important in the second-person, 'I-Thou' relationship, though they become less important in the third-person, 'I-It' relationship. Incidentally, people with autism, who have difficulty with pronouns, and often refer to themselves, or to others in their presence, in the third person, show right-hemisphere deficits in perspective-taking (Mizuno et al. 2011). The same right-hemisphere areas are involved in normal subjects when taking different perspectives during, for example, hearing or reading a story (Whitney et al. 2009).

Music and song are of fundamental importance in human relationships and societies, in bonding at work, in recreation, and in worship. There is no known society in which music does not play a pivotal part and in which it is not also thought of as a medium through which one may contact the divine (Nettl 1983). Birds use song to attract mates, but it is only humans that can synchronise the rhythm, or blend the pitch, of their utterances with that of their fellows. Human music is not, like birdsong, individualistic in intention and competitive in nature (birdsong, like other instrumental utterances, is grounded in the left hemisphere, not, like human music, in the right; Nottebohm 1970). Everything about human music suggests that its nature is sharing, non-competitive. It is the means of group bonding: for good or ill, the communal 'we' is also emotionally bound up with song and performance. There is a continuity in form and function with early poetry in preliterate societies, which was usually accompanied by music, was socially performative, and helped establish and expand common mythologies and narratives, confirming meaning in the deep structures of life, and consolidating the common purpose of the group.

It is also possible to see some fundamental features of religion, in particular, ritual, which is essentially a group phenomenon, in this light. Intrinsic to ritual are both linguistic utterances and musical utterances, either combined or alternating, embodied in necessarily poetic language, employing narrative, metaphor, and a form of symbolism that is diminished in meaning by being made explicit. In religious music and language, there is implied an 'I-thou' relationship between the utterer and the divine 'Other', and at the same time an 'I-we' relationship between the utterer and the fellow-believers with whom the divine is worshipped. At the root of this, from a purely linguistic point of view, is the nature of metaphor.

2 THE RIGHT HEMISPHERE, METAPHOR, AND RELIGIOUS EXPERIENCE

One of the most significant differences between the approach of the two hemispheres to language is that it is the right hemisphere that is best able to understand metaphor (Foldi 1987; Bottini et al. 1994). There is, however, some confusion over what is meant by metaphor. There is metaphoric content to almost everything we say—language is essentially metaphoric in nature, at the simplest level. In an extensive literature which otherwise consistently confirms the right hemisphere's key role in understanding metaphor, there stand out for comment a handful of studies which have suggested that it is the left hemisphere that is principally involved in the appreciation of metaphor. I will deal with this in section 3 below: for now let me say that I shall argue that we can conclude for all intents and purposes that metaphor is clearly the domain of the right hemisphere.

Metaphor reveals, and indeed creates, connections: it relies on openness to the fruitfulness of ambiguity, and the recognition of knowledge which is not propositional in nature but based on relations between forms. In fact, all the aspects of language that are peculiarly important to poetry—not just metaphor, but implied meaning of every kind, irony, connections between ideas not normally approximated, the connotative power of symbols, the 'music' of language (the movement of verse, its ictus, metre, and rhyme)—are all preferentially mediated by the right hemisphere, as are certain kinds of religious language. By common consent over generations, it is poetry which enshrines our profoundest insights into reality, and even philosophers such as Wittgenstein and Heidegger came to believe that philosophical discourse needed ultimately to cede to poetry, as Schopenhauer believed it needed to cede to music. Propositional discourse is limited in its ability to approach ultimate reality. Its very terms take us back, as left hemisphere discourse always does, to the familiar. In Nietzsche's words, language makes the uncommon common.

Additionally, and as might be expected from all the above, the right hemisphere is better able than the left to understand the meaning of symbols with implicit, multiple meanings (for example, the rose), as opposed to explicit meaning, or the one-to-one mapping, of 'red' onto 'stop' as in the case of a traffic light (Gloning et al. 1968; Goldberg 1990). In other words, it understands the complex of connotations and how they work to enrich meaning, whether this is in words, or images, or in symbolic enactment, such as ritual of all kinds. The left hemisphere sees in such phenomena only a lack of precision: it sees obfuscation, or at worst, untruth. Hence the Enlightenment view expressed by Locke that metaphors were 'perfect cheats' (Locke 1690). The right hemisphere is also more able to understand narrative (Ornstein et al. 1979; Mills and Rollman 1980; Swisher and Hirsh 1972; Carmon and Nachshon 1971; Nicholls 1994; Brown and Nicholls 1997; Hough 1990; Schneiderman et al. 1992; Vogeley et al. 2001): the unaided left hemisphere tends to categorise similar episodes of a story together and get them out of sequence, because it does not follow the overall meaning, the way in which a human story unfolds (McNeill 1992).

What does this tell us when we return to the question of how we may avoid the complacent belief that we know all there is to know? Every indicator is that the right hemisphere both grounds our experience of the world, at the bottom end, so to speak, and makes sense of it, at the top end. Broad vigilant attention is primary: though focussed attention may appear to its owner to be under conscious control, in reality it is already spoken for, since we direct attention according to what we are aware of, and for that we need broad, right-hemisphere attention. Then there is the primacy of wholeness: the right hemisphere deals with the world before separation, division, and analysis have transformed it into something else, before the left hemisphere has re-presented it. It is not that the right hemisphere connects—because what it reveals was never separated; it does not synthesise what was never broken down into parts; it does not integrate what was never less than whole. The right hemisphere also delivers what is new: it has the primacy of experience. And we must confront the fact that the left hemisphere's most powerful tool, referential language, has its origins in the body and the right hemisphere—a sort of primacy of means. Equally the implicit comes before the explicit. The right hemisphere is more in touch with both affect and the unconscious will, and neurological evidence supports what is called the primacy of affect and the primacy of unconscious over conscious will. Most remarkable of all, some subtle work by David McNeill shows that thought originates in the right hemisphere and is only 'worked up' by the left hemisphere (McNeill 1992). For understanding, what is then produced by the left hemisphere needs to be returned to the whole context known only to the right.

The left hemisphere may add—and it adds enormously much—but a return is required to the world that is grounded by the right hemisphere. The left hemisphere's world is a virtual world, one where we are no longer patient recipients, but powerful operators. The values of clarity and fixity are added through the processing carried out by the left hemisphere, making it possible for us to control, manipulate, and use the world. To this end, attention is directed and focussed; the wholeness is broken into parts; the implicit is unpacked; language becomes the instrument of serial analysis, and things are categorised and become familiar. In addition, affect is set aside and superseded by cognitive abstraction; the conscious mind is brought to bear on the situation; thoughts are sent to the left hemisphere for expression in words, and the metaphors are temporarily lost or suspended, the world being re-presented in a static and hierarchically organised form. This re-presentation enables us to have knowledge, to bring the world into resolution, but it leaves what it knows denatured and decontextualised. For understanding rather than efficient manipulation, there needs to be a process of reintegration whereby we return to the experiential world again. The parts, once seen, are subsumed again in the whole, as the musician's painful, conscious, fragmentation of the piece in practice is lost in the (now improved) performance. The part that has been under the spotlight is seen as belonging to a broader picture; what had to be conscious for a while becomes unconscious again; what needs to be implicit once again retires; the represented entity becomes once more present, and 'lives'; and even language is given its ultimate meaning by the right hemisphere's pragmatics—the understanding of the contextual whole.

All the evidence is that the right hemisphere 'sees' more than the left hemisphere. Perhaps it is for this very reason that it is more aware of the limitations of its knowledge. In neuropsychological studies, the right hemisphere exhibits a more tentative and self-depreciating style, whereas the left hemisphere is confident about matters of which it is ignorant, and overestimates its capacities (Gazzaniga and LeDoux 1978; Cutting 1997; Rausch 1985; Brownell et al. 1986; Henson et al. 2000; Kimura 1963; Phelps and Gazzaniga 1992; Schnider et al. 1996; Nebes 1974; Drake and Bingham 1985). Moreover, the left hemisphere is better able to inhibit the right than the right hemisphere is able to inhibit the left (Kinsbourne 1993; Oliveri et al. 1999), and transmission is faster from right hemisphere to left than from left hemisphere to right (Marzi et al. 1991; Bisiacchi et al. 1994; Brown et al. 1994; Saron and Davidson 1989). It seems that the cognitive processes of the right hemisphere allow it to appreciate the importance of *what it does not know*, whereas those of the left hemisphere do not permit such insight. And indeed, insight into one's capabilities is largely dependent on the right frontal region (Adair et al. 2003; Bisiach et al. 1986; Feinberg et al. 1994; Meador et al. 2000; Starkstein et al. 1992; Stuss 1991). The upshot is that if we ignore what alone the right hemisphere is able to tell us, we will radically limit the range of experience open to us, and misconceive the nature of reality.

Whatever we may mean by the realm of the divine, any apprehension of it would be rendered improbably difficult by a cognitive-perceptual style the aim of which was to narrow things down to a certainty, and to 're-cognise' them as examples of something already familiar. More particularly, such a realm would be recalcitrant to thought processes that require explicitness and see truth as a property of a set of syllogisms that exhibit internal coherence. Many—perhaps all—aspects of the human world that give meaning to life present such difficulties. To take just one example, the experience of love in all its many kinds is such that, despite its supreme importance, it cannot be well conveyed in language, especially not in propositional language. Such experiences are part of our embodied life taken as a whole. They can be conveyed best by poetry, or drama, or ritual, or image, or narrative, or music—by means, in other words, that are implicit, embodied, and contextually rich. They are resonant rather than declarative. The inherent weakness of the analytic method applied to theological matters has been described as 'cognitive *hemianopia*' (Stump 2009). This nicely hints that only half the visual field, and therefore one hemisphere's view, is being taken into account. It is not that we are using the proper faculties for the task, though they are half-blind, but that we are using the wrong faculties altogether. Trying to approach the divine using the serial, analytic methods of the left hemisphere is like trying to discover whether the sun is shining by listening for the noise it makes.

At the centre of the problem is that although it may be convenient, for some purposes, to pretend that some things are inert, distinct, and atomistic, everything actually exists in a network of relationships with everything else. Some things, such as music, exist only in relationships and yet have the power to mean as much as anything in the world. Music consists entirely of relations, 'betweenness'. The notes mean nothing in themselves: the tensions between the notes, and between notes and the silence with which they live in reciprocal indebtedness, are everything. Melody, harmony, and rhythm each lie in the gaps, and yet the betweenness is only what it is because of the notes themselves. Actually the music is not *just* in the gaps any more than it is *just* in the notes: it is in the whole that the notes and the silence make together. Each note becomes transformed by the context in which it lies. What we mean by music is not just any agglomeration of notes, but one in which the whole that is created is powerful enough to make each note live in a new way, a way that it had never done prior to this creation. Similarly, poetry cannot be just any arrangement of words, but one in which each word is taken up into the new whole and made to live again in a new way, carrying us back to the world of experience, to life: poetry constitutes a 'speaking silence'. Music and poetic language are both part of the world that is delivered by the right hemisphere, the world characterised by betweenness. Perhaps it is not, after all, so wide of the mark to call the right hemisphere the 'silent' hemisphere: its utterances are implicit.

Similarly we know that, while Newtonian mechanics operates at a purely local level, the physical universe is not precise, but probabilistic, that particles separated by a universe may exhibit entanglement, and that the act of observation affects the observed. I mention this not to make what may seem far-fetched comparisons between physics and psychology, but to demonstrate that the precision, isolation, stasis, linearity, and predictability of the Newtonian universe is a rough and ready approximation, which works well enough for practical purposes but is not actually true to the nature of reality, even of physical reality. Against a space-time background, we model the world as simple two-body systems close to equilibrium, systems which are idealised and only imperfectly representative of the real world: a model that the left hemisphere constructs to enable us to manipulate the world. This representation is opposed to the right-hemispheric apprehension of a world that is living, constantly flowing and changing, radically interconnected within itself, and unpredictable—a world that is truer not only to what contemporary physics tells us, but to what attentive reflection on the nature of the experienced world would tell us, were we not conditioned to think of physical reality in terms derived from the mechanical model of the universe discredited over a century ago.

In sum, we will never achieve even the starting point for an understanding of the divine by approaching it with the tools of the left hemisphere. Such tools have evolved for purely practical purposes—those of using and manipulating the world expediently. Instead, I suggest we need to approach purported revelations or self-disclosures of the divine principally with the tools of the right hemisphere, the one whose purpose is to be on the lookout for what is not suspected by the left hemisphere, busily engaged as this hemisphere is in the local matter of getting and using. The right hemisphere has evolved to help us be aware of what is going on in the world as a whole, to understand the nature of things in the context of the whole, and to guide our relationship with them. This means that any proposed theology that is articulated simply in terms of a set of specific propositions drawn from a self-enclosed, abstract model of the world, prizing clarity and internal consistency above all else, risks betraying, distorting, and misrepresenting its subject matter. As the apophatic tradition suggests, such propositions will be inevitably untrue, and stand between us and a purer understanding. Insights from contemporary neuroscience confirm that images, metaphors, and narratives are indispensable to theological knowledge, not just poor substitutes or intermediate steps in its evolution.

3 METAPHOR AS A PRIMARILY RIGHT-HEMISPHERE PROCESS

Let me elaborate a little on my assertion that it is the right hemisphere that understands metaphor. This is seen by some as a controversial area where, though much of the evidence might point to the role of the right hemisphere, other evidence casts doubt. I would contend that in reality the evidence points clearly, indeed overwhelmingly, to the crucial role of the right hemisphere. Why, then, the controversy?

Three issues tend to confound the picture. The first is simply a failure to be clear about what one is examining. The second is a matter of methodology. And the third is epistemological: how we go about understanding metaphor—by breaking it up into parts, or by seeing it as itself part of a much bigger phenomenon? Let me take each in turn.

3.1 What counts as metaphor?

Importantly, all language is metaphoric in nature. Verbal language originates in metaphor, and is grounded in the body.[1] This is a point made at length by Lakoff and Johnson in *Metaphors We Live By* (1980) and *Philosophy in the Flesh* (1999), and by myself in *The Master and his Emissary* (2009), where I point out that even words like 'abstract', 'virtual', and 'immaterial' take one back—sometimes by a circuitous route, but none the less—to the physical, embodied reality of a thing being dragged away, to a man's strength, and to a lump of wood. However, the metaphors here are dead: there is no felt gap between the use we make of each such word in daily life and the anchor in embodied reality from which it derives its meaning. The word has lost 'depth', become one-dimensional; it no longer respects its metaphorical nature (metaphor, from Greek *meta*, beyond, and *pherein*, to carry, means something that 'carries one beyond' an implied gap).

Poetry depends on live metaphor to circumvent this deadening effect of everyday language: as Nietzsche put it, 'Compared with music all communication by words is shameless; words dilute and brutalise; words depersonalise; words make the uncommon common' (Nietzsche 1968). What differentiates a live metaphor from literality is that the metaphor forms a link, in which the meaning is implicit, between two elements that in some respect bear a likeness but are clearly different, and there is therefore a felt gap between what is being stated and what is intended. The meaning lies in the whole, including the gap—in what I call the 'betweenness'. Making the intention explicit causes its richness and emotional impact to collapse, much as explaining a joke makes it fall flat, or paraphrasing a poem reduces it to a series of banalities. It returns us from the 'presencing' of the world in language (right hemisphere) to its 're-presentation' in language (left hemisphere). We do not use metaphor to decorate, and therefore obscure, something best conveyed literally (although that would be how the left hemisphere sees it), but to bring to life a deeper and broader set of meanings than could be conveyed by literal language. However, removing the meaning from its context in the poem or the joke, making it explicit, destroys it.

Thus there is not just a distinction to be made, but a polar opposition, between a fresh metaphor that still works as a metaphor and a cliché which does not. A poem cannot be composed of clichés, nor can the idea behind a joke be stale, if it is still to be funny. Distinguishing between true metaphor and cliché is of paramount importance: according to my understanding of hemisphere difference, the live metaphor should be appreciated by the right hemisphere while the well-worn idea should be available to the unaided left hemisphere. This distinction has not always been carefully enough made when the brain correlates of metaphorical understanding have been investigated. Success in determining the localisation of metaphor comprehension depends on using highly familiar *versus* unfamiliar, or conventional *versus* unconventional, metaphors as discriminatory (Schmidt and Seger 2009). Researchers using only conventional metaphors have, as might be expected, found little evidence of right hemisphere involvement in metaphor processing (Rapp et al. 2004; Eviatar and Just 2006; Lee and Dapretto 2006; Stringaris et al. 2007; Giora et al. 2000; Rinaldi et al. 2004). When the metaphor is new or imaginatively demanding, the kind encountered in poetry rather than cliché, it is clearly the right hemisphere that is involved (Faust and Mashal 2007; Foldi et al. 1983; Kaplan et al. 1990). Thus poetic phrases, such as 'rain clouds are pregnant ghosts', are understood by the right hemisphere, while clichés, such as, 'babies are angels', are understood by the left hemisphere (Schmidt et al. 2007). Familiar expressions activate the left hemisphere, whereas unfamiliar ones activate the right hemisphere (Bottini et al. 1994; Eviatar and Just 2006; Mashal et al. 2005, 2007). However, it is not the novelty effect alone, but specifically the combination of novelty with metaphorical content, that involves the right hemisphere (Mashal and Faust 2008).

3.2 How does methodology cause problems of interpretation?

The point here relates to the well-known limits of scanning as an investigative tool. Its findings should always be interpreted in the light of evidence from other sources. This is for a number of reasons. Imaging just shows a few peaks, whilst much of interest goes on elsewhere; one cannot assume that the areas that 'light up' are those fundamentally responsible for the 'function' being imaged, or that areas that do not light up are not involved; one cannot even assume that whatever 'peaks' is of primary importance, since only effortful tasks tend to register—the more expert we are at something, the *less* we will see brain activity (for example, people with higher IQs have *lower* cerebral metabolic rates during mentally active conditions). Worse still, activations we visualise in the brain may actually be *inhibitory*, not facilitatory, in nature. Small differences in the way the task is presented may make a large difference to the results; changes in novelty or complexity can mask relevant structures or falsely identify irrelevant ones; the more complex the task, the more widely distributed the networks involved are likely to be, and the harder it will be to know what it is that one is measuring; male and female subjects respond differently; handedness, race, and age also make differences; individual cases may be different because the way we experience the world individually is different; even the same brain varies in its response to the same task depending on the context—for example, what's happened previously. The upshot is that many such studies lack statistical power.

Not only this, but if an area of activity in one hemisphere is limited in extent but persistent over the time period of a scan, whereas the activity in the other hemisphere, though more significant, covers a larger area (remember that complexity leads to wider activation), with the precise area of maximum activity constantly varying over time, the first will falsely appear much more strongly correlated with the activity than the second, especially when the results from numerous studies are aggregated in an attempt to locate the 'key' area (Jung-Beeman 2005; Giora et al. 2007).

This point is well made by one of the best meta-analyses of imaging studies on metaphor to date (Bohrn et al. 2012). Having noted the frequent reports of right-hemisphere involvement in many imaging studies, the authors tried to account for the lack of any one right-hemisphere area's standing out in their meta-analysis. They concluded that this could be explained by the activation patterns in the right hemisphere being more widespread, and exhibiting less overlap, than those in the left. Making this adjustment to their interpretation brought their findings 'in line', as they put it, with results from other types of study (see below).

3.3 How should we approach an understanding of metaphor?

A lot of effort has been, and continues to be, directed at disentangling what it is that the right hemisphere is contributing when we say it is good at understanding metaphor. Is it an affinity for novelty? For complexity? For understanding utterances in context? Or for seeing the connection between superficially unrelated entities?

This is a little like asking what explains the cat's success in catching mice: Is it its swiftness? Its agility? Its visual acuity? The sharpness of its claws? Its habit of going out hunting at night? And so on. This, it seems to me, is the typical left-hemisphere approach: if we can break it up into bits, we will finally understand it. My view is that this will lead to a somewhat unproductive argument.

By contrast, we could approach this from the other direction, namely, that many things are better understood by observing, not the 'parts', but the whole of which they are themselves part. I see metaphor as one aspect of a wholly different way of understanding the world, the way that from other evidence—from other areas than language—stands out as the right hemisphere's world.

Let us leave language aside for a moment. There is ample evidence that the right hemisphere is the one that is adapted to appreciate the new and the unfamiliar (e.g. Goldberg and Costa 1981); that it is better at frame-shifting (e.g. Rausch 1977; Goel and Vartanian 2005); that it is better able to deal with the overall meaning of a complex whole (e.g. Yoshida et al. 2007); that it understands everything in a context (e.g. Kinsbourne 1988); and that it sees, and is able to make, more remote connections than the left hemisphere (e.g. Posner 1995). All this outside of language. Equally, it is better at understanding embodied (by contrast with abstract) meaning, emotional meaning, and is more in touch with the body in general (see McGilchrist 2009, pp. 55–59, 66ff., for discussion). It is also better than the left hemisphere at understanding implicit meaning. This includes interpreting incomplete or partially degraded stimuli in any modality, reading faces (Strauss and Moscovitch 1981), tone of voice, gesture and body language, as well as music: all of this, as I say, outside of language.

Turning to language—what is a metaphor if it is not something implicit, whose meaning is embodied in a new image, has to be understood as a whole and in context, increases emotional impact, forges new links, and deals with a broad complexity of meaning, not a simple, narrow one? We would therefore expect the right hemisphere to be better at implicit meaning in language; to understand new and unfamiliar meanings in language; to understand the meaning of a complex utterance as a whole (pragmatics); to be sensitive to emotional language; to understand words as modified by their context; and more readily to make remote connections in language.

It would, then, be odd indeed if the right hemisphere were not better at understanding metaphor. But does the evidence support this conjecture? I would argue it does.

Lesion studies clearly demonstrate that individuals with right-hemisphere damage exhibit inappropriate literal thinking, for which reason they often find it hard to understand ordinary conversation (Foldi et al. 1983; Kaplan et al. 1990). When presented with a metaphorical phrase such as 'she gave him a hand', or 'she's got him eating out of her hand', patients with right hemisphere brain lesions, but not left-hemisphere lesions, tend to select a picture representing the literal rather than the figurative meaning (Mackenzie et al. 1997; Mackenzie et al. 1999; Rinaldi et al. 2004; Winner and Gardner 1977; Kempler et al. 1999). One patient with a resection of a large part of his right hemisphere, when asked, a few months after the operation, 'How do you feel?', replied, without a trace of irony or humour, 'With my hands' (Bell and Karnosh 1949).

This prompts me to comment on a further difference between lesion studies and scanning studies. In most cases of right-hemisphere lesions that compromise language, there will be some damage to the capacity for pragmatics and contextual understanding. Under these circumstances, it can be seen that the unaided left hemisphere simply does not understand implied meaning, however hackneyed and familiar the phrase, as in 'she gave him a hand'. However, in scanning studies in the intact brain one is examining something different: the *relative* activity demonstrated in the right hemisphere compared with the left. Since the right-hemisphere pragmatics are intact, and are always functioning, in purported 'metaphor' cases as well as in control cases, there is little need for input from specifically metaphor-related areas of the right hemisphere if the meaning is banal and familiar.

Visual field studies confirm a right hemisphere advantage for metaphor comprehension (Anaki et al. 1998a, 1998b; Faust and Weisper 2000; Faust and Mashal 2007; Schmidt et al. 2007; Mashal et al. 2008).

Event-related potential studies also confirm the key role of the right hemisphere (e.g. Proverbio et al. 2009; Sotillo et al. 2005; Pynte et al. 1996).

Transcranial magnetic stimulation (TMS) of the right, but not the left, dorsolateral prefrontal cortex, caused improvement in understanding of metaphors in patients with Parkinson's disease (Tremblay et al. 2016). TMS demonstrates the critical involvement of right, but not left, posterior temporal cortex, in the understanding of novel metaphors (Pobric et al. 2008). Papagno and colleagues (2002) used TMS to confirm the left-hemisphere advantage in understanding stock phrases.

Meta-analysis confirms this impression. An overview of more than 60 behavioural and scanning studies to date found a coherent pattern: the right hemisphere is better wherever there is non-obvious, non-literal meaning—including, of course, metaphors (Mashal et al. 2008).

So what is it about *scanning studies* on their own? First of all, let us get the issue in proportion: in accord with all this evidence, most scanning studies do, in fact, also confirm right-hemisphere involvement in metaphor comprehension (Mashal et al. 2007; Mashal et al. 2008; Mashal et al. 2009; Schmidt et al. 2007). In particular, they confirm the role of the *right temporal lobe* (Pobric et al. 2008; Mashal et al. 2005;

Mashal et al. 2007; Mashal et al. 2008; Bambini et al. 2011; Diaz et al. 2011; Bottini et al. 1994), the *right temporo-parietal junction* (Prat et al. 2012), the *right parietal region* (Cardillo et al. 2012), and the *right insula* (Schmidt and Seger 2009), as well as the *right medial frontal and prefrontal cortex* (Bottini et al. 1994; Mashal et al. 2007; Mashal et al. 2008; Lee and Dapretto 2006; Ahrens et al. 2007; Schmidt and Seger 2009; Stringaris et al. 2006). In other words, metaphor comprehension is *widely distributed* throughout the right hemisphere—a point the significance of which I have already referred to in two contexts: one, with regard to the problems of finding a single consistent area emerging in a meta-analysis of scanning studies as *the* area of the right hemisphere involved in metaphor comprehension; and two, the futility of trying to break down metaphor into ever smaller parts, and seeing metaphor as a specialised, highly local, linguistic function, rather than as a *whole way of understanding reality*, intrinsic to the way of being in the world mediated by the right hemisphere.

It is obvious that metaphor induces more emotional impact than literal language, hence its use in poetry; unsurprisingly, therefore, it excites more deep-lying areas of the limbic system involved in emotional activity, including the amygdala and anterior hippocampus (Citron and Goldberg 2014). And the right temporal region is essential for the integration of two seemingly unrelated concepts into a meaningful metaphoric expression (Pobric et al. 2008; Sotillo et al. 2005). Unfamiliarity requires longer working memory, a feature of the right hemisphere (Kirsner 1980), so that the phenomenon may be held in suspension without collapsing it into something familiar: right (but not left) middle and inferior frontal regions have been specifically related to such activity (Wager and Smith 2003).

Studies of every kind examining *indirect meaning* in language—certainly metaphor (Winner and Gardner 1977; Anaki et al. 1998a, 1998b; Brownell et al. 1990), but also humour, irony, and sarcasm (Gardner et al. 1975; Brownell et al. 1983; Bihrle et al. 1986; Shammi et al. 1999; Shamay-Tsoory et al. 2005; Bohrn et al. 2012)—consistently report activity in regions of the right hemisphere. Sarcasm illustrates the limited use of trying to fillet out which particular aspect makes it conducive to being mediated by the right hemisphere: 'the right frontal lobe mediates understanding of sarcasm by integrating affective processing with perspective-taking', suggest the authors of one paper (Shamay-Tsoory et al. 2005). Once again, perspective-taking (e.g. Baron-Cohen et al. 1994) and affective processing (e.g. Shamay-Tsoory 2003) are both independently known to be superior in the right hemisphere, but so are many other aspects (Wapner et al. 1981). There is here a whole way of looking at the world, not just a narrow linguistic function—the modus operandi of the right hemisphere as a whole, not just a language module somewhere tucked away in the right hemisphere.

Despite all this, a small number of scanning studies still do not show a connection between the right hemisphere and metaphor. Why not?

Every study that I am aware of in which there has been a failure to find right-hemisphere recruitment during metaphor comprehension was *both* a scanning study *and* employed only familiar or conventional metaphors, which cannot be expected to recruit the right hemisphere (Rapp et al. 2004; Rapp et al. 2007; Lee and Dapretto 2006).

Thus, according to the authors of one such paper, 'the metaphors in our study were very simple statements, so-called predicate metaphors (e.g. "the alarm clock is a torturer")' (Rapp et al. 2004). Reference to 'torture' is an overused way of expressing displeasure—'it was torture having to drag myself out of bed this morning'. Bottini and colleagues (Bottini et al. 1994), who found a right-hemisphere pre-eminence, used phrases that still required the bringing together of two distinct ideas, e.g. 'the policeman who didn't give straight answers was jumping ditches'. Lee and Dapretto, who found no such right hemisphere pre-eminence in metaphor, used single word sequences to exhibit the so-called 'figurative' meaning of, for example, the word 'quick' ('slow—quick—fast' *versus* 'slow—quick—smart'), or 'cold' meaning unfriendly, examples which have little or no metaphoric status, lack context, and are banal (Lee and Dapretto 2006). The study of Stringaris and colleagues (2007) was similarly unlikely to test true metaphorical understanding: indeed, the paradigm 'metaphor' they report using—'some surgeons are butchers'—is hardly a metaphor at all (Stringaris et al. 2007). While such examples probably do involve some low-level right-hemisphere processing, there is no 'spike' in use, because the brain does not register anything to be 'worked out'—it's not experienced as different from saying 'some surgeons are brutal [or insensitive, or clumsy]'.

As predicted from knowledge of the left hemisphere's affinity for what is explicit and familiar, clichéd non-literal expressions should be (and are) dealt with in the left hemisphere. However, fascinatingly, in such cases it would be seeing the *literal*—not the *metaphorical*—meaning of the hackneyed phrase that refreshes it and makes it new. That is what now requires insight, a bit like seeing a joke (the comedian Milton Jones makes a career out of such insights: 'When my dad was ill, we rubbed his back with lard: after that he went downhill very quickly'). In such cases the literal meaning ('went downhill') becomes the non-salient (unfamiliar, because non-clichéd) meaning, which accordingly should get to be processed in the right hemisphere. And the evidence confirms exactly this (Mashal et al. 2008). But it still remains true that when the metaphor is of the kind encountered in poetry, rather than cliché, it is clearly the right hemisphere that is involved (Faust and Mashal 2007; Mashal et al. 2005; Schmidt et al. 2007).

The right hemisphere is more sensitive to discriminating unfamiliar *meaningful* from unfamiliar *meaningless* expressions than the left hemisphere (Mashal and Faust 2008). In fact, lexical semantics is crucial for the right-hemisphere involvement in metaphor processing (Argyriou et al. 2015; Forgács et al. 2014): how do we know if we are dealing with metaphorical meaning if there is no meaning to the phrase? The right hemisphere is involved in making sense of an utterance as a whole. Thus the right hemisphere is recruited when we have to generate, rather than just read, the last word of a sentence—when we have to understand meaning (Kircher et al. 2001). Again, when the words are unclear, partial, or degraded, so that they can be understood only in context, the right hemisphere is of critical importance (Sharp et al. 2004). And when the left hemisphere makes a mistake in contextual understanding, the interpretation is taken over by the right hemisphere (Rissman et al. 2003). In general, the right hemisphere becomes more involved as complexity of contextual understanding increases (Xu et al. 2005); indeed the harder it is, in general, to interpret a sentence, the more the right-hemisphere homologues of left-hemisphere language areas are recruited (Just et al. 1996). By contrast, the left hemisphere positively *disengages* when the meaning is metaphorical or unfamiliar (Cardillo et al. 2012; Lai et al. 2015). Here, as elsewhere, the hemispheres have a relationship of reciprocal inhibition, which it is part of the function of the corpus callosum to maintain.

In effect, the right hemisphere becomes crucially involved whenever the question involves meaning that is not revealed by simply following the rules: where the expression is unfamiliar, involves making new connections, requires understanding an utterance as a whole, in context, including tone, irony, humour, sarcasm, facial expression, and bodily posture—whenever the meaning does not, so to speak, come 'off the shelf'. This is demonstrated beyond doubt by lesion studies, and indeed every kind of non-scanning study.

In summary, it is worth bearing in mind two central points. First, the right hemisphere is always active *in people with normal brain functioning*—including contextual understanding, pragmatics, and retrieval of implicit meaning. No *excess* right-hemisphere activation is seen on scanning when the normal brain is presented with hackneyed phrases, whereas it is when the metaphoric content is 'active'. Second, when there is *brain damage* affecting the right-hemisphere's contribution to language comprehension, it is likely that all right-hemisphere language 'functions' will be affected, including what it contributes to understanding metaphor (because it understands meaning in context, overall meaning, and implicit meaning). Thus when the right hemisphere cannot be called on at all, meaning reverts to being literal.

4 RELIGIOUS EXPERIENCE AND THE BRAIN

A consensus is emerging from the literature that religious experience tends to be associated with the right hemisphere. This conclusion is supported by a book-length study of spirituality and the brain (Trimble 2007), by the comprehensive review of Devinsky and Lai (2008), and by McNamara (2009; cf. also McNamara and Giordano, chapter 5 of the present volume). McNamara largely implicates right fronto-temporal networks, a view supported by Trimble and Freeman (2006) and by Devinsky and Lai (2008), the latter of whom distinguish what they call the 'religion of the everyday man', with its characteristic ongoing belief pattern and set of convictions, predominantly localised to the frontal region, from ecstatic religious experience, more localised to the temporal region, both in the right hemisphere.

As this suggests, much depends on what is meant by religion. In some studies, what is measured is essentially a pathological hyper-religiosity; in others, an openness to ritual; in others, the holding of certain beliefs or practices; in others, experiences of a 'paranormal' kind. As if to demonstrate difficulties with generalisation, in one study the right hemisphere appeared foundational for aesthetic religious experience, while the left hemisphere was associated with ritual religious experience

(Butler et al. 2011), a distinction that, however it may work in the laboratory, falls short of the complexity of real-life experience: meanwhile, other studies have linked types of meditation in which self/other boundaries are blurred with *decreased* activity in the right inferior parietal lobule, an area known to be critical to the sense of the self (Johnstone and Glass 2008).

As regards ritual, I suspect that the hemisphere engaged depends on the degree to which it involves embodied symbolic actions and poetic language, both of which rely on known right-hemisphere 'functionality'. There is a tendency for Protestantism to eschew these aspects of worship, and its ritual is less likely to engage the right hemisphere (though the Anglican Book of Common Prayer—not, in any case, a truly Protestant creation—is rich in poetry) than, say, that of the traditional Roman Catholic or Eastern Orthodox churches. Outside of ritual, the language of mystics and religious poets depends heavily on those aspects of language subserved by the right hemisphere to evoke meaning that lies beyond normal experience.

Finally, some thoughts on the nature of religious belief may not be out of place. The word 'belief' has an interesting history, which tells us much about ourselves.

Nowadays belief is often viewed as simply a weaker form of knowing, as in 'I believe (but am not certain that) the train leaves at 6.13'. But this has not always been the case. The word 'belief' has nowhere buried in it the idea of signing up to a proposition, certain or uncertain. It is not a matter of cognition, but of recognition. It comes from the same Germanic root as the word 'love', a sense preserved in the now archaic word 'lief' with which one once described one's friend, sweetheart, or lord—someone in whom one believed.

Similar considerations apply to the German *glauben* (related to *lieben*, 'to love'), and to the French *croire* and other derivatives of Latin *credere*, a word which meant originally to 'entrust to the care of' (the sense lingers, in reduced fashion, in the idea of 'credit'). The word *credo* has indeed been traced to an origin in the expression *cor do*, 'I give my heart'. Belief is about a relationship, in which by definition, more than one party is involved. The believer needs to be disposed to love, but the believed-in needs to inspire another's belief. Whether this amounts to being worthy of that belief cannot be fully determined in advance. It emerges through commitment and experience. This transformative and reverberative relationship is what I have termed 'betweenness' (McGilchrist 2009).

Does belief historically, then, have nothing to do with truth? Indeed it does, but the word 'true' brings us straight back, not to a thing, but to a relationship. 'True' (cf. German *treu*, 'faithful') is related to 'trust', and is fundamentally a matter of what one trusts or believes. The Latin word *verum* (true) is cognate with a Sanskrit word meaning to choose or believe: like one's loved one, the one in whom one chooses to believe and place one's trust, to whom one is true. We still speak of two surfaces that 'marry' well as being 'true'. It is about fit—and fidelity. Etymology maps the slippage of thought. What it shows in this case is three revealing shifts.

First, the words 'truth' and 'belief' used to describe a reverberative or two-directional relationship, in which each party is 're-sponsible' for the fit. Truth and belief are no longer relational, but have become propositional. The causation is no longer distributed, but linear.

Second, it suggests that truth and belief used to be embodied actions or processes, involving commitment, not (as they are now conceived) detached, disembodied 'things'. Yet an understanding that enables evaluation of truth or belief cannot be achieved by simply sitting back and waiting passively for information to accumulate, since some truths become understandable only when we have made a move to meet them. They are incremental and come with experience.

Third, as processes, truth and belief derived their value from the context, could never be absolute, and were never single or static. The idea of truth as independent of us, immutable and certain, is a relatively recent invention.

Faith and belief are not optional. A true scientist can be certain of nothing. Science demonstrates no truths, but identifies only what is *not* true according to (an always provisional) paradigm. The most ardent atheist could not get out of bed in the morning without trust. In science, as in the rest of life, faith and belief depend ultimately on induction, namely, experience-guided, moulded, and interpreted by our beliefs, by the questions we ask or don't ask, what our assumptions allow us to see or prevent us from seeing. Logic is of vital importance along the way, but science is ultimately a form of pattern recognition.

Pattern *re*-cognition: one compares with a pattern *already seen*. Indeed, all understanding is of this nature. What we mean when we say we understand something is that it is like something else, of which we are already prepared to say 'I understand this'. Thus the can is kicked down the road, a road that, however, has no certain beginning or end.

When we say we believe, therefore, we are talking about what is more a disposition than a proposition. Belief is not the antithesis, but the complement, of reason; not the opposite of knowledge, but its inevitable basis. Our reasoning is bound up with the beliefs we are disposed to bring to it as much as beliefs are bound up with reasoning, in ways that cannot, in principle, be disentangled. Beliefs tend to actions and are embodied, not purely cognitive. They are not things, but relationships that leave the believer and the believed-in forever changed.

5 CONCLUSION

Understanding hemisphere differences helps to illuminate a number of aspects of language as it approaches the divine, especially metaphor, which we intuit as having depth of meaning but may otherwise find difficult to articulate in the face of the common assumption that truth is always clear and explicit. (Indeed, truth is probably never so.) It helps us understand why narrative, ritual, and symbolism are intrinsic to meaning in this area—as well as others where we feel ourselves to encounter ultimate meaning: in our relations with the natural world, in love, in appreciating life, and coming to terms with death. It helps us to avoid seeing belief as merely propositional, or indeed the divine as being, a proper realm for propositional thinking and language at all. The individual and society, mind and body, intellect and emotion, and ultimately our human selves and the realm of the sacred 'Other' beyond, are brought together in the music and richly poetic language of myth, ritual, and acts of worship, as well as in the writings of the great mystics of all traditions, where language will simply remain incomprehensible to the sort of mind that knows only how to adopt a literal approach.

NOTE

1. See the philosopher Jean Paul (Richter): 'metaphor . . . was the first word in spoken language, and only after losing its original colour could it become a literal sign' (Quoted in Biese 1893, p. 12).

REFERENCES

Aboitiz, F., A. B. Scheibel, and E. Zaidel (1992). Morphometry of the Sylvian fissure and the corpus callosum, with emphasis on sex differences. *Brain* 115(5), 1521–1541.

Adair, J. C., R. L. Schwartz, and A. M. Barrett (2003). Anosognosia. In K. M. Heilman and E. Valenstein (eds.), *Clinical Neuropsychology* (Fourth edition), pp. 185–214. Oxford: Oxford University Press,

Ahrens, K., H. L. Liu, C. Y. Lee, S. P. Gong, S. Y. Fang, and Y. Y. Hsu (2007). Functional MRI of conventional and anomalous metaphors in Mandarin Chinese. *Brain and Language* 100, 163–171.

Alexander, M. P., D. F. Benson, and D. T. Stuss (1989). Frontal lobes and language. *Brain and Language* 37(4), 656–691.

Allison, T., A. Puce, and G. McCarthy (2000). Social perception from visual cues: Role of the STS region. *Trends in Cognitive Sciences* 4(7), 267–278.

Anaki, D., M. Faust, and S. Kravetz (1998a). Cerebral hemisphere asymmetries in processing lexical metaphors (1). *Neuropsychologia* 36(4), 353–362.

Anaki, D., M. Faust, and S. Kravetz (1998b). Cerebral hemisphere asymmetries in processing lexical metaphors (2). *Neuropsychologia* 36(7), 691–700.

Andrew, R. J. and L. J. Rogers (2002). The nature of lateralisation in tetrapods. In R. J. Andrew and L. J. Rogers (eds.), *Comparative Vertebrate Lateralisation,* pp. 94–125. Cambridge: Cambridge University Press.

Argyriou, P., S. Byfield, and S. Kita (2015). Semantics is crucial for the right-hemisphere involvement in metaphor processing: Evidence from mouth asymmetry during speaking. *Laterality* 20(2), 191–210.

Bambini, V., C. Gentili, E. Ricciardi, P. M. Bertinetto, and P. Pietrini (2011). Decomposing metaphor processing at the cognitive and neural level through functional magnetic resonance imaging. *Brain Research Bulletin* 86(3–4), 203–216.

Banich, M. T. (2003). Interaction between the hemispheres and its implications for the processing capacity of the brain. In K. Hugdahl and R. J. Davidson (eds.), *The Asymmetrical Brain*, pp. 261–302. Cambridge, MA: MIT Press.

Baron-Cohen, S., H. Ring, J. Moriarty, B. Schmitz, D. Costa, and P. Ell (1994). Recognition of mental state terms: Clinical findings in children with autism and a functional neuroimaging study of normal adults. *British Journal of Psychiatry* 165(5), 640–649.

Bell, E. and L. J. Karnosh (1949). Cerebral hemispherectomy: Report of a case 10 years after operation. *Journal of Neurosurgery* 6(4), 285–293.

Bender, M. B., M. Feldman, and A. J. Sobin (1968). Palinopsia. *Brain* 9(2), 321–338.

Biese, A. (1893). *Die Philosophie des Metaphorischen*. Hamburg and Leipzig: Leopold Voss.

Bihrle, A. M., H. H. Brownell, and J. J. Powelson (1986). Comprehension of humorous and nonhumorous materials by left and right brain-damaged patients. *Brain and Cognition* 5(4), 399–411.

Bisazza, A., C. Cantalupo, M. Capocchiano, and G. Vallortigara (2000). Population lateralisation and social behaviour: A study with sixteen species of fish. *Laterality* 5(3), 269–284.

Bisiacchi, P., C. A. Marzi, and R. Nicoletti (1994). Left-right asymmetry of callosal transfer in normal human subjects. *Behavioural Brain Research* 64(1–2), 173–178.

Bisiach, E., G. Vallar, D. Perani, C. Papagno, and A. Berti (1986). Unawareness of disease following lesions of the right hemisphere: Anosognosia for hemiplegia and anosognosia for hemianopia. *Neuropsychologia* 24(4), 471–482.

Blakeslee, T. R. (1980). *The Right Brain*. London: Macmillan.

Blonder, L. X., D. Bowers, and K. M. Heilman (1991). The role of the right hemisphere in emotional communication. *Brain* 114(3), 1115–1127.

Bohrn, I. C., U. Altmann, and A. M. Jacobs (2012). Looking at the brains behind figurative language—a quantitative meta-analysis of neuroimaging studies on metaphor, idiom, and irony processing. *Neuropsychologia* 50(11), 2669–2683.

Bornstein, B. and D. P. Kidron (1959). Prosopagnosia. *Journal of Neurology, Neurosurgery and Psychiatry* 22(2), 124–131.

Bornstein, B., H. Sroka, and H. Munitz (1969). Prosopagnosia with animal face agnosia. *Cortex* 5(2), 164–169.

Borod, J. C. (1993). Cerebral mechanisms underlying facial, prosodic, and lexical emotional expression: A review of neuropsychological studies and methodological issues. *Neuropsychology* 7, 445–463.

Bottini, G., R. Corcoran, R. Sterzi, E. Paulesu, P. Schenone, P. Scarpa, R. S. Frackowiak, and C. D. Frith (1994). The role of the right hemisphere in the interpretation of figurative aspects of language: A positron emission tomography activation study. *Brain* 117(6), 1241–1253.

Bourgeois, M. J., S. Christman, and I. A. Horowitz (1998). The role of hemispheric activation in person perception: Evidence for an attentional focus model. *Brain and Cognition* 38(2), 202–219.

Breitenstein, C., I. Daum, and H. Ackermann (1998). Emotional processing following cortical and subcortical brain damage: Contribution of the fronto-striatal circuitry. *Behavioral Neurology* 11(1), 29–42.

Brown, H. D. and S. M. Kosslyn (1993). Cerebral lateralisation. *Current Opinion in Neurobiology* 3(2), 183–186.

Brown, S. and M. E. Nicholls (1997). Hemispheric asymmetries for the temporal resolution of brief auditory stimuli. *Perception and Psychophysics* 59(3), 442–447.

Brown, W. S., E. B. Larson, and M. Jeeves (1994). Directional asymmetries in interhemispheric transmission time: Evidence from visual evoked potentials. *Neuropsychologia* 32(4), 439–448.

Brownell, H. H., H. H. Potter, A. M. Bihrle, and H. Gardner (1986). Inference deficits in right brain-damaged patients. *Brain and Language* 27(2), 310–321.

Brownell, H. H., D. Michel, J. Powelson, and H. Gardner (1983). Surprise but not coherence: Sensitivity to verbal humor in right-hemisphere patients. *Brain and Language* 18(1), 20–27.

Brownell, H. H, T. L. Simpson, A. M. Bihrle, H. H. Potter, and H. Gardner (1990). Appreciation of metaphoric alternative word meanings by left and right brain-damaged patients. *Neuropsychologia* 28(4), 375–383.

Bugnyar, T., M. Stöwe, and B. Heinrich (2004). Ravens, *Corvus corax*, follow gaze direction of humans around obstacles. *Proceedings of the Royal Society of London, Series B–Biological Sciences* 271(1546), 1331–1336.

Butler, P. M., P. McNamara, and R. Durso (2011). Side of onset in Parkinson's disease and alterations in religiosity: Novel behavioral phenotypes. *Behavioural Neurology* 24(2), 133–141.

Cardillo, E. R., C. E. Watson, G. L. Schmidt, A. Kranjec, and A. Chatterjee (2012). From novel to familiar: Tuning the brain for metaphors. *Neuroimage* 59(4), 3212–3221.

Carmon, A. and I. Nachshon (1971). Effects of unilateral brain damage on the perception of temporal order. *Cortex* 7(4), 411–418.

Carmon, A. and I. Nachshon (1973). Ear asymmetry in perception of emotional nonverbal stimuli. *Acta Psychologica* 37(6), 351–357.

Chiarello, C. and L. Maxfield (1996). Varieties of interhemispheric inhibition, or how to keep a good hemisphere down. *Brain and Cognition* 30(1), 81–108.

Citron, F. M. and A. E. Goldberg (2014). Metaphorical sentences are more emotionally engaging than their literal counterparts. *Journal of Cognitive Neuroscience* 26(11), 2585–2595.

Conti, F. and T. Manzoni (1994). The neurotransmitters and postsynaptic actions of callosally projecting neurons. *Behavioural Brain Research* 64(1–2), 37–53.

Cook, N. D. (1984). Homotopic callosal inhibition. *Brain and Language* 23(1), 116–125.

Corballis, M. C. (1996). Hemispheric interactions in temporal judgments about spatially separated stimuli. *Neuropsychology* 10(1), 42–50.

Corballis, M. C. (1998). Sperry and the age of Aquarius: Science, values and the split brain. *Neuropsychologia* 36(10), 1083–1087.

Corballis, M. C., L. Boyd, A. Schulze, and B. J. Rutherford (1998). Role of the commissures in interhemispheric temporal judgments. *Neuropsychology* 12(4), 519–525.

Crow, T. J., L. R. Crow, D. J. Done, and S. Leask (1998). Relative hand skill predicts academic ability: Global deficits at the point of hemispheric indecision. *Neuropsychologia* 36(12), 1275–1282.

Csermely, D. (2004). Lateralisation in birds of prey: Adaptive and phylogenetic considerations. *Behavioural Processes* 67(3), 511–520.

Cummings, J. L. (1997). Neuropsychiatric manifestations of right hemisphere lesions. *Brain and Language* 57(1), 22–37.

Cutting, J. (1997). *Principles of Psychopathology*. Oxford: Oxford University Press.

Damasio, H., T. J. Grabowski, D. Tranel, R. D. Hichwa, and A. R. Damasio (1996). A neural basis for lexical retrieval. *Nature* 380(6574), 499–505. Erratum appears in *Nature* 381(6595), 810.

Denenberg, V. H., J. Garbanati, D. A. Sherman, D. A. Yutzey, and R. Kaplan (1978). Infantile stimulation induces brain lateralization in rats. *Science* 201(4361), 1150–1152.

Devinsky, O. and G. Lai (2008). Spirituality and religion in epilepsy. *Epilepsy and Behavior* 12, 636–643.

Dharmaretnam, M. and R. J. Andrew (1994). Age- and stimulus-specific use of right and left eye by the domestic chick. *Animal Behavior* 48, 1395–1406.

Dharmaretnam, M. and L. J. Rogers (2005). Hemispheric specialization and dual processing in strongly versus weakly lateralized chicks. *Behavioural Brain Research* 162(1), 62–70.

Diaz, M. T., K. T. Barrett, and L. J. Hogstrom (2011). The influence of sentence novelty and figurativeness on brain activity. *Neuropsychologia* 49, 320–330.

Dijksterhuis, A., H. Aarts, J. A. Bargh, and A. van Knippenberg (2000). On the relation between associative strength and automatic behavior. *Journal of Experimental Social Psychology* 36, 531–544.

Drake, R. A. and B.R. Bingham (1985). Induced lateral orientation and persuasibility. *Brain and Cognition* 4(2), 156–164.

Evans, C. S., L. Evans, and P. Marler (1993). On the meaning of alarm calls: Functional reference in an avian vocal system. *Animal Behavior* 46, 23–28.

Evert, D. L. and M. Kmen (2003). Hemispheric asymmetries for global and local processing as a function of stimulus exposure duration. *Brain and Cognition* 51(1), 115–142.

Eviatar, Z. and M. A. Just (2006). Brain correlates of discourse processing: An fMRI investigation of irony and conventional metaphor comprehension. *Neuropsychologia* 44(12), 2348–2359.

Fabre-Thorpe, M., J. Fagot, E. Lorincz, F. Levesque, and J. Vauclair (1993). Laterality in cats: Paw preference and performance in a visuomotor activity. *Cortex* 29(1), 15–24.

Faust, M. and N. Mashal (2007). The role of the right cerebral hemisphere in processing novel metaphoric expressions taken from poetry: A divided visual field study. *Neuropsychologia* 45(4), 860–870.

Faust, M. and S. Weisper (2000). Understanding metaphoric sentences in the two cerebral hemispheres. *Brain and Cognition* 43(1–3), 186–191.

Federmeier, K. D. and M. Kutas (1999). Right words and left words: Electrophysiological evidence for hemispheric differences in meaning processing. *Cognitive Brain Research* 8(3), 373–392.

Feinberg, T. E., D. M. Roane, P. C. Kwan, R. J. Schindler, and L. D. Haber (1994). Anosognosia and visuoverbal confabulation. *Archives of Neurology* 51(5), 468–473.

Fernández-Carriba, S., A. Loeches, A. Morcillo, and W. D. Hopkins (2002). Asymmetry in facial expression of emotions by chimpanzees. *Neuropsychologia* 40(9), 1523–1533.

Fink, G. R., J. C. Marshall, P. W. Halligan, and R. J. Dolan (1999). Hemispheric asymmetries in global/local processing are modulated by perceptual salience. *Neuropsychologia* 37(1), 31–40.

Foldi, N. S. (1987). Appreciation of pragmatic interpretations of indirect commands: Comparison of right and left hemisphere brain-damaged patients. *Brain and Language* 31(1), 88–108.

Foldi, N. S., M. Cicone, and H. Gardner (1983). Pragmatic aspects of communication in brain-damaged patients. In S. J. Segalowitz (ed.), *Language Functions and Brain Organisation*, pp. 51–86. New York: Academic Press.

Forgács, B., A. Lukács, and C. Pléh (2014). Lateralized processing of novel metaphors: Disentangling figurativeness and novelty. *Neuropsychologia* 56, 101–109.

Gainotti, G. (2002). The relationships between anatomical and cognitive locus of lesion in category-specific disorders. In E. M. E. Forde and G. W. Humphreys (eds.), *Category Specificity in Brain and Mind*, pp. 403–426. Hove, UK: Psychology Press.

Gardner, H. (1974). *The Shattered Mind*. New York: Knopf.

Gardner H., P. K. Ling, L. Flamm, and J. Silverman (1975). Comprehension and appreciation of humorous material following brain damage. *Brain* 98(3), 399–412.

Gazzaniga, M. S. and J. E. LeDoux (1978). *The Integrated Mind*. New York: Plenum Press.

Giora, R., O. Fein, D. Laadan, J. Wolfson, M. Zeituny, R. Kidron, R. Kaufman, and R. Shaham (2007). Expecting irony: Context versus salience-based effects. *Metaphor and Symbol* 22(2), 119–146.

Giora R, E. Zaidel, N. Soroker, G. Batori, and A. Kasher (2000). Differential effects of right- and left-hemisphere damage on understanding sarcasm and metaphor. *Metaphor and Symbol* 15(1–2), 63–83.

Gloning, I., K. Gloning, and H. Hoff (1968). *Neuropsychological Symptoms and Syndromes in Lesions of the Occipital Lobe and the Adjacent Areas*. Paris: Gauthier-Villars.

Goel, V. and O. Vartanian (2005). Dissociating the roles of right ventral lateral and dorsal lateral prefrontal cortex in generation and maintenance of hypotheses in set-shift problems. *Cerebral Cortex* 15(8), 1170–1177.

Goldberg, E. (1990). Associative agnosias and the functions of the left hemisphere. *Journal of Clinical and Experimental Neuropsychology* 12(4), 467–484.

Goldberg, E. and L. D. Costa (1981). Hemispheric differences in the acquisition and use of descriptive systems. *Brain and Language* 14(1), 144–173.

Grossman, M. (1988). Drawing deficits in brain-damaged patients' freehand pictures. *Brain and Cognition* 8(2), 189–205.

Güntürkün, O., B. Diekamp, M. Manns, F. Nottelmann, H. Prior, A. Schwarz, and M. Skiba (2000). Asymmetry pays: Visual lateralization improves discrimination success in pigeons. *Current Biology* 10(17), 1079–1081.

Haggard, M. P. and A. M. Parkinson (1971). Stimulus and task factors as determinants of ear advantages. *Quarterly Journal of Experimental Psychology* 23(2), 168–177.

Halpern, M. E., O. Güntürkün, W. D. Hopkins, and L. J. Rogers (2005). Lateralization of the vertebrate brain: Taking the side of model systems. *Journal of Neuroscience* 25(45), 10351–10357.

Hécaen, H. and M. L. Albert (1978). *Human Neuropsychology*. New York: Wiley.

Heilman, K. M., R. Scholes, and R. T. Watson (1975). Auditory affective agnosia: Disturbed comprehension of affective speech. *Journal of Neurology, Neurosurgery and Psychiatry* 38(1), 69–72.

Henson, R. N. A., M. D. Rugg, T. Shallice, and R. J. Dolan (2000). Confidence in recognition memory for words: Dissociating right prefrontal roles in episodic retrieval. *Journal of Cognitive Neuroscience* 12(6), 913–923.

Hoffman, A. M., P. E. Robakiewicz, E. M. Tuttle, and L. J. Rogers (2006). Behavioural lateralisation in the Australian magpie (*Gymnorhina tibicen*). *Laterality* 11(2), 110–121.

Hopkins, W. D. and L. Marino (2000). Asymmetries in cerebral width in nonhuman primate brains as revealed by magnetic resonance imaging (MRI). *Neuropsychologia* 38(4), 493–499.

Höppner, J., E. Kunesch E., J. Buchmann, A. Hess, A. Grossmann, and R. Benecke (1999). Demyelination and axonal degeneration in corpus callosum assessed by analysis of transcallosally mediated inhibition in multiple sclerosis. *Clinical Neurophysiology* 110(4), 748–756.

Hoptman, M. J. and R. J. Davidson (1994). How and why do the two cerebral hemispheres interact? *Psychological Bulletin* 116(2), 195–219.

Hough, M. S. (1990). Narrative comprehension in adults with right and left hemisphere brain-damage: Theme organization. *Brain and Language* 38(2), 253–277.

Hurford, J. R. (2007). *Language in the Light of Evolution I. The Origins of Meaning*. Oxford: Oxford University Press.

Hurford, J. R. (2012). *Language in the Light of Evolution II. The Origins of Grammar*. Oxford: Oxford University Press.

Hutner, N. and J. Liederman (1991). Right hemisphere participation in reading. *Brain and Language* 41(4), 475–495.

Ivry, R. B. and L. C. Robertson (1998). *The Two Sides of Perception*. Cambridge, MA: MIT Press.

Jäncke, L. and H. Steinmetz (2003). Anatomical brain asymmetries and their relevance for functional asymmetries. In K. Hugdahl and R. J. Davidson (eds.), *The Asymmetrical Brain*, pp. 187–230. Cambridge, MA: MIT Press.

Johnstone, B. and B. A. Glass (2008). Support for a neuropsychological model of spirituality in persons with traumatic brain injury. *Zygon* 43(4), 861–874.

Jung-Beeman, M. (2005). Bilateral brain processes for comprehending natural language. *Trends in Cognitive Sciences* 9(11), 512–518.

Just, M. A., P. A. Carpenter, T. A. Keller, W. F. Eddy, and K. R. Thulborn (1996). Brain activation modulated by sentence comprehension. *Science* 274(5284), 114–116.

Kaplan, J. A., H. H. Brownell, J. R. Jacobs, and H. Gardner (1990). The effects of right hemisphere damage on the pragmatic interpretation of conversational remarks. *Brain and Language* 38(2), 315–333.

Kempler, D., D. VanLancker, V. Marchman, and E. Bates (1999). Idiom comprehension in children and adults with unilateral brain damage. *Developmental Neuropsychology* 15(3), 327–349.

Kimura, D. (1963). Right temporal-lobe damage: Perception of unfamiliar stimuli after damage. *Archives of Neurology* 8, 264–271.

Kinsbourne, M. (1988). Hemispheric interactions in depression. In M. Kinsbourne (ed.), *Cerebral Hemisphere Function in Depression*, pp. 133–162. Washington, DC: American Psychiatric Press.

Kinsbourne, M. (1993). Orientational bias model of unilateral neglect: Evidence from attentional gradients within hemispace. In I. H. Robertson and J. C. Marshall (eds.), *Unilateral Neglect: Clinical and Experimental Studies*, pp. 63–86. Hove, UK: Lawrence Erlbaum.

Kircher, T. T., M. Brammer, N. Tous Andreu, S. C. Williams, and P. K. Mcguire (2001). Engagement of right temporal cortex during processing of linguistic context. *Neuropsychologia* 39(8), 798–809.

Kirsner, K. (1980). Hemisphere-specific processes in letter-matching. *Journal of Experimental Psychology: Human Perception and Performance* 6(1), 167–179.

Kitterle, F. L., S. Christman, and J. B. Hellige (1990). Hemispheric differences are found in the identification, but not the detection, of low versus high spatial frequencies. *Perception and Psychophysics* 48(4), 297–306.

Kosslyn, S. M. (1987). Seeing and imagining in the cerebral hemispheres: A computational approach. *Psychological Review* 94(2), 148–175.

Lai V. T., W. van Dam, L. L. Conant, J. R. Binder, and R. H. Desai (2015). Familiarity differentially affects right hemisphere contributions to processing metaphors and literals. *Frontiers in Human Neuroscience* 9, 44.

Lakoff, G. and M. Johnson (1980). *Metaphors We Live By.* Chicago: University of Chicago Press.

Lakoff, G. and M. Johnson (1999) *Philosophy in the Flesh: The Embodied Mind and its Challenge to Western Thought.* New York: Basic Books.

Landis, T., J. L. Cummings, D. F. Benson, and E. P. Palmer (1986). Loss of topographic familiarity: An environmental agnosia. *Archives of Neurology* 43(2), 132–136.

Landis, T. and M. Regard (1988). The right hemisphere's access to lexical meaning: A function of its release from left hemisphere control? In C. Chiarello (ed.), *Right Hemisphere Contributions to Lexical Semantics*, pp. 33–46. New York: Springer-Verlag.

Lee, S. S. and M. Dapretto (2006). Metaphorical vs. literal word meanings: fMRI evidence against a selective role of the right hemisphere. *Neuroimage* 29(2), 536–544.

Lippolis, G., A. Bisazza, L. J. Rogers, and G. Vallortigara (2002). Lateralisation of predator avoidance responses in three species of toads. *Laterality* 7(2), 163–183.

Lippolis, G., W. Westman, B. M. McAllan, and L. J. Rogers (2005). Lateralisation of escape responses in the striped-faced dunnart, *Sminthopsis macroura* (*Dasyuridae: Marsupialia*). *Laterality* 10(5), 457–470.

Locke, J. (1690). *An Essay on Human Understanding.* London: Thomas Bassett.

Mackenzie, C., T. Begg, M. Brady, and K. R. Lees (1997). The effects on verbal communication skills of right hemisphere stroke in middle age. *Aphasiology* 11(10), 929–945.

Mackenzie, C., T. Begg, K. R. Lees, and M. Brady (1999). The communication effects of right brain damage on the very old and the not so old. *Journal of Neurolinguistics* 12(2), 79–93.

Marsolek, C. J. (1995). Abstract visual-form representations in the left cerebral hemisphere. *Journal of Experimental Psychology and Human Perceptual Performance* 21(2), 375–386.

Martin, A., C. L. Wiggs, L. G. Ungerleider, and J. V. Haxby (1996). Neural correlates of category-specific knowledge. *Nature* 379(6566), 649–652.

Marzi, C. A., P. Bisiacchi, and R. Nicoletti (1991). Is interhemispheric transfer of visuomotor information asymmetric? Evidence from a meta-analysis. *Neuropsychologia* 29(12), 1163–1177.

Mashal, N. and M. Faust (2008). Right hemisphere sensitivity to novel metaphoric relations: Application of the signal detection theory. *Brain and Language* 104(2), 103–112.

Mashal, N., M. Faust, and T. Hendler (2005). The role of the right hemisphere in processing nonsalient metaphorical meanings: Application of principal components analysis to fMRI data. *Neuropsychologia* 43(14), 2084–2100.

Mashal, N., M. Faust, T. Hendler, and M. Jung-Beeman (2007). An fMRI investigation of the neural correlates underlying the processing of novel metaphoric expressions. *Brain and Language* 100(2), 115–126.

Mashal, N., M. Faust, T. Hendler, and M. Jung-Beeman (2008). Hemispheric differences in processing the literal interpretation of idioms: Converging evidence from behavioral and fMRI studies. *Cortex* 44(7), 848–860.

Mashal, N., M. Faust, T. Hendler, and M. Jung-Beeman (2009). An fMRI study of processing novel metaphoric sentences. *Laterality* 14(1), 30–54.

McGilchrist, I. (2009). *The Master and His Emissary: The Divided Brain and the Making of the Western World*. New Haven, CT: Yale University Press.

McGrew, W. C. and L. F. Marchant (1999). Laterality of hand use pays off in foraging success for wild chimpanzees. *Primates* 40(3), 509–513.

McNamara, P. (2009). *The Neuroscience of Religious Experience*. Cambridge: Cambridge University Press.

McNeill, D. (1992). *Hand and Mind: What Gestures Reveal about Thought*. Chicago: University of Chicago Press.

Meador, K. J., D. W. Loring, T. E. Feinberg, G. P. Lee, and M. E. Nichools (2000). Anosognosia and asomatognosia during intracarotid amobarbital inactivation. *Neurology* 55(6), 816–820.

Meyer, B.-U., S. Röricht, H. Gräfin von Einsiedel, F. Kruggel, and A. Weind (1995). Inhibitory and excitatory interhemispheric transfers between motor cortical areas in normal subjects and patients with abnormalities of the corpus callosum. *Brain* 118(2), 429–440.

Michel, E. M. and B. T. Troost (1980). Palinopsia: Cerebral localization with CT. *Neurology* 30(8), 887–889.

Mills, L. and G. B. Rollman (1980). Hemispheric asymmetry for auditory perception of temporal order. *Neuropsychologia* 18(1), 41–48.

Milo, R. G. and D. Quiatt (1993). Glottogenesis and anatomically modern *Homo sapiens*: The evidence for and implications of a late origin of vocal language. *Current Anthropology* 34(5), 569–598.

Mithen, S. J. (1996). *The Prehistory of the Mind. A Search for the Origins of Art, Religion, and Science*. London: Thames and Hudson.

Mithen, S. J. (1998). A creative explosion? Theory of mind, language and the disembodied mind of the Upper Palaeolithic. In S. J. Mithen (ed.), *Creativity in Human Evolution and Prehistory*, pp. 165–192. London: Routledge and Kegan Paul.

Mithen, S. J. (2005). *Singing Neanderthals: The Origin of Music, Language, Mind and Body*. London: Phoenix.

Mizuno, A., Y. Liu, D. L. Williams, T. A. Keller, N. J. Minshew, and M. A. Just (2011). The neural basis of deictic shifting in linguistic perspective-taking in high-functioning autism. *Brain* 134(8), 2422–2435.

Müller, T., T. Büttner, W. Kuhn, A. Heinz, and H. Przuntek (1995). Palinopsia as sensory epileptic phenomenon. *Acta Neurologica Scandinavica* 91(6), 433–436.

Mummery, C. J., K. Patterson, J. R. Hodges, and R. J. S. Wise (1996). Generating 'tiger' as an animal name or a word beginning with T: Differences in brain activation. *Proceedings of the Royal Society of London, Series B, Biological Sciences* 263(1373), 989–995.

Nagel, T. (1986). *The View from Nowhere*. Oxford: Oxford University Press.

Nebes, R. D. (1974). Hemispheric specialization in commissurotomized man. *Psychological Bulletin* 81(1), 1–14.

Nettl, B. (1983). *The Study of Ethnomusicology: Twenty-Nine Issues and Concepts*. Champaign, IL: University of Illinois Press.

Nicholls, M. E. R. (1994). Hemispheric asymmetries for temporal resolution: A signal detection analysis of threshold and bias. *The Quarterly Journal of Experimental Psychology. A. Human Experimental Psychology* 47(2), 291–310.

Nietzsche, F. (1968 [1906]). *The Will to Power*, transl. W. Kaufmann. New York: Vintage:

Nottebohm, F. (1970). The ontogeny of bird song. *Science* 167(3920), 950–956.

Oliveri, M., P. M. Rossini, R. Traversa, P. Cicinelli, M. M. Filippi, P. Pasqualetti, F. Tomaiuolo, and C. Caltagirone (1999). Left frontal transcranial magnetic stimulation reduces contralesional extinction in patients with unilateral right brain damage. *Brain* 122(9), 1731–1739.

Ornstein, R., J. Herron, J. Johnstone, and Charles Swencionis (1979). Differential right hemisphere involvement in two reading tasks. *Psychophysiology* 16(4), 398–401.

Papagno, C., M. Oliveri, and L. Romero (2002). Neural correlates of idiom comprehension. *Cortex* 38, 895–898.

Perani, D., S. F. Cappa, V. Bettinardi. S. Bressi, M. Gorno-Tempini, M. Matarrese, and F. Fazio (1995). Different neural systems for the recognition of animals and man-made tools. *NeuroReport* 6(12), 1637–1641.

Phelps, E. A. and M. S. Gazzaniga (1992). Hemispheric differences in mnemonic processing: The effects of left hemisphere interpretation. *Neuropsychologia* 30(3), 293–297.

Pobric, G., N. Mashal, M. Faust, and M. Lavidor (2008). The role of the right cerebral hemisphere in processing novel metaphoric expressions: A transcranial magnetic stimulation study. *Journal of Cognitive Neuroscience* 20(1), 170–181.

Posner, M. I. (1995). Attention in cognitive neuroscience: An overview. In M. S. Gazzaniga (ed.), *Handbook of Cognitive Neuroscience*, pp. 615–624. Cambridge, MA: MIT Press.

Prat, C. S., R. A. Mason, and M. A. Just (2012). An fMRI investigation of analogical mapping in metaphor comprehension: The influence of context and individual cognitive capacities on processing demands. *Journal of Experimental Psychology: Learning Memory and Cognition* 38(2), 282–294.

Price, C. J. and K. J. Friston (2002). Functional imaging studies of category specificity. In E. M. E. Forde and G. W. Humphreys (eds.), *Category Specificity in Brain and Mind*, pp. 427–447. Hove, UK: Psychology Press.

Proverbio, A. M., N. Crotti, A. Zani, and R. Adorni (2009). The role of left and right hemispheres in the comprehension of idiomatic language: An electrical neuroimaging study. *BMC Neuroscience* 10, 116.

Pynte, J., M. Besson, F. H. Robichon, and J. Poli (1996). The time-course of metaphor comprehension: An event-related potential study. *Brain and Language* 55(3), 293–316.

Querné, L., F. Eustache, and S. Faure (2000). Interhemispheric inhibition, intrahemispheric activation, and lexical capacities of the right hemisphere: A tachistoscopic, divided visual-field study in normal subjects. *Brain and Language* 74(2), 171–190.

Querné, L. and S. Faure (1996). Activating the right hemisphere by a prior spatial task: Equal lexical decision accuracy in left and right visual fields in normal subjects. *Brain and Cognition* 32(2), 142–145.

Rapp, A. M., D. T. Leube, M. Erb, W. Grodd, and T. T. Kircher (2004). Neural correlates of metaphor processing. *Brain Research: Cognitive Brain Research* 20(3), 395–402.

Rapp, A. M., D. T. Leube, M. Erb, W. Grodd, and T. T. Kircher (2007). Laterality in metaphor processing: Lack of evidence from functional magnetic resonance imaging for the right hemisphere theory. *Brain and Language* 100(2), 142–149.

Rausch, R. (1977). Cognitive strategies in patients with unilateral temporal lobe excisions. *Neuropsychologia* 15(3), 385–395.

Rausch, R. (1985). Differences in cognitive function with left and right temporal lobe dysfunction. In D. F. Benson and E. Zaidel (eds.), *The Dual Brain*, pp. 247–261. New York: Guilford Press.

Rinaldi, M. C., P. Marangolo, and F. Baldassarri (2004). Metaphor comprehension in right brain-damaged patients with visuo-verbal and verbal material: A dissociation (re)considered. *Cortex* 40(3), 479–490.

Rissman, J., J. C. Eliassen, and S. E. Blumstein (2003). An event-related fMRI investigation of implicit semantic priming. *Journal of Cognitive Neuroscience* 15(8), 1160–1175.

Rizzolatti, G., L. Fogassi, and V. Gallese (2001). Neurophysiological mechanisms underlying the understanding and imitation of action. *Nature Reviews Neuroscience*, 2(9), 661–670.

Robertson, L. C. and M. R. Lamb (1991). Neuropsychological contributions to theories of part/whole organisation. *Cognitive Psychology* 23, 299–330.

Robertson, L. C., M. R. Lamb, and R. T. Knight (1988). Effects of lesions of temporal-parietal junction on perceptual and attentional processing in humans. *Journal of Neuroscience* 8(10), 3757–3769.

Robins, A. and L. J. Rogers (2006). Complementary and lateralized forms of processing in *Bufo marinus* for novel and familiar prey. *Neurobiology of Learning and Memory* 86(2), 214–227.

Rogers, L. J. (2000). Evolution of hemisphere specialisation: Advantages and disadvantages. *Brain and Language* 73(2), 236–253.

Rogers, L. J. (2005). Cognitive and social advantages of having a lateralized brain. In Y. B. Malashichev and A. W. Deckel (eds.), *Behavioral and Morphological Asymmetries in Vertebrates*, pp. 129–139. Austin, TX: Landes Bioscience.

Rogers, L. J. and G. Kaplan (2006). An eye for a predator: Lateralization in birds, with particular reference to the Australian magpie. In Y. B. Malashichev and A. W. Deckel (eds.), *Behavioral and Morphological Asymmetries in Vertebrates*, pp. 47–57. Austin, TX: Landes Bioscience.

Rogers, L. J. and L. Workman(1989). Light exposure during incubation affects competitive behaviour in domestic chicks. *Applied Animal Behaviour Science* 23, 187–198.

Rogers, L. J., P. Zucca, and G. Vallortigara (2004). Advantages of having a lateralized brain. *Proceedings of the Royal Society of London, Series B—Biological Sciences*, 271(suppl 6), S420–S422.

Röricht, S., K. Irlbacher, E. Petrow, and B.-U. Meyer (1997). Normwerte transkallosal und kortikospinal vermittelter Effekte einer hemisphärenselektiven magnetischen Kortexreizung beim Menschen. *Zeitschrift für Elektroenzephalographie, Elektromyographie und verwandte Gebiete* 28, 34–38.

Ross, E. D., R. D. Thompson, and J. Yenkosky (1977). Lateralisation of affective prosody in the brain and callosal integration of hemispheric language functions. *Brian and Language* 56(1), 27–54.

Saron, C. D. and R. J. Davidson (1989). Visual evoked potential measures of interhemispheric transfer time in humans. *Behavioral Neuroscience* 103(5), 1115–1138.

Saron, C. D., J. J. Foxe, C. E. Schroeder, and H. G. Vaughan Jr. (2003). Complexities of interhemispheric communication in sensorimotor tasks revealed by high-density event-related potential mapping. In K. Hugdahl and R. J. Davidson (eds.), *The Asymmetrical Brain*, pp. 341–408. Cambridge, MA: MIT Press.

Saron, C. D., J. J. Foxe, G. V. Simpson, and H. G. Vaughan (2002). Interhemispheric visuomotor activation: Spatiotemporal electrophysiology related to reaction time. In E. Zaidel and M. Iacoboni (eds.), *The Parallel Brain: The Cognitive Neuroscience of the Corpus Callosum*, pp. 171–219. Cambridge, MA: MIT Press.

Schmidt, G. L., C. J. DeBuse, and C. A. Seger (2007). Right hemisphere metaphor processing? Characterizing the lateralization of semantic processes. *Brain and Language* 100(2), 127–141.

Schmidt, G. L. and C. A. Seger (2009). Neural correlates of metaphor processing: The roles of figurativeness, familiarity and difficulty. *Brain and Cognition* 71(3), 375–386.

Schneiderman, E. I., K. G. Murasugi, and J. D. Saddy (1992). Story arrangement ability in right-brain damaged patients. *Brain and Language* 43(1), 107–120.

Schnider, A., K. Gutbrod, C. W. Hess, and G. Schroth (1996). Memory without context: Amnesia with confabulations after infarction of the right capsular genu. *Journal of Neurology, Neurosurgery and Psychiatry* 61(2), 186–193.

Sergent, J. (1982). The cerebral balance of power: Confrontation or cooperation? *Journal of Experimental Psychology: Human Perception and Performance* 8(2), 253–272.

Shamay-Tsoory, S. G., R. Tomer, B. D. Berger, and J. Aharon-Peretz (2003). Characterisation of empathy deficits following prefrontal brain damage: The role of the right ventromedial prefrontal cortex. *Journal of Cognitive Neuroscience* 15(3), 324–337.

Shamay-Tsoory, S. G., R. Tomer, and J. Aharon-Peretz (2005). The neuroanatomical basis of understanding sarcasm and its relationship to social cognition. *Neuropsychology* 19(3), 288–300.

Shammi, P. and D. T. Stuss (1999). Humour appreciation: A role of the right frontal lobe. *Brain* 122(4), 657–666.

Sharp, D. J., S. K. Scott, and R. J. Wise (2004). Monitoring and the controlled processing of meaning: Distinct prefrontal systems. *Cerebral Cortex* 14(1), 1–10.

Sotillo, M., L. Carretié, J. A. Hinojosa, M. Tapia, F. Mercado, S. López-Martín, and J. Albert (2005). Neural activity associated with metaphor comprehension: Spatial analysis. *Neuroscience Letters* 373(1), 5–9.

Starkstein, S. E., J. P. Fedoroff, T. R. Price, R. Leiguarda, and R. G. Robinson (1992). Anosognosia in patients with cerebrovascular lesions: a study of causative factors. *Stroke* 23(10), 1446–1453.

Strauss, E. and M. Moscovitch (1981). Perception of facial expressions. *Brain and Language* 13(2), 308–332.

Stringaris, A. K., N. Medford, R. Giora, V. C. Giampietro, M. J. Brammer, and A. S. David (2006). How metaphors influence semantic relatedness judgments: The role of the right frontal cortex. *Neuroimage* 33, 784–799.

Stringaris, A. K., N. Medford, R. Giora, V. C. Giampietro, M. J. Brammer, and A. S. David (2007). Deriving meaning: Distinct neural mechanisms for metaphoric, literal, and non-meaningful sentences. *Brain and Language* 100(2), 150–162.

Stump, E. (2009). The problem of evil: Analytic philosophy and narrative. In O. D. Crisp and M. C. Rea (eds.), *Analytic Theology: New Essays in the Philosophy of Theology*, pp. 251–264. New York: Oxford University Press.

Stuss, D. T. (1991). Disturbance of self-awareness after frontal system damage. In G. P. Prigatano and D. L. Schacter (eds.), *Awareness of Deficit after Brain Injury: Clinical and Theoretical Issues*, pp. 66–83. Oxford: Oxford University Press.

Swisher, L. and L. J. Hirsh (1972). Brain damage and the ordering of two temporally successive stimuli. *Neuropsychologia* 10(2), 137–152.

Tootell, R. B., J. D. Mendola, N. K. Hadjikhani, A. K. Liu, and A. M. Dale (1998). The representation of the ipsilateral visual field in human cerebral cortex. *Proceedings of the National Academy of Sciences of the USA* 95(3), 818–824.

Tremblay, C., L. Monetta, M. Langlois, and C. Schneider (2016). Intermittent theta-burst stimulation of the right dorsolateral prefrontal cortex to promote metaphor comprehension in Parkinson disease: A case study. *Archives of Physical Medicine and Rehabilitation* 97(1), 74–83.

Trimble, M. R. (2007). *The Soul in the Brain: The Cerebral Basis of Language, Art, and Belief.* Baltimore, MD: Johns Hopkins University Press.

Trimble, M. and A. Freeman (2006). An investigation of religiosity and the Gastaut-Geschwind syndrome in patients with temporal lobe epilepsy, *Epilepsy and Behavior* 9, 407–414.

Vallortigara, G. (1992). Right hemisphere advantage for social recognition in the chick Right hemisphere advantage for social recognition in the chick. *Neuropsychologia* 30, 761–768.

Vallortigara, G., L. J. Rogers, A. Bisazza, G. Lippolis, and A. Robins (1998). Complementary right and left hemifield use for predatory and agonistic behaviour in toads. *NeuroReport* 9(14), 3341–3344.

van Kleeck, M. H. (1989). Hemispheric differences in global versus local processing of hierarchical visual stimuli by normal subjects: New data and a meta-analysis of previous studies. *Neuropsychologia* 27(9), 1165–1178.

Ventolini, N., E. A. Ferrero, S. Sponza, A. Della Chiesa, P. Zucca, and G. Vallortigara (2005). Laterality in the wild: Preferential hemifield use during predatory and sexual behaviour in the black-winged stilt (*Himantopus himantopus*). *Animal Behaviour* 69, 1077–1084.

Vogeley, K., P. Bussfeld, A. Newen, S. Herrmann, F. Happé, P. Falkai, W. Maier, N. J. Shah, G. R. Fink, and K. Zilles (2001). Mind reading: Neural mechanisms of theory of mind and self-perspective. *Neuroimage* 14(1, part 1), 170–181.

Vowles, D. (1970). Neuroethology, evolution and grammar. In R. Aronson, E. Tobach, D. Lehrman, et al. (eds.), *Development and Evolution of Behavior: Essays in Memory of T. C. Schneirla*, pp. 194–215. San Francisco: W. H. Freeman and Co.

Wager, T. D. and E. E. Smith (2003). Neuroimaging studies of working memory: A meta-analysis. *Cognitive, Affective and Behavioral Neuroscience* 3(4), 255–274.

Wapner, W., S. Hamby, and H. Gardner (1981). The role of the right hemisphere in the apprehension of complex linguistic materials. *Brain and Language* 14(1), 15–33.

Warrington, E. K. and R. A. McCarthy (1987). Categories of knowledge: Further fractionations and an attempted integration. *Brain* 110(5), 1273–1296.

Whitney, C., W. Huber, J. S. Klann, S. Weis, S. Krach, and T. Kircher (2009). Neural correlates of narrative shifts during auditory story comprehension. *Neuroimage* 47(1), 360–366.

Winner, E., and H. Gardner (1977). The comprehension of metaphor in brain-damaged patients. *Brain* 100(4), 717–729.

Wymer, J. H., L. S. Lindman, and R. L. Booksh (2002). A neuropsychological perspective of aprosody: Features, function, assessment, and treatment. *Applied Neuropsychology* 9(1), 37–47.

Xu, J. S., S. Kemeny, G. Park, C. Frattali, and A. Braun (2005). Language in context: Emergent features of word, sentence, and narrative comprehension. *Neuroimage* 25(3), 1002–1015.

Yoshida, T., A. Yoshino, Y. Takahashi, and S. Nomura (2007). Comparison of hemispheric asymmetry in global and local information processing and interference in divided and selective attention using spatial frequency filters. *Experimental Brain Research* 181(3), 519–529.

PART II
Investigating Metaphor in Religious Texts

The chapters in Part II all focus on the role of metaphor in religious thought and text, drawing on traditional scholarship, but using conceptual metaphor theory as a tool of analysis.

Some religious texts appear to produce their effects precisely by way of the metaphorical processing that they demand, generally within some kind of institutional setting. The first chapter of Part II, chapter 7, by Ellen Haskell, draws on philosophical and literary approaches to non-literal meaning as well as the more recent cognitive-science based theories of metaphor in order to elucidate the thirteenth-century *Zohar*, which is part of the Kabbalah, a belief system based on texts, teachings, and practices originating in Jewish mysticism. Haskell's analysis points to the potential effects of complex metaphor networks based on a central anthropomorphic source, the human face with all its deep-seated implications. In chapter 8, Glen Alexander Hayes introduces the reader to the various currents of Tantrism, represented in a variety of texts and languages, but focuses attention on the characteristic metaphor networks in local vernacular texts of Vaiṣṇava Sahajiyā, as distinct from Sanskrit-based traditions. He also introduces conceptual metaphor theory, conceptual blending, and embodied image schemas into the traditional scholarship, showing why it is essential to pay close analytic attention to the metaphorical conceptualisations embedded in linguistic detail. These conceptualisations create coherent felt realities, grounded in the body and its environment, that are the foundation of the religious experiences and ideas that these Tantric texts communicate. Chapter 9, by Hubert Kowalewski, continues this kind of exploration, turning to the sutras of the *Pali Canon*, the basic text of Theravadan Buddhism. Reference to kinds of emotion is recurrent in all religious discourse. Kowalewski addresses the distinctive ways in which emotions are conceptualized in Buddhist texts, thinking, and meditative practices, outlining the image schemas and metaphor networks involved and discussing key theoretical implications.

One of the tasks for cognitive-linguistic research into religion concerns the following questions: Is there a universal core of religious metaphors? Which themes attract metaphor? Which source domains get selected? Chapters 10 and 11 offer methodologies for the systematic investigation of religious text. In chapter 10, Xiuping Gao and Chun Lan examine metaphor choices in the *Heart Sutra* and the *Diamond Sutra*, two core texts of the Chinese version of Mahayana Buddhism. Gao and Lan make the case for extending the comparative analysis of religious metaphor within the framework of standard conceptual metaphor theory, applying the statistical approach developed in corpus linguistics (numerical analysis, generally computer-aided, of large data sets). Their findings show that highly abstract, counterintuitive, and paradoxical ideas, as well as those related to central doctrines, are dependent on metaphorical mappings from spatial image schemas. In chapter 11, a similar approach is adopted by Ahmad El-Sharif, who undertakes an investigation of the metaphorical patterns in the text corpus representing the Prophetic Tradition in Islam and affirms the centrality, even the indispensability, of metaphor in any religious thought formation. This view of the importance of metaphor, and the problems that attend it, is present from relatively early times in Islamic scholarship, where there are diverse strands of speculation and instruction around the matter. (There is a parallel here with other religions: cf. Chilton and Cram in chapter 16.). The results of El-Sharif's systematic corpus analysis indicate the presence of four major conceptual schemas, in which spatial schemas predominate.

Religious metaphor networks are not timeless unchanging structures. The final chapter of Part II examines in detail the crucial role that metaphorical re-conceptualisation can play in the historical transformation of systems of belief and organisation. As Ralph Bisschops shows (chapter 12), the emergence of Christianity from Judaism involved a radical revision of institutionalized practices, in particular circumcision. This in turn involved, as can be seen in the discursive struggles in which Paul of Tarsus was engaged, struggles in which metaphorical re-processing was crucial. In chapter 12, detailed historical and textual scholarship provides an account of the indispensable cultural context in which a cognitive perspective can demonstrate the potential of metaphor in historical transformations.

CHAPTER 7

A Composite Countenance

The Divine Face as Mixed Metaphor in Jewish Mysticism

ELLEN HASKELL

For you, my heart says, Seek My face!
O Lord, I seek Your face.

(Psalm 27:8)

In the Hebrew Bible and in Jewish rabbinic literature, the metaphoric image of God's face represents divine presence and beneficent attention. Likewise, in the sources examined in this chapter, the divine face's absence or turning away indicates disfavor.[1] Yet in the thirteenth-century Spanish Jewish mystical classic *Sefer ha-Zohar* (The Book of Splendor), the divine facial metaphor is transformed. No longer does it indicate simply presence or absence, favor or disfavor. Instead, the mystics invest this ancient metaphor with new meaning in order to redefine both divine and human faces as sites of revelation and spiritual transformation. In doing so, they take advantage of metaphor's interactive properties, allowing human and divine facial qualities to shape and influence each other.

Unlike traditional Jewish sources that liken the divine face to a single human face, the Zohar's authors restructure the facial metaphor's contiguity associations, manipulating the interplay of metaphor and metonymy to define a composite divine countenance. This composite countenance is described as many human faces at once and also in complex permutations of celestial, human, and natural images that displace normative human features. The mystics' goals in restructuring the divine facial metaphor are twofold. First, the mystics' own human faces are divinized, becoming vehicles of mutual revelation accessed through spiritual fellowship. Second, the divine face is simultaneously familiarized and defined as beyond human understanding, since human features are but one fragment of a whole that inspires contemplation through image juxtaposition. In this way, the kabbalists achieve an enhanced self-understanding while preserving the divine countenance's sacred uniqueness.

The analysis of divine facial metaphors that follows employs a cognitive approach to metaphor that is illuminated by engagement with anthropological literature. From a cognitive perspective, metaphors are complex tools for thinking that provide experiential understanding of that which they signify. As George Lakoff and Mark Johnson write, 'The essence of metaphor is understanding and experiencing one kind of thing in terms of another' (Lakoff and Johnson 1980, p. 5). When used to think about religion, metaphors become mediators of experience that complicate, define, and structure perceived reality for religious subjects. In this sense, they are the building blocks of religious culture, and therefore fertile ground for anthropological reflection.

Anthropologist James Fernandez explains that for religious participants a theology comprised of complex metaphors interacting in dynamic ways gives its adherents a sensation of cosmological coherence and effects a 'return to the whole,' a restoration of humanity's relative place within the ordering of the universe (Fernandez 1986, pp. 191, 208). This 'return to the whole' is reliant upon metaphor's ability to join disparate experiences into nuanced, holistic systems. Such systems, in turn, rely on complex networks of metonymies—contiguity associations that when linked become able to reference each other within the primary metaphorical statement. Deborah Durham and James Fernandez write, 'Metaphor does not simply juxtapose two domains, but ultimately joins them, uniting them metonymically in their parallel structures' (Durham and Fernandez 1991, pp. 197–198). The juxtaposed domains' boundaries become blurred as each acts reciprocally upon the other.[2] This interdependence 'creates a more concordant model of the world, a single, more encompassing organization' (Durham and Fernandez 1991, p. 198). These interactive characteristics allow metaphors to become powerful vehicles for cultural and personal transformation, because they construct new models that lead to changes in thought and behavior. It is just such an encompassing transformation of the universe and the individual's place within it that religious experience seeks to effect.

1 METAPHOR AND THE ZOHAR

Sefer ha-Zohar, the most influential text of the Jewish mystical movement called Kabbalah, is known for its elaborate divine imagery.[3] Produced during the last quarter of the thirteenth century in Castile, it is the product of group authorship, though pseudepigraphically attributed to the second-century sage Rabbi Shimon bar Yohai, who appears as one of the main characters in the text's narrative portions.[4] Perhaps because of its group composition, the Zohar contains an especially rich image vocabulary. Common images for God in its pages include anthropomorphic metaphors, animal metaphors, imagery of trees, watercourses, lights, prisms, flames, celestial bodies, human dwelling places, and much, much more. According to kabbalistic theology, God is both concealed from human understanding, a state represented by the title Ein Sof (Without End), and revealed to humanity in ten stages of divine life known as *sefirot*.[5] Each *sefirah* functions as a complex symbol that brings together related metaphoric images, including biblical references, emotional qualities, roles in transmitting divine energy, and more. These symbols shape religious experience by producing a contemplative and ultimately transformative spirituality for the mindful reader. In other words, kabbalistic metaphors play a critical role in the production of kabbalists.[6]

This production of mystics through the medium of mystical imagery is possible because of figurative language's ability to act upon the person. Both Jacques Lacan and Judith Butler emphasize language's role in informing and constructing self-understanding. For Lacan, language has a multi-directional effect on the human being. 'His nature is woven by effects in which we can find the structure of language, whose material he becomes' (Lacan 1985, p. 78). For Butler, language is '*performative*, inasmuch as this signifying act delimits and contours the body that it then claims to find prior to any and all signification' (Butler, 1993, p. 30).[7] Similarly, anthropologist James Fernandez defines the metaphoric image as 'a strategic predication upon an inchoate pronoun . . . which makes a movement and leads to performance' (Fernandez 1986, p. 8). Mary Carruthers explains how medieval Christian monastics used vivid metaphors as cognitive tools (Carruthers 1998, pp. 118–120). Together, these scholars' works explain how religious imagery functions as an important means by which religious practitioners like the Zoharic kabbalists construct models for their own self-transformation.

Zoharic divine facial imagery is useful for such contemplative transformation, since the face is a powerful anthropomorphic image that interacts closely with human experience and is thus especially fruitful for modeling thought and action. Indeed, Kabbalah relies heavily on the doctrine of *imitatio dei*, teaching that the human being as microcosm reflects the divine being as macrocosm. Because the kabbalists understand that macrocosm and microcosm are dynamic and responsive to each other, they believe that the person acts upon God even as God acts upon the person. In many ways, this theology resembles metaphor itself, in that it brings together two domains, each of which is used to understand the other. As Deborah Durham and James Fernandez explain, when domains are juxtaposed in a metaphor, the boundaries between them blur. 'Metaphor does not simply juxtapose two domains, but ultimately joins them, uniting them metonymically in their parallel structures. It creates a more concordant model of the world, a single, more encompassing organization' (Durham and Fernandez 1991, pp. 197–198). Such detailed models are created largely through manipulating the contiguous associations, or metonymies, associated with each metaphoric element, since metaphorization is not an act of simple word-replacement, but rather involves the broader conceptual structures that surround words.

Indeed, Durham and Fernandez note that one of the most effective ways to produce cultural transformation is to restructure the internal metonymic associations of culturally dominant metaphors (Durham and Fernandez 1991, pp. 209). The divine face, a Jewish trope reaching back to biblical literature, is an ideal example of such a transformative vehicle. Thus, when the kabbalists, with their advocacy of divine imitation, frame their model of revelation around the divine face, they are intentionally creating an interactive model that modifies their understanding of both divinity and humanity. For this reason, the details with which they invest and shape the divine facial metaphor are especially important.

2 A COMPOSITE COUNTENANCE

The Zoharic kabbalists describe the divine face as appearing through the vehicle of a human face, with macrocosm peering through microcosm. Such interactions often feature a composite countenance.

> *Sefer ha-Zohar* 2:94b[8]
> Rabbi Hiyya and Rabbi Yosi met one night at the tower of Tyre. They stayed there and rejoiced in each other. Rabbi Yosi said, How glad I am to see the face of the Divine Presence [*Shekhinah*]!

> *Sefer ha-Zohar* 2:163b
> Rabbi Yosi, Rabbi Yehudah, and Rabbi Hiyya were traveling on the road. They met Rabbi Eleazar. When they saw him, they all got down from their donkeys. Rabbi Eleazar said, Truly, I see the face of the Divine Presence [*Shekhinah*]! For seeing the pious and righteous of a generation and meeting them—truly they are the face of the Divine Presence. And why are they called the face of the Divine Presence? Because the Divine Presence is hidden within them. She is concealed and they are revealed. For those who are near to Her are called Her face.[9] And who are they? They are the ones with whom She adorns Herself to appear before the supernal King. And since you are here, truly the Divine Presence [*Shekhinah*] is adorned upon you, and you are her face. . . . For any realm with which a person is linked is revealed in his face.

While classical rabbinic literature also teaches that a person receiving a teacher or close friend is like one receiving the Divine Presence, there is more to these Zoharic passages than an affirmation of scholarship and friendship's holiness.[10] When the mystics meet, their faces constitute God's Presence, one of the ten divine gradations known as *sefirot*. Kabbalistic theology often considers this divine aspect to be female, adding some interesting gender implications to the passage. For the study at hand, however, it is the Divine Presence's composite countenance that demands greatest attention.

When Rabbi Yosi meets his mystical companion in Zohar 2:94b, he exclaims that he sees the Divine Presence's face. This revelation occurs as the two kabbalists come together and delight in each other's company, suggesting not simply that Rabbi Hiyya looks like the feminine divine presence, but rather that the interaction between the two men inspires the Presence's manifestation. Zohar 2:163b further elaborates this concept. There, Rabbi Eleazar remarks that seeing three of his mystical companions together constitutes seeing the Divine Presence's face. Notably, both texts employ metaphor, not simile. For Rabbi Yosi and Rabbi Eleazar alike, seeing their companions' faces is not *like* seeing the face of God. It *is* seeing the face of God. Although this face is normally concealed from humanity, it is revealed through the medium of the kabbalistic companions' faces in varying configurations. Furthermore, not just any faces reveal the divine countenance. The kabbalists encounter divinity through righteous faces. The passage goes on to assert that human faces display their spiritual allegiance by divulging the 'realm' (i.e. holy or unholy) with which they associate. This teaching is significant because the mystical companions named in the Zohar's narrative portions may represent the text's medieval Spanish authors.[11] The implication is that the kabbalists who wrote the Zohar understood their group to have revelatory capabilities grounded in the relations of the group itself, which together constituted and refracted the face of God.

In keeping with Kabbalah's interactivist theology, the righteous kabbalists' faces also reciprocally serve the Divine Presence in the heavenly realm, as the feminine Presence adorns Herself with them to appear before the masculine aspect of God as King—a common sexual metaphor for divine unification in Kabbalah. For the kabbalists, this meeting of masculine and feminine aspects within divinity both symbolizes and inspires redemption and correct world order. The kabbalists' faces adorn the divine at a critical moment for the world's continuation, becoming incorporated into a peak cosmological moment. Thus, the metaphor of God's composite countenance works on two levels at once. On earth among the mystics, the concealed divine face is made visible through human faces, while in heaven the mystics' faces appear as divine adornments that facilitate redemption. Heavenly and earthly realms integrate through the facial metaphor.

This understanding of divine and human countenances as mutually revelatory and transformative is grounded in the interactive qualities of metaphorization. Both the humans who constitute the divine face and the divine face itself modify each other through their juxtaposition. The divine face—a concept that cannot be known through direct experience—is humanized through the metaphor, though in a complex way that avoids the reductive pitfalls of likening it to a single human face. It is rendered capable of expressing emotion, communication, and all the complexities of identity and personality that are the metonymic entailments of a human face. These connotative associations give the divine facial metaphor conceptual structure and depth, transforming the divine into a relatable entity. As James Fernandez explains, 'The complexity of expressive experience lies in the interplay of contiguity and similarity associations in the predications upon the pronouns participating in this experience' (Fernandez 1986, pp. 43–44). Yet relationship to that entity is not as simple as relationship to a human being. The kabbalists, by intimating that the divine face is comprised of many human faces, indicate a multiplicity and complexity that extends beyond the merely human. The Presence's countenance is kaleidoscopic and ever changing. Its composition as a human image depends on the spiritual quality of the human beings in which it manifests, on which of the mystical companions are present, and on who is gazing at whom. In this way, the kabbalists avoid simplifying divinity or attributing an excessively human nature to God, a problem highlighted in medieval philosophical literature, though medieval philosophy preferred negative theology to the kabbalists' metaphor-rich strategy for understanding God.[12] In their teachings on the mystics revealing the divine face, the kabbalists perform the balancing act of humanizing God without limiting God to humanity.

At the same time as they humanize God, the kabbalists divinize themselves. Placed in a metaphoric relationship with the divine face, their own faces become part of the metonymic system developed by that relationship. No longer limited to the normal human facial associations, they reflect divinity in their countenances—a profound shift in recognition that constitutes a new understanding of themselves and their group.[13] As Fernandez explains, both metaphor and metonym advance statements regarding 'transformation or transcendence of state' (Fernandez 1986, p. 57). While the divine countenance itself is concealed, it is revealed through the medium of the kabbalists' own bodies, which are socio-religiously transfigured by the process. In the words of anthropologist Roy Rappaport, 'the actors themselves become terms in their own logic of the concrete' (Rappaport 1979, p. 136). When the kabbalists' countenances take on divine facial characteristics, they are elevated and transformed into vehicles of revelation. This transformation reinforces their desired group dynamic. Already members of an elite mystical fellowship, they become each other's path toward intimacy with and knowledge of God. Each time the kabbalistic companions meet becomes an opportunity for revelation, as spiritual fellowship allows access to divine encounter.

3 COUNTENANCE AND CONNOTATIONS

To further understand how the kabbalists associate divine revelation with face-to-face encounter, it is helpful to examine the ideas that structure their divine facial metaphor. The following passages demonstrate Zoharic understandings of the human face that extend beyond basic emotional and character expressions.

Sefer ha-Zohar 1:192a
Come and see: One who reflects on what he learned from his teacher and sees him in that wisdom is able to be increased greatly by that spirit. . . . Thus Joseph, in all that he did, would observe in the spirit of wisdom the image of his father. He would contemplate it, and so the matter prospered, and he was increased by another spirit of more exalted light.

Sefer ha-Zohar 2:70b
'This is the book of the generations of Adam' (Genesis 5:1). In the mysteries of human features are those generations revealed. Of the mysterious human features: in hair, in forehead, in eyes, in face, in lips, and in lines of hands, and in ears. By these seven are humans revealed.

Sefer ha-Zohar 2:73b
Mystery of the face for those masters of inner wisdom: For facial features are not in outward signs but rather in the signs of inner mysteries. For the face's features are changed by the mark of the features of the concealed face of the spirit that dwells within. And from within that spirit are seen outwardly the facial features that are revealed to the wise.

These passages present a conceptual framework for gazing at the faces of the wise, explaining what the mystical companions believed faces could reveal. The first passage, Zohar 1:192a, describes a contemplative practice performed by the biblical Joseph, a character known for his abilities to interpret dreams and to transform failure into success. The Zohar claims that to advance his cause, Joseph would gaze internally at the image of his father, the patriarch Jacob. This gaze brought him an additional heavenly spirit that allowed his endeavors to prosper. Significantly, the term for 'image' (*deyoqna*) in this passage is closely related to the word for 'features' (*deyoqnin*) in the other two passages. (*Deyoqna* is the singular form of the noun.) This word choice implies that Joseph did not contemplate Jacob's image in general, but rather that Joseph specifically contemplated his father's facial features. Thus the passage claims that through internal envisioning of a holy man's features, Joseph gained interior spiritual light that allowed him to succeed in life. While the biblical Joseph story attributes Joseph's success to God, the Zohar additionally attributes it to a contemplative process of internal gazing upon a patriarch's face.

The next two passages indicate how this technique might work. Both Zohar 2:70b and Zohar 2:73b are excerpts from a long section in *Sefer ha-Zohar* devoted to human physiognomy and chiromancy.[14] This section focuses not only on outward facial features, as demonstrated in Zohar 2:70b, but also on mysterious interior features understood to impress outer features, as described in Zohar 2:73b. The outward, accessible features signify characteristics such as a settled or unsettled mind, the ability to keep secrets, and potential success at Torah study.[15] Yet it is the interior concealed features that craft the outer revealed features, mirroring the tension between divinity as concealed and revealed in kabbalistic theology. The ability to perceive these concealed features depends on spiritual mastery.

Sefer ha-Zohar 2:74a

> When a person walks on the way of truth, those who know the mystery of their Lord look at him, because that spirit that is within is confirmed in him, and projects outside a figure of all. And that figure is the figure of a human, and thus it is a figure more complete than all [other] figures.[16] And this is the figure that passes briefly before the eyes of the wise of heart. This one, when they look at his outer face—a face that stands before eyes of the heart—they love it.

According to this passage, a face is more than its features and the lines etched upon it by time and personality. Instead, it is a window to the spirit within, which projects itself onto the outward features and shapes them, but also exhibits brief flashes of inner spiritual truth and reveals the soul's composition. This revelatory moment, which can only be perceived by the wise of heart (by which, of course, the kabbalists mean themselves), inspires love. Glimpsing this concealed human image within the revealed human face implies a further connection between microcosm and macrocosm, as the limited human face becomes an entry into the greater spiritual universe beyond it. Faces nest within faces, drawing the observer toward an inward journey of continuing revelation.

It is not only human faces that possess this nested character in the Zohar. One of the text's most famous passages recounts a face-to-face encounter between the Torah, which also represents the feminine Divine Presence, and her scholar-lover, who represents the kabbalist.

Sefer ha-Zohar 2:99a–b

A parable: To what may it be compared? To a beloved maiden who is beautiful in appearance and beautiful in form, and she is concealed in her palace. And she has a single lover who is unknown to people, except to her in concealment. This lover, for the love with which he loves her, passes constantly by the gate of her house, raising his eyes to every side. . . . What does she do? She opens a small window in that concealed palace where she is and reveals her face to her lover, and immediately pulls back and conceals herself. None of those who are near the lover see or understand—only the lover himself, and his inner being and his heart and his soul follow her. . . . Torah knows that the wise of heart circles her gate every day. What does she do? She reveals her face to him from within the palace and hints for him a hint, and immediately returns to her place and conceals herself. . . . As he comes near to her, she begins to speak with him from behind a curtain that she has spread, words suitable for him until he reflects little by little. . . . Then she converses with him from behind a fine veil, words of riddle. . . . Then when he is accustomed to her, she reveals herself to him face to face and tells him all her hidden secrets and all her hidden ways that were concealed within her heart from ancient days. Then he is a complete man, a husband of Torah and a master of the house, for she has revealed all her secrets to him, removing and concealing nothing.[17]

In this classic parable, face-to-face encounter again signifies revelation. Rather than a human face as revelatory mechanism, however, here the face is part of a metaphor applied to the Torah, described as a beautiful and beloved woman who draws her lover ever closer, removing curtains and veils until finally she meets him face to face. This movement inward is also a movement upward, with the face-to-face encounter representing the highest, most secret level of religious knowledge. As in Zohar 2:74a, such interior knowledge is accessible to the wise of heart, whose vision allows him both to see the interior face that spirit inscribes on the exterior human face, and to see the interior face of scripture with all of its curtains, veils, and safeguards removed. On the human level, this interior knowledge allows the kabbalists to recognize each other, to acknowledge their companions' spiritual merit, and ultimately to be transformed by this merit, which reveals the Presence of God. This interior knowledge also represents the esoteric Torah interpretations from which the kabbalists' religious understandings originate. Both the interior human face and the interior Torah-maiden's face grant admission to the Divine Presence, the most accessible aspect of divinity according to the kabbalists' theology. In addition to the image of a beautiful maiden or devoted wife, this aspect of God is often represented with metaphors of access points such as doors and gateways, refraction instruments like prisms and gathered waters, and chronological moments understood to grant heavenly access, such as the Sabbath.[18]

For the kabbalists who call themselves the wise of heart, the face is never simply a face. Through their rhetoric, the mystics craft and define facial contiguity associations, including the implications of face-to-face meeting. The face is the focal point for personal encounter, whether through a slow process of flirtation and unveiling that grants access to scriptural mysteries, or through its ability to allow interior spiritual traits to flash or shine forth permanently, marking mystical achievement. In both cases, momentary insight plays an important role. With the human facial encounter, flashes of insight reveal the person's spiritual qualities. A truly righteous person may eventually achieve a level of wisdom where his face constantly reveals his interior merit. In the encounter with the Torah-maiden, flashes of insight characterize the Torah's flirtations with her lover as she reveals her face briefly and tantalizes him to continue his pursuit so that he can converse at length face-to-face and receive Her secrets. In both cases, brief insights entice the viewer toward greater inner achievement. Thus, the face becomes both a vehicle for and an affirmation of personal spiritual transformation.

The composite divine face, with its complex plurality, conceptually facilitates this transformation. This is the face understood to manifest when kabbalists gather together, allowing them access to divine secrets. This face also contributes to the inner human face that impresses itself upon exterior features, providing insight into a person's spiritual composition and sometimes granting access to the Divine Presence. Beyond this, the composite countenance is also the face of Torah through which the Divine Presence peers to welcome the kabbalist. In each of these examples, participating in the composite facial metaphor modifies both human and divine countenances. The kabbalists are made holy as the divine manifests in their faces, and the divine face is humanized to the extent that it may manifest in human encounter, though in complex ways. Together, these aspects of the facial metaphor help to produce what James Fernandez calls a 'return to the whole'—a perceived restoration and affirmation of humanity's place within the greater ordering of the universe. As Fernandez explains, an important way to achieve this experience of cosmological coherence is to develop a theology that embraces dynamically interacting metaphors (Fernandez 1986, pp. 191–208). Through the metaphor of God's composite countenance manifested in human faces, the kabbalists teach themselves to inhabit a world transformed by access to God that is potentially present in the most common human meetings.

Emphasizing this point, the Zohar contains several stories in which the mystical companions encounter mysterious strangers who reveal divine secrets. Both Zohar 2:94b and Zohar 2:99a–b (presented above) derive from one such passage, *Sava de-Mishpatim* (The Old Man of Torah Portion Mishpatim), in which the companions encounter what at first appears to be an irritating old man who ultimately is revealed as a great sage and master of Torah. It is he who delivers the teaching on the maiden in the palace.

Read together, the Zohar's teachings on faces suggest that every face-to-face encounter may ultimately prove a vehicle for achieving spiritual transformation. Indeed, in *Sava de-Mishpatim* the kabbalists' own face-to-face encounter, which manifests the Divine Presence in Zohar 2:94b, leads to the mystics' recognizing the old man's spiritual merit through their face-to-face encounter with him. This interaction in turn reveals the process by which the wise of heart become lovers of Torah by encountering it face to face, approaching God's Presence in the process. The old man's first appearance as an annoyance teaches the Zohar's readers to seek divine encounter in every face-to-face encounter. In this way, the divine facial metaphor encourages the kabbalists to perceive God in the world around them, allowing daily experiences with other people to become lenses through which to view divinity. The kabbalists understand and experience God in the world in terms of encounters with others' faces.

4 THE DIVINE FACE AS COMPOSITE METAPHOR

For the kabbalists who composed the Zohar, applying anthropomorphic metaphors to God could be a risky endeavor that encouraged over-simplification of the divine and incorrect thinking about a spiritually critical topic. Although understanding God's face as composite helped to complicate a potentially reductive way of thinking about the divine, the idea that God's face could be too much like a human face was still troubling to the mystics. This concern echoed their tradition of understanding God as both revealed and concealed, which implied that while God could be understood to a certain extent, divinity remained ultimately mysterious. At the same time, metaphoric imagery was one of the kabbalists' most important cognitive tools. This creative tension led to an alternative method for describing the divine countenance: the kabbalistic mixed (or composite) metaphor.

In a typical kabbalistic mixed metaphor, diverse metaphoric images are blended to describe a divine attribute or activity. Such blending creates a complex contemplative model for the kabbalistic reader, who must situate himself in relation to each metaphoric element's distinctive connotations, as well as in relation to these images' interactions.[19] Using such images for contemplative purposes is possible because literary images encourage speculation on the connotative networks that structure them. Each figurative image stands in relation to this underlying network of connotations, which are present in the image's multi-layered texture. When an image is composed of many individual metaphors, it prevents any one image from becoming conceptually privileged, allowing each to stand as a corrective for the others and refining the concept expressed by broadening its range and expanding its serviceability (Kofman 1999, pp. 25, 29). James Fernandez describes such mixed images as 'polyvectoral—they move in several directions and often in such a counterposing manner as to result not in movement but in contemplation' (Fernandez 1986, p. 87).[20]

The kabbalists incorporate this dynamic into their mystical writings by describing the divine countenance not just as a face composed of many human faces, but as a face comprised of many mixed images and aspects—another type of composite countenance. Zohar 2:86a, for example, refers to the *sefirot* (divine aspects) as 'faces of the King, in which the Holy King manifests—and they are His Name, and He is they.' Each divine aspect is a face of God, and one face cannot be separated from the others—each is required to convey the divine Name. In further passages, the Zohar explains how these faces work together to express divine complexity. The following passage uses human imagery combined with light imagery to describe two interdependent faces of God.

Sefer ha-Zohar 2:51b–2:52a
This may be compared to a king who is entirely complete. His mind is entirely complete. What is the way of that king? His face shines always like the sun, because he is complete. And thus he judges. He judges for good and he judges for bad. And because of this one should try to be wary of him. One who is foolish sees the face of the king shining and smiling and is not wary of him. But one who is wise, even though he sees the face of the king shining, he says, Surely the king is complete. The king is complete. His mind is complete. I see that in that shining, judgment dwells and is hidden. Although it does not appear, without it the king would not be complete. And therefore one must be wary. Thus the Blessed Holy One is always complete, in this aspect and in that aspect, but only His shining face is seen. And therefore those wicked fools are not wary of Him. The righteous wise ones say, The King is complete. Although his face appears shining, judgment is hidden within it. Therefore one must be wary of Him.

Here, the text reminds its readers that the divine face encompasses all the complexities of a human face, including its many moods—both those moods that are apparent and the hidden thoughts that lie beneath the surface. For the unwary, these hidden thoughts can spell disaster, since the shining outward countenance may be misleading. As the Zohar explains in texts presented previously, even a human face is not merely its surface, but conceals an underlying complexity. With the divine face as well, a merciful countenance conceals the potential for harsh judgment, and therefore it is incumbent upon a wise person to remember that whatever a face may look like, it contains both aspects.[21] Humanity and divinity are two-faced. The mystics also describe the divine face as proceeding beyond the human condition, as in the following passage.

Sefer ha-Zohar 3:93b
Rabbi Yitzhak opened: 'For you, my heart says, Seek My face! O Lord, I seek Your face' (Psalm 27:8). . . . Seek my face, which is the Crowns of the King that are one with the King, and they are in Him and they are His Name. . . . Another thing: 'For you, my heart says, Seek My face!' . . . These are the appointed times and festivals, all of which are summoned to the place that is called Holy, in order to crown each and every one on its day and each and every one at its time.

In this passage, each divine aspect is a crown of God, and these several crowns together comprise the divine face. As in Zohar 2:86a, these faces together express the divine Name. Yet this passage goes a step farther, explaining that the sacred faces, which are also crowns, additionally encompass sacred time. The facial metaphor becomes multidimensional as it expands to reference not only human faces, but also crowns, cultural objects associated with richness and royalty, and time, the medium in which humanity lives. The divine countenance retains human facial connotations, but is also made unfamiliar through combination with rich material objects and the abstractions of temporality. Beyond this, since each face represents a sacred time, moments in the kabbalists' yearly ritual cycle become entry points into the face of God and thus invitations to divine encounter. This temporal facial metaphor functions similarly to texts that urge the kabbalists to seek God in each other's faces, because it transforms the cycle of holy days into a vehicle through which to seek the divine in daily experience. The divine face as sacred time creates opportunities to see God in ritual action.

Other Zoharic passages describe the divine countenance more explicitly. Zohar 2:122b–123a describes the head and face of the supernal King, including the divine hair, forehead, eyes, eyebrows, nose, ears, face, beard, lips, and mouth. Yet this vision of the divine countenance resembles a human face only in the categorical description of its parts, since these familiar features are composed of non-facial elements.

Sefer ha-Zohar 2:122b–123a
Face of the King: shining of Father and Mother and their stretching forth— brightening, surrounding, and glowing in this head of the King. And then testimony of the King is offered by them. . . . Lips of the King: Thus it is taught—when the shining of the Father is brightened, it shines with three lights. From one light shines supernal *Hesed* (Mercy). From one light glows a brightness that is called brain of the King. And one light is suspended until the brightness of the Mother glows, and then when illumined shines with five lights. With what is it illuminated? From one path that is hidden and concealed, to which Father clings, as it is written: 'A path unknown to a bird of prey (Job 28:7).[22] Then male cleaves to female and She becomes pregnant and bears five lights, and from those five lights are engraved fifty gates of many lights. They are fifty, received as forty-nine: forty-nine pure faces and forty-nine impure faces of Torah.[23] One remains, and this one is illuminated by all. And when that [light] of Father that is suspended unites as one and settles in the King, they are called Lips of the King. And therefore He decrees words of truth.[24]

In this passage, the divine countenance is composite in a manner different from the passages presented above. Even a single aspect of God's face, the divine lips, is expressed as a richly complicated mixed metaphor. The King's face, though still called a face, is not so much a countenance as a configuration of two divine aspects— the Father, also known as Wisdom (*Hokhmah*), and the Mother, also known as Understanding (*Binah*). In Kabbalah, these upper *sefirot*, considered less accessible than the Divine Presence, are sometimes understood as interior to the divine brain— another anthropomorphic metaphor. The face itself (or at least this portion of it) is thus a configuration of two entities that are ultimately one—a theme that extends through the description of the divine lips, where these two aspects' holy union is represented as sexual conjunction that produces offspring of light, which stand for further divine gradations and the paths of spiritual energy that flow between them.

The text's goal is to present divinity's different aspects as at once dynamic, varied, and unified.

Without getting too deeply into the passage's theology, it is helpful to examine the individual metaphors that comprise the divine lips—already a metaphor when applied to the ultimate unknown of God.[25] Yet quickly the passage shifts to describe those lips as configurations of light that also include Father, Mother, and offspring, which in turn branch out into gates of light—a typical kabbalistic way of describing the sefirotic structure. These images together define God as the source of truth. Contributing to this theme, the lips and lights are also called gates that simultaneously are faces of Torah interpretation—another mode of revealing sacred truth. Thus, a single aspect of the divine countenance, in this case God's lips, kaleidoscopically refracts to reveal multiple faces nested within it. As in the texts examined above, faces are nested within faces, and each face pulls the reader deeper into an inward journey toward spiritual knowledge that reveals further dimensions of divine encounter.

One way to approach such a text is as a synesthetic jumble whose meaning lies in the refusal to commit itself to meaning, implying a mystical experience ultimately beyond words. In this reading, the breakdown of comprehensibility among the metaphors' clashing components represents the ineffable divine nature. Yet these images also are deliberately chosen and crafted. Each element of the divine lips' description contributes its own associations to the overall face, drawing the reader into a web of meaning that includes human, parental, childbirth imagery, masculine and feminine gendered imagery, abstract light imagery, and material gateway imagery that is symbolic of entry, encounter, and transition. It also includes the sacred Torah text. These metaphors encompass nature, nurture, culture, access, and knowledge, while also expressing a general dynamicism as each image slips rapidly into the other. The tension between each of these metaphors' connotations creates a complex whole that prevents the reader from imagining God in overly simplistic or human terms, even as the text tells him that he is encountering the most relatable of anthropomorphic images, the human face. God is represented both as a culturally structured familiar being and as a shining abstraction beyond human nature.

Contemplating this image compels the reader to generate meaning from these tensions—on the one hand to perceive a connection with a human-like divine being, and on the other hand to understand that being as existing in a manner beyond human possibility. Such imagery both familiarizes and de-familiarizes divinity, encouraging readers to speculate on how these images blend together into a meaningful whole. As they do so, they are also compelled to contemplate their own relationship to this divine universality—especially since Kabbalah as a mystical movement is so deeply concerned with promoting *imitatio dei*. Thus the entire Zoharic description of the divine face can be read as a comment on divine universality and the mysterious ways in which this universality relates to humanity. For the mystics, God's face is and is not a human face. It is always shifting, becoming, dividing, uniting, and transforming into something more. The divine countenance is polyvectoral, promoting contemplation and the thoughtful reader's re-orientation within the greater universal order.[26]

5 CONCLUSION

Sefer ha-Zohar redefines the anthropomorphic metaphor of the divine face in a composite manner to invest it with new meaning. On the one hand, this kabbalistic text suggests that human faces together comprise the divine face, encouraging contemplative brotherhood among mystics who learn that they are to seek divine encounter in each other's faces, which become vehicles of mutual revelation. On the other hand, complex descriptions of the divine countenance as a mixed metaphor encourage the mystics to understand God as beyond human experience. This division of the divine face into knowable and unknowable aspects mirrors kabbalistic theology's greater structure, which describes God as both knowable and unknowable, both accessible and inaccessible. The kabbalists, committed to inhabiting such tensions, embed them in their writings as contemplative models for spiritual self-transformation. As they thoughtfully manipulate metaphors, they define the paths of revelation and redemption that they hope to follow.

NOTES

1. See Psalm 80:4; Psalm 44:24; and Babylonian Talmud Berakhot 7a–7b. Many other examples exist. Thoroughly exploring them requires a separate study.
2. Some scholars refer to this as an interactivist approach to metaphor. For example, see T. Turner (1991), pp. 128, 134.
3. For a review of literature on kabbalistic symbol and imagery, see Haskell (2008), pp. 337–342; and for further reflections on metaphor in Kabbalah, see Haskell (2013).
4. For an overview of the Zohar's composition and scholarship regarding it, see Green (2004, pp. 162–168). Most of the Zohar was composed between 1280 and 1286, although some sections may have been written earlier. The Zoharic authors continued writing and revising various textual sections throughout the early 1290s. Dating the Zohar's different parts with precision is a topic of scholarly debate. See Scholem (1941, pp. 163–168, 188); Tishby and Lachower (1989, vol. 1, pp. 91–96); Liebes (1993, pp. 11–12, 85–86). For theories regarding the Zohar's group authorship, see Liebes (1993, pp. 85–138); Meroz (2002, pp. 163–193); Huss (2008, pp. 43–44); Wolfson (2009, pp. 144–145, 173–175); and Abrams (2009, pp. 89, 111–113, 139).
5. These *sefirot* often are referred to as *Keter* (Crown), *Hokhmah* (Wisdom), *Binah* (Understanding), *Hesed* (Love), *Din* (Judgment), *Rahamim* (Compassion), *Netzah* (Eternity), *Hod* (Majesty), *Yesod* (Foundation), and *Malkhut* (Kingdom).
6. For a full discussion of how kabbalistic images produce kabbalists, see Haskell (2008, pp. 335–362).
7. The italics are Butler's.
8. The edition of *Sefer ha-Zohar* used in this study is Margaliot (1999). Translations of biblical and Zoharic texts are my own.
9. In Kabbalah, the Divine presence (*Shekhinah*) is generally gendered female. This emerges in part from the word's feminine form in Hebrew and Aramaic, but it is also an important aspect of kabbalistic theology's teachings on gender, completion, spiritual balance, and divine imitation. Gender in Kabbalah is the topic of much scholarly interest and debate. For an interesting reading of this passage that considers kabbalistic gender and sexuality, see Wolfson (1994, pp. 368–377). For further reflections on kabbalistic symbol, gender, and sexuality, including references to other scholars' works, see Haskell (2012, pp. 101–108).
10. For a brief overview of rabbinic passages that express these ideas, see Matt (2009, vol.5, pp. 1–2, n.3). Numerous rabbinic passages that describe human faces shining to

signify spiritual merit also exist. For an example, see Exodus Rabbah 47:6. This essay will focus only on the Zohar's teachings.

11. See the note above regarding Zoharic authorship for references.

12. Avoiding divine anthropomorphisms was a central concern of medieval Jewish philosophers, whose work was influential for the kabbalists. For example, the twelfth-century philosopher Maimonides writes of a need 'to refute the doctrine of the corporeality of God and to establish His real unity—which can have no true reality unless one disproves his corporeality' (Pines 1963 vol. 1, p. 21). While the kabbalists often embraced philosophical ideas, they enthusiastically described God in many and varying ways. Often, these multivocal divine metaphors seem to serve a similar purpose to negative theology, in that they seek to prevent oversimplifying the divine. For discussions of Kabbalah's relationship to philosophy, see Idel (1988, pp. 46–49); Huss (2001, pp. 125, 130–133); and Sendor (1994, pp. 28–35).

13. See T. Turner (1991, pp. 128, 134).

14. See Scholem (1941, p. 160). For a contextualization of physiognomic and chiromantic literature in relation to Kabbalah, see Matt (2007 vol. 4, pp. 392–393, n.76).

15. See Zohar 2:70b–2:73b.

16. The human figure in the passage refers to the prophet Ezekiel's vision in Ezekiel 1, which includes angelic beings with four faces: human, lion, ox, and eagle. For the Zoharic authors, the human face is the most complete and ideal of them all. See Zohar 2:73b–2:74a.

17. In this famous parable, the different levels of approach to the Torah-maiden represent different levels of scriptural interpretation ranging from the plain sense of the text through the most esoteric (kabbalistic) interpretation. For further reading on these interpretive levels and their Christian counterparts, see Talmage (1986, 313–355).

18. For an introductory essay on *Shekhinah*, see Tishby and Lachower (1989 vol. 1, pp. 370–422).

19. For more on the kabbalistic mixed metaphor, see Haskell (2008, pp. 349–356).

20. For similar reflections on the function of mixed images in ritual settings, see V. Turner (1967, pp. 103–106).

21. This comparison to a mercurial human king may have been especially relevant to the kabbalists who composed the Zohar. Relations between Jews and the Spanish rulers under whom they lived were often dangerously unpredictable. See Baer (1961, vol. 1, pp. 118–130).

22. The biblical citation is from the famous wisdom poem in Job 28, which reflects on wisdom's inaccessibility to human beings.

23. These numbers relate to traditional rabbinic teachings on how to derive pure and impure ritual categories by means of Jewish law. The passage's shift from the number fifty to the number forty-nine alludes to another traditional teaching, which is here applied to the interior divine passages among the *sefirot*. The concealment in this passage may have to do with the sexual aspect of the relation between the Father and the Mother, both of which are interior to divinity. For further sources and comments, see Matt (2009 vol. 5, pp. 154, n.42).

24. For reflections on a further section of this description of the divine countenance, see Haskell (2012, pp. 77–79).

25. Indeed, God can be thought of as a participant in a Derridean 'heliotropic metaphor,' in which 'one of the terms directly or indirectly implied in the substitution . . . cannot be properly known' (Derrida and Moore 1974, p. 52).

26. The Zohar also teaches that various sefirotic configurations form interdependent divine countenances, or *partzufim* (such as the Forbearing Face and the Impatient One), a theme greatly expanded upon in sixteenth-century Lurianic Kabbalah. Examining these divine countenances and their complex interactions is beyond the scope of the current study. For introductions to the topic, see Scholem (1941, pp. 268–273) and Fine (2003, pp. 138–141).

REFERENCES

Abrams, Daniel (2009). The invention of the *Zohar* as a book: On the assumptions and expectations of the Kabbalists and modern scholars. *Kabbalah: Journal for the Study of Jewish Mystical Texts* 19, 7–142.

Baer, Yitzhak (1961). *A History of the Jews in Christian Spain*, volume 1, *From the Age of Reconquest to the Fourteenth Century*. Translated by Louis Schoffman, with an introduction by Benjamin R. Gampel. Philadelphia: The Jewish Publication Society of America.

Butler, Judith (1993). *Bodies that Matter: On the Discursive Limits of 'Sex'*. New York: Routledge.

Carruthers, Mary (1998). *The Craft of Thought: Meditation, Rhetoric, and the Making of Images, 400–1200*. Cambridge Studies in Medieval Literature, no. 34. New York: Cambridge University Press.

Derrida, Jacques and F. C. T. Moore (1974). White mythology: Metaphor in the text of philosophy. *New Literary History* 6(1), 5–74.

Durham, Deborah and James Fernandez (1991). Tropical dominions: The figurative struggle over domains of belonging and apartness in Africa. In James Fernandez (ed.), *Beyond Metaphor: The Theory of Tropes in Anthropology*, pp. 190–210. Stanford, CA: Stanford University Press.

Fernandez, James (1986). *Persuasions and Performances: The Play of Tropes in Culture*. Bloomington: Indiana University Press.

Fine, Lawrence (2003). *Physician of the Soul, Healer of the Cosmos: Isaac Luria and His Kabbalistic Fellowship*. Stanford Studies in Jewish History and Culture, edited by Aron Rodrigue and Steven J. Zipperstein. Stanford, CA: Stanford University Press.

Green, Arthur (2004). *A Guide to the Zohar*. Stanford, CA: Stanford University Press.

Haskell, Ellen (2008). Metaphor, transformation and transcendence: Toward an understanding of Kabbalistic imagery in *Sefer hazohar*. *Prooftexts: A Journal of Jewish Literary History* 28(3), 335–362.

Haskell, Ellen (2012). *Suckling at My Mother's Breasts: The Image of a Nursing God in Jewish Mysticism*. Albany, NY: SUNY Press.

Haskell, Ellen (2013). Bathed in milk: Metaphors of suckling and spiritual transmission in thirteenth-century Kabbalah. In Shubha Pathak (ed.), *Figuring Religion: Comparing Ideas, Images, and Activities*, pp. 117–145. Albany, NY: SUNY Press.

Huss, Boaz (2001). Mysticism versus philosophy in kabbalistic literature. *Micrologus* 9, 125–135.

Huss, Boaz (2008). *Like the Radiance of the Sky: Chapters in the Reception History of the Zohar and the Construction of Its Symbolic Value*. Jerusalem: Mosad Bialik.

Idel, Moshe (1988). *Kabbalah: New Perspectives*. New Haven, CT: Yale University Press.

Kofman, Sarah (1999). *Camera Obscura of Ideology*, translated by Will Straw. Ithaca: Cornell University Press.

Lacan, Jacques (1985). The meaning of the phallus. In Juliet Mitchell and Jacqueline Rose (eds.), *Feminine Sexuality: Jacques Lacan and the* école freudienne, translated by Jacqueline Rose. New York: W. W. Norton and Pantheon Books, 1985.

Lakoff, George and Mark Johnson (1980). *Metaphors We Live By*. Chicago: The University of Chicago Press.

Liebes, Yehuda (1993). *Studies in the Zohar*, translated by Arnold Schwartz, Stephanie Nakache, and Penina Peli. SUNY Series in Judaica: Hermeneutics, Mysticism, and Religion, edited by Michael Fishbane, Robert Goldenberg, and Arthur Green. Albany: SUNY Press.

Margaliot, Reuven Moshe (ed.) (1999). *Sefer ha-Zohar al Hamishah Humshei Torah*. 3 vols. Jerusalem: Mosad ha-Rav Kook.

Matt, Daniel (ed. and transl.) (2007). *The Zohar: Pritzker Edition*, vol. 4. Stanford, CA: Stanford University Press for Zohar Education Project, Inc.

Matt, Daniel (ed. and transl.) (2009). *The Zohar: Pritzker Edition*, vol. 5. Stanford, CA: Stanford University Press for Zohar Education Project, Inc.

Meroz, Ronit (2002). And I was not there?: The complaints of Rabbi Simeon bar Yohai according to an unknown Zoharic story. *Tarbitz* 71, 163–193.

Pines, Shlomo (transl.) (1963). *The Guide of the Perplexed*, by Moses Maimonides, with an introduction by Leo Strauss. 2 vols. Chicago: University of Chicago Press.

Rappaport, Roy (1979). *Ecology, Meaning, and Religion*. Berkeley, CA: North Atlantic Books.

Scholem, Gershom (1941). *Major Trends in Jewish Mysticism*, with a foreword by Robert Alter. Jerusalem: Schocken Publishing House.

Sendor, Mark (1994). *The Emergence of Provençal Kabbalah: Rabbi Isaac the Blind's 'Commentary on* Sefer Yetzirah', vol. 1. Ph.D. dissertation, Harvard University.

Talmage, Frank (1986). Apples of gold: The inner meaning of sacred texts in Judaism. In Arthur Green (ed.), *Jewish Spirituality*, volume 1, *From the Bible through the Middle Ages*, pp. 313–355. World Spirituality no. 13. New York: Crossroad.

Tishby, Isaiah and Fischel Lachower (eds.) (1989). *The Wisdom of the Zohar: An Anthology of Texts*, translated by David Goldstein, 3 vols. Washington, D.C.: The Littman Library of Jewish Civilization.

Turner, Terence (1991). 'We are parrots', 'twins are birds': Play of tropes as operational structure. In James Fernandez (ed.), *Beyond Metaphor: The Theory of Tropes in Anthropology*, pp. 121–158. Stanford, CA: Stanford University Press.

Turner, Victor (1967). *The Forest of Symbols: Aspects of Ndembu Ritual*. Ithaca, NY: Cornell University Press.

Wolfson, Elliot (1994). *Through a Speculum that Shines: Vision and Imagination in Medieval Jewish Mysticism*. Princeton, NJ: Princeton University Press.

Wolfson, Elliot (2009). The Anonymous chapters of the elderly master of secrets: New evidence for the early activity of the Zoharic circle. *Kabbalah: Journal for the Study of Jewish Mystical Texts* 19, 143–194.

CHAPTER 8

The Guru's Tongue

Metaphor, Imagery, and Vernacular Language in Vaiṣṇava Sahajiyā Hindu Traditions

GLEN ALEXANDER HAYES[1]

The praises for Kṛṣṇa are the uterine blood, while the seed syllable is the semen.

The guru's tongue (guru jihvā) is the penis, while the ear of the disciple is the vagina.

So, your birth should result from these things.

You should really try to understand how you can be born through the grace of practitioners.

Ākiñcana-dāsa, Vivarta-vilāsa ('The Play of Transformation')2

These vivid passages from a 17th-century Vaiṣṇava Sahajiyā text provide us with a good example of the richness and complexity of metaphors and vernacular religious language (in this case, Bengali) as expressed in medieval Tantric literature. We will analyze these metaphors later in this essay, but they help to introduce us to some of the issues regarding the scholarly study of Tantra,[3] especially those concerning differences between South Asian Tantras composed in Sanskrit (the elite learned language of the high-caste Brahmins) and others composed in Bengali and other vernacular (local) languages. Most prior scholarship, especially in the area of Hindu Tantra, has emphasized the more abstract and elite Sanskrit-based texts; more recently, however, scholars of Tantra have demonstrated that important Tantric traditions have developed complex metaphors in vernacular languages such as Bengali, Hindi, and Malayalam.[4] In order to address the issues of religious language, metaphor, and mind which are the focus of this current volume, this essay has two objectives: (1) to briefly review modern metaphor theories and consider their use in the study of vernacular Tantra, and (2) to apply these insights to brief selections of 17th-century Bengali Vaiṣṇava Sahajiyā texts. But first we must consider the general background of vernacular or 'local' Tantra in Bengal.

1 METAPHOR, RELIGIOUS LANGUAGE, TANTRA, AND BENGAL

To begin with, the area of northeastern India including greater Bengal and Assam has historically been one of the most fertile arenas for the development and growth of Buddhist and Hindu Tantrism. It was, in many ways, a type of 'frontier area' removed from the more orthodox Brahmanical and Sanskritic areas of South Asia to the west and south. As such, it fostered a particular constellation of cultures, varieties of religious languages, and distinctive metaphorical expressions. The renowned Buddhist centers of Tamralipti and Nalanda were located here, and Buddhist Tantrics travelled throughout the region, including active exchanges between Bengal and Himalayan regions such as Nepal, Bhutan, Sikkim, and Tibet. As noted by Banerji (1978, p. 70) in his survey *Tantra in Bengal*, from 'the Tibetan Bstan-hgyur and Lama Tārānātha's history of Tibet, we learn about quite a number of other Buddhist Tantras by Bengali authors. Their Sanskrit originals are lost, and are preserved only in Tibetan versions and, in a very few cases, in Chinese.' But Tantrism was also being expressed in proto-vernacular languages like 'old Bengali' or Apabhraṃśa, surviving in manuscript form as collections called *caryāpadas* and *dohas* (ca. 950–1150 CE) by their discoverer, Haraprasad Sastri (see, for example, Mojumdar 1973). These important texts suggest a vital vernacular tradition of Buddhist Tantrism in Bengal, outside of the walls of universities and the elite, for the songs of the *caryāpadas* and *dohas* reveal aspects of domestic village life like dancing, cooking, music, and boating. As a result, their religious language and metaphors reflect the cultural contexts in which they developed. In contrast to the refined philosophy and abstractions of many Sanskrit- and Tibetan-based Tantras, these short Buddhist works focus more on the experiences of specific gurus and particular practices rather than developing a more general Tantric system.

Although the origins of Hindu Tantrism are as obscure as those of Buddhist Tantra, we also find many examples of both elite and popular expressions.[5] While this is not the place to examine the many important Tantric teachers and texts connected with Bengal, it should be noted that some of the most renowned works are the *Sarvollāsa* of Sarvānanda (ca. 1425 CE), the famous *Tantrasāra* of Kṛṣṇānanda Āgamavāgiśa (ca. 1580 CE), and the *Śyāmārahasya* of Pūrṇānanda (ca. 1575 CE).[6] But these texts tended to be written by, and intended for, upper-caste Hindus; as with Buddhist Tantrism, various Tantric movements flourished among village and rural people and among the lower castes and outcastes. It is especially among these groups that vernacular Tantric traditions developed. As with Buddhist Tantrism, in contrast to most Sanskrit-based Tantric traditions, Bengali vernacular Tantrics, such as the Vaiṣṇava Sahajiyās, the Bāuls, and the Kartābhajās, did not emphasize cosmic abstractions or complex philosophies.[7] Instead, these widespread movements and their gurus were concerned with the problems of everyday life, the human body, and desires. In their own ways, Sahajiyās, Bāuls, and Kartābhajās confronted the issues of cosmology, physiology, sexuality, and soteriology and came up with their own distinctive metaphorical worlds, conceptual blends, and vernacular expressions. Perhaps it is not surprising that they embraced the concept of *saṃdeha* or liberation 'with a body' far more than most Sanskrit-based texts, for whom the physical body was still regarded as less real than, for example, the subtle body (*sūkṣma-śarīra*, in Śaiva Tantras).[8] Although all Tantras regard some type of body as 'real' and useful for liberation, Bengali vernacular Tantras have placed great emphasis upon the physical body as the basis of *sādhana* (psychophysical ritual and meditative practices).

Perhaps as an extension of this *saṃdeha* worldview, Bengali vernacular Tantrics tended to embrace a cosmological continuum of substance and consciousness, as opposed to the more dualistic model proposed by Sāṃkhya and Sanskrit-based systems, for example, the contrast between *puruṣa* (consciousness) and *prakṛti* (matter). Although vernacular traditions employ classical South Asia homologies between the body and the cosmos, microcosm and macrocosm, these connections are not based so much upon the precise use of mantras as much as they are upon the use of specifically *bodily* rituals such as ritual sexual intercourse, ingestion of sexual and other substances, devotional singing, and visualization. This focus on embodiment and, in a way, the local and immediate world, led in turn to development of various religious metaphors dealing with 'taste,' 'touch,' and 'sight' (to name just a few). As a result, we find Bengali vernacular Tantric communities making use of esoteric discourses and rituals expressing these polyvalent metaphors to comprehend and achieve cosmic processes, beings, and liberation. Their religious language and metaphors reveal to us a type of 'sensuous cosmophysiology.'

Descriptions of the subtle inner yogic bodies and regions use imageries and metaphors from Bengali culture and the Gangetic delta, so that, for example, the better-known *cakras* and *kuṇḍalinī-śakti* of Śaiva and Śākta systems are often replaced in Vaiṣṇava Sahajiyā teachings by the more hydraulic and riverine images of enchanted ponds (*sarovara*) and winding rivers (*bāṅkānadī*). In the *Amṛtaratnāvalī* of Mukunda-dāsa (ca. 1600 CE) we find the following (verses 96–98):[9]

> Through the ninth door[10] is the Pond of Lust (*kāma-sarovara*).
>
> Thus has been proclaimed the story which all the *śāstras* discuss.
>
> There are the Pond of Lust (*kāma-sarovara*) [and] the Pond of Self-
>
> consciousness (*māna-sarovara*);
>
> The Pond of Divine Love (*prema-sarovara*) [and] the Pond of
>
> Indestructibility (*akṣaya-sarovara*).
>
> The four Ponds lie within the heart.
>
> If you have a body (*deha*), you can reach the other shore.[11]

In other Vaiṣṇava Sahajiyā, Bāul, and Kartābhajā texts we also find extensive uses of references to, and metaphors of, Bengali sweets, flowers, animals, villages, market-places, and even local coinage. To be sure, many of these have pan-Indian cognates, but they exist in these texts as specifically Bengali variants, located in, and expressing, Bengali culture and contexts.

In grappling with the fundamental Tantric issues of sexuality, ritual transformation, and cosmic powers, Bengali vernacular Tantras reflect not just a need to balance the feminine with the masculine, but, perhaps reflecting the prevalence of

Śaktism and other goddess traditions in the region, a frequent emphasis upon the cosmic feminine, the role of the female ritual partner (gopīs, nāyikās), and (especially with Sahajiyās) the necessity of the inner visualized female form (śrīrūpa-mañjarī) as prerequisites to final liberation. This emphasis is quite different than the more patriarchal and masculine emphases in much (although not all) of the higher Sanskrit traditions of orthodox Brahmins. In addition to this important valorization of the feminine, we find among the Vaiṣṇava Sahajiyās the process of what Joseph O'Connell calls 'anamnesia,' a ritual transformation whereby the practitioner seeks to 'remember' (smaraṇa) his/her 'true nature' (svarūpa) as a participant in the cosmic drama (dhāma-līlā) of Kṛṣṇa and Rādhā.[12] Understandably, this all has a dramatic influence upon the development of religious language and metaphor.

Finally, the academic study of Bengali vernacular Tantric traditions (as well as those from other regions) has been hampered not only by Orientalist strategies, terminologies, sanitizing, and censorship, as Padoux (2002), Brooks (1990), Stewart (2010) and Urban (2001a, 2003) have argued, but also by the problems of attempting to study 'local' and vernacular Tantra without having the discourse constrained by the generic reductionist concept of Sanskrit-based 'Tantra' or 'Tantrism' (itself an Orientalist and scholarly construct). This essay will demonstrate the vernacular 'Bengali' and local nature of Vaiṣṇava Sahajiyā Tantric traditions. Rather than understanding them from the perspective of Sanskrit-based, elite Tantric traditions, we will encounter them on their own terms, hopefully appreciating their richness and complexity.[13]

In this short essay I would like to consider some of these problems of studying 'local' and vernacular Tantric metaphors and religious language by referring to selections from two 17th century Vaiṣṇava Sahajiyā texts that I have translated.[14] Information gleaned from these wonderful, if challenging, esoteric texts can illustrate not only important aspects of vernacular Tantric literature, but also show how the use of modern conceptual metaphor theories (especially those developed by George Lakoff and Mark Johnson 1980, 1999; Lakoff 1987; Lakoff and Núñez 2000; and Lakoff and Turner 1989; see below) can help us to better understand the imaginative metaphorical worlds expressed by vernacular texts and traditions. One way to 'liberate' local Tantras from the constraints of the dominant Sanskrit-based model of 'Tantra' is to explore the vernacular language itself, to coax out the often-profound metaphors and entailments that 'live' in the texts.

Edward C. Dimock presented some of the basic beliefs and practices of Vaiṣṇava Sahajiyā traditions and discussed the problematics of determining their origins in his now-classic The Place of the Hidden Moon.[15] However, for the convenience of those readers not familiar with his work, I will provide a quick overview of these fascinating traditions. The Sahajiyās may be considered—in the very broad sense—an interaction of intricate Tantric yoga with Vaiṣṇava bhakti devotionalism, with the resultant a quite distinctive vernacular Tantric tradition.[16] First, Sahajiyās adapt classical devotional interpretations of Kṛṣṇa, transforming him from a supreme being (as Bhagavān, quite distinct from ordinary human beings) into the inner cosmic form (svarūpa) of every human male. Rādhā is transformed from the consort or hlādini-śakti ('bliss emanation') of Kṛṣṇa into the svarūpa of every woman. For

Sahajiyās, in other words, the goal is not to worship Kṛṣṇa or imitate Rādhā and the *gopīs* in a dualistic *bhakti* sense, but rather *to become* Kṛṣṇa or Rādhā themselves, in a monistic Tantric manner. Second, by expressing these alternative and antinomian notions of Kṛṣṇa and Rādhā in Bengali metaphors, language, and verse, and embedding these narratives in specific Sahajiyā teaching lineages, they move Kṛṣṇa and Rādhā even further from the Sanskrit-based and classical formulations into the local cultural and cognitive realities of Bengali men and women.

As Dimock has shown, Kṛṣṇa and his erotic encounters with Rādhā would seem to be natural choices for adaptations by late medieval Sahajiyā Tantrics as they sought to express the need to reverse the phenomenal flow of creation—engendered as the 'play' of male and female powers—'upwards against the current' (*sroter ujāna*) back to the unitive state of Sahaja, the 'Innate' or 'Primordial' condition. Of course, the popular notion of the religious leader Kṛṣṇa Caitanya (ca. 1486–1533 CE) as the dual incarnation of both Rādhā and Kṛṣṇa, developed by Kṛṣṇa-dāsa Kavirāja (ca. 1615 CE) in his *Caitanya-caritāmṛta*,[17] was also taken up by some Sahajiyā gurus as a clear reflection of their own belief that all Sahajiyās must themselves realize the indwelling of both male and female powers within their own physical bodies.

2 CONTEMPORARY METAPHOR THEORIES AND THE STUDY OF VERNACULAR TANTRA

If we can set aside the controversy of possible Sahajiyā influence on orthodox Vaiṣṇavism,[18] we can turn our attention to how vernacular Tantric metaphors are expressed in some Sahajiyā texts, such as the *Amṛtaratnāvalī* of Mukunda-dāsa (ca. 1600 CE) and the *Vivarta-vilāsa* of Ākiñcana-dāsa (ca. 1650 CE).[19] Of interest is the fact that, in contrast to most other Tantric traditions which have extensive written commentaries based on major subsequent or 'root' texts, there appears to be no such tradition of written commentaries in Vaiṣṇava Sahajiyā traditions. So the modern scholar is immediately challenged when dealing with the intricacies and details of the existing texts (many of which remain unstudied manuscripts in Bengali archives and libraries). We lack traditional guides to the texts, but we can turn to other methods. One fruitful way to do this is to explore the metaphors that lie at the heart of the texts. To begin with, the basic Vaiṣṇava notion of *avatāra* is itself a wonderful metaphoric process, for it enables an abstract, cosmic, divine being to be expressed in more earthly, concrete terms—one of the basic functions of either religious metaphor (such as 'God is love') or everyday metaphor ('Life is a journey'). Whether it is Viṣṇu taking form as a fish or a boar or a man-lion or Kṛṣṇa taking form as a baby, a friend, or a lover, it is this shape-shifting nature of Viṣṇu and Kṛṣṇa that lends itself to additional Tantric reinterpretation and metaphorical elaboration.

Until recent decades, metaphor has been studied by Western scholars primarily as a linguistic and poetic device. And, as scholars of South Asia know, metaphor is given extensive treatment in classical Indian aesthetics and dramaturgy in terms of *rūpaka*, *alaṃkāra*, and *dvani* (ideas which continue in Gauḍīya Vaiṣṇava and Sahajiyā aesthetics).[20] But over the past several decades a new theory of 'conceptual metaphor' has emerged, based on the efforts of a wide range of scholars, including linguists, philosophers, literary critics, folklorists, cognitive scientists, and anthropologists.[21] Many of these ideas are explored in other essays in this current volume. A methodology using concepts from this emerging field shows great promise in our efforts towards understanding religious texts and discourse. Vernacular religious traditions may be contrasted to classical and elite traditions not only because they are developed in (and responded to) different social, cultural, and historical contexts, but also because they make distinctive uses of conceptual metaphors in their attempt to construe and express sacred realities and beings. These are not metaphors just in the sense of literary and poetic devices; the modern understanding of conceptual metaphors connects metaphors to fundamental cognitive, physiological, and neurological processes, many of which we are only just beginning to understand (cf. Introduction to this volume and Feyaerts and Boeve, chapter 3).

As Lakoff and Johnson observe (1980, p.3), 'metaphor is pervasive in everyday life, not just in language but in thought and action. Our ordinary conceptual system, in terms of which we both think and act, is fundamentally metaphorical in nature.' According to Johnson (1987, pp. xiv–xv), metaphor is

conceived as a pervasive mode of understanding by which we project patterns from one domain of experience in order to structure another domain of a different kind. So conceived, metaphor is not merely a linguistic mode of expression; rather, it is one of the chief cognitive structures by which we are able to have coherent, ordered experiences that we can reason about and make sense of. Through metaphor, we make use of patterns that obtain in our physical experience to organize our more abstract understanding.

Following Lakoff and Johnson, other scholars applied their insights to culture and cognition, arguing that different languages and metaphors correspond to different cognitive models and worldviews. For our purposes it is worthwhile to note Palmer's (1996) argument that human communities operate with 'folk cognitive models,' models of reality that operate in the minds of speakers of a given language (p. 36). Thus, vernacular Tantric traditions like the Sahajiyās are not just using different languages to express the same basic Tantric worldviews; they are in fact expressing distinct cognitive, metaphorical, and cosmological models. That is one of the reasons why the Sahajiyā cosmophysiology of lotus ponds and rivers is so different from the Śaiva models of *cakras* and *nāḍīs*; although structurally similar, the metaphors used are different, as are the entailments, and the subtle meanings. In the terms used by Fauconnier and Turner (2002), the results are different 'conceptual blends' and 'emergent structure.'

According to Palmer, one of the major goals of language, especially metaphors, is to convey images from one person to another. This is also a major goal of Tantric *sādhana* and initiation, as gurus experience cosmic realities and bodily sensations, then share them with disciples using rituals, texts, metaphors, and discourses. But, just as Tantric imagery is always essentially secretive and esoteric (*gupta, rahasya, marma*), so are images never directly communicated by language; rather, to quote Palmer (1996, p. 47), they are 'mental representations that begin as conceptual analogs of immediate, perceptual experience from the peripheral sensory organs.' This is why we must pay close attention to the religious language and vernacularity of the traditions we study, for if the key to Tantric visualization and *sādhanas* are the images of deities and the disciples' connections with them, the shaping influence of vernacular language, metaphor, and culture must be understood. Although not referring to religious images per se, Palmer (1996, p. 47) observes that images are

> indirect conceptual analogs of the environment, broadly construed to include society, natural phenomena, our own bodies and their organic (and mental) processes, and the rest of what is often called 'reality' or 'the world out there.'

So, to summarize, we could argue that basically all imagery is structured by culture and what Palmer (1996, p. 49) calls 'personal history.' Thus, in order to understand and appreciate vernacular or elite Tantric imageries, metaphors, and religious language, we must understand the context of the culture and the language.

In an earlier essay (Hayes 2002) I suggested how modern conceptual metaphor theory can help us to understand Tantric visualization and ritual processes. Since other essays in this volume provide useful introductions to the concepts and methods of contemporary metaphor theory, it should suffice here to note that Tantric traditions have made extensive use of metaphors. This is due to the way that metaphors allow for the projections or 'cross-mappings' from a source domain (a relatively concrete image such as a pond or lotus flower) to a target domain, which is abstract and mysterious, such as a heavenly realm or a region of the 'yogic body.' These uses of metaphor are embedded in local, vernacular languages, as well as in the local topographical, geographical, botanical, and cultural contexts. By 'unpacking' the religious uses of metaphors in Vaiṣṇava Sahajiyā texts, we can better understand the cosmology and worldview expressed in such texts. An example from the *Amṛtaratnāvalī* helps to illustrate this complexity:

> That Pond is visualized as having a pleasing shape.
>
> I will tell you about it, please listen carefully!
>
> That Pond is adorned with precious gems (*maṇika*).
>
> That eternal Abode (*dhāma*) is inlaid with the Jewels (*ratna*).
>
> In the four directions there are four landing-stairs, connected to the
> path of the village leader.[22]
>
> The landing-stairs are redolent with the [scents] of musk, vermilion,
> and sandalwood.
>
> (verses 162–164)

This passage, which describes the visualization of one of the inner ponds of the yogic body, also contains images of stairs, villages, leaders, and ritual cosmetics. But beyond this basic level of simple description, there is a deeper underlying level of metaphorical process at work. When we examine Sahajiyā religious metaphors (and there are many), such as THE BODY IS A POND SYSTEM or REALITY IS FLUID or SAHAJA IS A CONTAINER or SADHANA IS A JOURNEY, we find that important aspects of the source domain (the relatively 'concrete' notions of a pond system, fluid, container, journey) tend to be applied to the target domains (the more abstract notions of body, reality, Sahaja, and *sādhana*) in ways that attempt to maintain metaphorical consistency. Thus, the local or 'folk' details of a river system (e.g. banks, landing stairs, waters, villages, ponds, current, boats) are connected to the body in a way that the Sahajiyās thus envision these details as part of the subtle inner body. In other words, the 'cognitive topology,' the 'nooks and crannies' as it were, of the source domains (the 'concrete' image) tend to constrain and structure how the target domain (the 'abstraction') is perceived and experienced. This is why we must pay attention to the specifically local images and vernacular Bengali expressions of religious language that are used to indicate cosmic abstractions like Kṛṣṇa, Sahaja, or the subtle body. This also suggests why the Sahajiyā subtle physiology is typically envisioned not as fiery energy centers and ascending *kuṇḍalinī-śakti* (more typically features of Sanskritic texts), but rather as the movement of fluids along a river, past villages, and into a series of inner ponds. There is a metaphorical and cognitive consistency that leads to what Tony Stewart calls 'coherent metaphoric worlds' and what Fauconnier and Turner (2002) call 'emergent structure.'[23]

Metaphors are thus useful because they enable what Johnson (1987) calls 'the imaginative structuring of experience' in human life, which consists of 'forms of imagination that grow out of bodily experience, as it contributes to our understanding and guides our reasoning' (Johnson 1987, p. 215). And it is here where we can gain an appreciation for the use of local, folk, and vernacular expressions, for it is this very function of metaphor that allows mystics such as the Sahajiyās to 'imaginatively structure' their yogic, emotional, and sexual experiences. This splendid feat of imagination is based upon what cognitive scientists and linguists call 'image schemas,' essentially 'a recurring, dynamic pattern of our perceptual interactions and motor programs that gives coherence and structure to our experience' (Johnson 1987, p. xiv). Casson (1983), for example, states that schemas are 'conceptual abstractions that mediate between stimuli received by the sense organs and behavioral responses' and that they 'serve as the basis for all human information processing, e.g. perception and comprehension, categorization and planning, recognition and recall, and problem-solving and decision-making.'[24] While this is not the place to explore the neurophysiological aspects of schemas[25] it is worth quoting Palmer on why they are essential to the study of language and culture:

> To understand a word as its speaker intended or to use it appropriately, it is necessary to know the schema or schemas to which it belongs in a particular context of use. Words evoke systems of meaning, and often, as in metaphor, they evoke two or more systems at once. Whole vocabularies pertaining to the landscape, the body, kinship, and other topics all have their own underlying schemas. Along such schemas, words and idiomatic phrases are distributed more or less systematically. (Palmer 1996, p. 66)

Some such schemas, such as the 'verticality schema' (and the meaning or value of 'up' versus 'down') or the 'container schema' (which can 'mark off' a mental space and turn an idea or experience into a 'vessel'), are perhaps universally found in humans, but it is likely that there are important local and individual variants—issues that cognitive linguistics continues to investigate.

Metaphors thus work together with bodily experience and image schemas to create 'coherent metaphoric worlds,' allowing us to interact with, and even to 'enter' those worlds. It is precisely this process of metaphorical 'mapping' that we can find in Sahajiyā notions of subtle physiology and ritual process, of identifying men with Kṛṣṇa and women with Rādhā. This 'mapping' allows for not just analysis and manipulation of the embodied condition and the material world, but for gradual transformation of the bodies of the male and female practitioners and the attainment of Sahaja.

Metaphors are deeply embedded in our ways of thinking about ourselves, others, and the world. Like the operating system of a computer that runs quietly 'in the background' of what we see on the screen, metaphors and image schemas exist underneath our words and thoughts and actions. They are at the heart of vernacular language. As Lakoff observes (1993, p. 241), 'metaphors impose a structure on real life, through the creation of new correspondences in experience. And once created in one generation, they serve as an experiential basis for that metaphor in the next generation.' This is precisely what seems to have happened in medieval Sahajiyā communities, as influential gurus like Mukunda-dāsa and Ākiñcana-dāsa developed distinctive metaphoric worlds based upon their own yogic experiences, expressed them orally and in written texts, and then passed them down to their own students. Through their development of such metaphoric worlds they were able to express and disseminate their experiences to others in greater Bengal. Some further examples of these visionary worlds from the Amṛtaratnāvalī will help to illustrate this metaphorical richness:

This *dharma* is the purest, without division or simple lust (*kāma*).
The abode (*dhāma*) beyond the heavenly Virajā river is transcendent.[26]
Along the far shores of the Virajā river is The Land (*deśakhāna*).
Sahajapur is that Village (*grāma*) which is called 'Eternal Bliss'
     (*sadānanda*).
To the west of that [river] is [a village called] Kaliṅga Kalikā;
The female partner (*nāyikā*) of that place is called Campaka Kalikā.[27]
[In that place are] the Tree of Emptiness,[28] and lotuses of one hundred
     and one thousand petals.
The Land surrounds that tree and the waters of the lotus Pond.
To the north [of the Virajā river] is the Village called 'Place of Bliss'
     (*ānandapura*).
[In that place are] mystics (*rasikas*), the grove (*kuñja*) of *rasa*, and the
     abode of the god of Love (*manmatha*, or kāmadeva).
Forever blissful, forever overwhelmed, forever desirous,

the Together-born Inner Person (*sahaja-mānusa*) always makes [its]
   home there.

To the east of that [Virajā river] is the heavenly Village of Sahajapura.

That is the eternal abode of the Together-born Person.

Forever blissful, forever overwhelmed, forever desirous;

the Together-born Person always makes [its] home there.[29]

To the south of that [river] is [the Village called] 'Place of Conscious
   Bliss' (*cidānandapura*);

a Land called 'Radiant Moon' (*candrakānti*) is not far away.

(verses 42–50)

When we consider such lovely inner worlds depicted in Sahajiyā texts, we need to bear in mind that these visionary worlds are connected to underlying metaphorical structures and experienced by Sahajiyās as very real—more 'real' than the outer realm of zamindars, geckos, and monsoons. Sahajiyās did not just attempt to construe their esoteric language so that it made sense in the ordinary world; rather, to paraphrase literary critic Samuel Levin, they construed the world to make sense of the esoteric language (Levin 1993, p. 121). It is thus this profound 'process of construal' that we must be sensitive to, by noting regional phrasings, local references, and above all metaphorical consistencies (or, in some cases, inconsistencies).

For esoteric mystical traditions like the Sahajiyās, ritual practices—ranging from the beginner's practices of singing and dancing adapted from Gauḍīya Vaiṣṇava *vaidhi-bhakti* to the Tantric sexual rituals practiced at the advanced stage of *siddha*—thus allow for a visualized inner cosmos and body that is construed in terms of the metaphors, be they 'rivers,' 'ponds,' 'flowers,' or 'villages.' There is, of course, a physical component, as parts of the human body and material world are homologized with the metaphors, such as the vagina with a lotus, the penis with a honeybee, the urethra with a river, and so forth. Verse 133 of the *Amṛtaratnāvalī*, for example, quoting another text by Mukunda-dāsa, 'The Garland of Bees' (*Bhṛngaratnāvalī*), compares men to bumblebees, allowing possible entailments such as taking honey, flitting from flower to flower, and so forth: 'Protected by the lotuses of the Pond which is a sea of Divine Love and nectar, men become bumblebees. How can the passionate ones, clinging to the feet of the blessed Body, enter the world inside the body?'[30] This esoteric 'process of construal,' then, allows for not just metaphoric language based upon concepts, but also for religious realities and concepts 'created' by the metaphoric language. The religious adept is thus 'projected into,' engages, and responds to, such metaphoric worlds as coherent reality, not at all fictive illusion.[31] For Sahajiyās, in a neurobiological sense, they really become bees, alight in floral realities.

Folklorist Barre Toelken, in his wonderful study of European and American folksongs and ballads, *Morning Dew and Roses* (1995), argues (p. 34) that 'We will not want to read meaning into a song, but rather attempt to read meaning out by carefully noting . . . the relationship of the metaphor to the assumptions in its culture and by charting its coherent relationships to the song in which it appears.' When reading such material (or listening to it), Toelken says (1995, pp. 35–36), the scholar should be sensitive to the 'range of metaphorical possibilities' within the text and the culture, and will discover that this range can span 'almost explicit metonymy to complex suggestive metaphor.'

In the case of Sahajiyā texts, which are often riddle-like in their use of uninflected language and esoteric vocabulary (which, along with the lack of written commentaries, makes their study quite vexing for modern scholars!), there is an interesting range of imagery and metaphor, much of which is 'hydraulic' in nature, based upon sexuality, fluids, rivers, ponds, and flowers. We find similar imageries and tropes in other Bengali vernacular Tantric traditions, such as Bāul, Śākta, and Kartābhajā songs.[32] This consistency suggests that such choices are neither coincidental nor random. In explaining the polysemy of Euro-American 'riddle songs,' Toelken (1995, p. 39) observes:

> The more fully we can perceive the vernacular system from which the song grows and in which such references make sense, the more we will realize that there is not a strict code of any sort, but rather a field of metaphorical possibility, a pool of culturally recognizable resources in the language and in everyday jokes and formulations.

Thus we return to an important point about metaphor that has emerged clearly within cognitive linguistics and cognitive science generally—that the relationship between target and source domains (for example, between the schemas for 'love' and 'journey,' or 'woman' and 'lotus flower') is not simple and predictable, and certainly not a simple or even predictable 'code.' But now we will turn to an examination of selected passages from Sahajiyā texts to apply some of these insights regarding metaphor and vernacular language.

3 METAPHOR AND VERNACULAR LANGUAGE IN SAHAJIYĀ TEXTS

3.1 Sacred jewels and fluids: The *Amṛtaratnāvalī* of Mukunda-dāsa

We have already examined some verses from the *Amṛtaratnāvalī* or 'Necklace of Immortality' of Mukunda-dāsa, which was composed around 1600 CE. In its over 300 couplets we find a rich trove of metaphors and Bengali cultural references—as well as the Tantric visualizations and ritual procedures that are its main focus. As with other Bengali vernacular Tantras, it expresses a worldview emphasizing embodiment, the transformative and salvific powers of ritual sexual intercourse, and the importance of 'substance' in the religious quest. The very title, 'Necklace (*ratnāvalī*) of Immortality (*amṛta*),' is itself a polysemic metaphor, for it suggests not only the uses of jewels and bodily ornamentation in Tantric ritual, but the more fundamental notion that the practitioner must 'fashion' and then figuratively 'wear' an encircling *mandala* made out of the 'jewels' or *ratna* which, in the esoteric language of the text, are yogically reversed sexual fluids. Called *vastu* or 'stuff' by Mukunda-dāsa, these fluids are created and joined when the male practitioner, as Kṛṣṇa, joins with his female partner who is visualized as Rādhā. The process is one in which the male is believed to draw the female sexual fluid (*rati*) from the woman's vagina into his penis, where it joins with his semen (*rasa*) and is then caused to move upwards along the 'crooked river' (*bāṅkānadī*), through four inner ponds (*sarovara*), and finally up to Sahaja itself.[33] (Some have playfully termed this the 'reverse-fountain-pen technique,' but it is a variant of the Tantric practice of 'reverse suction,' such as the *vajrolī-mudrā* of Siddha traditions; see White 1996.) As abstract and mystical as these inner places may be, they are all accessible through the fluids of the human body, connected to the very 'stuff' (*vastu*) of this world.

That Mukunda-dāsa and other medieval Vaiṣṇava Sahajiyās would use a substantive term like *vastu* in their description of subtle physiology is significant, for it illustrates the use of several different kinds of ontological metaphors identified by Lakoff and Johnson: entity, substance, and container metaphors. Abstractions like the experience of a 'divine body' (*deva-deha*) and associated states of consciousness are expressed and made more accessible through the use of such images. As Lakoff and Johnson (1980, p. 25) note:

> Our experience of physical objects and substances provides a further basis for understanding—one that goes beyond mere orientation. Understanding our experiences in terms of objects and substances allows us to pick out parts of our experience and treat them as discrete entities or substances of a uniform kind. Once we can identify our experiences as entities or substances, we can refer to them, categorize them, group them, and quantify them—and, by this means, reason about them.

Because of the use of such 'substantive' metaphors to express mystical experiences, the metaphoric world of the *Necklace* has a particular character or quality that distinguishes it from the metaphoric worlds of some Sanskrit-based Tantric or Kṛṣṇa traditions, which often use different kinds of metaphors. Whereas the metaphoric world of the *Necklace* is expressed primarily through metaphors of substances and fluids, other types of Tantric worlds, for example, those expressed using the better-known systems of *cakras* and *kuṇḍalinī-śakti*, use metaphors of energy, sound, power, and light.[34] Although this is not the place to explore the many fascinating issues arising from such differences (and similarities), it should be clear that, once a basic metaphorical world is established, certain entailments and outcomes are possible, while others are not. In other words, a cosmophysiology based primarily (though not exclusively) upon fluids and substances will probably have some dynamics or 'feel' (to use a modern sensory metaphor) that vary from one based primarily upon energy, sound, and light.

Mukunda-dāsa is quite clear about the importance of substance and fluid, for early in the text (verses 7–12), immediately after offering homage to notable Gauḍīya Vaiṣṇava authorities like Caitanya, Nityānanda, and the Gosvāmins, he discusses the importance of *rasa*, understood on several levels—as a religio-aesthetic experience, as a sexual substance, and even as an alchemical term (as mercury).[35] However, since the basic meaning of *rasa* is 'juice' or 'essence' (as from a sugar cane), this allows Mukunda-dāsa to develop entailments based upon the core image of a 'sweet fluid' that causes delightful sensations when 'tasted.' Thus, *rasa* may be the rapturous aesthetic or devotional experience of 'sweet' emotions, and it can also be the essence that derives, not just from a cane, but from the penis. Furthermore, those who experience *rasa* are called *rasikas* ('aesthetes,' 'connoisseurs,' or 'tasters'), and Mukunda-dāsa compares their experiences to floating upon a river (verses 8–9):

> Those devotees who are *rasikas* seek the subtle inner Body (*śrī-rūpa*).
>
> Their minds are constantly bobbing (*ḍubāya*) about in the *rasa*.
>
> With minds submerged (*magna*) in *rasa*, they float along.
>
> *Rasa* can only be produced by keeping the company of *rasikas*.

Both meanings of *rasa*—as aesthetic experience and sexual substance—share similar metaphorical entailments, for both 'experience' and 'semen' can 'flow' like a river. This riverine entailment or extended meaning of the basic substance/fluid metaphor also helps to suggest why the subtle physiology of the *Necklace* consists of a system of a river and ponds, and not the more familiar *suṣumṇā-nāḍī* and *cakras* of other traditions: fluids naturally run through rivers and streams and into ponds. Recalling the earlier metaphors of love and *sādhana* as a journey, which defines a path and surfaces, if mystical experience is being expressed in terms of fluidic metaphors, then the later stages of the process of liberation may be expressed as passage along a river, being contained by the two banks of the river, flowing into a pond, and leaving the waters through landing-stairs (*ghāṭ*) to enter neighboring celestial villages (*grāma*). Of course, much of this also reflects the natural topology and climate of deltaic Bengal, with its innumerable streams, rivers, and bodies of water. In other words, the experiences of substances, fluids, rivers, and bodies of water may have been adopted as metaphors and then projected in order to refer to, categorize, group, and quantify profound mystical and sexual experiences.

But Mukunda continues this use of substance metaphors as he introduces the importance of *vastu* as a 'cosmic substance' made out of yogically reversed sexual fluids, which are then used to generate the inner visualized form of the female ritual partner. Some relevant passages (verses 10–12) are:

> [Through the experience of] that *rasa*, you should internalize the principles of Substance (*vastu*).
>
> Indeed, the Together-born Substance (*sahaja-vastu*) and the principles of *rasa* are to be regarded like precious jewels (*ratna*).
>
> Influenced by the jewel [of Together-born Substance] the *rasa* [assumes] the shape of the Body (*rūpa*).
>
> The Body was born [by] the rituals of *rasa*.
>
> Then, in the company of *rasikas*, she who possesses the Body (*rūpavatī*) [must appear].
>
> Your own inner identity [requires] sporting as he who experiences *rasa* (*rasavati*).

We can detect many aspects of Sahajiyā ritual and religious discourse reflected in these few passages, especially the practice of ritual sexual intercourse, the yogic reversal of sexual fluids, and the use of those fluids to create the inner 'Body' (*rūpa*) of the female partner. Written in riddle-like vernacular Bengali, they help to illustrate the quite distinctive character of Sahajiyā worldviews and ethos.

3.2 The guru's tongue: The *Vivarta-vilāsa* of Ākiñcana-dāsa

In addition to their specifically religious usages, metaphors may also be used to claim authority and legitimation. Such examples may be found in the *Vivarta-vilāsa* ('The Erotic Sport of Transformation') of Ākiñcana-dāsa, an extensive treatise of several thousand couplets composed about 1650 CE. Much of this work is devoted to arguing that the renowned Bengali devotional leader Kṛṣṇa Caitanya (1486–1533 CE) and other notable Gauḍīya Vaiṣṇavas were in fact secretly practicing Sahajiyā sexual rituals (a claim hotly contested then as now by orthodox Gauḍīya Vaiṣṇavas).[36] Ākiñcana-dāsa quotes extensively from the *Caitanya-caritāmṛta* of Kṛṣṇa-dāsa Kavirāja and from other texts in order to argue for this 'privileged' Sahajiyā reading of Gauḍīya Vaiṣṇava history.[37] Most of the work is composed in Bengali, although there are some quotations from Sanskrit works like the *Bhagavad-gītā* and philosophical and aesthetic works by Gauḍīya scholars. Ākiñcana-dāsa had several goals in composing the *Vivarta-vilāsa*, including an outline of basic Sahajiyā worldview and ritual practices; however, it is clear from his extensive discourse with the mainstream Gauḍīya Vaiṣṇava tradition that issues of authority and legitimation were at the core of the text as well.[38] Thus, we can also find sophisticated uses of metaphors for these purposes; some, such as the first example below, are like Mukunda-dāsa's uses in the *Amṛtaratnāvalī*, essentially describing *sādhana* and *deha-tattva*. Others, like the vivid metaphor of the guru's tongue (*guru-jihvā*), are more complex, weaving issues of authority into those of cosmology, physiology, and *sādhana*.

Like Mukunda-dāsa and other Sahajiyā gurus, Ākiñcana-dāsa embraces a basically substantive and hydraulic cosmophysiology, and the metaphors help him to do this. One such example of a substance or ontological metaphor reflects not only traditions of ritual sexual intercourse and alchemy, but also the Bengali love of making candy and other sweets:[39]

> Without the help of experienced devotees, devotion to the
>   divine juice (*rasa*) cannot be understood.
> The alchemical candy (*bhiyāna*) is ritually prepared
>   using the instrument of divine love.
>
> *   *   *   *   *   *   *   *
>
> The alchemical candy was made by seizing the divine juice,
> and blending into that precious treasure the female and
>   the male principles.
> As many sugar-drops and candy pieces that can be made from the
>   juice of the sugarcane,

that much cosmic substance (*vastu*) and power (*śakti*) are to be
gained in the great mystical condition (*mahābhāva*).

In *The Immortal Acts of Caitanya* (2.23.23) it is said:

From the sugarcane plant come seeds, stalks, juice, and
molasses, but they share the same basic essence.

Sugar candy is really just the finest white sugar mixed with
spices.

Just as the flavor of these products of the sugarcane
gradually increases,

so does religious appreciation increase due to passion and
divine love.

The juice and cosmic substance are always present in a
special place.

If they remain, what happens? You must understand all of this.

Take the juice in that place and mix spices with it.

You must fashion the confection by transforming that juice.

Using the quaint and intriguing substantive metaphor of candy-making, this couplet clearly reflects the cultural context of Bengali village life. The underlying 'folk cognitive model' is that of transforming worldly substances like sexual fluids (*rasa*) into powerful alchemical substances or pills which, like candy (*bhiyāna*), can be ingested to achieve the higher stages of Sahajiyā *sādhana* and immortality. As with many Sahajiyā practices, there are additional devotional elements of bhakti and 'divine love' (*prema*) adapted from Gauḍīya Vaiṣṇavism; hence the citation from Kṛṣṇa-dāsa Kavirāja's great work in an attempt to legitimize this Tantric alchemical procedure and locate himself within the lineage of Caitanya and Kṛṣṇa-dāsa. Furthermore, all of this refers to the underlying hydraulic or fluidic metaphorical world found in most other Sahajiyā cosmologies. To the best of my knowledge, few if any other Tantric traditions use this metaphor of candy-making, which seems specific to vernacular Bengali texts.

The metaphor of the guru's tongue, although clearly connected to issues of cosmophysiology, initiation, and empowerment, also takes us to Sahajiyā attempts to claim authority and legitimation. As Urban has convincingly shown in his study of the 19th-century Kartābhajās, Bengali Tantric movements have attempted to deal with their marginal status by employing a number of strategies of appropriation, transformation, and concealment (Urban 2001a, especially chapters 3–5). In the case of the earlier Sahajiyās, we find not only attempts to claim the teachings and personalities of Gauḍīya traditions, but also the goal of achieving an entirely 'new birth' that would distinguish the Sahajiyās from others. These issues appear in the following key passage from the text, which has a number of metaphors, such as those of fluids, substances, and especially the basic 'container' metaphor in which THE BODY IS A CONTAINER. This is connected to a polysemic convergence of images of 'birth,' 'initiation,' and speaking/hearing,' all of which lead to the creation of the inner yogic body. It is worth quoting much of this passage to illustrate its richness:[40]

> Those rituals which deserve the highest praise involve childless
> asceticism.
> Please, I implore you, behold and understand the secret meanings!
> There is a full pitcher (*kumbha*) upon his head.
> When there is such a full pitcher, the practitioner becomes
> very powerful.
> Then divine love appears in his body:
> Thus everyone says: 'That inner country is truly a fine place.'
> Hear about the different kinds of birth from the manuals of the practitioners and from the mouths of practitioners.
> It is not even worth considering other viewpoints concerning the nature of devotion.
> The grace of the guru and the grace of practitioners come after the grace of mother and father.
> This tells you that there are two separate and distinct births.
> There is no birth at all without uterine blood, semen, vagina, and penis.
> How can that be? I will discuss its significance.
> At first there was a birth due to the bonding between mother and father.
> But behold how just a little grace from the guru can cause a rebirth (*punarjanma*).
> That also involves uterine blood, semen, vagina, and penis:
> Clear your mind and listen, for I speak the essence of this.
> The praises for Kṛṣṇa are the uterine blood, while the seed syllable is the semen.
> The guru's tongue is the penis, while the ear of the disciple is the vagina.
> So, your birth should result from these things.
> You should really try to understand how you can be born through the grace of
> practitioners.
> The eye and ear are some of the five organs of knowledge (*jñāna-indriya*).
> In the beginning and intermediate stages of practice, you must make them compassionate.
> Use the organ of knowledge that is the ear to hear about birth.
> Use the eye to see the grace of the practitioners and the eternal order (*nitya dharma*).
> You will then progress gradually through the three stages of practice: Beginner,
> Intermediate, and Perfected.
> Hear with the ear and see with the eye how these are all really one process.
> You must realize, brother, that everything has its uterine blood and semen.
> Semen and uterine blood will develop when one assumes the condition (*bhāva*) of Rādhā ('Prosperity').

The condition of being Rādhā I call the 'law of loving another's spouse' (parakīyā dharma).

All of the principles of greed and devotion can be found in that condition.

There is much to comment about regarding this interesting passage, which extols the virtues of 'childless asceticism,' an ironic (and seemingly oxymoronic) phrase, since this is an asceticism using ritual sexual intercourse.[41] However, whereas ordinary sexual intercourse, through the bodies of the father and mother, leads to the birth of the ordinary physical body of flesh and blood, the Sahajiyās seek a form of 'rebirth' (punarjanma) as the inner subtle body (śrī-rūpa). This passage makes use of various container metaphors: the pitcher upon the head, referring to the reservoir of semen, according to Bengali folk culture and, among Sahajiyās, to the uppermost pond (the akṣaya-sarovara), which is fashioned out of reversed sexual fluids.[42] But the most vivid couplets refer to the creation of this inner bodily container, which is made metaphorically from 'uterine blood, semen, vagina, and penis.' Instead of having a fleshly body born of mother's blood and father's semen (again based on the Bengali folk model), the Gauḍīya Vaiṣṇava praises (kīrtana) for Kṛṣṇa (used by Sahajiyās in early stages of practice) are equivalent to the blood (śoṇita), while the 'seed-syllable' or bīja-mantra used by the guru during initiation is compared to semen (śukra). Of note here is the transformation of sounds into substances and sexual fluids—yet another example of the core fluidic ontological metaphor. As far as the containers that hold these vital sound-fluids, the guru's tongue is creatively compared to the penis; metaphorically both share a similar function: they both deliver the female/male sound/fluid to what will be the 'womb' for the 'birth' of the yogic body. The disciple's ear is thus compared to the vagina/womb, as the receptacle for the conjoined principles. So, the guru's tongue and the disciple's ear serve as polysemic metaphors for initiation, epistemology, birth, and salvific passage. But beyond this the guru's tongue also expresses the Sahajiyā claim to authority and legitimation, and the disciple's ear (and, by extension, head) provides the 'vessel' within which both the 'new body' and the 'new power' are to grow.

Still, as the penultimate couplet notes: 'You must realize, brother, that everything has its uterine blood and semen,' meaning that the Sahajiyā worldview is grounded in substance, in stuff, in fluids—just as the surrounding world of medieval Bengal was based upon substances and sexuality. In contrast to the classical Sāṃkhya philosophy which valorizes the consciousness of puruṣa over the matter of prakṛti, Ākiñcana-dāsa and Mukunda-dāsa argued that even mystical experiences (bhāva, mahābhāva, rasa) are grounded in substance and stuff. Such is the 'folk cognitive model' that we find in the vernacular Tantric traditions of the Sahajiyās, a model made all the more vivid and 'real' through the skillful use of religious metaphors.

4 CONCLUSION

So what have we learned about vernacular religious metaphors in 17th-century Sahajiyā texts? To begin with, we must approach our understanding of such texts through the larger context of medieval Bengali culture and language. Sahajiyā Tantric texts express a worldview quite distinct from other Bengali Sanskrit Tantric texts, due at least in part to the vernacular language of Bengali. Behind the Sahajiyā cosmophysiologies we can find 'folk cognitive models' that are in turn connected to Bengali language and culture. Thus, using this methodology of modern metaphor theory and cognitive linguistics we can better understand the development and expressions of medieval Tantric discourse.[43] Although the goal of Sahajiyās is to become the indwelling cosmic being known as the *Sahaja-mānusa* (the 'innate' or 'together-born' Man), this soteriology is fully grounded in the physical bodies of the practitioners, promoted through their control of erotic energies and substances, and legitimated through the secretive power of the guru's tongue. Just as we are only beginning to appreciate the richness and diversity of vernacular Tantric traditions like the Vaiṣṇava Sahajiyās of medieval Bengal, we have only recently begun to understand the important role that metaphor and cognition play in the development of religious language and in the formation of culture and religion. Much of what I have written here must be considered at best as 'work in progress,' but I trust that it will inspire others to study vernacular texts and make further investigations into the fascinating worlds of metaphor. The 'guru's tongue,' so to speak, may have much to say to scholars of Tantric traditions.

NOTES

1. Portions of this essay were presented at a meeting of the Society for Tantric Studies at Flagstaff, Arizona, in October of 2002, and at the annual meeting of the American Academy of Religions in Toronto, Ontario, in November 2002. Other passages also appear in *Alternative Krishnas: Regional and Vernacular Variations on a Hindu Deity*, edited by Guy Beck (Albany: SUNY Press, 2005, pp. 119–132), and in *Yoga: The Indian Tradition*, edited by Ian Whicher and David Carpenter (London: Routledge, 2003, pp. 162–184). A full version (now modified for this current volume) appeared in *Pacific World*, 3rd series, no. 8, Fall 2006, pp. 41–71 (Hayes 2006). My thanks to Richard Payne and to The Institute of Buddhist Studies for their permission to revise that essay for this current volume.

2. Ākiñcana-dāsa, *Vivarta-vilāsa*, edited by Kṛṣṇa Bhattacharya (Calcutta: Taracand Dasa and Sons, n.d. [approx. 1988]), pp. 114–115. This text was composed around 1650 CE. All translations of this and other Bengali texts by the author, with thanks to the late Edward C. Dimock, Jr. and to Tony K. Stewart of Vanderbilt University for their tremendous help in working with such difficult texts. I would also like to thank Dr. Ramakanta Chakravarti of the University of Burdwan, The Asiatic Society, and the Bangiya Sahitya Parishad for his help during my studies in Calcutta in 1987–1988 and in 2007. Final responsibility, of course, remains with the author.

3. It has been well established, by scholars such as André Padoux, Douglas Brooks, and others, that the very categories of 'Tantra' and 'Tantrism' are Western Orientalist constructions. However, as Urban (2001a, p. 179) notes: 'Tantrism is perhaps much better understood as a product of the scholarly imagination, which we find it useful to employ as a tool or heuristic device.' In this essay I will also use the terms as heuristic devices, but look forward to continuing discussions with colleagues about the problematics associated with the terms. For a recent overview of the extensive bibliography and debates about the subject, see my entry on 'Tantra' in the 'Hinduism'

section of the *Oxford Bibliographies Online* at http://www.oxfordbibliographies. com/view/document/obo-9780195399318/obo-9780195399318-0090. xml?rskey=iGCYh5&result=83.

4. See, for example, Urban (2001a), as well as the companion volume of translations (Urban 2001b). The latter volume includes a superb introduction to the Kartābhajās and fine translations of many of their enigmatic vernacular songs. See also White (1996, 2003). Other regional expressions of Tantra are discussed in Caldwell (2001). I also address issues of vernacular expressions of Tantra in several of my own works, including Hayes (2003 and 2005). I have translated several Vaiṣṇava Sahajiyā texts, including lyrical poems and esoteric manuals. See Hayes (1995, 2000, 2012b). A useful study of various aspects of Tantra in both Asia and the West is Urban (2003). A superb recent study of modern Sahajiyās and other Bengali Vaiṣṇava traditions, based on fieldwork, may be found in Sarbadhikary (2015).

5. By using the terms 'elite' and 'popular' or 'vernacular,' I am not suggesting that these are two completely polar areas of culture; obviously, people who spoke Bengali and Sanskrit lived in the same region. However, as this essay will argue, the uses of elite or vernacular languages can often influence how one perceives and experiences the world. Still, in the broadest sense we should consider 'elite' and 'vernacular' as possibilities along a continuum of language, culture, and society. Some metaphors, such as the mind as a lotus flower, may be shared, while others, such as the channels of the yogic body as a river system, are more specific to riverine and deltaic Bengal.

6. For more on these and other texts see Banerji (1978, pp. 74–122).

7. For the Kartābhajās, see Urban (2001a) and Hayes (2015). For the Bāuls, see Salomon (1995), Openshaw (2002), and Hayes (2015).

8. For an excellent treatment of the issues regarding saṃdeha versus videha ('without a body'), see Fort and Mumme (1996).

9. My translations of the Necklace of Immortality are based upon a manuscript edition of the Amṛtaratnāvalī found in the collection of the Department of Bengali at the University of Calcutta, ms. #6451 ('M2'). Two other versions have been consulted and are often referred to when there are important variations or agreements: 'M1' refers to mss #595 in the University of Calcutta collection, while 'P' refers to the printed version found in Paritos Dasa (1972, pp. 131–159). See Hayes (1985, 1988, 1989, 1996). The author expresses his gratitude to the American Institute of Indian Studies for their support during 1979–80 and 1987–88. This work could not have been carried out without the assistance of the Registrar of the University of Calcutta, Archivist Tushar Mahapatra, and Department Heads Asit Kumar Bandhopadyaya and P. Dasa. During 1987–88, Dr. Ramakanta Chakravarti of the University of Burdwan, Asiatic Society, and the Bangiya Sahitya Parishad shared with me his great knowledge of Bengali religions and manuscripts. Deepest thanks are also extended to the late Professor Edward C. Dimock of the University of Chicago, who guided me in the translation of this difficult text and suggested many useful readings of obscure passages. Professor Tony K. Stewart of Vanderbilt University also suggested many useful changes and interpretations. The final responsibility for the translation, however, rests with the author.

10. The ninth door or orifice of the human body is widely known in yogic literature. It is often the last opening before the tenth door—which serves as the first opening to the yogic body. For a discussion of the Buddhist Tantric views, see Wayman, 'The Nine Orifices of the Body' in Wayman (1993, pp. 139–150). The Śrīvidyā school of Hindu Śaktism envisions a total of nine cakras; see Brooks (1990, pp. 56–58, 157–163).

11. On the importance of the symbol of the heart in the Kaula Tantric system of Abhinavagupta, see Muller-Ortega (1988). Line 98b is missing from M2 and is supplied from M1 and P.

12. See O'Connell (1989, 1993). A superb overview of Bengali Vaiṣṇava religion and textuality may be found in Stewart's (2010) magisterial *The Final Word: The Caitanya Caritamrita and the Grammar of Religious Tradition*.

13. These complicated issues have been addressed in a number of venues over the past few decades, including the University of Pennsylvania workshop in 1997; by the participants in the Tantric Studies Seminar of the American Academy of Religion (AAR; which ran from 1996–1999); the Tantric Studies Consultation of the AAR (2004–2006); and by colleagues in the Society for Tantric Studies, which has met several times, most recently in 2005 and 2010.

14. See notes 2, 4, and 9 above for information on the Bengali versions of the two texts. Standard scholarly works on the Vaiṣṇava Sahajiyās in English are Dasgupta (1969, especially pp. 113–156); Bose (1986 [1930]); and Dimock, Jr. (1966). My own works include those listed in the References at the end of this chapter and are referred to during the course of this chapter. Scholarly works in Bengali include Bose [Basu] (1932); Dasa (1972, 1978); and Kavirāja (1969, 1975), covering the Vaiṣṇava Sahajiyās in various places. Excellent introductions to Hindu Tantrism, as well as useful studies of specific traditions, may be found in Brooks (1990) and Muller-Ortega (1988). On the Kartābhajās, see Urban (2001a, 2001b).

15. Dimock, Jr. (1966).

16. As Hugh Urban (2001a) demonstrates, the Kartābhajās may be regarded as a later branch of the Vaiṣṇava Sahajiyās, also combining Tantra and Bhakti—but in distinctive ways that reflect the colonial context.

17. See the superb edition, including an introduction and commentary: Edward C. Dimock, Jr. and Tony K. Stewart (2000). The fruit of many years of labor, this volume will become the new standard work in the field. An invaluable study of the Bengali Vaiṣṇava traditions and the study of religion is found in Stewart (2010).

18. See O'Connell (1989) and also Hayes (1990) for debates concerning Sahajiyā influences on the Gauḍīyas. There is no debate about Gauḍīya influences upon the Sahajiyās.

19. Selections from these texts are translated in my contributions to three anthologies: see Hayes (1995, 2000, 2012b).

20. For a brief survey of Western views through the mid-twentieth century, see Hawkes (1972). On the basic traditions of Sanskrit aesthetics, see Ramanujan and Gerow (1974, pp. 115–143).

21. See the Introduction to the present volume. There have been many useful studies over the past few decades which examine metaphor and religious language from a range of disciplines, such as Pathak (2013). A classic collection of essays may be found in Ortony (1993). Another valuable collection is Sacks (1979). The URL for Mark Turner's website on conceptual metaphor and conceptual blending theory is http://markturner.org/blending.html. This has many links to other related sites.

22. Only ms. #6451 finishes the line this way; ms. #595 and the printed edition conclude with 'built with golden vessels' (bāndhā svarṇapuṭe). #6451 reads 'bāndhā sarddā pāthe.' However, the #595 and printed version makes more sense. This couplet also seems to describe the Rādhākuṇḍa in the Kuñjavarṇana of Narottama Dāsa, and suggests some of the preparations for mañjarī-sādhana. The cosmetics are used by the mañjarīs as they adorn themselves for the service of the divine couple in love play.

23. The concept of 'coherent metaphoric worlds' comes from Tony Stewart, personal correspondence (July 15, 1995). My thanks again to Tony Stewart for his guidance and inspiration over these many years.

24. Cited in Palmer (1996, p. 63). On body schema also see Gallagher (2005).

25. See, for example, McNamara (2009), a groundbreaking book, in which are presented exciting new findings and perspectives regarding studying religion using neuroscience, some of which I explored in my essay for Religions online (Hayes 2014). See also McNamara and Giordano's contribution to the present volume, chapter 5.

26. Verses 41b through 46 are found only in ms. #595 and #6451, not the printed text.

27. Kaliṅga Kalikā translates as 'Orissan Flower Bud,' while Campaka Kalikā is 'Magnolia Bud.' These obscure references to the flower buds may represent female ritual partners seated in a circle.

28. Śūnya-vṛkṣa is translated as 'tree of emptiness.' The usage of the term śūnya, 'void,' 'empty,' may reflect Buddhist Tantric ideas. It can also mean 'void,' or 'non-ejaculated' when applied to the term śukra, 'semen'; thus, this tree may be a metaphor for the phallus while in use during the ritual.

29. The first line of this couplet is found only in ms. #6451 and P, thus duplicating couplet 47. Such repetition suggests the possible use of this couplet as a mantra.

30. This passage refers to earlier references to bees, suggesting that the inner experiences of the sweet nectar of divine love transform humans into bees. Beyond the metaphorical connection to coitus, this possibly means the ability to fly about and such, reminiscent of the classical yogic powers known collectively as siddhis.

31. This is very much what goes on in the Gauḍīya Vaiṣṇava practice of rāgānugā-bhakti-sādhana, adapted by Sahajiyās for beginners. In this, one envisions, and gradually identifies with, a character in the mythical love-play of Rādhā and Kṛṣṇa. See Haberman (1988).

32. See, e.g., Urban (2001a, 2001b, 2003), and Openshaw (2002).

33. The four ponds are, in ascending order, the kāma-sarovara ('Pond of Lust'), the māna-sarovara ('Pond of Egotism'), the prema-sarovara ('Pond of Divine Love'), and the akṣaya-sarovara ('Pond of Indestructibility'). For more on these ponds, see my chapter in White (2000, pp. 313–314). On the uses of 'vastu' see Hayes (1988, 1989, 1996).

34. This is not to say that Mukunda does not make some use of these other metaphors, especially sound and color/light, or that other traditions eschew metaphors of fluid and substance. However, Mukunda clearly emphasizes the primacy of the substance/fluid metaphors over these others.

35. See Monier-Williams (1992, p. 869, cols. 2–3). On the Gauḍīya Vaiṣṇava and Vaiṣṇava Sahajiyā interpretations, see Dimock (1966, pp. 20–24). An extensive treatment of alchemy may be found in White (1996).

36. See note 18 above for works addressing this controversy.

37. See Urban (2001a) for ways in which the Kartābhajās also claimed that noted Gauḍīyas were practicing secret Tantric rituals.

38. See Stewart (2010) for an extensive discussion of the interactions between the two traditions on matters of textual interpretation and authority.

39. This passage appeared in my chapter in Lopez (1995, p. 348). I have used the seventh printed edition of the *Vivarta-vilāsa*, edited by Kṛṣṇa Bhattacharya (Calcutta: Taracand Dasa and Sons, n.d.). It was purchased in Calcutta in 1988. The excerpt comes from pp. 92–93.

40. This passage appeared in Lopez (1995), pp. 349–351, and is translated from the Bengali in *Vivarta-vilāsa*, pp. 113–114.

41. Compare this to the Kartābhajā phrase that men must become eunuchs and women must become castrated men. See Urban (2001a, e.g. pp. 98–100).

42. For a good overview of the basic Bengali model of procreation, which is transformed by the Sahajiyās, see Inden (1976), and Inden and Nicholas (1977).

43. For discussion of an updated approach to studying metaphors, known as 'conceptual blending theory,' see Hayes (2012a) and Turner (2014).

REFERENCES

Akincana-dasa. *Vivarta-vilāsa*. Edited by Kṛṣṇa Bhattacharya. Calcutta: Taracand Dasa and Sons, n.d. [purchased in Calcutta in 1988].

Banerji, S. C. (1978). *Tantra in Bengal: A Study in Its Origin, Development and Influence*. Calcutta: Naya Prokash.

Bose [Basu], Manindra Mohan (1932). *Sahajiyā Sāhitya*. Calcutta: University of Calcutta.

Bose [Basu], Manindra Mohan (1986 [1930]). *The Post-Caitanya Sahajia Cult of Bengal*. Delhi: Gian Publishing House.

Brooks, Douglas Renfrew (1990). *The Secret of the Three Cities: An Introduction to Hindu Śakta Tantrism*. Chicago: University of Chicago Press.

Caldwell, Sarah (2001). *Oh Terrifying Mother: Sexuality, Violence, and Worship of the Goddess Kali*. New York: Oxford University Press.

Casson, Ronald W. (1983). Schemata in cognitive anthropology. In Bernard J. Siegel, Alan R. Beals, and Stephen A. Tyler (eds.), *Annual Review of Anthropology*, pp. 429–462. Palo Alto, CA: Annual Reviews.

Dasa, Paritos (1972). *Caitanyottara prathama cāriṭi sahajiyā puṅthi*. Calcutta: Bharati Book Stall.

Dasa, Paritos (1978). *Sahajiyā o gauḍīya Vaiṣṇava dharma*. Calcutta: Firma K. L. M. Private Ltd.

Dasgupta, Shashibhusan (1969). *Obscure Religious Cults*, 3rd edition. Calcutta: Firma K. L. Mukhopadhyay.

Dimock, Edward C. Jr., (1966). *The Place of the Hidden Moon: Erotic Mysticism in the Vaiṣṇava-sahajiyā Cult of Bengal*. Chicago: University of Chicago Press.

Dimock, Edward C., Jr., and Tony K. Stewart (eds. and translators) (2000). *Caitanya Caritāmṛta of Kṛṣṇadāsa Kavirāja: A Translation and Commentary*. Harvard Oriental Series, 56. Cambridge: Harvard University Press.

Fauconnier, Gilles and Mark Turner (2002). *The Way We Think: Conceptual Blending and the Mind's Hidden Complexities*. New York: Basic Books.

Fort, Andrew O. and Patricia Y. Mumme (eds.) (1996). *Living Liberation in Hindu Thought*. Albany: SUNY Press.

Gallagher, Shaun (2005). *How the Body Shapes the Mind*. New York: Oxford University Press.

Haberman, David L. (1988). *Acting as a Way of Salvation: A Study of Rāgānugā Bhakti Sādhana*. New York: Oxford University Press.

Hawkes, Terence (1972). *Metaphor*. London: Methuen and Co.

Hayes, Glen Alexander (1985). *Shapes for the Soul: A Study of Body Symbolism in the Vaiṣṇava-sahajiyā Tradition of Medieval Bengal*. PhD dissertation: University of Chicago.

Hayes, Glen Alexander (1988). On the concept of Vastu in the Vaiṣṇava-sahajiyā tradition of medieval Bengal. In Purusottama Bilimoria and Peter Fenner (eds.), *Religions and Comparative Thought: Essays in Honour of the Late Dr. Ian Kesarcodi-Watson*, Sri Garib Dass Oriental Series No. 62, pp. 141–149. Delhi: Śrī Satguru Publications/Indian Books Centre.

Hayes, Glen Alexander (1989). Boating upon the crooked river: Cosmophysiological soteriologies in the Vaiṣṇava Sahajiyā tradition of medieval Bengal. In Tony K. Stewart (ed.), *Shaping Bengali Worlds, Public and Private*. South Asia Series Occasional Paper No. 37, pp. 29–35. East Lansing: Asian Studies Center/Michigan State University.

Hayes, Glen Alexander (1990). Vaiṣṇava Sahajiyā appropriations of Gauḍīya Vaiṣṇavism. *Journal of Vaiṣṇava Studies* 8(1), 77–90.

Hayes, Glen Alexander (1995). The Vaiṣṇava Sahajiyā traditions of medieval Bengal. In Donald S. Lopez, Jr. (ed.), *Religions of India in Practice*, Princeton Readings in Religions, pp. 333–351. Princeton, NJ: Princeton University Press.

Hayes, Glen Alexander (1996). Cosmic substance in the Vaiṣṇava Sahajiyā traditions of medieval Bengal. *Journal of Vaiṣṇava Studies* 5(1), 183–196.

Hayes, Glen Alexander (2000). *The Necklace of Immortality*: A 17th-century Vaiṣṇava Sahajiyā text on ritual sexual intercourse and the transformations of the body. In David Gordon White (ed.), *Tantra in Practice*, pp. 308–325. Princeton, NJ: Princeton University Press.

Hayes, Glen Alexander (2003). Metaphoric worlds and yoga in the Vaiṣṇava Sahajiyā Tantric traditions of medieval Bengal. In Ian Whicher and David Carpenter (eds.), *Yoga: The Indian Tradition*, pp. 162–184. New York: RoutledgeCurzon.

Hayes, Glen Alexander (2005). Contemporary metaphor theory and alternative views of Krishna and Rādhā in Vaishnava Sahajiyā Tantric traditions. In Guy Beck (ed.),

Alternative Krishnas: Regional and Vernacular Variations on a Hindu Deity, pp. 19–32. Albany: SUNY Press.

Hayes, Glen Alexander (2006). The guru's tongue: Metaphor, imagery, and vernacular language in Vaiṣṇava Sahajiyā traditions. *Pacific World: Journal of the Institute of Buddhist Studies*, 3(8), 41–71.

Hayes, Glen Alexander (2012a). Conceptual Blending Theory, 'reverse amnesia,' and the study of Tantra. *Journal of Hindu Studies*, 5(2), 193–209.

Hayes, Glen Alexander (2012b). Eroticism and cosmic transformation as Yoga: The Ātmatattva of the Vaiṣṇava Sahajiyās of Bengal. In David Gordon White (ed.), *Yoga in Practice*. Princeton Readings in Religions. Princeton, NJ: Princeton University Press, pp. 223–241.

Hayes, Glen Alexander (2014). Possible selves, body schemas, and Sādhana: Using cognitive science and neuroscience in the study of Medieval Vaiṣṇava Sahajiyā Hindu Tantric texts. *Religions* 5(3), 684–699. doi: 10.3390/rel5030684.

Hayes, Glen Alexander (2015). Exploring the uses of the term Sahaja in Hindu Tantra: Studying selected texts of the Vaiṣṇava Sahajiyās of Bengal. In Andrea Loseries (ed.), *Sahaja: The Role of Doha and Caryagiti in the Indo-Tibetan Interface*, pp. 125–137. Delhi: Buddhist World Press.

Inden, Ronald B. (1976). *Marriage and Rank in Bengali Culture*. Berkeley: University of California Press.

Inden, Ronald B. and Ralph W. Nicholas (1977). *Kinship in Bengali Culture*. Chicago: University of Chicago Press.

Johnson, Mark (1987). *The Body in the Mind: The Bodily Basis of Meaning, Imagination, and Reason*. Chicago: University of Chicago Press.

Kavirāja, Gopinath (1969, 1975). *Tantrik sādhana o siddhanta*. 2 vols. Burdhwan, India: Bardhaman Visvavidyalaya.

Lakoff, George (1987). *Women, Fire, and Dangerous Things: What Categories Reveal about the Mind*. Chicago: University of Chicago Press.

Lakoff, George (1993). The contemporary theory of metaphor. In Andrew Ortony (ed.), *Metaphor and Thought*, pp. 202–251. Cambridge: Cambridge University Press.

Lakoff, George and Mark Johnson (1980). *Metaphors We Live By*. Chicago: Chicago University Press.

Lakoff, George and Mark Johnson (1999). *Philosophy in the Flesh: The Embodied Mind and Its Challenge to Western Thought*. New York: Basic Books.

Lakoff, George and Rafael E. Núñez (2000). *Where Mathematics Comes From: How the Embodied Mind Brings Mathematics into Being*. New York: Basic Books.

Lakoff, George and Mark Turner (1989). *More Than Cool Reason: A Field Guide to Poetic Metaphor*. Chicago: University of Chicago Press.

Levin, Samuel R. (1993). Language, concepts, and worlds: Three domains of metaphor. In Andrew Ortony (ed.), *Metaphor and Thought*, 2nd edition, pp. 112–123. Cambridge: Cambridge University Press.

Lopez, Donald S., Jr. (ed.) (1995). *Religions of India in Practice*. Princeton Readings in Religion. Princeton, NJ: Princeton University Press, 1995.

McNamara, Patrick (2009). *The Neuroscience of Religious Experience*. Cambridge: Cambridge University Press.

Monier-Williams, Monier (1992). *A Sanskrit-English Dictionary*, revised edition. Oxford: Oxford University Press,

Mojumdar, Atindra (1973). *The Caryāpadas*, 2nd edition. Calcutta: Naya Prokash.

Muller-Ortega, Paul (1988). *The Triadic Heart of Siva: Kaula Tantricism of Abhinavagupta in the Non-Dual Shaivism of Kashmir*. SUNY Series in the Shaiva Traditions of Kashmir, ed. Harvey P. Alper. Albany: SUNY Press.

O'Connell, Joseph (1989). Were Caitanya's Vaiṣṇavas really Sahajiyās? The case of Rāmānanda Rāya. In Tony K. Stewart (ed.), *Shaping Bengali Worlds, Public and Private*, pp. 11–22. East Lansing, MI: Asian Studies Center.

O'Connell, Joseph (1993). Rāmānanda Rāya: A Sahajiyā or a Rāgānugā Bhakta? *Journal of Vaiṣṇava Studies* 1(3), 36–58.

Openshaw, Jeanne (2002). *Seeking Bāuls of Bengal*. New York: Cambridge University Press.

Ortony, Andrew (ed.) (1993) *Metaphor and Thought*, 2nd edition. Cambridge: Cambridge University Press.

Padoux, Andre (2002). *Vac: The Concept of the Word in Selected Hindu Tantras*. Delhi: Sri Satguru Publications.

Palmer, Gary B. (1996). *Toward a Theory of Cultural Linguistics*. Austin: University of Texas Press.

Pathak, Shubha (ed.) (2013). *Figuring Religions: Comparing Ideas, Images, and Activities*. Albany: SUNY Press.

Ramanujan, Attipate K. and Edwin Gerow (1974). Indian poetics. In Edward C. Dimock, Jr., et al. (eds.), *The Literatures of India: An Introduction*, pp. 115–143. Chicago: University of Chicago Press.

Sacks, Sheldon (ed.) (1979). *On Metaphor*. Chicago: University of Chicago Press.

Salomon, Carol (1995). Bāul Songs. In Donald S. Lopez (ed.), *Religions of India in Practice*, pp. 187–208. Princeton Readings in Religion. Princeton, NJ: Princeton University Press,

Sarbadhikary, Sukanya (2015). *The Place of Devotion: Siting and Experiencing Divinity in Bengal-Vaishnavism*. Berkeley: University of California Press.

Stewart, Tony K. (2010). *The Final Word: The Caitanya Caritāmṛta and the Grammar of Religious Tradition*. New York: Oxford University Press.

Toelken, Barre (1995). *Morning Dew and Roses: Nuance, Metaphor, and Meaning in Folksongs*. Urbana and Chicago: University of Illinois Press.

Turner, Mark (2014). *The Origin of Ideas: Blending, Creativity, and the Human Spark*. New York: Oxford University Press.

Urban, Hugh B. (2001a). *The Economics of Ecstasy: Tantra, Secrecy, and Power in Colonial Bengal*. New York: Oxford University Press.

Urban, Hugh B. (2001b). *Songs of Ecstasy: Tantric and Devotional Songs from Colonial Bengal*. Oxford: Oxford University Press.

Urban, Hugh B. (2003). *Tantra: Sex, Secrecy, Politics, and Power in the Study of Religion*. Berkeley, CA: University of California Press.

Wayman, Alex (1993). *The Buddhist Tantras*. Delhi: Motilal Banarsidass.

White, David Gordon (1996). *The Alchemical Body: Siddha Traditions in Medieval India*. Chicago: University of Chicago Press.

White, David Gordon (ed.). (2000). *Tantra in Practice*. Princeton Readings in Religions. Princeton, NJ: Princeton University Press.

White, David Gordon (2003). *Kiss of the Yoginī: 'Tantric Sex' in its South Asian Contexts*. Chicago: University of Chicago Press.

CHAPTER 9

Snakes, Leaves, and Poisoned Arrows

Metaphors of Emotion in Early Buddhism

HUBERT KOWALEWSKI

One of the basic assumptions of cognitive linguistics is that language is a symbol of thought or, to put it more technically, linguistic expressions are symbolizations of conceptual structures. If this claim is to be treated seriously, we are bound to admit that investigation into linguistic expressions is in fact investigation into human thought. From this point of view, comparative cross-cultural studies of linguistic data are not only studies of conventional ways of expressing concepts in different cultures, but, more importantly, studies of different ways of thinking about the world.

This paper investigates a relatively narrow, but very rich, area of language, namely, metaphorical expressions about emotions. My aim is to describe the main differences in conceptualizing emotions in early Buddhism and Western culture, as manifested in conceptual metaphors expressed linguistically in some of the most important Buddhist writings. I will also demonstrate that these differences are not arbitrary, but motivated by certain aspects of the two cultures.

The analysis focuses on expressions derived from suttas of the *Pali Canon*, a collection of the earliest surviving Buddhist writings. These texts are particularly useful for the purpose of this paper for two main reasons. First, they are relatively uncontroversial and can be considered as representative of the whole Buddhist philosophy, despite great diversity of modern and historical schools of Buddhism. While representatives of different schools of Buddhism may disagree about certain claims accepted in other schools, the ideas laid out in the *Pali Canon* are, to my best knowledge, universally accepted. Second, the suttas from the *Pali Canon* have a clear psychological focus, as they often include extended discussions on emotions and other mental phenomena, as well as the nature of the mind itself. Later texts frequently emphasize the philosophical, metaphysical, and religious aspect of Buddhist teachings, which are less relevant for the subject matter of this chapter.

1 CONCEPTUAL METAPHOR AND METONYMY

Conceptual metaphor theory (CMT) has already been outlined in detail by Feyaerts and Boeve in Part I of this volume, and is also referred to in the two chapters preceding the present one, in which Haskell (chapter 7) and Hayes (chapter 8) give detailed descriptions of metaphors in the sacred texts of two quite separate religious traditions. In the present chapter, I draw explicitly on CMT with the aim of outlining a cognitively explanatory analysis. It is therefore appropriate to recapitulate the key technical elements of the theory and its application to linguistic data. The present section, then, spells out some of the key methodological assumptions that the analysis relies on, assumptions that are also relied on in the two chapters that follow (chapters 10 and 11).

Emotion concepts are particularly prone to metaphorical conceptualization, but as Juliana Goschler (2005) notices, metaphors like ANGER IS HOT FLUID IN A CONTAINER are somewhat paradoxical. According to the canonical version of CMT advanced by Lakoff and Johnson (1980), the chief 'direction' of metaphorization is from abstract to concrete, that is to say, unfamiliar, abstruse, and complex ideas are typically construed as palpable physical objects (cf. TIME IS MONEY) or simple familiar events (cf. DEATH IS DEPARTURE). Yet emotions *are* familiar and directly experienced, which suggests that they should function as source concepts for conceptualizing more abstract and less directly experienced phenomena. Instead, emotion concepts are usually the target concepts, i.e. they are understood metaphorically as something else. Consider the following expressions:

(1)   The man was insane with rage. (ANGER IS INSANITY)

(2)   He unleashed his anger. (ANGER IS AN AGGRESSIVE ANIMAL)

(3)   The sight filled her with fear. (FEAR IS A LIQUID)

(4)   I'm in love. (LOVE IS A CONTAINER)

(5)   I found love. (LOVE IS AN OBJECT)

(6)   He drowned his sorrow in drink. (SADNESS IS A LIVING CREATURE)

(7)   I'm putting more into this than you are. (LOVE IS A CONTAINER, LOVE IS A FINANCIAL TRANSACTION)

Expression (1) is particularly peculiar in this context, since a familiar emotion concept ANGER is understood metaphorically in terms of the state that may be totally unfamiliar to the conceptualizer (INSANITY), but the metaphor remains meaningful and informative nonetheless. In short, ANGER IS INSANITY goes against the usual direction of metaphorization, since it construes the familiar in terms of the unfamiliar! There are several possible explanations of these unexpected metaphors. Perhaps the culturally entrenched representation of insanity is rich enough to function as a potential source concept, so that one does not have to experience insanity directly to be familiar with this state of mind. Perhaps LOVE IS INSANITY is used to highlight particular aspects of love, which happen to be stereotypically associated with insanity, so that the concept INSANITY is used as a 'filter' to highlight the aspects of love relevant in a particular situation. In this sense, LOVE IS INSANITY is meaningful and informative not because it 'familiarizes' the unknown, but because it draws attention to specific elements on the known. Perhaps construing unfamiliar in terms of the familiar is just prominent tendency rather than a strict law, and therefore it should not be expected to apply across the board. On this view, emotion metaphors would be, for some reason or no reason at all, principled exceptions to the general tendency. Fortunately, accounting for this unusual direction of metaphorical mappings is not a prerequisite for analysis carried out in this chapter, so we may accept any of the above explanations or leave the question open for the time being.

An important property of conceptual metaphors is systematicity. The systematicity of metaphorical mappings has at least two aspects. One of them is related to the way in which metaphors are organized in the human conceptual system. They rarely occur in isolation and tend to create larger configurations of interlocking, overlapping, and sometimes conflicting mappings. Another aspect concerns the fact that one metaphor can systematically give rise to different linguistic expressions. For instance, the metaphor LOVE IS AN OBJECT, which is evident in sentence (5), also appears in expressions like *I thought I'd never lose this love*. In this way, one metaphorical mapping is not exclusively bound to one linguistic pattern, but can become a basis for a potentially infinite number of expressions.

Metaphorical mapping is always partial and selective. Even though the conceptual metaphor in cognitive linguistics is often defined as a way of 'understanding and experiencing one kind of thing in terms of another' (Lakoff and Johnson 1980, p. 5), strictly speaking, a metaphor structures only some aspects of the target concept in terms of some aspects of the source concept. For instance, the metaphor FEAR IS A LIQUID compels us to think about the emotion as if it was a physical substance. Therefore, on the metaphorical plane it is possible for fear to 'fill' a person as a container can be filled with a liquid (compare sentence (3)). However, since not all semantic facets of the concept LIQUID are faithfully mapped onto respective facets of the concept FEAR, some possible inferences arising from this metaphor are blocked. Thus, while humans can typically be engaged in physical interaction with liquid substances, there are many actions that cannot be performed on emotions when the metaphorical understanding is activated. For example, despite the fact that many liquids can be stored in containers (in appropriate physical conditions) and used for some purposes in the future, it seems highly unlikely for anyone to say *I poured my fear in 10 bottles, then I gave 5 to Jane and stored the other 5 in a refrigerator*.

Another conceptual mechanism often discussed together with metaphor is metonymy. Lakoff and Johnson define metonymy as a device consisting in 'using one entity to refer to another that is related to it' (1980, p. 35). The word 'entity' appearing in the definition should not be understood in terms of material objects—since metonymy is a conceptual phenomenon, it operates in the realm of the human mind and links concepts rather than physical objects. Examples of metonymic expressions include *The ham sandwich is waiting for his check* and *The Times hasn't arrived at the press conference yet* (examples after Lakoff and Johnson 1980, p. 35). In the former sentence of this pair, *ham sandwich* metonymically stands for the client who ordered the sandwich, while in the latter sentence the title of the newspaper stands for the journalist working for the newspaper. In the religious context, a common metonymy is SYMBOL OF A RELIGION FOR THE RELIGION, by means of which the Christian Cross refers to Christianity, the Muslim Crescent refers to Islam, etc. Linguistic exponents of these metonymies include *I come to the cross seeking mercy and grace* (CROSS FOR (CHRISTIAN) GOD) and the title of Jerald Dirks's book *The Cross and the Crescent: An Interfaith Dialogue between Christianity and Islam* (2001).

Most basic statements about metaphor are also true for metonymy. Most pre-cognitive paradigms of linguistics treated metonymy as a purely linguistic device limited to certain types of discourses. It was cognitive linguistics that redefined it as a conceptual phenomenon manifested in linguistic expressions and emphasized the fact that metonymies surface in everyday language, not just in poetry and rhetorical speeches. Nonetheless, metonymy is different from metaphor, mainly because the former operates within one cognitive domain (i.e. relates concepts belonging to one and the same domain). Moreover, Lakoff and Johnson observe that '[metaphor] is principally a way of conceiving of one thing in terms of another, and its primary function is understanding. Metonymy, on the other hand, has primarily a referential function, that is, it allows us to use one entity to *stand for* another'[1] (1980, p. 36; original emphasis). An extended discussion on metonymy in the religious context is developed in chapter 14 of the present volume.

Metaphors and metonymies may form larger conceptual complexes and simultaneously motivate single linguistic expression. Expression (3) is an illustrative example of two metaphors shaping the understanding of one situation. In *The sight filled her with fear*, the metaphor of emotion is of course FEAR IS A LIQUID, but the metaphorical imagery would be incomplete and incomprehensible without the metaphor EXPERIENCER (OF AN EMOTION) IS A CONTAINER (FOR A LIQUID). The entire mental imagery makes sense only because the liquid and the container metaphors are activated together, which allows for conceptualizing a person experiencing fear as a container filled with a liquid. A similar 'cooperation' can be sometimes observed between metaphors and metonymies. In expression (2) (*He unleashed his anger*), the concept ANGER is understood in terms of an animal. The metaphor, however, is subsidiarily motivated by the general metonymy PHYSIOLOGICAL/BEHAVIORAL SYMPTOMS ACCOMPANYING EMOTIONS FOR EMOTIONS (cf. Kövecses 2000), involving the associations between emotions and physiological or behavioral responses accompanying them. In (3), the behavioral response metonymically associated with anger (violence) is used as an element of a larger metaphor ANGER IS AN (AGGRESSIVE) ANIMAL. This kind of metaphor-metonymy interaction in the construction of a single array of mental imagery is sometimes termed metaphtonymy (Goossens's 1990 term). Other examples of metaphtonymies of emotions include ANGER IS HEAT (*You make my blood boil*) and ANGER IS PRESSURE IN A CONTAINER (*When I told him, he blew up*; cf. Lakoff 1987, p. 381).[2]

1.1 Emotion-as-force metaphors

Conceptualizations of emotions are semantic structures which are particularly prone to metaphorization. In fact, most of the language used to talk about emotional processes in most (if not all) human languages relies heavily on various metaphorical mappings. This suggests that human beings understand, and consequently talk about, emotions mainly through systems of conceptual metaphors.

According to Zoltán Kövecses (2000), the most important system of that sort is built around a fairly abstract and general master metaphor EMOTION IS A FORCE. Even though not all metaphors of emotions can be viewed as realizations of this mapping, the number and diversity of expressions that instantiate it is substantial. Moreover, force-based metaphors of emotions can be found in many unrelated languages grounded in different cultural backgrounds,[3] which is a strong indication that human beings have a natural and universal tendency to conceptualize emotions as forces. The basic force schema underlying all force metaphors has been described by Leonard Talmy. Talmy (1988; after Kövecses 2000, p. 62) enumerates the following elements of this schema:

- Force entities
  - agonist
  - antagonist
- Intrinsic force tendency
  - toward action
  - toward inaction
- Balance of strength
  - stronger entity
  - weaker entity
- Result of force interaction
  - action
  - rest

A typical scenario built upon this schema develops in the following way: the antagonist is the active entity (i.e. has the intrinsic force tendency toward action) and the agonist is the inactive entity (i.e. has the intrinsic force tendency toward inaction). One of the entities in the configuration is stronger than the other. If the stronger entity happens to be the antagonist, the antagonist produces an action or there is a change on the part of the agonist. If the stronger entity happens to be the agonist, the agonist manages to 'resist' the influence of the antagonist and remains inactive or unchanged. Any metaphor involving the elements included in this basic scenario and organized in the same way as in the scenario can be considered a force metaphor. Instances of this mapping can be found in the following expressions; and the exact metaphors are given in the brackets and written with capital letters (adapted from Kövecses 2000):

(8)   You make my blood boil. (ANGER IS HEAT)

(9)   Jack was insane with fear. (FEAR IS INSANITY)

(10) He was engulfed by panic. (FEAR IS A NATURAL FORCE)

(11) It was an electrifying experience. (EMOTION IS AN ELECTRIC FORCE)

(12) That was a terrible blow. (SADNESS IS A PHYSICAL FORCE)

(13) He staggered under the pain. (SADNESS IS A BURDEN)

(14) Her whole body exploded with passion. (LUST IS PRESSURE INSIDE A CONTAINER)

Many of the force-based metaphors are grounded in human experience. As noted by Kövecses (e.g. 1990 and 2000), the source domain is often informed by physiological and behavioral effects which emotions produce in the experiencer. A good example of this is (8), in which anger is conceptualized in terms of heat. The choice of the source concept does not seem to be arbitrary—since anger is accompanied by increased body temperature and a subjective sensation of heat, it is heat rather than, for instance, the sensation of cold or relaxation that is naturally associated with this emotion. More technically, the metaphorical mapping ANGER IS HEAT can be viewed as a metaphtonymy involving the already mentioned metonymy PHYSIOLOGICAL/BEHAVIORAL SYMPTOMS ACCOMPANYING EMOTIONS FOR EMOTIONS.[4]

Let us now move on to force-based emotion metaphors in Buddhism. Since the force-based metaphorical system can be found in numerous unrelated languages and cultures, the first question to ask at this point is whether linguistic expressions instantiating the master metaphor are present in Buddhist writings. Not surprisingly, the answer is 'yes.' Expressions (15)–(25) feature several common emotion-as-force metaphors recurring throughout Buddhist suttas.

(15) Those chained by desire . . . aren't easily released for there's no liberation by others. (Sn 4.2)[5] (DESIRE IS BONDS)

(16) When anger arises, whoever keeps firm control as if with a racing chariot: him I call a master Charioteer. Anyone else, a rein-holder. (Dhp 17) (ANGER IS A CHARIOT)

(17) Conquer anger with lack of anger. (Dhp 17) (ANGER IS AN OPPONENT)

(18) 'The sixth fellow-traveling executioner with upraised sword' stands for passion & delight. (SN 35.197) (EMOTION IS AN OPPONENT)

(19) Guard against anger erupting in body. (Dhp 17) (ANGER IS PRESSURE IN A CONTAINER)

(20) Whoever avoids sensual desires—as he would, with his foot, the head of a snake. (Sn 4.1) (DESIRE IS A SNAKE)

(21) There's no fire like passion, no seizure like anger . . . no river like craving. (Dhp 18) (PASSION IS FIRE, ANGER IS SEIZURE, CRAVING IS A RIVER)

(22) The monk, when not loaded down, does not load himself down with pain. (MN 101) (EMOTIONAL PAIN IS A BURDEN)

(23) If this sticky craving overcomes you in the world, your sorrows grow like wild grass after rain. (Dhp 24) (CRAVING IS A STICKY OBJECT)

(24) With shame as his moat, the disciple of the noble ones abandons what is unskilful, develops what is skilful, abandons what is blameworthy. (AN 7.63) (SHAME IS A MOAT)

(25) Fields are spoiled by weeds; people, by aversion. (Dhp 24) (AVERSION IS A PLANT)

Even though the force dynamics embedded into these metaphors may not seem obvious, especially in the case of (24) and (25), after closer inspection the basic force schema can be found in all instances. Crucial elements of the schema as represented in expressions (15)–(25) are summarized in Table 1.

In most of the above cases, metaphors are used to highlight the 'active,' or even 'interactive,' aspect of emotion. This (inter)active aspect is related to the fact that emotional states may be conceptualized as phenomena exerting some kind of causal influence on the experiences and the experiencer may causally influence the emotion (e.g. by suppressing it). In the examples quoted above, some metaphors focus on the influence that emotion has on the experiencer, like in DESIRE IS A SNAKE, EMOTIONAL PAIN IS A BURDEN, and AVERSION IS A PLANT. On other occasions, it is the experiencer's attempt to influence the emotion that is emphasized—typically, the aim of such an action is to control or to eliminate the emotion (like in ANGER IS A CHARIOT, ANGER IS AN OPPONENT, and DESIRE IS BONDS). In this sense, force-metaphors construct the emotional state in terms of interaction between the emotion and the experiencer.[6]

The above scenario may be treated as prototypical, as it underlies an overwhelming majority of metaphors of emotions in Buddhism. However, other scenarios, although less typical, are available as well. One metaphor instantiating a different pattern is SHAME IS A MOAT. Here, the two entities involved in a force interaction are 'unskillful and blameworthy' actions and the emotion preventing the actions from influencing the experiencer. Even though the experiencer is present in the metaphorical scenario (as a participant 'attacked' by the unskillful and blameworthy actions and protected by the moat), the experiencer is not directly involved in the force interaction—the interaction takes place between the blameworthy actions and the emotion. In this sense, SHAME IS A MOAT deviates from the prototypical scenario, which features the experiencer as one of the force entities (either the antagonist or the agonist).

1.2 Emotion-as-object metaphors

Apart from emotion-as-force master metaphor, another extensive system of mappings is frequently used to conceptualize emotions, namely, EMOTION IS AN OBJECT. Similarly to EMOTIONS IS A FORCE, this metaphor does not merely structure an emotion in terms of another concept but evokes a whole schema embracing other

Table 1. FORCE-BASED EMOTION METAPHORS

Metaphor	Antagonist: Source → Target	Agonist: Source → Target	(Intended) Result: Source	(Intended) Result: Target
DESIRE IS BONDS	bound person → experiencer	bounds → emotion	person frees himself/herself from bonds	experiencer frees himself/herself from the influence of emotion
ANGER IS A CHARIOT	charioteer → experiencer	chariot → emotion	charioteer controls the chariot	experiencer controls emotion
ANGER/EMOTION IS AN OPPONENT	opponent → emotion	person assaulted → experiencer	person assaulted defeats/escapes the opponent	experiencer is not affected by emotion
ANGER IS A PRESSURE IN A CONTAINER	pressure → emotion	container → experiencer's body	pressurized container is not destroyed by the pressure	experiencer controls emotion
DESIRE IS A SNAKE	snake → emotion	person bitten by a snake → experiencer	person is not bitten by a snake	experiencer is not affected by emotion
PASSION IS FIRE	fire → emotion	burning object → experiencer	object is not destroyed by fire	experiencer is not affected by emotion
EMOTIONAL PAIN IS A BURDEN	burden → emotion	person carrying a burden → experiencer	person drops the burden	experiencer overcomes negative influence of emotion
CRAVING IS A STICKY OBJECT	person trying to detach from a sticky object → experiencer	sticky object → emotion	person detaches himself/herself from a sticky object	experiencer is not affected by emotion
SHAME IS A MOAT	person trying to cross a moat → 'unskillful and blameworthy' actions	moat → emotion	moat prevents someone from getting to the other side	emotion prevents experiencer from performing an action
AVERSION IS A PLANT	plants → emotion	field → experiencer	fields is not covered with plants (weeds)	experiencer is not affected by emotion

participants and establishing relationships between them.[7] The schema involves the following elements:

- Object(s)
  - affectant
  - base (optional)
- Initial state
  - affectant exists in a dominion *or*
  - affectant and base are in contact
- Change
  - affectant ceases to exist or is removed from the dominion, *or*
  - affectant and base are separated
- Factor causing the change (optional)
- Final state
  - affectant does not exist *or*
  - affectant and base are not in contact

The scenario evoked by the schema has two main variants. In the first variant, there is only one object called the affectant. The experiencer has a dominion in which affectants are located. The dominion[8] is a sphere of influence—the entities within the dominion are capable of entertaining some kind of cause-and-effect interaction with the experiencer and the entities outside the dominion are out of the range of any causal influence. Due to an intervention of some factor, a change occurs, so that the affectant ceases to exist. Since the dominion represents the entities exerting some sort of influence on the experiencer, the outcome of the scenario is the situation where the emotion is not experienced or at least it has no influence on the experiencer. In the second variant, there are two entities: the affectant attached or in close proximity to another object called the base. In this scenario, the base is identified with the experiencer of the emotion. Then, due to the intervention of some factor, the affectant is separated from the base, so that the two objects are not in contact anymore, so that the metaphorical image is that of an emotion becoming physically separated from the experiencer. Some instances of emotion-as-object metaphors in Buddhism include:

(26) Seeking your own happiness, you should pull out your own arrow: your own lamentation, longing, & sorrow. (Sn 3.8) (EMOTION IS AN ARROW)

(27) Cut down the forest of desire, not the forest of trees. (Dhp 20) (DESIRE IS A TREE)

(28) Slow would be the falling of the drops of water [on a hot pan], but they quickly would vanish & disappear. That is how quickly . . . anger ceases, and equanimity takes its stance. (MN 152) (ANGER IS A WATER DROP)

(29) [The wise man would] blow away any arisen grief, like the wind, a bit of cotton fluff. (Sn 3.8) (GRIEF IS A COTTON FLUFF)

(30)   aversion drops away from him—like a palm leaf from its stem. (Iti 3.88)
         (AVERSION IS A LEAF)

(31)   His passion, aversion, conceit, & contempt, have fallen away—like a mustard
         seed from the tip of an awl. (Dhp 26) (EMOTION IS A MUSTARD SEED)

(32)   Just as a ball of string, when thrown, comes to its end simply by unwinding,
         in the same way . . . the wise and the foolish alike will put an end to pain.
         (DN 2) (EMOTION IS A BALL OF STRING)

(33)   In him lamentation . . . like water on a white lotus, do not adhere. (Sn 4.6)
         (LAMENTATION IS A DROP OF WATER)

(34)   Your passion is stilled—like a pot of pickled greens boiled dry. (Thig 1.1)
         (EMOTION IS WATER IN A POT)

Similarly to the force metaphors, the typical scenario activated by object-based mappings involves some kind of interaction between the experiencer and the emotion. There are, however, significant differences that prevent us from classifying object metaphors as a subtype of force metaphors. First of all, in the former, emotion is conceptualized as a concrete entity which can be actively manipulated by the experiencer, while in the latter emotion is understood as a force influencing the experiencer. Consequently, even if the experiencer exerts some kind of influence on the emotion, this is conceptualized as a counterforce produced in response to a force, rather than manipulation of a physical object. To put it plainly, even though both scenarios involve interaction between the experiencer and the emotion, in the case of EMOTION IS A FORCE the experiencer interacts with a force, while in EMOTION IS AN OBJECT the experiencer interacts with an object; consequently, the nature of these interactions are very different.

Similarly to emotion-as-force mappings, the object-based metaphors display a clear prototype effect. In this case, the prototypical scenario embraces the experiencer performing some kind of action on the emotion-object, like in (26), (27), (29), and (32). Nonetheless, specific scenarios activated by particular instances of the master metaphor may differ significantly from the prototype. For example, in (28), (30), and (33) no action is performed by the experiencer and the emotion-object ceases to exist (or ceases to be in contact) without any intervention of an external factor (or at least the relevant factor is not explicitly included in the overall structure of the metaphor). Yet another deviation from the prototype is EMOTION IS A MUSTARD SEED as rendered in (31), where the experiencer is backgrounded and is a part of the target domain only implicitly. The most important elements of the mappings in (26)–(34) are summed up in Table 2.

EMOTION IS A FORCE and EMOTION IS AN OBJECT are two chief master metaphors in Buddhist conceptualization of emotional processes. While this is not to say that the two systems subsume *all* emotion metaphors, they do, however, embrace an overwhelming majority of mappings. Yet, a handful of metaphors cannot be accounted for in terms of any of the above systems, as they do not instantiate either force, or object schema, not even in highly non-prototypical versions. Apart from these few

Table 2. OBJECT-BASED METAPHORS

Metaphor	Affectant: Source → Target	Base: Source → Target	Action on the Part of the Experiencer?
EMOTION IS AN ARROW	arrow → emotion	wounded person → experiencer	yes
DESIRE IS A TREE	tree → desire	–	yes
ANGER IS A WATER DROP	water drop → anger	- *or* lotus → experiencer	no
GRIEF IS A COTTON FLUFF	cotton fluff → grief	–	yes
AVERSION IS A LEAF	leaf → aversion	palm tree → experiencer	no
EMOTION IS A MUSTARD SEED	mustard seed → emotion	awl → experiencer?	no
EMOTION IS A BALL OF STRING	ball of string → emotion	-	yes
EMOTION IS WATER IN A POT	water → emotion	pot → experiencer?	no

cases, there are several mappings which pose a greater classificatory problem, as they include crucial elements of both master metaphors discussed above. These mappings belong to the force-object type.

1.3 Force-object metaphors

The term 'force-object metaphors' may be slightly misleading—it should not suggest that the mappings form a different type because they belong to a separate metaphorical system independent of the two described above. Rather, in this case the two systems overlap at some points, and the force-object metaphors should be located in the area of this overlap. In this sense, the force-object type is a combination of the emotion-as-force and emotion-as-object mappings rather than a fully individuated and distinct class.

The best example of the mixed-type metaphor is EMOTION IS A POISONED ARROW, as instantiated in (35).

(35)   Suppose that a man were wounded with an arrow thickly smeared with poison. . . . Craving is said by the Contemplative to be an arrow. The poison of ignorance spreads its toxin through desire, passion, & ill will. (MN 105)

The metaphor clearly combines semantic components of both systems. The concept ARROW is an element of a well-known object-based mapping EMOTION IS AN ARROW appearing in numerous Buddhist texts (discussed in some detail in the previous section). An additional semantic component is POISON, which links the metaphor in (35) with the emotion-as-force mappings (interaction between poison and a poisoned organism can be successfully described in terms of force schema).

EMOTION IS A POISONED ARROW should not be considered as a loose mixture of unrelated threads of conceptualization; rather, the overall scenario evoked by the mapping features a unified and seamlessly integrated conceptualization of a certain action. The conceptualization is informed by the two master metaphors, but involves novel elements which are not directly derived from any of the component metaphors. Thus, the emotion-poison affects the experiencer in the same way any other emotion-force does, and the arrow can be pulled out just like any other emotion-object may be removed, destroyed, or detached from something. Yet, at the same time, removing the emotion-object results in the cessation of the emotion-force (i.e. pulling out the arrow puts an end to the spreading of the poison). Thus, there is a clear cause-and-effect connection between the force and the object scenarios, which integrates the contributions from both systems into a coherent and well-integrated conceptual complex.

2 MOTIVATION BEHIND TWO METAPHORICAL SYSTEMS

As demonstrated by Kövecses (1990, 2000), the EMOTION IS A FORCE metaphor is encountered in many cultures, which suggests that it reflects a way of thinking about emotions universal for all human beings. EMOTION IS AN OBJECT is far less common and rarely creates an extensive metaphorical system, at least in Western culture. A question that comes to mind at this point is why the emotion-as-object mappings have become so crucial in Buddhist texts that they yielded a vast metaphorical system and why this system is far less prominent in Western culture.

It is perhaps not surprising that the existence of culture-specific, object-based metaphor scenario in addition to more widespread force-based scenario is not a mere fancy of early Buddhist scholars. Paul Chilton (in a private conversation) noted the possibility that for some reason Buddhist thought has developed precisely because certain metaphors have been selected and selectively developed as the actual medium in which the Buddhist mind-set and discourse has been elaborated over time and via innumerable linguistic-conceptual communications in both speech and writing. One could also argue that the direction of development was the reverse, namely, that it is the Buddhist way of thinking about emotion crystallized into the two metaphor scenarios. However, since metaphors are inalienable elements of our way of thinking about the world, the question 'Which came first: the thought or the metaphor?' is void. In the light of Conceptual Metaphor Theory, it seems likely that the development described by Chilton is more similar to a continuous conceptual feedback loop rather than linear evolution: conceptual metaphors reinforce certain ways of thinking about emotions and are reinforced by these ways of thinking at the same time.

The cultural specificity of the object-based scenario can be partly explained by the fact that metaphorical mappings are selective and highlight only those elements that are considered to be the most relevant in a particular context and culture community. In Western culture, force metaphors tend to foreground the already mentioned interactive aspect of emotions, as this culture typically focuses on the influence of emotions on the experiencer or on the action taken by the experiencer in relation to the emotion (typically, an attempt to resist or control the emotion).

In Buddhism, the matter is slightly more complicated. In principle, force metaphors perform the same function as in Western culture, i.e. they point to the interactive aspect of emotions. The details of the conceptualization, however, are somewhat different. In the West, the axiological orientation of force-based mappings is fairly diverse—even though numerous metaphors suggest that the impact of emotion on the experiencer is negative (like in (9), (12), and (13)), instances of positive influence are common (e.g. in expressions (11) and (14)). In Buddhism, the influence of emotions is depicted as predominantly negative. As Padmasiri de Silva notes, '[emotions] are generally regarded in the mind of the Buddhist as aspects of our personality that interfere with the development of a spiritual life, as unwholesome states ethically undesirable, and roadblocks to be cleared in the battleground between reason and emotion' (2007). Yet there is an important caveat to this view (which de Silva acknowledges later in the article): certain emotions can serve as a powerful source of motivation for spiritual practice. In the introduction to *Salayatana-vibhanga Sutta: An Analysis of the Six Sense-media*, the translator Thanissaro Bhikkhu explains:

> In particular, this discourse counters a common misperception: that the distress that comes from having an unachieved goal is an obstacle in the practice, and that the antidote for that distress is to renounce any sense of goals. In actuality, that distress —termed "renunciation distress"—has an important role in the practice: to overcome the distress that comes with a sense of loss over sensual pleasures that have not been attained, or those that have been attained in the past but now no longer exist. Renunciation distress serves as a reminder that the loss of sensual pleasures is not a serious matter. As for renunciation distress, it is overcome, not by abandoning any sense of goal, but by following the path and realizing the joy that comes when the goal is reached. (Thanissaro Bhikkhu 2003)

Thus, the dissatisfaction from leading an unenlightened life and the joy after having achieved the goal of meditation are emotions which encourage spiritual practice of Buddhism. This point, however, is easily overlooked, which leads to what Thanissaro Bhikkhu calls 'a common misperception.' One source of this misperception may be the fact that this negative evaluation of emotion is far more frequent in metaphorical language of Buddhist suttas. The adverse and destructive aspect of passions is reflected in the selection of negatively evaluated source concepts in force-based metaphors (e.g. in DESIRE IS BONDS, DESIRE IS A SNAKE), the structure of scenario evoked by the metaphor (e.g. in EMOTION IS AN OPPONENT, like in (18)), and the choice of expressions which do not enter the metaphor directly (e.g. *Guard against anger erupting in body* in (19), where it is implicitly stated that anger is a threat to the well-being of the experiencer and thus it should be resisted).

Object metaphors, in turn, highlight another aspect of emotions, which is of great importance in Buddhism, but is virtually absent from Western philosophy. This type of metaphor conveys at least two important claims that the Buddha made about emotions. The first claim is that all phenomena are endowed with a property of 'essencelessness' (*anatta*). In Buddhism emotions are not treated as integral parts of the experiencer's mental constitution. Instead, they are viewed as transitory mental phenomena produced by a number of factors internal and external to the experiencer. Since emotions exist only as consequences of various events, they do not exist independently of either the events that produce them, or of the experiencer in whom they are produced. This means that in Buddhism emotions are considered to be purely relational phenomena which do not persist outside the cause-and-effect processes that create them. In other words, for Buddhists emotions 'happen' to human beings but do not 'constitute' their Selfhood, not even in the particular moment in which the emotion is experienced.

One of the aims of the Buddhist spiritual practice is the contemplation of this essencelessness (*anatta*) of mental states. One technique of Buddhist meditation, known as *vipassana*, is designed specifically to facilitate this sort of contemplation. One element of this technique is passive observation of mental and physical sensations, e.g. emotions, without getting involved in them. During *vipassana* meditation, instructors often advise disciples to observe how sensations arise, persist, and pass, but not to revel in them, resist them, or judge them in any way. It seems likely that this meditation technique and the states experienced during meditation sessions help to view emotions as objects, which in turn facilitates the meditation practice (in yet another 'conceptual feedback loop'). During *vipassana* meditation, it is explicitly forbidden to become engaged in any force interaction with the emotion; instead, the technique promotes passive, detached observation of emotional states. This, on the one hand, undermines the understanding of emotion in terms of interactive force dynamics and, on the other hand, encourages the experiencer to think of emotions as if they were observable entities, which do not, in and of themselves, engage the experiencer in any interaction. Since, as far as the metaphorical conceptualization of emotions is concerned, such properties are typical of objects rather than forces, it is the object that becomes a natural choice for source concepts in metaphorical mappings.

Another important aspect of emotions, and in fact all phenomena, is impermanence (*anicca*). Buddhism highlights the fact that everything from material objects to states of the mind is by nature unstable, changeable, and bound to disintegrate.[9] This is particularly true of emotions, both positive and negative, which are typically short-lived, and even if they do persist for an extended period of time, they change in quality and intensity. Similar to essencelessness, impermanence of emotional states is reflected in the object metaphor. Here, the crucial aspect of the general scenario evoked by emotion-as-object metaphors is the final stage, when the emotion-object disappears or is physically separated from the base. On the metaphorical level, the physical impermanence and disappearance of material objects is mapped onto psychological impermanence and cessation of the emotional processes. Thus, it appears that the structure of the object-based metaphors is founded on Buddhist thought and meditation practice, and at the same time supports and reinforces Buddhist thought and practice.

In the general scheme of things, the didactic work of suttas is skillfully distributed between force-based and object-based metaphors of emotions. The former type of metaphors employs imagery with predominantly negative axiological charge in order to demonstrate the adverse influence of passions on the experiencer's well-being. Even though de Silva and Thanissaro Bhikkhu explain that some emotions have a beneficial role to play, this positive aspect rarely surfaces in force-based metaphors. The main task of force-based metaphors is to encourage spiritual practice by painting a gloomy image of an unenlightened, passion-driven person. Once the image is established, object-based metaphors show that negative emotions can be eliminated just like things removed from a dominion or 'detached' from their base in the two main versions of the object-based metaphorical scenario. To use a medical analogy, force-based mappings are like a diagnosis of an illness of an unenlightened person, while the object-based mappings show that there is a cure for the illness.

The importance of FORCE and OBJECT as the master source concepts for Buddhist metaphors of emotions is hardly surprising in the light of Aleksander Szwedek's theory of objectification (cf. Szwedek 2000, 2008, 2011). According to Szwedek, humans have a natural tendency to metaphorically conceptualize abstract concepts as physical objects. While event metaphors (e.g. ARGUMENT IS WAR) and Lakoff and Johnson's orientational metaphors (e.g. GOOD IS UP) are common and form a great part of our human conceptual inventory, Szwedek holds that they are secondary. Object metaphors, in turn, are primary because '[it] is always a matter of the structure *and* orientation of objects, never *objects of structure or *objects of orientation. Before we can talk about structure and orientation, we have to have an object that has structure and orientation' (Szwedek 2008, p. 312). Szwedek agrees with Lakoff and Johnson (e.g. 1980) that metaphors and metonymies are embodied, i.e. grounded in basic bodily experiences of the conceptualizer,[10] and he claims that the most fundamental bodily experiences are tactile sensations. The sense of touch evolves and influences cognition already in the prenatal stage of human development. Thus, it is already at this stage that a human being has first basic experiences with properties of physical objects like softness, hardness, flexibility, etc., so that these experiences are formative for human cognition long before information from vision and other senses become important. Needless to say, the sense of touch provides cognitive access to solid physical objects rather than events or spatial orientation. If this view is accepted, it is anything but surprising that object-based metaphors are primary and more deeply rooted relative to event-based or orientational metaphors.

Szwedek's theory of objectification addresses at least two fundamental questions related to metaphorical understanding of emotions (not only in the context of Buddhism). First, the theory solves the problem noticed by Juliana Goschler (cf. 2005 and section 1 of this chapter), namely, the fact that familiar mental and physiological states (emotions) are often metaphorized in terms of something unfamiliar. Examples of such metaphors include the already mentioned ANGER IS INSANITY in *The man was insane with rage*, LOVE IS MAGIC in *I'm under her spell*, and in the context of Buddhism: EMOTION IS A CHARIOT in (16) and EMOTION IS A MUSTARD SEED (31).[11] Humans may have a preference for understanding the abstract and unfamiliar in terms of the concrete and familiar (as Lakoff and Johnson stipulate), but they also have a stronger and more fundamental preference for understanding non-things in terms of things. Since the preference for objectification is stronger than the preference for familiarity, conceptualizers are more likely to think about familiar processes as unfamiliar things, rather than to think about familiar processes in a literal non-metaphorical manner. This would explain why emotions in general are likely to be apprehended metaphorically rather than 'literally.'

This, however, does not provide a prima facie explanation of the popularity of force-based metaphors of emotions. At first blush, it may even seem that the large number of force-based metaphors run against the theory of objectification, because the theory predicts the predominance of object-based metaphors! I believe, however, that the problem is illusory and the popularity of force-based metaphors may even provide partial support for objectification. It is essential to bear in mind that for Szwedek the foundations for human cognition are laid in the prenatal stage of development, when the fetus explores her environment mostly through the sense of touch. Through tactile sensation the fetus familiarizes herself not only with physical properties of objects (softness, hardness, flexibility, shape, etc.), but also with basic force dynamics (pressure, release, resistance to pressure, etc.). Consequently, if we embrace the basic assumption of the objectification theory, according to which tactile sensations are the earliest and most fundamental formative factors of human cognition, it is quite easy to view force-based metaphors as a natural component of this theory.

3 CONCLUDING REMARKS

Let us recapitulate the story so far and discuss one possible objection to the conclusions presented in this chapter. The analysis carried out in this paper is by no means an exhaustive presentation of Buddhist conceptualization of emotions as manifested in metaphorical expressions. Two main points are worth highlighting. First, Buddhism makes extensive and systematic use of two master metaphors: one of them is organized around EMOTION IS A FORCE and the other around EMOTION IS AN OBJECT. These two systems overlap, giving rise to a more complex force-object metaphor, which seamlessly integrates semantic components from the two major systems. Mappings which are not covered by any of the systems are rare; most probably they cannot be reduced to any other 'master metaphor,' and do not seem to belong to any extensive network of metaphors. Second, the differences in the metaphorical conceptualization of emotion are not accidental; they are motivated by and intimately linked to certain aspects of Buddhist thought.

Comparative studies demonstrate that the metaphorical inventories used to facilitate conceptualization of emotions (and of other concepts) in different cultures are not entirely incompatible. A great number of both Western and Buddhist mappings can be reduced to a more primitive, and possibly universal, master metaphor EMOTION IS A FORCE. Moreover, even more idiosyncratic mappings found in Buddhist discourse, like the ones instantiating EMOTION IS AN OBJECT, are not entirely absent from the Western culture (cf. expressions in (5) and (6)). The difference between the two cultures lies in the fact that in Buddhism emotion-as-object metaphors are much more common, they are used more systematically (i.e. they evoke one complex scenario), and form extensive networks of mappings.

One possible objection[12] to the study carried out in the previous sections is whether all of the expressions analyzed in this chapter are metaphors. This objection is aimed specifically at the expressions suggesting a comparison or an analogy rather than a metaphor. The verbal markers of such expressions are words 'like,' 'as if,' 'in the same way,' etc. joining the alleged source and target concepts, for instance in expressions (16), (20), (21), (23), (29), (30), and (31). Moreover, this objection has some force against the expressions juxtaposing two 'images' without overtly identifying one concept with the other, e.g. expression (25). There is something to the objection, but I do not believe it seriously undermines the key conclusions of my analysis. First of all, the distinction between metaphor and comparison (or analogy) does not seem to be clear-cut, and the two conceptual devices share many important aspects. Both metaphors and comparisons rely on perceived or imagined similarities between concepts, they highlight these similarities and hide dissimilarities, and they are both conceptual (pertain to the way of thinking about the world) rather than purely verbal (they are not merely ways of talking about things). On the pragmatic level, both metaphors and comparisons may serve the same purposes. In early Buddhist suttas discussed in this chapter, the function of both of these devices is didactic: they are meant to show the effects of emotions on readers' minds and to teach the readers how passions should be handled in spiritual practice. More generally, the purpose of all the excerpts quoted in this chapter is to establish certain patterns of thinking about emotions through carefully constructed similarities between emotions and events or objects. The crucial difference between a metaphor and a comparison is that the former explicitly identifies the target concept with the source concept ('A is B'), while the latter juxtaposes the two concepts without showing them as identical ('A is like B'). Grady, Oakley, and Coulson (2007) raise a similar problem concerning the distinction between metaphors and counterfactuals (*I am a cloud* vs. *If I were a cloud*), concluding that one may employ some heuristic methods of telling the two devices apart, but on the whole 'metaphor is not a sharply delineated phenomenon' (p. 436). Any clear-cut distinction between a metaphor and a comparison (or a counterfactual) is bound to be somewhat arbitrary, and it would distract our attention from what I take to be the most important conclusion of this chapter, namely, the fact that the way of thinking about emotions in early Buddhist suttas is shaped primarily by two master scenarios: one in which an emotion is understood as a force and the other in which an emotion is understood as an object.

I may accept the objection and grant that not all of the expressions analyzed in this chapter are clear instances of metaphors (or even that they are not metaphors at all), but this only indicates that the two master scenarios can be instantiated in non-metaphorical expressions. Of course, this conclusion does not undermine the existence of the two scenarios.

NOTES

1. Radden and Kövecses add, however, that '[metonymy] does not simply substitute one entity for another entity, but interrelates them to form a new, complex meaning' (1999, p. 19).
2. For the purpose of this chapter I will not make a systematic distinction between metaphors and metaphtonymies. Consequently, all types of cross-domain mappings will be termed 'metaphor.' It is, however, worth remembering that some metaphors are built upon metonymic associations.
3. Kövecses (e.g. 1990 and 2000) describes metaphors belonging to this system in expressions from English, Hungarian, Zulu, Chinese, and Japanese just to name a few.
4. This, in turn, can be viewed as an instance of a yet more general and abstract metonymy EFFECT FOR CAUSE.
5. Sutta reference numbers are given after http://www.accesstoinsight.org.
6. Even though the pervasiveness of emotion-as-force metaphors may lead us to think that emotional process is indeed a type of interaction between am emotion and an experiencer, it must be remembered that such scenario is *constructed through metaphor* and has virtually nothing to do with psychological and neurological reality of the human mind. Actually, an emotion is not an entity, but rather a complex psychological, physiological, and neurological process, or even a set of processes. Similarly, we cannot reasonably claim that emotions are in any way distinct from the experiencer; on the contrary, an emotion is a way in which the experiencer's mind and body react to certain external stimuli. In this sense, the experiencer cannot be literally involved in any interaction with an emotion, since emotions cannot 'detach' themselves from the experiencer's bodies and mind. Such 'interactive' understanding of an emotional process is imaginable only on the metaphorical plane.
7. Contrary to the force schema, which is believed to be quite universal (i.e. shared by all human beings living in every culture) and relatively stable (i.e. fairly unchangeable in various actual instantiations), the object schema analyzed in this chapter is more local and culture specific. Obviously, this is not to say that the latter schema cannot appear in various metaphors outside Buddhism, but at least it does not seem to be the case that object-based metaphors of emotions are highly conventionalized in Western culture.
8. My use of the word 'dominion' is inspired, but perhaps not entirely compatible, with Langacker's, who defines the dominion as a 'sphere of control' (2008, p. 242).
9. Impermanence (*anicca*), essencelessness (*anatta*), and unsatisfactoriness (*dukkha*) are the so called three marks of existence, i.e. properties of all physical and mental phenomena which should be contemplated during *vipassana* meditation. The three marks of existence make all earthly goods and sensual pleasures valueless and unreliable; the only goal worth pursuing is developing spiritual qualities.
10. One example of this kind of embodiment is the metonymic connection between an emotion and bodily symptoms accompanying the emotion, mentioned in section 1. See also chapter 14 of this volume.
11. When I claim chariots and mustard seeds as source concepts are unfamiliar, I do not, of course, claim that no one ever has any direct experience with these objects. Instead,

I claim that direct experiential familiarity with these objects is not a prerequisite for understanding the metaphors. Thus, the metaphor in (16) (*When anger arises, whoever keeps firm control as if with a racing chariot . . .*) can be understood even by someone who has never ridden a chariot, but has some general cultural knowledge of what a chariot is.

12. This objection was raised by a member of the audience during a conference where a preliminary version of this chapter was presented.

REFERENCES

De Silva, Padmasiri (2007). *The Psychology of Emotions in Buddhist Perspective: Sir D. B. Jayatilleke Commemoration Lecture, Colombo, 1976. Access to Insight.* http://www. accesstoinsight.org/lib/authors/desilva-p/wheel237.html.

Dirks, Jerald F. (2001). *The Cross & The Crescent: An Interfaith Dialogue between Christianity and Islam.* Beltsville, MD: Amana Publications.

Goossens, Luis (1990). Metaphtonymy: The interaction of metaphor and metonymy in expressions for linguistic action. *Cognitive Linguistics* 1 (3), 323–340. doi: 10.1515/cogl.1990.1.3.323.

Goschler, Juliana (2005). Embodiment and body metaphors. *Metaphorik.de* 09/2005, 33–52.

Grady, Joseph, Todd Oakley, and Seanna Coulson (2007). Blending and metaphor. In Vyvyan Evans, Benjamin Bergen, and Jörg Zinken (eds.), *The Cognitive Linguistics Reader*, pp. 420–440. London-Oakville: Equinox.

Kövecses, Zoltán (1990). *Emotion Concepts.* New York: Springer-Verlag.

Kövecses, Zoltán (2000). *Metaphor and Emotion.* Cambridge: Cambridge University Press.

Lakoff, George (1987). *Women, Fire and Dangerous Things.* Chicago and London: University of Chicago Press.

Lakoff, George and Mark Johnson (1980). *Metaphors We Live By.* Chicago and London: University of Chicago Press.

Langacker, Ronald W. (2008). *Cognitive Grammar: A Basic Introduction.* New York: Oxford University Press.

Radden, Günter and Zoltán Kövecses (1999). Towards a theory of metonymy. In Klaus-Uwe Panther and Günter Radden (eds.), *Metonymy in Language and Thought*, pp. 17–55. Amsterdam: John Benjamins.

Szwedek, Aleksander (2000). Senses, perception and metaphors (of object and objectification). In Stanisław Puppel and Katarzyna Dziubalska-Kołaczyk (eds.), *Multibus Vocibus de Lingua*, pp. 143–153. Poznań, Poland: Motivex.

Szwedek, Aleksander (2008). Objectification: A new theory of metaphor. In Marianne Thormählen (ed.), *English Now: Selected Papers from the 20th IAUPE Conference in Lund 2007*, pp. 308–317. Lund, Sweden: Wallin & Dalholm.

Szwedek, Aleksander (2011). The ultimate source domain. *Review of Cognitive Linguistics* 9 (2), 341–366.

Talmy, Leonard (1988). Force dynamics in language and cognition. *Cognitive Science* 12 (1), 49–100.

Thanissaro Bhikkhu (2003). *Introduction to Salayatana-Vibhanga Sutta: An Analysis of the Six Sense-Media. Access to Insight.* http://www.accesstoinsight.org/tipitaka/mn/mn.137.than.html.

Website

All quotations from the suttas are derived from http://www.accesstoinsight.org. Accessed April 23, 2016.

CHAPTER 10

Buddhist Metaphors in the *Diamond Sutra* and the *Heart Sutra*

A Cognitive Perspective

XIUPING GAO AND CHUN LAN

In the field of religion, metaphor research from a cognitive perspective has focused heavily on the Christian and Hebrew Bibles (e.g. Basson 2006; Feyaerts 2003), while other religions such as Buddhism and Islam have been considerably underrepresented. In this study, we attempt to analyze metaphorical expressions identified in the *Heart Sutra* and the *Diamond Sutra*, both widely acknowledged as pivotal Buddhist scriptures with a long history and far-reaching influence. Both sutras belong to the Prajna Paramita (Perfection of Wisdom) class, one of the five classes of Mahayana Buddhism. The *Heart Sutra*, as Lopez (1988) puts it, is 'perhaps the most famous Buddhist scripture' (p. 3). First translated into Chinese by Master Xuan Zang in the year 649, it is the most concise sutra of the Prajna Paramita class and brings out the most essential points of the class in just 260 words (Chen and Shang 2010, pp. 59–64). The *Diamond Sutra*, as one of the earliest Mahayana scriptures, was first translated into Chinese by Kumarajiva in the year 402 (Chen and Shang 2010, pp. 3–9). As the outline of the Prajna Paramita class, it has exerted the most far-reaching influence on Buddhism in China and has evoked numerous discussions throughout the history (Master Hsing Yun 2008, p. 1).

Due to their importance and popularity, both sutras have more than one translation and abundant commentaries. In this study, we choose Chen and Shang's (2010) punctuated version of the *Heart Sutra* translated by Master Xuan Zang and of the *Diamond Sutra* translated by Kumarajiva. Both translations are the earliest and most popular version of the sutra concerned (Chen and Shang 2010). For each sutra, Chen and Shang provide a detailed introduction and a punctuated version of the translation in traditional Chinese, followed by a translation in modern Chinese and commentaries.

Needless to say, metaphor is to a certain extent subject to interpretative variation, especially in the domain of religion (Charteris-Black 2004, p. 180), and to add to the challenge, we are no Buddhism experts. To reduce subjective bias as much as possible, in identifying and analyzing the metaphorical expressions in the two sutras, apart from Chen and Shang's (2010) commentaries, we also refer to the commentary on the *Diamond Sutra* by Master Hsing Yun (2008), the commentary on the *Heart Sutra* by Master T'an Hsu (2000), and the cognitive linguistic study on the *Heart Sutra* by Lu and Chiang (2007). Our English translation of the examples cited from the two sutras is based on a selected combination of Lu and Chiang (2007), Master T'an Hsu (2000), Master Hsuan Hua (2002), and Chung Tai Translation Committee (2009). In a few cases, we take the risk of translating the examples into English ourselves to better illustrate the metaphorical meaning in the Chinese version, and in so doing, we refer to *A Chinese-English Dictionary of Buddhist Terms* (Chen and Li 2005) for the translation of some specific Buddhist terminologies.

1 THEORETICAL BACKGROUND

According to Conceptual Metaphor Theory, metaphor is not only a matter of language but fundamentally a matter of thinking, a cognitive mechanism by which we understand a more abstract concept via a more concrete one (Lakoff 1993, pp. 244–245). A metaphor has an internal structure, with mappings of slots, relations, properties, and knowledge of the source domain onto those of the target domain (Lakoff and Turner 1989, pp. 63–64). The mappings are motivated by our bodily, social, and cultural experiences and are systematic, unidirectional, and partial (Lakoff 1993, p. 245). Moreover, conceptual metaphors in our mind are manifested by ubiquitous metaphorical expressions in language (Lakoff and Johnson 1980, pp. 46–51). Therefore, we can observe linguistic metaphors and trace them back to an underlying metaphorical system in thinking.

For example, in the *Diamond Sutra* the Tathagata[1] says that 'you Bhiksus should know that my dharma is like a raft' (汝等比丘知我说法如筏喻者). This quotation contains a linguistic manifestation of the conceptual metaphor BUDDHIST PRACTICE IS A JOURNEY (ACROSS A RIVER), for in Buddhist belief, a Buddhist practitioner's life is often understood as a journey from this side of the river (i.e. reincarnation full of sufferings) to the other side (i.e. nirvana with pure peace and joy), and accordingly one needs a boat or raft to fulfill this journey (Lan 2012, p. 173). This conceptual metaphor activates systematic mappings from the source domain JOURNEY to the target domain BUDDHIST PRACTICE, projecting elements of the former to those of the latter, e.g. REINCARNATION as the STARTING POINT, NIRVANA as the DESTINATION, BUDDHIST PRACTITIONERS as TRAVELERS, BUDDHA as the GUIDE, BUDDHA'S DHARMA as the VEHICLE, DIFFICULTIES as OBSTACLES, and HETERODOX PRACTICES as CROOKED PATHS.

One of the major developments of Conceptual Metaphor Theory at the beginning of this century is Conceptual Blending Theory (Fauconnier 1994; Fauconnier and

Tuner 2002; Turner 2005), which extends the two-domain mapping to a multi-space blending. In this theory, conceptual blending is a pervasive cognitive mechanism where input spaces 1 and 2, both constrained by a shared generic space, are integrated to create a blended space. The blended space, also called the conceptual blend, integrates the characteristics of the two inputs and generates a new emergent structure. Popular Buddhist terms are often conceptual blends, such as 菩萨行 (*pu-sa-xing*, Bodhisattva's path), which integrates BUDDHIST PRACTICE with JOURNEY (cf. Lan 2012, p. 167).

2 PREVIOUS RESEARCH ON METAPHORS IN RELIGIOUS DISCOURSE

Religious discourse is abundant with signs, symbols, and metaphors (Yeo 2012, p. 3) and '[m]odern theologians agree that any religion is grounded in a network of metaphors' (Erussard 1997, p. 198), so much so that Tracy (1979, p. 104) claims that 'the study of metaphor may well provide a central clue to a better understanding of that elusive and perplexing phenomenon our culture calls religion.' Metaphor in religious discourse has been studied from a variety of perspectives, ranging from theology (e.g. Nielsen 1989, and Perdue 1991, on Christianity; Sugioka 2009, and Wayman 1974, on Buddhism), literature (e.g. Crain 2010, pp. 43–64, and Viberg 1994, on Christianity; Ding 1996, and Li 2009, on Buddhism), and feminism (e.g. Soskice 2007, Spencer 1996, and Talbert–Wettler 1995, on Christianity) to lexicology (e.g. Liang 1994, on Buddhism). A more recent perspective has been provided by cognitive linguistics, especially Conceptual Metaphor Theory. As Jäkel (2003) puts it, '[w]ith respect to metaphor in religious contexts, a cognitive–semantic approach after the manner of Lakoff and Johnson can provide valuable insights' (p. 55), to which we shall now turn.

2.1 Metaphors in the Christian and Hebrew Bibles

Within the framework of Conceptual Metaphor Theory, there has been extensive and systematic research on metaphors in the Christian Bible (the Old Testament and the New Testament) and the Hebrew Bible (equivalent to the Old Testament). These studies mainly fall into three paradigms: those which focus on source domains, on target domains, and on Biblical texts.

In the first paradigm, Charteris-Black (2004) adopts a corpus-based approach and conducts the most extensive survey on the source domains of metaphors found in the Old and New Testaments. According to his survey, ANIMALS, LIGHT, PLANTS, and FOOD AND DRINK are productive source domains in both the Old and New Testaments; BUILDINGS AND SHELTER, THE BODY, JOURNEYS, and FISHING AND HUNTING are more prominent in the Old Testament than in the New Testament; and CONFLICT, FIRE, and WEATHER as source domains are only found in the Old Testament. Some other studies focus on a specific source domain and analyze what it reveals of Christian or Jewish doctrines, e.g. HORTICULTURAL metaphors (Jindo

2010), JOURNEY metaphors (Jäkel 2002, 2003), PASTORAL metaphors (van Hecke 2005), SEXUAL AND MARITAL metaphors (Moughtin-Mumby 2008), and WEDDING metaphors (Bisschops 2003).

Studies in the second paradigm usually focus on a religious theme as a target domain and analyze how it is metaphorically conceptualized in Biblical texts. The themes that have been investigated include DISTRESS (King 2012), EVIL (Warren 2011), LOVE (Botha 1998), SACRIFICE (Gupta 2010), SIN (Lam 2012), WISDOM (Xu 2003), and WOMAN (Szlos 2001). In particular, GOD is the most thoroughly studied target concept and is found to be understood via a variety of metaphors, e.g. GOD AS KING (DesCamp and Sweetser 2005; Moore 2009), GOD AS FATHER (DesCamp and Sweetser 2005; Dille 2004; Harrison 2007), GOD AS SHEPHERD (DesCamp and Sweetser 2005; van Hecke 2003), and GOD AS HOST (Stallman 1999). Other source domains of GOD metaphors include POTTER, ROCK, BEAR, WOMAN, LANDOWNER, FEMALE HOUSEHOLDER, GATE, and PEARL (DesCamp and Sweetser 2005).

Studies in the third paradigm focus on specific Biblical texts and analyze how metaphors create meanings in them. The Biblical texts that have been examined include Psalms (Basson 2006) and Samuel (Weiss 2006) of the Old Testament, and Peter 1 (Howe 2003) and Epistles (Klingbeil 2006) of the New Testament.

There are also some Biblical metaphor studies that cannot be categorized into the above three paradigms but nevertheless adopt a clearly cognitive perspective, e.g. Long (1994) analyzing people's talk about God and Wang (2008) examining Jesus' parables as extended metaphors.

Roughly speaking, the present study of the Buddhist sutras falls into the second paradigm. We will identify the metaphorical expressions in the sutras and analyze the Buddhist themes underlying those expressions. The themes that we shall focus on include SPACE, TIME, LIFE, BUDDHIST PRACTICE, and EMPTINESS, for these concepts help construct the Buddhist world.

2.2 Metaphors in Buddhism

Compared with Christianity and Judaism, research on metaphors in Islam (cf. El-Sharif 2011, 2012; Selçuk 1998) and Buddhism from a cognitive perspective has been scarce. To set an immediate background for our study, in this section, we will review the few cognitive studies available on Buddhist metaphors.

Based on Conceptual Metaphor Theory, McMahan (2002, pp. 55–82) makes an early attempt on visual metaphors concerning the concept WISDOM in the sutras of the Prajna Paramita (Perfection of Wisdom) class of Buddhism. He finds that KNOWING IS SEEING is a pervasive conceptual metaphor supported by abundant metaphorical expressions in Buddhist discourse. For example, different levels of wisdom that Buddhist practitioners try to obtain are understood as eyes with different powers: flesh eye, divine eye, wisdom eye, dharma eye, and Buddha eye. Accordingly, eye diseases are used to conceptualize bewilderments of the mind such as greed, hatred, jealousy, and anger. Correct conceptualizations of the world are called 'awakening,' i.e. the state of being able to see, while wrong ones are called 'sleeping,' i.e. the state of being unable to see. Following this line, Buddha, who has supreme wisdom and who is able to see the world as it is, is referred to as the Awakened One (觉者, *jue-zhe*). In the sutras that he analyses, McMahan observes the working of a coherent system of metaphors centering around KNOWING IS SEEING, including KNOWING IS PENETRATION, KNOWING IS CUTTING, KNOWING IS ENTERING, KNOWLEDGE IS LIGHT, and KNOWLEDGE IS SPACE. He concludes that vision is key to understanding the wisdom of Buddhism and that KNOWING IS SEEING is a root metaphor of Buddhism.

Lu and Chiang (2007) conduct a word-by-word analysis of the *Heart Sutra* from a cognitive semantic perspective and summarize the conceptual metaphors in the sutra on both micro and macro levels. On the micro level, their analysis shows that the sutra is highly metaphorical, with two major groups of metaphors. The first group includes such perceptual (especially visual) metaphors as KNOWING IS SEEING, AN AID TO KNOWING IS A LIGHT SOURCE, IMPORTANT IS BIG, and DISTURBING IDEAS ARE DISTURBING FOOD. The second group is motion metaphors, e.g. STATES ARE LOCATIONS, PURPOSES ARE DESTINATIONS, LONG-TERM PURPOSEFUL ACTIVITIES ARE JOURNEYS, and DIFFICULTIES ARE IMPEDIMENTS TO MOTION. On the macro level, Lu and Chiang show how the sutra uses metaphors and oxymora to convey the pivotal Buddhist concept of EMPTINESS. They hold that FORM IS EMPTY and EMPTINESS IS FORM (色即是空，空即是色), arguably the best known lines of Buddhist doctrines, are the two overarching metaphors in the sutra.

The present study also intends to include the *Heart Sutra* in its data. We make this choice for two reasons. Firstly, Lu and Chiang's (2007) analysis of the sutra, although it provides valuable references for our study, is nevertheless not free of misinterpretations. Their semantic analysis of some lines in the sutra is meticulous but inaccurate. For example, in the line '无无明，亦无无明尽，乃至无老死，亦无老死尽' (There is no such thing as ignorance. Also, there is no ending of ignorance. Even there is no aging and death. Also, there is no extinction of aging and death), Lu and Chiang interpret 乃至 (*nai-zhi*, literally 'and thus reaching,' and even) purely etymologically, with 至 (literally meaning 'reaching') understood as an instance of STATES ARE LOCATIONS and PURPOSES ARE DESTINATIONS. In fact, 乃至 in this particular context is a sign of ellipsis, indicating the omission of 10 out of the 12 nidanas[2] (Chen and Shang 2010, pp. 69–70). Secondly, our approach to the metaphors in the *Heart Sutra* is different from that of Lu and Chiang. While they categorize micro metaphors according to the source domains, we will focus on the themes or target domains of the metaphors identified in the sutra.

The most recent cognitive exploration into Buddhist metaphors is made by Lan (2012) in a case study of the metaphorical expressions in the sutra 宝积经 (*Bao Ji Jing*, Treasure Accumulating Sutra, *Ratnakūṭa Sūtra*). Following Charteris-Black's (2004) Critical Metaphor Analysis, Lan identifies abundant metaphorical expressions in the sutra which center around three themes—singing praise to Bodhisattva's benefactions, looking on the emptiness and illusions of the mind, and concluding persuasions—and mainly involve such source domains as NATURAL PHENOMENON, ANIMAL, PLANT, HUMAN BEING, GHOST/SPIRIT, DREAM, and BOAT. Her analysis shows that the metaphorical expressions in the sutra are highly consistent in structure, with some appearing in parallel. The metaphors usually include mapping of the relationship between a major source domain and a minor source domain onto the relationship between a major target domain and a minor target domain, or mapping of the elements in a source story onto those of a target story. Lan also finds that in the sutra, metaphorical expressions typically play the role of legitimizing Buddhist doctrines and delegitimizing non-Buddhist doctrines by establishing the positive ethos of Bodhisattva, strengthening the pathos of the preaching, and establishing the boundlessness of Buddhist dharma with Buddhist legends (Lan 2012, p. 176).

Following the approach of Lan (2012), we will analyze the metaphorical expressions in the *Heart Sutra* and the *Diamond Sutra* to see what themes underlie those expressions and how metaphorical analysis can help us better understand those themes and the Buddhist doctrines they convey.

3 METHODS AND RESULTS

In data collection and analysis, we follow the approach of Critical Metaphor Analysis, developed by Charteris-Black (2004). As a combination of critical discourse analysis and Conceptual Metaphor Theory, Critical Metaphor Analysis is an approach to researching metaphor in three steps: metaphor identification, interpretation, and explanation. In the first step, metaphorical expressions are identified based on carefully reading a text according to the criterion of a semantic tension between a literal source domain and a metaphoric target domain (Charteris-Black, p. 35). The second step aims to work out the underlying conceptual metaphors and conceptual keys by establishing the relationship between metaphorical expressions and the cognitive and pragmatic factors that determine them (p. 37). In the third step, discourse functions of the conceptual metaphors are analyzed by identifying the social agency involved in the production of the metaphors and their social role in persuasion (p. 39). Since its proposal by Charteris-Black, Critical Metaphor Analysis has been applied by a number of researchers to metaphor analysis in a wide range of discourses, including metaphors about people's ideas, attitudes, and values in social science research writings (Cameron et al. 2009), culture war (i.e. struggle between cultural values) metaphors in legal instruments (Bruce 2009), terrorism metaphors in news reports (Hülsse and Spencer 2008; Spencer 2012), and collective memory metaphors in political speeches (Gavriely-Nuri 2013).

Regarding the identification of metaphorical expressions in Chinese texts, Lan (2012) justifies the need to include both metaphors (in Chinese 隐喻, *yin-yu*, implicit explaining) and similes (in Chinese 明喻, *ming-yu*, explicit explaining). Lan points out that 'in Chinese both metaphors and similes belong to a basic level category labeled as 比喻 (*bi-yu*, comparing explaining), which suggests that in the Chinese mind what is emphasized is not the difference between metaphors and similes, but the similarity' and that '[t]he rationale behind this practice is the assumption that both metaphorical expressions and simile expressions are motivated by conceptual metaphors in our cognition' (p. 158). Following this assumption, we identify three forms of metaphorical expressions in the *Diamond Sutra* and the *Heart Sutra*: (1) explicit metaphorical expression (i.e. *ming-yu*); (2) implicit metaphorical expression (i.e. *yin-yu*); and (3) transliterated metaphorical expression. Despite the difference in form, they all stem from an underlying system of conceptual metaphors.

In the two sutras, explicit metaphorical expressions are usually marked by the simile marker 如 (*ru*, 'like'), e.g.

(1)   ...... 若/菩萨/心住于法而行/布施/，如人入暗即无所见。
    ... if bodhisattva heart dwell in dharma PARTICLE walk give, **like** person enter darkness and no PARTICLE see.
    *A bodhisattva whose heart dwells in dharma when he gives is **like** a man who enters darkness, who cannot see a thing.*

According to this quotation from the *Diamond Sutra*, that a bodhisattva practicing charity with attachment to dharma cannot gain the genuine wisdom of giving is compared to a person unable to see anything in the dark, with the comparison marked by the word 如 ('like'). This simile evokes a pervasive visual metaphor in Buddhism: KNOWING IS SEEING (cf. section 2.2 in this chapter and McMahan 2002, p. 55–82). In other words, the ability to know and hence gain wisdom is understood as the ability to see and get views.

Implicit metaphorical expressions are not explicitly marked but imply a conceptual metaphor all the same, e.g.

(2)   若以色见我，以音声求我，是人行邪道，不能见/如来/。
    if with form see me, with sound voice seek me, this person **walk evil way**, not able see Tathagata.
    *If one sees me [the Tathagata] in forms, if one seeks me in sounds, he **walks along a deviant way** and cannot see the Tathagata.*

In this line from the *Diamond Sutra*, 'walking along a deviant way' metaphorically means 'practicing heterodox doctrines,' suggesting the conceptual metaphors BUDDHIST PRACTICE IS A JOURNEY (ON THE LAND) and HETERODOX PRACTICES ARE CROOKED PATHS. Moreover, obtaining the teaching and wisdom of the Tathagata is understood as 'seeing the Tathagata,' again reflecting the visual metaphor KNOWING IS SEEING.

By transliterated metaphorical expressions we refer to those cases where Chinese characters are used to represent the pronunciation of Sanskrit expressions with metaphorical meanings, e.g.

(3)   般若/波罗蜜多
    Prajna Paramita
    Wisdom, go to the other side (of the river)

As a phonetic representation of Sanskrit, the Chinese characters in example (3) do not have a metaphorical meaning in themselves, but the whole transliteration nevertheless inherits a metaphorical meaning from its Sanskrit counterpart, which means 'the wisdom of going to the other side of the river,' again an echo of the conceptual metaphor BUDDHIST PRACTICE IS A JOURNEY (ACROSS A RIVER).

Following the above formal categorization of explicit, implicit, and transliterated metaphorical expressions, we try to identify all the metaphorical expressions in the *Heart Sutra* and the *Diamond Sutra* based on a close reading of the two texts. During this process, we adhere to the two principles Charteris-Black (2004) puts forward for classifying and counting metaphorical expressions in the Bible: firstly, two metaphorical linguistic forms that evoke the same conceptual metaphor but appear in different verses in the Bible are counted as two metaphorical expressions; secondly, two metaphorical linguistic forms that appear in the same verse in the Bible but reflect two conceptual metaphors are also counted as two metaphorical expressions (pp. 178–179).

To adjust to the concrete contexts of the two Buddhist sutras, we add a third principle in identifying and counting metaphorical expressions, i.e. when a metaphorical expression is repeated in the same form with the metaphorical meaning remaining unchanged, the expression is counted only once. This usually happens with transliterated metaphorical expressions and some implicit metaphorical expressions. For instance, the transliterated 般若波罗蜜多 (Prajna Paramita) appears in the *Heart Sutra* five times and 阿耨多罗三藐三菩提 (Anuttara Samyak Sambodhi, or 'unexcelled complete enlightenment') appears in the *Diamond Sutra* twenty-eight times, all carrying the same metaphorical meaning; and 度众生 (*du-zhong-sheng*), an implicit metaphorical expression which means 'sending all sentient beings (to the other side of the river)' is repeated 10 times in the *Diamond Sutra* with the same metaphorical meaning. Following the third principle, we count these repeated occurrences only once.

The results of our metaphor identification in the two sutras are shown in Table 1.

From Table 1, it can be seen that implicit metaphorical expressions take up the majority in both sutras—79.41 per cent in the *Heart Sutra* and 82.80 per cent in the *Diamond Sutra*. Explicit and transliterated metaphorical expressions together account for only 17.80 per cent in the two sutras.

Table 1. METAPHORICAL EXPRESSIONS IN THE TWO SUTRAS

Category	Total		The *Heart Sutra*		The *Diamond Sutra*	
	No.	%	No.	%	No.	%
Explicit	17	8.90	0	0.00	17	10.83
Implicit	157	82.20	27	79.41	130	82.80
Transliterated	17	8.90	7	20.59	10	6.37
Total	191	100	34	100	157	100

Table 2. THEMES UNDERLYING THE METAPHORICAL EXPRESSIONS

Themes/ Target domains	The *Heart Sutra*	The *Diamond Sutra*	Total	
			No.	%
BUDDHIST PRACTICE	20	30	50	26.18
EMPTINESS	9	34	43	22.51
SCRIPTURE	4	21	25	13.09
HEART	0	18	18	9.42
LIFE	1	16	17	8.90
TIME	0	13	13	6.81
SPACE	0	13	13	6.81
Others	0	12	12	6.28
Total	**34**	**157**	**191**	**100**

To show to what extent the text of each sutra is metaphorical, we count the words of all the sentences that contain metaphorical expression(s). Chen and Shang's (2010) punctuated version of the Chinese translation of the *Heart Sutra* by Master Xuan Zang has 10 sentences and 260 Chinese characters. All of the 10 sentences are found to have metaphorical expressions. Chen and Shang's punctuated version of the Chinese translation of the *Diamond Sutra* by Kumarajiva has 226 sentences and 5,175 Chinese characters. Metaphorical expressions are found in 176 of the sentences (77.88 per cent of all the sentences), amounting to 4,332 Chinese characters (83.71 per cent of all the characters).

We then analyze all the 191 metaphorical expressions detected from the two sutras to reveal the underlying conceptual metaphors, the mappings between the source domains and the target domains, and the functions that the metaphors serve. The 191 expressions are found to center on seven major themes, as shown in Table 2.

From Table 2, we can see that the group BUDDHIST PRACTICE, EMPTINESS, SCRIPTURE, and HEART, which are concepts specific to Buddhism in general and the two sutras in particular, accommodate more metaphorical expressions than the group LIFE, TIME, and SPACE, which are more universal themes. Collectively, the former group accounts for 71.20 per cent of all the metaphorical expressions and the latter 22.52 per cent. In Table 2, the themes are listed according to the numbers of the metaphorical expressions that bear these themes. In the next section, however, we will analyze them in a different order, moving from more universal themes to more specific ones because the former are more fundamental and hence may serve as a basis to understand the latter. Since it is impossible to cover all the themes in a single paper, we will focus on SPACE, TIME, LIFE, BUDDHIST PRACTICE, and EMPTINESS, leaving SCRIPTURE and HEART for later research.

4 METAPHOR ANALYSIS

4.1 SPACE

We start our metaphor analysis with the concept SPACE because as Levinson (2004) puts it, '[s]patial cognition is at the heart of our thinking' (p. xvii), an observation which has been sustained by the prevalence of spatial metaphors in other domains, such as TIME, KINSHIP, SOCIAL STRUCTURE, MUSIC, and EMOTION, across different cultures and languages (p. 16). Moreover, in Buddhism SPACE and the associated concept WORLD have considerably different meanings from their modern counterparts, which might be revealed by our analysis in this section.

In Buddhist sutras in general and the two sutras that we are investigating in particular, SPACE is usually referred to as 虚空 (*xu-kong*, unsubstantial empty), e.g.

(4) '须菩提。于意云何？东方**虚空**可思量不？''不也，世尊。''须菩提，南、西、北方、四维、上下**虚空**可思量不？''不也，世尊。'

'Subhuti[3], what do you think? Is the **space** in the eastern direction measurable?' 'No, World Honored One, it is immeasurable.' 'Subhuti, is any of the **space** above or below, in the four cardinal directions, or in the four intermediate directions measurable?' 'They are immeasurable, World Honored One.'

According to Chen and Shang (2010), 虚空 means the space where all existences and phenomena exist and is thus named because it has no form or nature (hence unsubstantial) and no hindrance or obstruction (hence empty; p. 18). From the above quotation from the *Diamond Sutra* we can see that the Buddhist 虚空 is perceived to be immeasurable and has the features of being pervasive, stable, boundless, and eternal (Chen and Shang 2010).

The quotation also reveals the Buddhist frame of spatial references. In total, 虚空 encompasses 10 directions (十方, *shi-fang*, ten direction), including two vertical ones (上下, *shang-xia*, up/above down/below), four cardinal ones (四方, *si-fang*, four direction), and four intermediate ones (四维, *si-wei*, four dimension). The four cardinal directions refer to east, south, west and north; and the four intermediate directions refer to southeast, southwest, northeast, and northwest (cf. Chen and Shang 2010, p. 18).

Although 虚空 literally means 'unsubstantial empty,' it should not be understood as void of anything. Rather, it contains numerous fine dusts (微尘, *wei-chen*) and numerous worlds (世界, *shi-jie*) made of fine dusts and can be crushed into fine dusts, as shown in the following quotations:

(5) '须菩提，于意云何？三千大千世界所有微尘，是为多不？'

'Subhuti, what do you think? Are **all the fine dusts contained in this trichiliocosm** great in number?'

(6) '须菩提，若善男子、善女人，以三千大千世界碎为微尘，于意云何？是微尘众宁为多不？'

'Subhuti, what do you think? If a good man or good woman were to **take all the worlds of a trichiliocosm and crush them into fine dusts**, wouldn't these dusts be numerous?'

In both quotations, Buddha highlights the innumerability of fine dusts and the fact that worlds are made of and can be crushed back into fine dusts.

From examples (5) and (6), we can also infer that 世界 (*shi-jie*, world) in Buddhism has different meanings from its modern Chinese counterpart and its English counterpart. To avoid confusion, we will henceforth use *shi-jie* to refer to the Buddhist 'world' in the following analysis. According to Buddhist doctrines, there are numerous *shi-jie*, which are structured in a hierarchy of four levels to form a trichiliocosm. On the first level, a 'small *shi-jie*' (小世界, *xiao-shi-jie*) is constituted of Sumeru Mountain in the center, surrounded by four continents, nine mountains, and eight oceans. On the second level, a thousand 'small *shi-jie*' constitute one 'small thousand *shi-jie*' (小千世界, *xiao-qian-shi-jie*). On the third level, a thousand 'small thousand *shi-jie*' constitute one 'medium thousand *shi-jie*' (中千世界, *zhong-qian-shi-jie*). On the fourth level, a thousand 'medium thousand *shi-jie*' constitute one 'big thousand *shi-jie*' (大千世界, *da-qian-shi-jie*). As one 'big thousand *shi-jie*' includes $1{,}000^3$ 'small *shi-jie*,' it is also called 'three thousand big thousand *shi-jie*' (三千大千世界, *san-qian-da-qian-shi-jie*) or trichiliocosm. One trichiliocosm forms the realm that a Buddha indoctrinates and hence is also called one 'Buddha country' (佛国, *fo-guo*) or 'Buddha *shi-jie*' (佛世界, *fo-shi-jie*) (cf. Chen and Shang 2010, p. 23). Yet although a trichiliocosm or Buddha *shi-jie* includes such an enormous number of small *shi-jie*, this does not mean that there is only one trichiliocosm in the space (虚空). Rather, trichiliocosms or Buddha *shi-jie* exist in great numbers, e.g.

(7) '须菩提，如恒河中所有沙数，如是沙等恒河，于意云何？是诸恒河沙宁为多不？'须菩提言：'甚多，世尊！但诸恒河尚多无数，何况其沙。''须菩提，我今实言告汝：若有善男子、善女人，以七宝满尔所恒河沙数三千大千世界，以用布施，得福多不？'

'Subhuti, what do you think? If there were as many Ganges Rivers as the grains of sand in the Ganges, wouldn't the amount of sand contained in all those Ganges Rivers be great?' Subhuti said: 'Extremely great, World Honored One. If even the number of the Ganges Rivers is innumerable, how much more so their grains of sand?' 'Subhuti, now I tell you truthfully: If a good man or good woman filled as many **trichiliocosms** as the grains of sand in those Ganges Rivers with the seven jewels, and gave them away in charity, wouldn't this merit be great?'

(8)　'须菩提！于意云何？如一恒河中所有沙，有如是等恒河，是诸恒河所有
　　　沙数佛世界，如是宁为多不？'

'Subhuti, what do you think? If there were as many Ganges Rivers as there are
grains of sand in the Ganges River, and there were a **Buddha world** for each
grain of sand of all those rivers, would the number [of those Buddha worlds]
be great?'

In both quotations, Buddha makes an analogy between the number of grains of sand
in the Ganges River and the number of trichiliocosms/Buddha *shi-jie* in the space,
from which we can infer that the space contains innumerable *shi-jie*.

In addition, while WORLD in its modern sense is a fundamentally spatial concept,
the Buddhist 世界 (*shi-jie*), which literally means 'age boundary,' is a concept combining time and space, with 世 (*shi*, age) connoting time and 界 (*jie*, boundary) connoting
space (Chen and Shang 2010, p. 23). In the *Diamond Sutra*, *shi-jie* is also referred to as 世
间 (*shi-jian*, age interval). From the two terms we can infer that a Buddhist world exists
in a certain spatial boundary as well as in a time span. As we will show in section 4.2,
one *shi-jie* goes through four stages: formation, continuance, decline, and disintegration, which combine to form a kalpa—the longest time span according to Buddhism.
When one *shi-jie* disintegrates, another is formed, thus starting a new kalpa.

4.2 TIME

In the two sutras, we have identified three groups of metaphorical expressions
about TIME, concerning time passing, time sequence, and time span, respectively.
The first group, which mainly includes expressions referring to 'past,' 'present,'
and 'future' [collectively referred to as 三世 (*san-shi*, three age) in the *Heart Sutra*],
manifest the metaphor TIME PASSING IS MOTION, as shown in example (9) from the
Diamond Sutra:

(9)　须菩提/，过去心不可得，现在心不可得，未来心不可得。

Subhuti, **pass go** heart not able get, **now locate** heart not able get, **haven't
come** heart not able get.

*Subhuti, **past** thoughts are intangible, **present** thoughts are intangible, and
future thoughts are intangible.*

Altogether we find three terms referring to the past in the two sutras:

(10)　a. 过去 (*guo-qu*, pass go)
　　　b. 往昔 (*wang-xi*, gone past)
　　　c. 昔 (*xi*, past)

We find only one term referring to the present:

(11) 现在 (*xian-zai*, now locate)

And we find the future lexicalized in more diverse ways:

(12) a. 未来 (*wei-lai*, haven't come)
     b. 未来世 (*wei-lai-shi*, haven't come age)
     c. 来世 (*lai-shi*, coming age)
     d. 当来世 (*dang-lai-shi*, will come age)
     e. 当来之世 (*dang-lai-zhi-shi*, will come PARTICLE age)

From examples (9) to (12), it can be seen that 'time is conceptualized as objects moving toward and past the stationary Observer [i.e. the ego]' (Yu 1998, p. 132). Thus, the past is the time that has passed or gone by the ego, the present is the time where the ego is located, and the future is the time that has not come but is coming or will come towards the ego. In this metaphorical conceptualization of TIME, the ego not only plays the role of the stationary observer, but also serves as the reference point of the motion of time.

According to Lakoff and Johnson (1980; cf. Radden 2011), this moving time metaphor is only one of the two deictic versions of TIME PASSING IS MOTION. The other one is the moving ego metaphor, i.e. TIME PASSING IS MOTION OF THE EGO MOVING FROM THE PAST TO THE FUTURE. From the time expressions that we have collected in the two sutras, it can be observed that the moving time version plays a dominant role in the conceptualization of TIME in Buddhism. Nevertheless, the moving ego version is also demonstrated by one metaphorical expression found in the *Diamond Sutra*:

(13) 有 , 世尊。佛说如是甚深经典 , **我从昔来所得慧眼** , 未曾得闻如是之
      经。

      How rare, World Honored One, is this sutra so profoundly spoken by
      Buddha. **From the time I [Subhuti] obtained the wisdom eye until the
      present** I have never before heard such a sutra.

In this line, 我从昔来 (*wo-cong-xi-lai*, I from past come) indicates that what is moving is not time but rather the ego (in this case, Subhuti). Thus, the past is the time that has been left behind by the moving ego, the present is the time where the ego is located, and the future is the time that is lying ahead of the moving ego (Yu 1998).

The second group of metaphorical expressions concerns time sequence, i.e. the earlier- and later-than relationships of temporal landmarks (Núñez and Cooperrider 2013, p. 222). A typical example of this group is a line from the *Diamond Sutra*:

(14)   如来灭后, 后五百岁 , 有持戒修福者 , 于此章句能生信心 , 以此为实。

   After Tathagata's passing, in the last five hundred years [of the declining dharma age], there will be those who observe the precepts and cultivate merit, who have faith that these are words of truth.

In example (14), 后 (*hou*, back/behind) appears twice. In the first occurrence, 如来灭后 (*rulai-mie-hou*, Tathagata perish behind) marks the relationship between Tathagata's death and later events (i.e. people observing the precepts and cultivating merit). Here, 后 (back/behind) indicates that a later event is behind an earlier event, or a later event is the back while an earlier event is the front.

   In the second occurrence, 后五百岁 (*hou-wu-bai-sui*, back five hundred years) refers to the fifth 500 years after Tathagata's death (Master Hsing Yun 2008, pp. 63–64). According to Master Hsing Yun, there are five 500 years marking the development of Buddha's teachings. The first and second 500 years are the period of true dharma, the third and fourth 500 years are the period of semblance dharma, and the fifth 500 years mark the beginning of the period of declining dharma, which will last for 10,000 years. This fifth 500 years, later than the first four 500 years, is referred to as 'back 500 years' in example (14), again indicating that the later time is the back while the earlier time is the front.

   There is, nevertheless, a slight difference between the two occurrences of 后 (back/behind) in example (14) in that the first one involves a temporal event (i.e. Tathagata's death) while the second one has time itself as an entity or event. However, both occurrences suggest the same conceptual metaphor EARLIER IS FRONT/LATER IS BACK. This metaphor is also reflected by the terms used in the *Diamond Sutra* to refer to 'morning,' 'noon,' and 'evening'[4]:

(15)   a. 初日分 (*chu-ri-fen*, initial day division)
       b. 中日分 (*zhong-ri-fen*, middle day division)
       c. 后日分 (*hou-ri-fen*, back day division)

We can see that a day (日, *ri*) is divided into three parts, i.e. the initial, middle, and back parts. Apparently, the three parts are also sequenced according to EARLIER IS FRONT/LATER IS BACK.

   The third group of metaphorical expressions includes the terms of time scale which mark time spans, or 'perceivable or quantifiable temporal magnitudes' (Núñez and Cooperrider 2013, p. 223). In the two sutras, three time scales can be identified, i.e. day, year, and kalpa. The smallest scale, *day* (日, *ri*), has just been analyzed in example (15). The middle scale, *year* (岁, *sui*), which appears in example (14), has roughly the same meaning as its English counterpart. *Kalpa* (劫, *jie*), the largest scale, is, according to Chen and Li (2005), a transliteration from Sanskrit referring to the immeasurably long time between the creation and recreation of a Buddhist *shi-jie*. A single kalpa consists of four stages that a *shi-jie* goes through: 成 (*cheng*, formation), 住 (*zhu*, continuance), 坏 (*huai*, decline), and 空 (*kong*, disintegration). During a kalpa, a *shi-jie* is formed and destroyed. Then another kalpa starts and another *shi-jie* is formed. This cyclic process is ongoing and endless, as shown in example (16) from the *Diamond Sutra*:

(16)　须菩提，若有善男子、善女人，初日分以恒河沙等身布施，中日分复以恒河沙等身布施，后日分亦以恒河沙等身布施，如是无量百千万亿劫以身布施。

> Subhuti, suppose a good man or good woman should renounce their life for charity **in the morning** as many times as there are grains of sand in the Ganges, and do likewise **at noon** and **in the evening, continuing thus for immeasurable hundreds of thousands of millions of kalpas**.

This line demonstrates the cyclicity of time in general and of days and kalpas in particular. In the line, 如是 (*ru-shi*, like this) bridges the small cycle of a day and the big cycle of a kalpa, from which we can infer that the cyclic processes of days (and nights[5]) accumulate and constitute a kalpa, which is also a cyclic process itself and is forever accumulating and cycling. What is to be noticed is that the cycle of kalpas is a partial one in that the end of one kalpa also signals the beginning of the next kalpa (cf. Radden 2011, p. 12), i.e. when a *shi-jie* is destroyed and one kalpa ends, a new *shi-jie* is formed and a new kalpa begins.

Two conceptual metaphors for time span underlie the third group of metaphorical expressions of time scale. Firstly, the existence of time scales themselves manifests the metaphor TIME DURATION IS SPATIAL LENGTH, for when we refer to *day* as the smallest time scale and *kalpa* as an immeasurably long time, we are using spatial length to talk about temporal duration. Secondly, the cyclicity of days and kalpas and the relationship between them demonstrate the metaphor TIME IS AN ENDLESS CYCLE. Small day cycles accumulate and form a year, which accumulates and forms a kalpa, which in turn accumulates and forms an even bigger cycle.

To sum up, the metaphorical expressions under the theme TIME found in the two sutras bear out the following conceptual metaphors for time passing, time sequence, and time span:

(1) Time passing
    TIME PASSING IS MOTION (OF TIME MOVING TOWARDS THE STATIONARY EGO)
    TIME PASSING IS MOTION (OF THE EGO MOVING FROM THE PAST TO THE FUTURE)
(2) Time sequence
    EARLIER IS FRONT
    LATER IS BACK
(3) Time span
    TIME DURATION IS SPATIAL LENGTH
    TIME IS AN ENDLESS CYCLE

Two points need to be elaborated concerning these metaphors. Firstly, it is obvious that all the TIME metaphors have SPACE as their source domain, since *motion, front-back orientation*, *length* and *cycle* are all spatial terms. Therefore, the root TIME metaphor in Buddhism is in fact TIME IS SPACE, which has been attested in many of the world's languages (cf. Lakoff and Johnson 1980; Radden 2011) and has been extensively explored (cf. Núñez and Cooperrider 2013). Secondly, the three dimensions of TIME, i.e. passing, sequence, and span, are not conceptualized separately. Instead, TIME tends to be understood in more than one dimension at the same time, e.g.

(17)   须菩提，我念过去无量阿僧祇[6]劫，于然灯佛前，得值八百四千万亿那由他诸佛，悉皆供养承事无空过者。

Subhuti, I recall that **in the past for limitless asamkhyeya kalpas** prior to Burning Lamp Buddha, I encountered eighty-four thousands of millions of billions of nayutas of Buddhas, and made offerings to them all, and served them all without exception.

(18)   若当来世后五百岁，其有众生得闻是经，信解受持，是人即为第一希有。

In the ages to come, in the last five hundred years, if there are sentient beings who hear this sutra, believe, comprehend, and follow it, they will be most remarkable beings.

In example (17), 过去无量阿僧祇劫 (limitless asamkhyeya kalpas in the past) involves two dimensions, i.e. time passing reflected by 过去 (*guo-qu*, 'pass go,' the past) and time span reflected by 无量阿僧祇劫 (limitless asamkhyeya kalpas). In example (18), 当来世后五百岁 (back 500 years in the future) involves three dimensions, i.e. time passing reflected by 当来世 (*dang-lai-shi*, 'will come age,' the future), time sequence reflected by 后 (*hou*, 'back,' later), and time span reflected by 五百岁 (five hundred years).

4.3 LIFE

In the two sutras, the expressions under the theme LIFE concern two major aspects of life, *viz.*, lifetime and life form, which highlight the temporal and spatial dimensions of life, respectively. According to the *Diamond Sutra*, a living being may have an infinite number of lifetimes:

(19)   须菩提，又念过去于五百世作忍辱仙人，于尔所世无我相、无人相、无众生相、无寿者相。

Subhuti, I also recall that for **five hundred lifetimes** I was a rishi of tolerance. At that time, I was also free from the notions of a self, a person, a sentient being, or a life span.

In this quotation, Buddha recalls what he went through during five hundred lifetimes in the past. Not only has Buddha gone through an infinite number of lifetimes, a common living being goes through an infinite number of lifetimes as well:

(20) 须菩提，若有善男子、善女人，以恒河沙等身命布施，若复有人，于此经中乃至受持四句偈等，为他人说，其福甚多。

Subhuti, if a good man or good woman were to dedicate **lifetimes as numerous as the grains of sand in the Ganges River** to charitable acts, and another comprehended and followed even a four-line verse of this sutra and taught it to others, the merits gained by the latter would far exceed that of the former.

In this line, the limitless number of lifetimes a common person has to bear is compared to the grains of sand in the Ganges River.

Among the numerous lifetimes of a living being, the previous one is called 先世 (*xian-shi*, previous lifetime), the current one 今世 (*jin-shi*, present lifetime), and the following one 来世 (*lai-shi*, coming lifetime), as recorded in the following two quotations from the *Diamond Sutra*:

(21) 复次，须菩提。若善男子、善女人受持读诵此经，若为人轻贱，是人先世罪业应<u>堕恶道</u>，以今世人轻贱故，先世罪业则为消灭，当得阿耨多罗三藐三菩提。

Moreover, Subhuti, if a good man, or good woman, receives, holds, reads, and recites this sutra and if people ridicule him/her, that man/woman has karmic offences from **previous lifetimes** which destine him/her to **fall into the evil paths**. But because in his/her **present life** he/she is ridiculed by others, his/her karmic offences in his/her **previous lifetimes** are destroyed and he/she will attain Anuttara-samyak-sambodhi.

(22) 是故然灯佛与我授记，作是言，汝于**来世**当得作佛，号释迦牟尼。

Therefore, Burning Lamp Buddha gave me [Buddha] the prediction saying these words, 'Your will in **the future** attain Buddhahood and be named Sakyamuni.'

It can be seen that in example (21), a good man or woman may carry karmic offences from his/her previous lifetime (先世罪业) and may be ridiculed by others in his/her current lifetime (今世人轻贱). In example (22), the future lifetime of Buddha is referred to as the coming lifetime (来世). From these three expressions, we can see that lifetime in general is conceptualized as an object coming to the ego. Thus, the past lifetime (先世) is the one that has passed the ego, the present lifetime (今世) is the one that the ego is experiencing and observing now, and the future lifetime (来世) is the one that has not come but is coming to the ego. These inferences demonstrate the conceptual metaphor for time passing that we discussed in the previous section, i.e. TIME PASSING IS MOTION (OF TIME MOVING TOWARDS THE EGO). More specifically, we can summarize the LIFE metaphor as LIFE PASSING IS MOTION (OF LIFETIME MOVING TOWARDS THE EGO).

Moreover, 先世 (past lifetime) is also referred to as 前世 (*qian-shi*, front lifetime) (Ding 1922/2002, p. 461) and 来世 (coming lifetime) as 后世 (*hou-shi*, back lifetime) (Chen and Li 2005, p. 133) in Buddhism. While the sequence 先世-今世-来世 (past lifetime–present lifetime–coming lifetime) reflects the passing of time, the sequence 前世-今世-后世 (front lifetime–present lifetime–back lifetime) demonstrates the conceptual metaphor for time sequence that we discussed in the previous section, i.e. EARLIER IS FRONT/LATER IS BACK, in that an earlier lifetime is conceptualized as the front and a later lifetime as the back, with the current life in between. We may summarize the underlying LIFETIME metaphor as AN EARLIER LIFETIME IS FRONT/A LATER LIFETIME IS BACK.

Besides the past-future and earlier-later relationships, LIFETIME has also inherited another structure from TIME, namely, cyclicity. Since a living being has an infinite number of lifetimes, death can be understood as equivalent to rebirth. When one lifetime ends, another lifetime starts, leading to the metaphor LIFE IS AN ENDLESS CYCLE, which is a subordinate to the time span metaphor TIME IS AN ENDLESS CYCLE. Following Radden's (2011) differentiation of full and partial cycles, the lifetime cycle is also a partial one in that the end of a lifetime marks the beginning of a new one.

According to Buddhist doctrines, a living being bears a lifetime in a particular life form, and change of life form may take place at rebirth, a point illustrated in example (21) that we have just read. In that quotation, Buddha tells Subhuti that a person may be destined by the karmic offences from his/her previous lifetimes to 'fall into the evil paths' (堕恶道, *duo-e-dao*, 'fall evil path'), which means to be reborn into an inferior and more miserable life form. Fortunately, a person can also be saved from this destiny by his/her adherence to Buddhist practice and go on a good path and attain Anuttara-samyak-sambodhi.

The evil paths, as opposed to the good paths (善道, *shan-dao*), are those miserable places where a living being will be reborn due to karmic offences (Chen and Shang 2010, p. 40). In Buddhism, there are three evil paths (三恶道, *san-e-dao*) and three good paths (三善道, *san-shan-dao*), collectively referred to as the six paths (六道, *liu-dao*), on which living beings in different life forms endure endless lifetimes, as shown in Table 3.

It is particularly noteworthy that in example (21), the process of being reborn in an inferior life form is described as 堕恶道 (fall into the evil paths). From the word 堕 (fall) it can be inferred that the three evil paths are located under the three good paths. The conceptual metaphors behind the six paths and their relative locations may be summarized as follows:

GOOD/SUPERIOR LIFE PATHS ARE UPPER PATHS.
EVIL/INFERIOR LIFE PATHS ARE LOWER PATHS.
REBIRTH INTO A GOOD/SUPERIOR LIFE FORM IS RISING TO AN UPPER PATH.
REBIRTH INTO AN EVIL/INFERIOR LIFE FORM IS FALLING TO A LOWER PATH.

Table 3. LIVING BEINGS IN THE SIX PATHS OF LIFE

	六道 Six Paths		六道众生 Life Forms in the Six Paths	
三善道 **Three good paths**	天道 人道 阿修罗道	heavenly path human path asura path	天 人 阿修罗	heavenly beings human beings asuras
三恶道 **Three evil paths**	畜生道 饿鬼道 地狱道	animal path hungry ghost path hell path	畜生 饿鬼 地狱众生	animals hungry ghosts hell beings

These metaphors are coherent with the basic spatial orientation metaphor GOOD IS UP/BAD IS DOWN proposed by Lakoff and Johnson (1980; cf. also Lan 2003), for the three good paths and the three good life forms, with fewer miseries than the three evil paths and the three evil life forms, are conceptualized as occupying a higher position.

There is another fundamental conceptual metaphor that underlies the above metaphors, *viz.*, LIFE IS A JOURNEY, as specified by the word 道 (path). The use of 道 (path) indicates that life in a certain form is compared to traveling along a certain path. The six paths combine to form a wheel where the life journey takes place, which is nicely captured in the Buddhist saying 六道轮回 (*liu-dao-lun-hui*, six path wheel cycle), i.e. reincarnation in the wheel of rebirth. During a single lifetime, the journey takes place along a certain path. In the event of rebirth, when one lifetime ends and another starts, there is also a journey, and it can be a falling or rising one. Therefore, the life journey of a living being in his/her many lifetimes takes place both along and among the six paths.

The LIFE AS JOURNEY metaphor is vividly represented by the description of a Buddhist practitioner's life in the *Diamond Sutra*. Chapter 9 of the sutra mentions four phases in a Bodhisattva's practice and the achievement of each phase. The achievement of the second phase, in particular, is called 斯陀含果 (*situohan-guo*, Sakridagamin fruit), which is a transliteration of Sanskrit meaning 一往来 (*yi-wang-lai*, one go come). According to Chen and Shang (2010), 一往来 (one go come) refers to one return trip of going up to the heavenly path and then coming back to the human path, or being born as a heavenly being and then being reborn as a human being (p. 25). Apparently, 往 (go) and 来 (come) are both motion verbs that are normally used to describe a journey, with the former meaning going up there and the latter coming down here.

Based on the above analysis of the LIFETIME and LIFE FORM expressions in the two sutras, we can summarize the Buddhist LIFE metaphor as LIFE IS A CYCLIC JOURNEY IN THE WHEEL OF SIX PATHS. This metaphor captures both the temporal and spatial dimensions of life. Temporally, life is an endless cycle with an infinite number of lifetimes. Spatially, different life forms travel along and among the six paths located along an up-down orientation. The main entailments of this conceptual metaphor may be specified as follows:

LIFE IS A CYCLIC JOURNEY IN THE WHEEL OF SIX PATHS

(1) Temporal dimension: LIFETIME

    LIFE PASSING IS MOTION (OF LIFETIME MOVING TOWARDS THE EGO)
    AN EARLIER LIFETIME IS FRONT
    A LATER LIFETIME IS BACK
    LIFE IS AN ENDLESS CYCLE

(2) Spatial dimension: LIFE FORM

    LIFE IS A JOURNEY
    GOOD/SUPERIOR LIFE PATHS ARE UPPER PATHS
    EVIL/INFERIOR LIFE PATHS ARE LOWER PATHS
    REBIRTH INTO A GOOD/SUPERIOR LIFE FORM IS RISING TO AN UPPER PATH
    REBIRTH INTO AN EVIL/INFERIOR LIFE FORM IS FALLING TO A LOWER PATH

4.4 BUDDHIST PRACTICE

Among the seven major themes we identify, BUDDHIST PRACTICE accommodates the most metaphorical expressions (fifty). Underlying these expressions is the conceptual metaphor BUDDHIST PRACTICE IS A JOURNEY, which activates rich mappings from the more concrete and better structured source domain JOURNEY to the more abstract target domain BUDDHIST PRACTICE, as presented in Table 4.

Table 4. BUDDHIST PRACTICE IS A JOURNEY

Source		Target
Journey	→	Buddhist practice
Starting point	→	Reincarnation
Destination	→	Nirvana
Travelers	→	Living beings
Active travelers	→	Active practitioners
Passive travelers/passengers	→	Passive practitioners
Guides	→	Buddha/bodhisattvas/mahasattvas
Vehicle/draft	→	Dharma
Big vehicle	→	Mahayana
Small vehicle	→	Hinayana
Paths	→	Buddhist practices
Crooked paths	→	Heterodox practices
Obstacle	→	Difficulty

To start with, this JOURNEY metaphor is encoded in the Chinese term referring to 'Buddhist practice' itself, i.e. 修行 (*xiu-xing*, practice walk). As the term reveals, to cultivate oneself in Buddhist practice is to practice walking (along a Buddhist path), a point which is borne out by the first line of the *Heart Sutra*:

(23) 观自在菩萨，行深般若波罗蜜多时，照见五蕴皆空，度一切苦厄。

When the Bodhisattva Avalokitesvara was **coursing** in the deep Prajna Paramita, he saw by reflection that all five aggregates are empty. Thus, he overcame all ills and suffering.

Here, 行 (*xing*, walk/course) 'involves a conceptualization of the practice of meditation for wisdom as walking or traveling' (Lu and Chiang 2007, p. 340). The wisdom, referred to as 般若波罗密多 (Prajna Paramita; cf. section 3), means 'the wisdom of going to the other side of the river,' indicating that Buddhist practice is not just a journey, but a journey across the river of life.

Moreover, 波罗密多 (Paramita, go to the other side of the river) also implies the starting point and the destination of this Buddhist journey, that is, from this side of the river to the other side. This side is also known as reincarnation and is full of sufferings, while the other side is known as nirvana and is with pure peace and joy (cf. Lan 2012, p. 173), as reflected by the following lines from the two sutras:

(24) 以无所得故，菩提萨埵，依般若波罗蜜多故，心无挂碍。无挂碍故，无有恐怖。远离颠倒梦想，**究竟涅槃**。

Because there is nothing to be attained, the Bodhisattva, relying on the Prajna Paramita, has no obstruction in his mind. Because there is no obstruction, he has no fear; and thus, he passes far beyond confused imagination and **reaches ultimate nirvana**.

(25) 诸菩萨摩诃萨[7]应如是降伏其心：所有一切众生之类，若卵生，若胎生，若湿生，若化生；若有色，若无色；若有想，若无想，若非有想非无想，**我皆令入无余涅槃而灭度之**。

The bodhisattvas and mahasattvas should thus subdue their thoughts: All the different types of living beings, whether they are born from eggs, from wombs, from moisture, or by transformation; whether or not they have form; whether they have thoughts or no thoughts, or have neither thought nor non-thought, **I will liberate them by leading them to nirvana without residue**.

In example (24) from the *Heart Sutra*, Bodhisattva Avalokitesvara overcomes the obstruction, passes beyond confused imagination, and finally reaches ultimate nirvana (究竟涅槃, *jiu-jing-nie-pan*). Similarly, in example (25) from the *Diamond Sutra*, Buddha instructs that all bodhisattvas and mahasattvas should have the aspiration that they will liberate all living beings by leading them to nirvana without residue (无余涅槃, *wu-yu-nie-pan*). Both examples indicate that 涅槃 (nirvana) is the goal of Buddhist practice, or the destination of the journey.

The two examples also imply three different roles involved in the Buddhist journey, i.e. active traveler, guide, and passive traveler. In example (24), Bodhisattva Avalokitesvara cultivates himself in Prajna Paramita and finally reaches ultimate nirvana, thus playing the role of an active traveler. Example (25) is different in that bodhisattvas and mahasattvas lead living beings to nirvana. Thus the former plays the role of a guide and the latter the role of a passive traveler. The three roles are combined in the mantra at the end of the *Heart Sutra*:

(26)   揭谛，揭谛，波罗揭谛，波罗僧揭谛，菩提萨婆诃。
        Gate, gate, paragate, parasamgate, bodhi svaha.

        Go/send, go/send, go/send to the other side of the river, send all to the other side of the river, quickly get the wisdom.

As a mantra, this whole line is transliteration from Sanskrit and is meant to be chanted by Buddhist practitioners. In the line, 揭谛 (*gate*) is repeated twice. According to Chen and Shang (2010), the first time refers to *going* to the other side of the river while the second time refers to *sending* other living beings to the other side of the river (p. 74). Apparently, the 'go' sense indicates an active traveler while the 'send' sense involves both a guide and a passive traveler in the journey.

To fulfill the Buddhist journey of crossing the river of life,[8] one also needs a raft or boat, which is reflected by the following line from the *Diamond Sutra*:

(27)   以是义故，如来常说汝等比丘知我说法如筏喻者。法尚应舍，何况非
        法。

        For this reason, the Tathagata often teaches: Bhiksus, know that my dharma is like a raft. If the correct teachings (dharma) should be abandoned, how much more so the incorrect teachings (non-dharma)?

As we illustrated in section 1, in this line, Buddha's dharma is explicitly compared to a raft, a vehicle for crossing a river. What is implied is that as a raft takes one from this side of a river to the other side, Buddha's dharma helps a Buddhist practitioner become liberated from reincarnation and reach nirvana. However, in the context of this quotation, what is highlighted is not just that BUDDHA'S DHARMA IS A RAFT, but the relationship between 'raft' and 'traveling': When one goes ashore and thereby finishes one's traveling, one will not take the raft with him/her anymore. Similarly, a Buddhist practitioner should not be obsessed with dharma when he/she obtains nirvana, for it is nirvana, rather than dharma, that is the ultimate Buddhist goal.

Besides a raft, a land vehicle is sometimes used as well for the Buddhist journey, suggesting that the journey can also happen on the land:

(28) 须菩提，以要言之，是经有不可思议、不可称量无边功德。如来为发大乘者说，为发最上乘者说。……须菩提，若乐小法者，著我见、人见、众生见、寿者见。

In summary, Subhuti, this sutra carries inconceivable, immeasurable, limitless virtue, and the Tathagata teaches it for the benefit of the aspirants of **the great vehicle**, and the aspirants of **the supreme vehicle**. . . . Subhuti, those who are content with **inferior teachings** are attached to the views of a self, a person, a living being, and a life span.

In this line, 乘 (*sheng*), a term which originally means a chariot or vehicle, is used to refer to Buddhist dharma, for as a vehicle can carry people to their destination, Buddhist dharma can help Buddhist practitioners attain the pure peace and joy of nirvana. What is to be noticed is that in the above quotation two kinds of vehicles are mentioned: the first kind is 大乘 (*da-sheng*, big vehicle) and 最上乘 (*zui-shang-sheng*, most up vehicle), both of which refer to Mahayana, one of the two major Buddhism divisions, aiming to liberate not only oneself but also all living beings; the second kind is 小法 (*xiao-fa*, small dharma) or 小乘 (*xiao-sheng*, small vehicle), both of which refer to Hinayana, the other one of the two major Buddhism divisions, emphasizing self-cultivation and liberation (Chen and Shang 2010, p. 38). It is by no accident that the first kind is described as 大 (big) and the second as 小 (small), for as a bigger vehicle can carry more passengers, Mahayana can help liberate more people from reincarnation to nirvana.

Some metaphorical expressions in the two sutras also highlight the different paths followed by Buddhist practitioners to fulfill their journey. The paths are given a general term 道 (*dao*, path/road) in the *Heart Sutra*, where it is listed as the last of the four noble truths (四圣谛, *si-sheng-di*), namely, bitterness, origin, extinction, and path (苦集灭道, *ku-ji-mie-dao*). In particular, the noble truth of bitterness acknowledges the sufferings of all existences, the noble truth of origin explains the causes of sufferings, the noble truth of extinction deals with the extinction of sufferings, and the noble truth of path shows the way to fulfill the extinction and attain nirvana (cf. Chen and Shang 2010, p. 70; Ding 1922/2002, p. 828). Under this general way or path, some specific paths are mentioned in the *Diamond Sutra* that Buddhist practitioners can follow:

(29) 须菩提，于意云何？阿罗汉能作是念，我得阿罗汉道不？
Subhuti, what do you think? Can an Arhat[9] have the thought, 'I have obtained **Arhatship**.'?

(30) 以须菩提实无所行，而名须菩提，是乐阿兰那行。
Since Subhuti actually has no practice, he is called 'Subhuti, who delights in **practicing Arana**.'[10]

(31) 尔时，世尊而说偈言：'若以色见我，以音声求我，是人行邪道，不能见如来。'

At that time the World Honored One spoke a gatha, which says: 'If one sees me in forms, if one seeks me in sounds, he **walks along a deviant way**, and cannot see the Tathagata.'

Examples (29) and (30) mention two specific ways of Buddhist practice, *viz.*, the Arhat path (阿罗汉道, *a-luo-han-dao*) and the Arana walk (阿兰那行, *a-lan-na-xing*). The first one refers to the path leading to the supreme achievement of a Buddhist practitioner. The second one refers to the way of cultivating Buddhist practice by meditating in mountains and forests (Chen and Shang 2010, p. 26). In both cases, 道 (path/road) and 行 (walk) indicate the metaphor BUDDHIST PRACTICES ARE PATHS TO NIRVANA.

Example (31) is different in that it mentions a way of heterodox practice. As we analyzed the text in section 3, 行邪道 (*xing-xie-dao*, walk evil path) means 'walking along a deviant way' literally and 'practicing heterodox doctrines' metaphorically, suggesting the metaphor HETERODOX PRACTICES ARE CROOKED PATHS (TO INFERIOR LIFE FORMS).

To sum up, JOURNEY is a key concept to help us understand BUDDHIST PRACTICE. As shown in Table 4, a series of mappings have been established in the two sutras from the source domain JOURNEY to the target domain BUDDHIST PRACTICE, projecting the elements of the former to the latter.

4.5 EMPTINESS

EMPTY/EMPTINESS (空, *kong*)[11] is a key concept of Buddhism in general and of the *Heart Sutra* and the *Diamond Sutra* in particular. A major Buddhist doctrine is that all existences and phenomena, collectively referred to as form (色, *se*), are empty. Hence the doctrine can be succinctly presented as 'form is empty' (色即是空), i.e. all existences and phenomena are never absolute or fixed, but conditioned and illusory (cf. Chen and Shang 2010; Lu and Chiang 2007).

However, as Lopez (1988) points out, Buddhist emptiness 'does not negate the conventional appearance of form' and therefore should not 'be sought as something separate' (p. 58). In other words, Buddhist emptiness depends on the form that it qualifies in that 'the very essence of every phenomenon, EMPTINESS, produces FORM and needs to manifest itself in certain superficial ways' (Lu and Chiang 2007, p. 344). Thus the other side of the doctrine 'form is empty' is that 'emptiness is form' (空即是色).

Lu and Chiang (2007) regard FORM IS EMPTY and EMPTINESS IS FORM as the two overarching metaphors of the *Heart Sutra*, in which FORM and EMPTINESS serve as each other's source domain and target domain. The relationship between the two is stipulated in the *Heart Sutra* as follows:

(32)　舍利子，色不异空，空不异色，色即是空，空即是色，受、想、行、识，亦复如是。

Sariputra, form is no other than emptiness; emptiness is no other than form. Form is emptiness; emptiness is form. So are feeling, discrimination, compositional factors, and consciousnesses.

(33)　观自在菩萨，行深般若波罗蜜多时，照见五蕴皆空，度一切苦厄。

When the Bodhisattva Avalokitesvara was coursing in the deep Prajna Paramita, he saw by reflection that all five aggregates are empty. Thus, he overcame all ills and suffering.

In example (32), 色 (form), used in its narrow sense, refers to all material existences and phenomena. The other four aggregates, 受想行识 (shou-xiang-xing-shi), represent all immaterial existences and phenomena, including feelings, sensations, actions and reactions, and ideation and consciousness (cf. Chen and Shang 2010, p. 67; Chen and Li 2005, p. 360). Collectively, 色受想行识 are referred to as 五蕴 (wu-yun, five aggregate), which are all empty according to example (33).

Despite the emphasis on both FORM IS EMPTY and EMPTINESS IS FORM, both the *Heart Sutra* and the *Diamond Sutra* seem to focus more on the former. The emptiness of all forms is highlighted in the *Heart Sutra* by three pairs of polar modifiers:

(34)　舍利子，是诸法空相，不生不灭，不垢不净，不增不减。

Sariputra, in that way all phenomena are empty, neither beginning nor ending, neither pure nor impure, neither increasing nor decreasing.

In this line, three pairs of antonymous words, i.e. 生 (sheng, birth/produce) and 灭 (mie, perishing/cease), 垢 (gou, dirty) and 净 (jing, clean), and 增 (zeng, increase) and 减 (jian, decrease) are used in a row, and each of them is negated to illustrate the point that all existences and phenomena are empty. The main idea is that since all phenomena are empty, then what is being born is essentially not being born and what is perishing is essentially not perishing. This is also true with what is perceived as dirty and clean or as increasing and decreasing. It follows that one should not be obsessed with the distinctions between 生/灭 (birth/perishing), 垢/净 (dirty/clean), and 增/减 (increase/decrease).

The *Diamond Sutra* also seems to highlight the FORM IS EMPTY metaphor, the most apparent manifestation of which is a group of similes appearing at the end of the sutra:

(35)　一切有为法，如梦幻泡影，如露亦如电，应作如是观。

All conditioned phenomena, are like a dream, an illusion, a bubble, a shadow, like dew or a flash of lightning; thus we shall perceive them.

This verse demonstrates the emptiness of all forms by comparing them to six eva-nescent phenomena: dream, illusion, bubble, shadow, dew, and lightning. According to Chen and Shang (2010, p. 8), this verse captures the essence of the answer to the question put forward by Subhuti in the beginning of the sutra concerning Buddhist practice: 'when good men and good women resolve to attain unsurpassed complete enlightenment, how should they abide their heart, and how should they subdue their heart?' The answer is that Buddhist practitioners should realize that all existences and phenomena are empty and thus liberate themselves from obsession with their superficial manifestations.

Besides this verse, the FORM IS EMPTY metaphor is also reflected in the paradoxical use of VISION in the *Diamond Sutra*. On the one hand, we can find ample expressions in the sutra demonstrating the visual metaphor KNOWING IS SEEING. For example, a bodhisattva unable to obtain genuine wisdom is compared to a person unable to see anything (cf. section 3), and different levels of wisdom are referred to as eyes with dif-ferent levels of power: flesh eye (肉眼, *rou-yan*), divine eye (天眼, *tian-yan*), wisdom eye (慧眼, *hui-yan*), dharma eye (法眼, *fa-yan*), and Buddha eye (佛眼, *fo-yan*). On the other hand, the sutra repeatedly suggests that SEEING IS NOT KNOWING, because what can be SEEN is only FORM; thus if people are restricted by what they SEE, they cannot KNOW EMPTINESS and hence cannot obtain the wisdom of EMPTINESS, e.g.

(36) '须菩提，于意云何？可以身相见如来不？' '不也，世尊。不可以身相
      得见如来。何以故？如来所说身相即非身相。' 佛告须菩提：'凡所有
      相，皆是虚妄。若见诸相非相，即见如来。'

      'Subhuti, what do you think, can the Tathagata be **seen** by his physical
      appearances?' 'No, World Honored One. The Tathagata cannot be **seen**
      by his physical appearances. Why? It is because the physical appearances
      are spoken of by the Tathagata as no physical appearances.' Buddha said
      to Subhuti, 'All with appearances is empty and false. If you can **see** all
      appearances as no appearances, then you **see** the Tathagata.'

In this quotation, 见 (*jian*, see/look) is repeated four times. The first and second occurrences in 以身相见如来 (to see the Tathagata by his physical appearances) have a literal meaning. Yet the third and fourth occurrences seem to be used meta-phorically and mean 'understand' or 'conceptualize': 见诸相非相 (see all appear-ances as no appearances) means 'realize that all appearances are but superficial and hence empty' and 见如来 (see the Tathagata) means 'understand the Tathagata's dharma and find genuine wisdom' (cf. Master Hsuan Hua 2002, pp. 61–62). From these four occurrences of 见 (see), it can be seen that at a low level acquisition of the Tathagata's wisdom is compared to seeing the Tathagata, demonstrating the metaphor KNOWING IS SEEING. Yet at a high level the whole line suggests that SEEING IS NOT KNOWING in that if Buddhist practitioners try to see the Tathagata by his physical appearances, they would be attached to the Tathagata's form and would not be able to know the emptiness of the form and hence cannot obtain the absolute wisdom. This paradoxical use of 见 (see) is more straightforwardly captured in the following line, which we quoted in example (2) and analyzed in example (31):

(37)　若以色见我，以音声求我，是人行邪道，不能见如来。

If one **sees** me [the Tathagata] in forms, if one seeks me in sounds, he walks along a deviant way, and cannot **see** the Tathagata.

In this line, 'seeing the Tathagata' paradoxically results in 'not seeing the Tathagata,' with the first 'see' holding a literal sense and the second one a metaphorical sense. To put it briefly, the main argument behind the apparent paradoxical use of 见 (see) is that if one sees the Tathagata in form, then one cannot obtain the Tathagata's dharma and wisdom.

As Chen and Shang (2010) understand it, the main theme of the *Diamond Sutra* is the wisdom of EMPTINESS (p. 7). Under the overarching metaphor FORM IS EMPTY, the sutra illustrates the emptiness of SPACE, TIME, LIFE, and BUDDHIST PRACTICE, all of which are different FORMS. The emptiness of SPACE is first manifested by the fact that the concept itself is referred to as 虚空 (unsubstantial empty) in Buddhism (cf. section 4.1). Moreover, the two key spatial concepts DUST and WORLD (*shi-jie*) are also perceived to be empty:

(38)　佛说微尘众即非微尘众，是名微尘众。世尊，如来所说三千大千世
　　　界，即非世界，是名世界。何以故？若世界实有，即是一合相。如来说
　　　一合相，即非一合相，是名一合相。

The mass of fine dusts is spoken of by the Buddha as no mass of fine dusts. Therefore it is called a mass of fine dusts. World Honored One, all the worlds of a trichiliocosm are spoken of by the Tathagata as no worlds, therefore they are called worlds. Why? If worlds actually existed, then there would be a totality of appearances. The totality of appearances is spoken of by the Tathagata as no totality of appearances. Therefore it is called a totality of appearances.

This highly paradoxical line explains the emptiness of DUST and WORLD (*shi-jie*) in detail. According to Buddha, dusts do exist, yet their existence is but a superficial manifestation and their true nature is emptiness. This is because dusts are conditioned results of causes and effects and hence are transient and impermanent. In a word, dust is but a name. In turn, dusts constitute Buddhist worlds (*shi-jie*), which are also empty, for *shi-jie* constituted by numerous dusts is but a totality of appearances as well. Therefore, one should be not attached to the notions of DUST, WORLD, or SPACE.

As for TIME, the *Diamond Sutra* warns that one should not be attached to the notions of 'past,' 'present,' and 'future' either:

(39)　所以者何？须菩提，过去心不可得，现在心不可得，未来心不可得。

Why, Subhuti? Because past thoughts are intangible, present thoughts are intangible, and future thoughts are intangible.

According to Buddha, time is intangible because it is always passing. What is called the past is already gone, what is called the present is just passing by, and what is called the future has not arrived yet and hence cannot be taken hold of (cf. Master Hsuan Hua 2002, p. 159). Therefore, TIME is also apparently transient and hence empty.

The emptiness of LIFE and BUDDHIST PRACTICE is captured in the following line from the *Diamond Sutra*:

(40)   诸菩萨摩诃萨应如是降伏其心：所有一切众生之类，若卵生，若胎生，若湿生，若化生；若有色，若无色；若有想，若无想，若非有想非无想，我皆令入无余涅槃而灭度之。如是灭度无量无数无边众生，实无众生得灭度者。何以故？须菩提，若菩萨有我相、人相、众生相、寿者相，即非菩萨。

The bodhisattvas and mahasattvas should thus subdue their thoughts: All the different types of living beings, whether they are born from eggs, from wombs, from moisture, or by transformation; whether or not they have form; whether they have thoughts or no thoughts, or have neither thought nor non-thought, I will liberate them by leading them to nirvana without residue. When immeasurable, countless, infinite numbers of living beings have been liberated, in reality, no living beings have been liberated. Why is this so? Subhuti, if bodhisattvas abide in the notions of a self, a person, a living being, or a life span, they are not bodhisattvas.

The main idea of this quotation is that, as we discussed in section 4.4, in the Buddhist practice journey, the bodhisattvas and mahasattvas play the role of a guide and send all living beings to nirvana. After that, however, they should not cling to the notion of sending all living beings to nirvana anymore, for otherwise they would be attached to the following four notions. The first one is the notion of a self who can send living beings to nirvana. This self notion is the root of the other three notions—the notion of other persons to be sent, the notion of living beings to be sent, and the notion of a life that ends when a living being is sent to nirvana. In other words, to get the wisdom of emptiness, a Buddhist practitioner should not be attached to anything, not even to the life of Buddhist practice itself.

5 CONCLUSIONS

In section 4, we analyzed the Buddhist conceptualization of five themes: SPACE, TIME, LIFE, BUDDHIST PRACTICE, and EMPTINESS. The main conceptual metaphors involved in the conceptualization of these themes in the two sutras can be summarized as (1) TIME PASSING IS MOTION, EARLIER IS FRONT/LATER IS BACK, and TIME IS AN ENDLESS CYCLE; (2) LIFE IS A CYCLIC JOURNEY IN THE WHEEL OF SIX PATHS; (3) BUDDHIST PRACTICE IS A JOURNEY FROM REINCARNATION TO NIRVANA; and (4) FORM IS EMPTY and EMPTINESS IS FORM.

Our analysis also reveals the tangle of the five themes. Firstly, the centrality of spatial cognition is sustained by the spatial metaphors for TIME, LIFE, and BUDDHIST PRACTICE. Further, it can be observed that basic spatial image schemas underlie these metaphors (cf. Johnson 1987). To be specific, the PATH schema helps structure the metaphors TIME PASSING IS MOTION, LIFE IS A JOURNEY, and BUDDHIST PRACTICE IS A JOURNEY; the schemas of CYCLE, FRONT-BACK, and SCALE all play a role in the Buddhist conceptualization of TIME and LIFE; the UP-DOWN schema helps structure the Buddhist six paths of life in particular; and the CONTAINER schema, in a somewhat altered version, seems also involved in the Buddhist concept of EMPTINESS.

Secondly, we can see the intricate relationship between SPACE and TIME—the two 'central conceptual domains in human experience' (Filipović and Jaszczolt 2012, p. 1)—in the TIME AS SPACE metaphor and in the Buddhist conceptualization of the spatial concept WORLD (shi-jie) and the temporal concept KALPA. On the one hand, the spatial metaphors for TIME PASSING, TIME DURATION, and TIME SCALE reinforce 'the currently widely researched hypothesis that the human concept of time is (asymmetrically) dependent on the concept of space' (Filipović and Jaszczolt 2012, p. 2). On the other hand, our analysis of shi-jie and kalpa suggests that the relationship between SPACE and TIME is not totally asymmetrical, with the latter depending on the former. Rather, in the Buddhist mind there is a temporal dimension for SPACE as well, for the concept shi-jie itself denotes both TIME and SPACE, and shi-jie and kalpa seem to be 'inter-defined': a kalpa refers to the time span constituted by the four stages of a shi-jie, while a shi-jie goes through the four stages which combine to form a kalpa. Therefore, while acknowledging the dependence of temporal conceptualization on SPACE, we should also realize that 'there is no experience of space without time nor an experience of time without space' (Kronasser 1968, p. 158; cited in Radden 2011, p. 1).

Thirdly, as we analyzed in sections 4.3 and 4.4, Buddhist LIFE is confined by both SPACE and TIME, and accordingly, BUDDHIST PRACTICE aims at liberation from spatial and temporal confinement. In Buddhism, temporally, life is an endless cycle with an infinite number of lifetimes; spatially, different life forms travel along and among the six paths. This cyclic journey of life is confined by the wheel of reincarnation; and Buddhist practitioners, taking reincarnation as a starting point, travel along the path of BUDDHIST PRACTICE towards the destination of nirvana, where Buddhist practitioners are finally spatially freed from the six paths and temporally freed of endless death and rebirth.

Finally, the Buddhist wisdom of EMPTINESS proclaims that we should not be attached to the notions of SPACE, TIME, LIFE, or BUDDHIST PRACTICE, for none of them is permanent or fixed with a substantial nature. Rather, they are all conditioned results of causes and effects. Their true nature, in a word, is emptiness. Yet, paradoxically, to obtain the wisdom of EMPTINESS, a Buddhist should not even be attached to the notion of EMPTINESS itself. Otherwise it is not genuine EMPTINESS.

As for the role that metaphor plays in interpreting Buddhist sutras, the well-known finger-moon metaphor in Buddhism (cf. Wawrytko 2007) seems to be illustrative. The finger-moon metaphor is often used to demonstrate the relationship between Buddhist scripture and Buddha's dharma: As a finger is used to show the (visual) way to the moon, the scripture provides Buddhist practitioners with an access to Buddha's dharma. As the finger is of great use but not the ultimate goal, the scripture is significant but not the dharma itself. Borrowing this specific metaphor, we could perhaps explain the relationship between metaphor in general and Buddhist wisdom as follows. On the one hand, the power of metaphor is not to be ignored, for metaphorical expressions are pervasive in Buddhist sutras and play a crucial role in illustrating the underlying themes and wisdom (cf. Lan 2012, pp. 176–177). On the other hand, it should be realized that metaphor is not the essence of those themes or the wisdom itself. If, according to Buddhist doctrines, emptiness is the real nature of all forms, then metaphor and wisdom, both being forms, are also empty. Following the paradoxical tradition of Buddhism, we could thus tentatively conclude by saying that emptiness is metaphorical and metaphor is empty.

NOTES

1. Tathagata (如来) is one of the titles of Buddha. Another title frequently appearing in the examples cited from the *Heart Sutra* and the *Diamond Sutra* is World Honored One (世尊).
2. The 12 nidanas (十二因果) are also known as the 12 links in the chain of existence, i.e. 无明 (ignorance), 行 (volitional action), 识 (conditional consciousness), 名色 (name-and-form), 六入 (the six bases), 触 (sense-impressions), 受 (feelings), 爱 (desire), 取 (attachment), 有 (the life-or-rebirth process), 生 (birth), and 老死 (aging and death; Chen and Li 2005, p. 295). The line cited by Lu and Chiang from the *Heart Sutra* lists only the first nidana (ignorance) and the last nidana (aging and death), with 乃至 (and even) connecting the two and indicating the omission of the other 10 nidanas.
3. Subhuti (须菩提) is one of the 10 major disciples of Buddha and the best exponent of emptiness (Chen and Shang 2010, p. 13). In chapter 2 of the *Diamond Sutra*, he requests teaching from Buddha and in the subsequent chapters, the sutra unfolds in the form of the conversation between Subhuti and Buddha, mainly with Subhuti asking questions and Buddha answering them.
4. It should be pointed out that the initial, middle, and back day divisions are not exact equivalents to morning, noon, and evening. A day and a night are divided into six divisions, with each division covering four hours. Therefore, the three day divisions refer to the periods 6:00–10:00, 10:00–14:00, and 14:00–18:00, respectively (cf. Chen 1998, pp. 117–118; and Chen and Shang 2010, p. 38).
5. In Buddhism, as a day is divided into three parts, a night is similarly divided into the initial night division (初夜分, *chu-ye-fen*), the middle night division (中夜分, *zhong-ye-fen*), and the back night division (后夜分, *hou-ye-fen*) (Chen 1998, pp. 117–118).
6. 阿僧祇 (*a-seng-qi*) is a transliteration of the Sanskrit term 'asamkhyeya,' which means 'countless' and is often used to measure kalpas (Chen and Shang 2010, p. 40).
7. 摩诃萨 is a transliteration from the Sanskrit term *mahasattva*, which literally means 'great being' and refers to a bodhisattva, who is greater (*maha*) than any other being (*sattva*) except Buddha and has great compassion and energy to bring salvation to all beings (Chen and Li 2005, p. 217).
8. Lan (2012) observes that there are two versions of the LIFE IS A RIVER JOURNEY metaphor, one being LIFE IS A JOURNEY ALONG A RIVER, the other being LIFE IS A JOURNEY ACROSS A RIVER. With the former, an earlier time in one's life is a spot closer to the source of the river and a later time is a spot closer to the end of the river; one's life goal is to get somewhere further down the river. With the latter, one starts on one side of the river and wants to get to the other side. Sometimes this side of the river is understood as life and the other side as death.

9. *Arhat* is a Sanskrit word and is transliterated into 阿罗汉 (*a-luo-han*) in Chinese. It refers to a Buddhist practitioner who has obtained the supreme achievement of extinguishing all worries and getting liberated from endless rebirth (Chen and Shang 2010, p. 25).
10. *Arana* is also a Sanskrit word and is transliterated as 阿兰那 (*a-lan-na*) in Chinese. It literally means a forest or a remote and quiet place and metonymically refers to the Buddhist practice of meditating, which usually takes place in such a locale.
11. The Buddhist EMPTINESS is different from its modern Chinese counterpart and its English counterpart. As Paul Chilton points out (personal communication on April 4, 2016), the concept EMPTINESS in its modern sense is set up against the CONTAINER schema (usually thought of as an outside-boundary-inside structure), but what the Buddhist EMPTINESS emphasizes is the empty inside without the containing boundaries being assumed. We might also understand the Buddhist EMPTINESS as being set up against the boundless cosmos as the CONTAINER.

REFERENCES

Basson, Alec (2006). *Divine Metaphors in Selected Hebrew Psalms of Lamentation*. Tübingen, Germany: Mohr Siebeck.
Bisschops, Ralph (2003). Are religious metaphors rooted in experience? On Ezekiel's wedding metaphors. In K. Feyaerts (ed.), *The Bible through Metaphor and Translation: A Cognitive Semantic Perspective*, pp. 113–151. New York: Peter Lang.
Botha, Willem J. (1998). The love frame in the Bible: A cognitive linguistic analysis. In B. Biebuyck, R. Dirven, and J. Ries (eds.), *Faith and Fiction*, pp. 56–83. Frankfurt am Main: Peter Lang.
Bruce, Judy A. (2009). *A Supreme Battle in Metaphor: A Critical Metaphor Analysis of the Culture War in* Lawrence v. Texas. Doctoral dissertation. Denver: University of Denver.
Cameron, Lynne, Robert Maslen, Zazie Todd, John Maule, Peter Stratton, and Neil Stanley (2009). The discourse dynamics approach to metaphor and metaphor-led discourse analysis. *Metaphor and Symbol* 24(2), 63–89.
Charteris-Black, Jonathan (2004). *Corpus Approaches to Critical Metaphor Analysis*. Basingstoke: Palgrave Macmillan.
Chen, Guan-sheng and Pei-zhu Li [陈观胜、李培茱] (eds.) (2005). 中英佛教词典 [*A Chinese-English Dictionary of Buddhist Terms*]. Beijing: Foreign Languages Press.
Chen, Qiu-ping and Rong Shang [陈秋平、尚荣] (2010). 金刚经·心经·坛经 [*The* Diamond Sutra, *the* Heart Sutra *and the* Platform Sutra]. Beijing: Zhonghua Book Company.
Chen, Yi-xiao [陈义孝] (1998). 佛学常见词汇 [*A Buddhism Glossary*]. Taipei: Wen Chin Publishing Company.
Chung Tai Translation Committee (trans.) (2009). *The* Diamond of Perfect Wisdom Sutra. http://ctzen.org/sunnyvale/zhTW/images/pdf/2013sutra/2014sutra/diamond%20 sutra%20v1.9.17%2020131201%281%29.pdf.
Crain, Jeanie C. (2010). *Reading the Bible as Literature*. Cambridge: Polity Press.
DesCamp, Mary Therese and Eve E. Sweetser (2005). Metaphors for God: Why and how do our choices matter for humans? The application of contemporary cognitive linguistics research to the debate on God and metaphor. *Pastoral Psychology* 53(3), 207–238.
Dille, Sarah J. (2004). *Mixing Metaphors: God as Mother and Father in Deutero-Isaiah*. London: T&T Clark International.
Ding, Fu-bao [丁福保] (1922/2002). 佛学大辞典 [*A Comprehensive Dictionary of Buddhism*]. Shijiazhuang: Hebei Provincial Buddhism Association.
Ding, Min [丁敏] (1996). 佛教譬喻文学研究 [*Research on Buddhist Piyu Literature*]. Taipei: Dongchu Press.

El-Sharif, Ahmad (2011). *A Linguistic Study of Islamic Religious Discourse: Conceptual Metaphors in the Prophetic Tradition*. Doctoral dissertation. London: Queen Mary, University of London.

El-Sharif, Ahmad (2012). Metaphors we believe by: Islamic doctrine as evoked by the Prophet Muhammad's metaphors. *Critical Discourse Studies* 9(3), 231–245.

Erussard, Laurence (1997). From salt to Salt: Cognitive metaphor and religious language. *Cuadernos de Filología Inglesa* 6(2), 197–212.

Fauconnier, Gilles (1994). *Mental Spaces: Aspects of Meaning Construction in Natural Language*. Cambridge: Cambridge University Press.

Fauconnier, Gilles and Mark Turner (2002). *The Way We Think: Conceptual Blending and the Mind's Hidden Complexities*. New York: Basic Books.

Feyaerts, Kurt (ed.) (2003). *The Bible through Metaphor and Translation: A Cognitive Semantic Perspective*. New York: Peter Lang.

Filipović, Luna and Kasia M. Jaszczolt (2012). Linguistics, cultural, and cognitive approaches to space and time. In L. Filipović and K. M. Jaszczolt (eds.), *Space and Time in Languages and Cultures: Language, Culture, and Cognition*, pp. 1–11. Amsterdam and Philadelphia: John Benjamins Publishing Company.

Gavriely-Nuri, Dalia (2013). Collective memory as a metaphor: The case of speeches by Israeli prime ministers 2001–2009. *Metaphor Studies* 7(1), 46–60.

Gupta, Nijay K. (2010). *Worship that Makes Sense to Paul: A New Approach to the Theology and Ethics of Paul's Cultic Metaphor*. Berlin: de Gruyter.

Harrison, Victoria S. (2007). Metaphor, religious language, and religious experience. *Sophia* 46, 127–145.

Howe, Bonnie Tigner (2003). *Metaphor and Meaning in Christian Moral Discourse: The Role of Conceptual Metaphor in the Creation of Meaning in Christian Moral Discourse, with 1 Peter as Exemplar*. Doctoral dissertation. Berkeley, CA: Graduate Theological Union.

Hülsse, Rainer and Alexander Spencer (2008). The metaphor of terror: Terrorism studies and the constructivist turn. *Security Dialogue* 39(6), 571–592.

Jäkel, Olaf (2002). Hypotheses revisited: The cognitive theory of metaphor applied to religious texts. *Metaphorik.de* (2), 20–42.

Jäkel, Olaf (2003). How can mortal man understand the road he travels? Prospects and problems of the cognitive approach to religious metaphor. In K. Feyaerts (ed.), *The Bible through Metaphor and Translation: A Cognitive Semantic Perspective*, pp. 55–86. New York: Peter Lang.

Jindo, Job Y. (2010). *Biblical Metaphor Reconsidered: A Cognitive Approach to Poetic Prophecy in Jeremiah 1–24*. Winona Lake, IN: Eisenbrauns.

Johnson, Mark (1987). *The Body in the Mind: The Bodily Basis of Meaning, Imagination, and Reason*. Chicago and London: University of Chicago Press.

King, Phil (2012). Metaphor and methodology for cross-cultural investigation of Hebrew emotions. *Journal of Translation* 8(1), 9–24.

Klingbeil, Gerald A. (2006). Metaphor and pragmatics: An introduction to the hermeneutics of metaphors in the Epistle to the Ephesians. *Bulletin for Biblical Research* 16(2), 273–293.

Kronasser, Heinz (1968). *Handbuch der Semasiologie*. Heidelberg: Winter.

Lakoff, George (1993). The contemporary theory of metaphor. In A. Ortony (ed.), *Metaphor and Thought*, pp. 202–251. Cambridge: Cambridge University Press.

Lakoff, George and Mark Johnson (1980). *Metaphors We Live By*. Chicago and London: University of Chicago Press.

Lakoff, George and Mark Turner (1989). *More than Cool Reason: A Field Guide to Poetic Metaphor*. Chicago and London: University of Chicago Press.

Lam, Joseph Ching Po (2012). *The Metaphorical Patterning of the Sin-Concept in Biblical Hebrew*. Doctoral dissertation. Chicago: University of Chicago.

Lan, Chun (2003). *A Cognitive Approach to Spatial Metaphors in English and Chinese*. Beijing: Foreign Languages Teaching and Research Press.

Lan, Chun (2012). A cognitive perspective on the metaphors in the Buddhist sutra 'Bao Ji Jing.' *Metaphor and the Social World* 2(2), 154–179.

Levinson, Stephen C. (2004). *Space in Language and Cognition: Explorations in Cognitive Diversity*. Cambridge: Cambridge University Press.

Li, Xiao-rong [李小荣] (2009). 简论汉译佛典之'譬喻'文体 [A comment on the 'avadana' style in Chinese translation of Buddhist scriptures]. *Journal of Fujian Normal University (Philosophy and Social Sciences Edition)* 5, 65–73.

Liang, Xiao-hong [梁晓虹] (1994). 佛教词语的构造与汉语词汇的发展 [*Structure of Buddhist Lexicon and Development of Chinese Vocabulary*]. Beijing: Beijing Language Institute Press.

Long, Gary Alan (1994). Dead or alive?: Literality and God-metaphors in the Hebrew Bible. *Journal of the American Academy of Religion* 62(2), 509–537.

Lopez, Donald S. Jr. (1988). *The Heart Sutra Explained: Indian and Tibetan Commentaries*. Albany: State University of New York Press.

Lu, Louis Wei-lun and Wen-yu Chiang, (2007). Emptiness we live by: Metaphors and paradoxes in Buddhism's *Heart Sutra*. *Metaphor and Symbol* 22(4), 331–355.

Master Hsing Yun [星云大师] (2008). 金刚经讲话 [*Commentary on the* Diamond Sutra]. Beijing: New World Press.

Master Hsuan Hua (2002). *The* Vajra Prajna Paramita Sutra: *A General Explanation* (Buddhist Text Translation Society, trans.). Burlingame, CA: Buddhist Text Translation Society.

Master T'an Hsu (2000). *The Prajna Paramita Heart Sutra (Commentary)* (Master Lok To, trans.). New York: Sutra Translation Committee of the United States and Canada.

McMahan, David L. (2002). *Empty Vision: Metaphor and Visionary Imagery in Mahayana Buddhism*. London: RoutledgeCurzon.

Moore, Anne (2009). *Moving beyond Symbol and Myth: Understanding the Kingship of God of the Hebrew Bible through Metaphor*. New York: Peter Lang.

Moughtin-Mumby, Sharon (2008). *Sexual and Marital Metaphors in Hosea, Jeremiah, Isaiah, and Ezekiel*. Oxford: Oxford University Press.

Nielsen, Kirsten (1989). *There is Hope for a Tree: The Tree as Metaphor in Isaiah*. Sheffield: JSOT Press.

Núñez, Rafael and Kensy Cooperrider (2013). The tangle of space and time in human cognition. *Trends in Cognitive Sciences* 17(5), 220–229.

Perdue, Leo G. (1991). *Wisdom in Revolt: Metaphorical Theology in the Book of Job*. Sheffield: JSOT Press.

Radden, Günter (2011). Spatial time in the West and the East. In M. Brdar et al. (eds.), *Space and Time in Language*, pp. 1–30. Frankfurt: Peter Lang.

Selçuk, Mualla (1998). The use of metaphors in Islamic education. In B. Biebuyck, R. Dirven, and J. Ries (eds.), *Faith and Fiction*, pp. 99–114. Frankfurt am Main: Peter Lang.

Soskice, Janet Martin (2007). *The Kindness of God: Metaphor, Gender, and Religious Language*. Oxford: Oxford University Press.

Spencer, Aída Besançon (1996). Father-ruler: The meaning of the metaphor 'father' for God in the Bible. *Journal of the Evangelical Theological Society*, 39(3), 433–442.

Spencer, Alexander (2012). The social construction of terrorism: Media, metaphor and policy implications. *Journal of International Relations and Development* 15(3), 393–419.

Stallman, Robert C. (1999). *Divine Hospitality in the Pentateuch: A Metaphorical Perspective of God as Host*. Doctoral dissertation. Philadelphia: Westminster Theological Seminary.

Sugioka, Takanori (2009). The metaphor of 'ocean' in Shinran. Translated by Mark Unno. *Pacific World: Journal of the Institute of Buddhist Studies* 3(11), 219–228.

Szlos, Mary Beth Bruskewicz (2001). *Metaphor in Proverbs 31:10–31: A Cognitive Approach*. Doctoral dissertation. New York: Union Theological Seminary.

Talbert-Wettler, Betty (1995). Secular feminist religious metaphor and Christianity. *Journal of the Evangelical Theological Society* 38(1), 77–92.

Tracy, David (1979). Metaphor and religion. In S. Sacks (ed.), *On Metaphor*, pp. 89–104. Chicago: Chicago University Press.

Turner, Mark (2005). The literal versus figurative dichotomy. In S. Coulson and B. Lewandowska-Tomaszczyk (eds.), *The Literal and Nonliteral in Language and Thought*, pp. 25–52. Frankfurt: Peter Lang.

van Hecke, Pierre (2003). To shepherd, have dealings and desire: On the lexical structure of the Hebrew root r'h. In K. Feyaerts (ed.), *The Bible through Metaphor and Translation: A Cognitive Semantic Perspective*, pp. 37–53. New York: Peter Lang.

van Hecke, Pierre (2005). Pastoral metaphors in the Hebrew Bible and in its ancient Near Eastern context. In R. P. Gordan and J. C. de Moor (eds.), *The Old Testament in Its World*, pp. 200–217. Boston: Brill.

Viberg, Ake (1994). Wakening a sleeping metaphor: A new interpretation of Malachi 1:11. *Tyndale Bulletin* 45(2), 297–319.

Wang, Lei (2008). *A Cognitive Approach towards the Interpretation of Biblical Parables.* Doctoral dissertation. Shanghai: Shanghai International Studies University.

Warren, E. Janet (2011). *Cleansing the Cosmos: A Biblical Model for Conceptualizing and Counteracting Evil.* Doctoral dissertation. Birmingham: The University of Birmingham.

Wawrytko, Sandra A. (2007). Holding up the mirror to Buddha-nature: Discerning the ghee in the *Lotus Sutra*. *Dao* 6(1), 63–81.

Wayman, Alex. 1974. The mirror as a pan-Buddhist metaphor-simile. *History of Religions* 13(4), 251–269.

Weiss, Andrea L. (2006). *Figurative Language in Biblical Prose Narrative: Metaphor in the Book of Samuel.* Boston: Brill.

Xu, Chun-ying (2003). *The Study of Metaphor in the Bible: Cognitive Approach.* Master's thesis. Hangzhou: Zhejiang University.

Yeo, Khiok-khng [杨克勤] (2012). 庄子与雅各 [*Zhuangzi and James*]. Shanghai: East China Normal University Press.

Yu, Ning (1998). *The Contemporary Theory of Metaphor: A Perspective from Chinese.* Amsterdam and Philadelphia: John Benjamins Publishing Company.

CHAPTER 11

The Muslim Prophetic Tradition

Spatial Source Domains for Metaphorical Expressions

AHMAD EL-SHARIF

Religious discourse commonly involves covert and indefinite knowledge about abstract and metaphysical assumptions. These abstract assumptions, such as the existence of God, the creation of the universe, the definiteness of our destiny, the reality of death and the afterlife, are not easily comprehensible because they transcend our ordinary cognitive and sensual capacities. On the basis of the conceptual theory of metaphor, Olaf Jäkel makes significant predictions about the occurrence, frequency, and centrality of linguistic metaphors in texts which deal with religious issues (Jäkel 2002). Most importantly, he maintains that because of the high level of abstraction of the religious domain, it is likely that religious language will be largely (if not completely) dependent on metaphorical conceptualisation when mentioning concepts which are removed from our human sensual experience, such as God, the soul, the hereafter, and the freedom of moral choice (Jäkel 2002, p. 23).

1 METAPHOR AND RELIGIONS

Eva Kittay maintains that 'metaphor has cognitive value and this stems not from providing new facts about the world but from a reconceptualisation of the information that is already available to us' (Kittay 1987, p. 39). Metaphorical language can resolve ambiguous and incomprehensible arguments by bringing to the surface the most comprehensible aspects of the argument in question in reference to our familiar domains of experience. She further claims that 'Metaphor actually gives us "epistemic access" to fresh experience and, to the extent that we have no other linguistic resources to achieve this, metaphor is "cognitively irreplaceable"' (Kittay 1987, p. 39).

For these reasons, metaphorical language constitutes an indispensable linguistic tool in religious discourse. In her book *Metaphor and Religious Language* (1985), the Catholic theologian Janet Martin Soskice was among the pioneer researchers to draw attention to the relationship between metaphor and religious language. Soskice argues in her book that what is needed to study religious language is not a more literal theology but a better understanding of metaphor. She argues that the analysis of metaphor in religious language illuminates the way in which the clergy speak of God and contributes to revealing how our understanding of metaphors in religious language can facilitate the way we perceive sciences and other disciplines.

Soskice emphasises the idea that metaphors create new perspectives to increase humans' understanding of religious notions. She argues that by the creation of new perspectives, successful metaphors expand humans' descriptive powers when other types of linguistic expressions fail (Soskice 1985, p. 66). Furthermore, she suggests that metaphors in religious discourse involve an 'evocative' function where the range of associations evoked by metaphor genuinely tells the recipient of the religious discourse more about the metaphorised religious notion(s), especially if the religious notion is very abstract and difficult to recognise without the metaphor. For example, when perceiving the metaphor 'God is a father', the message of the metaphor acquaints the believer with different entailed propositions such as 'if God is our father, he will hear us when we cry to him; if God is our father, then as children and heirs we come to him without fear; if God is our father, he will not give us stones when we ask for bread' (Soskice 1985, p. 112).

Charteris-Black, who has studied metaphors in the Bible and the Quran, contends that the effectiveness of metaphor within religious discourse is related to the fact that

> [I]t [metaphor] is a primary means by which the unknown can be conceptualised in terms of what is already known [. . .] metaphors are a natural means for exploring the possible forms that [such] divinity might take and for expressing religious experiences. (Charteris-Black 2004, p. 173)

In many religions, perhaps in all, metaphors are the only means of representing religious concepts. The three major Abrahamic (monotheistic) religions, Judaism, Christianity, and Islam, generally express the concept of 'God' in the Old and New Testaments and in the Holy Quran by metaphorical transfer. In fact, theologians of all three traditions have argued that a believer's knowledge about God is deficient because of the lack of any direct experience (cf. Feyaerts and Boeve, chapter 3, this volume). This is why metaphorical language is the optimal tool to employ in religious discourse when referring to God.

Metaphorical language facilitates conceptualisation of the nature of God by directing attention to God's absolute intrinsic qualities by means of metaphor. For example, God is conventionally represented in Christianity and Judaism as a 'father', and in Islam He is represented using metaphors of 'light' (Charteris-Black 2004, p. 213). These images draw attention to particular symbolic qualities of God such as power, providential care, indispensability, and perfection.

In addition, metaphorical language may have an ideological function (cf. Fairclough 1992, p. 74), since it may invoke presupposed differences in power, social practices, principles, thoughts, and beliefs. Additionally, religious discourse may involve a system of ideas and beliefs which have ideological implications. Metaphors are used in religious discourse to associate aspects of people's experiential and social knowledge of the real world and society with the system of beliefs and values that their religion encompasses. For example, in relation to the concept of God in the three Abrahamic religions, one might argue that the two metaphoric representations of God as a 'father' and as 'light'[1] invoke ideological messages. On the basis of the religious beliefs of the three religions, the two metaphoric representations play an essential role within religious discourse in portraying the existence of God as a necessity for humanity. Humans, like children, are always in need of a father to whom they repair in moments of despair; the father represents power and authority in the eyes of his children regardless of his (the father's) own character and behaviour. Where God is represented using the metaphor of light, this image, in contrast to the image of darkness, is a means of conceptualising God's omnipotence and omniscience. Light, and its source in the sun and in fire, is understood as essential to life; God is thus metaphorised as the ultimate source of light. Light is also a cross-culturally common metaphor associated with knowledge, hence with omniscience in religious discourse. It is the network of emotions, evaluations, and ideas that follow from these two metaphorical representations of divinity that further involve concepts of power. There are, however, clearly important conceptual differences entailed by the two metaphors in the different religious traditions.

2 METAPHOR IN ARAB SCHOLARSHIP AND CULTURE

Ideas about, and attitudes toward, metaphor play a role in the fascination with meaning found in several religious traditions. Early Arab scholars referred to metaphor either as a (ʔesteʕaːra)[2] or as (madʒaːz), where the two notions share the concept of 'substitution'. The word (ʔesteʕaːra) is derived from the verb (ʔaʕaːra), which means 'to borrow' or 'to lend'. Al-Jurjani, the first Arab scholar to study metaphor distinctively, followed Aristotle's traditional characterisation of metaphor and defined it as a word that is temporarily 'lent'(ʔustuʕirat) and 'inserted' to refer to something that it does not designate conventionally in the system of language (Jurjani 1988). Al-Ghazali (c. 1058–1111), philosopher, referred to a metaphor as (madʒaːz), a word that roughly means 'passing over' or 'going beyond' and 'going through'. In fact, the word (madʒaːz) reflects early Arab rhetoricians' and philologists' views about metaphor, according to which a metaphor was a word or an expression not used in its original, or 'true' (ħaqiqi), place (Al-Ghazali 1904, pp. 341–342). In addition, metaphor was viewed as part of the study of rhetoric (albaːjn). Rhetoric, in the early stages of Arabic philology in the 11th century CE, was considered a science that allowed the conveying of ideas (Qalqila 1992, p. 37). Al-Jurjani (d. 1078 CE), for instance, maintained that a metaphor could only reveal deep insight into a few concealed relationships between different things (Jurjani 1988, p. 57). Al-Askari (d. 1004 CE) maintained that a metaphor is used to explain the intended idea for the purpose of emphasising its meaning (Askari 1981, p. 295). Both philologists Al-Rummani

(d. 994 CE) and As-Suyuti (d. 1505 CE) argued that a metaphor is capable of clarifying meaning in a way that could not be fully achieved by using everyday literal language (Al-Rummani 1968, p. 86; As-Suyuti 1973, p. 44). But metaphor was predominantly regarded as an ornamental device for poetry and speeches.

Nonetheless, metaphor was taken very seriously in the religious domain. The study of metaphors in Arabic religious texts has been driven mainly by the need to interpret the meanings of the Holy Quran and the Prophetic Tradition. In fact, the development in the science of interpreting and explaining the Holy Quran (tafsi:r) has significantly contributed to the development of Arabic studies, especially rhetoric. In this respect, the necessity for studying metaphors has developed from the need to deduce fundamental religious principles and commandments from the sources on a sound basis.

A number of early Arab philosophers and theologians questioned the existence of metaphors in Islamic religious discourse, especially in the Holy Quran, some because they believed that the word 'metaphor' denoted an untrue or false statement. Further, 'literalist' theologians affirmed that whatever the Quran says is (or should be) literally true because it is the word of God, and God does not say anything untrue. On the other hand, most early Arab philosophers recognised the inevitability of using metaphors in religious discourse. They argued that it is the incomparable nature of the divine communication that entails the existence of metaphors which can transmit the divine message into human language. In other words, since religion does not have a special language of its own, it must resort to ordinary language in accordance with society's conventions (ʕa:da) in which the given language operates as a means of conversation (muħawarah) (Al-Ghazali 1904, p. 35). Accordingly, a prophet easily expresses the distinguishing qualities of the divine language to his followers through similitude, since prophets have always been sent speaking the language of their people.

In spite of such justifications for the existence of metaphors in religious language, many Muslim theologians have persistently refused to 'blemish' the study of religion with philosophical arguments of this kind. Indeed, most early Muslim theologians feared that such speculations could lead to some metaphorical interpretations that would disagree with the well-established principles of faith and creed explicitly or implicitly. However, many moderate Muslim philosophers, and a few theologians, were influenced by the philosophical paradigms for the interpretation of metaphorical language in religious discourse by emphasising the fact that symbolic language in general, and consistent use of metaphors in particular, may have a deep and continuing impression on the 'heart', and give the religious texts more prestige and *divine* status.

Al-Ghazali, for example, argued that the immense weight of metaphors in Islamic religious discourse is a normal, and even necessary, phenomenon of religious language. So, the presence of metaphors in the Holy Quran cannot be ignored (Aydin Mehmet, 1997, p. 2). In spite of the fact that he emphasised in his treatises that no (kind of) language, especially religious, invariably means what it appears to mean in a literal sense, Al-Ghazali argued in favour of the existence of metaphors in the Quran, but he rejected the belief that all the divine words in the scriptures must be interpreted metaphorically. He maintained that metaphorical expressions in any given religious discourse require an interpretation (taʔwiːl) related to the overall exegesis (tafsiːr) of the religious text. Such metaphorical interpretation (taʔwiːl) should involve a process by which a transference from the original and literal (haqiːqi or lafðˤi) meaning to metaphorical (maӡaːzi) meaning takes place (Aydin Mehmet, 1997, p. 3). However, Al-Ghazali sustained the argument that no metaphorical interpretation will be accepted if it disagrees with the evidential principles of faith (or creed) which are explicitly mentioned in the Holy Quran or the Prophetic Tradition, and which constructs the 'narrated religious evidence' (daliːl naqli). Furthermore, he believed that a sound metaphorical interpretation must respect certain norms and regulations. First of all, an interpreter must possess a professional mastery of Arabic and its grammars and conventions. Secondly, the interpreter must look first for 'narrated religious evidence' (daliːl naqli) that supports the 'rational evidence' (daliːl ʕaqli) before adopting a particular metaphorical interpretation. Thirdly, and possibly most importantly, the interpreter should not accept any metaphorical interpretation that goes against the evident principles of religion and faith. From today's perspective, I would add to these norms that it is necessary for the interpreter to take into consideration the different settings and contexts where metaphors appear. The interpreter of the text and its metaphors must take into consideration that the meanings of words evolve over time. So, some metaphors may have had different implications in the Prophet's time. These metaphors may not necessarily have the same effect or implications in our days.

Consequently, interpreting instances of metaphors in any religious discourse, especially the Holy Quran and the Prophet Muhammad's Tradition (henceforth PT), requires the search for any potential and obvious literal interpretation. Those who are proficient enough in rhetoric, philology, and theology are best able to interpret the discourse and uncover its unseen meanings. Their efforts must be oriented towards making the interpretation of the metaphorical expressions transcend the limits of its literal sense to cover the way in which the Prophet and his companions used it, taking into consideration that the revealed meaning must be disregarded if it is judged absurd or against the fundamental beliefs of faith and Islamic doctrine. And if it happens that the exact metaphorical interpretation is inaccessible or difficult to the recipient because of some paucity in necessary pragmatic and contextual details, then the recipient of the religious message should adhere to the superficial literal interpretation without speculating about other controversial metaphorical ones. This approach is safe, especially when addressing an audience of laymen who do not have the well-founded knowledge and expertise to tackle controversial religious issues (Aydin Mehmet 1997, p. 7). In the research on which the present chapter is based, however, I am concerned purely with the linguistic manifestation and arguments regarding the existence of metaphorical language in the PT. Thus, I outline in my analysis the linguistic aspect of the interpretation and analysis of the metaphors, distinguishing that approach from the more sophisticated and debatable theological one. In this regard, I intend that my analysis will not be driven by a biased desire to prove how religious messages are consistently represented in the Prophetic discourse because of its divine nature.

The past two decades have witnessed the rebirth of research into metaphor from modern cognitive linguistic viewpoints. The pervasiveness of this linguistic phenomenon in ordinary language and discourse has been consistently demonstrated in many languages and for different types of discourse, especially political and ideological discourse. Still, the investigation of metaphor in religious language has been relatively rare (but cf. Aydin Mehmet 1997; Charteris-Black 2004; Jäkel 2002; Marston 2000). In addition, there has been comparatively little attention given to the cognitive theory of metaphor among Arab scholars. Apart from the study of the rhetorical aspects of language of the Holy Quran and its 'miraculous' value, few linguistic researchers have investigated any characteristics of early Islamic religious discourse, which includes the Holy Quran and the Prophet Muhammad's sayings and tradition, from a discourse-analytical viewpoint.

3 THE PROPHETIC TRADITION

The PT, also known as the *Hadith* (modern) or *Sunnah* (path), is considered in Islam the second source of legislation after the Holy Quran. This Tradition, or *Hadith*,[3] consists of an enormous body of texts that involves a range of laws, principles, and instructions taken from the sayings, actions, and approvals (consents) of the Prophet Muhammad. Muslims around the world believe that the laws and principles embedded within the PT, and which the Prophet Muhammad has provided, are of a divine source. In the Holy Quran, God (*Allah*) says:

- "وَمَا يَنطِقُ عَنِ الْهَوَى (3) إِنْ هُوَ إِلَّا وَحْيٌ يُوحَى (4) عَلَّمَهُ شَدِيدُ الْقُوَى (5)" (سورة النجم، 53:3-5)

'Nor does he [Muhammad] speak of (his own) Desire. It is only a Revelation revealed. He has been taught (this Qur'an) by one mighty in power [Jibril (Gabriel)]' (*An-Najm*, the Star, 53:3–5).

Thus Muslims are required to believe that both the Quran and the PT are the two main sources of Islamic laws (ʃariʕa). Although both the Quran and the PT are considered 'revelation' from God, it should be emphasised that Muslims perceive the Holy Quran as the actual word of God, whereas the PT is a revelation evoked by God but expressed through the words, ordinary actions and behaviour, consents and approvals of the Prophet Muhammad (Bearman et al. 1960–2005, Vol. 7: 'MuHaddeth').

The PT brings together a large number of sayings, speeches, and accounts of the Prophet's deeds and approvals, covering about twenty-three years of his life. The PT was narrated in extracts called *Sayings*, and each Saying is composed of two parts: a 'narrative' (ʔisna:d) and a 'body' (matn). The narrative (ʔisna:d) consists of the chain of people who narrated the Saying. It involves an ordered list of all those who have recited and transmitted the Saying of the Prophet beginning with the last transmitter in the chain (who is reciting the Saying to the Saying's collector) and ending with the 'Companions'[4] (sʕaħa:bah) who narrated it directly from the Prophet (Philips 2007, p. 43). The second part, the body (matn), involves the actual text of the narration, regardless of its nature; it can involve the Prophet's direct speech, accounts of his actions, his ethical values and morals, the actions which were performed before him that he approved (consents), and even his physical appearance (Philips 2007, p. 43).

Muslims consider the PT an essential supplement to the Quran and a clarification of its message. For example, the Quran explains in detail several laws and principles that regulate many matters essential to Muslims, such as the laws of household (alʔusra) and inheritance (almawa:ri:θ); however it does not talk in detail about other matters such as the performance of prayers, the manner of pilgrimage, or the amount of the obligatory charity (zaka:t). In addition to the Quran, Muslims believe that the PT constitutes an important source of religious knowledge materialised in the large body of laws and principles embodied in the PT.

It is impossible to identify the precise number of Sayings attributed to the Prophet. In addition, most of the Prophet's Companions (sˤaħa:bah) who heard the Prophet's Sayings and remembered them by heart moved from Medina after the Prophet's death. During the period of Islamic expansion many of them lived in the new conquered lands for the rest of their lives (Bin Ahmad 1984, p. 28). Naturally, centuries later the different narrations of the PT were spread throughout the vast Islamic world, so that it became very difficult to collect them entirely in one collection. Hence, different collections of the PT have emerged.

Around one century after the Prophet Muhammad's death, Muslims started to pay more attention to the PT and its transmission (Siddiqi and Murad 1993, p. 6). During the Umayyad Islamic state (in the second *Hijri* century), the PT was being narrated orally through many paths of transmission between the narrators on the one hand, and the teacher-student interaction on the other, though it is believed that the PT were initially preserved during the Prophet's life by his 'Companions' (sˤaħa:bah) in the same way that they preserved the Quran (Amin 1975, pp. 208–209; Siddiqi and Murad 1993, p. 24). Subsequently, the Companions' disciples, called the 'Successors' (tabeʕu:n), have passed on the *Hadith* from their teachers, the Companions, to their followers. Consequently, a chain of narration of the PT has been developed through successive narrations from teachers to students over the following centuries down to the present age (Philips 2007, p. 37; Siddiqi and Murad 1993, p. 86).

The process of collecting the Prophetic Tradition was not random. The seriousness of the task and its importance for keeping Islamic sources of legislation has strengthened the need to find out the most authentic Sayings of the Prophet. Accordingly, early collectors of the PT introduced rigid rules and criteria by which they managed to judge the authenticity of a given Saying. An authentic Saying will be marked as 'sound' (sˤaħi:ħ) if and only if the authenticity of the chain of the narrators of the Saying (ʔisna:d) is proved. A Saying will not be proved sound unless it meets four criteria that test the authenticity of the chain of the narrators. These criteria are as follows (As-Salah 1984, pp. 104–106). Firstly, the sound Saying must have a continuous chain of transmission (ʔisna:d) that is made up of trustworthy narrators narrating from other trustworthy narrators and which is found to be free from any irregularities or defects. Secondly, the narrators' integrity and authenticity must be put under investigation in order to distinguish the reliable narrator from the unreliable. Thirdly, the sound Saying must not contradict other well-known sound Sayings whose chain of narration is strong and correct. Finally, there must be no minor deficiency within the chain that can affect its truth.

The methodical and systematic compilation of the PT began around one century after the Prophet's death, and it continued through the following centuries during which many 'Traditionists'[5] (muħad.deθi:n) had been working exhaustively on collecting the sound Sayings. For example, Imam Al-Bukhari, a Sunni Islamic scholar who lived in Persia in the second century after the Prophet's death, was among the most prominent collectors of the sound PT, and he spent about sixteen years of his life in compiling his collection of the *Hadith*. His work, called al-dʒameʕ al- sʕaħiħ (the Sound Collection), involves most of the sound Sayings and deeds of the Prophet Muhammad. His method of classifying the sound Sayings is based on the scrutiny of each Saying's compatibility with the Holy Quran and on an examination of the veracity of the narrators' chain of the tradition. Al-Bukhari's firm criteria made him extract and refine about 7,265 sound Sayings from hundreds of thousands of alleged Sayings which he had collected (Abbott, 1967, p. 69), making his work regarded by the vast majority of Sunni Muslims as the second most authentic source of legislation after the Holy Quran (Philips 2007, p. 170).

This collection, in addition to many other collections of 'sound' Sayings, has been of great significance for the study of PT and Islamic legislation (ʃariʕah) and jurisprudence (fiqh). However, none of the earlier Traditionists has claimed to collect all the authentic and sound *Hadith* of their age. Later Traditionists have continued the work of collecting other sound Prophetic Sayings which could not be included in other collections because of particular impediments and limitations that hindered the earlier *Hadith* collectors; for example, the difficulties of travelling between the different regions of the Islamic state or the impossibility of finding and meeting a particular narrator of a particular Saying in a particular time.

4 METHOD
4.1 The research corpus

From the many collections of the Prophetic Traditions, the Arabic version of *Mishkat Al-Masabih* {pronounced: *Mishkat* al-masʕa:bi:ħ} (meaning: *The Niche of Lamps*) was selected.[6] This collection was originally compiled by Al-Baghawi (d. 1122 CE) and completed by Al-Tabrizi (d. 1340 CE); it includes a large number of Sayings which were initially mentioned in other collections of the Prophetic Tradition, such as Imam Bukhari's and Imam Muslim's collections of the sound Prophetic Sayings. The corpus was refined for systematic analysis by removing words and expressions that are not essentially part of the body of the Sayings—for example, names of the narrators, and the author's commentaries. In addition, I removed many Sayings which are not recognised as completely 'sound' Sayings by the many commentators and Traditionists.[7] This ensured that the analysis would be based on the most authentic Sayings attributed to the Prophet Muhammad. This process reduced the research corpus from about 390,000 words to about 320,000 words.

4.2 Identifying metaphors

Since there is currently no computer concordancing software currently capable of handling Arabic texts, it was necessary to find instances of metaphors in the corpus manually, that is, by close reading, supported by the 'Metaphor Identification Procedure' (MIP). This is a procedure developed by the Pragglejaz group[8] to judge the metaphoricity of a given keyword. This approach provides a systematic means of identifying metaphorical keywords that prevents the researcher from seeing 'concrete manifestations of conceptual metaphors everywhere' (Steen 2007, p. 27). In order to identify instances of metaphors in a given text, MIP suggests following these procedures (quoted from Pragglejaz 2007, p. 3).

1. Reading the entire text/discourse to establish a general understanding of the meaning.
2. Determining the lexical units in the text/discourse.
3. (a) Establishing meaning from context for each lexical unit in the text/discourse; this involves identifying how it applies to an entity, relation, or attribute in the situation evoked by the text (contextual meaning), and taking into account what comes before and after the lexical unit.
   (b) Determining whether each lexical unit has a more basic contemporary meaning in other contexts than the one in the given context. These basic meanings tend to be more concrete (what they evoke is easier to imagine, see, hear, feel, smell, and taste), related to bodily action, more precise (as opposed to vague), or historically older. It must be emphasised that basic meanings are not necessarily the most frequent meanings of the lexical unit.
   (c) Making a decision as to whether the contextual meaning contrasts with the basic meaning (but can be understood in comparison with it) if the lexical unit has a more basic current/contemporary meaning in other contexts than the given context.
4. Marking the lexical unit as metaphorical if step 3c is true.

Using these procedures, keywords were identified and subsequently classified in terms of source domain mappings already attested in language use by cognitive linguists, or classified as specific one-off metaphorical mappings. These keywords are content words (i.e. nouns, verbs, adjectives, etc.), and they are selected on the basis of their occurrence in the corpus more often than other words on the one hand, and on the other hand on the basis that they would be expected to appear in the Prophetic (or religious) discourse more than in other genres of discourse.

The Prophetic Tradition corpus shows a remarkable richness in the linguistic manifestation of a large set of underlying conceptual mappings. Amongst about 5,000 Sayings in the corpus, it was possible to distinguish some 826 instances of linguistic expressions of conceptual metaphors. The distribution of these expressions varies considerably: some Sayings involve only one instantiation of conceptual metaphor in their body, other Sayings may involve a cluster of more than two metaphors.

Most of the Prophetic metaphors show a large variation and productivity in their source domains in a manner that makes it unfeasible to categorise them in only a few sets of major categories.

My categorisation of the linguistic metaphors in the PT adopts the experientialist framework of the Conceptual Metaphor Theory (CMT) developed by George Lakoff and Mark Johnson. The labels and structure for the categorisation, however, draws on Kövecses's inventory of commonly used source (and target) domains (Kövecses 2002).[9] The results of systematically probing the PT along these lines showed the prominence of four major metaphorical mapping schemas corresponding to Kövecses's (2002) categorisation, plus a few other particular categories. These salient mappings involve the following source domains: (1) CONTAINER, (2) LOCATION, (3) DIRECTION and MOTION, and (4) THE GREAT CHAIN OF BEING. An overview of the major source domain categories and the target domain concepts onto which they map is presented in Figure 1 below.

For the purpose of discussion in the present volume, I have focused on metaphors in the PT grounded in the basic spatial cognition. This is because it is now widely claimed—and the claim seems plausible—that spatial structures have fundamental importance for linguistic meaning across languages and cultures. The interest here is with how a particular religious text, one of major cultural significance, selects from and uses this basic human endowment. It is, however, equally important to relate such structures to their context of production—that is, in the case of the PT, to the social, cultural, and religious experience of the early Arabs.

5 PROPHETIC METAPHORS: THE SPATIAL SOURCE DOMAINS
5.1 Container metaphors

Containment is a key concept in the tradition of Conceptual Metaphor Theory because of its noticeable presence in ordinary language as an ontological and epistemic image schema. In general, ontological metaphors have an explanatory function by which abstract concepts and intangible entities are conceptualised using physical substances and entities. Target domains, which mainly involve abstract entities, activities, emotional states, notions, and concepts, are represented using a CONTAINER and CONTAINED SUBSTANCE relationship. This analogy facilitates the conceptualisation of abstract concepts in the target domain because it assigns to them tangible qualities from features of the source domain. This process shows how the conceptualisation of events, actions, emotions, and states as entities and substances can be considered a basic conceptual structuring principle of human thinking (Lakoff and Johnson 1980, pp. 25–32).

The conceptual CONTAINER schema is deeply rooted in human thought and experience. Kövecses emphasises that the cognitive function of ontological metaphors (including CONTAINER metaphors) is to give an ontological status to general categories of abstract target concepts (Kövecses 2002, p. 34). These metaphors help language users to visualise (and probably also to 'feel' kinaesthetically) their experiences of using objects or substances that take the shape of a container or a substance

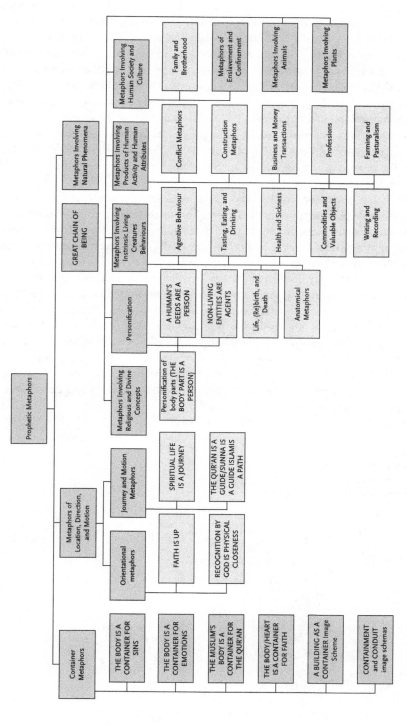

Figure 1 Categories of the major metaphoric source domains in the Prophetic Tradition.

within a container, and their experiences of actually being inside or outside, entering or exiting, various kinds of containing spaces. In most straightforward cases, metaphors from the CONTAINER conceptual domain can be easily recognised by the use of prepositions of location (in/out, inside/outside, into/out of). In most metaphoric expressions involving a CONTAINER metaphor, it is the metaphoric schema of 'containment' which is emphasised rather than the intrinsic qualities of the container or the thing contained. In public discourse, such an image schema makes CONTAINER metaphors used frequently to evoke ideas of membership of a particular group, as is reflected in such expressions as referring to 'in-group' and 'out-group' relationships (Charteris-Black 2004, 2005; Musolff 2003, 2004; Musolff et al. 1996; Rash 2006). The CONTAINER image schema carries a simple structure with it, as indicated in Figure 2.

CONTAINER metaphors in the Prophetic corpus are ubiquitous because of two facts: the ontological functions of these metaphors on the one hand, and the nature of Islamic religious discourse on the other. Islamic religious discourse is rich in abstract religious notions and ideas such as 'faith in One God' and 'obliteration of committed sins', which were not familiar to pre-Islamic Arabs. These notions involve a variety of qualities and attributes which needed to be conveyed to an audience regarded as ignorant. The understanding of such notions can be facilitated by using ontological metaphors which are based on human experiential knowledge. Furthermore, most of these metaphors are still used conventionally in contemporary Arabic language and culture. However, CONTAINER metaphors in the PT show discrepancies in terms of their degree of generality and specificity. Amongst the many metaphors that can be classified under the CONTAINER schema in the Prophetic discourse, I found the generic conceptual metaphor THE BODY IS A CONTAINER is elaborated in a multiplicity of specific-level metaphors, such as the metaphors THE BODY IS A CONTAINER FOR SINS or THE HEART IS THE CONTAINER FOR FAITH.

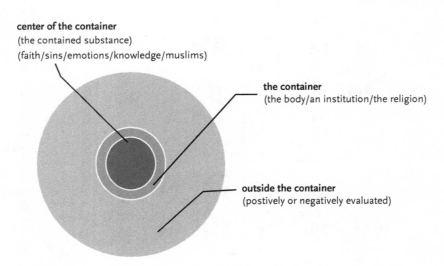

center of the container
(the contained substance)
(faith/sins/emotions/knowledge/muslims)

the container
(the body/an institution/the religion)

outside the container
(postively or negatively evaluated)

Figure 2 The CONTAINER metaphor schema applied to religion

5.1.1 THE BODY IS A CONTAINER FOR SINS

The metaphor THE BODY IS A CONTAINER FOR SINS is prolific in the PT. For example, one of its representations involves depicting sins as POLLUTION that is contained in the human body; the acts of repenting and obliterating sins are represented as an act of CLEANSING. This representation involves the juxtaposition of the metaphors MORALITY IS CLEAN and AMORAL IS DIRTY in the same context. Sins (xatˤaja:) are metaphorised as DIRT or POLLUTION which 'dwell' in the body, and they need to 'come out' (taxruʒa mina) by constant exposure to a cleanser. The Prophet Muhammad[10] says:

1. من توضأ فأحسن الوضوء <u>خرجت</u> <u>خطاياه</u> <u>من جسده</u>، حتى تخرج من <u>تحت أظفاره</u>.

(1) If anyone performs the ablution well, his **sins** {xatˤaja:hu} **will come out** {xaraʒat} from his **body**, even **coming out** {taxruʒa} from **under his nails**. (*Mishkat*, 284, p. 64)

2. إذا توضأ العبد المسلم، أو المؤمن، فغسل وجهه، <u>خرج</u> <u>من وجهه</u> كل <u>خطيئة</u> نظر إليها بعينيه مع الماء مع آخر قطر الماء، فإذا غسل يديه <u>خرجت</u> <u>من يديه</u> كل <u>خطيئة</u> بطشتها يداه مع الماء أو مع آخر قطر الماء، فإذا غسل رجليه <u>خرج كل</u> <u>خطيئة</u> مشتها <u>رجلاه</u> مع الماء أو مع آخر قطر الماء، حتى <u>يخرج نقيا</u> من الذنوب.

(2) When a Muslim, or a believer, washes his face in the course of ablution, every **sin** {xatˤij?a:} he contemplated with his eyes **will come forth from** {xaraʒa mina} his **face** along with the water, or with the last drop of water; when he washes his hands, every **sin** {xatˤij?a:} they wrought **will come forth from** {xaraʒa mina} his **hands** with the water, or with the last drop of water; and when he washes his feet, every **sin** {xatˤij?a:} towards which his **feet** have walked **will come out** {xaraʒa mina} with the water, or with the last drop of water, with the result that he **will come forth pure** {xaraʒa naqejan} from offences. (*Mishkat*, 285, p. 65)

In the two Sayings above, the human body is represented as a CONTAINER FOR SINS. The metaphor is elaborated by implicitly representing each body part as an 'outlet' from which sins leave. The act of performing ablution is metaphorised as a moral cleansing to the body, and the image schema of CONTAINMENT is evoked explicitly by the repetitive use of the keyword 'xaraʒa' (to come forth), which entails the flow of a substance (sins) from a CONTAINER (human body) to a place outside it. Part of the conventionality of this metaphor in Islamic religious discourse can be attributed to its ontological function; whereas 'sins', 'forgiveness', and 'obliteration' are abstract notions, their representation using a CONTAINMENT image schema aims to facilitate recognising the notion of 'forgiveness' for the believers.

5.1.2 THE BODY IS A CONTAINER FOR EMOTIONS

The Prophetic discourse also involves a range of conventional metaphors that conceptualise emotional states in terms of a substance contained in the human body, especially in the heart. Mercy (ar.raħma), for example, is an emotional attribute which is represented as a substance that can be 'tunzaʕu mina' (withdrawn from) the heart. The Prophet blamed a nomadic man for his uncompassionate treatment of his children by saying:

3. أو أملك لك أن نزع الله من قلبك الرحمة؟!.

(3) I cannot help you [to a nomadic Arab] since God **has withdrawn** {nazaʕa} <u>mercy</u> {ar.raħma} **from your heart** {qalbika}!!. (*Mishkat*, 4948, p. 1031)

The image in the Saying above is presented plainly by depicting the heart as the CONTAINER for the emotion of mercy. In addition, the metaphor is elaborated by assigning to God the role of an 'agent' who 'fills' the CONTAINER or makes it empty. This implicit message highlights God's might by which mercy is metaphorised as a 'substance' that is bestowed upon human beings by the will of God.

Additionally, excessive anger {alɣajðʕ} is conventionally metaphorised in ordinary language as a FLUID IN A CONTAINER (Kövecses 2002, 2005; Lakoff and Johnson 1980). In the PT, it is mentioned that a Muslim who finds himself exposed to a situation of excessive anger must 'restrain' (kaðʕama) his anger and 'swallow it back' (taʒaraʕa) when possible. The Prophet incites his follower that:

4.من كظم غيظا وهو يقدر على أن ينفذه دعاه الله على رؤوس الخلائق يوم القيامة حتى يخيره في أي الحور شاء.

(4) If anyone **restrains** {kaðʕama} <u>anger</u> {ɣajðʕan} when he is in a position to give vent to it God will call him on the day of resurrection over the heads of all creatures and let him choose whichever of the bright-eyed maidens he wishes. (*Mishkat*, 5088, p. 1055)

The metaphor of anger as A CONTAINED OBJECT WITHIN THE BODY is presented more specifically by representing the act of restraining anger as an act of preventing a substance, which was initially inside the body, from leaving the body; the act of restraining anger is represented as the act of re-swallowing a fluid substance by means of force (kaðʕama); and since the act of re-swallowing involves pushing the substance back inside of the body, then this substance was initially in the body. This scenario entails the metaphor THE BODY IS A CONTAINER FOR ANGER, a metaphor that is conventionally used in Arabic and in many other languages.

5.1.3 *THE MUSLIM'S BODY IS A CONTAINER FOR THE QURAN*

The CONTAINER metaphoric schema creatively metaphorises the Quran as a contained substance that diffuses a pleasant fragrance. This metaphor incites Muslims to memorise the Quran by heart, to recite it, and to apply it in their everyday life affairs. For example, the Prophet equates memorising the Quran with the act of keeping fragrance in a closed bag made from leather (ʒira:ban maħʃuwan meska). Accordingly, the body (or the heart) is conceptualised as the CONTAINER for the Quran, and the significance of the CONTAINED SUBSTANCE, the Quran, is invoked through the image of fragrance diffusing with reference to the metonymic representation THE FRAGRANCE FOR THE QUALITY OF ITS BEARER. The Prophet says:

5.تعلموا القرآن فاقراوه، فإن مثل القرآن لمن تعلم وقام به كمثل جراب محشو مسكا يفوح ريحه كل مكان. ومثل من تعلمه فرقد وهو في جوفه كمثل جراب أوكئ على مسك.

(5) Learn and recite the Quran {alqurʔaana}, for to <u>one who learns</u>, <u>recites</u> and <u>uses</u> it in prayer at night it is like **a bag filled with musk** {ʒira:ban maħʃuwan meska} whose fragrance **diffuses** {jafu:ħu} itself everywhere; and <u>he who learns it and goes to sleep</u> having it **within him** is like a **bag with musk tied up in it** {ʒira:ban ʔuki?a ʕala: mesk}. (*Mishkat*, 2143, p. 454)

The Saying above elaborates the image of the CONTAINER metaphor to involve fragrance and its scent as a source domain to stand for the qualities of the Muslim who memorises the Quran by heart, recites it, and works within its rules. However, the Prophet emphasises that the significance of the Quran should not be confined to its memorisation and recitation; instead, the Quran must be taught to others. Working with the Quran's teaching resembles the perfume that diffuses (jafu:ħu) its fragrance in the air so everyone enjoys its scent. This reflects the evaluative aspect of metaphors which involve images of FRAGRANCE in their source domains.

5.1.4 THE BODY/HEART IS A CONTAINER FOR FAITH

In Arabic, the heart is purportedly endowed with the cognitive capacities of the mind. For example, the intellect and consciousness, in addition to the experienced combinations of thought, memory, emotions, perception, imagination, desire, and will, and most other unconscious cognitive processes are conventionally attributed to the heart.

The Prophetic discourse, for the most part, conforms to the folklore beliefs of the society where it was first delivered, and its language supports the cultural and traditional linguistic system based on the people's beliefs. Thus, metaphors involving the heart are conventionally used in the Prophetic discourse (as in ordinary language too) to stand for the person's inherent qualities, such as his/her faith, moral values, traits, and attributes. For example, the Prophetic corpus involves sixteen instances of the metonymic representation THE HEART'S CONDITION FOR THE INDIVIDUAL'S FAITH. According to this schema, the heart is represented as a CONTAINER for human spiritual qualities. In most simple cases, this schema can be understood via the use of the preposition 'in' (fi:) to refer to the idea of CONTAINMENT. To illustrate, both faith (ʔi:ma:n) and pride (kebr) are represented in the PT as a contained substance whose presence in the person's heart may allow or prevent him/her from entering paradise. The Prophet declares that:

٦. لا يدخل النار أحد في قلبه مثقال حبة خردل من إيمان. ولا يدخل الجنة أحد في قلبه مثقال حبة من خردل من كبر. . .

(6) He who has **in his heart** {fi qalbehe} as much <u>faith</u> {ʔi:ma:n} as a **grain of mustard seed** {meθqa:la ħabate xardalen} will not enter hell, and he who has **in his heart** {fi qalbehe}as much <u>pride</u> {kebr} as a **grain of mustard seed** will not enter paradise. (*Mishkat*, 5107, p. 1058)

Similarly, as the heart is situated in the body, what is contained in it is essentially in the body too. Faith is represented dwelling in the Muslim's body, and it departs (xaraʒa mina) from the body when the Muslim commits the sin of fornication. The Prophet says:

٧. إذا زنى العبد **خرج منه** <u>الإيمان</u> فكان فوق رأسه **كالظلة**، فإذا خرج من ذلك العمل عاد <u>إليه الإيمان</u>.

(7) When a servant of God commits fornication <u>faith</u> **departs from** {xaraʒa mina} **him** and there is something like an **awning** over his head; but when he quits that action <u>faith</u> **returns to** {ʕa:da elaihe} him. (*Mishkat*, 60, p. 19)

Thus, the metaphor THE HEART IS A CONTAINER FOR FAITH or its generic representation FAITH IS IN THE HEART shows that faith is perceived as a SUBSTANCE that dwells in the heart, an image that can be attributed to the traditional belief that the heart is the centre of cognitive capacities.

5.1.5 A BUILDING IS A CONTAINER

The PT involves many metaphors whose source domains are derived from the conceptual domain of BUILDING and which in turn involve the metaphoric schema of CONTAINMENT. Its constituent image involves a building which has already been completed with its main components such as 'doors' and 'windows'. Generally, these images involve a few metaphoric keywords that entail the metaphor BUILDINGS ARE CONTAINERS, and amongst these metaphoric keywords we find nouns like 'door' (ba:b) or verbs like 'to open' (jaftaħ) and 'to close' (juɣleq). The CONTAINMENT schema in these metaphors is invoked by perceiving that what is inside the 'building' is different and isolated from what is outside. For example, in the PT, some of these metaphors are used to represent Islamic social forms to evoke images of shared aims and being under the protection against a threat. In some instances, these metaphors show the affluence of joining Islam and being affiliated to it. Thus, the metaphors suggest that being in a certain 'building' results in the acquisition of its qualities and the benefit of its provisions. For instance, God's mercy is implicitly represented in the PT as a BUILDING that opens its 'doors' (ʔabwa:b) for those who deserve it. GOD'S MERCY IS A BUILDING is the conceptual mapping which can be observed in the following Sayings:

٨. إذا دخل أحدكم المسجد فليقل: اللهم افتح لي أبواب رحمتك.

(8) When any of you enters the mosque he should say, 'O God, **open** to me **the gates** {ʔabwa:ba} of <u>Thy mercy</u> {raħmatek}.' (*Mishkat*, 703, p. 143)

٩. من ولي من أمر الناس شيئا ثم أغلق بابه دون المسلمين أو المظلوم أو ذي الحاجة أغلق الله دونه أبواب رحمته عند حاجته.

(9) If one who has been given any authority over the people locks his gate against Muslims, or one who has been wronged, or one who has a need, God **will lock the gates** {ʔylaqa allahu du:nahu ʔabwa:ba} of <u>His mercy</u> {raħmatehe} against him when he has a need. (*Mishkat*, 3729, p. 792)

In addition, poverty (faqr) and begging (suʔa:l) are among the notions which are represented using the BUILDING AS A CONTAINER metaphor. For example, the two notions are represented as BUILDINGS whose doors are (and must remain) closed. Here, the keywords 'open' (fataħa) and 'door' (ba:b) collectively map the conceptual metaphors BEGGING IS A BUILDING and POVERTY IS A BUILDING in the following Saying:

١٠ . . . . . ولا فتح عبد باب مسألة إلا فتح الله عليه باب فقر

(10) when a man opens **a door** {ba:b} towards <u>begging</u> {masaʔalaten} God **opens** {fataħa} for him **a door** {ba:b} towards <u>poverty</u> {faqr}. (*Mishkat*, 5287, p. 1095)

The metaphor of BUILDING AS A CONTAINER in Saying 10 above negatively represents 'poverty' (alfaqr) and what it may bring. However, the intrinsic nature and qualities of this CONTAINER are not explicitly mentioned in the Saying except that it has 'doors' (ba:b) which can be 'opened' (fataħa). This makes us infer that the container in the Saying above is more likely to be a building.

The PT involves many other instances of metaphors whose source domains involve the schema of BUILDING and which evoke the CONTAINMENT schemas. For example, the Prophet sees that good is contained within a BUILDING or a CONTAINER that has GATEWAYS (ʔbwa:ba) which can be opened through the correct religious practices (*Mishkat*, 29, p. 11). On the other hand, the Prophet represents evil deeds as a substance that is kept, or contained, within a firm CONTAINER, or a BUILDING, that could be opened (taftaħ) when the Muslim expresses his dissatisfaction and rejection of his fate by uttering the expression 'If I had done such and such, such and such would have happened' (*Mishkat*, 5298, p. 1098). Furthermore, usury, which is severely prohibited in Islam, is represented as a BUILDING which should not be approached by accepting a present for interceding for someone. The Prophet warns that if anyone intercedes for someone and that one gives him for it a present which he accepts, he has just passed through a great GATE of usury (*Mishkat*, 3757, p. 799).[11] In other Sayings, the Prophet represents marriage as a CONTAINER, more precisely a 'bowl' (sˤaħfa) where he (the Prophet) warns the woman against trying to ruin another married woman's life by taking her husband for herself; he says 'A woman must not ask to have her sister divorced [Original Arabic 'should not ask to empty her sister's bowl']' (*Mishkat*, 3145, p. 668). In another image, the Prophet metaphorises all sort of evils as being preserved in a box whose 'key' (mefta:ħ) is wine (*Mishkat*, 580, p. 117), in which we have the conceptual metaphors WINE IS A KEY FOR EVIL and EVIL IS A CONTAINED SUBSTANCE. Additionally, one's belly is depicted as a CONTAINER OR A VESSEL (weʕa:ʔ) and that man has never filled any vessel (with food) worse than it (*Mishkat*, 5192, p. 1077).

5.1.6 CONTAINMENT and CONDUIT image schemas

In another respect, CONTAINER image schemas reflect other relevant metaphoric schemas that conceptualise the interaction and transmission of ideas between humans. Conventionally, these metaphors, called the CONDUIT metaphors, conceptualise the exchange of ideas in terms of the transmission (or travelling) of a substance along a conduit as shown by expression 'his message came across' (Kövecses 2002, p. 74). The metaphorical image schema of any CONDUIT metaphor suggests that our language, and knowledge, describes a variety of abstract ideas, such as a theory, language, religious belief, or a piece of knowledge and information in terms of a substance. These ideas are structured using images such as THE MIND IS A CONTAINER, and IDEAS (OR MEANINGS) ARE (TRANSFERABLE) OBJECTS/SUBSTANCES, and COMMUNICATION IS SENDING (Kövecses 2002, p. 74). Consequently, the CONDUIT schema can be used to describe human verbal interaction; a speaker puts his ideas (objects/substance) into words (containers) and transmits them by a mutually understandable linguistic system (along a conduit) to a listener or reader (bearer) who in turn takes the idea (objects/substance) out of the word (containers). Generally, the source domains of these metaphors can be identified from the relevant processes (the verbs) in the expression. For example, in the expression 'his message came across' the conduit metaphor is implicitly deduced through the verb 'came across'.

CONDUIT metaphors occur on a large scale in the PT, and this can be attributed to their ontological and structural function in ordinary language. In the most straightforward cases of these metaphors, a range of abstract concepts, moral values, and attributes are defined and represented in the PT as substances that can be carried, given, and dropped. For example, 'faith' is an abstract religious concept that is conventionally conceptualised in religious discourse using conduit metaphors. Thus, 'faith' can be 'acquired', 'kept' or 'preserved', and 'bestowed upon', and in some cases it is represented as a 'transferable' and 'measurable' object as well. For example, 'faith' is represented metaphorically by using the conceptual mappings FAITH IS A SUBSTANCE THAT IS CONTAINED IN THE BODY and FAITH IS IN THE HEART. The combination of the two preceding metaphors entails the metaphor FAITH IS A TRANSFERABLE OBJECT, in addition to the predominant metaphor. The Prophet says:

11. يا معشر من أسلم بلسانه **ولم يفض الإيمان** إلى قلبه لا تؤذوا المسلمين، ولا تعيروهم، ولا تتبعوا عوراتهم

(11) You who have accepted Islam with your tongues but whose **heart** {qalbehe} **have not been reached by** {lam jafedʕ} <u>faith</u> {alʔi:ma:nu}, do not annoy the Muslims, or revile them, or seek out their faults . . . (*Mishkat*, 5044, p. 1047)

In Saying 11 above, the schema of transference is evoked through the metaphoric keyword 'reached by' (jafedˤu ela:) which literally means in Arabic 'to infuse' or 'to pour' a liquid substance into a container. This metaphorical representation carries the message that faith can be acquired and transferred from one place to another, namely, the believer's heart.

Knowledge is conventionally conceptualised using CONDUIT metaphors. Religious knowledge of Islamic principles and jurisprudence (ʃari:ʕa) is represented as an object that can be 'acquired', 'preserved, and 'given'; it is also represented as a 'transferable' and 'bearable' substance. So, the believers' mission is to deliver (ʔada:) it to the following generations. The Prophet says:

12. نضر الله عبدا سمع مقالتي فحفظها ووعاها وأداها، فرب حامل فقه غير فقيه، ورب حامل فقه إلى من هو أفقه منه

(12) God brighten [sic] a man who hears <u>what I say</u> {maqa:lati}, **gets it by heart**, **retains** {faħafeðˤaha:} it, and ***passes it on*** {ʔadaha:} to others! Many a **bearer of** {ħa:mele} <u>knowledge</u> {fiqh} is not versed in it, and many a **bearer of** {ħa:mele} <u>knowledge</u> {fiqh} conveys it to one who is more versed than he is. (*Mishkat*, 228, p. 55)

Sayings 11 and 12 above show CONTAINER metaphors serving an ontological function where the metaphors are used to give shape to abstract concepts and even contribute to the structure of concrete elements derived from the experiential knowledge of everyday life. The Prophet Muhammad, naturally, refers to these metaphors in order to facilitate the conceptualisation and understanding of the 'abstraction' that characterises religious discourse.

To conclude, all the above-mentioned Sayings and their metaphors show that CONTAINER image schemas are so basic to the Prophetic discourse that the discourse's recipient may hardly pay attention to these metaphors. However, in the cases where novel CONTAINER metaphors are employed creatively, it is clear that the Prophetic discourse encapsulates evaluative information implied from the Saying. This fact can be perceived by the metaphoric representation FAITH IS IN THE HEART. The centrality of the heart and its alleged conventional representation as the organ responsible for cognitive capacities suggests that 'faith' is central to the spiritual life of the believer as long as it remains within the believer's body; the quality of the container is recognised, to great extent, by the quality of the substance it contains; but when 'faith' leaves its container, then the quality of the container depreciates.

5.2 Metaphors of location, direction, and motion

Experiential and cultural knowledge helps the human cognitive system in conceptualising and transmitting ideas and thoughts by using metaphoric expressions which denote ideas with related to space and direction. These metaphors produce abstract concepts and notions with reference to a horizontal or vertical position that either moves or remains still relative to self, or in which self moves or is positioned. Kövecses notes that metaphors of location, direction, and movement serve a 'structural' cognitive function because their source domains provide a relatively rich knowledge structure for the target concept at hand (Kövecses 2002, p. 33). The PT employs a large number of such spatial metaphors, grounded as they are in human cognitive-motor systems concerning location, direction, and motion. The most striking aspect of these spatially grounded metaphors is their evaluative function: the different spatial concepts carry different evaluation associations, as outlined in Figure 3. In the following subsections, I present the different instantiations of this group of metaphors in the Prophetic corpus.

5.2.1 Orientational metaphors

Lakoff and Johnson argue that orientational or spatial metaphors such as GOOD IS UP and its opposite image BAD IS DOWN can be found at the most basic level of our human metaphoric conceptualisation (Lakoff and Johnson 1980, pp. 14–21). Many metaphors from this domain coincide with metaphors of MOVEMENT. In religious discourse, upward orientation tends to coincide with positive evaluation, and downward orientation with a negative one (Kövecses 2002, p. 36). For example, moral values and attributes are commonly represented in the PT using orientational relationships such as UP IS GOOD, DOWN IS BAD and NEAR TO GOD IS GOOD, FAR FROM GOD IS BAD, IMPROVEMENT IS UPWARD MOTION, and DETERIORATION IS DOWNWARD MOTION.

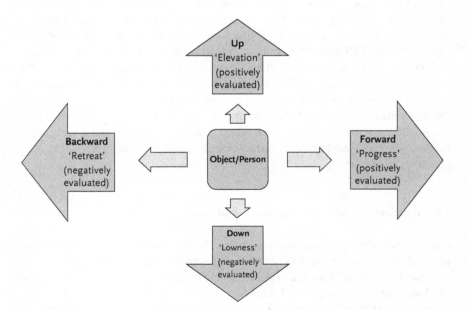

Figure 3 The conceptual schema of metaphors of location, direction, and motion.

It is argued that humans' attitude to show preference for UP metaphors over DOWN ones is culturally motivated in languages and societies which have a certain kind of social structure and organisation (Kövecses 2005, p. 262). In the case of Arabic and Islamic culture, this appreciation of upward positions coincides with the structural organisation of Arabic societies. For example, the head (raʔs) is always used to represent good qualities and high social status. Thus, we have the notion 'raʔs alʔamr' (the most important issue), 'raʔsul lqabila' (head of the tribe), and 'marfuːʕa alraʔs' (has the head always up, brave). From another perspective, the appreciation of upward positions can be attributed to the traditional belief that Heaven, with its pleasures, exists somewhere in the sky. On the other hand, the appreciation of down metaphor can be attributed to its association with the ideas 'ground', 'earth', and 'dirt'. One can also postulate that it is attributed to the concept of 'Hell' that is conventionally represented located in a lower place, as in the 'under-world'.

In Islamic religious discourse, and the PT in particular, favourable behaviours, traits, and attributes are assigned a high position. The appearance of metaphoric keywords such as 'raise' (jarfaʕ), 'exalt' (fadˤ.dˤʕalla), and high 'degree' (literally 'step') (daraʒa) with reference to the spiritual status of the individual invokes a religious moral message where the spiritual progress, achieved in the worldly life by the individual, will be rewarded by God. This reward consists of raising the believer's status up to a position near God and Paradise. In other words, a believer's spiritual improvement is metaphorised using the metaphor SPIRITUAL IMPROVEMENT IS MOTION UPWARD; a combination of the two metaphors FAITH IS UP and IMPORTANCE IS UP. This can be applied to many human deeds too where a good deed is the one that 'raises' the believer's status. For example, the Prophet urges his followers that human deeds in the worldly life are classified in a vertical hierarchy in terms of their goodness. He says:

.13 الإيمان بضع وسبعون شعبة: فأفضلها قول لا إله إلا الله، وأدناها إماطة الأذى عن الطريق.

(13) <u>Faith</u> {alʔiːmaːn} has over seventy branches, the **most excellent** [Original Arabic *'most exalted'*] {faʔafdˤaluha:} of which is <u>the declaration that there is no god but God</u>, and **the humblest** [Original Arabic *'lowest'*] {ʔadna:ha:} of which is <u>the removal of what is injurious from the road</u>. (*Mishkat*, 5, p. 6)

In Saying 13 above, 'faith' is represented using a hierarchical order where its most exalted (ʔafdˤal) sort of faith consists of the Muslim's confession that God is the only and absolute god. The image is more explicitly invoked by the contrast drawn from the metaphoric keyword 'humblest' (Original Arabic 'lowest') (ʔadna:), which is based on the metaphor TRIVIAL IS DOWN entailed from the more generic metaphor LOW IS BAD. Thus, the status of faith and the 'degree' (the rank) in Heaven which a believer will be rewarded are evoked in terms of a process of a gradual elevation within the hierarchy of both religion and Heaven. The metaphoric representation

SPIRITUAL IMPROVEMENT IS MOTION UPWARD is understood by the use of verbs and prepositions of motion. For example, the Prophet says:

14. ذلك أنه إذا توضأ فأحسن الوضوء ثم خرج إلى المسجد، لا يخرجه إلا الصلاة، لم يخط خطوة إلا **رفعت** له بها **درجة**، **وحط** عنه بها خطيئة . . .

(14) for when he [a man] performs ablution, doing it well, then goes out to the mosque, having no other reason than prayer for going out, he does not take a step without being **raised a degree** {rufeʕat lahu beha: daraʒa} for it and having a sin **remitted** {hutˤ.tˤa} for it. (*Mishkat*, 702, p. 143)

15.إن الله **يرفع** بهذا الكتاب أقواما **ويضع** به آخرين.

(15) By this Book [the Quran] God **exalts** {jarfaʕu} some peoples and **lowers** {jadˤaʕu} others. (*Mishkat*, 3685, p. 784)

For everyday practices, the Prophet emphasises in many Sayings the superiority, or the 'excellence', of having work over the act of begging. The Prophet compares a hand that can give alms and another hand that only takes alms by means of an orientational metaphor. The Prophet Muhammad says:

16. <u>اليد العليا</u> خير من <u>اليد السفلى</u>، واليد العليا هي <u>المنفقة</u>، واليد السفلى هي <u>السائلة</u>.

(16) The **upper** <u>hand</u> {aljadu alʕulja:} is better than the **lower** <u>one</u> {aljade alsufla:}, the upper being <u>the one which bestows</u> and the lower <u>the one which begs</u>. (*Mishkat*, 1843, p. 390)

In Sayings 14, 15, and 16 above, orientational metaphors evoke an evaluative judgement that is invoked by the constant use of the metaphors SPIRITUAL IMPROVEMENT IS MOTION UPWARD and IMPORTANCE IS UP/TRIVIAL IS DOWN, understood through the processes 'to raise a degree' (rufeʕa), 'to remit' (hutˤ.tˤa), 'to exalt' (jarfaʕu), 'to lower' (jadˤaʕu), and the adjectives 'upper' (alʕulja:) and 'lower' (alsufla:). This evaluative function is implicitly understood in Saying 16 where the hand that works and does not ask for alms is represented positively as an 'upper' hand. In this case, the hand, which metonymically stands for its bearer and stands also for labouring, is represented metaphorically as a reflection of the person's spiritual status. Furthermore, the metonym can be perceived as an illustration of the actual position of the hand in real-life experience where the position of a bestowing hand is generally spatially above a begging one.

5.2.1.2 RECOGNITION BY GOD IS PHYSICAL CLOSENESS

In addition to the UP/DOWN image schema, orientational metaphors and metaphors of LOCATION and MOTION in the PT sometimes represent the target domain with reference to a metaphorical spiritual and moral relationship with (the location of) God.

For example, people are represented in terms of their NEARNESS to and DISTANCE from God. The person who performs righteous deeds will be rewarded and brought spiritually 'nearer' to God. Thus, a person can be either NEAR to God or FAR from God according to the degree of his/her faith and the righteousness of his/her conduct, and this entails the metaphor RECOGNITION BY GOD IS PHYSICAL CLOSENESS. This metaphor emphasises that good deeds such as engaging in 'holy war' (dʒiha:d), performing ablution, praying on time, ruling justly, and mentioning God in prayers are highly esteemed in Islam. Muslims will be significantly rewarded on the Day of Resurrection by exalting their 'degree' (or rank) in Heaven NEAR to God. On the other hand, bad deeds and conduct cause the decline of the person's spiritual degree to position FAR from God and God's mercy. The Prophet says:

17.إن أحب الناس إلى الله يوم القيامة وأقربهم منه مجلسا إمام عادل... .، وأبعدهم منه مجلسا إمام جائر.

(17) The one who will be dearest to God and **nearest** {ʔaqrabuhum} **to Him** in station on the day of resurrection will be <u>a just imam</u> [ruler] {ʔima:mun ʕa:del}, ... and the one who will be **farthest** {ʔabʕaduhum} **from Him** in station will be <u>a tyrannical imam</u> {ʔema:mun ʒa:ʔer}. (*Mishkat*, 3704, p. 787)

18.لا تكثروا الكلام بغير ذكر الله، فإن كثرة الكلام بغير ذكر الله قسوة للقلب، وإن **أبعد** الناس من الله <u>القلب القاسي</u>.

(18) Do not speak much without mentioning God, for much talk without mention of God produces hardness of the heart, and the one who is **farthest** {ʔabʕada} **from God** is <u>he who has a hard heart</u> {alqalbu alqa:si}. (*Mishkat*, 2276, p. 480)

In Sayings 17 and 18 above, the metaphor of being close to God or far from him are evoked by the use of the adjectives 'nearest to' (ʔaqrabu) and 'far from' (ʔabʕadu). Like other metaphors which involve an upward orientation, these metaphors evoke an evaluative judgement by which the one who is near to God is positively evaluated, and this is explicitly invoked by the association between being seated 'near to' (qari:b) God on the Day of Resurrection and being 'dearest to' (ʔaħab.bu) God in Saying 17 above, which in turn conforms to the conventional metaphor NEAR IS GOOD.

5.2.2 Journey and motion metaphors

Metaphors of JOURNEYS and MOTION are commonly used in language and discourse to represent the idea of improvement and progress in social, political, or religious practices. The experiential bases of the metaphors from the domains of JOURNEYS and MOTION are characterised by the identification of a 'path', a point of departure, source(s) or means of movement, the path traversed, and the destination or goal, and most essentially, the travellers themselves (Kövecses 2002, p. 31). The cultural basis of this metaphorical domain can be reformulated as a mapping in which A PURPOSEFUL ACTIVITY is conceptualised as A PROCESS OF TRAVELLING ALONG A PATH TOWARDS A DESTINATION (Lakoff 1993). Charteris-Black argues that the rhetorical purpose of JOURNEY metaphors is to create solidarity so that positively evaluated purposes may be successfully attained (Charteris-Black 2005, p. 46). In addition, he finds that this extended version of the JOURNEY metaphor is preferable for analysing JOURNEY metaphors in political and religious discourses because the use of 'verbs of motion' indicates movement and the use of 'destination' indicates goal-orientation (Charteris-Black 2004, p. 74).

In the PT, different conventional and novel metaphors from the JOURNEY domain are employed to describe the religious life of people in terms of life's journey. These metaphors mostly draw attention to the fact that people have the freedom to choose the path of their religious life, but they must accept the consequences of their choices.

5.2.2.1 SPIRITUAL LIFE IS A JOURNEY

The PT repeatedly refers to the spiritual life of the individual in terms of a journey along a path. Generally, it is the idea of the path and its clarity and straightforward-ness which these metaphors highlight. In addition, the image of the destination in the metaphors SPIRITUAL LIFE IS A JOURNEY and ISLAM IS A PATH is creatively drawn in different Sayings in the PT within the conventional schema LIFE IS A JOURNEY. For example, the Prophet emphasises that the comparison of temporary worldly life to eternal future life is like a 'stranger' (ɣari:b) or a TRAVELLER 'passing through' (ʕa:beru sabi:l) who stops in a place temporarily before continuing his journey. The Prophet says:

19. كن في الدنيا كأنك غريب أو عابر سبيل.

(19) Be in the world as though you were a **stranger** {ɣarib} or one who is **passing through** {ʕa:beru sabi:l}. (*Mishkat*, 1604, p. 334)

In addition, many Sayings involve metaphors which represent the individual's spiritual life as a JOURNEY towards attaining God's forgiveness. For example, the Prophet represents the believer who is anxious about God's punishment and aspiring to God's forgiveness as a WAYFARER who does not sleep or who sets out at nightfall in order to reach his destination hastily and unharmed. Here, the Prophet elaborates the image by saying that a traveller who is afraid of a long journey must not sleep before arriving at his destination. The image follows the metaphor of the Muslim as A WAYFARER who does not set out at nightfall. The Prophet says:

20. من خاف أدلج، ومن أدلج بلغ المنزل

(20) He who fears **sets out at nightfall** {ʔdlaʒa}, and he who sets out at nightfall **reaches** {balaɣa} the **destination** {almanzel} (*Mishkat*, 5348, p. 1110)

In many other Sayings, the path which the believers have to follow is represented by the conceptual metaphor ISLAM IS A PATH, including other factors (such as people) who take the role of the GUIDES for the TRAVELLERS along the PATH. On the other hand, other factors may play the role of 'agents' who may lead the TRAVELLERS astray. For example, the Prophet draws a detailed metaphoric scenario in a parable in which the religious life of the individual is represented using a JOURNEY with its different metaphoric components. He says:

21.ضرب الله مثلا **صراطا مستقيما**، وعن جنبتي الصراط **سوران** فيهما **أبواب** مفتحة، وعلى الأبواب **ستور** مرخاة، وعند رأس الصراط **داع** يقول: **استقيموا على الصراط** ولا **تعوجوا**! وفوق ذلك داع يدعو كلما هم عبد أن يفتح شيئا من تلك الأبواب. . .

(21) God has propounded as a parable a **straight path** { sˁeraːtˁan mustaqiman} on the sides, of which are **walls** {suraːn} with open **doors** {ʔabwaːb} over which **curtains** {sutuːr} are hanging down. At the top of the path there is **one who calls** {daːˁen}, '**Go straight on the path** and do not **follow an irregular course**.' Above that one is another who calls out as often as anyone tries to open any of those doors . . . (*Mishkat*, 191, p. 48)

Saying 21 above represents a detailed scenario of the metaphor SPIRITUAL LIFE IS A JOURNEY which is conventionally used in the PT, and it provides a detailed account for the metaphor ISLAM IS A PATH, THE QURAN IS A GUIDE, FORBIDDEN DEEDS ARE DOORS, GOD'S LIMITS ARE CURTAINS, and THE HEART IS A GUIDE. Remarkably, metaphors are interpreted by the Prophet as he explains their different source and target domains. The Prophet continues:

· وفوق ذلك داع يدعو كلما هم عبد أن يفتح شيئا من تلك الأبواب قال: "ويحك لا تفتحه فإنك إن تفتحه تلجه ". ثم فسره فأخبر: " أن **الصراط** هو **الإسلام** وأن **الأبواب المفتحة** <u>محارم الله</u> وأن **الستور المرخاة** <u>حدود الله</u> وأن **الداعي على** رأس الصراط هو **القرآن** وأن **الداعي من** فوقه <u>واعظ الله</u> في قلب كل مؤمن".

'. . . calls out as often as anyone tries to open any of those doors: "Woe to you! do not open it, for if you open it you will go through It."' He then interpreted it telling that the **path** is <u>Islam</u>, **the open doors** are the <u>things God has forbidden</u>, **the curtains hanging down** are the <u>limits God has set</u>, **the crier at the top of the path** is the <u>Quran</u>, and the <u>one</u> above him is **God's monitor** in every believer's heart. (*Mishkat*, 191, p. 48)

In many other cases, the Prophetic discourse represents people as keen to 'follow' (*jatbaˁ*) the beliefs of their ancestors even if their ancestors were wrong. This metaphoric representation can be perceived from the combination of the metaphors SPIRITUAL LIFE IS A JOURNEY and ISLAM IS A PATH. The Prophet says:

22. من **دعا** إلى **هدى** كان له من الأجر مثل أجور من **تبعه**، لا ينقص ذلك من أجورهم شيئا. ومن **دعا** إلى **ضلالة** كان عليه من الإثم مثل آثام من **تبعه**، لا ينقص ذلك من آثامهم شيئا.

(22) If anyone **summons** {daˁaː} others to follow right **guidance** {hudaː} his reward will be equivalent to those of the people who **follow** {tabeˁahu} him without their rewards being diminished in any respect on that account; and if anyone summons others to **follow error** {dˁalaːla} the sin of which he is guilty will be equivalent to

those of the people who **follow** {tabeʕahu} him without their sins being diminished in any respect on that account. (*Mishkat*, 158, p. 42)

In Saying 22 above, the metaphor suggests a SPIRITUAL JOURNEY that involves the Prophet's divine message as the PATH and people as the TRAVELLERS who pass through along a well-designated path. The Saying implicitly highlights that God is the GUIDE who has provided the necessary 'guidance' (hedaja:) to all his people, but it is the task of people, mainly the believers, to guide the unbelievers to this sound path. The idea of 'following' and 'guiding' may implicitly refer to the privilege of precedence in joining Islam, some TRAVELLERS have preceded others, and those who come later shall 'be guided' and 'follow the tracks' of those who have preceded them.

5.2.2.2 THE QURAN IS A GUIDE/SUNNA IS A GUIDE/ISLAM IS A PATH

In most Sayings which involve the metaphor SPIRITUAL LIFE IS A JOURNEY and its elaborated image ISLAM IS A PATH in the PT, the Prophet emphasises that for this journey one requires a trustworthy guide or map: that is the Holy Quran and the *Hadith* (the Prophetic Tradition or *Sunna*). These two GUIDES provide the essential information that directs the TRAVELLER, the Muslim, to the sound destination, which is the attainment of God's forgiveness and the entering into Paradise. The Prophet says:

23. وقد تركت فيكم ما لن **تضلوا** بعده إن اعتصمتم به <u>كتاب الله</u> . . .

(23) . . . I have left among you something, i.e. <u>God's Book</u> {ketaba allah}, by which, if you hold to it, you **will never again go astray** {lan tadˤellu} . . . (*Mishkat*, 2555, p. 546)

24. أما بعد، فإن خير الحديث كتاب الله، **وخير الهدي** هدي <u>محمد</u>، وشر الأمور محدثاتها، وكل <u>بدعة</u> **ضلالة**.

(24) To proceed: the best discourse is God's Book, the **best guidance** {xaira alhadi} is that <u>given by Muhammad</u> {hadju muhammad}, and the worst things are those which are novelties. . . . Every <u>innovation</u> {bedˤaten} is **error** {dˤalala} (that **leads astray**). (*Mishkat*, 141, p.39)

Sayings 23 and 24 above explicitly refer to the idea that the path which a Muslim has to follow must be based on the principles of the Quran and Prophet's commandments. The metaphor is reflected by the idea that failure to follow these two 'guides' may cause the person to 'go astray' (tadˤellu) and deviates from the designated 'path'. This path is the one that keeps the believers safe from committing sinful deeds that can bring God's anger and afflict their societies with God's punishment.

In another respect, metaphors from the domains of the JOURNEY and MOTION are used in the Prophetic discourse to describe the quest for knowledge. For example, the Prophet illustrates in a (complex) image how important it is to seek knowledge, and he accentuates how the quest for knowledge is considered a good deed that deserves reward. The Prophet says:

٢٥. ومن **سلك طريقا** يلتمس فيه <u>علما</u> سهل الله له به **طريقا إلى الجنة**. . . ومن **بطأ به عمله لم يسرع به** <u>نسبه</u>.

(25) If anyone **pursues** {salaka} a **path** {tˤariːqan} in search of <u>knowledge</u> {ʕelman}, God will thereby make easy for him a **path** to paradise. But he who is **made slow** {batˤ.tˤaʔa} by his <u>actions</u> {ʕamaluh} **will not be speeded** {jusreʕ} by his <u>genealogy</u> {nasabuh}. (*Mishkat*, 204, p. 50)

Although the message of the Saying above can be interpreted literally, the metaphorical interpretation of the Saying cannot be ignored. The interpretation of the Saying is based on assigning a variety of mappings from the domain of JOURNEY and MOVEMENT in the sort of THE QUEST FOR KNOWLEDGE IS A JOURNEY, HUMAN DEEDS ARE A VEHICLE, and GENEALOGY IS A VEHICLE. Seeking any sort of knowledge is thus represented as a purposeful activity which can be represented in reference to the conceptual metaphor PURPOSES ARE DESTINATIONS.

In another example of the JOURNEY and MOTION domains, the Prophet makes it clear that he lives an unpretentious style of life because he sees himself as a mere RIDER (raːkeb) who shades (ʔestaðˤalla) himself under a tree, then goes off and leaves it (*Mishkat*, 5188, p. 1077). In addition, the Prophet urged Muadh, one of his followers, to accept being a judge on his behalf and that God will GUIDE his heart and keep his tongue true (*Mishkat*, 3738, p. 794). In another Saying, he represents the progress of Islamic society and its compliance to God's orders as a SHIP which has Muslims as its CREW and PASSENGERS (*Mishkat*, 5138, p. 1065).

The previous illustrations show that orientational metaphors and those from the domains of JOURNEY and MOTION vary considerably within the framework of Islamic religious discourse. For instance, it is clear that their instantiations vary in terms of their conventionality and novelty. While images of 'following' and 'guiding' frequently appear in the corpus as a reflection of their conventional use in everyday language, many other metaphors sound more 'discourse-specific'. These latter metaphors are easily recognisable by the discourse recipient(s). Thus, we see metaphors evoked by keywords intrinsically reflect the ideas 'spiritual progress and improvement' within the domains of JOURNEY and MOTION with respect to Islamic discourse such as 'guidance' (hedaja), 'leading astray' (dˤalala), 'path' (sˤeraːtˤ), 'to set free' (juʕteq), 'prison' (seʒn), and 'slave' (ʕabd). Metaphors of JOURNEY and MOTION also have an evaluative function in the Prophetic discourse. The Prophet outlines two kinds of people in his metaphors from the domains of JOURNEY and MOTION: those who follow the guidance of God and hold fast to the straight path of Islam and those who are led astray and deviate from the path. The evaluation is invoked through the juxtaposition between the qualities of the two paths on the one hand and the qualities of the travellers on the other. This relationship appears repeatedly in the Prophetic discourse.

6 CONCLUSION

In this chapter I have surveyed the major conceptual metaphorical source domains in the PT and their mappings with reference to CMT. It is clear that the Prophetic discourse makes great use of metaphors whose source domains vary considerably. I have put forward a way of classifying these metaphors, in particular spatial domains, but it should be noted that many instances of metaphor show overlap between different source domains.

The majority of the Prophetic metaphors in the corpus are common and this can be attributed to the ontological (explaining the nature of being, becoming, existence, or reality) and structural functions of most of the Prophetic metaphors. Since Islamic religious discourse is packed with abstract notions, metaphorical language naturally occurs as a means of conceptualising and facilitating the understanding of such religious abstraction (Soskice 1985, p. 112). The Prophetic metaphors show considerable discrepancy in terms of their degree of generality and specificity: many metaphoric schemas are generic in their mapping on the one hand (e.g. FAITH IS IN THE HEART; SPIRITUAL LIFE IS A JOURNEY; PEOPLE ARE SERVANTS/SLAVES OF GOD), and a large number of metaphors are very specific in their mapping (e.g. TALKING UNJUSTLY AGAINST A MUSLIM'S HONOUR IS USURY; PEOPLE ARE THE BEARERS OF KNOWLEDGE; QURAN RECITATION IS DIFFUSION OF FRAGRANCE) on the other.

With regard to their evaluative function, the Prophetic metaphors conform to the conventional belief systems of early Arabs who lived at the time of the Prophet. The discursive functions of the Prophetic metaphors, it may be surmised, depend on how the discourse recipients responded to a particular image; while positively evaluated metaphors evoke encouraging messages, negatively evaluated metaphors work on evoking a message of implicit threat to the discourse recipient. Some Sayings use the two evaluations within the same Saying, giving the discourse recipient the opportunity to compare the two metaphors and their implications. The Prophetic metaphors also vary considerably in terms of the target domains they involve. The variation in target domains suggests a comprehensive strategy so that all aspects of Islamic religious discourse can be delivered. Thus, the messages of unity, solidarity, brotherhood in Islam, the mutual relationship between the believers, and the association between people and their deeds all constitute target domains for the Prophetic metaphors.

NOTES

1. Metaphors involving the notion of 'light' have been a common motif for early Arabic and Islamic philosophy. This motif has augmented the philosophical debates about the nature of God in Islam and its 'transience' and 'emanation'. For a detailed account of the topic, see Netton (1989).
2. The author uses IPA symbols in transcribing Arabic words.
3. The notions 'the Prophetic Tradition' and Hadith and Sunna will be used interchangeably in this research; the three notions refer to the same text.

4. The 'Companions' were the disciples, scribes, and family of the Prophet Muhammad, and who lived during his life and saw him.
5. In early Arabic culture, those who studied the science of the *Hadith* were known as the 'Traditionists' (*muḥad.deθi:n*) (Bearman et al. 1960–2005, Vol. 7: 'MuHaddeth').
6. A Microsoft Word document can be downloaded online from *Meshkat Islamic Network* for Arabic digital books (www.almeshkat.net/books/open.php?cat=8&book=1762).
7. *Mishkat Al-Masabih* is considered to be one of the most authentic secondary collections of *Hadith*. However, it is not a 'primary source book' like Al-Bukhari or Muslim's Collections because it was intended as a revision and improvement to '*Masˤa:biḥ Al-Sunnah*' of Al-Baghawi. This latter's book (Al-Baghawi's) contained about 4,500 Sayings, over half of which were collected from the Al-Bukhari and Muslim's Collections of Sound Tradition. However, Al-Baghawi tried to classify most of his Sayings according to his knowledge, and he did not include the full *isnad* (chain of narrators) for the Sayings; thus it was difficult to know their exact reliability. Later, Al-Tabrizi added an additional 1,500 Sayings in his *Mishkat* and re-classified some others. He made some additions to the earlier work and most importantly, he made an effort to list the source of the Sayings which were left out in *Masˤa:biḥ Al-Sunnah*. In recent times, Sheikh Naser Aldin Al-Albaani meticulously investigated the collection, researched and reproduced its sources and authenticity wherever it is needed, and corrected many of what he perceived as deficiencies in the book.
8. The Pragglejaz Group (2007) is a group of researchers whose focus is on the study of metaphor in everyday language use. The acronym Pragglejaz derives from the first letter of the first names of the ten original members of the group: Peter Crisp (Chinese University of Hong Kong), Ray Gibbs (University of California, Santa Cruz), Alan Cienki (Vrije Universiteit, Amsterdam), Graham Low (University of York, England), Gerard Steen (Vrije Universiteit, Amsterdam), Lynne Cameron (the Open University, England), Elena Semino (Lancaster University, England), Joseph Grady (University of California, Berkeley), Alice Deignan (University of Leeds, England), and Zoltan Kövecses (Eötvös Loránd University, Hungary).
9. See also Lakoff and Turner (1989) and Lakoff and Johnson (1999), and it has been applied by many researchers in the field (Charteris-Black 2004, 2005; Deignan, 2003; Jäkel, 2002; Lundmark 2005; Musolff 2001, 2003, 2004; Rash 2006)
10. For purposes of elucidation, metaphoric keywords from the source domain are represented in bold and their Arabic transliteration are represented in *italic* between two curly brackets and quotation marks{*xxx*}, whereas elements from the target domain are represented underlined.
11. The provided English translation says 'If anyone intercedes for someone and that one gives him for it a present which he accepts, he has been guilty of a serious *type* [my italicisation] of usury' (Robson 1963, p. 799).

REFERENCES

Abbott, N. (1967). *Quranic Commentary and Tradition*. Chicago: University of Chicago Press.

Al-Ghazali, A. H. (1904). *kitab al-mustasˤfa min ʕelm al-usˤul*. Cairo: al-matbaʕah al-amirijah.

Al-Rummani, A. b. I. (1968). *al-Nakt fi iʕ ʒa:z al-Quran*. Cairo: dar al-Maʕrifa.

QuranAmin, A. (1975). *faʒru al-Islam*, 11th ed. Beirut: Dar alKetab alʕrabi.

Askari, A.-H. i.-A. (1981). *kita:b al- sˤina:ʕtain: al-kitabah wa-al-fiʕr*. Bayreuth: dar alKutub alʕilmjah.

As-Salah, I. (1984). *ʕlu:m al-Hadith*. Damascus: Daar AlFikr.

As-Suyuti, J. a.-D. (1973). *al-itqa:n fi ʕulum al-Quran*. Bayreuth: almaktaba alθaqafiya.

Aydin Mehmet, S. (1997). *Al-Ghazali on Metaphorical Interpretation*. Paper presented at the LAUD Symposium, Duisburg.

Bearman, P. J., T. Bianquis, C. E. Bosworth, E. van Donzel, W. P. Heinrichs, et al. (1960–2005). *Encyclopædia of Islam*. Second edition, 12 volumes. Leiden: E. J. Brill.

Bin Ahmad, T. A. a.-R. (1984). *al-Sunnah ʕabra al- ʕusur*. Algiers: diwan al-matbuʕa:t al-ʒamiʕija.

Charteris-Black, J. (2004). *Corpus Approaches to Critical Metaphor Analysis*. Basingstoke: Palgrave Macmillan.

Charteris-Black, J. (2005). *Politicians and Rhetoric: The Persuasive Power of Metaphor*. Basingstoke: Palgrave Macmillan.

Deignan, A. (2003). Metaphorical Expressions and Culture: An Indirect Link. *Metaphor and Symbol* 18(4), 255–271.

Fairclough, N. (1992). *Discourse and Social Change*. Cambridge: Polity.

Jäkel, O. (2002). Hypotheses revisited: The cognitive theory of metaphor applied to religious texts. *Metaphorik.de*. 2/2002, 20–42. Retrieved from metaphorik.de website on 10 Oct. 2010 via http://www.metaphorik.de/en/journal/02/hypotheses-revisited-cognitive-theory-metaphor-applied-religious-texts.html.

Jurjani, A. a.-Q. (1988). *Asrar Al-Balaghah*. Cairo: Al-Hayah Al-Ammah Al-Misriyah.

Kittay, E. F. (1987). *Metaphor: Its Cognitive Force and Linguistic Structure*. Oxford: Clarendon.

Kövecses, Z. (2002). *Metaphor: A Practical Introduction*. Oxford: Oxford University Press.

Kövecses, Z. (2005). *Metaphor in Culture: Universality and Variation*. Cambridge: Cambridge University Press.

Lakoff, G. (1993). The contemporary theory of metaphor. In A. Ortony (Ed.), *Metaphor and Thought*, pp. 202–251. Cambridge: Cambridge University Press.

Lakoff, G., and M. Johnson (1980). *Metaphors We Live By*. Chicago: University of Chicago Press.

Lakoff, G., and M. Johnson (1999). *Philosophy in the Flesh: The Embodied Mind and Its Challenge to Western Thought*. New York: Basic Books.

Lakoff, G., and M. Turner (1989). *More than Cool Reason: A Field Guide to Poetic Metaphor*. Chicago: University of Chicago Press.

Lundmark, C. (2005). *Metaphor and Creativity in British Magazine Advertising*. Doctoral dissertation. Luleå University of Technology, Luleå, Sweden.

Marston, G. (2000). Metaphor, morality and myth: A critical discourse analysis of public housing policy in Queensland. *Critical Social Policy* 20, 349–373.

Musolff, A. (2001). *Attitudes Towards Europe: Language in the Unification Process*. Aldershot: Ashgate.

Musolff, A. (2003). Ideological functions of metaphor: The conceptual metaphors of health and illness in public discourse. In R. Dirven, R. Frank, and M. Pütz (eds.), *Cognitive Models of Language and Thought: Ideology, Metaphors and Meanings*, pp. 327–352. Berlin: de Gruyter.

Musolff, A. (2004). *Metaphor and Political Discourse: Analogical Reasoning in Debates about Europe*. New York: Palgrave Macmillan.

Musolff, A., C. Schaffner, and M. Townson (1996). *Conceiving of Europe: Diversity in Unity*. Aldershot, VT: Dartmouth.

Netton, I. R. (1989). *Allah Transcendent: Studies in the Structure and Semiotics of Islamic Philosophy, Theology and Cosmology*. University of Exeter Arabic and Islamic Series. London: Routledge.

Philips, B. (2007). *Usool Al-Hadeeth: The Methodology of Hadith Evaluation*. Second edition. Riyadh, Saudi Arabia: International Islamic Publishing House.

Pragglejaz Group (2007). MIP: A method for identifying metaphorically used words in discourse. *Metaphor and Symbol* 22(1), 1–39.

Qalqila, A. A. (1992). *al-balaya al- ʔstilaħija*. Cairo: Dar Alfıkr Al A'rabi.

Rash, F. J. (2006). *The Language of Violence: Adolf Hitler's Mein Kampf.*
New York: Peter Lang.

Robson, J. (1965). *Mishkat Al-Masabih: English Translation with Explanatory Notes.*
Lahore: Sh. Muhammad Ashraf.

Siddiqi, M. Z., and A. H. Murad (1993). *Hadith Literature: Its Origin, Development and Special Features.* Cambridge, UK: Islamic Texts Society.

Soskice, J. M. (1985). *Metaphor and Religious Language.* Oxford: Clarendon.

Steen, G. (2007). *Finding Metaphor in Grammar and Usage.* Amsterdam/Philadelphia: John Benjamins.

CHAPTER 12

Metaphor in Religious Transformation

'Circumcision of the Heart' in Paul of Tarsus

RALPH BISSCHOPS

R eligious movements do not emerge out of nothing.[1] They tend to be born out of a previous religion and are the result of a theological re-shaping. Religious renewers incorporate the main notions and symbols of the mother religion into their doctrine. They need these ancestral notions to articulate their vision. Metaphoric speech and thinking, therefore, may connect the old with the new. In the present chapter I devote my attention to the gospel of St. Paul (Paul of Tarsus), who created, albeit roughly, the initial conceptual framework of Christianity.

Early Christianity was a faith highly dependent on Jewish lore. In Paul's time, there were no Christian gospels; hence a genuinely Christian text-based herme-neutic was not possible. The Hebrew Scriptures (and the Septuagint, their Greek translation) were the only sacred texts Paul and his fellow Christians could refer to. Paul, the apostle to the gentiles and a declared universalist, had to rely on his Jewish text-based tradition. His own cognitive instruments were the seman-tically highly dense words of the Hebrew Scriptures. He used these ancestral notions to voice things 'which no eye has seen and no ear heard'[2] and introduced ideas which subsequently would become core concepts in Christian ethics and metaphysics.

Metaphor, analogy, and allegorical reading were the tools Paul used to create a new domain of religious devotion,[3] namely, inwardness and spirituality, which were the cornerstones of his universalist, that is to say cross-ethnic,[4] outreach. I will con-fine myself to Paul's circumcision-metaphor in Romans (2:28–29), which is highly representative for Paul's metaphorical use of terms belonging to the Jewish canon. I have chosen this passage because it has far-reaching metaphysical and ethical implications. What is its semantic and cognitive mechanism? Can the insight in this mechanism be helpful in the ongoing exegetical debates?

1 METAPHOR IN RELIGIOUS DISCOURSE

Religious metaphor presents some difficulties which demand a specific approach. Source, target, and mapping present characteristics which are typically displayed in religious discourse. In some cases, the target domain is God, who is not only unknown to us but whose ontological nature differs fundamentally from things accessible to our empirical experience. This problem was already discussed at length in Scholasticism (Thomas Aquinas, Cajetan) and triggered a great many investigations of God-talk, also called 'theography', particularly since 1960, from various religious viewpoints. In 1981, Jean-Pierre van Noppen (Brussels) coined the term 'theolinguistics'[5] delineating a separate sub-discipline of linguistics devoted to the study of religious language.[6] Since 2000 the interest for Theolinguistics has shifted to Poland[7] and Germany.[8] Recently, the thread has been picked up by Sweetser and DesCamp (2014) in the United States, this time from the viewpoint of cognitive linguistics, which, postulating the experiential grounding of metaphor, has difficulties acknowledging the gap between human experience and the ineffable divine transcendence. Sweetser and DesCamp (2014, p. 18) write ' "good" or appropriate metaphors for the Divine-human relationship certainly express power differential, and that power differential (at least) is understood as "true" of God'. However, from a theological viewpoint, transcendence cannot be reduced to this-worldly (e.g. 'embodied') notions such as power differential. Van Noppen and earlier generations were sharply aware of the inadequacy of human language, experiences, and concepts to grasp the Divine, as were earlier scholars familiar with the Thomist tradition. Aquinas addressed this issue with unsurpassable clarity and a delicious touch of sarcasm (*Summa Theologiae*, art. 1, quest.9). To him it would be much better to use totally inappropriate metaphors for God, instead of beautiful images, in order not to incite the mind to idolatry. Attractive metaphors, Thomas Aquinas argued, do not prompt the mind to go beyond the image (i.e. 'source domain imagery'). Van Noppen (1999, p. 106) writes: 'if our theographic utterances convey any knowledge or report any experience of the divine, they can only refer to the believed or perceived aspect(s) of the total reality, while part of the divine "mystery" and transcendence remains beyond expression'.

To sum up: in cognitive linguistics the target domain (here: God) is viewed as capable of being conceptualised via a physical source domain, while the theological tradition (Aquinas, van Noppen) teaches that the transcendent divine can *never* be conceptualised in its entirety. Cognitive linguistics only investigates the way the mind conceptualises experiences de facto; theologians also want to assess whether these conceptualisations are appropriate. That does not only hold for theology: there will always be a tension between the *cognitive* and the *epistemic* approach.

Also with respect to the cognitive source, religious metaphors have some peculiarities. In some religious metaphors, the source lies in the domain of the holy and the sacred, notions which are extremely difficult to understand in themselves. Here frame semantics may be relevant. In the Jewish and early Christian scriptures, semantic and cultural *frames*[9] of 'holiness' can be clearly perceived and delineated, whereas the domain of Holiness itself lies beyond human knowledge and experience. The *frames* of 'holiness' pertain to religious ritual, consecrated things, and required states for participating individuals (such as purity, e.g. for the service of the Temple, or being circumcised, e.g. to be allowed to take part in the Seder of Passover). Metaphors borrowed from the service of the Temple in Jerusalem evoke such a frame.[10] The present investigation is about that kind of metaphor, i.e. metaphors whose source belong to the frame of the sacred (Temple, ritual) and which, by virtue of their provenance, are bearers of treasured values, since they are marked by the seal of the consecration to God.

It should be stressed right at the outset that in Judaism, the sacred and the profane are radically different domains which may not interfere with one another. As to the biblical notion of the Holy itself, an outline has been worked out by Israel Efros (1964), who states that the holy (*ha-kodesh*) is intimately interwoven with God's transcendence, in contrast to God's 'glory' (*ha-kavod*) which denotes His presence in this world. The Hebrew word for 'holy', *kadosh*, is rooted in the verb *le'kadesh*, which means 'to set apart'. Hence, holiness can refer to two notions: (1) God's transcendence, that is to say the idea that God stands apart from his creation, and (2) the consecration of all things which are used or performed in His service. It is worth emphasising that all things which are consecrated to the Divine service can no longer be used for profane purposes.

1.1 The value-ascribing function of metaphor

We can discern many functions of metaphor: descriptive,[11] explanatory, category-creating, heuristic, etc. An underestimated function which, however, matters much in religious discourse is the *value-ascribing* one. This function consists in assigning a positive or negative value (or even a set of positive or negative values) to the target—for example, *our finances are healthy, the leader of this rogue state is a new Hitler*. By appealing to values cherished by the audience or non-values abhorred by it, the speaker can influence decision-making processes, behaviours, and attitudes.

Seen from this angle, Lakoff's notion of metaphor as understanding one domain of experience via another[12] should also be seen as *evaluating* one domain of experience via another. Indeed, one of Lakoff's well-known examples of evaluative understanding involves a mapping of a financial frame onto a highly abstract target domain: TIME IS MONEY (Lakoff and Johnson 1980, p. 8). Lakoff and Johnson have also sought to outline the system of metaphors underlying morality concepts (Lakoff and Johnson, *Metaphors we Live by*, 2003, p. 250; Lakoff and Johnson 1999, pp. 292–331), and it is on this specific area of cognition that I wish to focus.

Lakoff and Johnson see value-ascription (a term they do *not* use) in terms of conceptualisation. In their investigation on the language of morality, they observe that the notion of well-being is 'conceptualised' in terms of wealth or financial transactions (Lakoff and Johnson 1999, p. 292). In this context, it is interesting to note that the source of morality (e.g. 'well-being' in Lakoff and Johnson) should not necessarily be 'moral' in itself. It's a value, but not a moral one. This being said, it is all the more important to note that well-being is not the only source of morality articulated via metaphors. The frames of Ritual and Holiness also convey moral values, without necessarily having any bearing on morality themselves.

1.2 Value, holiness, and words referring to sacred things

Let us pause a while on the notion of 'holiness'. In this frame, 'holiness' is a tremendous force. Moreover the 'Holy', albeit a supreme value, is not a mere moral notion: touching the Ark of the Covenant can be lethal, even if it is motivated by the best intentions.

> As the ark was being transported, the oxen pulling the cart stumbled, and a Levite named Uzzah took hold of the ark. God's anger burned against Uzzah and He struck him down and he died. (2 Samuel 6:1–7).

Holiness transcends well-being, yet it is one of the most central values of the Hebrew Bible. By the same token, ritual 'purity', which is the condition sine qua non for participating in the cult of the Temple, is not a moral one. A menstruating woman or a woman after childbirth is impure, although she cannot possibly be accused of immorality. A priest who touches her, even inadvertently, becomes impure too. He may not, among other things, partake in the priestly meals, although he is not necessarily in a state of moral deficiency or sinfulness (see also Klawans 2006, p. 54).

The world of religious life, more than any other, contains many sacred, and consequently value-laden, notions, such as 'priesthood', 'offering', 'purity', 'temple', and 'circumcision', which would provide a strong value to the target if used as metaphors. Impressive Pauline metaphors of this type are: *The body is a Temple of the Holy Spirit* (1 Corinthians 6:19)[13] and *'The body is the Temple of the living God'* (2 Corinthians 6:16–17).[14] Source, target, and mapping are easily discernible here: The body is a dwelling place of God, as is the Temple of Jerusalem. This metaphor also has a descriptive and heuristic function: it sketches (in a philosophically inarticulate way) the ontological nature of the human body. However, we cannot overlook the fact that in Paul's time, the Temple of Jerusalem, being most intimately associated with holiness, was the most central value in Israelite life. Paul bestows this value on the body of each individual. Incidentally, this metaphor also has strong ethical entailments with respect to sexual behaviour (1 Corinthians 6:18). In the same way as the Temple can be defiled, debauchery defiles the human body. It is crucial to note that statements about values also (or mostly) imply statements about *duties*. In Paul's case, the metaphor *the body is the Temple of the Holy Spirit* implies the duty of sexual restriction.

To be sure, value-laden sources for metaphors do not only appear in religious contexts. In all cases, they convey their value to the target (see below). In some cases, mapping and correspondences are just pretexts for bringing a source in the neighbourhood of the target, so that the source can project the values it embodies onto it (see Bisschops 1994, p. 118). It is important to note that the ascription of a value is an additional operation, once the mapping has been completed. In the case of metaphors operating through deliteralisation of sacred notions, the target comes to be 'hallowed' by its source.

1.3 Metaphor as deliteralisation of a sacred notion

1.3.1 Deliteralisation

Within the corpus of religious figures of speech, a separate category should be singled out on the basis of their specific performance, namely, deliteralisation (of course, these semantic processes are not specific to religious discourse: they also appear in other genres, but in religion their impact is highly decisive). Deliteralisation is a semantic process by which a word appearing in a given religious or doctrinal corpus, and usually understood in its literal sense, receives a non-literal meaning and a new referent, which under certain circumstances might be called 'target' (as in the case of metaphor). Christian readers might be particularly familiar with deliteralisations. One would immediately think of Matthew (15:10–11): 'Not that what goes into the mouth defiles the man, but what is going forth out of the mouth, this defiles the man'. This verse can be understood as the deliteralisation and subsequent redefinition of the Israelite notion of ritual impurity. Ritual impurity becomes moral impurity.[15] This, at least, is the way in which most readers unfamiliar with the polysemic Hebrew notion of impurity (*tumah*) would see it.

1.3.2 Deliteralisation of a sacred notion as a metaphor

In order to analyse the sometimes revolutionary performance of deliteralisation as a metaphor, let us consider the following verse of Isaiah:

> Is it such a fast that I have chosen? A day for a man to afflict his soul? [. . .] Is not this rather the fast that I have chosen? To loose the chains of wickedness, to undo the bands of the yoke, and to let the oppressed go free, and to break every yoke? Is it not to share thy bread with the hungry, and that thou bring the poor that are cast out to thy house? When thou seest the naked, that thou cover him; and that thou hide not thyself from thy own flesh? (Isaiah 58:5–7)

For the sake of clarity I shall oversimplify this passage, rephrasing it as CHARITY IS FASTING.

Isaiah's statement is unmistakably a metaphor. There is a source (fasting) and a target (charity). Both belong to radically different frames (holy vs. profane), and there is a mapping: sacrificing well-being to God can be mapped to giving wealth to the poor, the nexus between well-being and wealth being amply documented by Lakoff and Johnson (1999, p. 331) for metaphors in the field of ethics. We may call this figure a metaphor through deliteralisation of a sacred notion (fasting). Metaphors of this kind are often employed to challenge existing socio-religious values or to shift away from them. The fasting metaphor caused a religious and socio-cultural earth-quake whose consequences we still experience today. Isaiah's metaphor broke down the wall between the holy and the profane, and social empathy is endowed with the tremendous weight and gravity of holiness.

There is more, however: the ritual constraint of fasting on the Day of Atonement is projected upon our relationship with the needy and the oppressed. It becomes our *sacred duty* to help them. Within the biblical context, this metaphor sparked a revolution with consequences reaching all the way to Christian charity, socialism, communism, social democracy, and many other socio-cultural developments. Some of these movements are secular or even atheistic. Even if the source of holiness has faded away, its radiancy can still be felt.

1.3.3 *Value/duty extension versus value/duty shift*

If we follow Isaiah literally, fasting should be abrogated. Instead, we should help the poor and free the oppressed. It is important to note that rabbinical authorities would never accept such a reading and state that 'a verse cannot depart from its plain meaning'.[16] According to this meta-linguistic ruling, Isaiah's verse can only be understood as the *extension* of the original meaning, and hence of the duties it implies, not as a *shift*. If we accept this restriction, Isaiah's statement would mean that our obligations towards the underprivileged are at least as important as the ritual duty of fasting, without however advocating the abandonment of the latter. I would like to call this interpretation a 'duty extension', which of course is also a 'value extension'.

In his *Dialogue with Trypho* (2003, chapter 15), the Christian apologist Justin Martyr (100–165 CE) quotes Isaiah's verses, leaving, however, no doubt about the fact that he champions the abrogation of fasting, if this could make us more sensitive to the needs of the underprivileged. He introduces them with the following words: 'Learn to keep the true fast of the Lord (. . .)'. Justin's stance is indicated by the modifier 'true'. 'True' fasting means helping the oppressed, which, by the same token, implies that ritual fasting is 'untrue' and, hence, worthless. In this sense we are facing a *value-* and *duty-shift*.

This phenomenon can also be called an 'inversion' of values. Two evaluative processes are at work here: (a) the valuation of the target (charity) via the source (the sacred notion of the fast) and (b) the devaluation of the source itself. Such a *dual-phased* metaphorical process, departing from a classical theory of metaphor based on source domain and target domain correspondences, is difficult to comprehend. Fauconnier and Turner's Conceptual Integration Network Model (Fauconnier and Turner 1998), some implications of which have become an indispensable complement for the study of metaphor, might be more useful in such cases. In the Conceptual Integration Model, there is no direct projection/mapping from source to target. Source input and target input are (selectively) projected into the blending-space, which processes the information. Then the processed information is reprojected[17] onto the target and even to the source. Many things can happen in the blending-space: in the present case it is (1) the transformation of a ritual obligation into a social one, (2) the identification of man's partnership with God with that with his fellow beings, and (3) the inversion of the positive source-value into a negative one ('fast is good' into 'fast is bad').[18] This kind of reading would account for metaphors functioning as the tools of religious change. We now turn to the metaphor that is the focus of the present chapter, a metaphor, which like the fasting metaphor, also draws upon ritual practice for its source domain.

2 PAUL'S HEART CIRCUMCISION METAPHOR: THE QUESTIONS

In Romans 2:28 we find:

> For he is not a Jew, which is one outwardly; neither is that circumcision which is outward in the flesh. (Romans 2:28)

This is a clear case of a metaphorical expression, although it confronts us with the following problem: here 'circumcision' is apparently intended to denote an *inward* process. We may call it a target, but this target is created by the metaphor itself, which also contains an existential statement ('there is something like . . .' etc.). It is like a blank screen on which experiential elements and cultural assumptions can be projected. Is there any mapping? For the time being, there cannot be any correspon-dences, since the target is not known. Nonetheless, it seems Paul had both a target and correspondences in mind. Although the target cannot easily be identified and the mapping will be difficult to process by the reader, there still are an *intended* tar-get, presumed correspondences, and *intended* mapping. John Barclay (1998, p. 552) rightly observes that in this case 'the metaphorical sense is allowed to efface the significance of the circumcision of the flesh'. However, that is only one part of the cognitive process triggered by the metaphor. As we shall see, Paul's circumcision metaphor also effects a *duty shift*. The duty of physical circumcision is not only abro-gated, it is also superseded by a similar *duty*, which can only be fulfilled in the realm of inwardness.

This raises the following further question: which duties are shifted towards the target (i.e. inward circumcision)? The answer depends on our knowledge of the source. This knowledge not only includes information about the physical aspect of circumcision, but also about the way it has been perceived in Paul's time, about the religious legislations and folk theories surrounding it.

Thus, investigating Paul's metaphor presents us with the following particular issues:

(1) *Historical and religious context of the source*: What was the religious and cultural significance of the source (i.e. circumcision) in Paul's time and in his own thinking?

(2) *Precedents.* Historical precedents sometimes motivate the choice of a metaphor and can shed light on its meaning.[19] What are the precedents for Paul's metaphor in the Hebrew Bible? To what extent are they relevant for the reading of the metaphor under investigation? Does Paul refer to pre-existing (e.g. emblematic) notions of the source or does he deviate from them?

(3) *Target analysis.* What is the intended target, metonymically represented by the notion 'heart'?

(4) *Metaphorological analysis.* Is there a mapping? Which features of the source are mapped onto the target? What is the impact of religious dogma or creed on this mapping process?

(5) *Entailments.* What are the theological, ethical, and philosophical entailments of Paul's metaphor?

These are the considerations that we shall bear in mind in investigating Paul's circumcision metaphor. Before analysing it in detail, it is essential, given the importance of cultural and historical context in this case, to look closely at that context's major relevant dimensions.

3 HISTORICAL AND EXEGETICAL CONTEXT
3.1 The broad context

3.1.1 Paul of Tarsus (3–67 CE)

Paul was a contemporary of Jesus, and his epistles to Christian communities are the first extant written testimonies of the origins of Christianity. He stands at the heart of the transition from Judaism to Christianity. Paul, a Hellenised Jew, was religiously trained in the tradition of the Pharisees, who were the forerunners of Rabbinical Judaism. Initially he fought the Christian movement emerging among Jews, but after he experienced a sudden revelation ('Christophany'), he underwent a profound transformation and became a believer of Christ. In Jerusalem, he joined Peter and James, who restricted their own mission to evangelising the Jews. Paul took upon himself the spreading of Christianity among the gentiles throughout the Mediterranean. In the synoptic gospels, written from 70 CE onwards, Paul's firm belief in the universality of the Christian message is less adamantly expressed.

3.1.2 Circumcision in Judaism

Although circumcision was generally practised by the Near-Eastern peoples, including the Egyptians, it was nonetheless strongly associated with Jewish identity in the Mediterranean world. The Hebrew Bible enjoins circumcision on the eighth day after an infant's birth (there is no female circumcision/excision). According to biblical chronology, it is the first law recorded and was enjoined to Abraham and his descendants (it is also the last custom a Jew will ever abandon, even today). Until the rabbinical rulings on this matter (second century CE), which are recorded in the Talmud, there are no extant documents on the ritual accompanying the removal of the foreskin. As to the surgical details, we have, for pre-Talmudic times, to rely on the book of *Jubilees* (15:33), which stipulates that the entire foreskin is to be removed (Hebr.: *periah*). Possibly, it is with regard to this ruling that the prophet Jeremiah qualified the neighbouring peoples as 'uncircumcised' (Hebr.: *arel*),[20] even though they too practised some kind of circumcision.

Circumcision is generally seen as the sign of Abraham's covenant with God, but this view seems to be of a later date (fifth century BCE, priestly document). Men who wish to convert to Judaism are expected to undergo circumcision. This does not imply that circumcision automatically confers Jewish identity.[21] Whether conversion was regarded as possible by other Jewish traditions than the Rabbinical one is still heavily debated.[22]

Some people tend to think that circumcision has been motivated by hygienic concerns, others maintain that the practice of circumcision was believed to increase the fertility of the boy.[23] The ritual status of circumcision, however, is undeniable and clearly attested in Exodus 12:10 and Exodus 12:43–48. Being circumcised is a prerequisite to eat from the Pascal lamb on the evening of Passover.[24] The foreigners (Hebrew: *gerim*) and the slaves should undergo circumcision before partaking in the Passover meal.

These are the basics of the situation in which Paul's metaphor emerged and did its work. But to understand the role of contextual features in the pragmatic functioning of the metaphor in the short and in the long terms, it is important to investigate some of the finer details.

3.1.3 *The target group of evangelisation*

Paul's letters are permeated with Jewish lore and replete with references to the Hebrew Bible. For a gentile unfamiliar with the Hebrew Bible and Israelite religious practice, they would have been totally incomprehensible. Historical investigation, however, teaches us that in Roman antiquity there was a relatively great number of gentiles who felt attracted by Judaism and who practised Jewish rituals. We may, as most other scholars do, assume that they formed the initial target group of evangelisation. It can also be presumed that these Judaising gentiles attended synagogue services and received their religious initiation from Jews.

3.2 The debate about Paul and Judaism

The most obvious dependency of Paul's writings on Jewish lore (the Gospels were not yet written in his day) has preoccupied nearly all students of Paul and is also relevant for the present investigation. The details of these debates cannot be comprehensively discussed in this study. I restrict myself here to summing up the four main hypotheses in this problématique. They all gravitate around the issue of whether, in Paul's mind, Christianity should be included into Judaism or not.

3.2.1 The exclusivist answer

The *Anti-Judaic* hypothesis is that Paul did away with Judaism, claiming that a new era had begun where Jews and gentiles stand on an equal footing before God, and in which Torah-obedience has become obsolete once and for all with Jesus' crucifixion and resurrection. This summarises the classical, anti-Jewish (if not anti-Semitic) Christian and particularly Lutheran and Calvinist reading. Many of Paul's sayings can be adduced to underscore this approach (such as 1 Thessalonians 2:14–16).

There is, however also a hypothesis which I would like to call the *Judaic hypothesis* and which states that Paul remained a faithful Jew throughout his life, teaching that born Jews should abide by the Torah but that gentiles should gladly embrace the tremendous opportunity of salvation brought by Jesus. One of the most visible representatives of this view is Pamela Eisenbaum (2009), whose contention is that, according to Paul, Jews should remain Jews, and that gentiles should embrace the message of Christ without becoming Jews:

> Torah thus was God's answer for how humanity could be in relationship with God. Since gentiles could not follow it, God had to find an extrasystemic means of incorporating gentiles into God's family. That extrasystemic means was Jesus Christ. (Eisenbaum 2009, p. 240)

Closely related to Eisenbaum's hypothesis is Lionel Windsor's assumption that Israel is *not* the new (Christian) Church. Israel, however, is the recipient of the divine vocation to communicate the gospel to non-Jews (Windsor 2014, p. 45). Paul was a declared Jew, but he did not expect his communities to become Jewish. He only insisted on his Jewish identity to justify his apostolic ministry (Windsor 2014, p. 55).

3.2.2 The inclusivist answer

Christianity is the offshoot of Judaism, and Christians should be part of the Jewish people. Paul endeavoured to change Israel's boundary markers in order to include gentiles into the Jewish people. 'Salvation comes to the gentiles only through their being part in Israel'. This is an approach heralded by James Dunn (1998, p. 268).

All these hypotheses gravitate around the questions of how Paul saw himself and how he defined the relationship between Judaism and Christian faith. As a theorist of metaphor, I can only try to explore the role of metaphor, in particular the circumcision metaphor, in Paul's thinking. But, as we shall see, Paul's circumcision-metaphor can also be a point of departure for examining the way in which he incorporates Jewish teaching and identity.

4 THE ROLE OF METAPHOR IN PAUL'S SAYINGS ON CIRCUMCISION

In order to know which features of circumcision are salient for Paul in the construction of his metaphor, we must first gain solid knowledge about the way in which Paul viewed this ritual. Paul discusses circumcision, and through this approach his relation to Judaism, using both metaphorical and non-metaphorical language.

4.1 Paul's non-metaphoric sayings on circumcision: Paul's Letter to the Galatians

Among the fresh Jewish-Christian community, the debate raged whether gentile converts should undergo circumcision. Many Jewish Christians adamantly argued in favour of it. Among the gentile believers, the idea that circumcision was a prerequisite for becoming a Christian in good standing was also widespread (although circumcision was seen as an abomination in the Graeco-Roman world). However, we have already seen that the first gentile members of the early church were recruited among the relatively large group of Judaising gentiles. They practised Jewish customs—albeit selectively—and attended synagogue service. If we may trust our sources, these gentiles were prepared to undergo circumcision. Paul started discussing the issue of whether Christians should undergo circumcision in his letter to the Galatians, a group of Christian communities in Asia Minor which he had founded. After his departure, Jewish Christian missionaries urged them to undergo circumcision. Paul's epistle to the Galatians is a response to this interference with his own teachings.

To these Judaising gentiles he expounds the notions—characteristic for his theology—of justification by faith and not by works (i.e. obedience to the Jewish Law). Jewish religion, he argues, is focused on what people do ('their works'). The Torah enjoins people to behave in this or that way (keeping the festivals and the purity laws etc.), whereas Christianity demands faith. Through the advent and suffering of Christ, the obedience to Jewish Law has become irrelevant (albeit still binding for those who stand under it). It served provisionally as a fence against sin, but thanks to the indwelling spirit of Christ, proper behaviour no longer requires the precepts of Jewish Law. Christian living is inspired by impulses and virtues like 'love, joy, peace, patience, loving-kindness, goodness and faith' (Galatians 5:22–24).

Then Paul addresses the issue of circumcision. His admonition to the Galatians not to give in to the pressure of Jewish Christians is supported by the following arguments:

(1) In a Christian perspective there cannot be any distinction between Jews and Gentiles.[25]
(2) Circumcision as a sign of Jewish distinctiveness is no longer valuable and meaningful.[26]

(3) Undergoing circumcision is tantamount to denying the salvation brought by Jesus' advent and crucifixion. A man who does this is 'fallen from grace'.[27]

(4) Once a man is circumcised he stands under the rule of Jewish Law.[28]

(5) Those who abide under the Law must keep all the commandments lest they be doomed. Christ's salvation will be of no help in the case of failure to observe the Law in its integrity.

(6) Therefore Jewish Law, albeit useful in its time, has become a curse now that men can benefit by Jesus' grace.[29]

Paul thus leaves not the slightest doubt about the fact that he regarded circumcision as a non-value for Christians. In addition, Paul most obviously regarded circumcision as tantamount to being Jewish and standing under the Mosaic Law.

4.1.1 Circumcision and conversion to Judaism

Most puzzling is Paul's contention that circumcision *eo ipso* confers Jewish identity.

In this context the question arises about the significance of circumcision in the conversion procedure. There has been a Talmudic debate on this issue. The treatise *Yebamoth* (46a, *Babylonian Talmud*) records diverging opinions: some rabbis contend that ablution (a parallel to baptism) is to be regarded as ritually decisive but *not* circumcision, and vice versa. The discussion finally leads to the ruling that both, i.e. circumcision and the ritual ablution, are of equal importance.[30] If only circumcision has been completed, the children of a proselyte by a Jewish woman would be regarded as bastards (46a, *Babylonian Talmud*).

The following thing should absolutely be emphasised: circumcision is in no way an entry to Judaism; it's not a parallel to baptism. It is simply the first law to be applied. It's the father's duty to circumcise his sons. If he fails to do so, the son is expected to effect circumcision on his own body.[31] This implies that a man stands under Jewish Law by birth, even uncircumcised. The same holds for conversion to Judaism, which first and foremost is a commitment of the soul (Will and Orrieux 1992, p. 160). Since the (male) convert is regarded as a new-born person, he must undergo circumcision. To be sure, before 200 CE there was a Pharisaic tradition represented by Rabbi Eliezer ben Hyrkanos according to whom circumcision alone counts for conversion. It's possible that Paul was part of this tradition. However, the opposite view has also been expressed in that very period, saying that ritual bathing would be sufficient (b Sanhedrin, 68a, 101a; see also Will and Orrieux 1992, p. 163).

Whatever the case, all these rabbinical discussions deal with the legal formalisation of the conversion process, that is to say the sealing of the entry into Jewish peoplehood, not with religious conversion as such (Will and Orrieux 1992, p. 160), which, in any case, must be preceded by the solemn declaration to obey the Jewish laws.

Another question arises: for what reason the male Galatian converts to Christianity were eager to undergo circumcision? We have no record of what was going on in their minds. One might hypothesise that these non-Jewish Christians did not exactly want to become Jews but aspired to the 'imitatio Christi' (imitation of Christ). Jesus was circumcised, therefore they wanted to be circumcised too. The reason why I venture this hypothesis is a significant historical fact: Ethiopian converts in the sixteenth and seventeenth century vividly expressed the wish to undergo circumcision because they wanted to be like Jesus (Leonardo Cohen 2009, pp. 161, 181). There is also another interesting hypothesis put forward by Susan Elliot (1999, p. 679): circumcision reminded the Galatians of their ancestral cult of the Mother Goddess, whose priests were eunuchs. Whatever the case, Paul wanted to thwart by all means the emergence of ritualism among his communities.

In no way does circumcision automatically confer Jewish identity.[32] Paul's equation of circumcision with Jewishness was juridically based on weak ground and motivated by his will to dissuade his audience from converting to Judaism.

4.2 Circumcision as emblem for Jewishness

Metaphor is an important feature of human cognition and language, but it is not the only one. In this section, I use other theoretical tools from cognitive linguistics—metonymy and cognitive models—in order to probe the way Paul's mind may have been working with respect to the word 'circumcision' and the concept of Jewishness.

4.2.1 Some cognitive-linguistic instruments: Idealised cognitive models and metonymy

This situation can be understood further in terms of cognitive semantics. The human mind does not primarily think in terms of legal, philosophical, or logical definitions. It does not primarily form categories in this way—and what is at issue here is a category, the category of Jewishness. Rather, human minds form what Lakoff (1987) has called 'cognitive models' and 'idealised cognitive models' (ICMs). Cognitive models are mental chunks, generally unconscious, that contain understandings, perceptions, and feelings about the way different aspects of the world are. The term 'idealised cognitive models' recognises the fact that these models do not correspond with an objective reality 'out there'.

Lakoff argues that words are defined relative to a particular ICM, not to purely taxonomic or lexical criteria. For example, he shows that words that look like synonyms belonging to the same category when defined lexically do not in fact have the same meaning for their users, and are not in practice interchangeable. For example, 'unmarried man' and 'bachelor' are formally equivalent, i.e. they belong to the same formal category (whose necessary and sufficient conditions are + male and − married), but are not conceptually (including emotively) the same for speakers of English. There are separate cognitive frames for each word (Lakoff 1987, p. 130). In general, ICMs are categories that are formed all the time and can change; some become relatively fixed and become 'stereotypes' in social use—repeated models for social categories (Lakoff 1987, pp. 77–90). This is the way 'identities' are formed in the mind.

This is where metonymy also comes in. One of the ways we use ICMs is by way of metonymy—understood here as a core feature of the human cognition rather than as primarily a rhetorical device. Metonymy happens when one mental element in an ICM is used to stand for another (Lakoff 1987, pp. 77–79). In the case of the category (or ICM) Jew, included are presumably many kinds of knowledge and feeling concerning history, texts, laws, buildings, practices, even people's physical features, and of course the ritual of circumcision. Some of these can stand for the whole category, depending on what is relevant or salient in a particular context. They are called part-whole metonymies or frame metonymies (see Dancygier and Sweetser 2014, p. 101).

To stress the sometimes enormous discrepancies between the source-related ICM and the source as it 'really is' from an ontological (e.g. scientific) viewpoint, I introduced the notion of 'emblem' (see Bisschops 1994). In many if not most cases, the source of a metaphor or metonymy is associated with commonly accepted commonplaces, mythology, folk theories, and/or symbolism. All these elements constitute what I would like to call the *emblematic* meaning of the source. As Searle (1979, p. 102) observed: 'gorilla' in 'the doorkeeper is a gorilla' does not denote the animal from a zoological viewpoint but stands for a conglomerate of culturally determined assumptions and even imaginations (one might think of the effect of films such as King Kong). Gorillas are shy, doorkeepers not. In the doorkeeper's case, the 'gorilla' is not a gorilla at all.

Actually, the notions of circumcision and Jewish identity appear to alternate interchangeably in Paul's writings, as well as in the Hellenistic world. However, 'being circumcised' and 'being Jewish' do not refer to exactly the same categories of people, the same ICM; nor do they have the same conceptual and emotive connections in the mind (see also section 4.2.3).

This interchangeability, which, in principle, constitutes a clash of meanings, attests the metonymical character of the term 'circumcision' in Paul, both from a classical semantic and certainly from a cognitive viewpoint.

4.2.2 Circumcision as emblematic metonymy for Jewishness

It is an undisputable fact that in the Graeco-Roman world circumcision was regarded as the marker of Jewish identity par excellence, although many other Near-Eastern peoples also practised it. While such a view can be called 'stereotypical', Paul's equation of circumcision with Judaism and all the duties a Jew must observe (Torah) might be called idiosyncratic from a juridical (halakhic) angle. Both views, however, sustain each other in the socio-cultural context of Paul's language. In Paul's thought-world, circumcision appears as a metonymy for conversion to Judaism and Jewish (ritualistic) law-abidingness.

Paul's wholesale equation of circumcision with Jewish identity may be called emblematic: it functions as an emblem for Jewish law, Jewish identity, and law-abidingness. It has little bearing on the ritual and juridical relevance of circumcision as such in Judaism. Only from this stage onward can circumcision as an emblem, generated by a frame metonymical process, function as a metaphor in Pauline discourse (see Romans 2:28–29).

Generally, an orator presupposes a pre-existing emblem (and ICM background it is related to), shared by the audience and himself, to create his metaphors. In the absence of such emblematic notions, the metaphor would not be easily—and certainly not rapidly—understood (Bisschops 1994). But it is also imaginable that he or she constructs his/her own emblems before using them as sources for metaphors or metonymies. This seems to be the case with Paul, whose non-metaphoric sayings, as we have seen, are abundantly clear about the unconventional way he perceived circumcision. To substantiate this supposition we must first take a look at the biblical precedents of Paul's metaphor. Was Paul's use of it really so specific?

4.2.3 The covenantal meaning of circumcision

Some readers might object that the nexus between Judaism and circumcision may be justified by the 'covenantal' meaning of the latter. It is in the Priestly tradition, which arose in the fifth century BCE, that circumcision was bestowed with a covenantal meaning.[33] Since then it has figured as the sign of the Abrahamic covenant, while the Shabbat is the sign of the Sinaitic covenant. However, even in the Hebrew Bible the link between circumcision and covenant is not intrinsic. Abraham's first son, Ismael, was circumcised, but he was excluded from the covenant (Gen 17:20–21). A resident alien (Hebrew *ger*) was allowed to take part in the Passover meal, provided he underwent circumcision (Exodus 12:48). However, Bernat (2009, p. 48) shows that a *ger*, even circumcised, was still lower on the social ladder than born Israelites. As he puts it, circumcision as such 'does not effectuate a crossing or blurring of these boundaries [between outsiders and native Israelites]'.

At the same time, Paul downplayed the covenantal significance of circumcision, saying that Abraham received the commandment of circumcision *as a reward* for his righteousness (Romans 4:11). This is a reading which is perfectly defensible from a strictly Jewish viewpoint: the Torah is a gift, which one has to deserve. From this, Paul infers that righteously living people can claim Abraham as their ancestor *without* undergoing circumcision. Paul emptied the notion of circumcision from its covenantal meaning while establishing a link between this same notion and Torah-observance. He did not want the covenant with God to be sealed by rituals. And he certainly did not want his disciples to convert to Judaism, whose laws one could hardly observe in their minutiae. Paul's equation of circumcision and Jewish Law in its rigor serves as a deterrent.

5 BIBLICAL PRECEDENTS OF CIRCUMCISION AS A METAPHOR

We have now examined non-metaphorical processes involved in Paul's thinking about circumcision, noting in particular its metonymic functioning as an emblem for Jewishness. We now turn to metaphor, the projection of the whole cognitive complex surrounding the term circumcision onto new conceptual targets. The biblical tradition with which Paul was imbued had already begun this kind of metaphorical projection.

5.1 Observations

5.1.1 Biblical circumcision metaphors as value-extensions

The biblical precedents of Paul's circumcision-metaphor are well-known:

> Jeremiah (4:4): 'Circumcise (*himolou*) yourselves to the Lord and remove the foreskin of your hearts' (*hasirou orlot levavchem*).
> Deuteronomy (10:16): 'Circumcise the foreskin of your hearts' (*u-maltem et orlat levavchem*).

We may assume that Paul was familiar with these passages. And even more than that: Paul appeals to these verses to convey ancestral dignity to his own metaphorical statement, whose implications, in sharp contrast to their precedents, are strikingly heterodox. From the foregoing sections we can immediately note the following: according to the canonical interpretation of the verses, the injunction 'circumcise your hearts' does not imply that the ritual practice should be abrogated. In the context of Jeremiah, there is no doubt about it: his male audience was already circumcised.[34] Jeremiah stated that their 'heart' should be circumcised too. In this case, the metaphor represents a *value-extension*. Ritual circumcision is important, but the circumcision of the heart is of equal or even greater importance.

5.1.2 Contextual elements

In both verses, the illocutionary intention is admonition. The verses respond to the inclination towards idolatry among the children of Israel. In the verses preceding Deuteronomy 10:16, Moses recalls the incident of the worship of the golden calf. His metaphor is immediately followed by the warning: 'and do not be stiff-necked any longer' (*ve-arpechem lo takshou od*). In Jeremiah 4:4, the circumcision metaphor appears in exactly the same context; it is motivated by the idolatry of the Jews (Jeremiah 3:6–10 and 4:1). The illocutionary force is even more threatening, as it is immediately followed by the words 'lest My fury come forth like fire'.

5.2 Interpretations

5.2.1 Interpreting a Hebrew metaphor from its root-notion

The interpretive and exegetical effort which our metaphor demands is generally eschewed by pulpit paraphrases such as 'circumcision of the heart is a symbol of the devotion of the heart to its rightful Lord'.[35] They make the nexus between circumcision and the heart appear self-evident, while in reality it cannot be taken for granted at all. That a heart can be circumcised, even in a figurative way, is anything but obvious. In its original Hebrew wording the circumcision-metaphor is much more revealing than its Greek parallel in the Septuagint, where we read 'circumcise the hardness of your heart' (*peritemeiste tein sklerocardian*). This translation, incidentally, is already an interpretation. The Hebrew wording contains the clues for the interpretation of the metaphor: 'circumcise (*himolou*) and remove (*hasirou*) the foreskin (*orla*[t])[36] of your heart (*levavechem*)'. The metaphor is explicitly referred to as the 'cutting' and 'removal' of the 'foreskin', which are presented as the *salient* features of the source in its metaphorical use. Is that not self-evident? Certainly from a surgical viewpoint, but not from the viewpoint of historical semantics and metaphorology. Shaye Cohen (2010, p. 436) observes that in biblical times 'what mattered was the cut, not the blood'. The blood shed during the operation and which is sucked off by the *mohel* (circumciser)[37] has been much more vividly addressed in later Jewish (rabbinical) symbolism.[38] To put it in the vocabulary of cognitive linguistics: in the present examples, 'cutting' and 'foreskin' are metonymies in which parts of the cognitive model of 'circumcision' are used to stand for the whole model. The fact that in these cases we are possibly dealing with a standard locution does not alter this observation from a cognitive viewpoint.[39]

The Greek word *peritomè* ('cutting around') does not explicitly evoke the notion of foreskin and makes it easier to regard less surgical notions as salient (which, most visibly, is the case with Paul). The main reason why I insist on the Hebrew wording is the fact that *orla* (foreskin) goes back to the root-form *arel*, which means 'uncircumcised' if applied to people, but has other meanings as well. This word appears in contexts which are anything but related to ritual circumcision. *Arel* applies to the mouth (Exodus 6:12), designating a speech impairment, to the ears (Jeremiah 6:10), indicating deafness, and to the fruits of a tree within the first three years after it has been planted (Leviticus19:23). Finally, it applies to the heart as well. A common denominator for *arel* in the cases listed here is the notion of 'deficiency', or 'imperfection'. A mouth that cannot speak is deficient. So is an ear which cannot hear. As to the fruits, if there are any, it applies to products of trees which have not yet reached an age of three years:[40] they are inedible. Noteworthy is that one of the antonyms of *arel* brought forward in rabbinic writings is *tam*,[41] echoing Gen. 17:1 and meaning 'blameless'.[42] It is also noteworthy that the Septuagint translates *orla* (foreskin) as 'impurity' (*akatarsia*).[43] *Arel lev* ('uncircumcised' heart) would then mean a 'deficient, imperfect' heart. What can this mean? This leads us to the emblem of the heart in the Hebrew Bible.

5.2.2 'Heart' in the Hebrew Bible

The image of the heart presents us with an 'archetypical metonymy' (Norager 1999, p. 226). But what does this metonymy stand for? The bodily basis for the metonymy might be the close physical association between emotional states (fear, sadness, lust . . .) and physical sensations coming from heart rate, etc. What is the cognitive model it is related to? In the Western imaginary, 'heart' comes to be seen as the 'seat' of our emotions and is prominent in romanticising discourse. In most cases 'heart' also has this meaning in the Hebrew Bible, but there is more. In many biblical instances, the heart stands for mental capacities and performances such as understanding (Proverbs 8:5), judgement (Proverbs 24:30), and skill[44] (Exodus 35:25). The prophet Hosea says that 'prostitution and wine take away the heart' (Hosea 4:11). In this case 'heart' undeniably denotes, besides our corruptible feelings, also our mental capacities. In the Hebrew language, other body-based metonymies with similar meanings exist, including *kilyah* (kidney), which stands for intuition, and *kerev* (bowel), standing for our innermost perception of things. In none of these cases can the mind, seen as rational activity, and feelings be entirely dissociated. However, among the bodily-based metonymies 'heart' comes the closest to the notions of mind and understanding. The following example might provide an illustration of a definitely non-emotional meaning of 'heart'. In Hebrew, *la-sim lev* (literally: 'to *give* one's heart') means to take to heart (cf. 1 Samuel 4:20). But it also means to pay attention. In this sense, this locution appears in Ezekiel, where God asks the prophet to 'pay attention' to the architecture of the new Temple, shown to him in a vision (Ezekiel 40:4; 44:5).

A more philosophical question is whether 'heart' refers only to the psychosomatic part of the human being and not to the metaphysical notion of the soul as well. I think the former statement is true, since the Hebrew language has an array of notions designing more 'spiritual' concepts such as *rouach* (wind) standing for the 'breath of life', *nefesh*, and *neshama* meaning respiration, the latter word coming the closest to the notion of the soul. The Hebrew Bible is unspecific about the issue of soul and afterlife. Some Psalm verses (6:6 and 30:9)[45] seem to deny the existence of a soul that can be dissociated from the body, whereas Psalm 63:4 states that God's grace is more important than life. However, the Bible does not contain philosophical treatises. We must content ourselves with the provisional meaning of 'heart' as the seat of mind, thought, and feelings.

5.2.3 *Interpretative schemes from a receptive and a productive viewpoint*

From a *receptive* viewpoint, the interpretative scheme would then be:

(1) *arel* ('foreskinned') = imperfection, impurity, flaw, or abomination;
(2) *orla* ('foreskin') = the fact of being imperfect;
(3) *lev* ('heart') = understanding;
(4) *arel lev* ('foreskinned heart') = an imperfect, limited understanding;
(5) *moul be-orla* ('taking away the foreskin') = freeing the mind from its imperfection (torpor, absence of its capacity to differentiate, evil intentions, rebellion, etc.).

While the first four aspects of the understanding of the metaphor can be obtained from a literal reading, *moulah* (circumcision) can be regarded as a 'metaphor', provided that it is not only understandable via analogy but also via its groundedness in the polysemy of *arel*. From the viewpoint of *production*, the mechanism of the metaphor could then be described as follows:

(1) the mind of the Israelites is *arel* in the sense of imperfect, that is to say producing false, wrong, or rebellious thoughts;
(2) *arel* also means foreskinned;
(3) the rebellion must be taken away from their mind ('heart');
(4) resulting 'metaphor': The heart must be circumcised.

It is noteworthy that the line between metaphor and word-play is not easy to draw here.[46]

5.3 Source and target in the Hebrew circumcision-metaphors

Let us recapitulate our findings in the terminology of cognitive linguistics. The Hebrew circumcision metaphor is subdivided into two elements in the circumcision cognitive model that is the metaphor's source domain: (1) foreskin and (2) cutting, removing. The target of 'foreskin' is the 'rebellious ideas' of the Israelites, that is to say their inclination to idolatry.

The target of 'cutting' is the removal of these rebellious ideas. Hence, the 'circumcision of the heart' denotes *the process* of the extirpation of vicious and rebellious thoughts. Since both instances of the metaphor occur in admonishing (Deuteronomy) or even threatening (Jeremiah) verses, this process is a harsh and painful one, motivated by stern pedagogical concerns.

There is still one essential thing to be said about the target conceptual space. The circumcision metaphor does not refer to a clearly pre-existing target such as in schoolbook examples ('Richard is a gorilla', 'Man is a wolf', where stereotyped animal characteristics are mapped onto a rich existing conceptualisation of humans). The circumcision metaphor presupposes the possibility of the existence of a target space, that is to say the possibility of a circumcision on another, non-physical level. Whether this target really exists is an ontological issue and not a linguistic or cognitive one. The only thing we can observe is that the metaphor under consideration contains an *existential statement* about the target. It says: 'There is something in the mind which can be likened to circumcision'. Hence, the metaphor does not only *qualify* this inward process via projection, it also says that it *can and should exist*. Therefore, from a linguistic and cognitive[47] viewpoint, I would say that the circumcision metaphor is target-creating.[48]

5.4 Philo's analogical reading of the Biblical circumcision-metaphor

A systematic analogical reading has been undertaken by Philo of Alexandria (25 BCE–50 CE). He was a Hellenised Jew steeped in Greek philosophy and Homeric exegesis. He interpreted the Hebrew Scriptures systematically along analogical and allegorical lines. He was a contemporary of Paul, and his hermeneutics are believed to be a parallel of Paul's reading of the Hebrew Bible. I will show that this is not the case with respect to the circumcision metaphor.

I will present Philo's interpretation of Deuteronomy 10:16 in a concise form, since this issue has already been extensively discussed in Niehoff (2003). Philo departs from the Greek translation (the Septuagint). His interpretation runs as follows:

(1) The foreskin is 'superfluous with respect to procreation' (Niehoff 2003, p. 96) and therefore it should be removed. 'In this way circumcision emerges as a necessary perfection of Creation (Niehoff 2003, p. 96)'.
(2) The physical operation expresses a spiritual essence (Niehoff 2003, p. 95).
(3) The removal of the foreskin corresponds via analogy to the 'excision of superfluous accretions of the intellect', such as 'hard', 'rebellious', 'refractory thoughts', and 'arrogance' (cited by Niehoff 2003, p. 95).

It deserves attention that Philo's analogical reading leads to the same interpretation as the one I reached via lexical analogy: for Philo, the circumcision-metaphor also addresses rebellion and denotes the 'excision' (Philo, *The Special Laws I*) of all superfluous thoughts and excessive pleasures. Philo also goes back, albeit implicitly, to the notion of *arel* (meaning 'imperfect'), which he translates as 'superfluous'. This is in line with rabbinical thinking according to which Creation, which in principle should be perfect, still needs some corrections, one of them being circumcision.[49] In Philo's mind, all that is superfluous contradicts perfection. In keeping with this, Philo regards rebellious thoughts as 'superfluous' ones.[50] It is interesting to note that Philo, throughout his analogical interpretation, identifies circumcision of the heart as a metaphor in the full sense of the word. Source, target, and mapping are unmistakably clear here.

5.5 What about the experiential basis of the circumcision-metaphor?

Interpreted from an experiential, bodily perspective, 'circumcise your heart' could mean 'be more sensitive and hearken to God's word'.[51] The removal of the foreskin makes the glans more sensitive, and this experience might be projected onto the heart as the seat of thoughts and feelings and whose form resembles that of the glans.[52] The underlying metaphorical statement would then be: REVELATION IS LUST. In the light of the fact that the metaphor GOD IS THE HUSBAND OF HIS PEOPLE is widespread in the prophetic writings, this interpretation is not to be discarded wholesale. The problem with this approach, however, is that it does not square with the cultural construct around circumcision and sexual satisfaction: (1) According to all known Jewish folk-theories until Maimonides, the function of circumcision consists in weakening lust.[53] (2) In the Hebrew Bible, the motif of lust is exclusively developed with respect to worshipping alien gods (temple prostitution, wild pagan orgies). (3) The motif of the extirpation of rebellious thoughts connotes pain, as I have expounded, not lust.

6 THE PAULINE CIRCUMCISION METAPHOR

Now, finally, I return to Paul. Why did he retrieve a notion from the Jewish canon, which he seemingly no longer regarded as binding? One might presume that at least the metaphorical meaning of 'circumcision' in the verses of Deuteronomy and Jeremiah, to which he most obviously referred, was still precious to him. Even that seems not to be the case. Paul's intention was more specific, but also more difficult to uncover. Let us now focus on the following verses:

> For he is not a Jew, which is one outwardly; neither is that circumcision, which is outward in the flesh (Romans 2:28). But a Jew is inward/hidden; and circumcision is that of the heart, in the spirit, and not in the letter; whose praise is not of men, but of God (Romans 2:29).

In these verses, circumcision as metaphor appears within a cluster of notions referring respectively to ritual, anthropological, theological, and metaphysical entities. In my analysis, I shall first list those things which we can observe; subsequently, I will try to distil the possible messages from this highly complex passage. There are also other instances of circumcision of the heart in the Pauline oeuvre (Colossians 2:11 and Philippians 3:4), but these will not be discussed here: Paul's authorship of *Colossians* is heavily disputed. And regarding Philippians 3:4, as has been contended by Windsor (2014, p. 53), the words 'we are the circumcision', which might have been a feast for metaphorologists, do not include Paul's gentile audience but only apply to him and Timothy, who also was a Jew.[54] In that case there would be no metaphor.

6.1 Contextual and historical elements

Just as in the preceding instances, the circumcision metaphor appears in a polemic context (Romans 2:17–27). Paul addresses a so-called Jew for boasting of his being Jewish.[55] The fact that Jews appear in the third-person plural indicates that Paul is addressing Gentile Christians (see Jennings 2013, p. 55) In fact, Jewish presence in Rome at that time may not have been significant, Claudius (10 BCE–54 CE) having expelled the Jews in 49 CE (Smallwood 2001, p. 215). *Romans* appeared between 55 and 58. Claudius' successor Nero adopted a Jew-friendly policy. But the letter was written just at the beginning of his reign (54 CE).

Paul accuses his interlocutor of not keeping the law, while calling himself a Jew. He accuses him of blaspheming 'the Name of God among the Gentiles' (Romans 2:24). The wording of this reproach is typically biblical, echoing Leviticus 22:32: 'And ye shall not profane My holy name; but I will be hallowed among the children of Israel'.

The notion of *Chillul Ha-Shem*, desecrating the Name of God amidst the gentiles, is one of the harshest reprimands that can be formulated in Judaism. Up to the present times, it denotes a behaviour unworthy of a Jew in the presence of non-Jews. Then Paul says: 'For he is not a Jew, which is one outwardly; neither is that circumcision, which is outward in the flesh. But a Jew is inward/hidden; and circumcision is that of the heart' (Romans 2:28–29).

Unequivocally, the word 'Jew', immediately and repeatedly preceding the motif of heart circumcision, appears in a positive sense and clearly represents a strong value. It also serves as a clue to understand Paul's circumcision of the heart. The notion of the 'hidden Jew' seems to be equivalent to the 'circumcision of the heart'. In the light of the immediate context, circumcision clearly appears as a marker of Jewishness. As to the broader context, things are the same. After reprimanding the interlocutor, who was tremendously proud of his being circumcised, Paul launches a question which introduces his view on the destiny of the Jewish people:

> What then is the superiority of the Jew? Or what is the benefit of circumcision? (Romans 3:1)

Again, Paul seems to be using 'circumcision' and Jewishness as conceptually very closely connected, the former, as argued above, being emblematic of the latter. The rhetorical situation of *Romans* is fairly similar to that of *Galatians*. Paul faced a gentile audience which was more than willing to undergo circumcision. In Roman society, imitating Judaism was a fashionable thing to do. Thiessen (2014) believes that Paul's so-called Jewish interlocutor got himself circumcised without caring about any Jewish religious authority or ruling.

With respect to Paul's attitude towards Judaism, *Romans* contains new and surprising elements: Paul's straightforward identification with the Jewish people (Romans 11:1), his saying that Israel's election shall never be undone (Romans 11:29), and his admonition never to look down on the Jews (Romans 11:20)[56] have rarely been so sharply expressed in his work. A possible reason for Paul's public valorisation of Judaism in *Romans* is that it might have been animated by the plight of the Jews under Claudius and have stirred a spontaneous reflex of solidarity with his own brethren.

6.2 Paul's metaphor as a value-shift

In sharp contrast with the Biblical precedents discussed in section 5, Paul addresses the irrelevance of ritual circumcision, at least for Christians. In the light of the fact, however, that Paul already adamantly advocated the suppression of the rite in his non-metaphorical speech (cf. *Galatians*), the circumcision metaphor would be blatantly superfluous and merely ornamental if it performed no more than that.

Paul's circumcision metaphor effects a value-shift. Ritual circumcision does not make any sense, Paul says, but there is another level where it should be realised. The abrogation of circumcision is certainly not the sole and most important message of the metaphor.

Paradoxically, Paul dissuades his audience from undergoing circumcision using a specifically Jewish vocabulary: 'desecrating God's name' (*chillul ha-shem*), 'outer Jew' versus 'inner Jew'. The fact that he needed circumcision as a metaphor to abrogate genital circumcision is puzzling in itself. He introduces a supreme Jewish value to abolish it.

7 INTERPRETATION: WHICH VALUES ARE IMPORTED?
7.1 The source-referent

Our exegetical inquiry teaches us that in Paul's thought-world circumcision is a metonymy for the process of becoming a Jew and hence for law-abidingness (see also Dunn 2008, p. 315, and Windsor 2014, p. 45). I called this metonymy *emblematic* because this relation is not self-evident and was constructed in Paul's own work. Hence, the source domain of circumcision is the Torah, because in Paul's mind the most salient feature of circumcision is the fact that it is a law belonging to the Jewish written codex. This is not the case with the biblical precedents of the circumcision-metaphor, where other features need to be highlighted to understand the metaphor.

Contrary to some interpretations (Boyarin 1994, p. 80), Philo's analogy is not applicable in the case of Paul because it departs from the assumption that the foreskin is a mark of imperfection and something superfluous. This cannot be Paul's view, since he regarded circumcision as objectionable. On the inward, spiritual level, circumcision can *not* mean the extirpation of something evil, since the parallel (*analogon*) of that evil is absent in the source. Hence, the understanding of Paul's metaphor would *not* be advanced by highlighting the sub-units of 'cutting' and 'foreskin' in the source-domain cognitive model of 'circumcision'. In a word: Contrary to the biblical precedents and also to their Philonic reading, there is nothing to be cut off in Paul's case. The rhetorical situation in which circumcision of the heart appears is an additional argument for this view. The whole passage is about identity. Paul introduces the metaphor in order to suggest that Christian identity, though inspired by Jewish tradition, is not to be affirmed via external signs of commitment. This paradigm change has been overlooked in Pauline studies.[57]

The rhetorical situation of *Romans* (Paul talking to gentiles flirting with Jewish rituals) is also crucial to understand why he hints at the prophetic and toraic circumcision metaphors (Jeremiah 4:4; Deuteronomy 10:16), though he makes a totally different use of 'heart circumcision'. The reminiscence of this image, hallowed by its appearance in the Holy Writ, must have impressed his audience. Since 'circumcision' in Paul emblematically means 'being or becoming a Jew obedient to the Torah', it stands for a series of duties, that is to say the duties to be fulfilled by a faithful Jew. We noticed already that Paul was extremely uncompromising about that point: a Jew who fails to obey the minutiae of the Law is doomed. Paul, however, wanted Christianity to be freed from a codified system of duties the way Jewish legislation represents it. On the other hand, being a Jew is a value, particularly in *Romans*. How to uphold that value when the legal system it stands for is dismissed? There seems to be at least one solution, namely, to transpose the whole system of Jewish duties to another dimension, which in Paul's thought world is inwardness/hiddenness.

Three notions point towards this dimension: 'heart' (*kardia*), 'inwardness' (*to krypton*), and 'spirit' (*pneuma*). But what exactly is shifted towards that inward level? This brings us to the analysis of the target.

7.2 The target-referent

What is the target of the circumcision metaphor? As I have already argued with respect to the biblical precedents, the target is not obvious, unlike schoolbook cases ('man is a wolf'), but is presupposed by the circumcision metaphor, which, by the same token, also contains an *existential statement* ('there is—or must be—something like an inward circumcision'). Circumcision of the heart is an inward process which parallels physical circumcision. However, that inward process is a target which has just been created by the metaphorical statement. It is like a blank white projection screen which has been opened just a few moments ago. Or, to put it more philosophically, the target is an entity which is glaringly underdetermined. Consequently, it provides us with no clues for the mapping process. For this reason, Paul's metaphor can hardly be brought back to a conceptual metaphor in Lakoff's sense (such as TIME IS A VALUABLE COMMODITY), since in such a case the target is an entity or idea which already exists. This being said, acknowledging the cognitive performance of metaphors consisting in shaping extremely underdetermined (or even creating new) target domains seems to be essential for the study of philosophical and theological concepts.

7.3 The projection process

In Paul's case, this state of affairs is even more intricate, because, in the present metaphorical process, the source *loses* the values it initially stood for. Being abrogated, these values *cease to exist*. To put it simply: in Paul's circumcision metaphor, a target is *created* and the salient source elements *disappear*. In section 1.3.3 I described such a paradoxical phenomenon as the result of a *dual-phased* process with respect to evaluation: (1) the source stands for a positive value which is imported into the target (via the blending-space); (2) via inversion (operated in the blending space) the source gets de-valuated, which allows a value-shift (instead of a value-extension).

What, in this process, happens to the values that the source emblematically stands for? They are projected into the blending space, where they are transformed. Subsequently the outcome (transformed source-value) is projected upon the target. Only in a second move is the source affected by value-inversion. What matters now is the question of which source-elements are projected into the blending space and how they are transformed.

Two types of reading can emerge from this value-inversion: (1) The Torah is a supreme value which should be superseded by a new supreme value, that is to say faith. The Torah disappears and gives rise to Christian devotion. In that case, the target is an empty semantic space, which has to be filled in by something as valuable as Jewish law-abidingness in pre-Christian times. The sole foregrounded source element, then, is the notion of supreme value as such, nothing else. (2) According to the second reading the Torah, metonymically represented by circumcision, is the legal formulation of a set of values which should be rephrased within a Christian, cross-ethnic (universal) context. This reading, which points towards ethics, invokes cross-domain correlations between source and target and is more entitled to claim plausibility. However, as we have already seen, similarity between source and target is problematic in this case, the latter being underdetermined. Let me briefly discuss both avenues.[58]

7.3.1 First projection alternative: From law to faith

Many commentaries invoke the notions of faith and devotedness to God, which would supersede the former (Jewish) priority accorded to deeds. Their strength lies in their semantic simplicity: why project something from a source which is no longer needed?

The disadvantage of this approach is that it implicitly treats Paul's metaphor as a mere ornament of speech. If so, why did Paul choose a metaphor so heavily loaded with Jewish reminiscences? And why did he associate it with a notion even more heavily value-loaded, such as 'the inner Jew'?

7.3.2 Second projection alternative: From law to ethics

Since 'circumcision' in Paul stands for a set of duties, the target therefore can be a set of duties as well. The latter, however, should stand for something which is comparable to Israelite law. This can, in strictly semantic terms, only be something akin to this law, that is, ethics or justice. Therefore, one could argue, Paul's metaphor can only make sense if it effects the transformation of Jewish Law into ethics.

This brings up the question of Paul's ethics. Throughout his work, Paul insists on virtues, 'virtue' being the core notion out of which Greek and Roman ethics were developed. Paul, familiar with Hellenism, used virtue ethics as a model. Paul's virtues are rooted in Jewish Law but stripped of the legal formulation in which they are conveyed. They stress justice (Romans 8:10), fair business practice (1 Thessalonians 4:6), and attention to the poor (Galatians 2:10; 2 Corinthians 8:14). Pope Benedict XVI worded it thus (Ratzinger 2009, p. 40): in Paul 'love for the poor is liturgy'. Paul's transformation of Law into ethics culminates in the verse (Galatians 5:14): 'The entire Law, in one word, is fulfilled in this: you will love your neighbour as yourself'. This is a citation of Leviticus 19:18, but it appears here as a roundup of the whole Torah. In this sense, these words come straight from the 'tanna' Rabbi Hillel,[59] whose grandson, Rabban Gamaliel, was Paul's teacher in his youth. Asked by a proselyte to be taught the entire Torah while he was standing on one foot, Hillel (50 BCE–10 CE) answered: 'What is hateful to you, do not do to your neighbour. That's the whole Torah; the rest is the explanation of this. Go and study it!' (Talmud Babli, Shabbat 31a). The inward, motivational (instead of legal) character of Paul's ethics is reflected in his saying 'I delight [. . .] in the Law of God according to the inward man [*kato to eso anthropon*]' (Romans 7:22).

A Pauline metaphor which comes very close to that of the circumcision of the heart appears in a verse where gentiles who act rightfully are said to have the 'work of Law [*ergon tou nomon*] written on their hearts [*graphton en tais kardiais*]' (Romans 2:15). The fact that the '*work* of law' appears in this context lets us surmise that what is meant here is not mere faith, but an internal disposition towards action. Paul's moral advice reflects the Torah, albeit very selectively. From a modern perspective one would say that Paul focused on the *ratio legis*, the motivation of the Law, instead of its wording. In the light of the foregoing, one might conclude that Paul's circumcision-metaphor constitutes the cradle of Christian ethics.

Hence, Paul's circumcision-metaphor might answer the question: what are the Christian duties? They are duties of the heart, which does not mean that they are confined to nice thoughts and feelings. Paul was certainly not inimical to action, as many theologians have misread him. Paul posits justification by faith mainly in opposition to justification by works of the Law (*ergon nomoi*) in Galatians 2:16, which in Hebrew are called *mitzvoth*[60] or *ma-ase ha-torah*. What matters to him is the rootedness of our actions in an inward disposition which he calls 'faith' or 'love', and not in a written divine legislation which would entail that good deeds are performed out of fear. The rejection of fear as a motive for behaviour is explicitly worded in Romans 8:15.[61] The word 'fear' does indeed appear in the Hebrew notion of *irat shamayim* (the fear of Heaven) as the motive for right behaviour in Judaism.

7.4 Conclusion on Paul's circumcision metaphor

There are two possible answers to the question of which elements of the source (circumcision) are projected onto the target. Each response reflects a fundamental stance in Pauline exegesis: what is more fundamental in Paul? Religion or ethics? The first position is that of most religious interpreters. Protestants would tend to stress faith, Catholics both: faith and good works.[62] (This opposition between denominations, to be sure, is a bit stereotypical.) The second position is endorsed by the many secular and philosophical readers of Paul, such as Hobbes, Spinoza, Locke, Friedrich Engels, Jacques Derrida, and the liberation theologians. They all stress Paul's concern for justice, as Jennings (2013, pp. 2–8) observes. As to the circumcision metaphor itself, contextual elements and redundancies all over Paul's work make the ethical reading of it more plausible, although it has mostly been obscured by theologians. Last but not least, circumcision of the heart and the notion of the 'inner Jew' both point towards an inner Torah, by reason of the emblematic meaning they are endowed with by Paul. Hence Jewish law points first and foremost towards justice and ethical behaviour, as Jennings (2013) has convincingly expounded. However, in the light of the fact that law tends to legalism and religious law to legal fetishism, Paul wanted to free the original Jewish law from all aspects which might hinder the spontaneous solidarity and reciprocal loving kindness within his Christian community. Jennings calls it 'spirited solidarity' and 'improvisation of justice' (Jennings 2013, p. 12).[63] The fact that Paul uses Jewish law as a metaphor (circumcision being a metonymy for it) shows that, whilst rejecting it, he endeavours to *rescue* it in the context of his cross-ethnic outreach.

What are the implications for Pauline exegesis? Can the present metaphorologi-cal investigation shed some light on the ongoing discussion on whether Paul saw Christians as part of the Jewish people or not? The rootedness of Christianity in Judaism is the core message of Paul's highly elaborated parable of the two olive trees (Romans 11). The gentiles are the branches of a wild olive tree which are grafted now onto a cultivated one. The 'roots' of the latter are 'holy' (Romans 11:16) and represent the patriarchs (cf. Windsor 2014, p. 52). Paul sees Christianity as partak-ing of the Jewish historical destiny. Most theologians explain this away by focusing on the biblical oracles (Romans 3:2), announcing the advent of Christ and a new covenant. In the light of the passage of *Romans* studied here, Christianity is firmly rooted in Jewish history. And like all reformers (Luther, Mohammed), Paul hoped that Jews would one day join the movement he created (Romans 11:25–32). But as Windsor, Eisenbaum, Thiessen, and others observe, Paul in no way endeavoured to redefine ancient Jewish morality.[64] What we have seen so far in this investigation, then, is that Paul was a Jewish reformer with a cross-ethnic outreach. However, he was also—and even above all—the propagator of a new faith.

8 THE TARGET DOMAIN AND THE EMERGENCE OF METAPHYSICS
8.1 Inner and outer

The notions of 'spirit', 'inwardness', and 'heart' are part of a cognitive space, that is, in cognitive linguistic terminology, the target domain of Paul's metaphor. In its literal sense, circumcision is outward and not inward, physical and not spiritual, effected on the penis and not on the heart. The referents of these three notions, though they do not form a conceptual unity, make up the space wherein the source cognitive model ('circumcision') develops its metaphorical meaning.

Boyarin (1994, p. 78) rightly observes that Romans 2:28–29 establishes a three-fold set of interrelated binary oppositions: (1) 'outer' versus 'inner', (2) 'in the flesh (penis)' versus 'in the heart', (3) 'in the letter' versus 'in the spirit'. Correspondingly, the source domain is the whole material world. According to Boyarin, this set of oppositions, particularly between the 'inner' and the 'outer' world, reveals a dualistic philosophy. Boyarin's dualism has been criticised by Barclay (1998). The debate is oti-ose, since the issue of monism versus dualism can only be settled within a philosoph-ical discourse debating the metaphysical question of whether the soul is a substance. In Hebrew scriptures, however, the notion of 'substance' (Greek: *hypokeimenon*) is absent. One thing remains certain: if Paul was not a dualist, his rhetoric is unquestioningly dyadic.[65] Paul's language *points towards* dualism. His circumcision metaphor presupposes a concept of inner space. The same holds for his saying: 'Do you not know that you are God's temple and that God's Spirit dwells in you?' (1 Corinthians 3:16; see also 1 Thessalonians 4:8).

Paul turns inwardness into the locus of salvation, into the space of the soteriological process. Only metaphor has the power to effect such a venture into new dimensions of being, particularly within non-philosophical speech. Metaphor is not an ornament of speech, certainly not in Paul. It leads us very close to metaphysics.

8.2. The breakthrough of metaphysics

The intrusion of metaphysics in Paul's discourse is clearly to be traced on a textual level. Paul follows Jewish law, while simplifying it and abrogating its ritual components. At one point, however, he *adds* something, and this addition is highly surprising: according to Paul, sexual immorality (*porneia*) would be unfaithfulness towards the indwelling spirit of Christ (1 Corinthians 6:13–18). Paul therefore advises to refrain from sex, or, in the worst case, to stay within a strict monogamous relationship.[66] Jesus is seen as the partner of the faithful person in a physical sense. We are presented with a variation of the biblical metaphor GOD IS THE HUSBAND OF HIS PEOPLE, all-pervasive in the prophetic writings, with the difference that the prophets clearly understood it as a metaphor, while in Paul it is a naked, physical fact.

8.3 Re-framing holiness

Until now we have been studying circumcision in its connection to Jewish identity and law-abidingness. However, there are other cognitive frames (or 'models', to use an alternative term) of Jewish practices that contain circumcision as an element. Circumcision is also a prerequisite for eating the Passover lamb. This Jewish ritual still existed in Paul's time (it was abandoned after the destruction of the Temple). Paul, however, says in *Corinthians* (1 Corinthians 5:7–8):

> Purge out therefore the old leaven, that ye may be a new lump, as ye are unleavened. For even Christ our Passover is sacrificed for us: Therefore let us keep the feast, not with old leaven, neither with the leaven of malice and wickedness; but with the unleavened *bread* of sincerity and truth.

We have already seen that circumcision is first and foremost the prerequisite to eat from the Pascal Lamb. The fact that Jesus is seen as the 'true' and ultimate appearance of the Passover lamb and 'true' circumcision is that of the heart, presents us with a radical re-framing of the Passover-ritual. In Paul's view, the holiness of the Pascal lamb (which in the Hebrew Bible is regarded as a 'holy', i.e. as a consecrated meal) is reflected in the holiness of Christ. Finally, the evildoers, seen as leaven, should be separated from the dough, which is the community of the faithful. This is an unmistakable allusion to the prohibition of eating leavened foods during the Passover-week. If we leave the immediate contexts in which these new clusters of meaning appear (the Passover motifs in *Corinthians* and the circumcision motif in *Romans*), and adopt an overarching view, Paul's heart circumcision appears to be an element of the re-framed Passover frame and denotes the (inward) disposition necessary to approach Christ, who in this new frame is the centre of holiness. Taking part in the Eucharist symbolically supersedes the Passover-meal. Was Paul aware that he seamlessly replaced all frame-elements of the old sacrificial cult by new ones? We will never know. However, within a frame-based (or even structuralist) approach it would make sense to say that Paul's heart circumcision has a greater degree of sanctity than physical circumcision, because Christ, as the corresponding frame-element, is infinitely superior in holiness (see 2 Corinthians 3:11) than the consecrated Passover lamb. The above analysis can only be tentative. It opens up, however, the possibility of finding a strong religious motivation for Paul's dismissal of genital circumcision. Advocating the circumcision of the heart, Paul re-frames the ancient rite in a Christological sense.

9 GENERAL CONCLUSIONS

The results of the present investigation come close to the statement made by Lakoff and Johnson in *Philosophy in the Flesh* (1999, p. 7): 'metaphorical thought is the principal tool that makes philosophical insight possible'. I would like to emphasise the point that metaphor not only shapes pre-existing notions (such as 'time', 'love' and 'argument', paradigmatic examples in cognitive linguistics; see Lakoff and Johnson 1980). Metaphor is also a fundamental process of the human mind that can create new targets and thus new metaphysical concepts. The mechanism by means of which a new notion emerges can be described as follows: Some metaphors imply an existential statement (formulated in logic by the proposition 'there is/are . . .'). 'Circumcise your heart' implies the statement that there is (or must be) such a process as 'inner circumcision'. This new conceptual entity (i.e. the process of inner circumcision), pre-supposed (I would even say 'created') by the metaphor, is like an empty screen upon which source elements are projected.

As to the projection process, it is dependent on (a) contextual elements, and (b) the emblematic (metonymic) meaning of the source. In the case of the circumcision metaphor in Deuteronomy, Jeremiah, and Philo, the source-element of 'cutting away' is foregrounded and projected upon the target (i.e. the 'inner' circumcision). The metaphor expresses the injunction to extirpate rebellious (idolatrous) tendencies from the mind. Since the source (genital circumcision) is *not* abrogated by the Hebrew metaphor, circumcision of the heart represents a *duty-extension*, not a shift. It says: The circumcision of the flesh *remains* a duty, but there are also other types of circumcision.

In Paul's case, the circumcision metaphor takes on a fundamentally different meaning. Paul abrogates circumcision (at least for gentiles), and hence his metaphor represents a duty-*shift*. Given his opposition to genital circumcision, it is highly unlikely that Paul wanted the source element of 'cutting' to be projected upon the target. Paul's identification of circumcision with Jewishness, which has an emblematic character, and the context in which the metaphor appears, strongly suggest that he wants circumcision of the heart to be understood as a transformation of the notion of the Torah. In this way, the Torah, which, within Paul's cross-ethnical outreach, can no longer be followed in its present articulation, is transformed and thereby 'rescued' into an inward ethical disposition. The inward metaphorical 'space', which Paul metaphorically defines as 'God's temple', receives a distinction which it did not yet possess in Jewish and Greek antiquity: it becomes the locus by excellence where salvation is achieved. The ensuing centrality of inwardness will profoundly mark the Western conception of the self.

10 POSTSCRIPT

Only deeply rooted rituals can be used as a starting point towards internalisation. Without physical circumcision as a cognitive source model, Paul would never have opened up the inner dimension of devotion. Ritual and the interior life are 'interconnected' (Cavallin 2013, p. 13). We are living in a time marked by de-ritualisation, the valuation of interior life, moral feelings, good intentions, and authenticity. The individual's self, however, constituted by a long historical process of internalisation, has become diffuse (Cavallin 2013, p. 97). In religious studies, the pendulum is swinging to the other extreme point. Since a couple of years, we are witnessing a growing scholarly interest for material objects and rituals in religious practice: relics, rosaries, incense, ostensories, candles, Torah-scrolls, prayer shawls and skullcaps, devotional art, liturgical music, devotional necklaces and medals (Seland 2007), etc., which may be seen as 'the material or physical and expressive aspects of religion' being 'essential to our religious experience' (Laugerud and Skinnebach 2007, p. 10). These approaches might open new and complementary avenues of investigation.

NOTES

1. I must express my huge gratitude to all scholars who helped me in this interdisciplinary undertaking: Professor Paul Chilton, who, as the editor of the present volume, supervised my paper with greatest care and challenging questions; the late Professor René Dirven (Duisburg University); Rev. Professor James Francis (Sunderland University); Professor Jean Pierre van Noppen (Université Libre de Bruxelles); Professor Matthew Thiessen (Saint Louis University); Rabbi Mark Neiger M.A. (Leo Baeck College/King's College London); Rabbi Abraham Dahan (Synagogue Beth Hillel, Brussels) and the editors of Oxford University Press.
2. 1Cor 2:9. Note on the translations: generally I used the King James Version, which comes very close to the original text. In some cases I amended the extant translation to obtain a more precise rendering.
3. I refrain from using the expression 'religious experience' because so-called religious experiences rarely conflict with the theological framework of those affected by this

experience (see Bisschops 2003, p. 114). Our beliefs shape that which we call our religious 'experience'.

4. Barclay (1998, p. 556) rightly remarks that 'multi-ethnic' is a more appropriate term. The notion of 'universalism' is underdetermined. Recent scholarship insists on the Jewish 'self-apartness from the nations' (Dunn 2008, p. 380), which Paul is believed to have resisted. Actually, all peoples at that time maintained their 'self-apartness'.

5. See van Noppen, *Theolinguistics 1* (1981) and *Theolinguistics 2* (1983). Van Noppen's approach is presented in a concise way in his paper *Theographic Metaphors, Ordinary Words with Extraordinary Meanings* (1999). On theolinguistics, see also David Crystal's chapter in the present volume (chapter 1, 'Whatever happened to theolinguistics?').

6. Among the many scholars who have worked on theolinguistics, the following names might be mentioned: Jean-Pierre van Noppen, Wim De Pater, Eberhard Jüngel, Sallie McFague, Janet Martin Soskice, Anna Wierzbicka, and David Crystal.

7. See Mikolajczak and Rybka (2014).

8. See the book series *Theolinguistica* published by Bauer and Raspe.

9. The term 'frame' is used here in the following sense: 'Frames are (. . .) tightly linked chunks of conceptual structure which get evoked together. (. . .) Typically, complex frames have roles, and relations between those roles' (Dancygier and Sweetser 2014, p. 18). A very comprehensive development of frame-semantics with respect to metaphor has been elaborated by Sullivan (2013).

10. Robert von Thaden's chapter on Saint Paul (2014, p. 104) illustrates the usefulness of the notion of 'frame' when dealing with the Jewish priestly world.

11. That is, the description of the target with respect to appearance, condition, constitution, etc., e.g. 'The door-keeper of the *Tropical-Bar* is a gorilla'. In 'terrorism is the cancer of civilisation', the metaphor focuses on *the way* terrorism spreads (destroying from the inside via uncontrollable dissemination) and pretends to explain *why* it is so difficult to defeat it. The descriptive function of metaphor has received much attention following Hofstadter and Sander (2013), who focus on the heuristic function of metaphor and analogy in the elaboration of categories.

12. For instance the experience of love: 'The metaphor involves understanding one domain of experience, love, in terms of a very different domain of experience, journeys'. (Lakoff 1993, p. 206)

13. 'What? Know ye not that your body is the temple of the Holy Ghost which is in you (. . .)?' (1 Cor 6:19).

14. 'For ye are the Temple of the Living God (. . .)' (2 Cor 6:16).

15. In fact, the Hebrew word for impurity (*tumah*) has both meanings: ritual and moral impurity. Jesus' saying can also be interpreted as a word-play with homonymy conveying an ethical message.

16. 'R. Kahana said: "By the time I was eighteen years old I had studied the whole Shas, yet I did not know that a verse cannot depart from its plain meaning until today." What does he inform us? That a man should study and subsequently understand'. *Sabbath*, 63 a. (*Talmud Bavli*).

17. On 'reprojection' or 'projection backwards', see Fauconnier and Turner (2002, p. 44).

18. In this analysis I base myself on Fauconnier (2005).

19. The methodological importance of interpreting metaphors in the light of their historical precedents has been stressed by Friedrich Keller-Bauer (1984), Van Noppen (1988 and 1999), and Ralph Bisschops (1994).

20. See Steiner (1999).

21. This has convincingly been shown by Matthew Thiessen in *Contesting Conversion* (2011).

22. See Matthew Thiessen (2011, and 2014, pp. 373–391).

23. See Hoffman (1996, p. 39).

24. According to David A. Bernat (2009, p. 69), Exodus 12:10 is more foundational for circumcision than the covenant-idea.

25. 'There is neither Jew nor Greek (. . .) for ye are all one in Christ Jesus' (Galatians 3:28).

26. 'Behold, I Paul say unto you, that if ye be circumcised, Christ shall profit you nothing' (Galatians 5:2).
27. 'For I testify again to every man that is circumcised, that he is a debtor to do the whole law. Christ is become of no effect unto you, whosoever of you are justified by the law; ye are fallen from grace' (Galatians 5:3–4).
28. Galatians 5:3.
29. 'For as many as are of the works of the law are under the curse: for it is written, Cursed [is] every one that continueth not in all things which are written in the book of the law to do them' (Galatians 3:10).
30. Babylonian Talmud, *Yebamoth* (46a): 'The Sages, however, said, "Whether he had performed ritual ablution but had not been circumcised or whether he had been circumcised but had not performed the prescribed ritual ablution, he is not a proper proselyte unless he has been circumcised and has also performed the prescribed ritual ablution"'.
31. Samuel Holdheim (1806–1860) makes this clear in his book on circumcision (1844, p. 8): 'The one [i.e. non-circumcised man] who does not effect circumcision on himself, is a destroyer of the Covenant. Ergo: one can destroy the Covenant only if one is already part of it' [translation mine].
32. Surprisingly, Daniel Boyarin (1994, p. 112) writes that 'circumcision alone counts as conversion to Judaism'.
33. In early Israelite religion, as we know it from Deuteronomistic sources, circumcision was a custom but in no way the sign of a covenant (Hoffman 1996, p. 33).
34. Whether the children of Israel were circumcised while they were wandering in the desert is still a matter of rabbinical discussion.
35. Available at *Bible Hub* (online portal).
36. 'Orlat' is the *status constructus* for 'orla'.
37. Incidentally, it is precisely the blood which the liturgical text accompanying the circumcision evokes ('in your blood live!'). Blood is also the central motif in the enigmatic biblical passage where Zippora circumcises Moses' son and says 'a bloody husband thou art' (Exodus 4:26).
38. Marc Neiger (2011, p. 12) writes 'The biblical text does not give a specific role to the blood of circumcision, unlike sacrificial blood'. On the symbolism of blood in circumcision, see also Hoffmann (1996).
39. Cognitive linguistics focuses on metaphors which are part of everyday speech, including standard expressions, because they reveal the way we conceptualise our world view.
40. According to the rabbinical interpretation (Rashi, Sifra), the three years are counted from the time of planting. During such a short period, however, fruits grow only in rare cases, and the interdiction of their consumption would have a limited sense.
41. 'Now, he (Abraham) was ordered, WALK BEFORE ME, AND BE THOU WHOLE (Hebr. "tam"). If he circumcised himself at the ear, he would not be WHOLE; at the mouth, he would not be WHOLE; at the heart, he would not be WHOLE. Where could he circumcise himself and yet be WHOLE ("tam")? Nowhere else than at the "orla" (foreskin) of the body' (*Midrash Rabbah*—Genesis XLVI:5).
42. See Mark Neiger, *A Hill of Foreskins* (2011, p. 16).
43. Bernat (2009, pp. 83–114) endeavours to interpret *arel* (foreskinned) as a metaphor when applied to the mouth (Exodus 6:4–5) or the heart (Leviticus 26:41). His reading certainly deserves consideration. However, neither the Septuagint nor Philo sustain this reading (as Bernat himself observes).
44. In the locution *chacham lev*, meaning 'wise of heart' and denoting technical skillfulness.
45. 'For in death there is no remembrance of thee, who shall give thee thanks?' (Psalm 6:6); 'What profit is there in my blood when I go down to the pit? Shall the dust praise thee? Shall it declare thy truth?' (Psalm 30:9).
46. In another biblical context (Isaiah 25:6–8), a similar state of affairs has been noticed by Doyle (2003, pp. 153–184). He contends that some Hebrew word-play can also be

regarded as metaphor in that, of the evoked meanings, the least isotopic one functions as a metaphor of the other, more isotopic one.

47. It should be repeated once again that 'cognitive' does not imply that there actually is some verifiable or falsifiable cognition. Cognitive sciences deal with mental processes only, not with truth.

48. We can maybe understand the 'creation of a target domain' as the extreme case of underdetermination, where the verbal expression simply triggers the human cognitive processes to set up a blank conceptual domain ('space'), which is filled out by additional knowledge and inference.

49. 'Whatever was created in the first six days requires further preparation, e.g., mustard needs sweetening, vetches need sweetening, wheat needs grinding, and man too needs to be finished off [i.e. by circumcision]' (Midrash Rabbah—Genesis 11:6).

50. Niehoff (2003, p. 96) explains this in the following way: 'As much as Eve was a harmful addition to Adam, who until then had enjoyed perfect rationality and harmony with God, the passions are a harmful addition to the mind and therefore need to be cut off'.

51. The great medieval commentator Rashi sees it this way (cf. Rashi on Exodus 6:12 and Leviticus 19:23).

52. This more than obvious resemblance is noted by Philo (The Special Laws I). However, according to him, the mapping element is functionality: the penis is functional for procreation in the same way as the heart is functional for the working of the mind.

53. Maimonides (who was also a physician) writes: 'Circumcision simply counteracts excessive lust, for there is no doubt that circumcision weakens the power of sexual excitement, and sometimes lessens the natural enjoyment' (Moses Maimonides, Guide for the Perplexed, part 3, chapter 49). As to female pleasure during intercourse with non-circumcised men, see Midrash Rabbah: 'R. Hunia observed: When a woman is intimate with an uncircumcised person, she finds it hard to tear herself away' (Genesis Rabbah, 80:11).

54. 'For we are the true circumcision, who worship in the Spirit of God and glory in Christ Jesus and put no confidence in the flesh'.

55. Recent literature is unanimous about the fact that Paul addresses one single person (real or imaginary) in Romans 2:17–29. Thiessen is affirmative about the fact that Paul's interlocutor is a circumcised gentile (2014, pp. 378–379).

56. 'Has God cast away his people? God forbid. For I am also an Israelite of the seed of Abraham and the tribe of Benjamin'.

57. To start with John Calvin, who wrote: 'And what he subjoins with regard to true circumcision, is taken from various passages of Scripture, and even from its general teaching; for the people are everywhere commanded to circumcise their hearts, and it is what the Lord promises to do. The foreskin was cut off, not indeed as the small corruption of one part, but as that of the whole nature. Circumcision then signified the mortification of the whole flesh' (Commentary on Romans 2:28). In this reading Calvin is obviously inspired by Colossians 2:11. Colossians is not written by Paul, albeit attributed to him.

58. I will not deal with the many pulpit interpretations. Mostly preachers, but also exegetes, are quite careless interpreting biblical metaphors, seeing them as mere ornaments of speech.

59. A 'tanna' is one of the founding members of the Rabbinical tradition which led to Mishnah and Talmud.

60. I go along with Boyarin (1994, p. 112) that for Paul 'literal observance was merely irrelevant, being only in the flesh' and not 'a sinful striving for work-righteousness' in the sense of the Lutheran tradition.

61. 'For you did not receive the Spirit of slavery to fall back into fear, but you have received the Spirit of adoption as sons, by whom we cry "Abba, Father"'.

62. See Focant (2011, p. 51), who, from a Catholic viewpoint, stresses that both faith and ethics are important to Paul.

63. Jennings (2013, p. 54) goes even farther, asserting that Paul did not even care about the Christian community as such: 'there is no need to become in any way a Christian in order to become faithful of the messiah'.

64. This reveals an ambivalent attitude that was also typical for Reform Judaism in the nineteenth century. It wrestled with problems similar to Paul's. In the context of Jewish emancipation, the question arose of how to remain a faithful Jew whilst joining the gentile social tissue. Rabbi Samuel Holdheim (1806–1860), one of the great thinkers of that movement, endeavoured to extract the ethical core out of Jewish Law (*halakha*). He revealingly used a rhetoric very similar to Paul's, deliteralising and metaphorising canonical notions using the adjective 'true' ('true offering is . . .', 'true fast is . . .', etc.). It is no accident that his opponent Heinrich Graetz (1870, p. 565) goes so far as to say that 'since Paul of Tarsus, Judaism has never known such an enemy from within' as Holdheim. On the other hand, Holdheim never redefined Orthodox Judaism, neither did he define Reform Judaism in such a way that orthodox Jews would be excluded from it. To this day Reform Judaism welcomes Orthodox people (on Samuel Holdheim, see Bisschops 1999 and 2007).

65. Personally, I think that Paul's dualism is clearly attested in 2 Cor 5:1–10.

66. Sanders (1977, p. 455) extensively discusses the radical novelty and strangeness of this vision: 'We might expect an argument that a Christian should not behave in such and such a way, since immorality is not appropriate to being Christian, since it is forbidden in the Bible or since such a transgression would result in punishment from God; but to say that one should not fornicate because fornication produces a union which excludes one from a union which is salvific is to employ a rationale which today is not readily understood'.

REFERENCES

Barclay, John M. G. (1998). Paul and Philo on circumcision: Romans 2:25–9 in social and cultural context. *New Testament Studies* 44 (4), 536–556.

Bernat, David A. (2009). *Sign of the Covenant: Circumcision in the Priestly Tradition*. Atlanta: Society of Biblical Literature.

Bisschops, Ralph (1994). *Die Metapher als Wertsetzung*. Lang: Frankfurt.

Bisschops, Ralph (1999). Metaphor as the internalisation of a ritual, with a case study of Samuel Holdheim (1806–1860). In Ralph Bisschops and James Francis (eds.), *Metaphor, Canon and Community*, pp. 284–307. Bern: Peter Lang.

Bisschops, Ralph (2003). Are religious metaphors rooted in experience? On Ezekiel's wedding metaphors. In Kurt Feyaerts (ed.), *The Bible through Metaphor and Translation*, pp. 113–152. Bern: Peter Lang.

Bisschops, Ralph (2007). Samuel Holdheim and Sigismund Stern. In Christian Wiese (ed.), *Redefining Judaism in an Age of Emancipation*, pp. 241–277. Leiden-Boston: Brill.

Boyarin, Daniel (1994). *A Radical Jew: Paul and the Politics of Identity*. Berkeley: University of California Press.

Cavallin, Clemens (2013). *Ritualisation and Human Interiority*. Copenhagen: Museum Tusculanum Press.

Cohen, Leonardo (2009). *The Missionary Strategies of the Jesuits in Ethiopia (1555–1632)*. Aethiopische Forschungen 70. Wiesbaden: Harrassowitz Verlag.

Cohen, Shaye (2010). *The Significance of Yavneh and other Essays in Jewish Hellenism*. Tübingen: Mohr Siebeck.

Dancygier, Barbara and Eve Sweetser (2014). *Figurative Language*. New York: Cambridge University Press.

Doyle, Brian (2003). How do single isotopes meet? In Kurt Feyaerts (ed.), *The Bible through Metaphor and Translation*, pp. 153–184. Bern: Peter Lang.

Dunn, James D. G. (1998). Paul: Apostate or apostle of Israel? *Zeitschrift für die neutestamentliche Wissenschaft* 89 (3–4), 256–271.

Dunn, James D. G. (2008). *The New Perspective on Paul*. Cambridge: Eerdmans Publishing.

Efros, Israel (1964). *Ancient Jewish Philosophy: A Study in Metaphysics and Ethics*. Detroit: Wayne State University Press.

Elliot, Susan M. (1999). Choose your mother, choose your master: Galatians 4:21–5:1 in the shadow of the Anatolian mother of the gods. *Journal of Biblical Literature* 118(4), 661–683.

Eisenbaum, Pamela (2009). *Paul Was Not a Christian: The Original Message of a Misunderstood Apostle*. New York: HarpersCollins.

Fauconnier, Gilles (2005). Compression and emergent structures. *Language and Linguistics* 6.4, 523–538.

Fauconnier, Gilles and Mark Turner (1998). Conceptual integration networks. *Cognitive Science* 22(2), 133–187.

Fauconnier, Gilles and Mark Turner (2002). *The Way We Think*. New York: Basic Books.

Focant, Camille (2011). Paul, le Judaïsme et la Torah. *Revue Théologique de Louvain* 42, 35–52.

Graetz, Heinrich (1870). *Geschichte der Juden vom Beginn der Mendelssohnschen Zeit (1750) bis in die neueste Zeit (1848)*. Leipzig: Oskar Leiner.

Hoffman, Lawrence A. (1996). *Covenant of Blood: Circumcision and Gender in Rabbinic Judaism*. Chicago: University of Chicago Press.

Hofstadter, Douglas and Emmanuel Sander (2013). *Surfaces and Essences: Analogy as the Fuel and Fire of Thinking*. New York: Basic Books.

Holdheim, Samuel (1844). *Über die Beschneidung zunächst in religiös-dogmatischer Beziehung*. Schwerin: Verlag der Kürschner'schen Buchhandlung.

Justin Martyr (2003). *Dialogue with Trypho*. Edited by Michael Slusser, translated by Thomas B. Falls, revised by Thomas P. Halton. Washington, DC: The Catholic University of America Press.

Jennings, Theodore (2013). *Outlaw Justice: The Messianic Politics of Paul*. Stanford, CA: Stanford University Press.

Keller-Bauer, Friedrich (1984). *Metaphorisches Verstehen: Eine linguistische Rekonstruktion metaphorischer Kommunikation*. Berlin: de Gruyter.

Klawans, Jonathan (2006). *Purity, Sacrifice, and the Temple: Symbolism and Supersessionism in the Study of Ancient Judaism*. New York: Oxford University Press.

Lakoff, George (1987). *Women, Fire and Dangerous Things*. London: University of Chicago Press.

Lakoff, George (1993). The contemporary theory of metaphor. In Andrew Ortony (ed.), *Metaphor and Thought*. Second edition, pp. 202–251. Cambridge: Cambridge University Press.

Lakoff, George and Mark Johnson (1980). *Metaphors We Live By*. Chicago: University of Chicago Press.

Lakoff, George and Mark Johnson (1999). *Philosophy in the Flesh*. New York: Basic Books.

Lakoff, George and Mark Johnson (2003). *Metaphors We Live By*. With a new Afterword. Chicago: University of Chicago Press.

Laugerud, Henning and Laura Katrine Skinnebach (eds.) (2007). *Instruments of Devotion: The Practices and Objects of Religious Piety from the Late Middle Ages to the 20th Century*. Aarhus, Denmark: Aarhus University Press.

Mikolajczak, Stanislaw and Malgorzata Rybka (2014). *The Language of Religion, Past and Present*. Universyte im Adama Mickiewicza w Poznaniu.

Neiger, Mark (2011). *A Hill of Foreskins: Circumcision, Foreskin and Blood in Early Rabbinic Texts*. MA Dissertation, Leo Baeck College, London.

Niehoff, Maren R. (2003). Circumcision as a marker of identity: Philo, Origen and the rabbis on Genesis 17:1–14. *Jewish Studies Quarterly* 10(2), 89–123.

Norager, Troels (1999). 'Heart' as metaphor in religious discourse. In Lieven Boeve and Kurt Feyaerts (eds.), *Metaphor and God-Talk*, pp. 215–232. Bern: Peter Lang.

Ratzinger, Joseph A. (2009). *Saint Paul*. San Francisco: Ignatius Press.

Sanders, Ed Parish (1977). *Paul and Palestinian Judaism*. London and Philadelphia: Fortress Press.

Searle, John R. (1979). Metaphor. In Andrew Ortony (ed.), *Metaphor and Thought*, pp. 92–123. Cambridge: Cambridge University Press.

Seland, Eli Heldaas (2007). 19th century devotional medals. In H. Laugerud and L. K. Skinnebach (eds.), *Instruments of Devotion: The Practices and Objects of Religious Piety from the Late Middle Ages to the 20th Century*, pp. 157–172. Aarhus, Denmark: Aarhus University Press.

Smallwood, E. Mary (2001). *The Jews under Roman Rule: From Pompey to Diocletian: A Study in Political Relations*. Boston: Brill.

Steiner, Richard C. (1999). Incomplete circumcision in Egypt and Edom: Jeremiah (9:24–25) in light of Josephus and Jonckheere. *Journal of Biblical Literature* 118(3), 497–526.

Sullivan, Karen (2013). *Frames and Constructions in Metaphoric Language*. Amsterdam: John Benjamins.

Sweetser, Eve and Mary Therese DesCamp (2014). Motivating Biblical metaphors for God. In Bonnie Howe and Joel B. Green (eds.), *Cognitive Linguistic Explorations in Biblical Studies*, pp. 7–24. Munich: de Gruyter.

Talmud Bavli (the Babylonian Talmud) (1990). Edited by Isidore Epstein. New York: Soncino Press.

Thiessen, Matthew (2011). *Contesting Conversion: Genealogy, Circumcision, and Identity in Ancient Judaism and Christianity*. New York: Oxford University Press.

Thiessen, Matthew (2014). Paul's argument against gentile circumcision in Romans 2:17–29. *Novum Testamentum* 56, 373–391.

van Noppen, Jean-Pierre (ed.) (1981). *Theolinguistics 1*. Brussels: Studiereeks Tijdschrift Vrije Universiteit Brussel, New series No 8.

van Noppen, Jean-Pierre (ed.) (1983). *Metaphor and Religion. (Theolinguistics 2)*. Brussels: Studiereeks Tijdschrift Vrije Universiteit Brussel, New series No 12.

van Noppen, Jean-Pierre (1988). Metapher und Religion. In Jean-Pierre van Noppen (ed.), *Erinnern, um Neues zu sagen: Die Bedeutung der Metapher für die religiöse Sprache*. Frankfurt/Main: Athenäum Verlag.

van Noppen, Jean-Pierre (1999). Theographic metaphors: Ordinary words with extraordinary meanings. In Lieven Boeve andKurt Feyaerts (eds.), *Metaphor and God-talk*, pp. 95–111. Lang: Bern.

von Thaden, Robert H. Jr. (2014). Pauline rhetorical invention: Seeing 1 Corinthians 6:12–7:7 through conceptual integration theory. In Bonnie Howe and Joel B. Green (eds.), *Cognitive Linguistic Explorations in Biblical Studies*, pp. 99–120. Munich: de Gruyter.

Will, Edouard and Claude Orrieux (1992). *Prosélytisme juif? Histoire d'une erreur*. Paris: Les Belles Lettres.

Windsor, Lionel J. (2014). *Paul and the Vocation of Israel*. Berlin/Boston: de Gruyter.

PART III

New Perspectives

The thread running through the chapters of this book concerns the complex combining of mind, language, ideation, and emotion, with a focus on language itself. It is the ability of language to channel the metaphorising processes of the mind that has a particularly important place in Part II. Text has so far been the main object of attention, but as has been pointed out in Part I, religion involves various genres, written texts may not be central. We need to go further, both in terms of theories and methods, and in terms of the range of religious experience and behaviour. Besides the analysis of metaphor we need other instruments from cognitive linguistics, pragmatics, and discourse analysis. We need also to remember that religious language, especially that of ritual, occurs in strongly multimodal contexts.

In chapter 13, Christoph Unger applies Relevance Theory (see also Downes, chapter 4, and McNamara and Giordano, chapter 5), a framework that takes seriously the role of inferencing in linguistic meaning-making, including the processing of metaphor. The search for relevance is the search for cognitive payoff in return for cognitive effort, within particular cognitive environments—including those of religion. One such environment is that of religious art, within its wider religious framework of course, which includes the doctrinal. In chapter 14, Antonio Barcelona incorporates metonymy into an analysis of metaphor. Both underlie not only language but other modes of interpretative activity, including the production of, and making sense of, pictures. His analyses propose accounts of the ways in which both language and visual representation work in the processing of counterintuitive teachings such as the Christian notion of the Trinity. Many analyses of metaphor in this volume mention conceptual 'blending', especially when confronted with complex metaphorical expressions. In chapter 15, Mihailo Antović places conceptual blending in the forefront in analysing expressions that involve not only cross-domain mappings but various forms of conceptual association and integration. Conceptual blending is not peculiar to religious use of the mind or of language: it is intrinsic in the view of Antović to the evolution and cultural development of the human language ability, and to the historical transformation of religious mentalities. In particular, he proposes that conceptual integration models are able to capture complex religious states of mind that involve self-reflection, inner conflict, and self-transformation.

The study of religious ritual should not be obscured by a language-centric concern with text. In chapter 16, Chilton and Cram take two complementary perspectives.

One concerns a phenomenon that has already been reflected in other chapters—the presence in elaborated traditions of speculation concerning the very linguistic and cognitive processes that we have tried to put under the microscope in this volume. The other perspective applies a theory based on the fundamental importance of spatial cognition in language, in particular for what linguists call *deixis*, the subject-oriented representation of what is close and what is remote, including in metaphorical senses. Their analysis seeks to model some of the processes involved in what is, again, counterintuitive conceptualisation, in this case in the context of ritual. Chapter 17, by Monika Kopytowska, concerns the same religious ritual and applies a closely related theory developed for the analysis of discourse, in particular discourse in mediatised culture. Religious rituals have historically taken much of their power, in all religions, from the co-presence of individuals in special locations, from coordinated physical movements and vocalisations, and from the making present of gods. What happens, in terms of the relation between what is 'here and now' and what is 'there and remote', when participants, if that is the appropriate word, are alone watching a ritual transmitted to a TV screen or broadcast on the radio? How does the perceived distance impact on the audience's cognitive-affective responses? Combining cognitive linguistics, discourse analysis, and pragmatics, Monika Kopytowska concludes the volume by outlining a new framework that shows how language, the semiotic potential of the media, and the human mind co-construct religious realities and generate collective experience.

It happens that all the chapters in Part III analyse Christian material, but there is no reason to think that the same analytical methods and frameworks cannot be universally applied. Indeed, the extension of cognitive and linguistic approaches to all forms of religious experience and activity is a pressing need.

CHAPTER 13

Cognitive Pragmatics and Multi-layered Communication

Allegory in Christian Religious Discourse

CHRISTOPH UNGER

Allegory is a figure of speech employed frequently in Christian religious discourse throughout history. It has its place not only in the Christian Scriptures, but also in theological and homiletic literature. However, allegory and especially allegorical readings of scripture have also met with resistance in some schools of Christian thought. This raises the question of what it is about the nature of allegory that explains the undeniable attraction that it holds for use in Christian religious discourse, as well as the limitations that are often commented on. In this paper I want to explore whether an explanation might be found in the cognitive nature of allegory: is there perhaps anything in the way allegory is processed in the mind that may shed some light on the attractiveness and the limitations of allegory? Addressing this question is hampered by the fact that allegory has not yet been widely studied in its own right in cognitive-pragmatic approaches. Perhaps one reason for this is that there is a widespread intuition that allegory is closely related to, and perhaps even reduces to, extended metaphor. However, there are reasons to doubt this, and in this paper I will follow Unger (2017), where I propose a cognitive-pragmatic account based on the claim that allegory is not processed by the application of metaphorical processes. Rather, the comprehension of allegories involves our ability to detect multiple simultaneous layers of communication, all of which contribute individually and jointly to overall expectations of relevance in the sense of Sperber and Wilson (1995). I will argue that this account sheds light on the unique utility and limitations of allegory: because of its layered nature, allegory may be a useful tool to address a heterogeneous audience. Moreover, the layered nature of allegory makes it also a useful tool for persuasive or argumentative discourse. At the same time, the efforts involved in processing the communication layers involved in allegory increase risks, particularly of audiences overinterpreting the communication event. Thus, there are indeed cognitive causes for the attraction that allegory holds for practitioners of religious discourse and also for the caution against this figure of speech.

1 ALLEGORY IN CHRISTIAN RELIGIOUS LANGUAGE: A SURVEY

Christian religious language liberally makes use of allegory, a figure of speech classically described by Quintilian as a figure which 'presents one thing in words and another in sense, or sometimes a sense quite contrary to the words'. Allegories in this sense are found in the Bible and in extra-biblical texts. The most famous examples are perhaps the following: in the Old Testament, the prophet Nathan's parable for King David (2 Samuel 12:1–4), the Song of the Vineyard in Isaiah 5:1–7; in the New Testament, the parable of the sower (Matthew 13:3–9; Mark 4:3–9; Luke 8:5–8); other Christian writings employing allegory include John Bunyan's *Pilgrim's Progress* (Bunyan 1953); and C. S. Lewis' *The Chronicles of Narnia* (Lewis 1950, 1951, 1952, 1953, 1954, 1955, 1956).

Allegories need not be larger discourses such as these examples. In fact, Quintilian uses sentence-length examples. Such shorter allegories are found in the Bible as well:

(1) Jesus replied, 'No one who puts his hand to the plow and looks back is fit for service in the kingdom of God.' (Luke 9:62)

However, what is common to allegories in this sense is that the author intended the text to be understood allegorically in the first place. Allegory as a figure of speech requires allegorical reading to make sense of the text.

Distinct from the rhetorical figure allegory is *allegoresis* (*Allegorese* in the German hermeneutical literature), a method of interpretation that reads texts as allegories in search of a deeper, more profound meaning.[1] This method of interpretation has been highly controversial in the Christian church throughout history. Traces of this interpretation method can be found in the New Testament, for example in the apostle Paul's interpretation of the story of Hagar and Sarah resembling Christian believers and Jews, respectively (Galatians 4:21–31), and Paul's application of the law about muzzling oxen to the right of Christian teachers to financial support (1 Corinthians 9:9–12; 1 Timothy 5:18).

However, allegoresis came to be widely used only in the patristic period (around 150–400 AD) by church fathers of the Alexandrian school. In this school it was taught that every textual unit in Scripture has three levels of meaning: the literal meaning, a moral meaning, and a spiritual meaning. Allegoresis was the prime method of arriving at the moral and spiritual meanings. As an example, consider Origen's interpretation (around 244 CE) of the sexual relations between Lot and his daughters

(Gen. 19:30–38), discussed by Klein, Blomberg, and Hubbard (1993, pp. 34–35). The Biblical text reads as follows:

> Lot and his two daughters left Zoar and settled in the mountains, for he was afraid to stay in Zoar. He and his two daughters lived in a cave. One day the older daughter said to the younger, 'Our father is old, and there is no man around here to give us children—as is the custom all over the earth. Let's get our father to drink wine and then sleep with him and preserve our family line through our father.' That night they got their father to drink wine, and the older daughter went in and slept with him. He was not aware of it when she lay down or when she got up. The next day the older daughter said to the younger, 'Last night I slept with my father. Let's get him to drink wine again tonight, and you go in and sleep with him so we can preserve our family line through our father.' So they got their father to drink wine that night also, and the younger daughter went in and slept with him. Again he was not aware of it when she lay down or when she got up. So both of Lot's daughters became pregnant by their father. The older daughter had a son, and she named him Moab; he is the father of the Moabites of today. The younger daughter also had a son, and she named him Ben-Ammi; he is the father of the Ammonites of today. (Gen. 19:30–38, New International Version)

According to Origen (1982, pp. 112–120), the passage has a literal sense (it actually happened). But its moral meaning is that Lot represents the rational human mind, his wife the flesh inclined to pleasures, and the daughters vainglory and pride. Applying these three to people yields the spiritual (or doctrinal) meaning: Lot represents the (Old Testament) law, the daughters represent Jerusalem and Samaria, and the wife represents the Israelites who rebelled in the wilderness. Other church fathers in Antioch in Syria reacted strongly against this allegorical interpretation method. Among them were Theodore of Mopsuestia (ca. 350–428 AD), Theodoret (ca. 393–460), and John Chrysostom (ca. 347–407). In the Reformation period, Martin Luther and John Calvin added their voices to reject allegoresis in the interpretation of Scripture.

This controversy led some interpreters to not only reject allegoresis, i.e. allegorical reading as a method of interpretation, but to be wary of allegory as an overt figure of speech as well. Thus, Ethelbert Bullinger, who developed a highly elaborate taxonomy of figures of speech in biblical literature (Bullinger 1968), acknowledges the existence of allegory in the Bible but gives this warning: 'No figure requires more careful discrimination than *Allegory*. And it would be safer to say that there are no allegories in Scripture than to follow one's own judgment as to what is allegory, and what is not'. (Bullinger 1968, p. 749).

Adolf Jülicher (1899) came to an even more radical conclusion with respect to the parables of Jesus. After reviewing many different and divergent allegorical interpretations of Jesus' parables, he concluded that these parables are not allegories at all and should be treated to advance only one point of teaching about spiritual truths, rather than establishing various allegorical resemblances between elements of the parable and its intended meaning. Meanwhile, many interpreters have moved away from this extreme position, among them Dodd (1935) and Jeremias (1947), and Klein et al. (1993, p. 337) observe that '[a] growing minority of interpreters once again regards as appropriate a limited amount of allegorical interpretation. . . . At the same time, few have been willing to abandon the quest for one central truth per passage'.

This short and no doubt selective review of the role of allegory in Christian religious language highlights a paradox: on the one hand, allegory occurs extensively in Christian religious discourse, both in the Scriptures and in other forms of religious discourse. On the other hand, allegory is met (at least in certain traditions) with a lot of suspicion, bordering on the denial of its existence. This raises the question of whether there is something in the essence of allegory as a figure of speech that explains both the enormous utility of allegory in religious discourse, and also its limitations. In this paper I want to address this question from a cognitive pragmatic point of view: do the cognitive processes involved in interpreting allegory shed light on both the utility and the limitation of allegory?

2 ALLEGORY AND METAPHOR

Since both allegory and metaphor appear to involve relating two domains of meaning, we need to clarify the relation between them. Consider the following definitions of allegory:

> *Allegory,* which is translated in Latin by *inversio,* either presents one thing in words and another in meaning, or else something absolutely opposed to the meaning of the words.[2] (Quintilian, translated in Butler 1922, chapter 6, section 44)

> Allegory . . . is metaphor . . . continued as a trope of thought . . . and consists in the exchange of the intended thought with another thought which is in a similarity relation . . . to the intended thought.[3] (Lausberg 1984, section 423, p. 139)

> Few figures have been the subject of greater controversy than *Allegory*; or, have been more variously defined. One class of Rhetoricians declare that it is a continued metaphor: and another class declare that it is not. But, as is often the case under such circumstances, neither is quite correct, because both have a part of the truth and put it for the whole. Neither of the contending parties takes into consideration the existence of *Hypocatastasis.* And this fact accounts for the confusion, not only with regard to *Allegory,* but also with regard to *Metaphor.*

> All three figures are based on *comparison. Simile* is comparison by *resemblance; Metaphor* is comparison by *representation; Hypocatastasis* is comparison by *implication.*

> In the first the comparison is *stated;* in the second it is *substituted;* in the third it is *implied.*
> Thus *Allegory* is a continuation of the latter two, *Metaphor* or *Hypocatastasis;* while the *Parable (q.v.)* is a continuation of the *Simile.* (Bullinger 1968, p. 748)

What these definitions have in common is that they define allegory in relation to metaphor, and that they presuppose the substitution theory of metaphor, which claims that metaphor is the result of the substitution of one word with another one. However, there is a progression: while the classic definition of allegory given by Quintilian clearly distinguishes allegory from metaphor and is designed to cover instances of allegory 'unmixed with metaphor' (Butler 1922), the other two definitions bring into focus the idea that allegory is some sort of continuation from metaphor. In Lausberg's case, it is not entirely clear what kind of continuation he has in mind, as he still distinguishes clearly between metaphor as 'word substitution trope' and allegory as 'thought substitution trope'. However, Bullinger's definition borders on claiming outright that allegory is essentially extended metaphor and what he calls extended hypocatastasis (where the distinction between hypocatastasis and metaphor remains unclear).

This comparison reveals a central theme in the discussion of allegory: how does this figure of speech relate to metaphor? This question remains current even for modern pragmatic theory approaches to allegory that have long ago parted from the substitution theory of metaphor. Prominent among modern pragmaticists working on allegory is Peter Crisp (Crisp 2001, 2005, 2008). Other valuable contributions have been made by Harris and Tolmie (2011), Gibbs (2011), Thagard (2011), Kasten and Gruenler (2011), and Oakley and Crisp (2011). These researchers are working in the framework of cognitive linguistics, according to which metaphor is a basic principle of human cognition, a figure of thought, not of speech. This idea was introduced by Lakoff and Johnson (1980), who made two important observations on metaphor, as already noted by a number of contributors to the present volume. First, metaphor is ubiquitous in everyday speech. Thus, it is not credible to claim that metaphor is an artistic device for rhetoric embellishment of speech, or a deviation from a norm. Second, the metaphors used in everyday speech appear to centre around certain types of mappings between abstract conceptual domains and concrete domains, based on our experience of persons and things moving through a three-dimensional space. An example for such domain mappings is one that can be called LOVE IS A JOURNEY. Lakoff (1993) cites many examples in English where a love relationship can be talked about and reasoned about in terms of comparing it to a journey:

(2)   Look how far we've come. It's been a long, bumpy road. We can't turn
       back now. We're at a crossroads. We may have to go our separate ways.
       The relationship isn't going anywhere. We're spinning our wheels. Our
       relationship is off the track. The marriage is on the rocks. We may have to bail
       out of this relationship. (Lakoff 1993, p. 206)

Lakoff takes this as evidence that domain mappings such as LOVE IS A JOURNEY are instantiated in cognitive structure, and these cognitive domain mappings underlie our ability to comprehend metaphors.

Crisp (2001, 2005, 2008) and Gibbs (2011) claim that the interpretation of metaphor and allegory makes use of the same cognitive principles of metaphorical mapping and which involve creating a blended conceptual space from concepts belonging to the source and target domain of the figurative utterance. This does not mean that there is no distinction between allegory and metaphor: Gibbs claims that allegory comprehension involves applying the processes of metaphor comprehension to utterances that do not obviously involve metaphorical language (Gibbs 2011, p. 122). Crisp (2008, pp. 293–294) argues that in allegory, the metaphorical mappings are applied in a more radical way: not only are the mappings more extensive than in metaphor, but separate more clearly the literal source domain and the figurative target domain. Allegory, unlike metaphor, does not mix language relating to these domains but relates directly only to the source domain. Moreover, allegory describes fictional situations by way of referring directly to possible situations, whereas metaphor (and extended metaphor) creates new blends between unrelated concepts of the source and target domains and uses this blended conceptual space to refer directly to an entity within this space.

Another influential approach to metaphor in modern pragmatic theory is the relevance theory account of Sperber and Wilson (1990, 1995, 1998, 2008; Wilson and Carston 2007; Wilson and Sperber 2002; Carston 2002). Sperber and Wilson agree with Lakoff and Johnson (1980) that metaphor is ubiquitous in everyday speech and cannot be regarded as a special device, a departure from a norm. But unlike Lakoff and Johnson, Sperber and Wilson do not claim that it is necessary to postulate the existence of metaphor-specific cognitive principles or processes in order to account for metaphor comprehension. An empirical motivation for this claim is that there seems to be a continuum between literal uses, approximation uses (loose uses), hyperbole, and metaphor. The following examples illustrate this:

(3)   Would you please take the kettle off the fire, the water is boiling.

(4)   Ouch, I burned my tongue, this coffee is boiling.

(5)   I had to wait for half an hour before I could take my bath, the water was boiling.

(6)   John was boiling with anger.

(7)   Peter: What did you think of Angela Merkel's reaction to the news that the NSA listened to her mobile phone?
       Mary: Oh, she was boiling with anger.

In (3), the word *boiling* is used literally. In (4), *boiling* is used in an approximate sense: the coffee poured out for the speaker to drink was definitely not literally boiling, but hot enough to burn her tongue. Example (5) is a case of hyperbole. The bath water was not even approximately boiling, but hotter than comfortable for the speaker. Example (6) is a typical metaphorical use of the word *boiling*. There is no sense in which *boiling* in this example can be said to involve a temperature at all. Rather, it conveys the idea that John was showing his anger in an agitated manner, and this agitation is of a sort that reminds one of the agitation of boiling water. With respect to (7), it is necessary to know that German Chancellor Angela Merkel normally does not show much emotion in her public speech. However, in a statement she made after the revelation that the United States intelligence service listened to her mobile phone, she used a slightly more emotional wording and manner for her style. Thus, when Mary answers Peter as in (7), she is engaging in a hyperbolic metaphor.

Sperber and Wilson claim that the linguistic meaning of utterances falls far short of conveying the speaker's meaning. Rather, the linguistic meaning of utterances merely provides clues for the audience inferring the speaker's meaning. For inferring the speaker's meaning, audiences follow a heuristic procedure that can be paraphrased as follows:

(8)   Accept the first hypothesis about explicit meaning, implicit import, and contextual assumptions that is most easily accessible. Check if the utterance, on this interpretation, is at least relevant enough to be worth the audience's attention. If so, the audience is entitled to accept this interpretation as the one the speaker intended. If not, follow a path of least effort in accessing interpretations and checking them for relevance, stopping at the first interpretation that satisfies the audience's expectations of relevance, or abandon the process if processing effort becomes too high.[4]

Relevance is a technical notion. It is a property of inputs to cognitive processes (for example, utterances) and is defined in terms of positive cognitive effects and cognitive processing effort. Positive cognitive effects are true improvements in the individual's representation of the world. Such improvements may be achieved by strengthening previously held assumptions, by eliminating assumptions that turn out to be false, or by acquiring information that leads to further true implications. The more cognitive effects an input to cognitive processes yields, the more *relevant* it is. On the other hand, the more processing effort is needed for getting these effects, the less relevant the input is.

In example (3), the easiest accessible assumption about the explicit meaning of the utterance includes the assumption that the word *boiling* communicates the concept BOILING which is standardly encoded by the word. This is because the first part of the utterance conveys the request made of the audience to move a kettle full of water off the fire. This raises the question of which relation the second part bears to the first. A highly accessible context is that the fact that the water in a water kettle is boiling is a good reason for taking the water kettle off the fire. On this interpretation the utterance achieves relevance because it provides a good reason for the request being made in the first part of the utterance. But this presupposes that the word *boiling* is understood as conveying the concept BOILING.

In (6), *boiling* is predicated of a person, but the concept BOILING cannot be predicated of people. The phrase *with anger* indicates that *boiling* is more narrowly predicated of a person in a specific emotional state, namely, that of anger. This means that a relevant interpretation of the utterance can only be found if the word *boiling* can be understood as conveying a context specific concept BOILING* that can be predicated of a person in the emotional state of anger, but that nevertheless is best conveyed by using the word *boiling*. An easily available contextual assumption is that people in anger typically show an agitated behaviour. Also, boiling water is moving in an agitated way. Thus, it is easy to construct a context-specific concept BOILING* that differs from the concept BOILING in that it does not refer to a temperature of substances at all, but that does refer to agitated states of persons and gives an idea what this kind of agitation may helpfully be compared to.

Thus, whether a word is used in a metaphorical, literal, approximation, or a hyperbolic sense can be comprehended simply by following the relevance-theoretic comprehension heuristic in (8). The intended interpretation must be the most easily accessible combination of hypotheses about explicit meaning, implicit import, and contextual assumptions. On this account, metaphor as such has no special theoretical significance, nor does it require special interpretive mechanisms. It is, in Sperber and Wilson's words, a 'deflationary' account of metaphor (Sperber and Wilson 2008).

However, Wilson (2012) points out that it is unclear how this account of metaphor could explain utterances such as the following ones, which are often identified as typical instances of allegories:

(9) O ship, new waves will bear thee back to sea. What dost thou? Make the haven, come what may.[5] (Horace, quoted by Quintilian in Butler 1922, chapter 6, section 44)

(10) You can't put the toothpaste back in the tube. (Wilson 2012)

(11) When you walk through a storm, hold your head up high. (Wilson 2012)

The relevance theory account of metaphor argues that metaphors communicate ad hoc concepts, concepts that are not encoded in the word that is used. But in allegories such as (9), it appears that the concept ordinarily encoded by the word (e.g. SHIP encoded by ship) is still communicated along with the contextually adjusted concept (e.g. SHIP* referring to the institution of the state).

A similar point has been made by Carston (2010) and Carston and Wearing (2011). These authors point to examples such as the following, where the literal meaning appears to remain transparent to the audience along with the figurative meaning:

(12) Life's but a walking shadow, a poor player
That struts and frets his hour upon the stage
And then is heard no more: it is a tale
Told by an idiot, full of sound and fury,
Signifying nothing. (Shakespeare, *Macbeth* V. v. 24–30, quoted from Carston 2010, p. 306)

(13) Depression, in Karla's experience, was a dull, inert thing—a toad that squatted wetly on your head until it finally gathered the energy to slither off. The unhappiness she had been living with for the last ten days was a quite different creature. It was frantic and aggressive. It had fists and fangs and hobnailed boots. It didn't sit, it assailed. It hurt her. In the mornings, it slapped her so hard in the face that she reeled as she walked to the bathroom. (Zoë Heller, *The Believers*, 2008, p. 263, quoted from Carston 2010, p. 307)

(14)   Love is the lighthouse and the rescued mariners. (Oskar Davičo, 'Hana', 1979, quoted from Carston 2010, p. 295)

(15)   My Life had stood—a Loaded Gun—In Corners—(Emily Dickinson in Franklin 2005, quoted from Carston 2010, p. 309)

Note that this transparency of the literal meaning appears not only in cases of extended metaphor, (12) and (13), but also in some instances of creative metaphors with a strong image-like feel to them, (14) and (15). Carston and Wearing (2011) argue that these examples motivate the postulation of a second path to metaphor comprehension in addition to the one described in the standard relevance theory account of metaphor, a path that leads to a more conscious and effortful interpretation process that is induced in instances where the more general, intuitive process of metaphor comprehension doesn't return satisfactory results without incurring unreasonable processing effort. However, Carston and Wearing do not provide an explicit account of what this second path based on conscious inference processes consists of.

These observations about the limitations of the standard relevance-theoretic account of metaphor comprehension with respect to allegory (and arguably, other types of extended and basic metaphors as well) converge with observations made by literary theorists. Kurz (1997) points to a long tradition among literary theorists who point out that the one characteristic feature of allegory is the transparency of the literal meaning alongside the allegorical meaning. In fact, Kurz points out the literal descriptive meaning of allegory and the allegorical meaning stand side by side, as it were: they are coherent in themselves, and are interconnected. This is different from metaphor: even though in some metaphors the literal meaning may be transparent, metaphor identifies the topic with the source domain of the metaphor. For example, in the metaphorical use of 'boiling' in (6), the communicator conveys the idea that John's emotional state has some properties that can also be attributed to boiling water. Unger (2017) picks up this observation that the transparency of the literal meaning in allegory is most fundamental for understanding the essence of allegory and develops an account of allegory within relevance theory that breaks with the longstanding tradition of seeking to understand allegory in terms of (extended) metaphor. In the following section, I will review this account in more detail and outline reasons for preferring this one over others.

Breaking with the tradition that characterises allegory in terms of metaphor has important consequences for understanding the utility of allegory for religious discourse, and Christian religious discourse in particular. For example, it might be claimed that metaphor is a particularly useful device for talking about mysterious concepts such as occur frequently in religious thought. If the essence of allegory is not rooted in metaphorical processes at all, then none of these considerations would apply to the discussion of the utility of allegory for religious discourse. The utility of allegory for (Christian) religious discourse will have to be sought along other lines of thought. In section 4 I will discuss this issue in somewhat more detail.

3 A RELEVANCE THEORY ACCOUNT OF ALLEGORY

Unger (2017) argues that allegory comprehension does not involve any cognitive processes that are not independently necessary to account for comprehension in general, and which are not already explained in relevance theory. In particular, the following insights are crucial to account for allegory comprehension:

- Verbal communication may involve several simultaneous layers of communicative acts. Each of these layers may achieve relevance individually within its layer, and the layers contribute jointly to the overall relevance of the total communication act.
- The meanings conveyed at these various layers of communication are related by *interpretive resemblance*.

The first of these insights—that ostensive communication (i.e. overtly intentional communication that provides only partial evidence of the speaker's meaning) may be layered—was first pointed out by Sperber and Wilson (1987), and commented on by Wilson (2012). Sperber and Wilson discuss the question of how texts of fiction can be relevant, when relevance is defined in terms of positive cognitive effects, that is, true thoughts about the world. They propose that in works of fiction, there are (at least) two layers of communication. In the first layer, the narrator, or implied author, describes situations in a fictive world, and this is relevant for the implied audience in terms of the cognitive effects achieved relative to this fictive world. At the same time, the interpretation of the first layer of communication is capable of inducing positive cognitive effects in the audience in the real world, for example by spotting similarities between life experiences the reader has had and experiences that the characters in the fiction are described as going through. Wilson (2012) calls the kind of relevance achieved in the first layer *internal relevance* and the relevance achieved at the second layer *external relevance*. Internal and external relevance combine to satisfy the overall relevance expectations created by works of fiction, and since external relevance is due to positive cognitive effects in the real world, works of fiction can be accounted for in relevance theory.

It is obvious that this notion of communication layering may be helpful to account for the observation that in allegory, the descriptive (literal) meaning is transparent and coherent in itself. Indeed, Wilson (2012) suggests that accounting for allegory along these lines is more promising than attempting to widen the ad hoc concept account of metaphor. However, the question remains how to account for the intuition that the descriptive meaning of allegories is intended to provide an example for the implied point (the allegorical meaning). Wilson (2012) points out that we do this spontaneously in everyday speech of the kind exemplified in (10) and (11), but it is not obvious how to explain this ability. Are there perhaps dedicated cognitive mechanisms? Unger (2017) argues that in order to interpret the relation between the descriptive meaning of allegories and their intended point, the mind must evaluate interpretive resemblance relations between propositions conveyed in the descriptive meaning of allegories and assumptions implicitly conveyed in the allegorical meaning.

According to Sperber and Wilson (1995), two mental representations interpretively resemble each other to the extent that they share logical properties. In particular, mental representations that yield overlapping implications in the same context share logical properties. For example, given the context IF SUNSHINE INCREASES THEN THE WEATHER WILL GET WARMER, both THE CLOUDS CLEAR and THE SUN COMES OUT OF THE CLOUDS MORE AND MORE yield the logical implication THE WEATHER WILL GET WARMER. Therefore, the representations THE CLOUDS CLEAR and THE SUN COMES OUT OF THE CLOUDS MORE AND MORE interpretively resemble each other.

The ability to process and exploit interpretive resemblances underlies our capacity to engage in what Sperber and Wilson (1995) call *interpretive use* and Wilson (2000) refers to as *metarepresentational use* of utterances: when communicators use utterances not to describe states of affairs in the world but to represent other public or private representations (i.e. utterances or thoughts). Wilson (2000) surveys a wide range of varieties of metarepresentational or interpretive use of utterances and shows that this type of utterance use is ubiquitous in verbal communication. Reported speech, interrogatives, and irony are only some examples. A crucial factor in the metarepresentational use of utterances is that the representations represented by the utterance interpretively resemble the propositions conveyed by the utterance. Thus, the ability to recognise interpretive resemblance relations is an important component of our ability to comprehend utterances.

Unger (2017) does not claim that allegory is an instance of metarepresentative use of utterances. The claim is merely that the recognition of interpretive resemblance relations is crucially involved in comprehending allegories. To see how interpretive resemblance enters into allegory interpretation, consider a paradigm case of allegory in the Bible: the parable of the sower.

'A farmer went out to sow his seed. As he was scattering the seed, some fell along the path; it was trampled on, and the birds of the air ate it up. Some fell on rock, and when it came up, the plants withered because they had no moisture. Other seed fell among thorns, which grew up with it and choked the plants. Still other seed fell on good soil. It came up and yielded a crop, a hundred times more than was sown.'

When he said this, he called out, 'He who has ears to hear, let him hear.' (Luke 8:5–8, New International Version)

The parable describes a scene which presumably was very familiar to the audience: a farmer sowing seed, and the seed falling on different ground. It is a coherent story and may be relevant to the audience in terms of accurately recalling some of their life experience. However, the fact that Jesus is telling this story sets higher expectations than this: the people expect him to say something about God and their relationship to God. These relevance expectations are blatantly not met. It is mutually manifest[6] that the story falls short of meeting these expectations. Hence the audience continues to interpret this text to find out how it could be understood as having relevance for spiritual matters. This is not necessarily a straightforward matter and involves some effort. A little later, Jesus is reported as helping his disciples to understand the intended interpretation:

> This is the meaning of the parable: The seed is the word of God. Those along the path are the ones who hear, and then the devil comes and takes away the word from their hearts, so that they may not believe and be saved. Those on the rock are the ones who receive the word with joy when they hear it, but they have no root. They believe for a while, but in the time of testing they fall away. The seed that fell among thorns stands for those who hear, but as they go on their way they are choked by life's worries, riches and pleasures, and they do not mature. But the seed on good soil stands for those with a noble and good heart, who hear the word, retain it, and by persevering produce a crop. (Luke 8:11–15, New International Version)

This explanation builds bridges to help the audience understand how the story of the sower can exemplify spiritual realities. But notice that these bridges do not provide a full interpretation of the parable. It does say that the various types of ground the seed falls onto resemble types of audiences that differ in the way they listen to the word of God (which is represented by the seed). But in order to understand the spiritual truths that this parable intends to convey, more inference is necessary.

Let us consider the kind of inferences necessary for comprehension by focusing on the first type of soil (Luke 8:5; cf. also Luke 8:12). Simplifying somewhat, the descriptive meaning conveys the propositions in (16), and the canonical interpretation given in Luke 8:12 conveys the propositions in (17):

(16)   A sower threw seed. Some fell along the path. The birds ate it.

(17)   Someone came to tell God's word. Some listeners hear and Satan makes them not believe it.

Notice that the propositions in (16) and those in (17) are both entailments of a proposition such as the following:

(18)   The success of even beneficial and desirable activities does not depend on the agent alone.

Thus, (16) and (17) share logical properties and interpretively resemble each other to some degree. In the process of recognising this interpretive resemblance relation, the mental mechanism responsible for processing interpretive resemblance relations raises the activation level of (18), so that this mental representation becomes accessible as part of the context for interpreting the text. When it is accessed as a contextual assumption for interpreting this text, it raises an implicit question: on what factors does the success of the activities of the agent depend on each layer of meaning? In other words, the addition of this assumption to the context for interpretation raises a specific expectation of relevance: the story is relevant to the extent that the audience can identify such factors for success of the respective agent's activity. (On the relation between implicitly raised questions and relevance expectations, see Unger 2006, pp.143–155.) Indeed, it is easy to see how the various steps of the story converge to give rise to a conclusion such as (19), and the corresponding application (allegorical) layer related by interpretive resemblance to the descriptive layer jointly produce the conclusion in (20):

(19)   The success of a sower depends on the soil.

(20)   The success of a preacher depends on how people listen to God's word.

Thus, arriving at the conclusion in (19) is a cognitive effect that contributes to the internal relevance of the descriptive layer of the allegorical story, and arriving at the conclusion in (20) is one that contributes to the external relevance of the allegorical story on the second layer, what could be called the application layer of the story. But notice that (20) does not only satisfy some relevance expectations, it also creates others. It may raise the question in the audience: if the benefit of eternal life depends on how I listen to God's word and believe, then what can I do to ensure I listen well enough? One aspect of answering this question would be to make sure to listen to a reliable source for God's word. And indeed, an answer suggests itself once the audience is willing to entertain yet another bridge for interpretation: to assume that Jesus is the one who is conveying the word of God, and it is Jesus whom the sower in the story represents. Once the audience is willing to entertain this interpretation, there is a further layer of application available, which, if processed in the context of (20), yields cognitive effects such as:

(21)   The success of Jesus' conveying the word of God to me, an individual
        member of the audience, depends on how well I listen to him.

The claim expressed in (21) was (and is) a controversial claim to make. It is highly relevant for members of the audience who are sceptical about the truth of this claim: it contradicts many of their previously held assumptions and raises the question of whether there is sufficient reason to revise their beliefs or to reject this claim. It is also relevant for those members of the audience who are inclined to accept this claim: it will confirm their intuition that what Jesus says has lots of personal relevance for them. Thus, the audience that is willing to entertain this third layer of allegorical application will receive a much larger cognitive reward, and this may well be worth taking the risk of going even beyond the level of allegorical interpretation explicitly sanctioned in Luke 8:11–15.

Recall the pattern underlying this interpretation: the allegorical utterance or text raises expectations of relevance which are blatantly only partially fulfilled. In other words, it is mutually manifest that a first intuitive interpretation is only partially relevant. This overt withholding of relevance in turn functions as a salient property of the communicative act that calls for comprehension. Thus, the relevance-theoretic comprehension procedure is entered again, this time seeking to understand why relevance was deliberately withheld in the first run. This leads to the recovery of a second layer of interpretation, an allegorical interpretation. The recovery of this interpretation is conditioned by the search for interpretive resemblances between propositions conveyed on this second layer and those conveyed on the first. This cycle is entered again until relevance expectations are satisfied. Unger (2017) argues that his pattern of interpretation underlies the comprehension of allegories in general and supports this claim by applying it to both very complex allegories such as the Song of the Vineyard in Isaiah 5:1–7 and simple, everyday allegories such as (10) above.

This interpretation pattern for allegory claims that the relevance-theoretic comprehension procedure is passed through at least twice, if not several times. As Mercier and Sperber (2009) point out, such recursive applications of intuitive inference heuristics to their own output can shed light on the distinction between spontaneous, unconscious inference processes and reflective, conscious ones. With respect to argumentation processes, Mercier and Sperber argue that all argumentative inferences are executed by intuitive, subconscious cognitive processes. However, the same processes may be applied to the output of earlier applications of the same process, thus leaving intermediate steps of which the reasoner may become conscious. Mercier and Sperber claim that the more intermediate results a reasoning process produces, the more we feel that the overall process was a reflective, conscious one. My claim is that cases of layered communication such as are found in allegory (and fiction) produce a similar effect: the more layers of communication are recovered in the interpretation process, the more we feel that the comprehension process was of a reflective, non-spontaneous or conscious nature. But this does not mean that comprehension makes use of different processes. On the contrary, the same relevance-theoretic comprehension heuristic is applied in all cases; only when this process is called upon again and applied to its own output do we become conscious of the existence of intermediate comprehension results, and the more intermediate interpretation results there are, the more we feel that the comprehension process was of a reflective nature. In this way we can account not only for the transparency of the literal meaning in allegories, but also for the intuition that allegory interpretation is a more conscious process than what is required for non-allegorical speech.

Before moving on to consider the role of allegory in discourse in the next section, a few remarks are in order on the role of interpretive resemblances in allegory comprehension. The proposed pattern of allegory interpretation states that the allegorical layer(s) of interpretation are related to the descriptive meaning by interpretive resemblance relations. This distinguishes allegory from general cases of fiction. As a quick illustration, consider another of Jesus' parables, the parable of the Good Samaritan:

On one occasion an expert in the law stood up to test Jesus. 'Teacher,' he asked, 'what must I do to inherit eternal life?'

'What is written in the Law?' he replied. 'How do you read it?'

He answered: ''Love the Lord your God with all your heart and with all your soul and with all your strength and with all your mind'; and, 'Love your neighbor as yourself.'

'You have answered correctly,' Jesus replied. 'Do this and you will live.'

But he wanted to justify himself, so he asked Jesus, 'And who is my neighbor?'

In reply Jesus said: 'A man was going down from Jerusalem to Jericho, when he fell into the hands of robbers. They stripped him of his clothes, beat him and went away, leaving him half dead. A priest happened to be going down the same road, and when he saw the man, he passed by on the other side. So too, a Levite, when he came to the place and saw him, passed by on the other side. But a Samaritan, as he traveled, came where the man was; and when he saw him, he took pity on him. He went to him and bandaged his wounds, pouring on oil and wine. Then he put the man on his own donkey, took him to an inn and took care of him. The next day he took out two silver coins and gave them to the innkeeper. 'Look after him,' he said, 'and when I return, I will reimburse you for any extra expense you may have.'

'Which of these three do you think was a neighbor to the man who fell into the hands of robbers?'

The expert in the law replied, 'The one who had mercy on him.'
Jesus told him, 'Go and do likewise.'

(Luke 10:25–37, New International Version)

This parable is told as an answer to the question 'Who is my neighbour'? The answer is given in the form of a fictive story that overtly does not provide an answer. Thus, the audience is induced to process the story further to see if it gives rise to cognitive effects that provide an answer. However, in this case interpretive resemblance relations between the descriptive meaning of the story and the intended implicit meaning do not play a role. Rather, the story as a whole can be interpreted to support implicatures such as the following:

(22)   My neighbour is any human being who is in need of my acting
        compassionately to him or her.

This provides a relevant answer to the question the parable is designed to answer.

4 THE VIRTUES AND VICES OF ALLEGORY

The relevance theory account of allegory reviewed in the previous section claims that allegory is a relatively costly use of language. It requires several applications of the comprehension heuristic to interpret several layers of communication. Furthermore, it requires the ability to process interpretive resemblance relations.

This ability matures hand in hand with that of metarepresentation processing, and Wilson (2012) reviews evidence that this ability fully matures only at about four to six years of age, after basic communicative competence has been acquired. Because it is a relatively costly use of language to process, allegory differs noticeably from metaphor, which according to the standard relevance theory account is a natural by-product of the relevance-theoretic comprehension heuristic. In virtue of this, it seems surprising at first that allegory should be as widespread as it is. Obviously, the use of allegory must provide benefits for communication.

One of these benefits can be seen from the nature of the complexity found in allegory comprehension: the audience has to comprehend various layers of communication involved in the utterance. Certain relevance expectations are met on each of these layers. This means that even audiences who expect fairly low levels of relevance from the communicative act may be sufficiently rewarded, even though they miss the full range of meaning in the allegory. Moreover, audiences who are not capable of gaining sufficient relevance on all these layers may still get enough relevance on lower levels of communication that they are willing to engage again with the text at a later time, knowing that they are not yet able to understand the full meaning of the text. Thus, allegory appears to be a good communicative tool to address a heterogeneous audience.

Another benefit is that allegory may be a good tool for persuading audiences to accept a controversial claim. Recall that in the analysis of the parable of the sower in the previous section it was shown that on a higher layer of communication, the parable can be understood to make a controversial claim (the claim that it is Jesus to whom people need to carefully listen to and believe his words so that they may get eternal life). Notice two points here: first, the audience must arrive at this claim completely by means of their own inferencing. Thus, the audience carries a lot of responsibility for attributing this claim to the communicator. Second, the audience can infer this controversial claim only after already having inferred motivations for accepting this controversial claim. In the parable of the sower, this motivating factor is the idea that the one who listens to God's word and believes it will reap a great benefit (eternal life), just as the seed that falls on the fertile ground grows to produce much grain. Given these two factors, it appears that allegory may be a useful tool in argumentative or persuasive discourse.

But allegories can easily misfire. Notice that the guiding factor for the audience to engage in re-application of the comprehension heuristic in order to interpret higher layers of communication is the relevance expectations of the audience. If an audience has unjustifiably higher expectations of relevance than the communicator has envisaged, then this audience will be tempted to over-allegorise the utterance or text. Moreover, since allegory interpretation requires at least the comprehension of two layers of communication, it involves a certain degree of reflectivity or consciousness in the interpretation. The more conscious the interpretation is, the easier it is for an audience to assume that they have not yet exhausted the intended meaning, and the less resistance there is to put in more effort in seeking more relevance on additional layers of communication. Thus, allegory may be doubly prone to overinterpretation, especially by audiences who are frequently re-reading a text.

Thus the relevance theory account of allegory reviewed here provides a cognitive explanation for the observation recalled in section 1: that allegory has a firm place in Christian religious language, even though allegory and allegoresis are treated with suspicion. Moreover, this account allows a more general prediction to be made for the use of allegory in religious discourse in general: since allegory is a useful tool in argumentative discourse, and appears to be used frequently in persuasive discourse, it should be expected that allegory occurs primarily in the religious discourse of religions where truth-claims are prevalent (such as in Christianity, Judaism, or Islam) and markedly less so in religions that focus more on mysticism and are of a more integrative if not syncretistic nature (such as, arguably, Hinduism or Yezidism). Future research must show whether this prediction is true.

5 CONCLUSION

In this paper I have discussed the question of what light, if any, the relevance-theoretic account of allegory of Unger (2017) sheds on the use of allegory in Christian religious discourse. This account of allegory breaks with a long-standing tradition of seeing the nature of allegory as intricately linked to the nature of metaphor. Rather, allegory is seen as related to fiction: a multi-layered communication event, where relevance is optimised jointly over these various layers. Moreover, the communication layers are related by interpretive resemblance relations between the propositions conveyed at the various layers. Thus, allegory comprehension utilises fairly sophisticated cognitive abilities such as the ability to process interpretive resemblance relations and the ability to process multi-layered communication events, necessitating the re-application of the relevance-theoretic comprehension procedure on its own output. This explains the intuition that allegory comprehension is often a reflective, conscious process, where the descriptive meaning of the allegory is transparent throughout the comprehension process. The multi-layeredness of communication events employing allegories provides interesting insights into the usefulness and the limitations of allegory. For one thing, since some relevance relations are satisfied on each communication layer, even at the lowest one, the descriptive meaning, an audience that has rather low levels of relevance expectations may still be cognitively rewarded, enough to pay attention. Moreover, an audience that does not get all their relevance expectations fulfilled may get sufficient cognitive reward to be willing to attend to the text later on and hold out for an eventual deeper understanding, instead of breaking off the comprehension effort completely. Thus, allegory may be a good way to address a heterogeneous audience.

The same multi-layeredness of allegory also suggests that it can be a good tool to indirectly communicate controversial claims to cautious or unsympathetic audiences. This is because the controversial claim is conveyed by means of implicatures that are recoverable only in processing higher layers of communication that become accessible as a result of processing the basic layers of the communication event. Moreover, before the audience can process the level where the controversial claim is made, the audience is induced to process lower levels of communication, which typically carry thoughts that would motivate the acceptance of that controversial claim. In fact, many if not most of the allegories in the Jewish and Christian Scriptures appear in argumentative contexts. Thus, it appears that allegory is a device closely linked to argumentative discourse. If this is true, then one might expect allegory in religious language to be used primarily when (religious) truth claims are discussed. This prediction then leads to another one: that allegory in religious discourse is primarily used in religions that place a high value on truth claims, and less frequent in religions that are more centred on mystic experiences.

The cognitive processes involved in processing multi-layered communication make allegory comprehension a mostly reflective, conscious inference process. As such, there is little that prevents audiences from trying to find more layers of meaning than the communicator envisaged. Thus, the use of allegory comes with an inherent risk of communication failure. In this way, the relevance-theoretic account of allegory given in Unger (2017) simultaneously sheds light on the advantages and limitations of allegory as a communicative device.

ACKNOWLEDGEMENTS

I warmly thank Robyn Carston for stimulating discussions of allegory and extended metaphor. I am also indebted to Paul Chilton for helpful comments.

NOTES

1. See for example Zhang (2005) for an intensive cross-cultural discussion of allegoresis as an interpretation method.
2. Allegoria, quam inversionem interpretantur, aut aliud verbis aliud sensu ostendit aut etiam interim contrarium.
3. Die allegoria . . . ist die als Gedanken-Tropus . . . fortgesetzte Metapher . . . und besteht im Ersatz des gemeinten Gedankens durch einen anderen Gedanken, der zum gemeinten Gedanken in einem Ähnlichkeits-Verhältnis . . . steht.
4. See Sperber and Wilson (2004) for an authoritative statement of this comprehension procedure on page 613, and a fully worked-out example of an application of this procedure on pages 615–617.
5. O navis, referent id mare te novi fluctus; o quid agis? fortiter occupa portum.
6. A piece of information is *manifest* to an individual to the extent that he or she is capable to represent it mentally and accept it as true or probably true. When it is manifest to communicator and audience that a certain piece of information is manifest to them both, this piece of information is *mutually manifest* to communicator and audience. See Sperber and Wilson (1995, pp. 38–46) for a detailed exposition, and Sperber and Wilson (2015) for discussion.

REFERENCES

Bullinger, Ethelbert W. (1968). *Figures of Speech Used in the Bible*. Grand Rapids, MI: Baker Book House. First edition, 1898, London: Eyre and Spottiswode.

Bunyan, John (1953 [1684]). *The Pilgrim's Progress*. London: Collins.

Butler, Harold Edgeworth (1922). *Quintilian. Institutio Oratoria, Book 8. With an English Translation*. Cambridge, MA: Harvard University Press. http://data.perseus.org/texts/urn:cts:latinLit:phi1002.phi0018.perseus-lat1

Carston, Robyn (2002). *Thoughts and Utterances*. Oxford: Blackwell.

Carston, Robyn (2010). Metaphor: Ad hoc concepts, literal meaning and mental images. *Proceedings of the Aristotelian Society* CX(3), 295–321.

Carston, Robyn and Catherine Wearing 2011. Metaphor, hyperbole and simile: A pragmatic approach. *Language and Cognition* 3(2), 283–312.

Crisp, Peter (2001). Allegory: Conceptual metaphor in history. *Language and Literature* 10(1), 5–19. http://lal.sagepub.com/content/10/1/5 (Accessed 29 January, 2013).

Crisp, Peter (2005). Allegory and symbol—A fundamental opposition? *Language and Literature* 14(4), 323–338. http://lal.sagepub.com/content/14/4/323.short (Accessed 21 June, 2012).

Crisp, Peter (2008). Between extended metaphor and allegory: Is blending enough? *Language and Literature* 17(4), 291–308. http://lal.sagepub.com/content/17/4/291.short (Accessed 21 June, 2012).

Davičo, Oskar (1979). Hana. In Oskar Davičo, *Pesme: Hana*. Belgrade: Prosveta.

Dodd, Charles Harold (1935). *The Parables of the Kingdom*. Volume 44. London: Nisbet.

Franklin, R. W. (ed.) (2005). *The Poems of Emily Dickinson: Reading Edition*. Cambridge, MA: Harvard University Press.

Gibbs, Raymond W. (2011). The allegorical impulse. *Metaphor and Symbol* 26(2), 121–130. http://www.tandfonline.com/doi/abs/10.1080/10508406.2011.556498 (Accessed 21 June, 2012).

Harris, Randy Allen and Sarah Tolmie (2011). Cognitive allegory. *Metaphor and Symbol* 26(2), 109–120.

Heller, Zoe (2008). *The Believers*. London: Penguin.

Jeremias, Joachim (1947). *Die Gleichnisse Jesu*. Zürich: Zwingli-Verlag.

Jülicher, Adolf (1899). *Die Gleichnisreden Jesu*. Volume 1, *Die Gleichnissreden Jesu im Allgemeinen*. Revised edition. Freiburg: J. C. B. Mohr (P. Siebeck).

Kasten, Madeleine and Curtis Gruenler (2011). The point of the plow: Conceptual integration in the allegory of Langland and Voltaire. *Metaphor and Symbol* 26(2), 143–151. http://www.tandfonline.com/doi/abs/10.1080/10508406.2011.556502 (Accessed 29 January, 2013).

Klein, William W., Craig C. Blomberg, and Robert L. Hubbard (1993). *Introduction to Biblical Interpretation*. Dallas: Word Publishing.

Kurz, Gerhard (1997). *Metapher, Allegorie, Symbol*. Fourth edition. (Kleine Vandenhoeck-Reihe 1486.) Göttingen: Vandenhoeck & Ruprecht.

Lakoff, George (1993). The contemporary theory of metaphor. In A. Ortony (ed.), *Metaphor and Thought*. Second edition, pp. 202–251. New York: Cambridge University Press.

Lakoff, George and Mark Johnson (1980). *Metaphors We Live By*. Chicago: Chicago University Press.

Lausberg, Heinrich (1984). *Elemente der literarischen Rhetorik*. Eighth edition (First edition 1963). Munich: Max Hueber Verlag.

Lewis, Clive S. (1950). *The Lion, the Witch and the Wardrobe*. London: Geoffrey Bles.

Lewis, Clive S. (1951). *Prince Caspian: The Return to Narnia*. London: Geoffrey Bles.

Lewis, Clive S. (1952). *The Voyage of the Dawn Treader*. London: Geoffrey Bles.

Lewis, Clive S. (1953). *The Silver Chair*. London: Geoffrey Bles.

Lewis, Clive S. (1954). *The Horse and His Boy*. London: Geoffrey Bles.

Lewis, Clive S. (1955). *The Magician's Nephew*. London: The Bodley Head.

Lewis, Clive S. (1956). *The Last Battle*. London: The Bodley Head.

Mercier, Hugo and Dan Sperber (2009). Intuitive and reflective inferences. In J. Evans and K. Frankish (eds.), *In Two Minds: Dual Processes and Beyond*, pp. 149–170. Oxford: Oxford University Press.

Oakley, Todd and Peter Crisp (2011). Honeymoons and pilgrimages: Conceptual integration and allegory in old and new media. *Metaphor and Symbol* 26(2), 152–159. doi: 10.1080/10508406.2011.556507. http://www.tandfonline.com/doi/abs/10.1080/10508406.2011.556507 (Accessed 29 January, 2013).

Origen (1982 [after 244 ce]).*Genesis Homily V*. In *Origen: Homilies on Genesis and Exodus.* In volume 71 of *The Fathers of the Church*, pp. 112–120. Washington, DC: Catholic University of America Press. https://www.unifr.ch/bkv/kapitel3208-2.htm (Accessed April 29, 2016).

Sperber, Dan and Deirdre Wilson (1987). Presumptions of relevance. *Behavioral and Brain Sciences* 10(04), 736–754.

Sperber, Dan and Deirdre Wilson (1990). Rhetoric and relevance. In David Wellbery and John Bender (eds.), *The Ends of Rhetoric: History, Theory, Practice*, pp. 140–156. Stanford, CA: Stanford University Press.

Sperber, Dan and Deirdre Wilson (1995). *Relevance*. Second edition. Oxford: Blackwell.

Sperber, Dan and Deirdre Wilson (1998). The mapping between the mental and the public lexicon. In Peter Carruthers and Jill Boucher (eds.), *Language and Thought*, pp. 184–200. Cambridge: Cambridge University Press.

Sperber, Dan and Deirdre Wilson (2004). Relevance theory. In Laurence R. Horn and Gregory Ward (eds.), *The Handbook of Pragmatics*, pp. 607–632. Oxford: Blackwell.

Sperber, Dan and Deirdre Wilson (2008). A deflationary account of metaphor. In Raymond W. Gibbs (ed.), *The Cambridge Handbook of Metaphor and Thought*, Volume 18, pp. 84–105. Cambridge: Cambridge University Press.

Sperber, Dan and Deirdre Wilson (2015). Beyond speaker's meaning. *Croatian Journal of Philosophy* XV(44), 117–149.

Thagard, Paul (2011). The brain is wider than the sky: Analogy, emotion, and allegory. *Metaphor and Symbol* 26(2), 131–142. http://www.tandfonline.com/doi/abs/10.1080/10926488.2011.556509 (Accessed 21 June, 2012).

Unger, Christoph (2006). *Genre, Relevance and Global Coherence: The Pragmatics of Discourse Type*. Palgrave Studies in Pragmatics, Language and Cognition. Basingstoke: Palgrave Macmillan.

Unger, Christoph (2017). Towards a relevance theory account of allegory. In Agnieszka Piskorska and Ewa Walaszewska (eds.), *Applications of Relevance Theory: From Discourse to Morphemes*, pp. 152–174. Newcastle-upon-Tyne: Cambridge Scholars Publishing.

Wilson, Deirdre (2000). Metarepresentation in linguistic communication. In Dan Sperber (ed.), *Metarepresentation*, pp. 411–448. Oxford: Oxford University Press.

Wilson, Deirdre (2012). Relevance and the interpretation of literary works. Paper presented at the 5th Symposium on Intercultural, Cognitive and Social Pragmatics (EPICS V), Sevilla, Spain, March 14–16, 2012.

Wilson, Deirdre and Robyn Carston (2007). A unitary approach to lexical pragmatics: Relevance, inference and ad hoc concepts. In Noel Burton-Roberts (ed.), *Pragmatics*, pp. 230–259. Palgrave Advances in Linguistics. Basingstoke: Palgrave Macmillan.

Wilson, Deirdre and Dan Sperber 2002. Truthfulness and relevance. *Mind* 111, 583–632.

Zhang, Longxi (2005). *Allegoresis: Reading Canonical Literature East and West*. Ithaca, NY and London: Cornell University Press.

CHAPTER 14

Metaphor and Metonymy in Language and Art

The Dogma of the Holy Trinity and Its Artistic Representation

ANTONIO BARCELONA

Religious language is highly metaphorical and metonymic; so is visual art in general and religious visual art in particular. In this chapter I will concentrate on just a few basic theographic metaphors involved in the formulation of the dogma of the Holy Trinity, in order to be able to contrast their linguistic with their pictorial manifestation. That is, the aim is to study the operation of theographic metaphor and metonymy across two different expressive modes: religious *language* and religious *painting*. More specifically, I aim to study the extent to which the same or other conceptual metaphors and metonymies that I have identified in the linguistic formulation and discussion of the dogma are also present in its artistic representation, and how they are expressed and exploited in this mode. This is an initial and exploratory approach to such questions, questions that will require much more research before they can be given fully satisfying answers.[1]

1 THE CHRISTIAN DOGMA OF THE HOLY TRINITY: THE ROLE OF METAPHOR AND METONYMY IN ITS UNDERSTANDING

The Christian dogma of the Holy Trinity states that there are three real Divine Persons (the Father, the Son, and the Holy Spirit), with their own identities and different from each other. But it also states that there is only one God. However, each of the Persons is at the same time the whole of God. The dogma also states that there exists an 'order of procession' among the Divine Persons, which is not temporal but ontological: The Son 'proceeds' ontologically from the Father (who is the ontological 'origin' of the Trinity), and the Holy Spirit 'proceeds' from both the Father and the Son (*filioque*). The Orthodox Church upholds a slightly different version of the dogma, where The Holy Spirit proceeds from the Father *through* the Son; this is considered by most theologians to be a minor difference.

Christian theology acknowledges the fact that the trinitarian dogma is definitely beyond (but not necessarily against) human reason. Therefore the dogma is at the same time a *mystery*: 'God has left some traces of his Trinitarian being' in his *oikonomia*, that is his 'works,' but 'his inmost Being as Holy Trinity is a mystery that is inaccessible to reason alone' (Catechism of the Catholic Church, henceforth CCC, 1994 p. 56). It is only partly intelligible to Christian believers, thanks to Revelation and the Christian tradition of theological reflection (especially as represented by the so-called Fathers of the Church, who wrote in the early Christian period).

Christians cannot fully comprehend God in his own terms, because he is not fully apprehensible by the human mind, theologians claim. Human beings can only know about him what he has revealed, and then elaborate on this Revelation (the term 'Revelation,' with initial capital, is used to designate the Christian's main source of information about God; this information is contained in the Christian Bible and in the Christian Church's 'Tradition,' embodying the teachings of the Apostles to the earliest Christian communities). Despite their limited understanding of the dogma, Christians are supposed to respectfully believe in it. To them the Trinity is the manifestation of God's inner nature in human history.

The manner in which believers (including the author of this chapter) understand and interpret the Revelation underlying the dogma and the actual formulation of the latter (carried out gradually in the first centuries of the history of Christianity) is inevitably metaphorical and/or metonymic (Soskice 1985, p. 96), i.e., by projecting our human categories onto the divine. However, for Christian believers, dogmatic statements are true. Their *comprehension* of those truths is largely metaphorical and metonymic, but to them, the truths are such, independently from the way they mentally access them. As Lakoff and Johnson (1980) pointed out long ago, metaphoricity (and figurative thought in general) should be carefully distinguished from 'fictivity': a metaphorical expression may be assessed as true or false on the basis of its context (including its cognitive context). A metaphorical expression about God (such as *God is our Father*) is judged true by the community of Christian believers because it metaphorically predicates of God a property (fatherhood), which presupposes a further set of properties (God's creative activity, love and care, protective attitude, patience, etc.) that Christianity has attributed to God since its inception.

The justification for this chapter should thus be obvious: irrespective of personal beliefs or attitudes, the study of the metaphors, metonymies, and other figurative means used to present this mystery and to 'explain' it constitutes a fascinating research topic. The research reported in this chapter is a detailed exercise in cognitive semantics and in cognitive semiotics, as it moves beyond language into another semiotic system: figurative art.

2 SUMMARY OF MY EARLIER STUDIES ON CONCEPTUAL METAPHORS AND METONYMIES IN THE TRINITARIAN DOGMA

This section is devoted to summing up (and inevitably oversimplifying) earlier detailed studies (Barcelona 1997a, 1997b, 1999; especially the latter) which were concerned with the linguistic formulation of the dogma of the Trinity. I deal separately with metaphor and metonymy.

2.1 Metaphor and metaphor networks

Only an overview and a few examples can be provided here. Two 'root' metaphors[2] are proposed in these studies: GOD IS HUMAN and HUMAN IS GOD. The first metaphor is the fundamental overarching metaphor used in talking and thinking about God, that is, the mapping of human experience onto our limited understanding of God's nature. It consists of an enormous number of *submetaphors* or *submappings*, as will be shown below.

The second metaphor, HUMAN IS GOD, is directly based on the Bible, which tells us that man was created *in the image of God* (Genesis 1:27), but I have not yet been able to study in depth the artistic representation of this metaphor. Some discussion is to be found in Barcelona (1999), where I claim that HUMAN IS GOD implies that although, to a believer, man is not a possible model for God (since God is the *wholly Other*), God is really a model for man. In a mysterious way, the model of notions like progeneration, family, love, life, light, etc. is ultimately God the Father's parenthood, the community of Life in the Holy Trinity, their Love, their Life, their Light, etc.[3] Thus, although Christian believers can understand metaphorically (GOD~HUMAN), and very imperfectly, what it is for the Father to eternally beget the Son, they can be certain that this eternal divine progeneration is the origin and standard of human progeneration (CCC 1994, p. 57). Therefore, there has to be some mysteriously profound truth to a statement that regards God as a father or as a loving husband.

Let us now examine GOD IS HUMAN in some detail, by briefly discussing some of the submappings in the metaphor. These submappings are summed up in Table 1 (reproduced from Barcelona 1999).

For the sake of brevity, I will just comment on a few examples of each of the various groups of submappings that make up the root metaphor under discussion.

As regards the *submappings onto the divine of experiential models of spatial concepts*, such notions as VERTICALITY and PLACE or LOCATION are often mapped onto God, as in the Nicene Creed (NC hereafter), which proclaims that Jesus 'came *down from* Heaven'; or in Mark 16:19, where we are told that Christ 'was taken *up into* heaven' (English version of NC in the CCC 1994, pp. 47–48). That is, Heaven is conceived of as a place in space ('from/up into Heaven'). But we know from other biblical passages that Heaven is not necessarily confined to any spatial co-ordinates.

Table 1. HUMAN CONCEPTUAL SOURCE DOMAINS METAPHORICALLY
MAPPED ONTO THE DOMAIN OF THE DIVINE

(a) *Experiential folk notions of tri-dimensional space as source domains*: verticality, place, movement, container, boundary, light, etc.

(b) *Metaphorically understood abstract notions as source domains*: existence, being, essence or substance, time, events, action, causation, etc.

(c) *Metaphorical and nonmetaphorical notions of the human person as source domains*: personhood, emotions, the human body, etc.

(d) *Metaphorical and nonmetaphorical notions of human interpersonal relationships as source domains*: power, authority, status, family relationships (father/mother, son), love (as a relationship), language and communication, groups of individuals, social roles

Another well-known example is the mapping of LIGHT onto the divine. Light occurs in space. It is often treated in non-religious language as a physical entity which can move, be seen, measured, etc.: *The light* went *out, there is* too much *light here*, etc. In Christian religious language, LIGHT and DARK are also conventional metaphorical sources for GOOD and EVIL. This is part of the basis for the mapping of LIGHT onto Christ in the Prologue of the Fourth Gospel (John 1:9): 'The true *light*, which *enlightens* everyone, was *coming into* the world,' where the spatial character of the source concept is preserved.

Finally, a fundamental submapping in this group is the mapping of spatial origin onto 'ontological precedence,' the so-called ontological 'order of procession' of the three Divine Persons: we are also told by the NC that the Holy Spirit 'proceeds from the Father and the Son,' and is the mutual love of the Father and the Son.

The *submappings onto the divine of metaphorically understood notions of abstract, non-emergent concepts* can be exemplified by the notions of GRACE and TRUTH, which are conceptualized as physical entities, of which the Father's only Son is 'full' (John 1:14). The theological notion of grace derives from the human notion of grace as gratuitous help, favor, or special benefit. This human notion is metaphorically understood as an object that can be transferred to a recipient, and this is also represented in Biblical language: 'From his *fullness* we have all *received, grace upon grace*' (John 1:16). Truth is also understood metaphorically as a physical entity which can be measured, given, etc., as in *She gave me the whole truth*; this metaphorical understanding of truth is also mapped onto the Christian notion of divine truth.

The *submappings onto the divine of metaphorical and nonmetaphorical notions making up or related to the notion of the human person* (such as personhood, emotions, the human body) could in part have been included in the preceding group (such notions as that of personhood are also abstract). The fundamental metaphor is A PERSON IS A CONTAINER, whereby a person is understood in terms of the container image schema, which includes that person's mental and emotional life (Barcelona 1986; Kövecses 1990). This metaphorical understanding of personhood is then further projected onto the understanding of the divine Persons, who are also conceptualized as containers.

If divine grace is treated by St John, in the above quotation from the Prologue to his Gospel (John 1:16), as a metaphorical object that can be transferred to a recipient, the metaphorical spatial origin of that transfer is Jesus, regarded as a 'full' container (an infinitely 'full' one): 'From his fullness'. . . . In the same Gospel (John 14:10–12; see also John 16), Jesus is reported as saying 'the Father who dwells *in me* does his works. Believe me that I am *in the Father* and the Father is *in me*,' treating the Father and Himself as containers. The CCC (1994 p. 60) uses the same conceptualization of the Divine Persons in this statement: 'We do not confess three Gods, but one God *in three persons*,' that is, the divine 'substance' (as Christian theology has used this term since patristic times) is presented as being all of it in three different metaphorical containers.

Finally, the *submappings onto the divine of metaphorical and nonmetaphorical notions of human interpersonal relationships* is manifested by the application of 'human-sized' conceptualizations of these relationships to some of the relationships among the Divine Persons and to the relationship between God and men. For example, the Holy Spirit is attributed such *social roles* as 'Consoler' (CCC 1994, p. 160). And Christ and the Holy Spirit are often called 'Teacher.' *Family relationships* deserve special mention for our purpose, since the human notion of family is projected onto the notion of the Holy Trinity. On the one hand, the human notions of FATHERHOOD and SONHOOD are source domains applied to the Holy Trinity to gain some understanding and to grasp an essential truth about the nature of the First Person and that of the Second Person and about their relationship to each other. Part of our knowledge of human fatherhood and sonship can thus be analogically applied to God the Father and God the Son and to their relationship:

- The progeneration of a son by his father is mapped onto the eternal begetting of the Son by the Father (the NC states that 'our Lord Jesus Christ' is 'eternally begotten of the Father').
- The sharing of a son in his father's biological endowment is mapped onto the sharing of the same divine 'substance' by the Father and the Son.
- The (imperfect) mutual love to be expected between a human father and his son, the (imperfect) obedience of a son to his father, etc. are mapped onto the perfect mutual love between Father and Son, onto the perfect obedience of the Son to the Father, etc.

There are multiple New Testament passages where this father-son relationship is revealed: Jesus' Baptism ('A voice from heaven said, 'This is *my* Son, the Beloved, with whom I am well pleased,' Matthew 3:17); his Transfiguration (Matthew 17:5); Peter's confession that Jesus is the Son of God (Matthew 16:17); and Jesus' formal statement of his divine Sonship before the high priests (Luke 22:70).

Of the enormous number of submappings in GOD IS HUMAN, the most relevant ones in the structure, limited understanding, and discussion of the dogma are these:

- Within group (a) in Table 1:
  - The mapping onto God of the notion of spatial movement.
  - The mapping of light onto divine Light and its personification in Christ.

- Within group (b) in Table 1:
  - The mapping of the human philosophical (and metaphorical) notion of 'substance' onto the notion of 'divine substance.'
- Within group (c) in Table 1:
  - The mapping of the metaphorical notion of human personhood onto the notion of divine personhood.
- Within group (d) in Table 1:
  - The mapping onto Christ of the Father's Word and its personification in Christ [this process also involves a submapping from group (b) in Table 1].
  - The mapping of the parent-child relationship onto God.

These submappings have been used to illustrate the dogma, especially at the time when it was being formed (Kelly 1968). Most of them have already been illustrated above, except for the mapping of the human philosophical notion of 'substance' onto the notion of 'divine substance' and the mapping onto Christ of the Father's Word and its personification in Christ.

'Substance' is used in philosophy in an abstract sense, denoting something like 'essential nature,' 'essence.' This philosophical notion, which was incorporated into Christian theology from Greek philosophy, is probably a metaphorical projection from the experiential notion of a mass object. Lakoff and Johnson (1999) talk about the metaphor ESSENCE IS MATERIAL SUBSTANCE as underlying Aristotle's notion of essence. The metaphorical understanding of the notions of essence and substance is present in the NC: 'true God from true God, begotten, not made, of one Being with the Father,' where of, which has a partitive value, evokes the idea of a material component. It is also present in theological discussions of the trinitarian dogma that talk about the *consubstantiality* of the three divine Persons (CCC 1994, pp. 57–59).

The mapping onto Christ of the Father's Word and its personification in Christ requires a more complex discussion. Firstly, the understanding of the notion of God's Word is naturally rooted in our experience of human communication. Whenever we are told that God or any one of the Divine Persons spoke, we are assuming a nonmetaphorical human model of communication as a source domain mapped onto God. This assumption is involved in our understanding of the NC's statement that the Holy Spirit 'hath spoken through the Prophets'; of Jesus' promise to the Apostles that the Spirit of truth 'will not speak on his own, but will speak whatever he hears, and he will declare to you the things that are to come' (John 16:13); and of the biblical passages where we are told that the Father spoke during the Baptism of Christ and during his Transfiguration, that God spoke to Moses, or the theological statement that God speaks to each of us. When Christian theology attempts to investigate the nature of God's communicative activity, it has to resort to human linguistic categories like those of 'word' and 'utterance,' which are projected onto the transcendental Word and Utterance: 'Through all the words of

Sacred Scripture, God speaks only one single Word, his one Utterance in which he expresses himself completely' (CCC 1994, p. 29). This Word is the Second Person (the Son).

Secondly, God's transcendental Word is personified and eventually identified with Christ. Again, this metaphorical process is itself understood from a deep-rooted metaphorical model of human communication, which treats utterances (i.e. linguistic actions) as physical entities. One of the specific cases of Lakoff's (1993) EVENT STRUCTURE metaphor regards events and actions, as physical entities which can, inter alia, be acquired and handled (as in *I gave my son a hug*, or *Take my word*). In the domain of linguistic action, utterances and linguistic expressions tend to be seen as physical containers for meaning; this is Reddy's (1993) well-known CON-DUIT metaphor. On the other hand, the 'objectification' of events is a common metaphor in many languages (just consider eventive nouns like *dance, destruction, fall, death*), which occurs independently from, but is consistent with, the event structure metaphor. It is not uncommon for some of these objectified events to be personified (cf. expressions like *I saw the face of Death*, or artistic conventions like representing the event of victory as a woman). This tendency explains in part why God's Word (his 'linguistic action') is often personified in the Old Testament, a personification which paves the way for the later identification of the Word as one of the Persons in the Holy Trinity, the Second Person (see Gerard and Nordon-Gerard 1995, p. 1471), as revealed in the New Testament. The personification of the Word can, therefore, be claimed to be also understood as a projection from the metaphorical understanding of human-sized actions and events [that is, as one of the submappings in group (b) of Table 1].

The above six submappings can be shown to cohere with each other, thus lending some strictly *metaphorical coherence* to the dogma, by noting that the image schema (Johnson 1987) of CONTAINER operates in all of them. The PERSON~CONTAINER metaphor is closely allied to a set of other metaphors that are also applied to the divine. Each of the Divine Persons is conceived of as a container, and God himself, the Divine Being, is also conceived of as a container. The notions of uttering speech, of giving off light, of progeneration, of emo-tions, especially love (part of the mapping of the human notion of person onto the notion of the Divine Persons), of ontological 'substance' (which, according to Lakoff and Johnson 1999, is a metaphorical projection from the notion of a physical core), moral attributes, and of spatial motion, especially of spatial origin (mapped onto the ontological 'order of procession' of the Divine Persons) are all closely connected to that of container. This is so because a person, an utterer, a light-source, a parent, or an experiencer of an emotion can be regarded as a container, with ontological substance, words, light, offspring, or emotions as the content coming out of it. And a spatial origin may be precisely the container (the Father and the Son) from which the moving entity (the Spirit) proceeds. Thus these metaphorical conceptualizations are all consistent with each other because they are all compatible with the container image schema.

2.2 Metonymy, metonymic networks, and their interaction with metaphor

Another, complementary, level of figurative coherence of the dogma is *metonymic coherence*. In my earlier writings on this topic (especially Barcelona 1999), I suggested these four coherence-creating metonymic relationships:

- The relationship between God and his word, his linguistic action.
- The relationship between a light and its radiance.
- The relationship between a parent and her/his offspring.
- The relationship between the initial or the final point of a path and the mover along this path.

These connections are claimed to offer some 'figurative intelligibility' to the dogma. The second of them was used in patristic writings as a way of illustrating the mysterious coherence of the dogma. There exists a specific metonymic relationship between action and agent, whereby the action (the word) can stand for the agent (God). There are numerous conventional examples in many languages of this specific ACTION FOR AGENT metonymy. We can often use referring expressions where the agent is identified by his action: 'The man that helped you has come.' We often simply nominalize the action and use the nominalization to refer to the agent characterized by that action: 'Your help came' (meaning 'the person that helped you'). Note that the action refers to the whole of the agent, not just to an aspect of it.

Similarly, God's word can stand in our minds for the whole of God himself. This metonymic substitution of the action for the whole of the agent might provide a metonymic bridge between the oneness of God and the fact that both the First and the Second Persons are wholly God.

There is also a metonymic mapping of effects onto causes (see Radden and Kövecses 1999). The relationship between a light-source and the light that it gives out can be seen as an instance of the cause and effect relationship. When a light stands for its source, the EFFECT FOR CAUSE metonymy is at work. In English the noun *light* is often used to denote a match or a torch (both light-sources). Consider examples like *Turn on/off the light* (what is actually turned on or off is the electric power which brings about light). Similarly, if God is the cause of all Light (he is Light himself) and gives off Light, his Light can metonymically stand for the whole of God. As stated earlier, the example of light and light radiance (both are light) has been exploited since the earliest times in Christian theology to make it imaginable how the Second Person can be different from the First, and at the same time be exactly like it, and, therefore, have the same divine substance (Kelly 1968, chapter 3).

It is not clear in which type of metonymic relationship of those proposed by Radden and Kövecses (1999) the relationship between a parent and his/her offspring should be included. But the fact is that the children are often conceptualized from the perspective of their parents, typically from the perspective of their father. The very conventions of naming often use the father's family name or last name as the distinctive surname for the children. We normally refer to someone whose father's name we know as *the son of* X. And we often use the father's forename as a way of referring to a male child whose forename we may not know—we may (in the appropriate circumstances) intelligibly say *Here comes Mike* to refer to Mike's son, even though he has a different forename. So it is with the Second Person. He came to be known as the *Son of God*. The concept GOD is a distinguishing attribute in the expression, and it overshadows the concept SON. Therefore GOD (as a whole) metonymically stands for SON OF GOD, and the Son can thus be God and yet be different from God the Father.

There is finally a metonymic connection between the initial or the final point in a path and the mover along this path. Expressions like *the Birmingham train* can refer to the train bound for or coming from Birmingham. We are concerned here with the metonymy in which the initial point in the path stands for the mover along the path. Among other examples of this metonymy we can cite those in which the origin of a mover is foregrounded, as when we say 'the doctor *that came from Durham*' to refer to a doctor whose name we do not know but whose provenance we do know, or even colloquial uses in which a locative expression is used with personal reference, almost like a personal name, as in '*Durham* is sitting over there,' referring to the same doctor. Similarly if the Holy Spirit proceeds from the Father and the Son, both of whom are God, he proceeds from God. And God, the initial point of his path, can wholly stand metonymically for him. This would then be a metonymic bridge between the oneness of God and the individuality of the Holy Spirit.

In fact, in the realm of the divine, these four metonymies could be regarded as special cases of the CONTAINER-AND-CONTAINED metonymic relationship, which, in Radden and Kövecses's (1999) view, can also yield two types of PART FOR PART metonymies: CONTAINED FOR CONTAINER (as in their example *The milk tipped over* for the 'The milk container tipped over'), or CONTAINER FOR CONTAINED (as in *John ate the whole box* [of chocolates]). As we saw above, the metaphorical conception of people as containers is also mapped onto the Divine Persons. The Father is regarded as a container for his Word, his Light, his Son, and his Spirit. The Word and the Light that, being contained in the Father, come out of him, can stand for him. The Father is God. So his Word and his Light can stand for God; that is, God, the Container, can be mentally accessed and identified via his Word and his Light, the Contained. In fact, the Word and the Light become in this way a name for, and are equated with, the whole of God, just as *your help* becomes a name for someone characterized by helping you, or just as *light* (radiance) becomes a name for a light-source.

The WORD FOR GOD and the LIGHT FOR GOD metonymies can thus also be regarded as CONTENT FOR CONTAINER metonymies. The two other metonymies proposed above can be regarded as instances of the CONTAINER FOR CONTAINED metonymic pattern. The Father-Container can stand for his Son-Contained. The Father is God. Therefore the Son-Contained can be mentally accessed and identified via his Father-Container, who is the one God, and can thus be called, not Father, but the Father's name, which is that of 'the one God.' And as before, the metonymy creates a conceptual network that leads to the identification of Son and God: the Son is the whole of God. However, outside the metonymy, the Father is still different from the Son. It is quite frequent for a container to be the initial point of the path followed by a mover. In the case of the Second Person, this initial point is the Father. In the case of the

Holy Spirit, there are two initial points, because he proceeds from the Father and the Son, both of whom are one God, as we know from the preceding metonymies.

As we can see, the container image-schema constitutes a link between the metonymic and the metaphorical coherence of the dogma. This kind of conceptual coherence is by no means an explanation of the dogma, which—from both a religious and a strictly logical-referential perspective—is beyond human intelligence in man's earthly existence, but it seems to show that the dogma is compatible with human cognitive abilities that are part also of human linguistic abilities.

3 THE ROLE OF METAPHOR AND METONYMY IN ARTISTIC REPRESENTATIONS OF THE TRINITARIAN MYSTERY

Throughout the Christian era, artists have attempted to represent graphically the Holy Trinity or some of its aspects in different ways. We will focus our attention in this chapter on those paintings that represent the three Divine Persons, or at least one of them, in the form of a human being, accompanied with other visual elements symbolizing their individual character. We will leave out abstract types of representation trying to stress the compatibility between the oneness of God and the individuality of each of the Persons, such as the equilateral triangle, the three interwoven circles, the six-pointed star, the triquetra, the shield of Trinity, etc., unless they are incorporated into the mainly anthropomorphic iconographies we will be concerned with. As a non-specialist in religious iconography, I have had to consult specialized works (Allenov et al. 2000; Atienza Ballano 2009; and most particularly, Maquívar 2006; Réau 1995; and Statsny 1994, pp. 10, 35–45) that classify these anthropomorphic representations into several types on the basis of several criteria. The criteria and the resulting iconographic types are as follows:

Criterion 1: Degree of similarity of the figures representing the Divine Persons (as is known, it is normally the Father and the Son that are given an anthropomorphic representation, with the Holy Spirit represented as a dove; but sometimes the Holy Spirit is also represented as a human figure or the Son as a lamb, etc.).

Iconographic types:
- *Heteromorphic*: Representations where those figures have a markedly different appearance.
- (wholly or partially) *Isomorphic:* representations where those figures have the same or similar appearance. An extreme, special case of isomorphic representation is constituted by so-called 'three-faced Trinities' (see below).

Criterion 2: Spatial arrangement of the images.

Iconographic types:
- vertical arrangement: The figures corresponding to the Persons are displayed at different heights in the spatial arrangement of the scene represented in the painting.
- horizontal arrangement: The figures corresponding to the Persons are displayed approximately on the same level.

Criterion 3: Orthodoxy from the perspective of Christian theology.
Iconographic types:
- orthodox
- deviant.

Both heteromorphic and vertical representations have historically been regarded as orthodox, whereas homomorphic and horizontal representations have normally been associated with varying degrees of theological deviance (in Roman Catholicism, not in the Orthodox churches).

The above classification of iconographic types is, admittedly, an oversimplification, but it is useful for my purposes as a general classificatory scheme. The iconography of the Holy Trinity is richer and more complex, however, with several highly specific iconographic patterns such as the *Compassio Patris*, the *Thronum Gratiae*, the 'Three-Faced Trinities,' The Trinity with the Globe, etc., which often combine with each other. There are also different iconographic traditions in Western (especially Catholic) and Orthodox churches. The general iconographic types established above on the basis of criteria 1–3 combine in several ways. These are exemplified below with one painting for each combination; at the same time, some of these paintings constitute examples of some of the more specific iconographic types mentioned above.

An example of an *orthodox heteromorphic horizontal* representation is *The Trinity*, by Antonio de Pereda (Spain, 17th century), which is kept in the Budapest Museum of Fine Arts. A good image of the painting can be viewed at https://es.wikipedia.org/wiki/Archivo:Antonio_de_Pereda_y_Salgado_-_The_Holy_Trinity_-_WGA17176.jpg (last accessed February 28, 2017). This painting also follows the specific iconographic pattern that displays the Trinity with the Globe, which is being blessed by Christ and God the Father. In the painting, the three divine Persons appear on the same level in a left-to-right arrangement, with Christ as a young man on the left, the Holy Spirit in the shape of a dove above the Globe in the middle, and the Father as an old man on the right.

The *orthodox-heteromorphic-vertical* combination is exemplified by means of the *Allegory of the Holy Eucharist*, whose author was Miguel Cabrera (Mexico, 17th century). See Maquívar (2006). The image can be viewed at https://es.pinterest.com/pin/123637952247002599/ (last accessed February 28, 2017). The painting arranges the three divine Persons vertically in a top-bottom arrangement, with the Father as an old man at the top, the Holy Spirit as a dove immediately below, and the Cross with a Host inserted in its center and the Lamb, both symbols of Christ, right below the Holy Spirit. This painting also represents the specific iconographic pattern where Christ is presented as a lamb on an altar.

An *orthodox isomorphic horizontal* representation is Figure 1.

The painting is theologically orthodox from the perspective of the Catholic Church and at the same time it represents the Trinitarian beliefs of the Orthodox Church. This richly symbolic icon, kept at the Tretyakov Gallery, Moscow, constitutes at the same time an excellent example of the 'Hospitality of Abraham' iconographic type, based on the Biblical passage with the story of the so-called

Figure 1 *Holy Trinity Icon.* Attributed to Andrei Rublev, 1411 or 1425–1427.
Source: Allenov, Dmitrieva, and Medvedkova (2000). Image downloaded from Wikipedia Commons, where it is declared to be in the public domain in the United States and copyright free.

'Mamre theophany' (Genesis 18:1–3), where the three Divine Persons seem to have manifested themselves to Abraham in the shape of three equal Angels, whom Abraham addressed in the singular ('Lord, . . .'). The various analyses of the icon agree that the central figure corresponds to Christ, who is flanked by the Father on the left of the painting and by the Holy Spirit on the right, each figure wearing different garments and colors allusive to their character. This Father-Son-Holy Spirit arrangement is normally interpreted as a reminder of the doctrine of the Orthodox Church regarding the order of procession of the Holy Spirit (from the Father through the Son).

A *deviant isomorphic horizontal* combination is illustrated by Figure 2.

This painting constitutes an example of the 'three-faced' iconographic type, in which the Trinity is represented as one human figure with three (often partly

Figure 2 *Trinity*. Anonymous. Church of the Saints Justo (Justus) and Pastor. Cuenca de Campos, Valladolid, Spain.
Source: Atienza Ballano (2009). Image provided and reproduction permission granted at no cost by *Fundación Las Edades del Hombre*, Valladolid, Spain.

overlapping) human faces, all of them of course on the same level. It was regarded as theologically unorthodox.

The image of the cloth in the painting of the *Veronica*, an 18th century anonymous painting kept at the Virgin of the Pilar Church, San Isidro, Lima, exemplifies the rare pattern (particularly rare in Europe) *deviant-isomorphic-vertical* (most isomorphic representations tend to be horizontal). On this painting, see Statsny 1994: 16, 41. The painting can be viewed at http://bibliotk.iep.org.pe/bib_img/5945-8-1.pdf, from where Statsny's study can be downloaded; the image is in page 41 (last accessed February 28, 2017). This representation is regarded as theologically deviant because three heads (each corresponding to a Divine Person but all with Christ's appearance) appear on the cloth on which, according to a popular Christian tradition, Christ's face was imprinted after Veronica wiped his face with it and because the three heads bear the Crown of Thorns, a (metonymic) attribute of Christ. This is a way of suggesting that the three Persons had suffered the Passion, a claim that had already been considered heretical in early Christian theology (Kelly 1968, p. 123).

Finally, Figure 3 constitutes a special case, where the three Persons are represented by a single human figure. It is a *deviant blended* representation in which criteriaons 1 (similarity among the individual representations of the Divine Persons) and 2 (relative spatial arrangement of those representations) cannot apply.

Although the main purpose of this section is simply to illustrate the main iconographic tendencies in the pictorial representation of the Holy Trinity rather than to analyze them in terms of conceptual metaphor or metonymy, I will devote a few paragraphs here to point out at least some of the main metonymies and metaphors involved in the creation and understanding of this painting. This simple analysis also constitutes a transition to the fuller analyses presented in section 4.

Figure 3 *Trinity. Saint Elizabeth Monastery.* Medinaceli, Soria, Spain. Anonymous painting (early 18th century).

Source: Atienza Ballano (2009). Image provided and reproduction permission of granted at no cost by *Fundación Las Edades del Hombre*, Valladolid, Spain. Permission to reproduce the image was additionally granted by the Abbess of Saint Elizabeth Monastery.

Compared to the painting in Figure 2 (and to that in Figure 6), the 'fusion' of the three Persons in the image is more complex. It constitutes an instance of *conceptual blending*, in Fauconnier and Turner's sense (Fauconnier and Turner 2002; see Feyaerts and Boeve, chapter 3 in this volume) and as applied by Antović in chapter 15, this volume. And, theologically, Figure 3 is even more unorthodox, even though it is not aesthetically disgusting. Apart from the various trinitarian metaphors and metonymies mentioned in section 2, which are also represented in this painting and in others presented earlier, this painting is rich in *metonymy-driven allusion*, which is the cognitive means used to carry out the fusion, the blending of the conventional representations of the three Persons into one single figure. The three Divine persons are represented through one sitting male figure with certain elements of the figure alluding to each of the Persons. The Father is represented by:

- The head with the tiara and by the pontifical cape (each of these elements are metonymic allusions to conventional metaphorical representations of the Father's primacy and power, and they have traditionally been used as his iconographic attributes).
- The left arm, with the scepter on the globe, both metonymy-based attributes of the Father's power over the Creation.
- The grey beard, a metonymic indication of old age, in turn a metaphor for the Father's primacy as the ontological origin of the Trinity.

Christ, the Son of God, is represented by:

- The rest of the body (the body of a younger man, a metaphorical representation of the Son's ontological provenance from the Father), naked to the waist, with ulcers on its right side, its right foot and its right hand, which holds the Cross. The ulcers and the Cross are metonymic allusions to Christ's Passion, hence to Christ himself.

The Holy Spirit is represented by the two powerful dove wings[4] spreading out from behind the shoulders, a metonymic allusion to the appearance the Holy Spirit took at the Baptism of Christ in the Jordan River.

Both this representation of the Holy Trinity and the isomorphic 'three-faced' representations in Figures 2 and 6 are motivated by a metaphor that maps the notion of SHARING THE SAME BODY onto the notion of SHARING THE SAME SPIRITUAL SUBSTANCE. The purpose of these representations was to emphasize God's unity, but this was done at the expense of iconographically (i.e. metaphorically) blurring the distinction between the three Persons and of downplaying the fundamental issue of the 'order of procession' of the three Persons. Therefore these paintings were considered unorthodox by many Catholic theologians and church authorities, since the paintings could be interpreted as supporting the *modalist* heresy (which stated that each Person is just a 'mode' of Divinity, but not fully God), the heresy of *subordinationism* (the Son and the Spirit are subordinate to God the Father in essence), or the errors known as *Sabellianism, Patripassianism,* or *Priscillianism,* some of which, besides upholding modalism, claimed that the Father had experienced human suffering.

4 A FEW DETAILED ANALYSES IN TERMS OF CONCEPTUAL METAPHOR AND METONYMY

This section includes a relatively detailed conceptual analysis of four paintings representing three of the iconographic types described and illustrated in section 3. Many of the metaphorical submappings in GOD IS HUMAN, briefly discussed in section 2, are also represented in these paintings and in Christian art in general. In order to keep the discussion within reasonable length, it will be focused mainly on these highly relevant submappings:

- *Three-dimensional space as a source domain*, especially the mapping of container, position, and motion onto aspects of the Trinity.
- *Abstract notions as source domains*, especially the human-sized notions of essence and substance mapped onto the Holy Trinity.
- *The notion of human personhood as a source domain* mapped onto the Holy Trinity.
- *Human interpersonal relationships as source domains*, especially that of family (and within it the notion of human progeneration in particular) mapped onto the Holy Trinity.

4.1 An *orthodox heteromorphic vertical* representation of the Holy Trinity: José de Ribera's *Trinity* (Figure 4)

A brief comment on this painting is to be found on the website of the Museo del Prado (https://www.museodelprado.es/coleccion/obra-de-arte/la-trinidad/91fb4e51-f5ad-47a7-adb2-9d0410c159bf). This painting had two clear, complementary *iconological purposes* in the spirit of the Counter-Reformation stimulated by the Council of Trent (1545–1563): to extoll Catholic dogma against heresy and to 'teach' an illiterate audience one of the pillars of dogmatic theology, the Holy Trinity dogma.

4.1.1 *Analysis of the expression in this painting of the four submappings in* GOD IS HUMAN *selected*

The *vertical arrangement* of the scene was considered to be the most convenient way of conferring the necessary unity on the group and to emphasize Christian monotheism. There have been numerous variants of this arrangement in Christian art like the *Throne of Grace*, the *Compassio Patris* as in this case, etc. In this arrangement, the position of the dove representing the Holy Spirit varies widely, adding to the number of variants. The representation of the Persons is anthropomorphic, except for the one of Holy Spirit, which is zoomorphic.

As regards the *mapping of spatial relation concepts onto the Trinity*, the embodied notions of *height* and *place* are mapped onto the notion of HEAVEN and POWER (or

Figure 4 *Trinity 1635–1636* by José de Ribera. Museo del Prado, Madrid.
Source: ©Museo Nacional del Prado. Image provided and reproduction rights granted by Museo Nacional del Prado, Madrid, Spain.

rather, AUTHORITY, since Christ, the Son, obeyed the Father) by way of the metaphors HEAVEN IS UP and AUTHORITY IS UP. The latter understanding of power and authority is simultaneously mapped onto divine power. These metaphorically understood notions are visually and metonymically expressed by means of the upper location of the golden area (also a conventional representation of Glory and Heaven) and the position of the Father with respect to the Son. The position of the Dove, between the Father and Son, metonymically evokes the metaphorical understanding of the

Spirit's ontological provenance from both in terms of spatial provenance (this is the *filioque* doctrine, which differs from the doctrine of the Orthodox church, according to which the Spirit proceeds from the Father *through* the Son). Another important metaphor prompted in the painting is SPIRITUAL IS UP: the dove *flies* and the Father is in *Heaven*. By contrast, Christ is not *purely* spiritual (he is also a man), and is thus presented on a lower plane.

A fundamental metaphor in GOD IS HUMAN is the mapping of the spatial notion of (three-dimensional) CONTAINER onto the Holy Trinity, either directly or via the mapping of the human-sized notions of PERSONHOOD or GROUPS (OF PEOPLE) onto the Trinity (see below). In language, the notion of containment is expressed by such expressions as *in, inside, out, outside, container, include,* etc. In painting this notion is expressed by means of visual bi-dimensional configurations that represent three-dimensional containers. This way the painting expresses concepts which were first expressed linguistically, and it does so in the context of shared religious knowledge. That is, religious painting is an instance of *intertextuality* operating across two different texts, one linguistic and another (fundamentally) pictorial. The same applies to the imagistic representation of the mapping of other spatial relations onto the divine or onto other abstract targets (expressed in language, for example, by such expressions as *being seated at the right hand of the Father*).

The metaphorical projection of the human notion of LIGHT onto the notion of God, onto the notion of divine Light, and onto Christ, who is said by the Gospels to be the personification of God's Light, is imagistically and metonymically represented in the painting by means of the strong light falling on Christ's body and shroud, on the Father, on the Holy Spirit, and on the angels. This light contrasts with the dark lower background (a metonymic pointer to the human-sized metaphors GOOD IS UP/ BAD IS DOWN and GOOD IS LIGHT/EVIL IS DARK). These metonymies could be called METAPHORICAL SOURCE FOR METAPHORICAL MAPPING. This light is also a metonymic reminder of LIFE IS LIGHT/DEATH IS DARK, which seem to have been used to suggest to the spectator Christ's imminent victory over evil and death. This interpretation is reinforced through the activation of two metaphorical understandings (HEAVEN IS LIGHT and HEAVEN IS UP) of Heaven. This metonymic activation of the metaphors is achieved by means of the strong golden light (as coming from the Sun, i.e., 'from above') in the upper background. These metaphors are a hint at Christ's eventual rise to Heaven after Resurrection.

With respect to *metaphorically understood abstract notions as source domains* mapped onto the divine, we have already commented on the pictorial representations of the indirect mapping of some abstract notions (Heaven, Goodness) onto the divine. Another possible set of metaphorically understood abstract notions may be mapped onto the conventional linguistic and pictorial symbolization of the Holy Spirit as a dove. The Dove was the form under which the Holy Spirit manifested itself on the occasion of the baptism and transfiguration of Jesus (Matthew 3:17; 17:5). The image of a Dove as a symbol for the Holy Spirit in Christian art is rooted in the New Testament, which, as part of Revelation, is believed by Christians to have been inspired by God; therefore the choice of that symbol is believed by Christians to have been made by God himself. But since Revelation constantly uses metaphor and metonymy to communicate its message to humans, we may wonder whether the choice of this form of self-revelation has a metaphorical basis itself. Apart from the human-sized metaphorical representation of an attribute of the Holy Spirit (SPIRITUALITY) in terms of physical space (ability to fly/being up; see above), another attribute of the Holy Spirit that may have been metaphorically presented is MORAL PURITY, understood as CLEANNESS, which is in turn understood metonymically as WHITENESS (the white color of the dove evokes cleanness, and the latter is often connected metaphorically to moral purity). GOOD IS LIGHT (see above) is also probably involved, as whiteness is connected to intense light in our experience. As stated in relation to Figure 3 (section 3), the Dove is also a metonymic allusion to the manifestation of the Father and the Holy Spirit in the Baptism of Jesus, and is therefore also an allusion to the manifestation of the Holy Trinity. The metonymy could be called ENTITY FOR ASSOCIATED EVENT.

The *mapping of metaphorical and nonmetaphorical notions of the human person as source domains* is clearly represented in the painting, where the images of two different human male persons are metaphorically mapped onto the First and the Second Person of the Trinity (DIVINE PERSON AS HUMAN PERSON). In all anthropomorphic representations of the divine Persons, the HUMAN PERSON notion is *metonymically* activated by means of the human body (BODY FOR PERSON), in this case by means of two heteromorphic male human bodies. This mapping is highlighted by the naturalistic treatment of the nude and of the Father's hands.

Another domain included in the HUMAN PERSON domain is that of emotions. The human notions of pity and sadness are mapped onto the Father's pity and sadness, a product of his paternal love. These emotions are metonymically suggested by the old man's solemn demeanor (BEHAVIORAL EFFECT FOR EMOTION).

The *mapping of metaphorical and nonmetaphorical notions of human interpersonal relationships*, such as those of GROUPS OF INDIVIDUALS, POWER, AUTHORITY, FAMILY RELATIONSHIPS and LOVE, is expressed in the painting by several means. The application of the metaphorical understanding of POWER and AUTHORITY to God's power and authority is expressed, as stated above, by the relative vertical arrangement of the figures.

Groups of people, like groups of entities in general, are often metaphorically conceptualized as containers (cf. 'got *into* a new club,' 'Mary is not *in* our society anymore; she got *out of* it,' 'she *entered* an *enclosed* order,' 'the UK may *exit* Europe'). This metaphorical human understanding of groups is also mapped onto the conceptualization of the Holy Trinity. The CONTAINER image schema is visually evoked in this painting by the cloak that embraces the three Persons, and by the spatial region they configure together. The mapping of CONTAINER onto groups of people is a way of highlighting their moral unity and their similarity in a given respect (their common interests, ideology, etc.). The mapping of this metaphorical notion of human groups onto the Holy Trinity also highlights its *essential unity* and may also be a way of highlighting the essential similarity between the Divine Persons, i.e. their *consubstantiality*.

Another submapping within the mapping of human interpersonal relationships onto the Holy Trinity is that of *human language and communication* onto the divine

Word. Human linguistic expressions are often understood as physical entities and may in some cases be personified. As stated in section 2, this metaphorical understanding of human communication is projected onto the understanding of God's linguistic action as an entity, specifically a personal entity, i.e. Christ. This metaphorically understood theological knowledge is pictorially activated by means of the Father's gesture: the Father's mouth seems to me to be slightly open; if my impression is correct, this gesture would metonymically activate the notion of speaking [PRECONDITION (OPENING MOUTH) FOR ACTION (SPEAKING)] and the fact that his hands seem to be showing Christ to the observer seems to be a metonymic source for his handing of Christ over to us [again a PRECONDITION (SHOWING ITEM TO BE TRANSFERRED) FOR ACTION (TRANSFERRING AN ITEM) metonymy], thus activating the source domain TRANSFER OF PHYSICAL ENTITIES of the conventional metaphor COMMUNICATION IS TRANSFER OF PHYSICAL ENTITIES. The target domain (COMMUNICATION) of this metaphor is activated by the above-mentioned metonymy PRECONDITION (OPENING MOUTH) FOR ACTION (SPEAKING). The metaphor, in the context of theological knowledge, is applied to the notion that Christ is the Father's message, his Word. And if the personification of the Word is 'metaphtonymically' (Goossens 1990) alluded to in the painting, so is perhaps also the divine nature of the Word itself ['And the Word was God' (John 1:1)]; see section 2, where it was suggested that one of the elements of the understanding of the coherence of the dogma at a figurative level is the ACTION FOR AGENT metonymy.

Another key subdomain within the domain of human interpersonal relations that is mapped onto the Holy Trinity is that of the FAMILY, more specifically the subdomain of human progeneration manifested as a *parent-child relation*. This relation is mapped onto the *ontological (not temporal) precedence* of Second from First Person in the theological formulation of the dogma. In the painting, this metaphorical mapping is imagistically represented by means of the contrast between two males of different ages (a white-bearded old man and a younger man), which *metonymically* maps onto the notions of human fatherhood-sonship and metaphorically onto the ontological relation between God the Father and God the Son. This mapping also highlights the *consubstantiality* between these two different Persons, since the biological endowment shared by human parents with their children maps onto the divine 'substance' shared by the Father and the Son ('God from God,' as stated by the NC).

4.1.2 Identificational metonymies in the painting

The painting in Figure 4 is rich in metonymy, like all the paintings we are examining in this essay. Some of them have an identificational purpose and, as suggested above, reinforce some of the metaphorical mappings intended in the picture. Most of the metonymies are related to Christ and his Passion and Resurrection. The image of the seemingly unconscious or lifeless young man with his eyes closed below the older man is a metonymic representation of a *dead* man, and at the same time (in the context of the painting, with the aid of the metonymies to be mentioned below, and by virtue of the intertextuality with the Gospel), it is a metonymy for Christ dead after Crucifixion. Background knowledge is almost always involved in understanding both verbal and visual representations. The other metonymies related to Christ are:

- INSTRUMENT (CROWN OF THORNS) FOR EVENT (CHRIST'S PASSION) and his Passion is in turn a property identifying Christ. (The Crown of Thorns is hardly visible due to the chiaroscuro.)
- OBJECT INVOLVED (HOLY SHROUD) FOR EVENT (CHRIST'S DEATH), his death being another property identifying Christ.
- EFFECT (WOUNDS) FOR CAUSE (CHRIST'S PASSION), with a similar identificational role.
- ENTITY (CHERUBS SURROUNDING CHRIST'S BODY) FOR CONVENTIONAL FUNCTION (GLORIFYING GOD) FOR EVENT (JESUS' GLORIFICATION AFTER DEATH). Again a further identificational trait, but at the same time a reminder that Christ's death is inseparably connected to his resurrection.

We have already mentioned the metonymic activation of the notion of older age by means of the image of the grave, *grey-bearded* man in the metaphorical mapping of human fatherhood onto divine Fatherhood and have commented on the image of the Dove as a conventional metaphor-based metonymy for the Holy Spirit.

Finally, the metonymy ESSENTIAL PROPERTY (TRINITARIAN CHARACTER) FOR ENTITY (THE HOLY TRINITY) underlies the presence on the older man's head of the triangular (an equilateral triangle) halo, since this is a conventional symbol for the Holy Trinity. This abstract symbol, on the other hand, involves the mapping of the CONTAINER image schema onto the Trinity. The trinity is represented directly as a container (see 4.3.3 on the 'Trinitarian Shield'). Therefore, this is at the same time one more instance of the metaphorical mapping of spatial notions onto the divine. The choice of an equilateral triangle maps the fact that all the sides are equal, that the triangle can be observed from any angle, and that all sides contain and are contained in the triangle onto the diversity of the divine Persons, their equality in dignity, and the oneness of God (each Person is the whole of the one God).

The remaining analyses in this section will be less detailed. They deal with relatively deviant instances of pictorial representations of the dogma. The analyses will stress the main differences between these unorthodox representations and orthodox representations in terms of the exploitation of trinitarian metaphors and metonymies.

4.2 A *deviant (near-)isomorphic horizontal* representation of the Holy Trinity: The miniature of the *Trinity* (Figure 5)

Figure 5 is an anthropomorphic representation of Father and the Son, and a zoomorphic representation of the Holy Spirit. Its *iconological purpose* is to emphasize the essential oneness of God despite the diversity of the divine Persons. However, in this attempt, the artist somehow downplays the true individuality of the three Persons and unintentionally comes close to the positions held by certain heresies (the Patripassianists, the Sabellians, and others) already condemned in early Christianity.

Figure 5 *Trinity*. Miniature (15th century). National Library of France.
Source: Réau (1995). Image (Latin 18014–Fol. 183) provided and reproduction rights granted by Bibliothèque Nationale de France.

4.2.1 Analysis of the expression in this painting of the four selected submappings in GOD IS HUMAN

As regards the mapping of *human-sized spatial notions of tri-dimensional space*, CON-TAINER is an overarching image schema in the painting, which metonymically activates the metaphorical understanding of the Holy Trinity as a container. The visual container is created by the two human figures clasping their hands and joining their clothes, and by the spread-winged dove, which closes the container at its top. This metaphorical understanding of the Trinity highlights the consubstantiality of the three Divine Persons and the oneness of God, as in Ribera's *Trinity*. The spatial position of the figures metonymically activates the metaphorical understanding of the ontological order of procession as spatial position and motion. The Father holds and supports the Son's hand (the Son is on the left of the painting where the Father is on the right of the image; that is, the Son is 'at the Father's right'). The Son holds the World (so it seems that the Son receives his power from the Father, and in turn, via the Globe, he transfers it to the Spirit, represented by the Dove. But both of them actually hold the Globe where the Dove is standing). The spatial motion metonymically activated by the spatial arrangement of the figures is 'visual motion' or 'visual scanning,' if we scan the image from the Father's hand supporting and joining the Son's hand, which in turn supports the Globe and the Holy Spirit. This visual scanning in space is metaphorically mapped onto the ontological order of procession from Father to Son and from both to the Holy Spirit. On the other hand, the position of the Dove in this painting and in Ribera's (in both it is placed *between* the Father and the Son, whether on a vertical or a horizontal arrangement) is a clear metaphtonymic reminder of the *filioque* doctrine prevailing in the Catholic and Protestant churches. Let us compare the position of the Dove in those two paintings with the position of the angel representing the Holy Spirit in Rublev's painting (see section 3, comment on Figure 1) at the right of Christ (who is in turn seated at the right of the Father), a reminder of the traditional position in the Orthodox Church that the Holy Spirit proceeds from the Father via the Son.

As stated above, the Dove closes the container and at the same time is situated between the Father and the Son, metonymically hinting at the provenance of the Holy Spirit from both of them. The metonymy involved is the one connecting the initial or the final point of a path and the mover along this path (see section 2.2); in this case, the relevant variant of the metonymy is ENTITY FOR ORIGIN, and it highlights both the divinity of the Holy Spirit and the oneness of God.

As for the mapping of *abstract notions onto God and the Trinity*, the joined hands and the corresponding arms, together with the spread-winged dove, create an inner container enclosing the Globe, thus perhaps suggesting that Creation is under God's protection and control. These two abstract notions, PROTECTION and CONTROL, are often understood metaphorically [PROTECTING IS (SPATIALLY) COVERING and CONTROLLING IS HOLDING IN/WITH THE HANDS], and this understanding is often expressed in idiomatic language ('We were sheltered by our government,' 'I'm in your hands'). In the picture, the inner container covers the Globe, which is also under the Holy Spirit and in the Father and the Son's arms. At the same time, the Son's left hand holds the Globe. This holding of the Globe is a metonymic conventional attribute of the Father in Christian iconography, but it was later extended to the Second Person.

In the painting, the fact that the Dove's wings seem to connect the Father's and the Son's lips can be seen as a further metonymic hint to the doctrine of the Holy Spirit's provenance from both of them (*filioque*), that is to the metaphorical formulation of the abstract notion of divine ONTOLOGICAL PRECEDENCE in terms of SPATIAL ORIGIN. The fact that the wings seem to touch the *lips* of Father and Son is also a metonymic reminder of the complementary metaphorical formulation of the nature of the HOLY SPIRIT as the FATHER'S AND THE SON'S BREATH. This metonymic reminder is possible because the LIPS are in turn connected metonymically, as a PART, to the mouth, which is in turn connected metonymically, as the SOURCE, to the BREATH (SOURCE FOR MOVING ENTITY).

The mapping of *metaphorical and nonmetaphorical notions of the human person* onto God, which is involved in the understanding of the dogma, is *metonymically* activated by means of the figures of two human males, as in Ribera's and most other pictorial representations of the Trinity. An important difference from Ribera's painting is that in this miniature the two figures have similar, almost identical bodies, including their faces. Both figures have the same relatively greyish beard, which is a metonymy for sameness of age. Their bodily identity constitutes an attempt at metaphorically presenting the notion of SAME DIVINE ESSENCE AND NATURE (i.e. CONSUBSTANTIALITY) as SIMILAR BODY, whereas the notion of SAME HUMAN AGE is mapped onto the same divine 'age,' that is, ETERNITY. The painting is an attempt at presenting both divine Persons, the Father and the Son, as equally eternal, thus echoing the NC: 'true God from true God, begotten, not made, of one Being with the Father.'

The bodily identity is *metonymically* reinforced in the painting by means of almost complete *identity in attitudes and with identical divine attributes and clothes.* Both figures slightly bend their heads and place their hands in the same way. Both wear the *Cruciferous halo*, with a *red cross*; this attribute is a symbol that metonymically stands for Christ's blood and passion, also exhibited by the Dove. And they also wear the *same clothes* with the *same deep blue* color (this choice of color perhaps being a metonymy for the skies and the skies for the metaphor HEAVEN IS UP, i.e. in the skies). These additional levels of sameness thus reinforce the overall mapping of sameness of bodily appearance and of age onto, respectively, consubstantiality and equal eternity.

The *mappings of metaphorical and nonmetaphorical notions of human interpersonal relationships* onto the Trinity do not include the mapping of the human notion of FAMILY or of the FATHER-SON RELATIONSHIP in this painting. The figures corresponding to the Father and the Son seem to be indirectly distinguished from each other in terms of the equal *power* and *authority*, two interpersonal relationships that the NC attributes to both of them by means of a spatial metaphor expressed linguistically by stating that Christ is 'seated *at the right hand of the Father*.' Therefore, although both figures are standing, the male figure that has the other male figure at its right presumably represents the Father (who appears on the right of the painting), and the male figure at the right of the first figure presumably represents the Son (who thus appears on the left of the painting). This spatial arrangement in the painting is thus a metonymy for the above-mentioned complex spatial metaphor in the NC (and in the Bible), which maps the complex metaphor for equal human power and authority BEING AS POWERFUL AS A POWERFUL PERSON IS BEING AT THE RIGHT OF THAT PERSON onto the equal divine power and authority of Father and Son. That complex human metaphor is in turn a combination of two more basic metaphors. One of them is the understanding of EQUALITY/SIMILARITY (in power in this case) in terms of SPATIAL CLOSENESS (SIMILARITY IS SPATIAL CLOSENESS, a metaphor in turn rooted in the metonymy SPATIAL CLOSENESS FOR SIMILARITY; see Barcelona 2000 and Radden 2000). The other metaphor is RIGHT IS GOOD/MOST VALUABLE, manifested in the frequent use of the notion of a SPATIAL RIGHT LOCATION to designate 'positive' notions in many languages ('being one's right hand'; *ser el ojo derecho* 'being one's right eye,' a metaphorical idiom used in Spanish to say that someone is highly valued and appreciated by the speaker).

Other metaphorically understood human interpersonal relationships mapped onto the Holy Trinity by the dogma and represented in the painting (Figure 5) are attitudes such as solidarity and love. These metaphors for solidarity [SOLIDARITY IS CLOSENESS as when people express their solidarity to/from others by means of expressions such as 'I'm with you in this struggle,' 'You are always there (to help)'] and love (LOVE IS EXTREME CLOSENESS, as when people express their love to each other with such expressions as 'We are one,' 'She's my other half') are evoked metonymically by means of the spatial closeness of the three figures to each other, especially by the joining of the hands between Father and Son and by the closeness of the Dove to both of them, with its wings apparently touching their lips. This human understanding of solidarity and love is mapped onto inter-trinitarian solidarity and love. The metonymic evocation of the notions of solidarity and love are also evoked metonymically in the painting by means of the action the Father and the Son perform with their left hands: they seem to be blessing each other, the Holy Spirit, and the world (represented by the Globe) at the same time. The Globe metonymically stands both for mankind and for the whole of creation, and both figures look at it, so their solidarity and love seems to be extended to it.

4.2.2 Identificational metonymies in this painting (Figure 5)

Apart from the metonymic connection of the *image* of a dove with a God-chosen symbol of the Holy Spirit (with all its complex metaphorical basis), hence with the Holy Spirit itself (see 4.1.1), the shape of the clothes worn by the Father and the Son can be seen as having a potentially metonymic function. They are evocative of the shape of a shroud [SALIENT PROPERTY OF AN OBJECT (SHAPE) FOR THE OBJECT (SHROUD)]. This metonymy is directly suggested by the painting. With the help of the religious topic of the painting (the Trinity), the above metonymy chains to a further metonymy [CATEGORY (SHROUD) FOR SALIENT MEMBER (THE HOLY SHROUD)] to enable the inference that the clothes are evocative of the *Holy Shroud*. In turn this metonymy is chained to the metonymy OBJECT INVOLVED IN AN EVENT (THE HOLY SHROUD) FOR THE EVENT (CHRIST'S PASSION) in the interpretation of the images. The fact that Christ and the Father wear the same shroud-like clothes seems to suggest that it had been the Father that had become incarnate as Christ, and had died and resurrected.

As stated at the beginning of 4.2, this way of representing the Trinity is part of a metaphorical strategy on the part of the artist to highlight the consubstantiality and oneness of Father and Son, and also of the Spirit, who also wears the red cruciferous halo. But this goal is achieved at the *expense* of downplaying the distinct personal character of the three Divine Persons, a fact that lent itself to heretical readings (such as Patripassianism), which had claimed that it was the Father that had become incarnate as Christ, and had died and resurrected, or Sabellianism, which claimed that a divine 'Monad' had manifested itself in different roles: Father and Creator, Son and Redeemer, Holy Spirit and Grace-Giver (see Kelly 1968). This was the reason why this type of representation was later disfavored and regarded as theologically unorthodox after the Council of Trent.

4.3 A deviant (fully) isomorphic (three-faced) horizontal representation of the Holy Trinity: The Panel of the Holy Trinity (Figure 6)

On this painting, see Maquívar (2006) and Martínez (2013). A few remarks on this special iconographic type are necessary before the analysis. The attempts at highlighting the oneness of God and the consubstantiality of the three Persons, the main *iconological purpose*, both of this painting and of those in Figures 2, 3, and 5, and in the *Veronica* briefly commented on above, was carried to an extreme in the so called 'three-faced Trinities,' illustrated in section 3 by Figure 2). In these representations, the Holy Trinity is normally presented by means of an image purported to be that of Christ, but with a blended head resulting from the fusion of three identical heads and their faces. This iconography derives from the Greco-Roman system of *gryllas* (Baltrusaitis 1994) and was known as a representation of the Holy Trinity in the British Isles and France (due to Celtic influence) as early as the twelfth century, its use becoming quite frequent in the fifteenth and sixteenth centuries.

This representation of the Holy Trinity had already been denounced in the Middle Ages by the French theologian Jean de Gerson (1369–1429) as sacrilegious and monstrous, and it was later condemned by the Council of Trent in the sixteenth century. In 1628, Pope Urban VIII formally prohibited it as decidedly heretical and had its images burnt. This decision was later confirmed by Pope Benedict XIV in 1746. But these images were still frequent in the Spanish American colonies between the sixteenth and the eighteenth centuries (Maquívar 2006).

Artistic representations of the Holy Trinity were supposed to inspire love, respect, and adoration of God, and at the same time to give a glimpse of God's spiritual beauty. But these three-faced Trinities, apart from being theologically incorrect, caused repulsion to the observer. If man is made in God's image (HUMAN IS GOD), it was considered that these monstrous human images could not be used

Figure 6 The Holy Trinity, by Jerónimo Cósida (c. 1570). Panel in the Monastery of Santa María de la Caridad, Tulebras, Navarre, Spain.

as adequate images of God, notwithstanding the honest purpose guiding their creation. This was a fundamental motivation in the prohibition of these images (Ramos Domingo 2004) and explains the small number of this type of paintings that has come down to us.

4.3.1 Analysis of the expression in this painting of the four submappings in GOD IS HUMAN selected

The mapping of *human-sized notions of three-dimensional space* onto the Holy Trinity (THE HOLY TRINITY IS A CONTAINER) is activated metonymically by means of the image of a sitting single human body with a three-faced head; this body and the faces are meant (as we will see in 4.3.2) to represent the body and the face of Christ. Therefore, the metaphor is *deviantly exploited* in this case, by *superimposing* the image of one of the Persons (Christ) as the container for the others, thus near-eliminating their individuality, except for the splitting of Christ's face into three partially fused faces. The image had a well-meant purpose, to highlight the *consubstantiality* and *oneness* of God and perhaps also to highlight the fact that Christ is, to the New Testament, the face of God. But in more orthodox representations, the spatial position of the three Persons, who are represented by means of a separate image for each of them, configures a container that includes them all.

As for the mapping of *metaphorically understood abstract notions* onto the Holy Trinity, the mapping onto the Trinity of the human-sized notion of substance, understood metaphorically as physical substance (ABSTRACT SUBSTANCE IS PHYSICAL SUBSTANCE), is elaborated in a way similar to that in Figure 5, that is, SAME ABSTRACT SUBSTANCE IS SAME PHYSICAL SUBSTANCE, i.e., SAME BODY (but in Figure 5 the two male bodies are separate although identical, and in any case, they are not fused into the *same* body). This elaboration could alternatively be called SHARING IN SPIRITUAL SUBSTANCE IS SHARING THE SAME BODY. The elaboration is in fact a counterfactual elaboration, because its source (a body shared by three different individuals) is itself counterfactual. The above elaboration of this metaphorical understanding of 'substance' and of 'consubstantiality,' and its mapping onto the divine, are activated metonymically, in the religious context of interpretation of the painting,[5] by the image of Christ with three overlapping heads.

Regarding the mapping of *metaphorical and nonmetaphorical notions of the human person* onto the Holy Trinity, the nonmetaphorical notion of HUMAN PERSONHOOD is mapped onto the notion of DIVINE PERSONHOOD, i.e. onto the three Persons, not just onto two of them, as in most of the paintings reproduced in this chapter. But the mapping does not proceed, as in theologically orthodox homomorphic representations (like that of Figure 1) or even in other partly deviant homomorphic representations (like those in *Veronica* and Figure 5), by mapping one human person onto one divine Person. Here, as stated above, the source is a counterfactual, almost total blend of three different human persons into one person (the blend is total in Figure 3). As stated above, too, the metaphor and the blend are activated metonymically by the three-faced human body within the religious context of interpretation of the painting.

The painting does not activate metonymically the projection onto the Holy Trinity of *metaphorical and nonmetaphorical notions of human interpersonal relationships*, especially the notion of the FAMILY and within it, that of PROGENERATION, by visual, i.e. imagistic, means. It does so only verbally, by means of the legend in the *trinitarian shield* that the sitting male figure holds in his hands, which includes the Latin words *PATER* ('Father') and *FILIVS* ('Son'). The Holy Spirit is also referred to verbally, not imagistically, by means of a conventional abbreviation of his full Latin name (*SPIRITUS SANCTUS*).

4.3.2 Identificational and other metonymies

The metonymy CONVENTIONAL SYMBOL FOR ENTITY/EVENT motivates the representation of the *cruciferous halo*, a symbol for Christ and for his Passion. Therefore, it serves a mainly *identificational* purpose. This symbol, incidentally, is itself metonymically motivated by ENTITY SALIENTLY INVOLVED IN AN EVENT FOR THE EVENT (the Cross and Christ's blood were physical entities that stand out in the narration of his Passion). The fact that the cruciferous halo (a metonymic reminder of Christ's passion) is worn by the triune head can be, and in fact was, interpreted as a (probably unintentional) heterodox suggestion that the *whole* Trinity suffered the Passion.

The metonymies that partly motivate this iconographic type are SALIENT MEMBER (CHRIST) FOR SET (THE WHOLE HOLY TRINITY). To a Christian, Christ, the Second Person, is naturally salient in his experience, because although he is regarded as having the same 'rank' and dignity as the two other Persons, he is God made human; and because the Christian religion is founded on his teachings, Death and Resurrection. Another metonymy that may be claimed to motivate this iconographic type is IMAGE FOR ENTITY (Christ's, God's image, is chosen to activate the whole of the Trinity, i.e. God). These two metonymies motivate homomorphic iconographies of the Trinity that represent it as three full-body images of Christ (there is no example of this subtype in any of the paintings mentioned in this essay, but there are many instances in the History of Art; see Maquívar 2006, which reproduces some of them). An additional metonymy that partly motivates both the homomorphic iconographies of the Trinity that only represent it by means of three separate faces of Christ (as in the Lima *Veronica* briefly discussed in section 3) and three-faced Trinities is FACE FOR PERSON. This metonymy is allied to the identificational metonymy mentioned above (CONVENTIONAL SYMBOL FOR ENTITY/EVENT) to activate the notion of CHRIST, but its main role in the motivation of the three-faced iconographic type (together with the metaphor SHARING IN SPIRITUAL SUBSTANCE IS SHARING THE SAME BODY) is to activate the notion of three human persons (metaphorically mapped onto the three Divine Persons, as stated in 4.3.1) by means of three human faces. The purpose is to distinguish (minimally) the Divine Persons from each other, despite their sharing of the same substance and despite each of them constituting the one God.

4.3.3 Attempted muting of unwanted implications: The trinitarian shield

The trinitarian shield is a visual device frequently used in Christian Art to illustrate pedagogically the fact that there is only one God and that each of the Persons of the Holy Trinity is the whole of God while being entirely different Persons with the same rank and dignity.

The trinitarian shield in this painting, apart from this didactic purpose, has the function of muting, or at least counterbalancing, the unwanted implications that might be perceived in homomorphic iconographies in general and in three-faced iconographies in particular. Those implications were, as stated above, the apparent support these images lent to heretical positions like *modalism* and others, since they appeared to blur the distinction between the three Persons, in this case by (unintentionally, probably) suggesting that the Father and the Son were 'modalities' of Christ. In addition, as noted earlier, the images were found aesthetically offensive and irreverent.

The use of the trinitarian shield was probably thought by Jerónimo Cósida and by the creator of the painting in Figure 2 to be an adequate way to preserve the orthodoxy of their images while taking advantage of their well-meant pedagogical purpose (that is, to stress the oneness of God despite the distinction among the Divine Persons, and the fundamental role of Christ in the economy of salvation). The purpose of the trinitarian shield is explicit in its shape and in the texts reproduced in it.

The shield is an inverted equilateral triangle because the triangle is a conventional symbol of the Holy Trinity. A chain of two metonymies must have historically motivated the choice of this symbol: ENTITY (TRIANGLE) FOR ESSENTIAL PROPERTY ('THREENESS') + ESSENTIAL PROPERTY ('THREENESS') FOR ENTITY (THE HOLY TRINITY). On the other hand, the shield suggests the metaphorical understanding of the Holy Trinity as a container since the names of each of the Persons appear at the vertices of the triangle and *DEUS* ('God') appears in the center of the incircle of the triangle. Perhaps the metaphor mapping SIZE onto IMPORTANCE motivated the choice of an equilateral rather than an irregular triangle, to indicate that the three Persons are equal in rank and dignity.

The artist, Jerónimo Cósida, is aware of the blurring of the distinctness of the Persons due to the triune face and uses the trinitarian shield to make it clear (in Latin) that the Father, the Son, and the Holy Spirit are clearly different from each other but that the three are the one God at the same time. The Latin texts on the top side (from vertex to vertex) of the triangle say, when read from left to right, *PATER NON EST FILIVS* ('FATHER IS NOT SON'), and *FILIVS NON EST PATER* ('SON IS NOT FATHER'), when read from right to left. The left side of the triangle, when read from top to bottom says *PATER NON EST SPIRITUS SANCTUS* ('FATHER IS NOT HOLY SPIRIT') and when read from bottom to top it says *SPIRITUS SANCTUS NON EST PATER* ('HOLY SPIRIT IS NOT FATHER'). The right side of the triangle says from top to bottom *FILIVS NON EST SPIRITUS SANCTUS* ('SON IS NOT HOLY SPIRIT') and from bottom to top *SPIRITUS SANCTUS NON EST FILIVS* ('HOLY SPIRIT IS NOT SON'). Finally, the lines connecting each of the vertices to the central node containing the word *DEUS* ('GOD') can also be read bi-directionally, resulting in the following six propositions (skipping the Latin original): THE FATHER IS GOD, THE SON IS GOD, THE HOLY SPIRIT IS GOD, GOD IS THE FATHER, GOD IS THE SON, GOD IS THE HOLY SPIRIT.

However, the use of this ingenuous visual and verbal device did not clarify in what respect the Father 'is not' the Son and the Son 'is not' the Holy Spirit or the latter 'is not' the Father: just in 'personality' or also in 'nature,' 'substance'? This imprecision, long ago noted by theologians commenting on this traditional device, added to the monstrosity of the three-faced image, and it led the Church's authority to remove the table from public display in the seventeenth century and to reserve it only as a supplementary instrument in catechesis; that is, it was considered adequate only as a teaching instrument, not as an image aimed at inspiring devotion and adequate for prayer.

5 CONCLUSIONS

These art works make use of the same metaphors identified in the biblical texts, especially the New Testament, and in the theological discussion of the dogma which inspired the painting, plus some other traditional theographic metaphors in Christianity and their corresponding traditional iconographic representation (see Barcelona 1997a, 1997b, 1999). The lack of conformity to tradition and Scripture explains why certain iconographic types were deemed to be unorthodox.

A great advantage of artistic representations of complex notions over a purely linguistic discussion is that it allows the synthetic, synoptic presentation or evocation of an enormous network of conceptual metaphors and metonymies underlying the biblical revelation of the dogma and its theological discussion. The level of understanding of Trinitarian theology underlying these artistic representations ranges from the basic, superficial understanding of the layman with elementary religious education to that of the professional theologian.

When religious thinking and language apply metaphorically understood concepts onto the Holy Trinity, it is understood on the basis of a double-level mapping:

1. The metaphors which, drawing on directly perceivable human experience, motivate in part the creation and often the understanding of these human abstract concepts (especially highly abstract notions like essence, similarity, person, emotion, but also more concrete notions like family or social group).
2. The application of these inherently metaphorical human notions to the realm of the divine, which constitutes in itself a second level of mapping.

This double metaphorical mapping is preserved in religious painting, but is regularly activated metonymically by means of the physical, visual representation of a token of the source of the mapping at the first level. This token, in the right cognitive-cultural context (i.e. the knowledge of at least the basic trinitarian doctrine and its biblical basis) activates the source at the first level and triggers the mapping onto its target and the mapping of the latter onto the target at the second level. For instance, the visual representation of two identical male bodies activates the source of the first-level metaphor SAME ABSTRACT 'SUBSTANCE' IS SAME PHYSICAL SUBSTANCE, which is mapped onto SAME DIVINE 'SUBSTANCE.'

When religious painting maps nonmetaphorical concepts onto their counterparts in the realm of the divine (i.e. a spatial concept like SPATIAL ORIGIN mapped onto a theological concept like ONTOLOGICAL PROVENANCE), the mapping is also activated metonymically, by representing a spatial position metonymically connected to SPATIAL ORIGIN: In the miniature of the Trinity (4.2.1) and in Ribera's painting (see 4.1.1.), the notion of SPATIAL ORIGIN is the metonymic target of the GOAL reached by the trajector, the Dove in this case, which activates the origin of the motion (the figures of the Father and the Son). And this metonymic activation of the notion of SPATIAL ORIGIN again leads to the activation of the metaphorical connection between this notion and that of ONTOLOGICAL PROVENANCE.

Figurative art in general and religious figurative art in particular normally have to resort to metonymies activating salient visual elements of the source domains of the metaphors involved. In religious *language,* this is not always the case. The source of the first-level mapping does not have to be expressed metonymically from a notion connected to the source of a metaphor partly structuring the target abstract concept, since there are a number of conventional linguistic labels for many abstract notions (such as *eternity, substance, power*) that enable speakers to denote them non-metonymically. Although the structure and properties of these abstract notions are ultimately structured and understood metaphorically by means of mappings from concrete domains, these *terms* are used to activate the corresponding abstract notion *directly*, without the mediation of any metonymic reference point. This is not normally possible in figurative art, where the interpretation of these abstract notions necessarily depends on the metonymic activation of the source (SAME PHYSICAL SUBSTANCE) of the first-level mapping (SAME ABSTRACT 'SUBSTANCE' IS SAME PHYSICAL SUBSTANCE).

NOTES

1. The present paper is based on my brief presentation on this topic at the eighth conference of the Researching and Applying Metaphor society (RaaM) at the Vrjie Universiteit of Amsterdam in 2010 and my longer invited presentation at the International RaaM Seminar held at the University of Castilla La Mancha, Spain, in 2011. I include (section 2) a brief summary of my earlier detailed studies of the metaphorico-metonymic network partly underlying the linguistic formulation and theological discussion of the Trinitarian dogma and the language of some of the biblical passages that led to it (Barcelona 1997a, 1997b, 1999).
2. A root metaphor 'serves as the basic assumption underlying the way in which we describe the entire enterprise of science or religion' (Mac Cormac 1976, pp. xii–xiii).
3. The initial capital in these words is meant to signal the conceptual difference between the non-theological sense of these words (e.g. *light*) and their theological sense. Whenever I feel this contrast should be highlighted, I will use the same device.
4. The wings are not clear in the reproduced image because the original is damaged.
5. Any Catholic observer aware of the basic catechetic teaching that the Holy Trinity is three different Persons but one God would have easily understood the purpose of this three-faced representation, especially if reminded about the doctrine by a religious educator to help them interpret the painting correctly (I'm grateful to Paul Chilton for pointing out the likely influence of preachers). As stated later, the painting was eventually reserved for catechetic purposes.

REFERENCES

Allenov, Mikhail, Nina Dmitrieva, and Olga Medvedkova (2000). *Arte ruso*. Volume 44 of *Summa Artis: Historia General del Arte.* Madrid: Espasa Calpe.
Atienza Ballano, Juan Carlos (ed.) (2009). *Paisaje interior: Soria 2009. Catálogo.* Soria: Fundación Las Edades del Hombre.

Baltrusaitis, Jurgis (1994). *La Edad Media fantástica: Antigüedades y exotismos en el arte gótico*. Madrid: Cátedra.

Barcelona, Antonio (1986). On the concept of depression in American English: A cognitive approach. *Revista Canaria de Estudios Ingleses* 12, 7–33.

Barcelona, Antonio (1997a). Constitutive metaphors in the trinitarian dogma. *Linguistic Agency, University of Duisburg Series A: General and Theoretical*, 1–25.

Barcelona, Antonio (1997b). ¿Es el de Dios un concepto literal en el cristianismo? Ensayo de teolingüística. *Revista Española de Lingüística Aplicada*, 12, 141–154.

Barcelona, Antonio (1999). The metaphorical and metonymic understanding of the trinitarian dogma. In Lieven Boeve, Kurt Feyaerts, and James Francis (eds.), *Metaphor and God-Talk*, pp. 187–213. Bern: Peter Lang.

Barcelona, Antonio (2000). On the plausibility of claiming a metonymic conceptual motivation for metaphorical mappings. In Antonio Barcelona (ed.), *Metaphor and Metonymy at the Crossroads: A Cognitive Perspective*, pp. 31–58. Berlin: De Gruyter.

Catechism of the Catholic Church (1994). English Edition. London: Geoffrey Chapman-Libreria Editrice.

Fauconnier, Gilles and Mark Turner (2002). *The Way We Think: Conceptual Blending and the Mind's Hidden Complexities*. New York: Basic Books.

Gerard, André-Marie and Andrée Nordon-Gerard (1995). *Diccionario de la Biblia*. Spanish translation by Antonio Piñero. Madrid: Anaya and Mario Muchnik.

Goossens, Louis (1990). Metaphtonymy: The interaction of metaphor and metonymy in expressions for linguistic action. *Cognitive Linguistics* 1 (3), 323–340.

Johnson, Mark (1987). *The Body in the Mind: The Bodily Basis of Meaning, Imagination, and Reason*. Chicago: University of Chicago Press.

Kelly, J. N. D. (1968 [1958]). *Early Christian Doctrines*. London: Adam and Charles Black.

Kövecses, Zoltán (1990). *Emotion Concepts*. New York: Springer Verlag.

Lakoff, George (1993). The contemporary theory of metaphor. In Andrew Ortony (ed.), *Metaphor and Thought*, Second edition, pp. 202–251. Cambridge: Cambridge University Press.

Lakoff, George and Mark Johnson (1980). *Metaphors We Live By*. Chicago: University of Chicago Press.

Lakoff, George and Mark Johnson (1999). *Philosophy in the Flesh*. Chicago: University of Chicago Press.

Maquívar, María del Consuelo (2006). *De lo permitido a lo prohibido: Iconografía de la Santísima Trinidad en la Nueva España*. México: Instituto Nacional de Antropología e Historia y Grupo Editorial Miguel Ángel Porrúa.

Martínez, Francisco José. 2013. Trinidad trifacial y milenarismo Joaquinita. *Acta/Artis. Estudis d'Art Modern* 1, 51–67.

Mac Cormac, Earl R. (1976). *Metaphor and Myth in Science and Religion*. Durham, NC: Duke University Press.

Radden, Günter (2000). How metonymic are metaphors? In Antonio Barcelona (ed.), *Metaphor and Metonymy at the Crossroads: A Cognitive Perspective*, pp. 31–58. Berlin: De Gruyter.

Radden, Günter and Zoltán Kövecses (1999). Towards a theory of metonymy. In Klaus-Uwe Panther and Günter Radden (eds.), *Metonymy in Language and Thought*, pp. 17–59. Amsterdam/Philadelphia: John Benjamins.

Ramos Domingo, José (2004). Arte y preceptiva: Del rigor, la propiedad y el decoro en la iconografía de la Trinidad. *Estudios Trinitarios* 39, 371–399.

Réau, Louis (1995). *Iconografía del arte cristiano: Iconografía de la Biblia; Antiguo Testamento*. Book 1, volume 1. Spanish translation. Barcelona: Ediciones del Serbal.

Reddy, Michael J. (1993). The conduit metaphor: A case of frame conflict in our language about language. In Andrew Ortony (ed.), *Metaphor and Thought*, Second edition, pp. 164–201. Cambridge: Cambridge University Press.

Stastny, Francisco (1994). *Síntomas medievales en el 'barroco americano'*. Documento de trabajo no 63. *Serie Historia del Arte no 1*. Lima: Instituto de Estudios Peruanos.

Soskice, Janet Maryord: Clarendon Press.

CHAPTER 15

Waging War against Oneself

A Conceptual Blend at the Heart of Christian Ascetic Practice

MIHAILO ANTOVIĆ

This chapter aims to analyze the metaphor of 'struggle against oneself' as elaborated in the classic Orthodox Christian book *Unseen Warfare* (St Nicodemus the Hagiorite ca. 1801). The purpose of the analysis will be to provide a contribution in three domains: (1) cognitive linguistics, where I attempt to show that the metaphor in question is better explicable by applying the tenets of the Conceptual Blending Theory than by using the Conceptual Metaphor Theory alone; (2) cognitive science—where I attribute the emergence of this metaphor to a specific instance of double-scope blending, one which may have occurred with the advent of Christianity in the early centuries AD; and (3) theology—where I discuss the problem of *causality* behind this changed 'warfare' concept, claiming that it may not have been merely a consequence of cognitive pressure, but may also have emerged from deeper ontological human needs.

To this end, in section 1 I present some fundamental facts about Orthodox Christianity and basics of its theology and attempt to draw some unrecognized parallels between its foci and research in modern cognitive science. I conclude this overview with the presentation of the 'unseen warfare' concept. Section 2 lists three groups of examples where this metaphor is used in the book, and analyzes them in terms of Conceptual Metaphor Theory, Conceptual Blending Theory alone, and Conceptual Blending Theory, involving fictive interaction supported by elements of Force Dynamics. I suggest that this third variant provides the clearest explanation of the cognitive mechanisms involved in producing the given construct. Then I discuss the implications of the existence and use of this metaphor for cognitive science and theology, and try to reach a tentative conclusion on how, in this domain, the two fields may complement, rather than exclude, one another (section 3).

1 ORTHODOX CHRISTIANITY AND COGNITIVE SCIENCE: SOME UNRECOGNIZED CONNECTIONS

Orthodox Christianity is the second largest Christian denomination in the world, with principal strongholds in modern Greece and Russia, but also dominant in much of the Balkans and Eastern Europe, and visibly present in parts of the Middle East, North Africa, and the Americas. While it naturally shares the main tenets of faith with its Catholic and Protestant sister churches (e.g. God as the Trinity; adherence to the Scriptures; the Holy Sacraments; the primacy of concepts such as sin, repentance, and forgiveness; belief in the Resurrection . . .), Orthodoxy has in many respects traveled its own path—from the official recognition of Christianity by Constantine the Great in AD 313, through its golden age in Byzantium up to the Ottoman conquest of Constantinople in 1453, to the romantic, national liberation movements in the nineteenth century Balkans. An immediately visible formal peculiarity of the Orthodox Church, for Western observers, is the lack of strict hierarchy as present in the Church of Rome: rather than having just one center, the Orthodox churches operate relatively independently along mostly national borders. Likewise, although they exert comparatively little political influence, they are inextricably linked to the culture and national heritage of many countries with the majority population belonging to this religion. This can be illustrated by the fact that, in the ninth century, it was two monks from Thessaloniki that provided a decisive impetus to the cultural development of Balkan Slavs, or by the historical role of the Orthodox church in preserving practically the entire heritage of a number of Slavic nations during the Ottoman reign (for a good general introduction into Orthodox Christianity, see Tyneh 2003; for an in-depth comparison with Roman Catholicism, see Brown and Anatolios 2009). In spite of what Western minds sometimes interpret as a cheerful outward appearance (church interiors painted in bright colors) and even apparent liberalism (priests allowed, indeed required, to marry), in fact, when penetrated a bit deeper, Orthodoxy proves to be a very strict religion. This is seen, for example, in its insistence on frequent, if possible incessant, praying; its stringent fasting regulations (four periods of Lent accompanied by every Wednesday and Friday, more than half a year of veganism altogether); disallowance of the Eucharist unless it has been preceded by strict fasting, prolonged self-reflection, extended prayer, repentance, and confession; the encouragement for believers to choose a spiritual father, an experienced guide to whom one should be fully obedient, not as an act of submissiveness but rather of supreme freedom to gradually renounce one's own will; and prescription to constantly struggle against *all* major sins, from gluttony to pride, and not only their outward, physical manifestations, but even more their internal, mental causes (for a comprehensive introductory study of the principal theological positions of Byzantine Christianity, see Meyendorff 1974).

Perhaps most of all, Orthodox Christianity is about this last point: the mental struggle of resisting sin and temptation at their very onset—in the mind of the believer. This is especially the tradition of the autonomous monastic state on Mount Athos, the 'Holy Mountain' in northeastern Greece, which represents the last living trace of the once powerful Eastern Roman Empire. Yet, the concept of spiritual advancement as an exercise in mental activities is very prominent in all Orthodoxy: to the extent possible, this strict routine of appeasing the mind is required not only of experienced ascetics in monasteries but also of lay practitioners. The difference between an 'ordinary' believer and a monk in this feat is more a matter of degree than kind. Thus, while other Christian virtues, from almsgiving to modesty, from diligence to compassion, are also commendable, it is the focus on the mind that is given most attention, especially in ascetic Orthodox literature. In an approachable form, this was succinctly presented by an influential, recently deceased, Serbian monk in his book entitled *Our Thoughts Determine Our Lives*: 'Our life depends on the kind of thoughts we nurture. If our thoughts are peaceful, calm, meek, and kind, then that is what our life is like. If our attention is turned to the circumstances in which we live, we are drawn into a whirlpool of thoughts and can have neither peace nor tranquility' (Elder Thaddeus 2009, chapter 1). The believer is, thus, asked to keep his or her mind constantly directed toward God, and not allow anything to interfere with this process: the more often he or she is successful in this effort, the more he or she gains the most valuable of states—inner peace, from which all other virtues emerge. Importantly, this does not imply passivity or the believer's renunciation of legitimate earthly needs. Rather, the belief is that to the practitioner who always strives to preserve the connection with God everything else that he needs will be added (cf. Matthew 6:33). This view of Christianity as primarily a mental exercise provides a natural, though rarely acknowledged, connection between the Orthodox faith and modern cognitive science. Some of its facets may include the Orthodox *holistic, systematic* view of *theology*, which is understood not as a mere intellectual investigation into the 'truths' of faith, but rather as a practice requiring the unity of mind. Here the 'inner heart' (intellect), will, and passions always act together in the believer's quest for Divine presence. This early differentiation into the 'three powers of the mind,' well expressed by the seventh-century ascetic St Maximus the Confessor, strongly resembles the modern psychological classification into the cognitive, conative, and affective realms (cf. Antović 2012, p. 101). Moreover, the very insistence on the 'holism' of the mind reminds one of what some schools belonging to the so-called second generation cognitive science have been attempting in the last fifteen or so years. On this view, piecemeal, analytical approaches, such as those from early artificial intelligence, modular theories of the brain, and localizationist neuroscience, are slowly giving way to connectionism, constructivism, and, generally, more synthetic attempts. Some parallels with Orthodox thought can undoubtedly be drawn here. Secondly, while remaining chiefly a spiritual activity, perhaps slightly more than its Western sister churches, Orthodox Christianity insists on *the link with the bodily*: though the body is often depicted as an adversary, which must be stifled in order for the soul to develop, for instance through fasting and temperance, it is also understood as an indispensable tool in the process of salvation. Hence, many Orthodox practices, such as prostrations during an evening prayer, can be very physical, while the liturgy itself is filled with sensory impressions—icons, choral music, incense. This request that the body help the soul has been rightly observed by some to reflect the rather 'psychosomatic' nature of Orthodox theology: 'Orthodoxy sees the human being [. . .] as an embodied soul or an ensouled body' (Smith 2006, p. xi). A connection between the theories of embodiment, as put forward by Lakoff and Johnson (1999), is quite strong here. In a related phenomenon, Orthodox theology commonly embraces a specific kind of mysticism, which usually goes under the label of *hesychasm*. This practice of 'stillness' requires that the practitioner rid the mind of all images, enter deeply into his or her own heart, and seek union with God, through a number of techniques, notably by uttering the Jesus prayer: 'Lord Jesus Christ, Son of God, have mercy on me, a sinner' (Ware 1995). These words are meant to be constantly repeated, to the point of automaticity—during daily activities, conversations, even sleep. While the technique may resemble the mantric practices of religions further east, one should note the mind-body connection in this act, too. This prayer is repeated frequently so that it becomes synchronized with heartbeat and thus literally *embodied*. However, in addition, Orthodox authors insist on the *meaning* of its words, since the semantic level is equally important—the invocation of the name of Jesus, followed by the expression of our sinfulness, and the plea with him to be merciful. Thus this prayer could be viewed as a typical 'form-meaning template,' a phenomenon of central interest in cognitive approaches to grammar. For a final possible connection, one should mention the enormous attention that Orthodox theology pays to the concept of *conscience*. This faculty is rooted so deeply in our minds that we should be better off if we followed it in all matters: 'The judgments of conscience tend to be all-embracing, to the point and indisputable. So it should not be evaded,' according to St. Philoteos of Sinai.[1] More importantly, Orthodox authors claim that our intuition of right and wrong is often blurred, as a consequence of the Fall. Thus, in anything we do, we must never rely on our own judgment, but should seek divine assistance, by a means such as prayer and the advice of elders. While interest in the cognitive origins of morals, most notably empathy, has grown among scientists in recent years (Ramachandran 2004; Churchland 2011; Decety and Wheatley 2015), the relevance of the phenomenon of 'conscience' and its unreliability have not been given direct attention in cognitive science so far (but see De Oliveira-Souza, Zahn, and Moll 2015).

As can be seen from the previous paragraph, potential connections with modern cognitive studies are numerous. In what follows I shall restrict the discussion to one phenomenon that may be of broad interest to cognitive science, but which is more particularly related to cognitive linguistics: the metaphorical language of Orthodox religious discourse. In particular, I concentrate on the metaphor of 'struggle against oneself,' whose principal idea is that a Christian should always wage battle, but not a battle against external enemies. Rather, he or she is invited to conduct a spiritual, internal war against the sin in him- or herself, so that, if victorious, he or she could earn spiritual perfection. This process has been described by Orthodox theologians as 'theosis' or 'deification'—gradual personal maturation that results in one's complete unity with God. The rigorous, lifelong program of mental self-control and renunciation of evil leading to theosis is often represented as an 'internal struggle' in Orthodox Christian literature: from the Bible itself (e.g. Ephesians 6:12; Hebrews 12:4) to the influential collection of monastic texts known as *The Philokalia* ('love of the good').[2]

The metaphor seems to be most prominent, however, in the work exclusively dedicated to the idea of internal struggle: *Unseen Warfare*. This textbook on the leading of a good spiritual life, aimed at beginner monks and laics, was originally written in Italian in the late sixteenth century by the Venetian priest Fr. Lorenzo Scupoli as *Spiritual Combat*. It was later translated into Greek, adapted and elaborated by the eighteenth-century Mount Athos monk St Nicodemos the Hagiorite, and, once again, translated and further adapted by the nineteenth-century Russian ascetic, St Theophan the Recluse. Today, the book is especially cherished in the Eastern Church; its Greek and Russian versions deviate from the original in some chapters (e.g. there were practically no references to the Jesus Prayer in the original text). That said, one cannot but notice that, given its tripartite origin (Italian, Greek, Russian), the book may stand as a reminder that the rift between Western and Eastern Christianity is not as big as adherents sometimes claim.

Unseen Warfare contains twenty-seven chapters whose purpose is to instruct the beginner ascetic into the basics of the Christian struggle. The purpose of this 'war' is for the practitioner to attain true Christian virtue and, ultimately, receive full grace and reward in the afterlife. Some of the topics include the signs of Christian perfection, the reasons why not to trust our own will or judgment, control of our senses and the tongue, correction of imagination and memory, the art of inner prayer, the order of acquiring virtues, and temptations in the hour of death. In all these chapters, the metaphor of internal battle is used, as, for instance, in the following paragraph:

> Do you now see what all this means, brother? I presume that you are longing to reach the height of such perfection. Blessed be your zeal! But *prepare yourself also for labor, sweat and struggle* from your first steps on the path. You must sacrifice everything to God and do only His will. Yet you will meet in yourself as many wills as you have powers and wants. Therefore, to reach your desired aim, it is *first of all necessary to stifle your own wills and finally to extinguish and kill them altogether*. And in order to succeed in this, you must constantly oppose all evil in yourself and urge yourself towards good. *In other words, you must ceaselessly fight against yourself and against everything that panders to your own wills, that incites and supports them. So prepare yourself for this struggle and this warfare and know that the crown—attainment of your desired aim—is given to none except to the valiant among warriors and wrestlers.* (*Unseen Warfare*, p. 7, italics mine)[3]

The central thesis is, therefore, given already at the beginning of the book: the advancement toward perfection is represented as a *path* that needs to be *traversed*. However, one cannot simply walk along it and expect no *obstacles*. Rather, it is a road filled with *labor* and *sweat*, where one must first *stifle*, and then *kill* one's own will. If the goal—i.e. salvation—is to be reached, one must prepare oneself for a lot of *struggle* and must know that only the bravest, *most valiant, warriors* are given the *crown of victory*.

In the following section, I shall investigate some actualizations of this metaphor in the original text, in the hope of showing that cognitive linguistics can provide appropriate analytical tools for studying certain religious phenomena occurring in the mind of readers.

2 THE STRUGGLE AGAINST ONESELF—THROUGH THE LENSES OF CONCEPTUAL METAPHOR AND CONCEPTUAL BLENDING

Metaphors with the source domain of 'war' have been well studied in the cognitive linguistic literature. The best known case in the field is certainly the ARGUMENT IS WAR conceptual metaphor originally introduced by Lakoff and Johnson (1980, chapter 1). This was the primary example chosen to introduce the theory of pervasive metaphorization in everyday discourse. Accordingly, the connection between metaphor and war has been given a lot of attention in the past thirty years: both in terms of metaphors used in times of war (Lakoff 2008) and, more in the vein of the present article, in terms of various instances of metaphorization in which 'war' could serve as an appropriate source domain (e.g. Romaine 1996; Steinert 2003; Johnson 2005; Chiang and Duann 2007; Coe and Winter 2013). Using ARGUMENT IS WAR as an example, some authors have also proposed the enhancement of, or even the abandoning of the Lakoff-Johnson model (Vervaeke and Kennedy 1996; Ritchie 2003; Howe 2007; McGlone 2007).

Along such lines, in this section I hope to provide a contribution to the analysis of war metaphors by looking into the concept of the 'struggle against oneself' given in *Unseen Warfare*, drawing on recent developments in cognitive semantics that represent theoretical and technical elaborations of the original Lakoff-Johnson approach. More particularly, I present three typical paragraphs from the original text in which the metaphor is realized, and analyze them using three alternate methodological frameworks from cognitive linguistics: Conceptual Metaphor Theory (CMT); Conceptual Blending Theory (CBT) using a mirror network; and Conceptual Blending Theory using a mirror network supported by elements of Force Dynamics and invoking identity connections, compression, and fictive interaction. I will suggest that, of the three approaches, the latter blending analysis provides the most comprehensive account of what may be going on in the mind during the processing of the metaphors of *Unseen Warfare*.

2.1 Conceptual Metaphor Theory

Before engaging in the CMT analysis, it is of interest to note some historical precursors that suggest an awareness of metaphor as a phenomenon within the intellectual, and indeed the theological, tradition. The Lakovian approach to investigating metaphor is not as new as we tend to think. Jäkel (1999) in particular has noted some prominent, seldom mentioned, precursors to the paradigm as proposed in cognitive linguistics, such as Giambattista Vico, Hermann Paul, Hans Blumenberg, and Harald Weinrich. From my own cultural milieu, I mention here the book *Metaphors and Allegories* by the Serbian mathematician and philosopher Mihailo Petrović (1868–1949), who proposed a phenomenological theory of metaphor based on the mathematical mapping concept, in many ways announcing what Lakoff and Johnson would publish forty years later (Petrović, 1968 [1942]). Unfortunately, due to the linguistic barrier, this work has remained largely unknown to the Western audience. While not developing the *theoretical* notion of metaphor, St Nicodemus of the Holy Mountain (1749–1809) seems to use a proto-cross-domain-mapping system in the beginning of his book, too:

> This book [. . .] is justly named *Unseen Warfare* [. . .] for it teaches not the art of visible and sensory warfare, and speaks not about visible, bodily foes, but about the unseen and inner struggle, which every Christian takes from the moment of his baptism [. . .]
>
> This book teaches that the warriors who take part in this unseen war are all who are Christians; and their commander is our Lord Jesus Christ, surrounded and accompanied by His marshals and generals, that is, by all the hierarchies of angels and saints. The arena, the field of battle, the site where the fight actually takes place is our own heart and all our inner man. The time of battle is our whole life.
>
> With what weapons are warriors armed for this warfare? Listen. Their helmet is total disbelief in themselves and complete absence of self-reliance; their shield and coat of mail—a bold faith in God and a firm trust in Him; their armor and cuirass—instruction in the passion of Christ; their belt—cutting off bodily passions; their boots—humility and a constant sense and recognition of their powerlessness; their spurs—patience in temptations and repudiation of negligence; their sword [. . .]—prayer with the lips or within, in the heart; their three-pronged spear [. . .]—a firm resolve never to consent to the passion which assails them. . .
>
> (Foreword to the Greek translation of *The Spiritual Combat*,
> Scupoli 1997 [1589] pp. 71–72)

But for the schematic representation, this eighteenth-century excerpt provides an almost complete analysis by means of the CMT, 200 years before its formulation. What a metaphor theorist today usually tries to indirectly infer from the text is given here quite explicitly and systematically. First, the name of the metaphor—'unseen warfare'; then the definition of its source and target domains—the 'visible and sensory warfare' and the 'unseen and inner struggle'; after this follow the particular mappings which elaborate the specific conceptual elements allowing for the connection between the source and the target, as given in the following Figure 1.

Not only does St Nicodemus speak of unseen warfare as a predominantly mental struggle, providing a foretaste of what cognitive science would be studying a few centuries later, he additionally presents this concept to the reader in such a way as to make sure they fully understand the metaphor that he is using. For this reason, he first names the metaphor, then defines its principal mapping, and finally specifies in considerable detail the correspondences between the constituent elements of the two domains. While perhaps he is not proposing a theory in the modern sense of the word, what is striking is that there is an unusually high degree of explicit detail in his presentation of two domains of experience. There also seems to be conscious

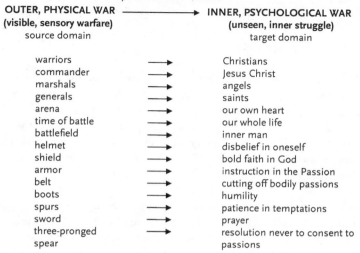

CMT Analysis
Metaphor: 'Unseen Warfare'

OUTER, PHYSICAL WAR (visible, sensory warfare) source domain		INNER, PSYCHOLOGICAL WAR (unseen, inner struggle) target domain
warriors	⟶	Christians
commander	⟶	Jesus Christ
marshals	⟶	angels
generals	⟶	saints
arena	⟶	our own heart
time of battle	⟶	our whole life
battlefield	⟶	inner man
helmet	⟶	disbelief in oneself
shield	⟶	bold faith in God
armor	⟶	instruction in the Passion
belt	⟶	cutting off bodily passions
boots	⟶	humility
spurs	⟶	patience in temptations
sword	⟶	prayer
three-pronged spear	⟶	resolution never to consent to passions

Figure 1 St Nicodemus' correspondence schema for armed conflict and mental conflict.

deliberation in using a concrete domain (warfare and details associated with it) to think about a highly abstract one (non-visible psychological and ethical conflicts experienced by human minds). In most cases, the mappings that are outlined appear natural, and seem to follow the 'optimality principles' claimed to be operative in conceptual blending (Fauconnier and Turner 1998, pp. 170–171; cf. Grady, Oakley, and Coulson 1999, p. 108). The impression remains that St Nicodemus' writing is remarkable in its attempted analytical precision.

Conceptual Metaphor Theory has been instrumental in the past thirty years in answering the following question: *what* is globally going on during the creation of metaphors, i.e. specifying the concrete mappings which naturally lead from source to target domain? However, the other two relevant questions—*how* and *why*—seem difficult to answer by using this approach alone. In the remainder of this section I try to address the first of these two problems: *How* is it possible for the human mind to conceptualize the contact between the physical and metaphysical worlds, and even more, to view one person as two warriors in a battlefield?

In Christian theology, there is a spiritual 'war' raging all around us—that between angels and demons, the armies of God and the Evil One. Patristic literature is not always clear about whether this thesis is to be interpreted as a metaphor for the struggle within us or whether it is to be viewed more literally, as the actual influence of metaphysical forces on our psychological and spiritual well-being. Retaining some of this ambiguity, *Unseen Warfare* contains both groups of examples. The following two belong more clearly to the latter, rather literal group (*Unseen Warfare*, p. 8):

Accustom yourself to be wary and to fear your innumerable enemies whom you cannot resist even for a short time. Fear their long experience in fighting us, their cunning and ambushes, their power to assume the guise of angels of light, their countless wiles and nets, which they secretly spread on the path of your life of virtues.

Similarly (*Unseen Warfare*, p. 76):

Watch yourself with all diligence, lest the enemy steals near and robs you, depriving you of this great treasure, which is inner peace and stillness of soul. The enemy strives to destroy the peace of the soul, because he knows that when the soul is in turmoil it is more easily led to evil. But you must guard your peace, since you know that when the soul is peaceful, the enemy has no access to it; then it is ready for all things that are good and does them willingly and without difficulty, easily overcoming all obstacles.

In these two examples, St Nicodemus clearly speaks of 'the enemy' (he means evil counterparts to angels, i.e. demons), who are numerous, experienced, and cunning, and whose only purpose is to disturb the peace of the believer's soul. A CMT analysis of these paragraphs would likely again invoke the metaphor PSYCHOLOGICAL CONFLICT IS PHYSICAL WAR, which would motivate a number of particular mappings. I argue, however, that this conceptual structure is more complex than CMT methods can capture. It is not the case here that the physical world conceptually *turns into* its metaphysical counterpart. Rather, we seem to have a conceptualization of an implicit *connection* between the two worlds: when they come into contact, the human and the demonic mind produce novel qualities—such as the struggle whose result is that one's soul can fall deeper into sin or rise toward the heavens.[4]

2.2 Conceptual Blending Theory: A mirror network

Conceptual Blending Theory (CBT, as outlined by Fauconnier and Turner 2002) has been instrumental in functionally approaching these apparently 'impossible' connections. In their numerous analyses of metaphorical or counterfactual expressions in the last fifteen years, applications of CBT have shown that new semantic features may *emerge* from putting together apparently disparate conceptual information. In a classic example (Fauconnier and Turner 2002, pp. 59–63), a modern American philosopher may say that he 'has been debating with Kant all night.' While we understand that this is physically impossible, we are still able to provide a semantic interpretation of the expression: we may allocate the professor's share in the debate, produced last night somewhere in the United States, to one conceptual packet, or 'mental space,' and Kant's portion, for instance something from one of his *Critiques* written in Königsberg in the eighteenth century, to another. Only when elements of these two mental spaces start interacting can we get a 'blended' space, i.e. an imaginary situation in which the modern professor and Kant are actually talking and discussing a philosophical problem. Similarly, the contact between the Christian and a demonic mind may be presented by the following blending network (see Figure 2).

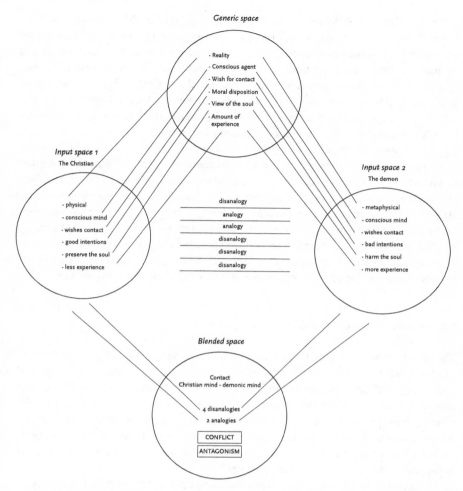

Figure 2 Conceptual Blending model: the Christian mind fights the demonic mind as an integration network.

As in any classic blending analysis invoking 'minimal networks' (Fauconnier and Turner 2002, p. 47), we have a generic space which hosts preconceptual topologies common to the two input spaces—in this case, the idea of the world from which the agents are coming, of there being conscious minds in this world, and of the minds being able to interact with one another (perhaps having a desire, an ontological need, to communicate). The agents moreover have moral dispositions, a view of the soul, and a degree of experience. There are also two input spaces—in one, we find the conscious mind of the Christian, which feels the necessity of contact, has good intentions with regard to its own fate, cherishes virtues, and strives to preserve the soul. In the second input, the demonic mind is also conscious, feels the need for contact, but cherishes vice and has evil intentions. The particular conceptual elements contained in the input spaces are mapped onto one another by what blending theorists call 'vital relations' (Fauconnier and Turner 2002, p. 101). In this particular case, we seem to have the connection of 'analogy' relating some conceptual elements (the conscious minds, the need for contact) and 'disanalogy' connecting others (physical vs. metaphysical, virtues vs. vices, good vs. evil intentions, less vs. more experience).

An important phenomenon occurs in conceptual integration which would not be easily explicable by means of CMT alone: *emergence* in the blended space, where the interaction motivates a novel feature, which was not originally present in the inputs. Here it seems that the four disanalogy relations mentioned above outweigh two analogical connections, creating a cognitive tension between the two input spaces. As these spaces host the representations of two conscious agents/minds, the semantic construct of 'struggle' between them emerges from this cognitive pressure. Blending theorists would call this type of conceptual integration a *mirror network*, since the structures of the input spaces are almost identical, but the disanalogous relations between some conceptual elements in the inputs give rise to the notion of the struggle. The tension that emerges in the blended space is foremost a cognitive construct, but it may quickly develop into a more holistic psychological phenomenon, integrating the cognitive and affective components into a rich conceptual experience.

2.3 An extended CBT analysis: Force dynamics

The structure we are trying to analyze, and the experience itself of cognitive blends of this kind, might involve conceptual elements that have been termed 'agonist' and 'antagonist,' in the force-dynamic modelling of linguistically encoded meanings (see for instance Mandler 1992; Talmy 2000). Force dynamic theories claim that the physical perception of forces being exerted on or by our bodies provides the underlying experiential motivation for numerous structures occurring across languages, on both literal ('The wind made the pages turn') and more metaphorical levels ('His arguments made me reconsider my position').

The analysis in the previous section has suggested what might be happening in the conceptual construction of the struggle between a practicing Christian and a metaphysical, evil-intending mind. Yet there is a deeper ontological sense, a sense even of tragedy which may emerge from a further theological appreciation of this network: the demonic mind's failure to realize that its 'success' in the battle would lead not only the Christian soul, but also itself, to further descent. The analysis of this additional twist would require a further blending network, showing the disanalogy between the demon's belief that his intentions are good for himself, and the actual fact that they are as bad for him as they are for the Christian he is struggling with, as evil can only bring more evil. I do not go into details here, but one should keep in mind that the deeper the theological explanation, the more complex the underlying conceptual integration.

As we have just seen, more radical adherents of the monastic tradition of Mount Athos would likely favor a literalist interpretation of the mind's struggle, as offered above. A more psychologically oriented theologian would rather interpret these examples as metaphors, where 'the enemy' is coming from the believer's mind, while of course the 'Christian warrior' is equally a part of that same mind. In this case, we have the clearest instance of struggle against oneself, as explicitly given in paragraphs such as the one that follows (*Unseen Warfare*, p. 7):

> But if this is the hardest of all wars—since in fighting against ourselves it is in ourselves that we meet opposition—victory in it is the most glorious of all; and, what is the main thing, it is most pleasing to God. For if, inspired by fervour, you overcome and put to death your unruly passions, your lusts and wills, you will please God more, and will work for Him more beautifully, than if you flog yourself till you draw blood or exhaust yourself by fasts more than any ancient hermit of the desert.

In this excerpt, there is no doubt that St Nicodemus is taking the struggle metaphorically, and that the adversaries are both located in the single mind of the believer. Since only one conscious agent is involved, CMT cannot provide a satisfactory account, as it remains unclear where the 'source' and 'target' originate from. A blending analysis can approach this conceptualization in a more integrated way, suggesting that the underlying mental process is now considerably more complex than in the analyses outlined in sections 2.1 and 2.2. The metaphorization 'allocates' the same person, the believer, to *both* input spaces. For this to be achieved, this person first needs to be mentally 'replicated' from one input space to the other, through a process which Fauconnier (1997, p. 15 et passim) refers to as *identity connection*. This results in what blending theorists call *decompression* of the network, where, through the process of identity, the contents of one mental space, with all their conceptual elements, are mapped onto another space. Thus, we now have in both spaces the person with all of their characteristics, where the salient ones for this particular integration are those representing their 'virtues and vices,' i.e. positive and negative moral qualities. So it is the 'moral disposition' element from the generic space from the previous network that becomes more elaborated here. We may conveniently present the required elements in the inputs by means of Eight Major Virtues, as opposed to Eight Deadly Sins,[5] which nicely stand in full opposition to one another. It can be assumed for the sake of analysis that an Orthodox mind processing the text will draw on this additional relevant religious knowledge in order to achieve satisfactory conceptual integration via the blending process. In this integration network, the virtues and vices from input 1 and input 2 interact, resulting in the emergent *fictive interaction* (Pascual 2008), in which the person is fighting him- or herself in the blend (see Figure 3).

This blending diagram is simplified for reasons of clear graphic presentation. In the part targeting the vices and virtues in the inputs, it represents only the (global) disanalogy connections between their respective groups in the two spaces, which result in fictive interaction (two intersecting lines between the inputs). In actuality, each of the sixteen elements from input 1 (a virtue or a vice) may map onto each of the corresponding sixteen elements in input 2. Identity connections between elements of equal name (e.g. 'chastity' + 'chastity' or 'wrath' + 'wrath') result in uniqueness, and the emergent property is that this trait becomes stronger in the blend (i.e. the soul is more virtuous, or sinful). Many other combinations of two virtues or two vices are also possible, for instance that of 'charity' linking with 'meekness' or

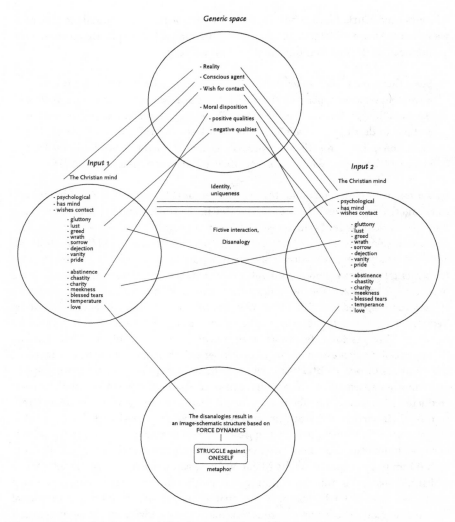

Figure 3 Extended Conceptual Blending model drawing on force-dynamic cognition.

'wrath' connecting with 'sorrow.' These mappings are analogical, and they result in the enhancement of total virtue or sin in the soul.[6] In opposition to this enhancement, the metaphor of conflict emerges from the disanalogical connections. They may be weaker in intensity, when a sin and a virtue interact which are not complete opposites (e.g. 'gluttony' and 'meekness').[7] Finally, they reach their full strength when a sin and a virtue which are total counterparts interact: 'gluttony' and 'abstinence,' 'wrath' and 'meekness,' 'pride' and 'love.' So we seem to have here a total of 256 possible connections, which can have two valences (analogical or disanalogical), and which are ranked by intensity. Assuming the valence is different, the greater the intensity, the stronger the force-dynamic effects between the agonist and the antagonist, and the clearer the metaphor of 'struggle' which emerges in the blend.

Thus, while reading the text containing the metaphor, we create a blended space in which we 'see' the person fighting with him or herself, based on the valence and intensity of the mappings between his or her vices and virtues from the inputs. Of course, this 'seeing' process does not necessarily result in a rich visual image. Yet there still seems to be a special cognitive effect emerging from the interaction, one which is more intense and integrated than in, for example, explicit analogy. This fight is of course impossible in the physical reality, but the reader has little if any problems in correctly interpreting the intended message. The blending process results in a novel, emergent image of some kind, which becomes *compressed* again, so that we can easily understand it at the most natural level—what Fauconnier and Turner (2002, p. 323) call the *human scale*. In this case, it is an image of two conscious, probably anthropomorphized minds, fighting one another.[8] Thus, the entire integration process involves cognitive mechanisms which are arguably more complex than the ones in the previous two analyses. Again, this is a *mirror* network, in which the elements of both input spaces and the blend share the topology of their organizing frame. Yet, there is a distinct geometric elegance to this one: in a perhaps more fundamental sense, the vices and virtues given in the inputs as conceptual elements likewise 'mirror' one another, as, theologically, some of them stand as full opposites.

It appears, then, that 'the struggle against oneself' requires a conceptual blending analysis for the cognitive linguist to postulate, on a functional level, what may be happening in the mind of the reader while he or she processes this metaphor. In order to conceptualize the construct, one needs selective projection, compression, and emergent structure, which can then be further reinforced by the invocation of agonists and antagonists from force-dynamic concepts. This, I hope, provides some support to using CBT rather than CMT alone in analyzing the metaphors from *Unseen Warfare*.

3 IMPLICATIONS OF THE USE OF THE METAPHOR FOR COGNITIVE SCIENCE AND THEOLOGY

Conceptual Metaphor Theory nicely shows that metaphor is not a linguistic, but a broader cognitive phenomenon, and explains how elements of source and target domains systematically map onto one another. It thus answers the question *what* the elements of a metaphorical construction are. Conceptual Blending Theory can well explain processes such as compression or emergence, which account for *how* some apparently impossible elements of metaphorical expressions occur—for instance, how a single person can be viewed as occupying two positions, or assuming two semantic roles, at the same time. This final section attempts to go one step further and provide some thoughts on *why* the metaphor involving internal, psychological antagonism may have emerged in the first place.

A common tendency of metaphor theorists is to analyze the materials from various types of discourse, including theology, as a handy corpus for proving or disproving some technical thesis in linguistics. While this is of course a perfectly valid method which yields new insights in the theory of language, it is often accompanied by implicit deconstruction—the conclusion that the only interesting thing in the (religious) discourse is the metaphors it is using, and how the human mind creates such fanciful, but factually impossible images. On such views, deeper insights, ontologies, or moral messages behind a metaphorical construct are just ignored. I would like to argue here that the mere analysis of metaphors is not enough; that their presence indicates a deeper meaning rather than just revealing the secrets of how the mind may formally or functionally work; that the quest for a possible *causation* behind the occurrence of some metaphors, though quite speculative, is perhaps a more laudable task than just assuming that they appear 'automatically,' through endless concentric circles of emergence, constrained, if at all, by adaptational pressure. In short, I believe the analysis of religious metaphors remains only halfway done unless the ultimate question is *ontological*. So, *why* internal struggle?

In relation to cognitive science, this question is directly related to the problems of *morality* and *empathy*. In a previous article (Antović 2012), I have tried to make some connections between the Orthodox concept of deification and theories of morality in modern cognitive science, including the braintrust theory of Patricia Churchland (Churchland 2011) and mirror neuron theory of Giacomo Rizzolatti and Vittorio Gallese, adapted for the discussion of morality by Vilayanur Ramachandran (Ramachandran 2004). The two approaches have proposed to view empathetic behavior, respectively, as a consequence of biochemical and neurophysiological evolutionary pressure. I here wish to call upon the functionalist theory of conceptual blending again—this time not as a technical tool for analyzing unusual linguistic expressions, but rather as a hypothesis on the origins of modern human cognition.

According to this view (cf. Fauconnier and Turner 2002, p. 183 et passim; Turner 2006) human beings are special, as, historically, they evolved the most complex type of conceptual integration, *double-scope blending*. In mirror networks, the mental spaces which interact with one another share a single organizing frame. Such was the case with two instances of unseen warfare analyzed in the previous section, where features such as 'type of reality,' 'conscious agency,' 'wish for contact,' and 'moral disposition' underlay both the generic space and the two input spaces, motivating the emergent sense of 'struggle' in the blend. In double-scope networks, on the other hand, the frame and identity properties valid for the entire network come from *each of the two input spaces*, even in situations in which input 1 and input 2 seem to be structurally very different. Double-scope blending therefore allows for the integration of fully disparate conceptual content—human beings and lions in mythology (the Sphinx), space and time in theoretical physics, frozen water and consciousness in personality psychology (Freud's 'tip of the iceberg' metaphor), or complex numbers in mathematics. Thus, in humans, even fully diversified input spaces may merge to create a powerful novel blend, and this is arguably the central source of human creativity. Fauconnier and Turner speculate that this newly evolved mental capacity was that one key spark which allowed the emergence of the 'cognitively modern human being' some fifty to eighty thousand years ago, as reflected in our increased capacity to manipulate symbols, exercise ritual behavior, create expressions of art, and use language. Once it came onto the scene, the argument goes, double-scope blending went on and on, through history, resulting in ever more complex products of human creativity.

In connection with Christianity, many events narrated in the Bible may be interpreted as blends, and some of them are of central importance. We witness double-scope blending when a snake and a mind possessing evil intentions combine to create the one malicious being responsible for human metaphysical torment. We find an even more complex case, a series of double-scope blending networks ultimately compressed into one powerful megablend, when we reduce every sin of every single person in history and its every single redemption to the human-scale event of just one man, Christ the Redeemer, the Lamb of God, suffering and resurrecting in three human days (Turner 2003). While Fauconnier and Turner do not press the connection with Christianity this far, my thesis is that after the beginning of the present era there may have been another, so far unrecognized, instance of blending. In addition to earlier sequences of double-scope blends, a mirror network may have emerged in this period akin to the one presented in Figure 3, in which the object of the human moral struggle was gradually replaced—from an external enemy to the foe within. Perhaps it all went this way: with the first cognitively modern humans, physical struggle with others slowly transformed into mental struggle with others; with elaborate double-scope blends everywhere, this mental struggle was slowly turned into a struggle against evil metaphysical beings; around AD 1, the object of the struggle in input space 2 became fully replicated from input space 1, and thus internalized. This provided a new instance of blending which gave rise to morality as reflected in Christianity, strikingly in Orthodox Christianity, but certainly also in other religious traditions of that time. One could add that, after such a historical development, the struggle against oneself with the purpose of personal maturation is today part of the human condition, not necessarily related to the religious realm.

Naturally, how new this concept was is open to debate. Precursors to this transformed ethics had certainly been numerous, where one can recall at least a few Hellenic elements—the dialectic and agonistic nature of Greek literature and philosophy; the many conquest metaphors of the Greeks cutting across poetry, politics, and religion; Hellenistic ethics, with its views of the human being as a universe in itself, as the measure of all things; and Neo-Platonism, often present in Christian mystic thought. Thus, the concept of internal struggle need not have been that new when it appeared in Christianity. What was new, though, was its *impact* and *radical interpretation*. The message was so powerful that it spread rapidly and widely throughout Late Antiquity—a world quite slow and informationally handicapped by our twenty-first-century standards. And it was there to stay. Millions accepted this apparently radical idea: not just the observance of the Commandments; not just practical empathy for persons dear to us; but love of all beings, particularly enemies, followed by the uncompromising effort to kill all evil in ourselves, at all times, throughout our lives. Millions remain trying today. Naturally, 'Christ's dangerous idea' (to paraphrase Daniel Dennett 1996) has had a powerful impact on secular life, too. If we consider just one example, in the West and, consequently, most of the world, we organize the entire calendar, spanning all history and prehistory, around the birth of Christ: it is therefore perceived as a historical, but perhaps also a cognitive turning point, presented as the 'center' in the image schematic construct of the 'historical timeline.' Whether or not one affiliates with the religion, the fact remains that many things changed in the West with its arrival.

So what may have been the *cause* that sparked this additional postulated wave of blending? Was it cognitive pressure alone? An accident? A complex adaptation to environmental conditions, which, though it looks empathetic on the surface, just reveals deeply ingrained selfish motives? Was it an increased computational complexity of the cognitive system which somehow resulted in radically new forms of thought? Naturally, provided those thoughts are radically new at all, i.e. that our introspective sense of their fundamental difference from what we had before is not another illusion of the endlessly looping cognitive system. Or could it be it was God that was behind this change, as believers might feel?

These questions touch upon the point of bitter divergence, but paradoxically also of strong connections between theology and cognitive science. While of course assuming the God-as-the-cause position, there are highly respected, psychologically oriented Orthodox theologians who claim that human beings have an *ontological need* to find an antagonist. Thus, if this need is so deeply ingrained in us, then it is much better if we target the enemy in ourselves than in others (Jerotić 2010). It is of course the meaning of 'ontological' that presents the key problem here. For a theologian, it means provided by God. For a cognitive scientist, there are typically two possibilities. One answer is that this 'antagonistic urge' is inborn, part of our genetic heritage, i.e. biology. An Orthodox theologian should have no problems with this position, as it may only support the thesis that our Christian morality is God-given, since our teeth, stomach, or brains are also biological, and supplied by God so we can put them to good use (the fact that we tend to *abuse* these biological givens is of central theological concern). An evolutionary scientist might not agree with the invocation of God, but for him or her, too, the connection between biological evolution and higher cognitive capacities, such as mental moral conflict, may be plausible.

There is a growing research literature on the evolutionary basis of morality in general. One line of argument is that the proscription of asocial behavior evolved in order to enhance group survival. This might be an evolutionary source for concepts of the conflict between good and evil, subsequently elaborated in culture, perhaps in part by evolved cognitive abilities such as metaphorical projection described by CMT and creative complexity as approached by CBT, further facilitated via the emergence of language and elaborated over generations by writing. Yet the radical variant of (Christian) struggle against the evil in us remains a puzzle. For instance, how can there be an evolutionary basis behind a Christian morality, if it encourages chastity to the point of abstinence, or self-negation to the point of sacrifice? There is, of course, at least one more possibility in the cognitive sciences to explain the emergence of the inner-struggle construct, and it may sound attractive to cognitive linguists: that this 'moral antagonism' which we feel as a given is not inborn, but constructed out of sensory experience. For instance, a child's early familiarization with forces exerted on or by the body, and the emergent sense of 'disbalance' and urge for 'equilibrium,' may later map onto numerous psychological constructs, perhaps through the process of metaphorical extension. In this respect, force-dynamic concepts may not just *emerge* from the blends of Christian internal struggle, but alternatively or also *cause* them. In this case, in the network diagram for inner struggle, it would perhaps be appropriate to represent the agonist and antagonist into the generic space, too. While not necessarily excluding the Divine element (for instance in our very propensity to sense forces and admit them such metaphorical importance), this option might be acceptable for supporters of more materialistic positions, as well.

Naturally, there is also the believer's explanation: that moral antagonism has been 'ontological' since the early days of civilization, the birth of cognitively modern humans, or the Fall—i.e. that unseen warfare is a very real, ontic category, where metaphors and blends are its *consequence*, rather than cause. In other words, for people like the Mount Athos monks, and indeed many Orthodox Christians, the metaphysical battle is quite concrete—in it there are external, unseen forces impacting our mind, and the only real act of freedom that we have is to embrace or reject them. The rest is not ours. If this is the case, some expressions that we consider metaphorical, such as 'The idea crossed my mind' or 'I'm struggling with the temptation' are not only metaphors, but, in part, also literal descriptions of what may be going on at the intersection of the physical and metaphysical worlds. None of us can tell for sure—not, as a believer might say, until we shuffle off this mortal coil. Strange as it may sound to a rational, analytical mind, this literalist view has been held, and practiced, by numerous monks in monasteries to whom, today as in the past, thousands in Orthodox countries flock for spiritual advice. When one encounters some of those wise, serene and loving men, their profound insights often leave one in awe. To abuse the blending jargon once again, after meeting these people, what 'emerges' from the contact is only peace.

4 CONCLUSIONS

I have tried to show in this paper that metaphors permeate Orthodox Christian literature; that they are better formally explicable by means of Conceptual Blending than Conceptual Metaphor Theory alone; that they occur for a reason, which may have its cognitive, ontological, and, for a believer, perhaps also metaphysical roots; and that cooperation, rather than conflict, between cognitive science and theology should result in their better appreciation in the future.

Whatever our ultimate position may be, and this depends on the presence or absence of faith, the cultural background, intellectual affiliations, and many things more, as a linguist I will always plead that we beware of simplifications, e.g. in claiming that some expressions are mere metaphors, interesting for formal analysis but devoid of deeper meaning. Quite the contrary, my stand remains that the presence of a metaphor is just an indicator, and that without a deeper meaning, we would not find the metaphor in the discourse at all. It remains my hope that the true meaning of unseen warfare may be found in the synergy of theology, cognitive science, and linguistics.

NOTES

1. See Volume 3 of *The Philokalia*, translated and edited by G. E. H. Palmer et al. 1979–1999, [V3]27, para. 28.
2. e.g. St Mark the Ascetic [V1] 119, paras. 134, 139; [V1]140, para. 170; St Hesychios the Priest [V1] 170, paras. 34, 44; in G. E. Palmer et al. 1979–1999, volume 1.
3. Online version http://www.stnicholasdc.org/files/Orthodoxy/Unseen-Warfare.pdf. All page numbers cited are from this version.
4. The image-schematic metaphor GOOD IS UP is rooted in, indeed constitutive of, discourses relating religion and morality; it is frequently linked with the warfare conceptualization that we are considering.
5. The number, names, and precise meanings of deadly sins and virtues vary across religious cultures. While Catholic sources usually list seven in both categories, Orthodox ascetic authors typically name eight. The list in the network above follows the nineteenth-century Russian Orthodox author St Ignatius Brianchaninov (2012).
6. Descriptions of such connections can also be found in Orthodox spiritual literature. Authors often claim that a virtue/sin never occurs alone, but that it is strongly interrelated with others, sometimes generating more complex [emergent] ones, for instance: 'Overeating and gluttony cause licentiousness. Avarice and self-esteem cause one to hate one's neighbor. Self-love, the mother of vices, is the cause of all these things' (St Maximus the Confessor, Four Hundred Texts on Love, *The Philokalia* [V2] 84, para. 7; Palmer et al. 1979–1999).
7. Virtues in combination can sometimes defeat a sin, for instance: 'Dejection [. . .]can be healed by prayer, hope in God, meditation on Holy Scripture, and by living with godly people' (St John Cassian, On the Eight Vices, *The Philokalia* [V1] 88; Palmer et al. 1979–1999).
8. There might be even more compression involved here. When one of the two selves wins, the result is a decision made by the unified self. Thus, after each battle, the two selves are compressed back into one, which gives us the sense of sustained struggle against oneself. I am thankful to Cristóbal Pagán Cánovas for providing this insight.

REFERENCES

Antović, M. (2012). Evolutionism and creationism: Arguments from cognitive science. In D. B. Djordjević, D. Gavrilović, and D. Todorović (eds.), *Religion, Religious and Folk Customs on the Border*, pp. 85–102. Niš: Yugoslav Society for the Study of Religion.

Brown, S. F. and K. Anatolios (2009). *Catholicism and Orthodox Christianity*. New York: Infobase Publishing.

Chiang, W. Y. and R. F. Duann (2007). Conceptual metaphors for SARS: 'War' between whom? *Discourse and Society* 18(5), 579–602.

Churchland, P. (2011). *Braintrust: What Neuroscience Tells Us about Morality*. Princeton, NJ: Princeton University Press.

Coe, C. and B. Winter (2013). ARGUMENT IS WAR metaphors in current politics. Paper presented at the *12th International Cognitive Linguistics Conference*, University of Alberta, Canada.

Decety, J. and T. Wheatley (eds.) (2015). *The Moral Brain: A Multidisciplinary Perspective*. Cambridge, MA: MIT Press.

Dennett, D. C. (1996). *Darwin's Dangerous Idea: Evolution and the Meaning of Life*. New York: Simon and Schuster.

De Oliveira-Souza, R., R. Zahn, and J. Moll (2015). Neural correlates of human morality: An overview. In J. Decety and T. Wheatley (eds.), *The Moral Brain: A Multidisciplinary Perspective*, pp. 183–196. Cambridge, MA: MIT Press.

Elder, T. (2009). *Our Thoughts Determine Our Lives: The Life and Teachings of Elder Thaddeus of Vitovnica*. Platina, CA: St Herman Press.

Fauconnier, G. (1997). *Mappings in Thought and Language*. Cambridge: Cambridge University Press.

Fauconnier, G. and M. Turner (1998). Conceptual integration networks. *Cognitive Science* 22(2), 133–187.

Fauconnier, G. and M. Turner (2002). *The Way We Think: Conceptual Blending and the Mind's Hidden Complexities*. New York: Basic Books.

Grady, J., T. Oakley, and S. Coulson (1999). Blending and metaphor. In R. Gibbs and G. Steen (eds.), *Metaphor in Cognitive Linguistics*, pp. 101–124. Amsterdam: John Benjamins.

Howe, J. (2007). Argument is argument: An essay on conceptual metaphor and verbal dispute. *Metaphor and Symbol* 23(1), 1–23.

Jerotić, V. (2010). *Drawing Closer to God*. Belgrade: Ars Libri.

Johnson, E. (2005). WAR in the media: Metaphors, ideology, and the formation of language policy. *Bilingual Research Journal* 29(3), 621–640.

Jäkel, O. (1999). Kant, Blumenberg, Weinrich: Some forgotten contributions to the cognitive theory of metaphor. In R. Gibbs and G. Steen (eds.), *Metaphor in Cognitive Linguistics*, pp. 9–28. Amsterdam: John Benjamins.

Lakoff, G. (2008). *The Political Mind: A Cognitive Scientist's Guide to Your Brain and Its Politics*. New York: Penguin.

Lakoff, G. and M. Johnson (1980). *Metaphors We Live By*. Chicago: University of Chicago Press.

Lakoff, G. and M. Johnson (1999). *Philosophy in the Flesh: The Embodied Mind and Its Challenge to Western Thought*. New York: Basic Books.

Mandler, J. M. (1992). How to build a baby: II. Conceptual primitives. *Psychological Review* 99(4), 587–604.

McGlone, M. S. (2007). What is the explanatory value of a conceptual metaphor? *Language and Communication* 27(2), 109–126.

Meyendorff, J. (1974). *Byzantine Theology: Historical Trends and Doctrinal Themes*. New York: Fordham University Press.

Palmer, G. E. H., K. Ware, and P. Sherrard (transls. and eds.) (1979–1999). *The Philokalia: The Complete Text, Compiled by St Nikodemos of the Holy Mountain and St Makarios of Corinth*, 4 volumes. New York: Faber & Faber.

Pascual, E. (2008). Fictive interaction blends in everyday life and courtroom settings. In T. Oakley and A. Hougaard (eds.), *Mental Spaces in Discourse and Interaction*, pp. 79–107. Amsterdam: John Benjamins.

Petrović, M. (1968 [1942]). *Metafore i alegorije*. Belgrade: Srpska književna zadruga.

Ramachandran, V. (2004). *A Brief Tour of Human Consciousness: From Impostor Poodles to Purple Numbers*. New York: Pi Press.

Ritchie, D. (2003). 'ARGUMENT IS WAR'—Or is it a game of chess? Multiple meanings in the analysis of implicit metaphors. *Metaphor and Symbol* 18(2), 125–146.

Romaine, S. (1996). War and peace in the global greenhouse: Metaphors we die by. *Metaphor and Symbolic Activity* 11(3), 175–194.

Scupoli, Fr. L. (1997[1589]). *The Spiritual Combat*. New York: St. Vladimir's Seminary Press.

Smith, A. (2006). *Philokalia: The Eastern Christian Spiritual Texts: Selections Annotated and Explained*. Woodstock, VT: SkyLight Paths Publishing.

St Brianchaninov, I. (2012). *The Arena: Guidelines for Spiritual and Monastic Life*. Chicago: Holy Trinity Publications.

St Nicodemus the Hagiorite (ca. 1801). *Unseen Warfare*, available online at: http://www.stnicholasdc.org/files/Orthodoxy/Unseen-Warfare.pdf

Steinert, H. (2003). The indispensable metaphor of war: On populist politics and the contradictions of the state's monopoly of force. *Theoretical Criminology* 7(3), 265–291.

Talmy, L. (2000). *Toward a Cognitive Semantics*, Vol. 1: *Concept Structuring Systems*. Cambridge, MA: MIT Press.

Turner, M. (2003). Double-scope stories. In D. Herman (ed.), *Narrative Theory and the Cognitive Sciences*, pp. 117–142. Stanford, CA: CSLI Publications.

Turner, M. (2006). The art of compression. In M. Turner (ed.), *The Artful Mind: Cognitive Science and the Riddle of Human Creativity*, pp. 93–114. New York: Oxford University Press.

Tyneh, C. S. (ed.) (2003). *Orthodox Christianity: Overview and Bibliography*. New York: Nova Science Publishers.

Vervaeke, J. and J. M. Kennedy (1996). Metaphors in language and thought: Falsification and multiple meanings. *Metaphor and Symbol* 11(4), 273–284.

Ware, Fr. Kallistos (1995). Act out of stillness: The influence of fourteenth-century Hesychasm on Byzantine and Slav civilization. In Daniel J. Sahas (ed.), *The Byzantine Heritage Annual Lecture*, pp. 4–7. Toronto: The Hellenic Canadian Association of Constantinople and the Thessalonikean Society of Metro Toronto.

CHAPTER 16

Hoc est corpus

Deixis and the Integration of Ritual Space

PAUL CHILTON AND DAVID CRAM

The purpose of this study is to present a cognitive analysis of the liturgical language involved in the celebration of the Eucharist,[1] with particular focus on the words *hoc est corpus meum* ('this is my body'), which form part of the consecration formula. Although our approach is a narrowly linguistic one, it is not 'hermeneutic' in the traditional sense of being focused primarily on word-meaning. It draws on recent thinking in cognitive semantics and pragmatics and is built in particular on the model developed in the book *Language, Space and Mind* (Chilton 2014). This model is a 'radical' pragmatic one in the technical sense that it takes deixis—pragmatic orientation in space and time—as the primitive dimensions which provide the starting point for our construction of meaning, rather than taking word-meaning as a primitive notion and modulation of meaning in context as a derivative process.[2] In this way, the analysis attempts to give a multidimensional account of how the consecrational formula is imbued with meaning by virtue of the way the words employed interact with other cognitive components of the liturgical event—spatial, temporal, gestural, and so on—all of which are anchored in the primary deictic matrix.

The interpretation of the consecration formula 'this is my body' has been grounds for intense theological controversy over many centuries. In the Reformation and the early modern period, the interpretation of these words came to be viewed as a pivotal point defining the larger-scale doctrinal differences between Catholic and Protestant thinkers, and further gave rise to finer-grained differentiation both within the Protestant camp and, to some degree, within anti-Reformation theology. Any modern academic view about how the liturgical formula works cannot avoid being informed by a pressing awareness of these ramified doctrinal differentiations. However, we wish to draw attention to the fact that even where doctrinal differences were in themselves theologically clear-cut, the historical debates inevitably involved hermeneutic appeals to ideas concerning word-meaning and sentence-meaning which were anchored in early modern grammatical and rhetorical theory, the basis of which may be unknown or out of focus for the modern lay person.

In presenting this radical pragmatic analysis, in which we aim to be as explicit and as rigorous as possible about the linguistic assumptions being made, it is not our intention to align ourselves with, nor indeed distance ourselves from, any particular doctrinal position. Some readers will, of course, approach the hermeneutic issues involved from a firm doctrinal perspective, but we hope that those who do so will follow us in focusing on the strictly linguistic and cognitive aspects of the way in which the hermeneutic issues are articulated. Coming from a theoretical linguistic background, as both authors do, we would like to suggest that the received framework for hermeneutic analysis in the early modern period is underpinned by assumptions about the way meaning in language works which are largely unattended to by sophisticated religious thinkers, both lay and clerical, who are not linguistically informed. We do not claim that a radical pragmatic perspective will in itself serve to confirm or corroborate any particular doctrinal position, but we do argue that it affords a cognitive-linguistic perspective on the hermeneutic issues that is fundamentally different from the received framework. A secondary purpose of this chapter, therefore, is to defamiliarise the received hermeneutic framework by contrasting it, in an introductory section, with the quite different medieval framework which preceded it. This framework is broadly similar to our own analysis in that it can be characterised as *radically pragmatic*, and we hope this approach will offer a way of grasping the nub of the contrast with the *radically semantic* received framework.

The salient characteristic of the received early modern hermeneutic approach to the consecrational formula 'this is my body' is that it focuses on the predicate of the expression, i.e. the expression with the head noun 'body'; it is thus *radically semantic* in the sense that it starts out from the lexical meaning of the word 'body' and goes on to investigate how, if at all, this may be contextually modulated, e.g. taken metaphorically rather than literally. The approach of the medieval theologian, informed by the theory of the period known as 'speculative grammar', focuses, by contrast, not on the predicate but on the deictic element which is in the position of grammatical subject, that is, on the word 'this'. Using an elaborate logical-grammatical apparatus developed for these purposes, the medieval analysis investigates what the deictic term 'this' is pointing at, and does so quite independently of the reference of the word 'body' in the predicate. The formula is thus interpreted by taking for granted that the predicate 'body' is interpreted quite literally but enquiring how the deictic 'this' is to be construed.

These two contrasting perspectives can be illustrated with an everyday example. Imagine someone saying 'This is my home'. From one perspective (the radically semantic one), we focus on the predicate, and construe what the speaker means by working out what is intended by the word 'home'. Looking this up in our mental lexicon, we may take it in a 'basic' or 'default' sense as 'my fixed residence, my abode, my dwelling'. Checking further, we may entertain more 'extended' senses, either equally concrete but less immediately local (my locality, my town, my country), or less concrete (involving dimensions such as 'where I was born/grew up', 'where I feel I belong', etc.). Indeed the context of the utterance may well suggest an interpretation of the word which in some way overrides a literal meaning: the whole point of declaring this to be 'my home' may be precisely that it is *not* one's habitual residence, but nevertheless is 'where I feel I belong'. And there are more distantly constructed interpretations which are possible: for example, a couple going round an art gallery may enter a room full of impressionist paintings, and one may turn to the other and say '(Now), this is my home'. The alternative perspective (the radically pragmatic one) is to focus not on the lexical item 'home' but on the deictic term 'this', which does not have any lexical context (in the way that 'home' does) but is used simply as a pointing word. On this basis, we construe what the speaker means by saying 'This is my home' by working out what he or she is pointing at (or drawing attention to) by using the word 'this'.

The difference between these two perspectives is not their scope or flexibility; but while the radically semantic approach immediately triggers controversy about literal versus metaphorical meaning, the radically pragmatic approach does not: the person in the room of impressionist painting is using the word 'home' in its default or literal sense, but is applying it in a local and immediately relevant way. In what follows, we are inviting the reader to follow us in approaching the liturgical formula 'this is my body' from these two complementary perspectives: the radically semantic one focuses on the word 'body' and the debate between its literal and metaphorical interpretation; the radically pragmatic one focuses on the deictic word 'this' and enquires what it points to.

The structure of the paper is as follows. In section 1.1 we will show how the doctrinal differences in the interpretation of the eucharistic formula in the early modern period are *both* standardly articulated from what we are identifying as a radically semantic perspective; in other words, a common language became established in which these differences were to be expressed—one which, we argue, still informs modern theological debate in fundamental ways. In section 1.2 we contrast this framework with one that prevailed during the Middle Ages, one which is grounded in a radically pragmatic theory of meaning, in which deixis (or pointing words) plays a central and substantial role. We hope that the broad contrast between the two approaches will prepare the ground for the cognitive-linguistic model which will be developed in the sections that then follow. This model is fairly technical in its detail, but is based on a set of fundamental cognitive principles which we believe are in themselves not inaccessible for the non-specialist.

1.1 The intertwining of theological and rhetorical dimensions in disputes about the Eucharist

In this section we will look in some detail at the statements of position by Reformation and Counter-Reformation theologians, and attempt to show that although the positions are diametrically opposed, their articulation is formulated in a common grammatical language. A useful starting point is to take the wording of the decree relating to the sacrament of the Eucharist issued at the Council of Trent at its thirteenth session on 11 October 1551, in the Waterworth translation, which reads as follows:

> If any one denieth, that, in the sacrament of the most holy Eucharist, are contained truly, really, and substantially, the body and blood together with the soul and

divinity of our Lord Jesus Christ, and consequently the whole Christ; but saith that He is only therein as in a sign, or in figure, or virtue; let him be anathema.[3]

The positive theological doctrine asserted here (that of the Real Presence, elaborated further in the following seven decrees) is situated explicitly by reference to the counter-doctrine 'that Christ is present in the Sacrament only as in a *sign* or *figure*', as taught by Calvin and Zwingli.

The Protestant counter-doctrine to which this decree refers is explicitly articulated in seventeenth-century English Bible commentaries on the primary New Testament texts relevant to the institution of the Eucharist: Matthew 26:26–30; Mark 14:12–31; Luke 22:17–20; John 6:32–35, 47–58; and 1 Corinthians 11:23–25. All of these are interpreted as indicating that the eucharistic bread and wine stand as a metaphor or sign for flesh and blood, rather than constituting their sacramental Real Presence.[4] The interpretive terminology used here is uniformly a grammatical-rhetorical one, and Christ himself is described as using 'sacramental language' in uttering the eucharistic formula 'hoc est enim corpus meum'.

A representative Protestant Bible commentary of this sort is the one compiled by the Welsh non-conformist minister Matthew Henry (1662–1714), a six-volume work entitled *An exposition of the Old and New Testaments* (1721–1725), which provides a synthesis of English biblical exegesis of the late seventeenth century.[5] The sections relating to the interpretation of the consecrational formula are quoted below, under the headings used by Henry:

On Matthew 26:26–30
The body of Christ is signified and represented by bread; he had said formerly (John 6:35), I am the bread of life, upon which metaphor this sacrament is built;
This is my body, spiritually and sacramentally; this signifies and represents my body. He employs sacramental language, like that, Ex. 12:11. It is the Lord's passover. Upon a carnal and much-mistaken sense of these words, the church of Rome builds the monstrous doctrine of Transubstantiation, which makes the bread to be changed into the substance of Christ's body, only the accidents of bread remaining.

On Mark 14:12–31
The institution of the Lord's supper. It was instituted in the close of a supper, when they were sufficiently fed with the paschal lamb, to show that in the Lord's supper there is no bodily repast intended; to preface it with such a thing, is to revive Moses again. But it is food for the soul only, and therefore a very little of that which is for the body, as much as will serve for a sign, is enough. [. . .]

On Luke 22:7–20
[T]he Lord's supper is instituted to be a commemorative sign or memorial of a Christ already come [. . .]
The shedding of Christ's blood, by which the atonement was made (for the blood made atonement for the soul, Leviticus 17:11), as represented by the wine in the cup; and that cup of wine is a sign and token of the New Testament, or new covenant, made with us.

On John 6:29

To feed upon Christ is to do all in his name, in union with him, and by virtue drawn from him; it is to live upon him as we do upon our meat. How our bodies are nourished by our food we cannot describe, but that they are so we know and find; so it is with this spiritual nourishment. Our Saviour was so well pleased with this metaphor (as very significant and expressive) that, when afterwards he would institute some outward sensible signs, by which to represent our communicating of the benefits of his death, he chose those of eating and drinking, and made them sacramental actions. [. . .]

Christ, having thus spoken of himself as the bread of life, and of faith as the work of God, comes more particularly to show what of himself is this bread, namely, his flesh, and that to believe is to eat of that, v. 51–58, where he still prosecutes the metaphor of food.

The common interpretative dimension which connects these various textual comments by Matthew Henry is usefully pinpointed by a near-contemporary, the Baptist preacher Benjamin Keach (1640–1704), author of *Tropologia: A Key to Open Scripture-Metaphors*, an equally successful devotional work which was published in 1681, reprinted several times during the compiler's lifetime, and is still accessible at the present day in a number of religious websites. The aim of Keach's work is to give a systematic inventory of the rhetorical devices used in the Old and New Testaments. These he divides first under two principal heads, *tropes* and *figures*: tropes concern the sense of words, 'When they are drawn from their proper and genuine signification to that which is different or contrary'; figures are rhetorical devices which do not alter or vary the sense of words, but serve simply to 'embellish, beautify, or adorn them' (Keach 1681: book 1, p. 1). The various scriptural manifestations of these devices are then assembled under ramified sub-divisions within these two primary headings. In effect, Keach's work is a rhetorical Bible commentary turned inside out, with the materials presented in a systematic and classified fashion rather than by their textual order.[6]

The consecrational formula is classified by Keach under tropes, as distinct from figures, and appears in book 1, chapter 3, sub-section 5, which deals with cases of metonymy 'When the thing *Signed* is put for the *Sign*'. This is explained and exemplified as follows (Keach 1681, p. 20):

Sometimes the *thing signified* is *formally* put for the *Sign*, that is, for the term or appellation of the sign, as *Exod.* 8.23. *And I will put Redemption between my people and thy people*, that is, the *sign* or token of Redemption. [. . .] By this *Trope* Bread is called the *Body of Christ*, and *Wine* is called *his Blood*, Matth. 26.26, 28. Mark 14.22, 24. 1 Cor. 11.24, 25. that is, a Sacramental sign and symbol of his Body and Blood, instituted in remembrance of him.

The hermeneutic approach which, as we have seen, is deployed by Matthew Henry and others in the Bible commentaries is given a theoretical foundation by Keach in terms of contemporary grammatical and rhetorical thinking; the key to understanding a scriptural passage, or form of words, is based first and foremost on an understanding of word-meaning and the tropes and figures which modulate the literal meaning of a word in a particular context.[7] Furthermore, the principles which are here deployed in biblical and liturgical exegesis were being developed in parallel to those being adopted to govern the use of English for scientific purposes, particularly in the network of the Royal Society. In this secular context, the key to proper usage is summarised by the ideal of the 'plain style'.[8] The sense of a 'plain' manner of speaking' and writing, in this context, is one in which the literal meaning of words is not cluttered by 'ornamental' rhetorical devices, and where the use of figures and tropes, for the purposes of explanation and clarification, is under full rational control. It was likewise assumed that literal meaning itself could be placed under rational control, by means of newly developed taxonomic systems and by the logical analysis of complex ideas into their simplex component elements.[9]

The linguistic assumptions which underpinned these various activities were not without their critics. Indeed, following Locke's critique of language in his *Essay* of 1690 it became evident that the notion of 'literal' meaning was theoretically no less problematic than that of lexical usage rhetorically modulated by tropes and figures.[10] However, for the purposes of comparison in what follows, it is fair to say that what determines the focus both for hermeneutic analysis and for prescriptions about scientific style at this period is the issue of word meaning. In the case of the consecrational formula, this narrows the focus for debate to the status of the lexical items in the formula 'hoc est corpus meum': how is the word 'body' to be construed? Is it to be understood literally or metaphorically, and in either case, how do we arrive at our understanding of the word?

1.2 The interpretation of the Eucharist in the framework of medieval grammatical and logical traditions

It can come as quite a surprise to those not familiar with medieval hermeneutics to encounter for the first time an approach to the consecrational formula where the focus is not on the lexical item in the predicate, 'body', but on the deictic expression in subject position, 'this'. From this perspective, our starting point is not to understand what the word 'body' means, but rather what the demonstrative 'this' is pointing to.

As with the early modern approach we have just been looking at, this medieval perspective is one which has its own theoretical underpinnings, most elaborately developed in what is known as 'speculative grammar', speculative in the sense of the Latin *speculum* (mirror), because language was held to 'reflect' the structures of reality and the mind.[11] The way in which such grammars were applied in liturgical contexts has been investigated in a series of studies by Irène Rosier-Catach, most notably in the volume *La parole efficace: Signe, rituel, sacré* (2004). A distinctive feature of speculative grammar is the way in which grammatical concepts are systematically linked with those in logic, which makes access to the central notions (including the key term 'suppositio' in the explanation of deixis) difficult for the modern reader. For our present purposes, however, it is not essential to familiarise ourselves with the full panoply of speculative grammar, but merely to *de*familiarise ourselves from received ideas about meaning in language sufficiently well to put ourselves in the shoes of the medieval liturgist. One way of doing this, at the risk of anachronism, is to set the medieval view off against the early modern view, as exemplified in the narrative of Adamic naming which figured prominently in projects for a philosophical language.

This account starts out from the verse in *Genesis* (2:19) which relates how, having formed every beast in the field and every fowl of the air, God subsequently 'brought them unto Adam to see what he would call them: and whatsoever Adam called every living creature, that was the name thereof'. From this, it was concluded, firstly, that names were a human rather than a divine invention and that the process of naming amounted to a two-way match: for each single thing there was to be one appropriate name, and also vice versa. For the seventeenth-century taxonomist, this provided the basis for a fully adequate theory of how words mean, with accompanying theories of ontology and epistemology (how things exist in the outside world and how we have knowledge of them) to support and buttress this view of language.

What it does *not* provide, however, and indeed does not even provide room for, is an adequate account of deictic words, words whose semantic function is to point at things rather than name them: words such as 'this' in the sacramental formula. Deictics do have a broad meaning of a language-specific sort; the English word 'this' contrasts with 'that' to indicate proximity versus non-proximity, and other languages differ in having three- and four-way rather than a two-way distinction. But deictics do not 'name' things. What we understand a deictic such as 'this' to be pointing to depends not on the word's lexical content (as with nouns and verbs) but on context. If I point at our cat in the presence of my wife, then by default I will be drawing her attention to a member of the cat species.[12] But the situation could also be such that I am drawing attention to the creature more specifically as a Burmese—a variety of cat; or, again, I could be drawing attention to this feline object as 'your birthday present'; or, to the colour of the cat's coat so as to indicate the colour of cardigan I would like my own birthday present to be; or, I could be seeking to identify the putative culprit responsible for the recent breaking of a vase. Thus not only do deictics not name things, their use does not carry the assumption that what is being pointed to is a 'thing' in a taxonomic or Adamic sense.[13] The process of lexical naming is of course one *part* of how we seek to establish what an interlocutor is aiming to point at by means of a deictic word, but, from this larger perspective, it plays only a subsidiary role.

Let us return at this point to the seventeenth-century controversies surrounding the words pronounced by the priest at the centre of the Catholic mass. As Rosier-Catch (2014) shows, one group of Catholic scholars (though seen as heretical by some contemporaries) took up the logic- and grammar-based thread of the medieval thinkers and focused on the logic and grammar of the deictic words in the formula 'this is my body'. It is arguable they did so in a way that remarkably foreshadows the modern cognitive approach to human language, quite irrespective of what their religious beliefs and commitments were.

We first summarise briefly the central points about the two works analysed by Rosier-Catch, the *Logique* of Port Royal (Arnauld and Nicole [1662] 1683) and

Arnauld's *Perpétuité de la foi de l'eglise catholique touchant l'eucharistie* (1781 [1667]).

1. The authors focused on the words spoken *by Jesus* according to biblical accounts (quoted above), while their medieval predecessors, in their logical, grammatical, and rhetorical analyses, focused also on the same words as spoken *by the priest* performing the eucharistic rite—which is what we do in our cognitive account in section 3 below.

2. The authors consistently speak to what is happening *in the minds* of the participants in the supper narrated in the biblical passages, rather than speaking of words as if words had direct reference to referents (cf. Rosier-Catach 2014, pp. 544–548, 552–554). In this sense, the analysis offered in the *Logique* and the *Perpétuité*, although aimed primarily to prove a doctrinal point, is nonetheless cognitivist in orientation. Moreover, the authors assume universal cognitive operations that are applicable to the minds of Jesus and his disciples just as much as to those of any other human mind. It is an approach that has a decidedly modern ring. In our analysis, we shall, however, be focused primarily on what may be going on in the minds of participants in the Eucharist ritual, and on what are the potential cognitive (including emotional) effects.

3. The central question, both for the scholars of the high Middle Ages and, more prominently, for the Reformation and Counter-Reformation, was the question of metaphoricity: was Jesus (and the priest in the mass who was reporting/repeating and narrating Jesus's words) saying 'this [bread] is my body' in a metaphorical ('figurative') way? The Port Royal texts are determined to assert, *contra* the Protestants, that these words are not metaphorical but literal, claiming to demonstrate this by logical and linguistic analysis. They thus continued to maintain the truth of the Catholic doctrine that there was a real change of one thing (bread) into another (my body). As is well known, this claim depends on the conceptual framework of Aristotelian physics, which entailed a distinction between an appearance or *species*, which you can see, touch, etc., and a *substance*, an inner essence, which you can't. Nonetheless, Arnauld and his colleague seem on track toward a cognitivist account, according to which the change from bread to body (which they assume to be stated in the biblical text) *arises in the mind*, and is thus 'metaphorical' (in their terminology) and not 'figurative' (in the Protestants' sense). Rosier-Catach spells out the burden of this observation more explicitly as follows:

   > It is not of [primary] importance that the bread remain in its [proper] nature (consubstantiation), or that it ceases to exist in its [proper] nature, like a rainbow (transubstantiation). The emphasis is [here] placed solely on *the persistence of the image of the bread*, which allows other ideas to be stimulated, so as to represent the way in which the body of Christ is the food of the soul, and the way in which the faithful are gathered in. (2014, p. 552; translation by David Cram)

4. It is the analysis of deixis, however, that concerns us most here. Apart from the fact that the seventeenth-century Port Royal scholars are riding on the back of the medieval accounts, they also point forward to the cognitive deixis-based theory outlined below (section 2). The way the authors of the *Logique* and the *Perpétuité*

approach the meaning of the Latin word *hoc* (translated as French *ceci*, roughly 'this thing here') is in line with a cognitive account of meaning, in which the meanings of words are conceptual schemata that can be filled in by ideas relevant in the particular context in which they occur. Furthermore, the *Logique* approaches the whole sentence 'hoc est enim corpus meum' as an utterance produced and understood in real time. The word *hoc*, it is explained, raises an 'idea' that is 'vague' [French: 'idée confuse']—or, as we might nowadays say, '[semantically] underspecified' (Sperber and Wilson 1995; Pustejovsky 1998). As the utterance proceeds through time, according to the authors, *hoc* will, at t_1, be linked with the bread that is on the table in the scene—and may or may not persist (the doctrinal argument hinges on this, but need not detain us) as a mental *image* till the speaker gets to the words *corpus meum*, at which moment, t_2, the word *hoc* is understood as also linked to the idea 'body'. Now given the general emphasis on mental representation in this part of the *Logique*, the suggestion that two concepts are merged in real time in response to a linguistic utterance brings us rather close to the theory of cognitive blending in cognitive linguistics.[14] The fact that the approach serves doctrinal propaganda need not detract from its interest as an early example of a cognitivist account. The explanation developed in the next sections of this paper is not, of course, concerned with theological justification but with furthering scientific understanding of ritual and ritual language in relation to the workings of the human mind.

A final note about the medieval approach to the consecrational formula might be helpful for extrapolating to the modern deictic one to which we now turn. Although the pivotal element to the medieval viewpoint can be narrowed down to the deictic point where linguistic and logical frameworks intersect, the larger discussion of liturgical practice and liturgical 'meaning' with which it is associated is strikingly multidimensional and involves equal attention to the significance of dress, posture, and gesture. This should not, on reflection, be surprising if one considers that the situational effects that apply to the semantics of linguistic deixis will apply also, *mutatis mutandis*, to aspects of gesture and ritual which are not verbal. A deictically anchored approach to hermeneutics such as the medieval one will thus, by its very nature, have a broader semiological scope than a lexical-semantic one. In modern terms, it can be better characterised as a 'cognitive' approach rather than a narrowly 'linguistic' one, as is the case also for the modern deictic framework, to which we now turn.

2 A MODERN COGNITIVE APPROACH TO DEIXIS: DEICTIC SPACE THEORY

The general theoretical framework is that of cognitive linguistics and more broadly that of cognitive science—outlined in the Introduction to the present volume. We extend familiar cognitive-linguistic topics (metaphor, grammatical constructions) and outline a cognitive theory of deixis (Chilton 2014) that is based on spatial cognition. In section 3 of this chapter, we use this framework to account for the cognitive effects, in their multimodal ritual context, that may be produced by the 'hoc est corpus meum' formula. In the analysis of the ritual itself, we also draw on conceptual integration (blending) theory and emphasise that conceptual integration is not only linguistic—it may also involve a combination of linguistic and non-linguistic representations. We try to show how one little piece of the ritual of the mass blends 'material anchors' with language, using the blend to structure the consciousness of participants.

Deictic Space Theory (DST) is based on an extended theory of deixis that builds on the human ability for metaphor. The theory takes orientation of self in experienced space-time as its starting point and integrates it with the self's experiences of and judgements about what is real and 'irreal'.[15] The advantage of this model is that it is the basis for modelling highly abstract concepts, without losing touch with their bodily basis, and also linking them to linguistic and other semiotic input from a context. The diagram below (Figure 1) is the basic diagram for a very abstract 'deictic space'. It is a conceptual space, not a physical one. It is the conceptual space that language systems use to represent many kinds of conceptualisations by way of words, parts of words, and grammatical constructions—conceptualisations that need not be literally to do with spatial objects at all but which are derived from our brain's representation of them. In the diagram, the point where the three axes converge, the geometric origin S, is the experiential self, the 'I' who represents the world around it in terms of three *concep-tual* dimensions. The *a*-axis (the attention axis) puts entities (not necessarily concrete objects) relatively close to or distant from S, in the foreground or in the background.

The *t*-axis represents the way human minds mainly think of time and talk about it—as extending in two directions, into the future (abstracted from planning and antici-pation systems of the brain) and into the past (abstracted from memory systems).[16] The *m*-axis (modal axis) is special and important. It represents our sense of what is most real (true), generally that which is closest to us, 'present' and 'here', literally and metaphorically within our grasp. What is more distant is progressively less real, more uncertain epistemically, and ultimately unreal. So we have degrees of distance from self on axes of attention, temporal ordering, and epistemic judgement. These are abstrac-tions, used by language and other semiotic systems, for building complex ideas and communicating them. They are based in what cognitive psychologists call peripersonal

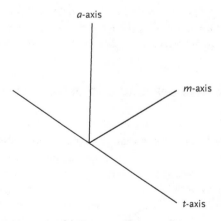

Figure 1 Basic diagram for abstract deictic space.

space (roughly the space that extends as far as our reach) and extrapersonal space, which is 'further out', though within the distance within which we can move about and control our environment (Previc 1998, 2006, 2009). Language and other semiotic systems go beyond this, however, to associate remote distance, when one 'reaches' both to the horizon and into the sky, with what is increasingly uncertain and unknown. Different brain systems and different neurotransmitters may be involved in these different distance attention systems, whether it is the concrete or the abstract world that is being attended to (as suggested for physical space in Previc 1998, 2009). Previc (2006) argues that distance attention, and the dopaminergic systems associated with distance attention, can be closely connected with religious experience.[17]

There is another component in the DST apparatus. This component models the *relations* between linguistically denoted referents, e.g. an object positioned in a place, an entity moving from one place to another, an agent moving an object, changing an object, and so forth. What is basically involved here is directedness, conventionally notated by an arrow. DST uses arrows in roughly the way elementary geometry uses arrows to symbolise the mathematical idea of a vector—'roughly' because what is needed are intuitive natural vectors rather than the axiomatised mathematical kind, though the latter may have their bodily origin in the former. Sometimes the operations defined for formal vectors also seem to have their source in intuitive combinations of intuitive vectors. A sentence such as 'he gave the bread to the disciples', structured round the transfer verb *give*, is modelled in DST—at least so far as its most basic conceptual structure is concerned—as in Figure 2.[18] What is important to

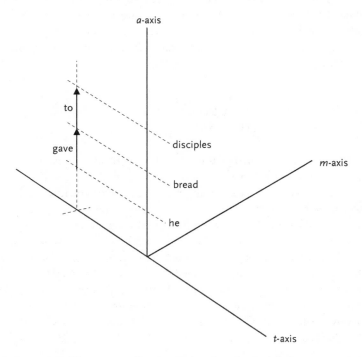

Figure 2 Structure of the sentence 'he gave the bread to the disciples'.

remember is that the three axis systems in which the vectors are positioned constitute a reference frame relative to a speaker S.

All this may seem reductive and mechanistic. However, theoretical modelling can be a way of getting at concrete roots. DST gives us some clarity about the physical and physiological basis of the psychic sensations that we think are entirely abstract. The important point is that conceptualisations experienced through language structure (and other semiotic structure) are *abstractions* from human perception of the spatial environment, particularly the structure of the visual field and the experience of reaching, grasping, and manipulating objects in front of us. Space-based abstractions can be spatially manipulated in the mind—referents can be moved 'closer' or 'further away', axis systems can be added, embedded within one another, linked, and merged.

In psychology, the roots of DST lie in the theories of Bühler (1990/1934; see Chilton 2014), and a related recent approach is MacWhinney (2005). In recent neuroscience, imaging evidence points to the involvement of specific brain regions in the processing of deixis and deictic shift.[19] In anthropology, Bühler's conception has been clarified and adapted to the analysis of religious ritual. Hanks (2005) elaborates on Bühler's notion of the *Zeigfeld* (pointing/showing field, or 'deictic space'), emphasising that the deictic space is embedded in social situation and social practice within a culture. Hanks demonstrates this 'embedded' idea of deixis in detailed analyses of social activities across cultures, including religious ritual, specifically the situated words and gestures of shamanic ceremonies that are relevant to the present example.[20] The DST-based cognitive approach seems to be compatible with Hanks's framework. It is also compatible with the principles of CSR, outlined in the Introduction, which take natural cognitive processes to be the source of religious effects—when modified by institutionalised context and interpretation.

3 APPLYING DST TO A RITUAL STRUCTURE: DEIXIS IN THE TRIDENTINE MASS

It is time to take a look at the ritual itself and the central formula about which so much ink has been spilled. Ritual verbal formulae are embedded in live multimodal performances, experienced in the minds and bodies of participants. We are particularly concerned with the little word *hoc*, which is usually translated as 'this' in English and in other languages, by 'this' and its equivalents. But the semantics of the Latin morpheme *hoc* are better glossed as 'thing or stuff here' (cf. above section 1.2). By 'semantics' here we mean the bare bones of conventionally understood meaning, before they receive contextual flesh. When you utter this or other deictic words, you and your hearers can only know what you fully mean and refer to, if you are in a context, or know about a context, reciprocally known among two or more participants. There are ways to ensure this, and collective ritual is one of them. Consider first the text alone. This is one of the high points, if not *the* high point of the ritual.[21]

[priest]. Qui pridie quam pateretur, accepit panem in sanctas ac venerabiles manus suas, et elevatis oculis in coelum ad te Deum Patrem suum omnipotentem tibi gratias agens, bene+dixit, fregit, deditque discipulis suis, dicens: Accipite, et manducate ex hoc omnes:	[priest]. Who, the day before He suffered, took bread into His holy and venerable hands, and having raised His eyes to heaven to you, God, His Almighty Father, giving thanks to You, He blessed+it, broke it, and gave it to His disciples, saying: "Take and eat of this, all of you,
HOC EST ENIM CORPUS MEUM.	FOR THIS IS MY BODY."

The meaning of the deictic word HOC (*this thing*) depends on its integration in the actually performed ritual—a lived mental event in the minds of the participants. Here we can only examine an instance of such an event indirectly, conveying only bare indications of the expressive effects in non-linguistic modalities. The integrated experience includes vision, relative positioning of participants, clothing, bodily postures, and lighting. In addition, there are auditory and olfactory effects: the ringing of bells and the diffusion of incense at the moment when the sacred object is revealed.

The gestures and postures are specified in extraordinary detail, and synchronised with the speaking of the text in the rubrics of the *Missale Romanum* of 1962. The speaking of the capitalised words is inserted into a sequence of ritual actions that have cognitive and affective functions:

with his elbows placed upon the Altar, standing with his head inclined, he pronounces distinctly, reverently, and secretly the words of the consecration over the Host [. . .], and holding his own Host with his thumbs and finger, he says:

HOC EST ENIM CORPUS MEUM

When this has been said, the Celebrant, holding the Host between his aforementioned thumbs and index fingers upon the Altar, with the remaining fingers of the hand extended, and at the same time [. . .], genuflecting, he adores It. Then he arises, and as much as he can comfortably do, elevates the Host in the air, and directing his eyes toward It [. . .], shows it reverently to the people, for their adoration. And soon he reverently replaces It upon the Corporal with his right hand only, in the same place from which he raised It, and without interruption. He does not disjoin his thumbs and index fingers up to the ablution of the fingers after the Communion, except when he must touch or handle the consecrated Host.
When the consecrated Host has been replaced on the Corporal, he genuflects and venerates It. [. . .]

The minister warns the faithful a little before the Consecration with a ring of the small bell.[. . .] and with his right hand rings the small bell three times at [the] elevation of [the Host] . . .[22]

The prescribed gestures are concerned with manipulation of the object or with hand movements close to it. Manual actions on or close to an object are intuitively connected with altering it. Doctrinally, this alteration is expounded in the theory of transubstantiation. One particular effect of the text in combination with actions is to bring the priest manipulating the bread in present time into alignment with the mental representation of Jesus in the past-time narrative that he is reciting—'taking' into his hands and 'blessing' the bread (marked by + in the rubrics).

The next action is the priest bending low over the wafer that he is holding close to his body and focusing his downward gaze on. These actions are not totally visible to the participants in the Tridentine mass; they are executed in the priest's personal space.[23] Of central importance here is the action of 'elevation'—the bringing of the wafer out of the priest's invisible personal space into the upper visual field of the observers: 'he arises and, as much as he can comfortably do, elevates the Host [i.e. the now consecrated wafer] in the air . . . directing his eyes toward It', as depicted in Figure 3. This sub-event of the ritual has the cognitive and social effect of 'showing'—that is, directing collective attention to the ritual object, in the relatively high (and thus metaphorically superior) region of shared physical space, causing a vertical saccade and mental effects entailed by that switch. Attention is further drawn to the object by bells and incense. The action is not simultaneous with the word 'hoc', but it immediately follows the sentence in which 'hoc' is uttered, thus leaving no doubt about the most immediate material referent intended—though the text makes the associated cognitions potentially more complex, as will be seen.

The required anchoring of the uttered 'hoc' is also ensured by the architectural space, the ritual building, which constructs height and 'depth' effects for the people inside it—depth in the sense of successive containing spaces nested within one another on the horizontal axis, at increasing distance, from nave to sanctuary to tabernacle (the box on the altar to contain the wafer). The entire structure constrains the attention space of the participants. The contribution of raised and nested spaces, enclosures, and seating orientation can be seen from the example given in Figure 3. The probable angle of gaze of the participants can be guessed from the positions and angles of the heads: eyes and minds converge on the object held aloft by the priest.

Although the non-linguistic elements are carefully constructed and coordinated for their effects, neither their full ritual impact, nor their codified doctrinal implications, can be accounted for unless one also accounts for their integration with language. It is the blending of non-linguistic context with the further cognitive effects achieved specifically by linguistic manipulation that produces concepts of change and transformation. The scholars of Port-Royal were, we have suggested in section 1.2, aware of this fact. We use the DST tool in an attempt to model the likely cognitive mechanisms involved in the conceptual processing of the verbal part of this ritual high point.

3.1 Ritual reference frames

Deictic expressions are relative to reference frames, whose centre is located at a speaker, or at some point contained in the speaker's reference frame—for example,

Figure 3 Hoc est corpus meum.
https://disqus.com/by/TotusTuusFamily/

deictic expressions may be related to a point in the past that is itself relative to a speaker, to a point in space close or distant to the speaker, or to a point that for the speaker is real and present or perhaps imaginary or even avowedly counterfactual. In the case of the speech event constituted by the eucharistic formula spoken by the priest, we have, on the face of it, a straightforward embedded narrative—that is, a reference frame located at a second speaker, Jesus, positioned in the past relative to priest and people, in their real here-and-now reference frames. However, it is important to emphasise that reference frames are not simply physical and spatial; they are constructed mentally with reference to evoked vantage points in space, time, and reality; and reference frames can be cognitively combined and shifted.

But we want to show that in its ritual context and in the performance itself the narrative can deliver more complicated cognitive effects that help to explain the nature of the ritual experience itself, the ideas surrounding it, and the variety of rationalisations that theology has thrown up. The context, that is, the reference frames for *this*, the tense/time marker *is*, and the pronoun *my*, is given by the piece of narrative preceding the crucial eucharistic formula *hoc est corpus meum*.

The hearers are aligned and oriented as we have described, facing a raised distant table with the speaker's back to them facing the table; his voice, it is worth noting, may be a distant reverberating mumble. Let us not exclude such theatrical effects. The deictic space in the here and now is partly—only partly—defined by this arrangement. The deictic space is a mental construct, including a mental construct of the physical surrounding space, and further mental 'spaces' are triggered by the words, combining with background knowledge frames and the liturgical episodes being performed. In the present case, lexical 'space builders' (Fauconnier 1994) construct 'mental spaces' that include at least the following: (1) temporal points in sequential narrative of the Passion, t_1 the day he suffered (*pateretur*) and t_2 the day before (*pridie quam*) he suffered, and (2) the word 'saying' (*dicens*) which signals words spoken by a new speaker, Jesus. The mental representations triggered in this way depend on and prompt cognitive frames stored in memory—the narrative sequence of the Passion and Crucifixion, and the visual representation of one episode in particular, the 'last supper', influenced by traditional images.

Figure 4, using DST format (outlined earlier, section 2), models the base deictic space for the piece of text above. For clarity, only focal elements of the sentence are modelled.

The diagram works like this. The thick axes are anchored in the here-now-real of the priest and people. In this space are times in the remote past, marked on the t-axis: the time point t_1 when 'Jesus suffered' (*pateretur*) and time t_2, the day before t_1. On the attention axis, there are three discourse referents to which the utterance is drawing attention: Jesus, the disciples, and the bread, each with positions of relative attentional 'closeness' to S, and coordinates running through the discourse space, as usual in DST. Jesus, unsurprisingly, is the most foregrounded referent by grammatical structure (word order). The arrows are directed actions that take place at t_1 and relate the agent Jesus to the bread (*panem*) and to the disciples by two natural vectors, one (a force vector) exerting a 'giving' force on the bread, the other (a displacement vector) transferring it from one place to another (from Jesus to the disciples)—all shown schematically.[24] Note that all this is drawn as 'located' in the reality plane of the base coordinate system, that of the performing priest S_1 and the participants.[25] If S_1 were representing the actions as a 'maybe' or a falsehood or a fantasy, they would have coordinates at the mid-point on the m-axis (horizontal axis) or at its end point. While the taking, blessing, breaking, and giving are all actions of Jesus in the past, it is important to note that in the *present* the priest is, simultaneously with the words he is speaking to report (and cause his hearers to mentally represent) Jesus's actions, taking, blessing, and breaking the white wafer disk on the square cloth ('corporal', basically Latin for 'the thing to do with the body') on the altar.

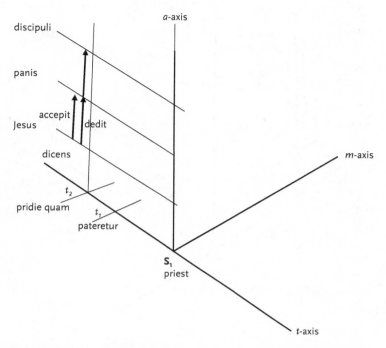

Figure 4 Jesus, the day before he suffered, took bread . . . and gave it to his disciples.

Then we come to the word *dicens* (saying), a crucial space builder, prompting any human hearer processing language to set up a mental space in which there is another speaker uttering their own words, bracketed off, as it were, from the words of the main speaker, here S_1. That may seem a pretentious way to describe a simple bit of 'direct speech', but it is something that only humans do, a type of metarepresentation. Figure 5 below shows this embedded direct speech in an idealised form in dashed lines as an embedded set of coordinates located at Jesus, new speaker S_2. It is this space, as we shall see later, that is capable of slippage during processing.

In Figure 5 the direct speech space is an embedded deictic space anchored at Jesus as speaker in the remote past relative to the 'now' of S_1 in the base deictic space. It is a present-in-the-past space, in which Jesus's words appear in the present tense, referring to *his* 'now'.

The performative dimension of the base speech event is important: while Jesus is immediately understood as the grammatical subject of *dicens*, and as the S_2 of the embedded space relative to him, the priest himself is speaking the very words introduced by *dicens*. Furthermore, in the written script, the conventional `+´ marks the moment at which the priest moves his right hand slightly above the wafer tracing the shape of a cross, though Jesus did not (one assumes) make that specific sign (see Figure 3). So the priest's action is in the present base coordinates even though the narrated action of Jesus is in a narrated past, where the exact blessing act is not

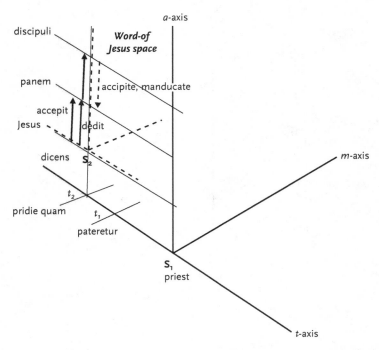

Figure 5 Jesus, the day before he suffered, took bread . . . and gave it to his disciples, saying: 'Take, eat . . .'

specified. Note that all actions are represented in the plane at m = 0 on the *m-axis*, that is, as *real* and factual rather than as possible or probable or counterfactual.

This may sound complicated but is only part of the complexity the mind constructs as it represents a conceptualisation prompted by the words in their context. This is the sort of thing the human mind/brain does with language all the time. It is all we need before moving ahead to examine what the brain constructs next for the crucial words *hoc est enim corpus meum*. . . . We will look specifically at *this, my*, and *you*.

3.2 The deictic expressions *hoc/this* and *meum/my*

In this next part of the sentence, the relative salience of the referents changes slightly: we still have *Jesus*, but now the *disciples* are not in focus—rather the relation between Jesus and the loaf of bread assumed to be in front of him, in his hands. Figure 6 attempts to model the essential deictic elements of the focal sentence, 'this is my body' (*hoc est corpus meum*), which is spoken in the verbal context modelled in Figure 5 above. Here all the relations between referents are in the embedded present-in-the-past space anchored on the referent *Jesus*.

It is essential to note, as the Port-Royal *Logique* did, that *hoc/this* is understood as referring to *the loaf*. Not any old loaf but the one in Jesus's hands. Linguistically *hoc/*

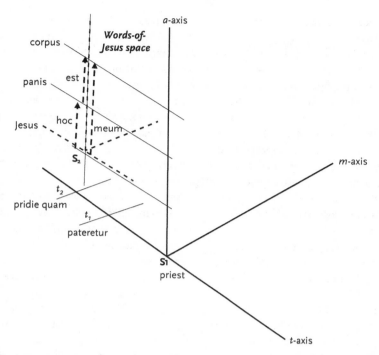

Figure 6 *hoc est enim corpus meum/for this is my bo*dy, in its verbally triggered context: conceptualization of embedded present-in-past space.

this is taken to be textually part of a chain: *panem . . . ex hoc . . . hoc.* This is not simply a linguistic link—there is no *actual* linkage, only sequencing of words and cognitive inferencing by a hearer of the text following principles of relevance.[26] This combines crucially with a second semantic element of *hoc*, namely, that, as opposed to say *ille* or *iste, hoc/this* anchors a referent primarily in the peripersonal space of a speaker S.

The three dashed upward pointing arrows in the embedded direct speech space at t_2 are natural position vectors that DST uses to model such basic deictic relations. Thus, in Figure 6, the tail of the arrow labelled *hoc* (this thing) locates the loaf in Jesus's peripersonal space (not by a grammatical reference back to *panis* but to this thing understood to be the loaf of bread). The longer dotted arrow, labelled *meum* (my), is also a position vector,[27] modelling the meaning of the possessive pronoun *meum/my*, namely, its anchorage at S_2, i.e. at Jesus.

The crucial point for our analysis is that the embedded space of S_2 provides a sealed reference frame within which the word *hoc* (this) refers; it refers only to the space around S_2, the origin of that space. The same is true for *meum* (my); it can refer only to the speaker in the same embedded reference frame. However, as we noted earlier, direct speech spaces can be unstable, and we return to this point below. Before doing so, something needs to be said about the word *est* (is).

This verb *est* is also deictic, temporally deictic, in the sense that it ties the *x-be-y* relation to the moment of speaking. Importantly, this 'copula' verb has very little by way of conventional semantics and is always interpreted as a function of context; many languages (e.g. Russian, Chinese) do not bother with it for most contexts. Nonetheless there are two broad semantic relations associated with the copular verb: existence ('there is a tree in the garden'), attribution of properties of different types including class membership ('the tree is an oak', 'the tree is tall' . . .), roles ('she is the boss'), and the like. All these relations, it can be argued, are derived from (*not* reduced to) location relations and modelled by natural position vectors: there are objects and people, and they can appear in particular places relative to other objects, and can have properties, roles, and functions 'attached' to them. That is fine for existence or presence, and for properties and roles, provided the two objects can be meaningfully related with an acceptable degree of cognitive effort. But in the case of *bread* and *body*, to make sense of them in an *is* sentence actually requires considerable cognitive effort. This is not the main object of the present enquiry. Suffice it to say that it may be precisely this requirement that qualifies it as a 'mystery', provided it occurs within a coherent ritual construct that that is both social and cognitive. The contextual approach gives us some idea of what may be going on to bring the mind to a quasi-coherent representation in which such 'mysteries' are entertained.

Embedded deictic spaces may be typically unstable, and deictic expressions within them may be cognitively costly to keep track of. Occasionally, even in ordinary speech, the various elements, especially the referents of pronouns, in the two different spaces (the base space and the direct speech space), may lose their anchorage within an embedded deictic space.[28] In the ritual context, the embedded deictic space of which S_2 is the deictic centre may be similarly unstable and slide into alignment with the base frame of reference of S_1: there are many non-linguistic devices that seem to encourage that.

3.3 Frame shifting, deixis, and 'real presence'

The idea of embedded deictic spaces acting as secondary reference frames related to the base reference system is not an ad hoc description but a technical idea needed to describe the working of other operations found in the human linguistic-conceptual apparatus (see examples in Chilton 2014). Religious rituals, including their verbal element, exploit these natural neurological capacities for the shifting of deictic reference frames (Whitney et al. 2009; Mizuno et al. 2011). In the present case, the time shifting of the past narrative space is brought about by concurrent non-linguistic factors. At the same time, the cognitive effects of the time shift combine with another well-studied phenomenon in both linguistic and non-linguistic processing, namely, conceptual blending (Fauconnier and Turner 2002). Using these tools, two relevant analyses suggest themselves.

Focusing first on the most mystifying part of the wording, it is possible that in processing the eucharistic formula the mind may perform a conceptual blending operation *within the embedded narrative space*, anchored on S_2 at time t_2, a remote time point relative to S_1—in other words, within the present-in-the-past space. How would such a conceptual blending work? Let us assume the participant's mind (not to mention the theologians' theorising) is struggling to process the *est/is* and conceptualising the relation is delayed; working memory still holds *bread* (both the perceived wafer displayed by the priest and the concept triggered by the word) and a conceptualisation of *my body* triggered by the linguistic input. Without explicit resolution of the *x-is-y* relation, it is possible that a cognitive compression *bread/body*, a conceptual blend in the sense of Fauconnier and Turner, might arise, aided by various props and bits of background knowledge. That is to say, the sentence *hoc est corpus meum* is only superficially a logical proposition, in its ritual setting, and is only indirectly a product of the elucubrations of theologians. Those present see a wafer and hear 'my body'. The copula *be* may be cognitively redundant: the cognitive product may simply be synchronous firing of representations of bread (visual) and body (abstract mental representation based on the heard word). Rationalised accounts such as transubstantiation, consubstantiation, and so forth result from this ritual experience, and may be thought of as the rational mind seeking to make sense of a cognition that is playing by different rules.

A second analysis involves the time-shifting of S_2's deictic space, which also results in a blend (of past and present). In terms of DST diagrams, the embedded (dashed) axes are translated, as shown in Figure 7, so that the origin of the embedded space is not positioned in the remote past at t_2, but coincides with the 'now' point $t = 0$ of S_1, the priest (and the participants in the ritual). It carries with it, of course, the

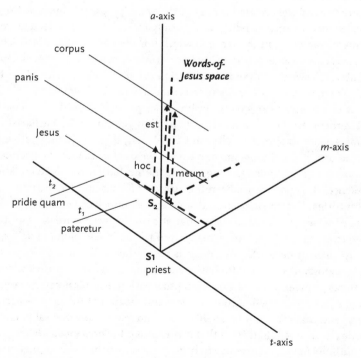

Figure 7 *hoc est enim corpus meum, for this is my bo*dy, frame shifted conceptualization.

blending operation on the concepts of bread and body described above. So we have simultaneously the bread-body blend and the past-present blend.

As one would expect, blending two separate deictic reference frames produces interesting effects. The most obvious cognitive yield after the shifting of the S_2 reference frame into alignment with the S_1 frame (the base frame) is that *hoc/this* now refers into two spaces simultaneously. As the authors of the Port-Royal *Logique* understood, *hoc* would be expected—from a logical viewpoint—to refer into Jesus's mental space: *hoc* refers to the object in front of Jesus on a particular evening, as shown in Figure 6. After the transformation diagrammed in Figure 7, the result is a kind of referential double vision. The demonstrative pronoun *hoc* refers to Jesus's bread in Jesus's time frame, when Jesus (performed by the priest) mysteriously asserts the bread-body blend.[29] At the same time, because the priest is miming Jesus's actions and voicing the words he is reporting, the *hoc* expression can refer to the altar bread in S_1. Normally, or in strictly logical terms, the deictic expression *hoc* can only refer to one thing at one time, but the elaborately triggered time-shift blend, in itself simply a process of the human mental apparatus, can give rise to such experiential phenomena.

In more general terms, the prevailing cognitive effect of this frame-shift blend is a temporal *compression*—perhaps experienced as something more like a temporal suspension, or better, dissolution of temporal deixis. The present in the past becomes the past in the present: the presence of Jesus in the embedded past-anchored axis system becomes *a presence* in the base space of priest and hearers. This is not simply a play on the two closely related senses of the word 'presence'. The effecting of the conceptual structure analysed diagrammatically in Figure 7 can indeed be regarded as a cognitive *presencing*, in the sense in which it is discussed by Iain McGilchrist; in this case, it is conceivable that the ritual performance brings about (or is capable of bringing about) a switch to predominantly right-hemispheric systems of the brain.[30] As noted earlier, all this is mentally represented in what DST geometry calls the *realis* plane at $m = 0$. This brings us to several other possible cognitive effects that are reflected in theological rationalisations about what goes on in the Eucharist.

The frame-shift account, modelled in DST format, might explain another important feature of the ritual phenomenon we are looking at, together with one of the most important of Catholic teachings about the Eucharist: the doctrine known as 'Real Presence'. This notion has been the attractor for discussion, dispute, and conflict for centuries. The core idea promulgated at the Council of Trent is that when the bread and wine are presented in the eucharistic rite with the words and gestures we have been examining, they change 'really' into the body and blood of Jesus, who is thus 'really' present here and now. What is meant by 'really' is another part of the story. It is impossible to do justice to the enormous range, and centuries-long intellectual efforts to make sense of this conceptualisation. Even if it can never be made sense of in some intellectual frame, this does not mean that it has to be accepted as a 'mystery' and that it cannot be scientifically understood *qua* mental phenomenon (unless one rejects out of hand that that is what it is). The present cognitive-linguistic account outlined here is an attempt to begin to describe this mental phenomenon.

One possible way in which Jesus and priest merge, though not the precise way described in the diagram of Figure 7, would result from actually co-locating S_1 (priest) with S_2 (Jesus) at the same deictic centre (the one in the base space for S_1). Even the version in Figure 7, where Jesus and priest have separate discourse referent coordinates, would bring S_1 and S_2 into cognitive proximity.[31] This effect emerges from the presencing operation brought about in the context of the ritual.[32] In theological and doctrinal commentaries, the priest is said to be acting *in persona Christi*, that is, 'in the persona, or role, of Christ'. (In Latin, *persona* is the character mask worn by actors in classical theatre.) What this suggests is that ritual performance precedes theology and doctrine, which are rationalisations after the fact based on intuitively experienced ritual experiences. Over time the influence is not one way, since rationalisations can feed back into performance.

As already suggested, the most abstruse and historically most contested of theological theories, transubstantiation, may be an attempt to rationalise a cognitive experience generated by a ritual device that is both linguistic and non-linguistic. What might a general cognitive-linguistic explication of the eucharistic transformation look like? Here is an outline. Jesus' deictic present is transformed (as the geometrical transformation of DST shows) into the present of priest and people; his temporal coordinate is now that of the priest and the priest's hearers. Also, the relations between all referents in Jesus's S_2 space are simply transferred across into the present, including the *est* relation vector that produces the bread-body compression blend, as outlined earlier. At the point where the verbal input *hoc est corpus meum* occurs, it combines with the non-verbal ritual apparatus, and is indeed already contextualised by it. The non-verbal apparatus prompts the 'presencing' frame shift in the mental representation set up by the verbal input. A key bit of the non-verbal action is the handling of the wafer by the priest in his peripersonal space on the altar table followed by 'elevation'—the priest raises the wafer into the upper visual field. As you see the wafer aloft, the cognitive-linguistic 'presencing' shift takes place: both Jesus and host are 'present' cognitively. In cognitive terms, we have a complex 'blend' mentally constructed from linguistic and structured sensory prompts. As a doctrine, the theory of transubstantiation may have emerged over time as an attempt to rationalise intricate liturgical effects that have, largely, their own prior evolution.

4 OVERVIEW

We have introduced some novel procedures in the study of religious ritual, procedures that focus on language as an integral constituent, while taking the overall position that the nature of contextualised cognition is fundamental. There are two main perspectives: understanding the mechanisms of ritual language at a micro-analytic level and taking account of the historical meta-representations of ritual in doctrinal discourses.

4.1 Analysing ritual language

In this chapter, particularly in the second half, we have aimed to demonstrate how ritual language is integrated with physical actions and settings—or, more precisely, with the ways in which the human mind entertains conceptualisations and emotions stimulated by such integration. An implication of this approach is that the human language system depends on and accesses the same cognitive systems as other forms of human action and mentation. To do this we need an appropriate kind of linguistics. What tools are available? Neither traditional descriptive linguistics nor a linguistics based on the postulate of an autonomous faculty modelled in terms of formal rules have this capability perspective—it is simply not built into their goals and assumptions. It should go without saying, incidentally, that the assumption, still rife among sociologists and anthropologists, that language is about information transfer, needs to be dropped.

Cognitive linguistics is a paradigm that connects language knowledge to other cognitive systems. It is a set of linked research paradigms and theories that broadly incorporate the findings of cognitive science and make links with experimental psychology and neuroscience. Cross-disciplinary concerns such as action schemata (frames), categorisation, and concept formation are central; motor systems, spatial cognition, and vision play a particularly important role in modelling both lexical and grammatical structures. The particular theory we have applied in section 3 of this chapter is a recent cognitive-linguistic model (Deictic Space Theory) that focuses on the fundamental phenomenon of deixis and deictic reference frames that is ultimately based on the probably unique human ability to point meaningfully to establish joint attention in spatial coordinates (Tomasello 2006). What we have aimed at, then, in the second part of this chapter is to apply this perspective to understanding a specific piece of religious ritual language in its ritual context. Specifically, we focus on potential cognitive effects (and potential emotional effects) yielded by words interwoven with actions and objects in particular kinds of physical spaces. In fact, of course, specific uses of language are themselves forms of action. It is possible, in principle at least, to trace back these multiple-source effects to neural processes. This is why we have from time to time noted important neurological studies directly relevant to the phenomenology.

The micro-level approach, particularly at the level at which linguistic minutiae are processed, is uncommon in disciplines concerned with religious experience, belief, and practice, even those with a declared cognitive orientation. Linguistic micro-analysis can, however, be justified as a means of gaining insight into underlying mental (and also physiological) processes. There is a further justification. Ritual behaviour is highly detailed (whether in religious performance, doctrinal prescriptions, or pathological conditions such as OCD). Some of the detail of compulsive and compelled action may be arbitrary, a type of (self-)control, but equally it may be *motivated* in the sense of intentionally generating conceptual representation integrated with effects such as reduction of cognitive vigilance, refocusing of attention, emotional arousal or damping, and self-monitoring (cf. McNamara 2014; Schjoedt et al. 2013). This is why a cognitive-linguistic and generally cognitive-semiotic micro-analysis is justified. We recognise, however, that routinisation has cognitive effects in a participant's attention to detail, as discussed by Whitehouse (2004).

4.2 Historical and doctrinal perspectives

Religious rituals are culturally complex human institutions that are embedded in histories of cultural evolution. This is why the first part of this chapter began with a historical perspective. There is an enormous amount of writing devoted to the history of the Christian eucharistic ritual, and it was certainly not our purpose to add to this or even to draw on it. We do, however, think that it is important in studying any ritual in its detailed form to treat it in the historical context of the religious institutions in which it is set, and that includes internal histories of the discourses of those institutions.

In section 1 of the present chapter, we entered into the long history of Christian ritual at the point where doctrinal conflicts concerning the interpretation of the Eucharist came to the fore. It is important to note that this involves attending to non-ritual religious discourse, specifically doctrinal discourse, sharpened by internal conflicts, themselves a product of exegetic reflection (as well as socio-political factors). This distinction is recognised by a number of authors working in the paradigm of cognitive science of religion (cf. Introduction, this volume). In particular, Whitehouse (2004) outlines a theory of 'modes of religiosity' that distinguishes between two 'attractor positions': ritual action (ranging from high-arousal episodes to routinised) and doctrinal (ranging from 'spontaneous exegetic reflection' to institutionalised religious experts). Exegetic reflection, such as we find in the historical analyses examined in section 1, can feed back into the structure of rituals, or, depending on the degree of institutional control, be used to maintain existing ritual practice. Whether ritual is historically prior to doctrine in the development of any religion, or the reverse, is another question; it seems more plausible to assume the prior evolution of ritual. The two halves of our chapter reflect the dynamic interaction between these two poles at a particularly critical moment in Western religious thinking, albeit one that was continuous with earlier periods. The doctrinal mode is essentially a form of language-dependant metarepresentation.

When exegetic conflict emerges, as in the early modern period in Europe, it can yield, within the religious community itself, descriptions, analyses, and claims that are focused particularly on language, though also on actions, objects, and spaces. And what emerges from that strand of European-Christian exegetic thinking, influenced by humanistic philosophical tendencies, is a strand that that pays attention to the mental processing of the world, including the narrated biblical world and the world of religious activity. Intriguingly, early modern approaches to religious disputes about the interpretation of ritual, while continuing medieval enquiries into the relation between language, mind, and world, seem to foreshadow modern cognitive approaches to verbalisation, both cognitive and pragmatic. What these early modern thinkers did not do, of course, and were unable to do, was stand back sufficiently far to be able to extend the cognitivist line of argument as a way of explaining the disputed ritual (and indeed the practice of exegesis itself) as products of the human mind and human institutions.

In conclusion, we repeat that in order to understand ritual practices, we need an integrated view of language, appropriate tools to analyse their cognitive effects, and a due consideration of modes such as exegetic reasoning in their institutional and cognitive environments. Incorporating language into the study of human religions in general could have important consequences. Religious practices may, for example, vary, across cultures and over time, in terms of the degree to which language is involved. More fundamentally, it is still not clear to what extent religious experience itself is actually dependent on language, either evolutionarily or culturally.

NOTES

1. We use this name to refer to the Christian ritual also known as the Lord's Supper, Holy Communion, and the Mass, among other names.
2. The term 'radical pragmatics' is used here in the robust sense thus indicated; in recent pragmatic theory, the term covers a range of more specific positions on the relation between sentence meaning and utterance meaning, the details of which are not of immediate relevance. For discussion and further references, see Cole (1981), Jaszczolt (2002), and Huang (2014a and 2014b).
3. Council of Trent, ed. and trans. by J. Waterworth (1848), p. 82: Session the Thirteenth, Being the third under the Sovereign Pontiff, Julius III., celebrated on the eleventh day of October, 1551. Decree Concerning the Most Holy Sacrament of the Eucharist. Canon 1.
4. Since we are contrasting metaphorical with 'deictic' readings, we do not here explore the different understandings of the term 'metaphor', including the modern cognitive theories of metaphor and conceptual 'embodiment', which are referred to in several chapters of the present volume. On the use of the term 'metaphor' in a seventeenth-century hermeneutic context, see the discussion of Keach (1681) below.
5. The enormous popularity of Henry's commentary superseded that of an earlier three-volume compilation by English non-conformist Matthew Poole, which had appeared first in Latin (Poole 1669–1676) and subsequently in an English translation (Poole 1683–1685).
6. This type of hermeneutic tool originated in Protestant circles on the continent in the sixteenth century; the broad structure of Keach's work is derived from the pioneering classification by German theologian and biblical critic Salomon Glass (1593–1656), whose *Philologia Sacra* first appeared in 1623 and was augmented and revised in multiple subsequent editions.
7. Keach's tract was aimed at the general lay reader; a similar theoretical orientation, but one aimed more specifically at the clerical reader, can be found in John Wilkins's manuals on preaching (1646) and on prayer (1651).
8. For a detailed discussion of the role of the 'plain style' in the methodological ethos of the Royal Society, and for further references to the extensive recent literature on the topic, see Hüllen (1989). The notion of a 'plain style' is deployed by Robert Boyle both in his scientific work and also in his discussion of the style of the New Testament (Boyle 1663).
9. On linguistic engineering of this sort, under the rubric of the philosophical language scheme devised by John Wilkins under the auspices of the Royal Society, see Slaughter (1982) and Lewis (2007).
10. For a useful and accessible discussion of the problematic status of 'literal meaning' within modern linguistic theory, see Recanati (2003).

11. A representative example of such grammars is that of Thomas of Erfurt, of which there is an edition and translation by Bursill-Hall (1972); this includes one of the best available short introductions to speculative grammar for the non-specialist reader. On the larger context of medieval theories of the Eucharist, see Adams (2010).

12. This is what those employing Prototype Theory call a 'basic level' category, on which see Taylor (1989, chapter 3).

13. For an accessible account of deixis from the viewpoint of language acquisition, see Roger Brown's aptly entitled study 'How shall a thing be called?' (Brown 1958). For a discussion within a more formal linguistic framework, see the critique of the 'code' model of language in the introductory chapters of Sperber and Wilson (1995).

14. See Fauconnier and Turner (2002) and on religious conceptualisation Turner (2003); see also the Introduction to the present volume and Antović, chapter 15, this volume).

15. The term 'irreal' is intended to reflect the technical term 'irrealis mood' used in linguistics to refer to morphologically marked semantic categories such as 'subjunctive', 'conditional', and many others that are used to express states of affairs not asserted to be (yet) true. Their existence testifies to an underlying cognitive category that we label 'irreal' here. Morphological marking is not the only way it is expressed cross-linguistically.

16. Whether the direction in relation to the body is conventionally up-down, front-back, back, back-front, etc. varies across languages. In English we speak of the past being behind us and the future in front; speakers of Aymara do the reverse. The left-right orientation of the t-axis in the diagrams is not significant in itself, but the bi-directionality centred on self is.

17. Dopamine activity in religious experiences including ritual and reduced serotonin activity are noted also by McNamara (2014, pp. 139–141, 216–217; also chapter 6 of the present volume), who links such 'transient' changes with a suspension of subjective agency and intentionality at the onset of a religious experience (2009, pp. 143–144)—a point that may be linked further with the hypothesis of 'cognitive depletion' during ritual proposed by Schjoedt et al. (2013).

18. On this modelling of the verb give, see Chilton (2014), pp. 75–79.

19. For pronouns I and you, right anterior insula and precuneus (Mizuno et al. 2011). Deictic shifts in narrative comprehension involve the right temporal gyrus, precuneus, and bilaterally posterior/middle cingulate (Whitney et al. 2009). See also references in Chilton (2014, pp. 284–305).

20. One of his examples involves a Mayan shaman, whose ritual practices involve deictic phenomena somewhat similar to those of a priest in the ritual of the Catholic mass (Hanks 2005, pp. 201–204).

21. Quoted here in the Latin form in which it was authorised by the Council of Trent in the Missale Romanum in 1570 and again in the 1962 edition. Referred to as the Tridentine Mass and now also known as 'the extraordinary form'. The printed words themselves are products of an institutional chain of authorisation that establishes their validity. The text used here is taken from the website of the Fordham University Internet History Sourcebooks Project: http://sourcebooks.fordham.edu/basis/latinmass2.asp.

22. The Rubrics of the Missale Romanum 1962, translated into English by Rev. Dennis Duvelius, taken from http://www.sanctamissa.org/en/rubrics/.

23. In the 'ordinary' form of the mass, the entire ritual is performed facing the participants, as in the performances analysed in chapter 17 by Monika Kopytowska. The semiotic and cognitive effects are significantly different, but the role of the wafer as the deictic anchor of hoc or its vernacular equivalent, is the same.

24. Note that 'take' (accipere) is the converse of 'give' (dare). Strictly speaking, 'take' involves two vectors, one directed toward the object and one toward the same actor as receiver of the object.

25. Subscripts are used to distinguish one S from another if there are more than one, as is the case in the emerging deictic space model here.

26. There is also no grammatical linkage: *hoc* (neuter) is not the same gender as *panis* (masculine), so there is no link via the word form per se. In fact *hoc/this* in the text functions as a noun, something like 'this thing here'. The reference to the loaf can only be established by inference and, if one is present, perception of the object and perhaps a pointing or showing gesture. All this was pointed out by the Port-Royal writers (cf. Rosier-Catach 2014, pp. 542–544).
27. Possession is conceptually related to position: see Chilton (2014), pp. 57–58.
28. This happens occasionally in spoken sentences, where quotation marks cannot be clearly spoken—as when a hearer may be unsure, without context, of who the 'I' is in an ordinary sentence like *John said this will do the job* or *John said I will do it*. We cannot be sure to what or to whom exactly 'this' or 'I' refer, if markers of embedding are unclear or lost; hearers probably rely mainly on context to infer the intended referent.
29. In terms of speech act theory (Searle 2010), *assertives* are propositional (they are taken as intended to be true or false). Within a framework of belief, this may be the case, or it may cause a cognitive challenge yielding further cognitive effects (cognitive suspension and search for interpretation). The utterance could also be thought of as a *declaration* (in Searle's sense) creating a represented 'reality'. It seems likely that religious speech acts of this kind are special; they certainly require further cognitive investigation.
30. McGilchrist (2010), pp. 56, 93, 197, 232, 244, 255, and chapter 6 this volume. Compare the notion of 'presencing' as a linguistic-cognitive operator (Chilton 2014, pp. 124–132, discussing cognitive effects in the English tense system). There is more than one type of presencing operator in language; the frame shift discussed in the present chapter is one of them.
31. Compare Figure 3: the ritual space provides vertical alignment of priest, wafer, and Jesus, the latter in three-dimensional representation (the crucifix).
32. The point may be generalised. Sørensen (2007, p. 289): 'The structural presence of gods, spirits, ancestors, and holy figures is exactly the defining characteristic of magical and religious rituals'. McCauley and Lawson (2002) use a cognitive event frame approach that distinguishes between the agent and patient slots in the ritual action frame. In the Eucharist, the god is present in the patient slot: the priest transforms bread and wine into the god's body and blood. They also claim that if the god is in the patient role, the ritual is likely to be a frequently repeatable one, and also that in rituals in which the god is more immediately present the ritual is likely to be more central to the participating community; broadly speaking, the cognitive characteristics of the Eucharist bear out these claims.

REFERENCES

Adams, M. M. (2010). *Some Later Medieval Theories of the Eucharist: Thomas Aquinas, Gilles of Rome, Duns Scotus, and William Ockham*. Oxford: Oxford University Press.
Arnauld, A. (1781 [1667]). *La perpétuité de la foi de l'eglise catholique touchant l'eucharistie*. A Paris, & se vend à Lausanne: Chez Sigismond d'Arnay & compagnie.
Arnauld, A. and P. Nicole (1662). *La logique, ou l'art de penser*. Paris: Jean Guignart, Charles Savreux, & Jean de Lavnay.
Boyle, R. W. (1663). *Some Considerations Touching the Style of the H. Scriptures*. London: Henry Herringman.
Brown, R. (1958). How shall a thing be called? *Psychological Review* 65 (1), 14–21.
Bühler, K. (1990 [1934]). *The Theory of Language: The Representational Function of Language*. Translated by D. F. Goodwin. Amsterdam: John Benjamins. [Translation of Bühler, K. 1934. *Sprachtehorie. Die Darstellungsfunktion der Sprache*. Stuttgart: Fischer Verlag.]
Bursill-Hall, G. L. (1972). *Grammatica Speculativa of Thomas of Erfurt*. London: Longman.

Chilton, P. (2014). *Language, Space and Mind*. Cambridge: Cambridge University Press.

Cole, P. (1981). *Radical Pragmatics*. New York: Academic Press.

Council of Trent (1848 [1551]). *The Canons and Decrees of the Sacred and Oecumenical Council of Trent*. Edited and translated by J. Waterworth. London: Dolman.

Fauconnier, G. (1994). *Mental Spaces: Aspects of Meaning Construction in Natural Language*. Cambridge: Cambridge University Press.

Fauconnier, G. and M. Turner (2002). *The Way We Think: Conceptual Blending and the Mind's Hidden Complexities*. New York: Basic Books.

Glass, S. (1623). *Philologiæ sacræ, qva totius sacrosanctæ Veteris & Novi Testamenti scripturæ, tum stylus & literatura, tum sensus & genuinæ interpretationis ratio expenditur, libri duo*. Jena: Typis & Sumtibus Tobiæ Steinmanni.

Hanks, W. (2005). Explorations in the deictic field. *Current Anthropology* 46(2), 191–220.

Henry, Matthew (1721–1725). *An exposition of all the books of the Old and New Testament: wherein the chapters are summ'd up in contents*. London: printed for J. Clark and R. Hett, J. Knapton, J. and B. Sprint, J. Darby, D. Midwinter [and 13 others].

Huang, Y. (2014a). *The Oxford Dictionary of Pragmatics*. Oxford: Oxford University Press.

Huang, Y. (2014b). *Pragmatics*. Second edition. Oxford: Oxford University Press.

Hüllen, W. (1989). *'Their Manner of Discourse': Nachdenken über Sprache im Umkreis der Royal Society*. Tübingen: Gunter Narr.

Jaszczolt, K. (2002). *Semantics and Pragmatics: Meaning in Language and Discourse*. London: Longman.

Keach, B. (1681). *Tropologia: A Key to Open Scripture-Metaphors*. London: Enoch Prosser.

Lewis, R. (2007). *Language, Mind and Nature: Artificial Languages in England from Bacon to Locke*. Cambridge: Cambridge University Press.

Locke, J. (1690). *An Essay Concerning Human Understanding*. London: Thomas Basset.

McCauley, R. N. and E. T. Lawson (2002). *Bringing Ritual to Mind*. Cambridge: Cambridge University Press.

McGilchrist, I. (2010). *The Master and His Emissary: The Divided Brain and the Making of the Western World*. New Haven: Yale University Press.

McNamara, P. (2014 [2009]). *The Neuroscience of Religious Experience*. Cambridge: Cambridge University Press.

MacWhinney, B. (2005). The emergence of grammar from perspective. In D. Pecher and R. A. Zwaan (eds.), *Grounding Cognition: The Role of Perception and Action in Memory, Language and Thinking*, pp. 198–223. Cambridge: Cambridge University Press.

Mizuno, A., Y. Liu, D. L. Williams, T. A. Keller, N. J. Minshew, and M. A. Just (2011). The neural basis of deictic shifting in linguistic perspective-taking in high-functioning autism. *Brain* 134, 2422–2435.

Poole, M. (1669–1676). *Synopsis criticorum aliorumque S. Scripturæ interpretum*. London: Cornelius Bee.

Poole, M. (1683–1685). *Annotations upon the Holy Bible*. London: Thomas Parkhurst, Dorman Newman, Jonathan Robinson, Bradbazon Ailmer, Thomas Cockeril and Benjamin Alsop.

Previc, F. H. (1998). The neuropsychology of 3D space. *Psychological Bulletin* 124, 123–164.

Previc, F. H. (2006). The role of the extrapersonal brain system in religious activity. *Consciousness and Cognition* 15, 500–539.

Previc, F. H. (2009). *The Dopaminergic Mind in Human Evolution and History*. Cambridge: Cambridge University Press.

Pustejovsky, J. (1998) The semantics of lexical underspecification. *Folia Linguistica* 32, 323–347.

Recanati, F. (2003). *Literal Meaning*. Cambridge: Cambridge University Press.

Rosier-Catach, I. (2004). *La Parole efficace: Signe, rituel, sacré*. Paris: Seuil.

Rosier-Catach, I. (2014). Les médiévaux et Port-Royal sur l'analyse de la formule de la consécration eucharistique. In S. Archaimbault, J. M. Fournier, and V. Raby (eds.), *Penser l'histoire des savoirs linguistiques: Hommage à Sylvain Auroux*, pp. 535–555. Paris: ENS Editions.

Schjoedt, U., J. Sørensen, K. L. Nielbo, D. Xygalatas, P. Mitkidis, and J. Bulbulia (2013). Cognitive resource depletion in religious interactions. *Religion, Brain & Behavior* 3(1), 39–86.

Searle, J. R. (2010). *Making the Social World*. Oxford: Oxford University Press.

Slaughter, M. M. (1982). *Universal Languages and Scientific Taxonomy in the Seventeenth Century*. Cambridge: Cambridge University Press.

Sørensen, J. (2003). The question of ritual. *Scripta Instituti Donneriani Aboensis* 18, 207–220.

Sørensen, J. (2007). Acts that work: A cognitive approach to ritual agency. *Method and Theory in the Study of Religion* 19, 281–300.

Sperber, D. and D. Wilson (1995 [1986]). *Relevance: Communication and Cognition*. Second edition. Oxford: Blackwell.

Taylor, J. R. (1989). *Linguistic Categorization: Prototypes in Linguistic Theory*. Oxford: Clarendon Press.

Tomasello, M. (2006). Why don't apes point? In N. J. Enfield and S. C. Levinson (eds.), *Roots of Human Sociality: Culture, Cognition and Interaction*, pp. 506–524. Oxford and New York: Berg.

Turner, M. (2003). Double-scope stories. In D. Herman (ed.), *Narrative Theory and the Cognitive Sciences*, pp. 117–142. Stanford, CA: CSLI.

Whitehouse, H. (2004). *Modes of Religiosity: A Cognitive Theory of Religious Transmission*. Walnut Creek, CA: Rowman Altamira.

Whitney, C., W. Huber, J. Klann, S. Weis, S. Krach, and T. Kircher (2009). Neural correlates of narrative shifts during auditory story comprehension. *Neuroimage* 47, 360–366.

Wilkins, J. (1646). *Ecclesiastes: or, A Discourse Concerning the Gift of Preaching as It Fals under the Rules of Art*. London: Samuel Gellibrand.

Wilkins, J. (1651). *A Discourse Concerning the Gift of Prayer: Shewing What It Is, Wherein It Consists, and How Far It Is Attainable by Industry*. London: Samuel Gellibrand.

CHAPTER 17

The Televisualization of Ritual

Spirituality, Spatiality, and Co-presence in Religious Broadcasting

MONIKA KOPYTOWSKA

The objective behind this chapter is to develop a theoretical framework for understanding the interface between religion, media, and social cognition, and to explain the role which language along with other semiotic resources—as they are used in the media—play in mediating religious experience and transforming the notion of *sacred space, sacred time*, and a sense of *communion* based on collective emotion. Churches have ceased to be the only centres of collective worship and prayer, and physical presence is no longer the prerequisite to participate in ceremonies, events, and other religious activities. Technology allows seekers of communion and spiritual experience to satisfy the *compulsion of proximity* by 'transporting' them into 'worship spaces' co-created by broadcasting media and offering mediated communal experience (Hoover 2006). The particular case we are considering here is that of the central ritual of the Roman Catholic Church (cf. also Cram and Chilton in chapter 16, this volume).

The analytic approach, which draws heavily upon the insights from Cognitive Critical Discourse Analysis, Deictic Space Theory, and Searle's theory of social ontology, places in the focus of its attention the notion of *distance* between the believers and spiritual reality as it is mediated for them by the institution of the Roman Catholic Church (hereafter 'the Church') and the media. The underlying assumption here is that while the intention and mission of the Church is to, firstly, *proximize* (bring epistemically and affectively 'closer') such spiritual reality to its believers through the genres of preaching, prayers, and rituals and secondly, to build up the 'body of Christ' (1 Corinthians 12:13) and create a community of the faithful, the media have become an important intermediary in this process.

The chapter focuses specifically on mediated rituals and discusses the role of metaphor and metonymy and other cognitive operations within discourse space (in their verbal and visual dimension) used to mediate spiritual experience and enrich the sense of community. We will demonstrate that both TV and radio, with their liveness and immediacy, provide the audience with a sense of participation and interaction as the semiotic properties of both media enable various types of spatial, temporal, and epistemic proximization and the resulting cognitive-affective responses. While the audio capability of the radio has been often linked to the *fides ex auditu* principle ('faith comes from hearing', Romans 10:17; see Lepa 2000, p. 79), it is also argued that the act of looking 'contributes to religious formation, and, indeed, constitutes a powerful practice of belief' (Morgan 1998, p. 3); and Antonio Barcelona in chapter 14 of this volume has examined the cognitive effects of traditional images in religious doctrine. In the case of mediated images, it is their indexical quality on the one hand and their constructed character on the other that are significant when it comes to understanding the perceptions, emotions, and value judgements of the viewer-believer. The indexical quality of images has to do with the 'true-to-life' quality that photographs and live TV have, and which other types of visual images do not have (Messaris and Abraham 2003). Acting as 'direct pointers', they carry with them 'an implicit guarantee of being closer to the truth than other forms of communication' (Messaris and Abraham 2003, p. 217), which 'could diminish the likelihood that viewers would question what they see' (p. 217). Yet, although images tend to be viewed by audiences as 'direct evidence', the 'constructed nature' of broadcast data, resulting from the choice of filming and editing techniques, can hardly be denied. For example, unlike the direct experience of the believer physically present in the church, the mediated experience of a TV viewer will be partly shaped by camera techniques and angles.

Combining the cognitive and the social aspects of the religion-communication interface, the present chapter brings together various themes discussed so far in this book, namely, a web of correlations between religious beliefs and religious practices, the nature of religious experience and its time-space embedding and conditioning, cognitive-affective aspects, as well as the axiological dimension. While accepting language as the main mediating tool and the constitutive character of cognitive operations within discourse space, we argue that yet another dimension should be added to the process of forming and shaping religious experience seen as part of social reality construction, namely, its mass-mediated character. Contemporary 'media culture' has transformed the way we understand, experience, and communicate religion. The semiotic properties of various media and their affordances have not only blurred time-space boundaries and changed the nature of individual and collective experience, but also fundamentally enhanced the emotional and axiological potential of religious messages. Various structural and functional aspects of this process, along with its social implications, will be addressed in the following sections.

1 SOCIAL COGNITION, SOCIAL CONSTRUCTION, AND CONCEPTUALIZATION

Religion and *social cognition* are increasingly prominent themes in the cognitive science of religion, which seeks to explain the origins and workings of religions.

Typically associated with the field of social psychology, the latter covers the processes involved in the perception, judgement, and memory of various social stimuli, the impact of social and affective factors on information processing, and the behavioural consequences of cognitive processes. Social schema theory, for example, places particular emphasis on how concepts are represented in the brain and categorized, along with interest in the processes that increase accessibility of schemas, namely, *salience* and *priming*. Rather than going into the details of this approach, my main aim here is to look at some aspects of the interface between the cognitive and the social which are relevant to the study of mediated religious experience. The dialectics of the two seems to be partly addressed in the questions posed by Searle (1995, pp. xi–xii): 'How does a mental reality, a world of consciousness, intentionality and other mental phenomena, fit into a world consisting entirely of physical particles in fields of force?'; and Berger and Luckmann (1991/1966, p. 30), 'How is it possible that subjective meanings *become* objective facticities?'. In an attempt to create the link between the objective and subjective aspects of social reality, the latter coined the term 'social construction' (Berger and Luckmann 1991/1966, p. 149), placing 'culture, language, discourse, and knowledge' in the centre of this process (Elder-Vass 2013, p. 8). For Berger and Luckmann (1991/1966), language indeed is a major society-forming tool, as it enables objectivization, institutionalization, and legitimization, merging the subjective mental representations of individuals into the fabric of social reality. Searle (1995) also argues that the construction of social reality is possible thanks to language, which according to him (Searle 2006, p. 14) has far more fundamental functions than simply allowing us to categorize, enable rational agreement, assert power, and so forth. The symbolic nature and the constitutive potential of language make it possible to explain why and how 'X counts as Y in context C'. Consequently, we see things as having a certain status, and in virtue of the collective acceptance of that status, they can perform functions that they could not perform otherwise. The very performance of speech acts creates social phenomena, provided people accept the declarations (Searle 1995, 2006, 2010).

Discourse theorists see *discourse* as the main society-forming agent, underlining its socially constitutive and socially constituted nature (Fairclough and Wodak 1997, p. 258). Fairclough (1992, p. 64) considers discourse the 'practice of not just representing, but signifying, constituting and constructing the world in meaning'; while van Dijk (1997, p. 8) regards discourse as a form of action, i.e. an intentional, controlled, purposeful human activity. The latter, in his socio-cognitive approach, argues that 'it makes sense to include in the concept of discourse not only observable verbal or non-verbal features, or social interaction and speech acts, but also the cognitive representations and strategies involved during the production or comprehension of discourse' (van Dijk 1990, p. 164). And this is where the notions of *conceptualization* and *construal*, discussed extensively within cognitive linguistics, gain particular relevance. Langacker (1988, p. 50) understands the former in terms of cognitive processing, and treats it 'in a maximally inclusive way comprising the domain of mental experience, sensory, emotive and kinesthetic sensations and extending to our awareness of the physical, social and the linguistic context'. Construal is for him the level of specificity at which the situation is characterized, background assumptions and expectations, the relative prominence accorded to various entities, as well as the perspective taken on the scene. Since 'linguistic coding is highly selective', a particular construction implies a selection of a particular image to structure the conceived situation for communicative purposes (Langacker 1990, pp. 214, 315). A language user, both in the process of production and the process of reception, can thus 'construe' a conceived situation in alternative ways, using different 'mental imagery' (Langacker 1987, 1988, 1990). The choice of a particular conceptualization depends on the speaker's purpose in a particular context. Langacker (1987, pp. 116–137) mentions the following construal operations: (1) selection—concerning the language users' capacity to selectively attend to some facets of a structure and ignore others; (2) perspective—concerning the choice of the position from which a conceived situation is viewed, and including four subtypes (figure/ground distinction, viewpoint, deixis, subjectivity/ objectivity); and (3) abstraction—related to our ability to establish commonalities between distinct phenomena, thereby organizing concepts into categories.

It is our argument here that another mediated dimension, or meta-level, should be added to Searle's model (1995, 2010) of social ontology because a substantial number of material and abstract social entities acquire meaning, 'quasi status functions', and 'deontic powers' in and through the media-generated context.[1] Also, we believe that it is the integration of cognitive linguistics that makes it possible to hypothesize about how both (religious) discourse producers and audiences make use of cognitive resources in their construal of time, space, knowledge, and values, in particular in the case of phenomena and events which are beyond the audience's immediate experience. Salience, achieved by selection and metonymic conceptualizations, is an important aspect of construal. So are judgement/comparison involving categorization (framing), metaphor, figure/ground, and perspective/situatedness encompassing deixis along with their spatiotemporal (including spatial image schemas), epistemic (common ground), and empathy dimensions (Croft and Cruse 2004). While we accept Searle's constitutive rule in the form 'X counts as Y in context C' (Searle 1995, p.28), we posit that construal operations are central to this process, especially in the case of mediated experience when the choices of discourse producers are likely to influence the conceptualizations of the audience, along with resulting value judgements and emotions. A new model explicating this process will be presented in section 4.

2 MEDIATED EXPERIENCE AND MEDIATIZATION OF RELIGION

Recent years have seen a growing interest in the interface of media and religion (Lyon 2000; Lynch 2005, 2007; Ammerman 2007; Mazur and McCarthy 2001; Mahan 2014). In 1922, Walter Lippmann wrote about media creating pictures in our minds, while in the 1970s Real (1977) introduced the term 'mass-mediated culture' to describe societies in which media provide our primary picture of people, places, and ideas. As pointed out by Newman (1996, p. 130), they have enabled 'new forms of perception and understanding'. One might even go as far as to claim that in the contemporary mediatized world Thompson's observation that '[o]ur experience of events which take place in contexts that are spatially and temporally remote [. . .] is an experience largely mediated by the institutions of mass communication' (1995, p. 216) could well be applied to various forms of *religious experience* related to *ritualized actions*. According to Hepp and Krönert (2010, p. 268) '"the media" are central mediators of "faith" in the present'. Following up on Couldry's (2003) assumption that they are the 'unquestioned centre of society', they claim that 'any form of religion and spirituality that wants to be in the "center" of societies has to be staged by "the media"' (Hepp and Krönert 2010, p. 268).

This fact seems to have been noticed by the Roman Catholic Church itself. While in the Vatican II decree on the means of social communication (*Inter Mirifica*) issued by Pope Paul VI on December 4, 1963, it was already acknowledged that 'technological discoveries [. . .] have most direct relation to men's minds' and 'have uncovered new avenues of communicating', three decades later another pastoral instruction concluded that 'human experience itself is an experience in media' (*Aetatis Novae*, Pontifical Council for Social Communications 1992, section 2). The Pontifical Council for Social Communications was thus established in 1989 and entrusted with the task of dealing 'with questions concerning the instruments of social communications, so that also by these means the message of salvation and human progress may serve the growth of civilization and morality' (John Paul II, Apostolic Constitution *Pastor Bonus*, 1988, article 169).[2] The objective has been to make 'the teaching of Christianity more interesting and effective' (*Communio et Progressio*, Pontifical Council for Social Communications 1971, section 131) and to identify 'new strategies for evangelization and catechesis through the application of communications technology and mass communications' (*Aetatis Novae*, Pontifical Council for Social Communications 1992, section 28). The Council has created a number of instructional documents for Catholics dealing with media use and effects. Since 1967, various media-related issues have been discussed by the pontiffs during the World Communications Days, celebrated annually. Despite its pro-media stance, however, the Church made a clear distinction between physical participation in religious rituals and communal life on the one hand and virtual presence on the other:

> Virtual reality is no substitute for the Real Presence of Christ in the Eucharist, the sacramental reality of the other sacraments, and shared worship in a flesh-and-blood human community. There are no sacraments on the Internet; and even the religious experiences possible there by the grace of God are insufficient apart from real-world interaction with other persons of faith. [. . .] At the same time, pastoral planning should consider how to lead people from cyberspace to true community and how, through teaching and catechesis, the Internet might subsequently be used to sustain and enrich them in their Christian commitment. (Pontifical Council for Social Communications, 2002)

It is precisely the difference between physical and mediated participation in religious events and rituals, and the cognitive-affective character of the latter, that is of interest to us in the present chapter. According to Stout and Buddenbaum (2008, p. 227), 'religion is increasingly mediated and the examples are ubiquitous: televangelism, religious radio, mega-churches, emergent churches, church-sponsored advertising campaigns, religious magazines, spiritual films and faith blogs to mention but a few'. Religion has thus more and more frequently been discussed from the perspective of *mediatization*, a dynamic process which is said to have fundamentally transformed the contemporary media-society interface (Hepp 2013; Hjarvard 2013). Hjarvard (2013, p. 17) defines mediatization as:

> the process whereby culture and society to an increasing degree become dependent on the media and their logic. This process is characterised by a *duality*, in that the media have become *integrated* into the operations of other social institutions and cultural spheres, while also acquiring the status of social institutions in *their own right*. As a consequence, social interaction [. . .] increasingly takes place via the media.

Being considered a special case of mediation (Livingstone 2009; Agha 2011), mediatization can be discussed along two lines: its role in creating a common spatiotemporal, epistemic, and axiological sphere of shared experience (Krotz 2007, 2009; Kopytowska 2013, 2014, 2015a, 2015b, 2015c: Kopytowska and Grabowski 2017), and its function of replacing social activities, which previously took place face-to-face (Schulz 2004). According to Hjarvard (2013, p. 83), mediatization 'entails a multidimensional transformation of religion that influences religious texts, practices and institutional relationships and, eventually the very nature of belief in modern societies'. Indeed, when discussing the interface between media and religion, Hjarvard (2013, p. 80) states that modern media not only represent and report on religious issues but also 'change the very ideas and authority of religious institutions and affect how people interact with each other when dealing with religious issues'. Both religious imaginations and practices are thus transformed (Hjarvard 2011, p. 120), with the resulting change in the nature of the 'sacred space' of communication, co-presence, and immediacy of spiritual experience.

Hjarvard (2008, p. 14) points to both direct and indirect forms of this process. The former takes place when non-mediated activities and events are changed into mediated ones, e.g. televangelism, in the case of which preaching is performed through interaction with the medium. The latter is manifest in the fact that symbols, forms, and content generated by the media shape everyday practices and activities. Both direct and indirect forms have attracted the interest of scholars exploring the interface of society and religion (Hjarvard 2008, 2013; Hjarvard and Lövheim 2012; Hoover and Clark 2002; Meyer and Moors 2006). It has been argued that the media have changed perception, attention, and understanding, and thus the very experience of both faith itself and a sense of belonging to a community of believers (Hoover 2006; Sa Martino 2013).

Hjarvard (2013) suggests looking at the mediatization of religion taking as a point of departure Meyrowitz's (1993) metaphors of (1) media as conduits, (2) media as languages, and (3) media as environment. The first one means examining how media transport religious messages and symbols across time and space. The second one evokes interest in the aesthetics of media, the format of religious messages, and the construction of communicative relationships between the sender, content, and the receiver, or 'how the choices of medium and genre influence features like narrative construction, reality status and reception of particular messages; how media adjust religious representations to the modalities of the specific medium and genre' (Hjarvard 2013, p. 82). The third one entails a focus on how media systems and institutions facilitate and structure human interaction and communication by generating a sense of community and belonging (Anderson 1991; Morley 2000), ritualizing small transitions of everyday life and events in the wider society, e.g. official funerals and commemorations (Dayan and Katz 1992).

It could thus be argued that the media transformation of the religion-related sphere and of religious communication has had both vertical and horizontal directions. Horizontally, mediatization has changed the character of interaction between believers and other members of religious communities (altering the institutionalized format of religion), while vertically it has facilitated in some sense a bringing closer of spiritual reality. As a result, 'a new sense of presence and community' (Hjarvard 2013, p. 85) has been created and, at the same time, the media have encouraged 'believers to adopt a more individualized stance towards religious texts and institutions' (Hjarvard 2013, p. 85). According to Sa Martino (2013), in consequence of this transformation followers and potential followers 'are understood as followers not only of a particular religion but as "followers-receivers" of a discourse in which their particular beliefs are linked to the public space'. This is to some extent reflected in the term 'electronic church' created in the 1980s.

What is of particular interest to us in the present chapter is the triad of media, religion, and cognition. The main question we would like to address is how the media impact on people's mental schemata and emotional responses, how their discourse (in its verbal and visual dimension) through manipulating the salience of issues, perception of time and space, transforms religious experience, whether it is about interacting with the spiritual or with other members of the religious community. Martelli and Capello (2005, p. 254) argue that 'religion is interpreted [. . .] through the cognitive and expressive schemes moulded by television and the media'. Hence, it seems justified to examine how visuality, intertextuality, emotivity, and immediacy of media discourse can potentially influence the religious audience's perceptions of sacred time, place, and thus experience of rituals. Media's social/interpersonal role in the context of religion should be considered too, as the media impact on the interactions among members of religious communities, both at the in-group and out-group level, and on the attitudes of believers towards religious leaders, authorities, and, more generally, institutions. How is a sense of community and presence created and altered as a result of transcending spatial boundaries? How do media spaces and identities impact on spaces and identities (both individual and collective) in the real world? How does participation in rituals change due to the semiotic affordances of various media? These are some of the questions that we will try to address in the following sections.

3 RITUALS: TIME/SPACE-MAKING, COGNITIVE NEEDS, VALUE MANAGEMENT, AND COLLECTIVE EMOTION

Being 'humanity's basic social act' (Rappaport 1999), ritual lies at the very heart of religion (Durkheim 1969/1915; Eliade 1958, 1959; Turner 1967, 1969), and it is participation in rituals that creates believers (Alcorta and Sosis 2005; Sosis 2003). While most cognitive scientists and evolutionary psychologists have focused primarily on the nature of religious beliefs and the psychological mechanisms involved in the creation of supernatural agents in all cultures (Atran 2002; Barrett 2000; Boyer 2001; Guthrie 1993), evolutionary anthropologists, drawing on the insights of Durkheim (1969/1915), Turner (1967, 1969), and Rappaport (1999), have concentrated on religious practices, linking religious ritual to socially adaptive behaviours and seeing it as having an important social cohesion-building function (Cronk 1994; Sosis and Alcorta 2003; Alcorta and Sosis 2005; Sosis 2003). The intention of the present section is to look at ritual from four vantage points, namely, time-space (spatiotemporal dimension), knowledge (epistemic dimension), norms and values (axiological dimension), and emotions (emotional dimension), as shown in Figure 1. We argue here that religious rituals are both constituted by and constitutive for these notions, and that these notions themselves are correlated and interdependent.

Rituals are both embedded in time and space and constitutive for them. The location of religious practice becomes sacred to a given religion (Eliade 1959), and such places themselves became tangible representations of the sacred, offering a symbolic bridge between the physical and spiritual worlds. Due to the repetitive nature of the ritual, for believers of Judeo-Christian religions sacred space provides a level of continuity that improves the religious experience (Eliade 1959). According to Rappaport (1999), ritual creates the sacred—whether it is about time, space, or values—by investing it with emotional meaning. In a similar vein, Otto (1950) linked the perception of holiness to religious emotion, insisting that sacred places ought to have the potential to evoke an affective response.

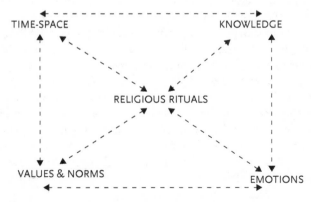

Figure 1 Constituted and constitutive character of religious rituals.

Time also plays a central role in and for rituals. For Willerslev, Christensen, and Meinert (2013, p. 5), who analyse the function of time in death-related rituals, ritual 'is not a given and neutral phenomenon. It is moulded, grasped and transformed in various ways'. Hence, following up on Flaherty's (2011, p. 12) concept of 'timework' (along with a range of analytical categories including duration, frequency, sequencing, timing, allocation, and taking time), they refer to ritual as one of the 'social technologies of time through which humans preclude, craft and produce certain temporal experiences'. Rituals are time-bound but, simultaneously, structure time and daily functioning.

Importantly, mediated religious rituals transform the notions of (sacred) time and space and their perception. The place of worship is extended to encompass the homes of viewers or listeners of religious broadcasts, or rather it is *brought* to these homes, as will be argued in the next section. This is what we will call the 'inclusivity of mediated space'. Time-space compression enabled by the technological affordances of various media, and their semiotic properties is one of the factors which are key to the construction of mediated experience related to indirect participation in rituals, and also key to what such a participation entails, namely, a sense of communion, presence, and collective emotion.

The relationship between knowledge and religious ritual is also two-directional. On the one hand, if we follow the 'cognitive need' explanation for religion, people want to understand events and phenomena taking place around them and the reasons behind them (Johnstone 2015, p. 28). Religious discourse thus becomes a source of knowledge, and provides continuity between the past, the present, and the future. On the other hand, for such discourse to appeal to religious audiences, it has to draw on what is already known and familiar. This epistemic dimension is well highlighted in the following fragment:

If part of the pastoral task of the Church is to communicate God's mercy and God's freedom in a way that people can understand, then you have to use the language that they are using, you have to use the metaphors and forms of experience that are already familiar to them. You can't ask people to believe in something their own experience forbids them to believe. . . . (Beaudoin in Nickell 2006, pp. 18–19)

As pointed out by Alcorta and Sosis (2005, p. 332), 'the meaning of abstract religious symbols must be created, both cognitively and emotionally'. While sacred symbols have distinct cognitive schema, their sacred status is highly contingent on their emotional meaning. The act of imbuing them with attributions of 'awe', 'purity', and 'danger' (Douglas 1966) constitutes an integral part of religious ritual everywhere (Douglas 1966; Durkheim 1969/1915; Rappaport 1999; Turner 1969). For Pyysiäinen (2001, p. 71) religious experience can be understood as 'emotional reaction to religious representations'; people's belief in religious ideas has a strong emotional basis (p. 72). Unsurprisingly, the importance of emotions has been emphasized in homiletics within the Catholic Church where emotion, seen as the 'creation of an affective experience for the audience of a sermon' was identified as a feature of the New Homiletic (Reid 1995, p. 7).

Others have underlined emotional needs, claiming that people seek to maintain emotional stability in the face of danger, instability, and disruption (also death; Lowie 1924). Goodenough (1965) thus describes the need for religion as a response to threats to safety, security, and future existence. Clark (1958) claims that people's four drives (or needs)—security, response, recognition, and new experience—explain the psychological need and appeal of religion; while for psychologists like Fromm (1950), it is the need for an object of devotion and allegiance. According to Alcorta and Sosis (2005, p. 339), the fact that communal ritual invests previously neutral stimuli with deep emotional significance enables the creation of a shared symbolic system that motivates behaviour and determines individual choices (Dehaene and Changeux 2000). In this way religious ritual, through the elicitation of neurophysiological responses, may coordinate social behaviours (Alcorta and Sosis 2005, p. 345), thereby impacting on identity construction and negotiation, involving in-group/out-group formation across both space and time (Rappaport 1999). Because of their emotional salience and motivational force, religious rituals are 'biologically significant events' (Alcorta and Sosis 2005, p. 344, 336). Neuroimaging studies show that memories of emotion-invested experiences (e.g. those related to religion) generate brain patterns similar to those which appear when events are experienced for the first time (Keltner and Haidt 2003).

Emotions and values seem to be closely related in the case of religious rituals. Durkheim (1969/1915), who saw religion as legitimizing values and norms and binding the members of society more closely, distinguished four social functions of a religious ritual: (1) disciplinary/preparatory function; (2) cohesive function; (3) revitalizing function—'we have a shared past'; and (4) euphoric function. Consequently, for him ritual was linked with the sacred and with collective emotion. Likewise, Collins (2004) argued that rituals have special significance in social life because they induce and commemorate times of great individual and collective emotion.

Catherine Bell (1997, p. 168) defines ritualization as 'the simple imperative to do something in such a way that the doing itself gives the acts a special or privileged status'. This is in line with Humphrey and Laidlaw (1994) and Seligman et al. (2008), who see ritual as a certain framing of actions. In their book *Ritual and its Consequences: An Essay in the Limits of Sincerity*, Seligman et al. claim that ritual and ritualistic behaviour 'are not so much events as ways of negotiating our very existence in the world' (p. 8) and that ritual 'addresses the relational aspects of role, and of self and other' (p. 12). Rituals are thus invested with values and emotions, but at the same time they attribute values to individuals, groups, objects and phenomena (axiological dimension), and condition emotional responses (emotional dimension).

Focus on the lived experience of people of faith, on religious practices, rather than doctrine as such has become the preoccupation of 'practical theology', which argues for the 'performative' character of theology, manifested in the liturgical, evangelistic, sacramental, and practical actions of faithful communities (Graham 1996; see also Miller 2003). According to Ward (2007, p. 92), 'doctrine should be seen as performative'. Giving an example of the Eucharist, he argues that both theological reflection and the study of religion should bring under scrutiny 'the complex and multi-layered interplay' (p. 92) between the production of religious meanings, their representation, and the way they transform and are transformed by congregations. We could rephrase his postulate by saying that religious discourse should be seen and analysed as both a process and product. The former entails interest in the production and reception of religious texts practices. Seeing them as a product means analysing them in terms of their verbal and visual aspects—indeed, their broader multimodal character, as we should also consider ritual sounds, scents, and gestures. The mediatization of religion adds another dimension to rituals understood in this way, impacting on the spheres of production and consumption as well as on the level of representation. Already in 1999, Mitchell made a theological case for a discourse which engages the listener multi-sensorially (pp. 6–7). With their liveness and multimodal (albeit limited) resources, media offer a conducive environment for that. Live broadcasts of religious events make it possible for an entire community to both witness and participate. Hepp and Krönert (2010) point to the hybrid character of religious media events. As they demonstrate with the example of the Catholic World Youth Day, religious celebrations are often intentionally staged as media events. With audiences gathered in front of TV screens, religious communication is no longer confined to churches and thus loses its 'sacred space' of communication/ 'exclusive space' in the traditional sense (Hepp and Krönert 2010, p. 269).

Durkheim's theory (1969/1915) of the role of ritual in the establishment of social life along with other anthropological studies on ritual helped to recontextualize communication theory in general (Rappaport 1999; Rothenbuhler 1998, 2006, 2010). The concept of ritual itself became very prominent in media studies after Dayan and Katz (1992) demonstrated that media themselves perform collective rituals with a highly integrative social function and thus facilitate the construction of collective emotions. Drawing on Durkheim as well as Dayan and Katz's (1992) 'media events', Couldry introduced the notion of 'media rituals', which he defined as 'formalised actions organised around media-related categories and boundaries' (2003, p. 29). These encompass ritual forms of media work, ritualized forms of media content, and ritualized activities of media audience members (Cottle 2006; Couldry 2003). Cottle even termed mediated events 'mediatized rituals' and emphasized the 'performative agency of the media' in 'staging, enacting, and propelling certain events and processes forward' to 'sustain and/or mobilize collective sentiments and solidarities' (2008, p. 139). As in the case of religious rituals, the media construction of events has as its main purpose bringing about 'social togetherness'.

According to Rothenbuhler (2010, p. 71), the study of ritual highlighted the importance of communicative form, which reduces ambiguity and uncertainty, is easy to recognize, to teach, to imitate, and is likely to cultivate expectations more rapidly, thereby producing patterned outcomes and predictable relationships. He illustrates this with an example of a radio broadcast. In *The TV Ritual*, Goethals (1981) went as far as to claim that television has become a substitute for sacraments. Indeed, the ritual nature of communication with the active participation of television audience members constructs a symbolic world in which they are not ordinary viewers of television but 'witnesses and participants' (Rothenbuhler 2010, p. 65; see also Kopytowska 2015b). The ritual character of mass communication, in particular TV and radio, is also connected with temporal orientation because of the role these media have in making transitions in the course of the day, week, month, or year (Rothenbuhler 1998). As section 5 will show, such transitions are of considerable importance in religious broadcasting.

Rituals are a form of symbolic action based on convention which involves ways of saying things that produce meanings, cognitions, and emotions (Rappaport 1979, 1999; Rothenbuhler 2010). In the words of Rothenbuhler:

> Rituals provided examples of how communication can produce effects . . . by the logic of speech acts, by symbolic implication, by entailment, acceptance, and other such modes the mass communication effects literature could not recognise. Rituals provided examples of how communication creates realities, and thus the way in which communication is part of the foundation of the social world. (Rothenbuhler 2010, p. 65)

Such an observation takes us back to the role of language and its performative character, mentioned in section 1. Austin's and Searle's speech act theories have been attempts to explain how 'in saying something we do something' (Austin 1962, p. 91). Searle (1972, p. 145) points out that meaning is a matter of convention and, drawing on speech act theory, develops his theory of social ontology (Searle 1995, 2010) where he explains the role of collective agreement, status functions, and deontic powers (see section 1) in the construction of social reality. Seuren's (2009, p. 140) 'principle of social binding' seems to be of particular relevance to rituals too. For him, 'all speech acts . . . are performative in that they create a socially binding relation or state of affairs' (2009, p. 147). Creating and stabilizing social relations is indeed one of the most important functions of rituals (Senft 2014, p. 86). The final point to be made here is that 'ritual communication is artful performed semiosis, predominantly but not only involving speech, that is formulaic and repetitive and therefore anticipated within particular contexts of social interaction' (Basso and Senft 2009, p. 1).

4 PROXIMIZATION: CO-PRESENCE, SALIENCE, AND EMOTIONS

A claim made in the present chapter is that the institutions of mass communication play such an important role in mediating religious experience because they reduce the perceived *distance*—mental and physical—between the members of the audience and the elements of a supernatural 'reality' and the spiritual objective reality (understood as religious events and rituals performed in the remote space) they have no direct access to, thus influencing their cognitive-affective involvement and, as a result, perceptions, judgements, and actions. The process happens simultaneously along the vertical and horizontal axes (Figure 2). In the first case, the media bring closer the spiritual reality and the doctrine. In the second case, they reduce the distance between the Self and other members of religious community. The audience's conceptualizations of religious rituals (and other events), and the resulting

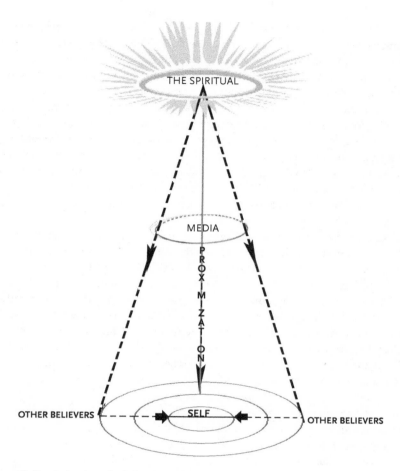

Figure 2 Proximization of religious experience.

understanding and judgements, are thus arguably influenced by which aspects of reality are 'proximized', that is, made perceptually more salient.

It seems important here to refer to the typology proposed by Kaid et al. (1991, cited in McNair 2003, p. 12). This is a typology allowing us to distinguish three dimensions of social reality, namely, (a) an *objective* reality, comprising events and phenomena as they actually occur; (b) a *subjective* reality—the 'reality' of events as they are perceived by social actors (including in our case the institution of the Church and its representatives, for example); and (c) a *constructed* reality—events along with material and abstract phenomena as they are covered/mediated by the media. In the case of religious discourse, we need to add to the objective dimension of reality the believer's spiritual dimension, connected with both religious doctrine and religious events. However, here we are primarily interested in the mediated dimension of religious experience, which we consider part of 'mediated social reality'. Reformulating Searle's statement, we are interested in how the media (in mediated religious discourse) make X (religious beliefs and practices, religious entities and values) count as Y in a certain context. The questions we will thus attempt to address here are as follows: (1) How is it possible that certain phenomena, events, groups, or individuals—related to the domain of religion and spirituality—acquire their axiologically and emotionally imbued representations within the sphere of collective consciousness? (2) How do the media transform human experience of religion in its both cognitive (understanding religion) and interactive (interacting with other believers) dimensions? (3) How is conceptual salience, necessary to bring particular aspects of religious reality closer (proximize them), constructed in mediated religious discourse? (4) What are the mechanisms underlying proximization work—key to mediated experience? (5) What is the role of language and discourse in this process? (6) How is this process linked to social cognition, and what is cognitive about it?

To answer these questions and offer the rationale behind the proximization model that we present below, we need to refer to Chilton's discourse-cognitive perspective. In his Discourse Space Theory (2004, 2005, 2010) and Deictic Space Theory (2014), Chilton argues that, in discourse, communicators position various entities (people, objects, events, etc.) in relation to themselves (the self—'I' or a variable 'we'—and a more distant 'other'), being in the deictic centre. While this process has its discursive manifestations, it is essentially cognitive in nature and related to the cognitive linguistics notion of 'conceptualization' defined by Langacker (1990, p. 18) as 'the cognitive activity constituting our apprehension of the world'. The perception of time and space are key here, as they are 'basic categories of human experience' (Harvey 1990, p. 201), or as Langacker (1987, pp. 147–154) puts it, 'basic domains', i.e. primitive representational fields. Chilton further argues that, using background assumptions and indexical cues, communicating individuals position various entities along three intersecting axes within discourse space: time, space, and modality. Spatial distance relative to S (self, speaker, subject) is reflected metaphorically on all three axes. The modal dimension involves both degrees of truth and deonticity.

In further developments of the theory, Hart (2010) and Cap (2006, 2008, 2010, 2013, who adds the axiological dimension in his spatial-temporal-axiological model) demonstrate how the perception of distance from the Self can be skilfully manipulated in political discourse to legitimize the actions to be taken by political actors. Chilton and Cram (chapter 16, this volume) apply Deictic Space Theory to explain the dynamics of religious ritual and the performative potential of language during the Eucharist. The Media Proximization Approach (MPA) presented here, when it comes to motivations behind it and its implications, goes far beyond the legitimizing function suggested by Cap (2013); it constitutes another meta-level in the process of constructing social reality, as suggested by Searle (see section 1), and is inherent to the process of 'mediatization' (see section 2).

At the heart of these two processes—that is, mediatization and proximization—lie the notions of co-presence and mediated experience. Using the term 'response presence', Goffman (1983, p. 2) defines social interactions as occurring between physically co-present individuals, where presence means being 'accessible, available, and subject to one another' (p. 22). According to Urry (2002), who sees all interactions as complex combinations of proximity and distance, or absence and presence, people aim for proximity within three dimensions: with other people in face-to-face interactions, with unique locations in face-to-place interactions, and with special events in face-to-moment interactions. Boden and Molotch (1994, pp. 258, 277) refer to this need to achieve a state of co-presence as 'compulsion of proximity'. In the case of religion, we can thus mention the proximity with the Spiritual (God), sacred places, religious events and rituals, and other believers—members of a religious community.

Media space in its various forms and genres, thanks to its semiotic potential, provides its users with a possibility to satisfy this compulsion, thereby offering a chance for 'mediated experience', defined by Giddens as 'the involvement of spatially/temporally distant influences with human sensory experience' (1991, p. 243) or 'the intrusion of distant events into everyday consciousness' (p. 189). Harvey (1990) links such experience to 'space-time compression', while in the words of Thompson (1995, p. 9) media users 'become space-time travellers who are involved in negotiating between different space-time frameworks and relating their mediated experience of other times and places back to the context of their everyday lives'. What can thus be seen is that spatial and temporal dimensions of distance are key in this proximization process due to the fact that the abstract or material entities or individuals accessed are 'located' out there in the world, beyond the audience's immediate reach. The epistemic distance results from the fact that the audience is to various degrees unfamiliar with the events and phenomena presented to them; it is thus related to media users' experience-based cognitive schema of interpretation and gains particular prominence in the case of religious discourse. The axiological distance is contingent on values and norms, while the emotional distance is connected with various degrees of emotional involvement on the part of the audience (Figure 3).

As already mentioned, operations within the spatiotemporal dimension constitute the basis for proximization process and will be a prerequisite for other types of distance-related work (Figure 4).

For Berger and Luckmann (1991/1966, p. 40) 'the world of everyday life is structured both spatially and temporally' and it is the capacity to transcend the 'here and now' that makes language a powerful tool in the social construction process:

> language bridges different zones within the reality of everyday life and integrates them into a meaningful whole. The transcendences have spatial, temporal and social dimensions. [. . .] As a result of these transcendences language is capable of 'making present' a variety of objects that are spatially, temporally and socially absent from the 'here and now'. (Berger and Luckmann 1991/1966, p. 64)

Combined with images and media capacity for instant transmission, language thus makes it possible to bring selected aspects of distant objective reality closer to media users, both spatially and temporally. Temporal and spatial dimensions of distance are related to the fact that the events presented happened or happen in a physically distant space, beyond the audience's immediate experience. This mechanism is of particular relevance in the case of religious live broadcasting. The public is given a feeling that events are happening right *now*, and *here*, in front of their eyes (see

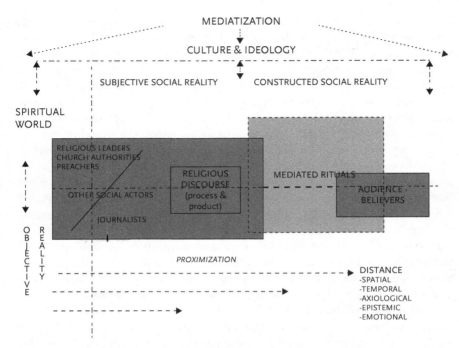

Figure 3 Constructed social reality and mediated rituals: Media Proximization Approach.

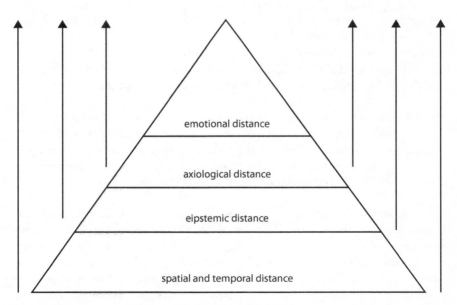

Figure 4 Dimensions of distance (Kopytowska 2015c: 141).

Kopytowska 2014, 2015b). Due to the primacy of visual perception, the lack of other sensory input (e.g. smell of incense) is largely compensated for by moving images accompanied by verbal commentary. Hence, Hoskins and O'Loughlin (2007, p. 37) speak of 'an ongoing present', with various elements being proximized from the past (recency), present (currency), and future (imminence), not only temporarily, but also spatially (and, in consequence, epistemically and axiologically).

Recency is 'generated' and enhanced both visually, through camera techniques and editing, and verbally, through deictic expressions as well as the use of tenses, progressive and perfective aspects, and other lexical expressions (see Kopytowska 2014, 2015a, 2015b). With 'home and world [put] into temporary co-presence' (Corner 1999, p. 40), the viewers are given a sense of being 'right there, right now', a sense that television connects them 'live' to important events, and thus guarantees a potential connection to shared social realities as they are happening (Couldry 2004, pp. 355–356). Moving images have, as Corner (1995, p. 12) puts it, an 'indexical quality', that is to say, prompt the audience to take their truth for granted.

The epistemic distance is connected with the audience's knowledge/familiarity with the events presented. This is achieved, among other ways, by providing and repeating certain words and visual images and putting them in a particular context, which results in drawing attention to some elements of reality while obscuring others. Since the audience will understand an event better if they are able to 'incorporate' it into their 'mental map', that is, culturally determined knowledge about the structure of reality (Hall et al. 1978), in order to proximize such an event or phenomenon epistemically media will refer to the already existing scenarios of representation, ideological patterns, and cultural stereotypes (which they will assume the audience to be familiar with). In order to reduce this dimension of distance, media will rely on metaphors. Additionally, events and phenomena will often be simplified, re-contextualized, and interpreted in terms of the already familiar ones.

Berger and Luckmann (1991/1966, p. 111) argue that 'knowledge precedes values in legitimation of institutions'. Accordingly, we espouse the view that the axiological dimension of distance is, to a large extent, contingent on the epistemic one. As claimed by philosophical, anthropological, and psychological theories, the self has a natural tendency to position itself vis-à-vis others within the environment and to group or classify surrounding entities as spatially and thus epistemically and axiologically close/distant (similar/different).

Cognitive-discursive operations in this context can thus be characterized by three functions (see also Kopytowska 2015a, 2015c):

(1) establishing axiological status: 'our' religious and moral values/norms;
(2) delineating axiological conflict: incompatibility of 'our' values/norms with other values/norms;
(3) conveying axiological urgency: responding to a threat posed to 'our' values/norms and accepting moral responsibility to act.

Finally, proximization work also concerns emotional distance. Increasing the emotional involvement of media users seems to be one of the ways of making selected aspects of objective reality more salient than others, and, at the same time, a factor enhancing persuasiveness of media messages. Emotions are inherent to religious broadcasting. While we assume in MPA that emotional proximization is highly contingent on, and very often the result of, operations on other dimensions of distance, it has to be acknowledged that there seems to be a strong correlation between beliefs, judgements, and emotions. Frijda and Mesquita speak of the 'emotion-belief spiral' (2000, p. 49), arguing that emotions can give rise to new beliefs, change the existing beliefs, and reduce or amplify the strength with which beliefs are held (Frijda and Mesquita 2000, p. 45; see also Frijda, Manstead and Bem 2000, p. 5). Metaphor and metonymy, in their verbal and visual dimensions (as will be demonstrated in the following sections) will be an important proximization trigger in this case. Other triggers include, for example, positively or negatively loaded words, hyperboles and quantity expressions, comparison and contrast, etc. Likewise, presenting events from the perspective of individual experience (value of 'personalization'), which at the level of discourse brings forth personal narratives and, visually, high frequency of close-up shots and zooming in camera movements, has a highly proximizing function.

5 MEDIATING RELIGIOUS EXPERIENCE: ETERNAL WORD TELEVISION NETWORK, RADIO MARYJA, AND TV TRWAM

The objective of the previous section was to elaborate the notion of proximization and to propose the main lines of a theoretical model explaining the mediatization of religion. But how is the perceived distance reduced? What are the cognitive-discursive and the semiotic mechanisms of proximization? Not surprisingly, metaphor and metonymy play a major role in the proximization of remote mediated ritual. Other proximizing strategies involve the use of deixis and motion verbs. In this section, I thus attempt to demonstrate some of the cognitive operations that may be involved by looking at the examples of two religious broadcasters, namely, the Eternal Word Television Network (henceforth EWTN), based in the United States, and Radio Maryja (along with TV Trwam), based in Poland.

EWTN, launched on 15 August 1981, is the largest religious media network in the world, broadcasting twenty-four hours a day and reaching more than 250 million homes in 140 countries and territories. Started by Mother M. Angelica, a Poor Clare nun, it has become a state of the art audiovisual complex and religious centre funded totally with donations from individuals and groups and visited annually by thousands of pilgrims.

Radio Maryja (henceforth 'RM') was founded in Toruń, Poland, on December 9, 1991, by a Redemptorist, Father Tadeusz Rydzyk. The name of the radio station, 'Maryja', is a traditional Polish form of the name 'Mary', and a reference to the Virgin Mary. It is owned by the Warsaw Province of the Congregation of the Most Holy Redeemer, and financed through donations from its audience. The foundation of the radio was also the beginning of a religious movement, called the Radio Maryja Family, with hundreds of clubs and offices across Poland. Radio Maryja Family holds a pilgrimage to Częstochowa every year, which is said to attract thousands of people. TV Trwam (henceforth 'TVT'), a sister station of Radio Maryja, and targeted at the same audience, launched its terrestrial broadcast on 13 May 2003, as well as regular broadcasting via satellite. It is also largely funded by donations from viewers and listeners of Radio Maryja.

5.1 Conceptualizing the audience: Family metaphor and its proximizing function

Metaphors are an intrinsic part of human cognition and communication, and, along with the development of cognitive linguistics and Conceptual Metaphor Theory, it became a well-established view that they play a key role in framing issues and experience. In *Metaphors We Live By* (1980), Lakoff and Johnson argued that 'most of our ordinary conceptual system is metaphoric in nature' (p. 4) and 'conceptual metaphors are mappings across conceptual domains that structure our reasoning, our experience and our everyday language' (Lakoff and Johnson 1999, p. 47; see also Gibbs 1994; Johnson 1987). This allow us 'to see one highly structured and clearly delineated concept in terms of another' (Lakoff and Johnson 1980, p. 61), or as posited by Sweetser and DesCamp (2014, p. 10), to conceptualize 'a relatively *less intersubjectively accessible* domain or frame in terms of a *more intersubjectively accessible* domain or frame [original italics]' (see also Sweetser 1990; DesCamp and Sweetser 2005; Dancygier and Sweetser 2014). They are useful in simplifying complex problems and events, making them relevant, accessible, and understandable to the general public.

We argue here that metaphor, due to its epistemic, axiological, and emotional potential, serves as a major trigger in the proximization process. Firstly, as already mentioned, it enables people to think about the situations that are new, complex, and remote (Chilton 1996, p. 47), thus reducing, what we call in our model, the epistemic distance. The unfamiliar and the abstract are presented in terms of what the audience already knows, in terms of what is very often based in bodily experience (embodiment) and culturally embedded. For this reason, as several authors in this volume demonstrate, metaphor constitutes an integral and crucial part of language and thinking related to religious experience. It is present in sacred texts and writings, sermons and religious education, and ritual practices and forms of worship, and is used to conceptualize the experience of both everyday worshippers and mystics or prophets (Sweetser and DesCamp 2014, p. 11).

Its axiological and emotional proximizing potential is of key importance too. Transferring positive or negative associations from the source domains to a target domain metaphor provokes affective responses (Charteris-Black 2005, p. 20), as 'certain intuitive, emotionally linked mental schemas are being evoked', and 'emotions that can be regarded as in some way basic are evidently stimulated' (Chilton 2004, p. 17). The relationship between metaphor and values has also been frequently emphasized, in particular in Lakoff's 'moral politics' framework (Lakoff 1996, 2004, 2006, 2008; see also Johnson 1993; Goatly 2007). We can thus look at metaphor from the perspective of its both cognitive and interactive function. While increasing the perceptual salience of issues, they contribute to creating the situation in which one understanding of reality is privileged over others (Chilton

1996, p. 74), and—to use Searle's terms—X is more likely to become (or rather be perceived/understood) as Y in a certain context. In this way, they can evoke and consolidate group solidarity and entail a range of community-related roles, responsibilities, and benefits.

Two metaphorical conceptualizations are of particular interest to us in the present chapter, as we argue that they have played a major role in establishing and maintaining the social status and impact of the radio/TV stations in question. These are the FAMILY metaphor and the RELATIONSHIP IS PROXIMITY/COHESION metaphor. The cognitive-affective potential of the former has been frequently emphasized in both secular (e.g. NATION IS A FAMILY) and religious contexts (CHURCH/CONGREGATION IS A FAMILY; e.g. Baab 2008; Frambach 2003). We argue that these metaphors perform a proximizing function along both vertical (Self-God) and horizontal axes (Self-other believers). As pointed out by Sweetser and DesCamp (2014), who explore the biblical meanings of the GOD IS FATHER metaphor, metaphors of parental care are so powerful because they relate to our first and deepest experience of a positive power-asymmetric relationship. It seems relevant to our discussion to refer here to Lakoff's (1996) comparison of strict father versus nurturant parent conceptualizations. The former is the moral authority in the family, someone who knows right from wrong and is inherently moral. He is in control of the household, and his authority and decisions are not to be challenged. Obedience to the father is moral, while disobedience is immoral. The latter is the empathic parent, someone who understands, cares, and provides for children's basic needs. Sweetser and DesCamp (2014) point out that in Orthodox and Catholic traditions God typically emerges as a strong paternal figure while the need for nurturance is filled by the conceptual and emotional frame built up around the figure of the virgin-mother Mary.

The family metaphor has its long-established presence in conceptualizing the community of believers and aspects of congregational life. What the two religious media networks do is apply it, successfully, as a way of conceptualizing their target audiences. In so doing, through metaphorical entailments, the two media networks attribute deontic powers and status functions (to use Searle's [1995, 2010] terms) to a spatially dispersed set of individuals—the Self and other believers, the TV audience members, God, Virgin Mary, and also the networks' founders and directors. The effect is to legitimate all these dispersed participants as a virtually co-present congregation. We thus have to do with 'EWTN Family' and 'Radio Maryja Family'. Listener/viewer-believers are conceptualized as siblings who get guidance and support, but also are expected to be obedient and support the family in both material and moral terms. Much depends on the background family model (strict father or nurturant mother, for example) that is drawn on the metaphorical mapping (see below).

Both media institutions organize pilgrimages and gatherings for their 'family' members, e.g. 'EWTN Family Celebration' and 'the Pilgrimage of the Radio Maryja Family'. The metaphor is used to create unity and motivation for action as in, for example, 'We come together here as a family' (EWTN), or 'We want you to come back because we're a family' (EWTN). Radio Maryja and TV Trwam regularly air a programme called 'In our family', and the metaphor is constantly activated, as in 'Today we have very interesting guests in our family. The Radio Maryja Family—all the people who create this radio, who listen to it, who pray for us'.

Two interesting shifts in the mappings of the family structure and difference in the attribution of parental roles within the metaphor can be observed in the way the discourse is developed. The metaphorical concept THE CHURCH IS A FAMILY, where GOD IS FATHER and VIRGIN MARY IS MOTHER, is merged with the metaphorical concept of (MEDIA) INSTITUTION IS A FAMILY. Since EWTN was established by Mother Angelica, in her own broadcasts as well as in programmes about her, she emerges as a nurturant parent figure taking care of her children, providing guidance (rather than admonitions) and solutions to problems. In one of her broadcasts she says: 'Now I have a family business we need to discuss', only to proceed to discuss some faith-related issues.

In the case of the Radio Maryja Family, the dominant parental role of a strict father is attributed to the founder and director of the station, Father Rydzyk (often called 'Father Director'). He is the moral authority whose duty is to teach his children right from wrong. At the same time, the role of Virgin Mary as mother is constantly made salient, both verbally and visually. While the most common greeting in the Roman Catholic Church is, 'Praised be Jesus Christ', the Radio Maryja Family uses 'Praised be Jesus Christ and Mary, ever Virgin'. The radio station's logo features Virgin Mary with baby Jesus, placed in the centre of circles which seem to have a double function: firstly, they stand metonymically (and perhaps metaphorically) for the radiating waves of the broadcast signal, and secondly, they represent motherly protection and care (Figure 5).[3] While her motherly pose acts as an emotional proximization trigger, the fact that she is placed in the centre has an axiological dimension.

The protective and caring role of the virgin mother is also underlined in the words of John Paul II, which have become the audience's daily prayer: 'Mary, the Star of Evangelisation, lead us, lead Radio Maryja and take care of it'.[5]

Inherent in the family conceptual framework is the notion of proximity as a naturally motivated indication of good relationship (Kövecses 1990) and, as mentioned in section 4, a basic human need (see discussion on the 'compulsion of proximity' concept). Goatly (2007, p. 178) refers to this as physical closeness, physical attachment, or indivisibility of a unit, while Chilton (1996, pp. 54–55) underlines the importance of the LINK schema (on this image schema, see Johnson 1987) based on physical closeness between bodies and objects. The schema is frequently evoked in the words of one of the most popular songs of the Radio Maryja Family: 'So that we are one, let's hold our hands, so that we are together and have one heart'; or in the statement that is often repeated by its founder, 'Don't let them divide us'. Of course isolated viewers cannot literally hold hands, so this phrasing is activating an entailment of the family metaphor. It is further activating the metaphorical entailment 'unity/togetherness is strength', as evidenced in the following:

Family, a prayer we pray united together is a powerful prayer. So please, pray together with me our EWTN prayer. Today we pray for EWTN. Lord Jesus Eternal Word, Splendour of the Father, we adore You! We thank You for the Eternal Word

Figure 5 The logo of Radio Maryja.

Television Network which began to defend Your glory. Use EWTN to bring faith to non-believers and to help those of other Religions to discover You, the Way, the Truth and the Life. Use EWTN to bring conversion to sinners and to those who are indifferent or hostile to the Faith. Bless EWTN that it may be Your Instrument of mercy. Amen. (EWTN)

Interestingly, here it is the figure of Jesus, not the Virgin Mary as in the Radio Maryja case, that becomes the agent and focal element. While the Virgin Mary led and protected the radio audience, Jesus is expected, and requested, to use the network according to his divine plans. Also, if we consider the vertical axis God–believers (Figure 2), the EWTN is conceptualized as making distant spiritual reality closer to people, in part by using orientational motion verbs ('bring faith', 'bring conversion').

We may now go back to Searle's (1995) question about what makes it possible for institutions to function and apply it to these two religious media institutions and their audiences. The answer that such functioning is contingent on collective agreement and the attribution of status functions and deontic powers can be further elaborated (and validated) with a reference to the proximizing potential of metaphorical conceptualizations. The cases of the two media networks (their financial status and position on the market) are a clear example of how and why carefully selected and consistently applied metaphors can result in emotional (a feeling of bonding and loyalty), behavioural (collective participation in actions and initiatives), and material (financial support) effects.

5.2 Timework, spatial inclusiveness, and collective (spiritual) experience

'Timework' in the context of mediated religious rituals has several dimensions. The first dimension is related to media potential for immediacy, liveness, and interactivity and inextricably connected with spatial proximization. Thanks to real-time broadcasts, listeners and viewers can indirectly participate in religious events and rituals as they actually occur. The effect of liveness and co-presence is constructed primarily through merging various deictic centres, including those of journalists and guests in the studio, on-site participants of the events, and members of the audience watching or listening to broadcasts at home. This is achieved by means of lexical items, grammatical constructions, and, on a visual level, camera movement and editing techniques. Verbal proximization triggers include expressions such as 'now', 'shortly', 'just', and 'live', as well as the present tense along with progressive and perfective aspects. The perception and processing of spatial distance is also reduced by proximal spatial deictic expressions, such as 'here' and 'this', together with deictically structured verbs of oriented movement dependent on the PATH schema such as 'arrive', and those dependent on the LINK schema, such as 'join', in the following examples:

> You *have arrived* at Call me Catholic. (EWTN)
> Tune in *now*! We invite all of our EWTN family to *join us live* 11:30. (EWTN)
> Please, *join us* for the opening prayer given by EWTN chaplain, Father Joseph Mary Wolfe. (EWTN)

The use of such verbs in this way is essentially metaphorical (nobody is literally arriving anywhere, or joining anybody). The use of *now* is not metaphorical, but is a temporal deictic that really does reflect and prompt simultaneity.

In the case of Radio Maryja and TV Trwam, each broadcast of daily mass or other religious events or celebrations starts by linguistically presupposing and conceptually evoking the co-presence of listeners and viewers, using the same techniques— activating cognitive frames of the family, and metaphorically representing movement into a communal space:

> Dear listeners and viewers joining us now . . . (TVT)
> Dear pilgrims gathered here in front of the Jasna Góra hill, as well as those who are joining us via the broadcast of TV Trwam and Radio Maryja. I invite you to our joint Rosary prayer here on the Jasna Góra square of prayer by the heart of the Queen of Poland. In the community of the Radio Maryja Family we want to thank . . . (TVT/RM)
> I would like to cordially greet people who join us in this prayer in front of their radio sets in our country and abroad. (RM)
> Brothers and sisters in Christ gathered here in the Radom cathedral and joining us via the service of mass-media, radio, TV and the press. (TVT)

I'm very happy to welcome all the guests who arrived at this meeting, the meeting of the Radio Maryja Family. [. . .] I cordially welcome and greet all listeners of Radio Maryja and viewers of TV Trwam. I extend my greetings to our fellow citizens in our country and abroad. (TVT/RM)

The 25th pilgrimage is just starting. We cordially greet everybody on the square [. . .] but also those who since early morning hours have been gathering in front of Radio Maryja and TV Trwam. (TVT/RM)

Here and in many places of prayer and rest. . . . (RM)

'Joining us [here] in front of your TV set [there]' is indeed a conceptual paradox, but its resolution is coerced in the combination of cognitive devices in the discourse. Co-presence is also constructed with directive speech acts in the first-person plural form, calling for joint action:

Uniting with the pilgrims of the radio Maryja Family let's now all take the Rosary into our hands so that we could recite it. . . . (RM)

Let's listen now to the words of. . . . (RM)

These directives do indeed prompt simultaneous actions by dispersed individuals, but also evoke a concept of *joint* action ('let us . . .). And from the studio the viewers are taken to various other locations, where either the live broadcast or (more often) video footage comes from. Shifts to another deictic centre are triggered both verbally and visually. On the verbal level, the triggers are spatial adverbs with directional prepositions ('and now to') or, as is most often the case, spatial verbs such as 'move' combined with the first-person plural verb form (pronoun 'we' in English), demanding the inclusive interpretation):

After the rosary we *will move* immediately *to*. . . (RM)

Interactivity is also an important spatiotemporal proximization trigger. Viewers and listeners can call in and participate in the on-air prayer. This prayer—like the 'Our Father'—is always antiphonal, divided into two parts, the first being recited by people in the studio and the other one by those who are calling. The following exchange is a typical example of the radio prayer-related conversational routine, in which participants introduce themselves by their names and place they are calling from:

'Thank you for the joint prayer. From London – Arkadiusz'. – 'Thank you very much and greetings to all Poles in the UK.' (RM/TVT)

Such a routine involves the remote worshiper in a real-time liturgy, creating a sense of reduced spatial distance (bringing in distant locations), and has an emotionally proximizing function (personalization) produced by the very act of verbal interaction between two persons.

Another important aspect of 'timework' is that TV/radio religious broadcasting is both constitutive for and constituted by daily, weekly, and monthly routines. The programme schedule in both networks is organized according to the Liturgy of the Hours, includes daily mass, meditations, Gospel readings, but also news bulletins, live coverage of religious events, and call-in programmes with a community-bonding function. The mutual interface between the radio/TV schedule (mediated participation in religious rituals and events) and daily functioning, including direct participation in such events, is emphasized in the following fragment by Father Rydzyk, who during the pilgrimage inaugural mass in Częstochowa refers to the radio programme:

> The Radio Maryja Family is a family which sanctifies each day with a prayer, and this is how the programme schedule of Radio Maryja is constructed. And we know very well that the morning programme starts with a song 'When the morning dawn breaks', so let's sing it now. (TVT/RM)

Importantly, we can also speak here of both time and space inclusiveness, manifested in the fact that listeners or viewers can tune in at any given moment and from any place (e.g. listening to the radio at home or in the car). What is more, they can watch or listen to the coverage not only live but also *post factum* since the videos and audio files are uploaded online. Sacred time and sacred space are thus 'extended' beyond the actual here and now. Sacred space-time can be brought forth in real time, or be displaced and become atemporal or even super-temporal.

5.3 Mediating knowledge, values, and emotions

The sensation of co-presence satisfying the compulsion of proximity, discussed in the previous sub-section, enabled by the semiotic properties of the broadcasting media and time-space manipulation, is just one aspect of mediated religious experience. As already mentioned (see Figure 4), the spatiotemporal proximization, contingent, among others, on media's capacity for liveness and simultaneity, forms the basis for other forms of proximization. Here, we would like to discuss them in the context of the visual dimension, which takes particular prominence if we consider 'ocularcentrism' (Jay 1993, cited in Rose 2007, p. 2), that is, the centrality of the visual to contemporary social life. As emphasized in the extract below, the power of the television image lies in the feeling of authenticity it generates and, as a result, the fact that viewers take the 'reality' of presented events for granted.

> Since one of the main characteristics of the television image is its capacity for the instantaneous transmission of electronically produced images and therefore for extending our own senses into simultaneously occurring situations without apparent intervention or manipulation, television, like the photograph carries with it a sense of authenticity that no other media can match. (Barry 1997, p. 174)

The on-screen caption 'live' denoting a simultaneous occurrence connotes 'contemporaneity', while actuality footage signifies 'observed reality' (Bignell 2002, p. 111). In this way, moving images act as evidence, and this perceived realism influences social judgements, attitudes, and emotions (Rubin and Perse 1987; Potter 1988; Busselle and Greenberg 2000). Since in 'mediated images such as television pictures [. . .] the camera stands in for us' (Barry 1997, p. 115), the viewers are encouraged to adopt the perspective offered by the medium, and very often do so subconsciously. For example, Lombard (1995) found out that television audiences' responses to interpersonal distance cues (manipulated via image size and viewing distance) were similar to responses demonstrated in interpersonal communication studies. And, we have to remember here that 'images are also subject to construal' (Hart 2014, p. 72). Since the visual language is grounded in perceptual experience, Kress and van Leeuwen (2006) and, more recently, Hart (2014) argue that the visuo-grammatical properties of images invite particular evaluations and emotional responses. In the words of Barry (1997, p. 126):

> Because perception encompasses spatial relationship, color and three-dimensionality, and because perception is neurologically routed directly through the amygdala as well as to the neocortex or 'thinking brain', visual language can speak directly to the emotions and has a dynamic complexity and multiplicity of meaning that escapes verbal language.

Hence, Barry (1997, p. 178) speaks of 'a universal visual language of shots, angles, and distance that is readily understood by viewers'. We make a claim here that visual distance and angle manipulation acts as a powerful axiological and emotional proximization trigger in the process of mediating religious experience. Following Hart (2014, p. 71), we relate camera angles to orientational metaphors: being located above an object or entity (high camera angle) may correlate with our being more easily able to control it or having power over it, while being located beneath an object or entity (low camera angle) may imply a lack of power and control.

In the TV coverage of religious rituals, a priest during certain points of the Eucharist as well as religious symbols (statues or paintings) are often filmed with various degrees of a low camera angle (Figures 6, 7, 8,). If we assume that the viewer is encouraged to adopt the camera's perspective, such an angle is likely to command both respect (and admiration) and a sense of subjugation. As in the FAMILY metaphor, the perspective of the child is imposed on the believer, while the figure looking down on him/her is vested with both parental authority and capacity to protect.

At the same time, people gathered at religious celebrations are often filmed with a high camera angle (Figures 9, 10,), which has two important consequences. Firstly, especially in its extreme version of a bird's-eye view shot, this makes it possible to convey the scale and impact of the event. The view of hundreds or thousands of believers contributes to strengthening a sense of collective experience. Secondly, there is a symbolic metaphorical meaning attached to it (especially as high-angle shots like this often precede or follow low-angle shots described earlier), namely,

Figure 6 The Radio Maryja Family pilgrimage mass: the statue of Virgin Mary (low camera angle).

Figure 7 The Radio Maryja Family mass: church carving with Jesus on the cross (low camera angle).

Figure 8 The Radio Maryja Family mass: a priest during the elevation of the chalice (low camera angle).

Figure 9 The Radio Maryja Family mass: pilgrims participating in the ritual (high camera angle).

Figure 10 The Radio Maryja Family mass: priests and believers gathered inside the church (high camera angle).

the believers gathered appear as if presented from the perspective of God or Virgin Mary, as children, full of both trust and respect.

When distance is added to low- or high-angle shots, the emotional impact is enhanced. 'Near' may be associated with intimacy in the conceptual metaphor SOCIAL RELATIONS ARE DISTANCE (Hart 2014; see also section 5.1). When distance is reduced, as in a close-up, the object within the frame is likely to evoke stronger emotions. If it is another individual, 'facial features seem to reveal internal thoughts and emotions, and we feel ourselves in a one-on-one relationship of empathy with the person' (Barry 1997, p. 137). Very often during religious celebrations, the camera, which first shows the altar from the distance (Figure 11), zooms in on the face of the priest or other believers (Figure 12). Such close-ups along with the zooming-in

Figure 11 The Radio Maryja Family mass: the altar from the distance (long shot).

Figure 12 The Radio Maryja Family mass: the priest celebrating the mass (high camera angle combined with a close-up).

movement connote increasing proximity and the unity of experience. A similar effect is achieved with close-ups of religious symbols (Figure 13). In this case, however, we could speak about proximization along the vertical axis, in relation to spiritual reality (rather than communal experience, which happens in the case of horizontally oriented proximization), being brought 'closer' to viewers-believers.

We argue here that the media coverage of religious ritual on the one hand enriches and on the other shapes the experience of indirect participants by both enabling and, at the same time, imposing certain conceptualizations. While for someone physically present in the actual place of worship it would be possible to change the focus of attention and the object of gaze, he/she would not be able to

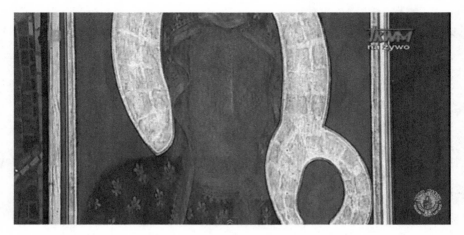

Figure 13 The Radio Maryja Family mass: the painting of the Black Madonna of Częstochowa (high camera angle combined with tilting camera movement ending in a close-up).

continually change the distance between himself/herself and, for example, the altar (and other religious objects) or assume a bird's-eye perspective allowing him/her to see the whole community. Perhaps then such possibilities of changing distance and angle are meant to compensate for the lack of other perceptual stimuli and have an empowering function for the viewer. Yet, the choice of the sequence of camera movements and the objects of camera focus, which entails a certain construal of a given situation, is likely to influence viewers' conceptualizations and thus, potentially, emotions.

6 CONCLUSIONS AND QUESTIONS

As argued by constructivists, social reality is to a large extent co-constructed by discourse. In his book on social ontology, Searle argues that 'there are things that exist because we believe them to exist' (1995: 1) and explains the role of language in attributing status functions and deontic powers, which he believes is key to the functioning of social institutions. Adding a cognitive dimension to it, Chilton in his Deictic Space Theory demonstrates how, by positioning various entities within discourse space, we can shape the Self's perception of both material and abstract entities along with their embedding in time, space, and epistemic-deontic status. What we have tried to demonstrate in this chapter is that mediatization has added yet another dimension to this process of social construction. With the media becoming integrated into the functioning of other social institutions and spheres of life, they have had a major say in how 'X counts as Y in context C'. One of the reasons behind it is that they have acted as an intermediary between the members of the audience and aspects of reality which cannot be experienced by them directly, bringing these aspects perceptually closer. We have argued here that it is this work on distance, in all its dimensions, starting with the spatiotemporal dimension, that makes the phenomenon of mediatization possible, also in the context of mediatization of religion.

The process of reducing the perceived distance can be viewed both horizontally and vertically. In the former case, it results in what we could call, following Anderson (1991), the construction of 'imagined communities' contingent on mediated presence and collective experience. In the latter case, certain metaphorical conceptualizations (expressed both verbally and visually), for example, make selected aspects of the spiritual reality more cognitively and affectively accessible.

DesCamp and Sweetser argue that '[i]f a liturgy is intended to help worshippers reach an appropriate state of mind for [a] spiritual relationship with God, it is important to consider what we know about [the] human mind and how it may be affected by particular kinds of input' (2005, pp. 207–208). It seems that with the presence of the media (and mediated ritual experience) another key issue should be addressed here, namely, how media's semiotic potential and the cognitive affordances they offer (enabling visuality, intertextuality, emotivity, and immediacy) may transform this input and its perception and reception, how it may impact on the relationship with both God and other believers. Also, from a theological point of view, how does this new mediated form of experience correlate with the doctrine of the 'real presence'? Even if it is not likely to supersede it in the near future, maybe it still does seem a viable alternative for those who, for various reasons, cannot afford direct physical participation in religious rituals. It undoubtedly does make 'Church reality' more inclusive both space- and time-wise, by generating super-time and super-space within which religious practices can be embedded. It also allows religious media (and the institutions behind them) to have greater control over cognitive and affective responses of the audience, since, as demonstrated by cognitive science and many authors in this volume, certain (verbal and visual) forms of construal can potentially shape, or at least considerably influence, human reactions. In other words, cognitive effects can bring about behavioural effects and have material consequences. In this way, mediated (and mediatized) religious experience becomes an example of the interface between the cognitive and the social, the abstract and the material, individual and collective, belief and practice, an interface within which language (and discourse in its multimodal dimension), as this book has attempted to show, plays an instrumental and constitutive role.

NOTES

1. According to Searle (1995), the social status of objects, people, and institutions is not naturally inherent to them but granted by the society as a result of collective agreement. Status functions, conferred by the community by means of speech acts and other symbolic acts, entail deontic powers, e.g. authorization to marry people.
2. Its origins, though, go back to 1948 when Pope Pius XII created the Pontifical Commission for the Study and Ecclesiastical Evaluation of Films on Religious or Moral Subjects (see Pontifical Council for Social Communications 1999).
3. They may also suggest the spatial image schema of CONTAINER.

4. The slogan 'The Catholic voice in your home', while it fits very well within the family and home conceptual framework, also performs a spatially proximizing function through deictic reference to the Self's space.
5. Fragments from Radio Maryja and TV Trwam broadcasts, originally in Polish, have been translated by the author of this chapter.

REFERENCES

Agha, A. (2011). Meet mediatization. *Language & Communication* 3, 163–170.
Alcorta, C. S. and R. Sosis (2005). Ritual, emotion, and sacred symbols: The evolution of religion as an adaptive complex. *Human Nature* 16(4), 323–359.
Ammerman, N. (ed.) (2007). *Everyday Religion: Observing Modern Religious Lives*. New York: Oxford University Press.
Anderson, B. (1991). *Imagined Communities: Reflections on the Origin and Spread of Nationalism*. London: Verso.
Atran, S. (2002). *In Gods We Trust: The Evolutionary Landscape of Religion*. Oxford: Oxford University Press.
Austin, J. L. (1962). *How to Do Things with Words*. The William James Lectures at Harvard University in 1955. Edited by J. O. Urmson and Marina Sbisa. Oxford, UK: Clarendon Press.
Baab, L. M. (2008). Portraits of the future church: A rhetorical analysis of congregational websites. *Journal of Communication and Religion* 31, 143–181.
Barrett, J. L. (2000). Exploring the natural foundation of religion. *Trends in Cognitive Science* 4, 29–34.
Barry, A. M. S. (1997). *Visual Intelligence: Perception, Image and Manipulation in Visual Communication*. Albany: State University of New York Press.
Basso, E. B. and G. Senft (2009). Introduction. In G. Senft and E. B. Basso (eds.), *Ritual Communication*, pp. 1–19. Oxford, UK: Berg.
Bell, C. 1997. *Ritual Perspectives and Dimensions*. New York: Oxford University Press.
Berger, P. and T. Luckmann (1991/1966). *The Social Construction of Reality: A Treatise in the Sociology of Knowledge*. London: Penguin Books.
Bignell, J. (2002). *Media Semiotics: An Introduction*. Manchester: Manchester University Press.
Boden, D. and H. L. Molotch (1994). The compulsion of proximity. In R. Friedland and D. Boden (eds.), *NowHere: Space, Time, and Modernity*, pp. 257–286. Berkeley: University of California Press.
Boyer, P. (2001). *Religion Explained: The Evolutionary Origins of Religious Thought*. New York: Basic Books.
Busselle, R. W. and B. S. Greenberg (2000). The nature of television realism judgments: A reevaluation of their conceptualization and measurement. *Mass Communication and Society* 3, 249–268.
Cap, P. (2006). *Legitimisation in Political Discourse: A Cross-Disciplinary Perspective on the Modern US War Rhetoric*. Newcastle: Cambridge Scholars Press.
Cap, P. (2008). Towards the proximization model of the analysis of legitimization in political discourse. *Journal of Pragmatics* 40, 17–41.
Cap, P. (2010). Axiological aspects of proximization. *Journal of Pragmatics* 42, 392–407.
Cap, P. (2013). *Proximization: The Pragmatics of Symbolic Distance Crossing*. Amsterdam: Benjamins.
Charteris-Black, J. (2005). *Politicians and Rhetoric: The Persuasive Power of Metaphor*. New York: Palgrave Macmillan.
Chilton, P. (1996). *Security Metaphor: Cold War Discourse from Containment to Common House*. New York: Peter Lang.
Chilton, P. (2004). *Analysing Political Discourse: Theory and Practice*. London: Routledge.

Chilton, P. (2005). Discourse Space Theory: Geometry, brain and shifting viewpoints. *Annual Review of Cognitive Linguistics* 3, 78–116.

Chilton, P. (2010). From mind to grammar: Coordinate systems, prepositions, constructions. In V. Evans and P. Chilton (eds.), *Language, Cognition and Space: The State of the Art and New Directions*, pp. 499–514. London: Equinox.

Chilton, P. (2014). *Language, Space and Mind: The Conceptual Geometry of Linguistic Meaning*. Cambridge: Cambridge University Press.

Clark, W. H. (1958). *The Psychology of Religion*. New York: Macmillan.

Collins, R. (2004). *Interaction Ritual Chains*. Princeton, NJ: Princeton University Press.

Corner, J. (1995). *Television Form and Public Address*. London: Edward Arnold.

Corner, J. (1999). *Critical Ideas in Television Studies*. Oxford: Clarendon Press.

Cottle, S. (2006). Mediatized rituals: Beyond manufacturing consent. *Media, Culture and Society* 28(3), 411–432.

Cottle, S. (2008). 'Mediatized rituals': A reply to Couldry and Rothenbuhler. *Media, Culture and Society* 30(1), 135–140.

Couldry, N. (2003). *Media Rituals: A Critical Approach*. London: Routledge.

Couldry, N. (2004). Liveness, 'reality' and the mediated habitus from television to the mobile phone. *The Communication Review* 7(4), 353–361.

Croft, W. and A. D. Cruse (2004). *Cognitive Linguistics*. Cambridge: Cambridge University Press.

Cronk, L. (1994). Evolutionary theories of morality and the manipulative use of signals. *Zygon* 29, 32–58.

Dancygier, B. and E. Sweetser (2014). *Figurative Language*. New York: Cambridge University Press.

Dayan D. and E. Katz (1992). *Media Events: The Live Broadcasting of History*. Cambridge, MA: Harvard University Press.

Dehaene, S. and J. P. Changeux (2000). Reward-dependent learning in neuronal networks for planning and decision-making. In H. B. M. Uylings, C. G. van Eden, J. P. D. deBruin, M. G. P. Feenstra, and C. M. A. Pennartz (eds.), *Cognition, Emotion, and Autonomic Responses: The Integrative Role of the Prefrontal Cortex and Limbic Structures*, pp. 219–230. New York: Elsevier.

DesCamp, M. T. and E. Sweetser (2005). Metaphors for God: Why and how do our choices matter for humans? The application of contemporary cognitive linguistics research to the debate on God and metaphor. *Pastoral Psychology* 53(3), 207–238.

Douglas, M. (1966). *Purity and Danger*. New York: Frederick A. Praeger.

Durkheim, E. (1969/1915). *The Elementary Forms of the Religious Life*. New York: Free Press.

Elder-Vass, D. (2013). *The Reality of Social Construction*. Cambridge: Cambridge University Press.

Eliade, M. (1958). *Rites and Symbols of Initiation: The Mysteries of Birth and Rebirth*. Dallas: Spring Publications.

Eliade, M. (1959). *The Sacred and the Profane: The Nature of Religion*. New York: Harcourt Brace Jovanovich.

Fairclough, N. (1992). *Discourse and Social Change*. London: Polity Press.

Fairclough, N. and R. Wodak (1997). Critical Discourse Analysis. In T. A. van Dijk (ed.), *Introduction to Discourse Studies*, pp. 258–284. London: Sage.

Flaherty, M. G. (2011). *The Textures of Time: Agency and Temporal Experience*. Philadelphia: Temple University Press.

Frambach, N. (2003). Congregations in mission: Rethinking the metaphor of "family." *Currents in Theology and Mission* 30, 210–218.

Frijda, N. H. and B. Mesquita (2000). Beliefs through emotions. In N. H. Frijda, A. S. R. Manstead, and S. Bem (eds.), *Emotions and Belief: How Feelings Influence Thoughts*, pp. 45–77. Cambridge: Cambridge University Press.

Frijda, N. H., A. S. R. Manstead, and S. Bem (2000). The influence of emotions on beliefs. In N. H. Frijda, A. S. R. Manstead, and S. Bem (eds.), *Emotions and Belief: How Feelings Influence Thoughts*, pp. 1–9. Cambridge: Cambridge University Press.

Fromm, E. (1950). *Psychoanalysis and Religion*. New Haven: Yale University Press.

Gibbs, R. W. (1994). *The Poetics of Mind*. Cambridge, UK: Cambridge University Press.

Giddens, A. (1991). *Modernity and Self-Identity: Self and Society in the Late Modern Age*. Stanford, CA: Stanford University Press.

Goatly, A. (2007). *Washing the Brain: The Hidden Ideology of Metaphor*. Amsterdam & Philadelphia: John Benjamins.

Goethals, G. (1981). *The TV Ritual: Worship at the Video Altar*. Boston: Beacon Press.

Goffman, E. (1983). The interaction order: American sociological association, 1982 presidential address. *American Sociological Review* 48(1), 1–17.

Goodenough, E. R. (1965). *The Psychology of Religious Experiences*. New York: Basic Books.

Graham, E. L. (1996). *Transforming Practice: Pastoral Theology in an Age of Uncertainty*. Eugene: Wipf and Stock.

Guthrie, S. E. (1993). *Faces in the Clouds: A New Theory of Religion*. New York: Oxford University Press.

Hall, S., C. Critcher, T. Jefferson, J. Clarke, and B. Roberts (1978). *Policing the Crisis: Mugging, the State and Law and Order*. London: Macmillan.

Hart, C. (2010). *Critical Discourse Analysis and Cognitive Science: New Perspectives on Immigration Discourse*. Basingstoke: Palgrave.

Hart, C. (2014). *Discourse, Grammar and Ideology: Functional and Cognitive Perspectives*. London: Bloomsbury.

Harvey, D. (1990). *The Condition of Postmodernity: An Enquiry into the Origins of Cultural Change*. Cambridge, MA: Blackwell.

Hepp, A. (2013). *Cultures of Mediatization*. Cambridge: Polity.

Hepp, A. and V. Krönert (2010). Religious media events: The Catholic 'World Youth Day' as an example of the mediatization and individualization of religion. In N. Couldry, A. Hepp, and F. Krotz (eds.), *Media Events in a Global Age*, pp. 265–282. London: Routledge.

Hjarvard, S. (2008). The mediatization of religion: A theory of the media as agents of religious change. *Northern Lights* 2008. Bristol: Intellect.

Hjarvard, S. (2011). The mediatisation of religion: Theorising religion, media and social change. *Culture and Religion* 12(2), 119–135.

Hjarvard, S. (2013). *The Mediatization of Society*. New York: Routledge.

Hjarvard, S. and M. Lövheim (eds.) (2012). *Mediatization and Religion*. Gothenburg: Nordicom.

Hoover, S. M. (2006). *Religion in the Media Age*. London: Routledge.

Hoover, S. M. and L. S. Clark (2002). *Practising Religion in the Age of the Media: Explorations in the Media, Religion and Culture*. New York: Columbia University Press.

Hoskins, A. and B. O'Loughlin (2007). *Television and Terror: Conflicting Times and the Crisis of News Discourse*. Basingstoke: Palgrave.

Humphrey, C. and J. Laidlaw (1994). *The Archetypal Actions of Ritual: A Theory of Ritual Illustrated by the Jain Rite of Worship*. Oxford: Clarendon Press.

Jay, M. (1993). *Downcast Eyes: The Denigration of Vision in Twentieth-Century French Thought*. Berkeley: California University Press.

John Paul II (1998). *Pastor Bonus*. Apostolic Constitution. Retrieved July 1, 2015 from: http://w2.vatican.va/content/john-paul-ii/en/apost_constitutions/documents/hf_jp-ii_apc_19880628_pastor-bonus.html

Johnson, M. (1987). *The Body in the Mind: The Bodily Basis of Meaning, Imagination and Reason*. Chicago, IL: University of Chicago Press.

Johnson, M. (1993). *Moral Imagination: Implications of Cognitive Science for Ethics*. Chicago, IL: University of Chicago Press.

Johnstone, R. L. (2015). *Religion in Society: A Sociology of Religion*. London: Routledge.

Kaid, L. L., J. Gerstlé, and K. R. Sanders. (eds.) (1991). *Mediated Politics in Two Cultures: Presidential Campaigning in the United States and France*. New York: Praeger.

Keltner, D. and J. Haidt (2003). Approaching awe, a moral, spiritual, and aesthetic emotion. *Cognition and Emotion* 17(2), 297–314.

Kopytowska, M. (2013). Blogging as the mediatization of politics and a new form of social interaction. In P. Cap and U. Okulska (eds.), *Analyzing Genres in Political Communication*, pp. 379–421. Amsterdam: Benjamins.

Kopytowska, M. (2014). Pictures in our heads: Crisis, conflict, and drama. In Y. Kalyango and M. Kopytowska (eds.), *Why Discourse Matters: Negotiating Identity in the Mediatized World*, pp. 89–109. New York: Peter Lang.

Kopytowska, M. (2015a). Covering conflict: Between universality and cultural specificity in news discourse genre and journalistic style. *International Review of Pragmatics* (Special Issue on *Communicative styles and genres: between universality and culture-specificity*) 7, 308–339.

Kopytowska, M. (2015b). Ideology of "here and now": Mediating distance in television news. *Critical Discourse Studies* 12(3), 347–365.

Kopytowska, M. (2015c). Mediating identity, ideology and values in the public sphere: Towards a new model of (constructed) social reality. *Lodz Papers in Pragmatics* 11(2), 133–156.

Kopytowska, M. and Ł. Grabowski (2017). European security under threat: Mediating the crisis and constructing the Other. In C. Karner and M. Kopytowska (eds.), *National Identity and Europe in Times of Crisis Subtitle: Doing and Undoing Europe*, pp. 83–112. Bingley: Emerald Publishing.

Kövecses, Z. (1990). *Emotion Concepts*. New York: Springer-Verlag.

Kress, G. and T. van Leeuwen (2006). *Reading Images: The Grammar of Visual Design.*, 2nd ed. London: Routledge.

Krotz, F. (2007). The meta-process of mediatization as a conceptual frame. *Global Media and Communication* 3, 256–260.

Krotz, F. (2009). Mediatization: A concept with which to grasp media and societal change. In K. Lundby (ed.), *Mediatization: Concept, Changes, Consequences*, pp. 21–40. New York: Peter Lang.

Lakoff, G. (1996). *Moral Politics: How Conservatives and Liberals Think*. Chicago, IL: University of Chicago Press.

Lakoff, G. (2004). *Don't Think of an Elephant: Know Your Values and Frame the Debate*. White River Junction, VT: Chelsea Green.

Lakoff, G. (2006). *Whose Freedom? The Battle over America's Most Important Idea*. New York: Farrar, Straus and Giroux.

Lakoff, G. (2008). *The Political Mind: Why You Can't Understand 21st Century Politics with an 18th Century Brain*. New York: Viking.

Lakoff, G. and M. Johnson (1980). *Metaphors We Live By*. Chicago, IL: University of Chicago Press.

Lakoff, G. and M. Johnson (1999). *Philosophy in the Flesh: The Embodied Mind and Its Challenge to Western Thought*. New York: Basic Books.

Langacker, R. W. (1987). *Foundations of Cognitive Grammar: Theoretical Prerequisites*. Stanford, CA: Stanford University Press.

Langacker, R. W. (1988). A view of linguistic semantics. In B. Rudzka-Ostyn (ed.), *Topics in Cognitive Linguistics*, pp. 49–90. Amsterdam: Benjamins.

Langacker, R. W. (1990). *Concept, Image and Symbol: The Cognitive Basis of Grammar*. Berlin: Mouton de Gruyter.

Lepa, A. (2000). *Pedagogika mass mediów*. Łódź: Archidiecezjalne Wydawnictwo Łódzkie.

Lippmann, W. (1922). *Public Opinion*. New York: Harcourt, Brace and Co.

Livingstone, S. (2009). On the mediation of everything. *Journal of Communication* 59(1), 1–18.

Lombard, M. (1995). Direct responses to people on the screen: Television and personal space. *Communication Research* 22, 288–324.

Lowie, R. (1924). *Primitive Religion*. New York: Boni & Liveright.

Lynch, G. (2005). *Understanding Theology and Popular Culture*. London: Routledge.

Lynch, G. (ed.) (2007). *Between Sacred and Profane: Researching Religion and Popular Culture*. London: I. B. Tauris.

Lyon, D. (2000). *Jesus in Disneyland: Religion in Postmodern Times*. Cambridge: Polity Press.

Mahan, J. H. (2014). *Media, Religion and Culture: An Introduction*. New York: Routledge.

Martelli, S. and G. Capello (2005). Religion in the television mediated public sphere. *International Review of Sociology* 15(2), 243–257.

Mazur, E. and K. McCarthy (eds.) (2001). *God in the Details: American Religion in Popular Culture*. New York: Routledge.

McNair, B. (2003). *An Introduction to Political Communication*. London: Routledge.

Messaris, P. and L. Abraham (2003). The role of images in framing news stories. In S. D. Reese, Oscar H. Gandy, Jr., and A. E. Grant (eds.), *Framing Public Life: Perspective on Media and Our Understanding of the Social World*, pp. 215–226. Mahwah, NJ: Lawrence Erlbaum Associates.

Meyer, B. and A. Moors (eds.) (2006). *Religion, Media and the Public Sphere*. Bloomington: Indiana University Press.

Meyrowitz, J. (1993). Images of media: Hidden ferment—and harmony—in the field. *Journal of Communication* 43(3), 55–66.

Miller, V. J. (2003). *Consuming Religion*. New York: Continuum.

Mitchell, J. (1999). *Visually Speaking: Radio and the Renaissance of Preaching*. Louisville: Westminster John Knox Press.

Morgan, D. (1998). *Visual Piety: A History and Theory of Popular Religious Images*. Berkeley: University of California Press.

Morley, D. (2000). *Home Territories, Media, Mobility and Identity*. London: Routledge.

Newman, J. (1996). *Religion vs. Television*. Westport, CT: Praeger.

Nickell, J. (with Beaudoin, T. and Lynch, G.) (2006). Meaning, spirit and popular culture: An interview with Tom Beaudoin. *Crucible* (July–Sept), 17–23.

Otto, R. (1950). *The Idea of the Holy*. Oxford: Oxford University Press.

Pontifical Council for Social Communications (1971). *Communio et Progressio: On the Means of Social Communication; Written by Order of the Second Vatican Council*. Retrieved July 1, 2015 from http://www.vatican.va/roman_curia/pontifical_councils/pccs/documents/rc_pc_pccs_doc_23051971_communio_en.html

Pontifical Council for Social Communications (1992). *Aetatis novae: Pastoral Instruction on Social Communications on the Twentieth Anniversary of Communio et Progressio*. Retrieved July 1, 2015 from http://www.vatican.va/roman_curia/pontifical_councils/pccs/documents/rc_pc_pccs_doc_22021992_aetatis_en.html

Pontifical Council for Social Communications (1999). A brief outline and history of the Pontifical Council for Social Communications. Retrieved July 1, 2015 from http://www.vatican.va//roman_curia/pontifical_councils/pccs/documents/rc_pc_pccs_pro_14101999_en.html

Pontifical Council for Social Communications (2002). *The Church and Internet*. Retrieved July 1, 2015 from http://www.vatican.va/roman_curia/pontifical_councils/pccs/documents/rc_pc_pccs_doc_20020228_church-internet_en.html

Potter, W. J. (1988). Perceived reality in television effects research. *Journal of Broadcasting and Electronic Media* 32, 23–41.

Pyysiäinen, I. (2001). Cognition, emotion, and religious experience. In J. Andersen (ed.), *Religion in Mind: Cognitive Perspectives on Religious Belief, Ritual and Experience*, pp. 70–93. Cambridge: Cambridge University Press.

Rappaport, R. A. (1979). *Ecology, Meaning and Religion*. Berkeley: North Atlantic Books.

Rappaport, R. A. (1999). *Ritual and Religion in the Making of Humanity*. London: Cambridge University Press.

Real, M. (1977). *Mass Mediated Culture*. Englewood Cliffs, NJ: Prentice Hall.

Reid, R. S. (1995). Postmodernism and the function of the New Homiletic in Post-Christian congregations. *Homiletic* 20(2), 1–13.

Rose, G. (2007). *Visual Methodologies: An Introduction to Interpretation of Visual Materials*. London: Sage.

Rothenbuhler, E. W. (1998). *Ritual Communication: From Everyday Conversation to Mediated Ceremony*. Thousand Oaks, CA: Sage.

Rothenbuhler, E. W. (2006). Communication as ritual. In G. J. Shepherd, J. John, and T. Striphas (eds.), *Communication as . . .: Perspectives on Theory*, pp. 13–21. Thousand Oaks: Sage.

Rothenbuhler, E. W. (2010). From media events to ritual to communicative form. In N. Couldry, A. Hepp, and F. Krotz (eds.), *Media Events in a Global Age*, pp. 61–75. London: Routledge.

Rubin, A. and E. Perse (1987). Audience activity and soap opera involvement. *Human Communication Research* 14(2), 246–268.

Sa Martino, L. M. 2013. *The Mediatization of Religion: When Faith Rocks*. Ashgate Publishing Company

Schulz, W. (2004). Reconstructing mediatization as an analytical concept. *European Journal of Communication* 19, 87–101.

Searle, J. R. (1972). What is a speech act? In P. P. Giglioli (ed.), *Language and Social Context*, pp. 136–154. Harmondsworth: Penguin.

Searle, J. R. (1995). *The Construction of Social Reality*. London: Penguin.

Searle, J. R. (2006). Social ontology: Some basic principles. *Anthropological Theory* 6(1), 12–29.

Searle, J. R. (2010). *Making the Social World: The Structure of Human Civilization*. Oxford: Oxford University Press.

Seligman, A. B., R. P. Weller, M. J. Puett, and B. Simon (2008). *Ritual and Its Consequences: An Essay on the Limits of Sincerity*. New York: Oxford University Press.

Senft, G. (2014). *Understanding Pragmatics*. London: Routledge.

Seuren, P. A. M. (2009). *Language from Within*, Vol. 1: *Language in Cognition*. Oxford, UK: Oxford University Press.

Sosis R. (2003). Why aren't we all Hutterites? Costly signaling theory and religious behavior. *Human Nature* 14, 91–127.

Sosis, R., and C. S. Alcorta (2003). Signaling, solidarity and the sacred: The evolution of religious behavior. *Evolutionary Anthropology* 12, 264–274.

Stout, D. A. and J. M. Buddenbaum (2008). Approaches to the study of media and religion: Notes from the Editors of the *Journal of Media and Religion* with recommendations for future research. *Religion* 38, 226–232.

Sweetser, E. (1990). *From Etymology to Pragmatics: Metaphorical and Cultural Aspects of Semantic Structure*. Cambridge: Cambridge University Press.

Sweetser, E. and M. T. DesCamp (2014). Motivating biblical metaphors for God: Refining the cognitive model. In B. Howe and J. B. Green (eds.), *Cognitive Linguistic Explorations in Biblical Studies*, pp. 7–23. Berlin: Walter de Gruyter.

Thompson, J. B. (1995). *The Media and Modernity*. Cambridge: Polity Press.

Turner, V. (1967). *The Forest of Symbols*. New York: Cornell University Press.

Turner, V. (1969). *The Ritual Process*. Chicago: Aldine.

Urry, J. (2002). Mobility and proximity. *Sociology* 36(2), 255–274.

van Dijk, T. A. (1990). Social cognition and discourse. In H. Giles and P. H. Robinson (eds.), *Handbook of Language and Social Psychology*, pp. 163–183. London: Wiley and Sons.

van Dijk, T. A. (1997). *Discourse as Social Interaction*. London: Sage.

Ward, P. (2007). The Eucharist and the turn to culture. In G. Lynch (ed.), *Between the Sacred and Profane: Researching Religion and Popular Culture*, pp. 82–93. London, I. B. Tauris.

Willerslev, R., D. R. Christensen, and L. Meinert (2013). Introduction. In R. Willerslev and D. R. Christensen (eds.), *Taming Time, Timing Death: Social Technologies and Ritual*, pp. 1–16. Burlington, VT: Ashgate Publishing.

INDEX

Bible (*cont.*)
  King James Bible, 12
  metaphors in, 232, 321, 264, 325n43,
    325n46, 326n58, 377
  Revised Version, 39
  Tyndale New Testament, 13–15
  Vulgate, 14, 38
  Wycliffe, 13–15
biblical criticism, xix
  exegesis, xviii, xxvi–xxix, 267, 312, 319,
    320, 326n58, 410, 412, 432 (*see also*
    allegory and allegorical interpretation)
  expressions, 35
  idiom, 14–16
  language, 4, 5, 12, 356
  metaphor, 232, 312, 321, 326
  studies, 45
  texts, xliv, 231, 232, 325, 334, 335, 383
Black, Max, xviii
blessing, xl, 17, 92, 118, 377, 420, 422–423.
    See also speech acts, blessings
Boyer, Pascal, xx–xxv, xxxiii, xxxix, 444
brain, xxi, xxv, xxix–xxxv, xliii, xlvi, 2,
    99–102, 113, 125–126, 128–131,
    136–137, 139, 147–148, 150,
    152–153, 388, 416–418, 424, 428
  amygdala, xxxii, 130, 151, 462
  Broca's and Wernicke's areas, xxxv, 129
  caudate nucleus, 126
  corpus callosum, 136, 153
  hippocampus, xxii, xxxiv, xliii,
    129–130, 151
  lateral hypothalamic area, 101
  limbic system, xxxiv, xliii, 151
  nucleus accumbens, 126
  prefrontal cortex, xxxii, xxxiv, 126–128
  putamen, 126
  substantia nigra, 126
  temporal lobe, xxxiv, xliii, 126, 129, 131
  thalamus, 126
Buddha, 223, 230, 232, 233, 239–242,
    244–246, 248–250, 254–258, 258n1,
    258n3, 258n5, 258n7
Buddhism, vii, 20, 167, 206n28, 215–216,
    218, 222–227, 227n7, 229–233, 235,
    237–241, 244, 246, 251–252, 255,
    257–258, 258n5

Cajetan, Thomas, 295
Calvin, John, 326, 326n57, 335, 410
Calvinist, 303
Carmelite nuns, 130
categories, 24, 29, 32, 34, 39, 63, 70, 76,
    78, 272, 306, 324, 354, 358, 433,
    440, 450

church, xlii, 16, 24, 45, 48, 303, 304, 365,
    388, 437, 438, 442, 447, 449, 456,
    457, 467
  Catholic, 32, 34, 36, 39, 41, 154, 354,
    363, 375, 387, 437, 441, 445, 457,
    459, 468n4
  Christian, 334
  Eastern Church, 390
  electronic, 443
  Orthodox, 154, 354, 363, 364, 370,
    375, 387
  Protestant, 375, 387
Chomsky, Noam, xx, xxv, xxxi, 5
Christ, 79, 97, 301, 303–306, 320–322,
    355–359, 364, 365, 367, 369, 370,
    372, 373, 375, 378, 380–382, 389,
    392, 393, 401, 402, 410, 411, 414,
    429, 437, 457, 459
Christianity, vii, xviii, xxxiv, xlii, 22, 23, 26,
    45, 53, 168, 213, 231, 232, 264, 294,
    301, 316, 320, 349, 383, 388, 390,
    401, 441
  Christian art, 368
  Christian concept of God, 30–32, 74
  Christian Creed, 19, 45
  Christian doctrine, xliv, 34
  Christian dogma, 353
  Christian eschatology, 44, 47
  Christian ethics, 35, 294, 319
  Christian iconography, 376
  Christian missionaries, 24, 304
  Christian morality, 402
  Christian petitionary prayer, xxxix, 90,
    93, 110
  Christian Scriptures, 333, 350
  Christian theologians, xviii
  Christian theology, 31, 354, 357, 358,
    360, 363, 365
  Christian tradition, xvii, 1, 19, 40, 78,
    123, 354, 365
  Orthodox Christianity, 387
chronocentrism, 48. *See also*
    Anglocentrism; Eurocentrism
Chrysostom, John, 335
circumcision, 7, 168, 297, 300–326
co-presence, 91, 332, 427, 448, 450–451,
    453, 456, 459–461
cognition, xxiii, xxiv, xxv, xxx, xxxii, xxxix,
    xlii, xlv, 63, 89, 90, 99, 101, 116, 117,
    126, 154, 203, 224, 225, 234, 296,
    306, 307, 326, 337, 398, 400, 427,
    429, 443, 448, 455
  cognitive effects, xxiii, xxxix, 97, 110,
    130, 339, 345, 399, 420, 422, 428,
    431, 432, 434, 438

Counter-Reformation, 368, 409, 414.
    See also Reformation
creativity, xxi, xxxvi, xli, 400, 401
culturally postulated supernatural agents
    (CPS-agents), xxi, xxv–xxx, xxxix–xl,
    115, 117, 127, 444

Darwin, Charles, 141
decentering, xxxiv, xxxv, 120–123, 129
deixis and deictic words, 408, 409, 412,
    413, 419, 420, 421, 424, 426, 428,
    430, 453, 459, 468
  deictic centre, 429, 450, 459, 460
  deictic space, 416, 418, 422, 423, 426,
    427, 433, 437, 450
  deictic space theory (DST) also discourse
    space theory, 416, 430, 466
deliteralisation, 298, 299, 327
Dennett, Daniel, xx, xxiv, xlvin, 401
deontic powers, xli, 440, 456, 458,
    466, 467
Derrida, Jacques, 57, 58, 319
dialogue, xxix, xxx, 91
Diamond Sutra, 167, 229, 230, 234,
    235–238, 240–245, 247, 249–256,
    258n1, 258n3
Dionysius the Areopagite
    (Pseudo-Dionysius), xviii, 55–56,
    58, 79, 80
disanalogy, 396–398. *See also* analogy
discourse, xxiii, xxviii–xxx, xxxii, xxxix,
    xli, 4, 7–9, 11, 47, 57, 58, 59, 65, 136,
    143, 188, 189, 191, 199, 203, 213,
    221, 222, 226, 271, 285, 311, 321,
    346, 348, 391, 399, 403, 439, 443,
    450, 454, 460, 466–467
  interactional discourse, 62
  political discourse, 64
  prophetic discourse, 274–275, 277, 281,
    287–289
  public discourse, 274
  religious discourse, xlii, 6, 9, 52, 53,
    74, 167, 198, 231–232, 263–268,
    274–275, 280–283, 286, 289–290,
    295–296, 298, 333–334, 336, 341,
    349–350, 389, 400, 431, 445, 447,
    449–452
  theological discourse, 59, 73, 75, 76
discourse analysis, xxiv, 7, 66, 331–332
  Critical Discourse Analysis, 7–8, 11, 234
    (*see also* Cognitive Critical Discourse
    Analysis)
discourse marker, 105
discourse referent, 422, 429
discourse space, 422, 437, 438

discourse space theory, 450
distance, xliii–xliv, 9, 28, 66, 80n2, 285,
    332, 416–417, 420–422, 437, 448,
    450–455, 458–460, 462, 464–467.
    See also proximity; proximization
dopaminergic system, xxxiv, xliv, 417
Douai-Rheims, 13–14

emblem, 306–308, 310, 315–317, 319,
    322–323
embodiment, xxxvi, 188, 196, 227, 389,
    432, 455
emotion, affect, xvii, xx, xxxv, xliii, xlvi, 1,
    62, 64, 99, 100–102, 105, 108, 113,
    121, 123, 125, 128, 130, 141, 155,
    167, 173, 197, 211, 214, 220–225,
    226n, 227n, 265, 272, 274–277, 311,
    331, 339, 356, 359, 371, 383, 430,
    437, 438, 440, 444–448, 454, 461,
    462, 464, 466
  emotional needs, 446
  metaphors for, 212–227
empathy, xxxvi, 100, 299, 389, 400, 401,
    440, 464
Engels, Friedrich, 319
epilepsy, xxxii
eschatology, 44–48, 78
Eternal Word Television Network (EWTN),
    454, 456–459
Eucharist, xlii, 322, 387, 407, 410, 412,
    414, 428, 431, 432, 433, 434, 441,
    446, 450, 462
Eurocentrism, 20, 29, 48
evolution, xxviii, xxxvii, 70, 102, 136, 141,
    146, 221, 429, 431

feminism, xix, 8, 79, 231
folk religions, xxiv, 92, 98–99, 104, 112,
    191, 277, 300, 307, 313
frame, xxx, xli, xlii, 78, 238, 295, 296–298,
    306, 321, 324n9, 324n10, 420–422,
    425, 428, 459
  frame-shifting, 149, 426–427, 429,
    430, 434n30
  reference frame, 418–422, 425–426,
    428, 430
Frege, Gottlob, xviii-xix

gamma-amino butyric acid (GABA), 136
Gandhi, Mahatma, 111
gender, 172, 181
gender studies, 8
genre, xxvii–xxix, xxxix, xliv, xlvin, 17, 44,
    92–93, 102–103, 108, 113, 271, 298,
    437, 443, 451

Spinoza, Baruch, 319
status functions, xli, 440, 448, 456, 458, 466, 467
  quasi-status functions, 440
Sunnah, 268. See also *Hadith*; Prophetic Tradition
supernatural agents, xi, xxix–xxx, xxxix–xl, 115, 117, 127, 444. *See also* CPS-agents
Swinburne, Richard, xviii, xix
symbol, 7, 21, 120, 123, 124, 130, 143, 171, 210, 213, 231, 294, 363, 370, 373, 376, 381, 382, 400, 443, 445, 462, 465
symbolic language, 122, 266
symbolic signaling, xxxvii
symbolism, 142, 155, 307, 310

Talmud, 302, 305, 319
Tantra, 186–190, 196, 203–205
Tao, 20, 21
Teilhard de Chardin, Pierre, 49
television, 443, 447, 453, 454, 458, 467, 462
temporal lobe epilepsy (also TLE), xxxii
theology, xix, xxix, xlii, 1, 6–8, 23, 24, 26, 29, 31, 32, 53–59, 73–77, 79, 92, 97, 103, 105, 11, 112, 146, 171, 231, 264, 267, 295, 304, 368, 383, 386, 399, 402, 403, 407, 422, 429
  apophatic, xviii, 52–58, 73, 76, 83n59, 146 (see also *via negative*)
  Christian, 31, 354, 357, 358, 360, 363, 365
  Kabbalistic, 172, 173, 175–177, 182
  neurotheology, xxxi
  Orthodox, 389
  practical, 446
Tillich, Paul, 22–23, 34–36, 116
time, xliii, 66, 211, 237, 238, 240–248, 255–258, 296, 317, 416, 420–422, 426, 428, 438, 440, 444–446, 450, 467
time-shifting, 426–428
time-space compression, 445, 451
timework, 445, 459, 461
Torah, 175–181, 303, 304, 307, 308, 316, 318, 319, 323

translation, 9–12, 24, 26, 31, 70, 77, 78, 229, 230, 294, 310, 313. *See also* Bible, Bible translation
transubstantiation, doctrine and ritual, 410, 414, 420, 429
Trinity, doctrine of, 331, 353–355, 387
  representation of, 357, 359, 362–364, 366–384
truth-conditional semantics, xviii, xix
TV Trwam, 454, 456, 459–460, 468n5
Tyndale, William, 13, 14

universal semantic primes, 28, 29, 34, 41, 48

values, xxxv, 90, 115–118, 120–125, 129–131, 234, 265, 277, 280, 282, 296, 297, 299, 305, 309, 316, 318, 440, 444, 446, 450, 451, 453, 455, 461
  shift in , 299, 315, 317, 322, 323
Vatican II, 5, 10, 441
vectors, 417, 418, 422, 425, 426, 433
Vedic scriptures, xviii, 297
via negativa, xviii, xxiv, xlvin7, 57, 80n11
vision, visual system, xxi, xliii, xliii, 149, 224, 233, 254, 419, 427, 430, 453–454, 461–462
  visual field, xliii, 145, 150, 418, 420, 429
  visual image, xlii, 129, 399, 453, 461
  visualization, 188–189, 192, 195–196, 198, 272
visual art, visual representation, 353–384, 422, 438, 443, 447
  visual salience, 457
  visual scanning, 375
visual shifts, 460

Wittgenstein, Ludwig, 90, 111, 112, 143
worship space. *See* space, ritual
Wycliffe, John, 13–15

Yezidism, 349
yoga, 189

Zohar, 167, 169–183
Zwingli, Huldrych, 410